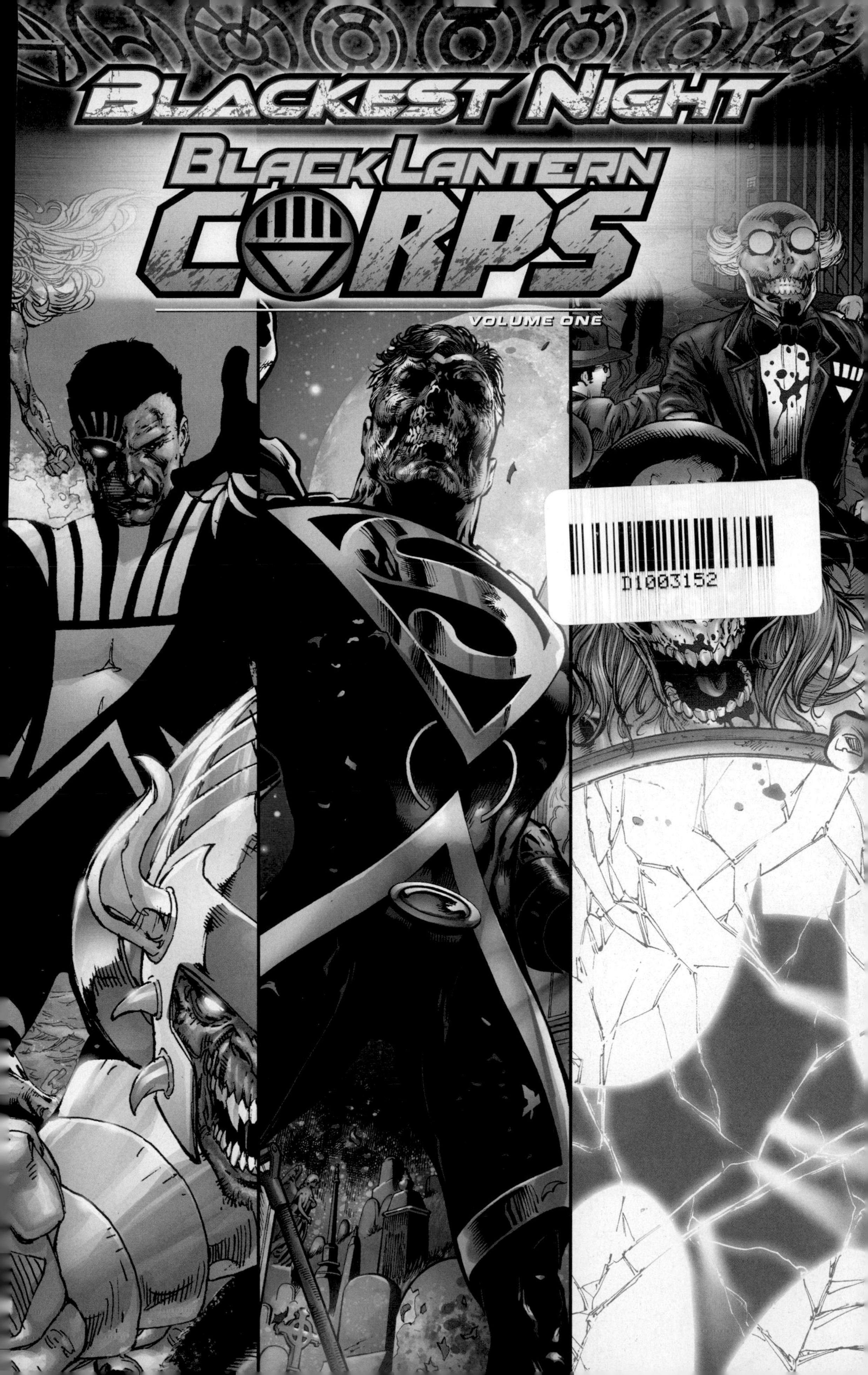
BLACKEST NIGHT
BLACK LANTERN
CORPS
VOLUME ONE

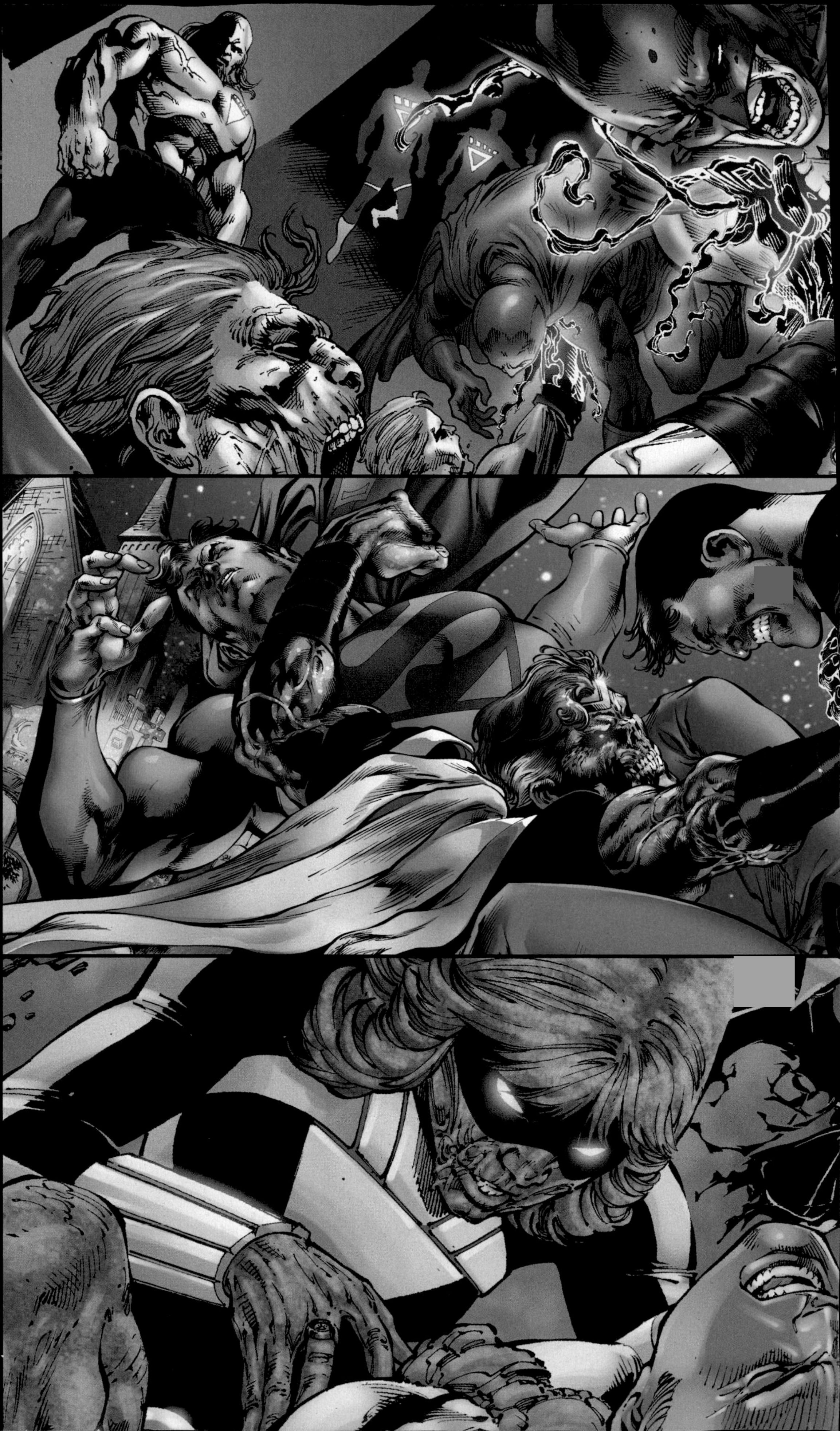

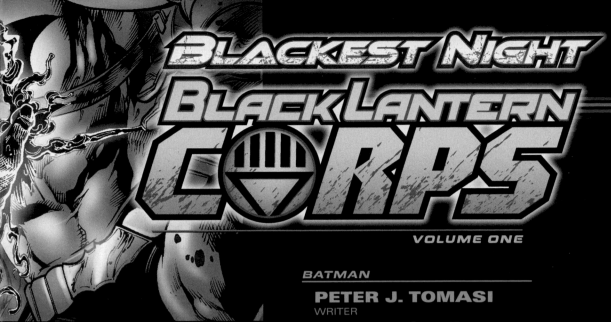

BLACKEST NIGHT
BLACK LANTERN CORPS

VOLUME ONE

BATMAN

PETER J. TOMASI
WRITER

ARDIAN SYAF
PENCILLER

VICENTE CIFUENTES
JOHN DELL
INKERS

NEI RUFFINO
COLORIST

JOHN J. HILL
LETTERER

SUPERMAN

JAMES ROBINSON
WRITER

EDDY BARROWS
ALLAN GOLDMAN
PENCILLERS

RUY JOSÉ
JULIO FERREIRA
EBER FERREIRA
INKERS

ROD REIS
COLORIST

STEVE WANDS
LETTERER

TITANS

J.T. KRUL
WRITER

ED BENES
PENCILLER

ROB HUNTER
JON SIBAL
JP MAYER
SCOTT WILLIAMS
ED BENES
INKERS

HI-FI DESIGN
COLORIST

ROB CLARK JR.
LETTERER

BATMAN CREATED BY **BOB KANE**

SUPERMAN CREATED BY **JERRY SIEGEL & JOE SHUSTER**

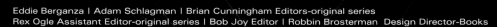

Eddie Berganza I Adam Schlagman I Brian Cunningham Editors-original series
Rex Ogle Assistant Editor-original series I Bob Joy Editor I Robbin Brosterman Design Director-Books

Bob Harras Senior VP – Editor-in-Chief, DC Comics

Diane Nelson President I Dan DiDio and Jim Lee Co-Publishers
Geoff Johns Chief Creative Officer I John Rood Executive VP – Sales, Marketing & Business Development
Amy Genkins Senior VP – Business and Legal Affairs I Nairi Gardiner Senior VP – Finance
Jeff Boison VP – Publishing Planning I Mark Chiarello VP – Art Direction & Design
John Cunningham VP – Marketing I Terri Cunningham VP – Editorial Administration
Alison Gill Senior VP – Manufacturing & Operations I Hank Kanalz Senior VP – Vertigo & Integrated Publishing
Jay Kogan VP – Business & Legal Affairs, Publishing I Jack Mahan VP – Business Affairs, Talent
Nick Napolitano VP – Manufacturing Administration I Sue Pohja VP – Book Sales
Courtney Simmons Senior VP – Publicity I Bob Wayne Senior VP – Sales

Cover by Rodolfo Migliari

BLACKEST NIGHT: BLACK LANTERN CORPS VOLUME 1 Published by DC Comics.
Cover, text and compilation Copyright © 2010 DC Comics. All Rights Reserved.

DC COMICS 4000 Warner Blvd., Burbank, CA 91522 A Warner Bros. Entertainment Company

Printed by Transcontinental Interglobe, Beauceville, QC, Canada. 4/17/15. Fourth Printing
ISBN: 978-1-4012-2804-0

SUSTAINABLE Certified Chain of Custody
FORESTRY Promoting Sustainable Forestry
INITIATIVE www.sfiprogram.org
SFI-00507

This Label only applies to the text section

Library of Congress Cataloging-in-Publication Data

Tomasi, Peter J.
            Blackest Night. Volume one, Black Lantern Corps / Peter J. Tomasi, James Robinson, J.T. Krul, Ardian Syaf ... [et al.].
         p. cm.
    "Originally published in single magazine form in Blackest Night: Batman 1-3, Blackest Night: Superman 1-3, Blackest Night: Titans 1-3."–Tp
verso.
    ISBN 978-1-4012-3164-4 (alk. paper)
    1. Graphic novels. 2. Comic books. 3. Strips. I. Tomasi, Peter J.. II. Title. III. Title: Blackest night volume one black lantern corps
  PN6728.G742 T59 2010
  741.5'973–dc23
                                        2012372947

THE STORY SO FAR...

Billions of years ago, the self-appointed Guardians of the Universe recruited thousands of sentient beings from across the cosmos to join their intergalactic police force: the Green Lantern Corps.

Chosen because they are able to overcome great fear, the Green Lanterns patrol their respective space sectors armed with power rings capable of wielding the emerald energy of willpower into whatever constructs they can imagine.

Hal Jordan is the greatest of them all.

When the dying Green Lantern Abin Sur crashed on Earth, he chose Hal Jordan to be his successor, for his indomitable will and ability to overcome great fear. As the protector of Sector 2814, Hal has saved Earth from destruction, even died in its service and been reborn.

Thaal Sinestro of Korugar was once considered the greatest Green Lantern of them all.

As Abin Sur's friend, Sinestro became Jordan's mentor in the Corps. But after being sentenced to the Anti-Matter Universe for abusing his power, Sinestro learned of the yellow light of fear being mined on Qward. Wielding a new golden power ring fueled by terror, Sinestro drafted thousands of the most horrific, psychotic and sadistic beings in the universe, and with their doctrine of fear, burned all who opposed them.

When the Green Lantern Corps battled their former ally during the Sinestro Corps War, the skies burned with green and gold as Earth erupted into an epic battle between good and evil. Though the Green Lanterns won, their brotherhood was broken and the peace they achieved was short-lived. In its aftermath, the Guardians rewrote the Book of Oa, the very laws by which their corps abides, and dissent grew within their members.

Now Hal Jordan will face his greatest challenge yet, as the prophecy foretold by Abin Sur in his dying moments finally comes to pass...

The emotional spectrum has splintered into seven factions. Seven corps were born.

The Green Lanterns. The Sinestro Corps. Atrocitus and the enraged Red Lanterns. Larfleeze, the avaricious keeper of the Orange Light. Former Guardians Ganthet and Sayd's small but hopeful Blue Lantern Corps. The Zamarons and their army of fierce and loving Star Sapphires. And the mysterious Indigo Tribe.

As the War of Light ignited between these Lantern bearers, the skies on every world darkened. In Sector 666, on the planet Ryut, a black lantern grew around the Anti-Monitor's corpse, using his vast energies to empower it.

The first of the Black Lanterns, the Black Hand, has risen from the dead, heralding a greater power that will extinguish all of the light—and life—in the universe.

Now across thousands of worlds, the dead have risen, and Hal Jordan and all of Earth's greatest heroes must bear witness to Blackest Night, which will descend upon them all, without prejudice, mercy or reason.

BLACKEST NIGHT: BATMAN 1

Cover by Andy Kubert with Alex Sinclair

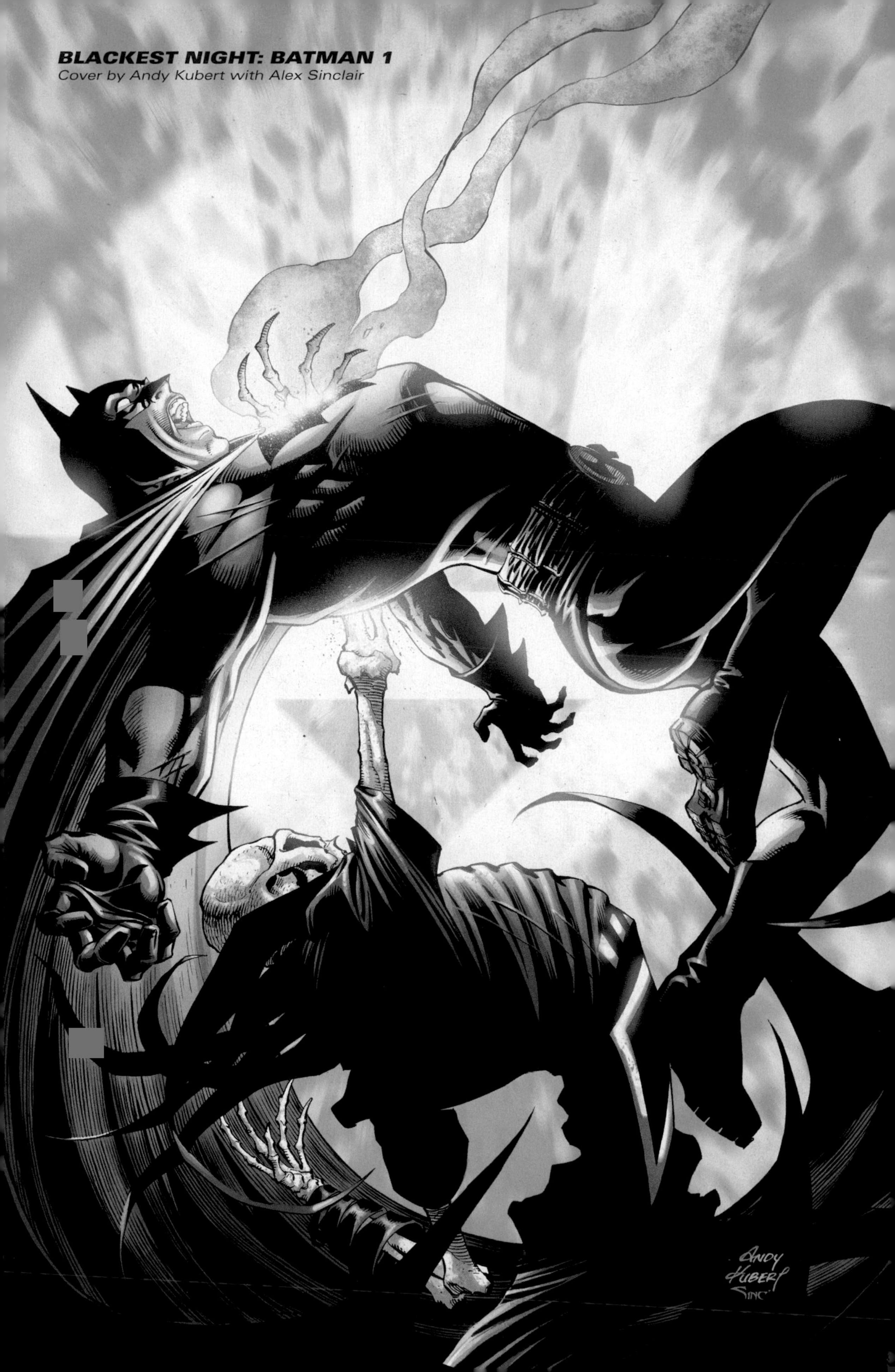
ANDY
KUBERT
SINC

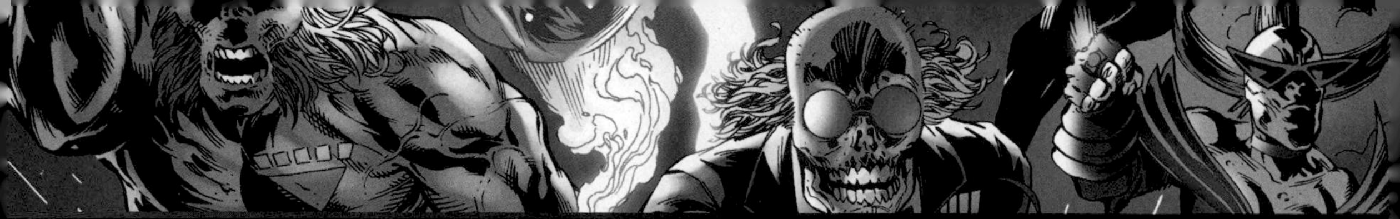

WHO BURNS WHO
PART ONE

PETER J. TOMASI
WRITER

ARDIAN SYAF
PENCILS

JOHN DELL
VICENTE CIFUENTES
INKS

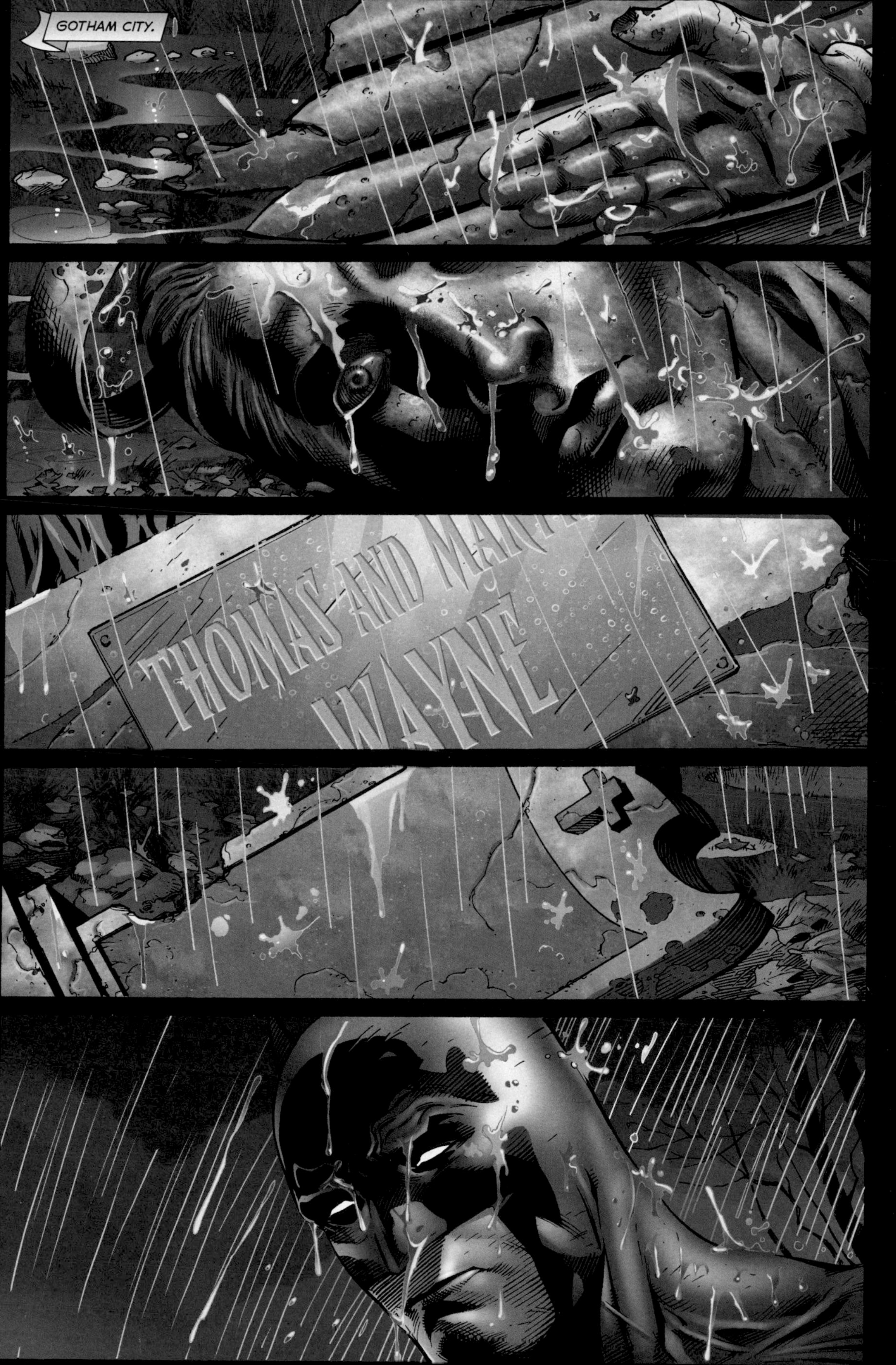
GOTHAM CITY.
THOMAS AND
WAYNE

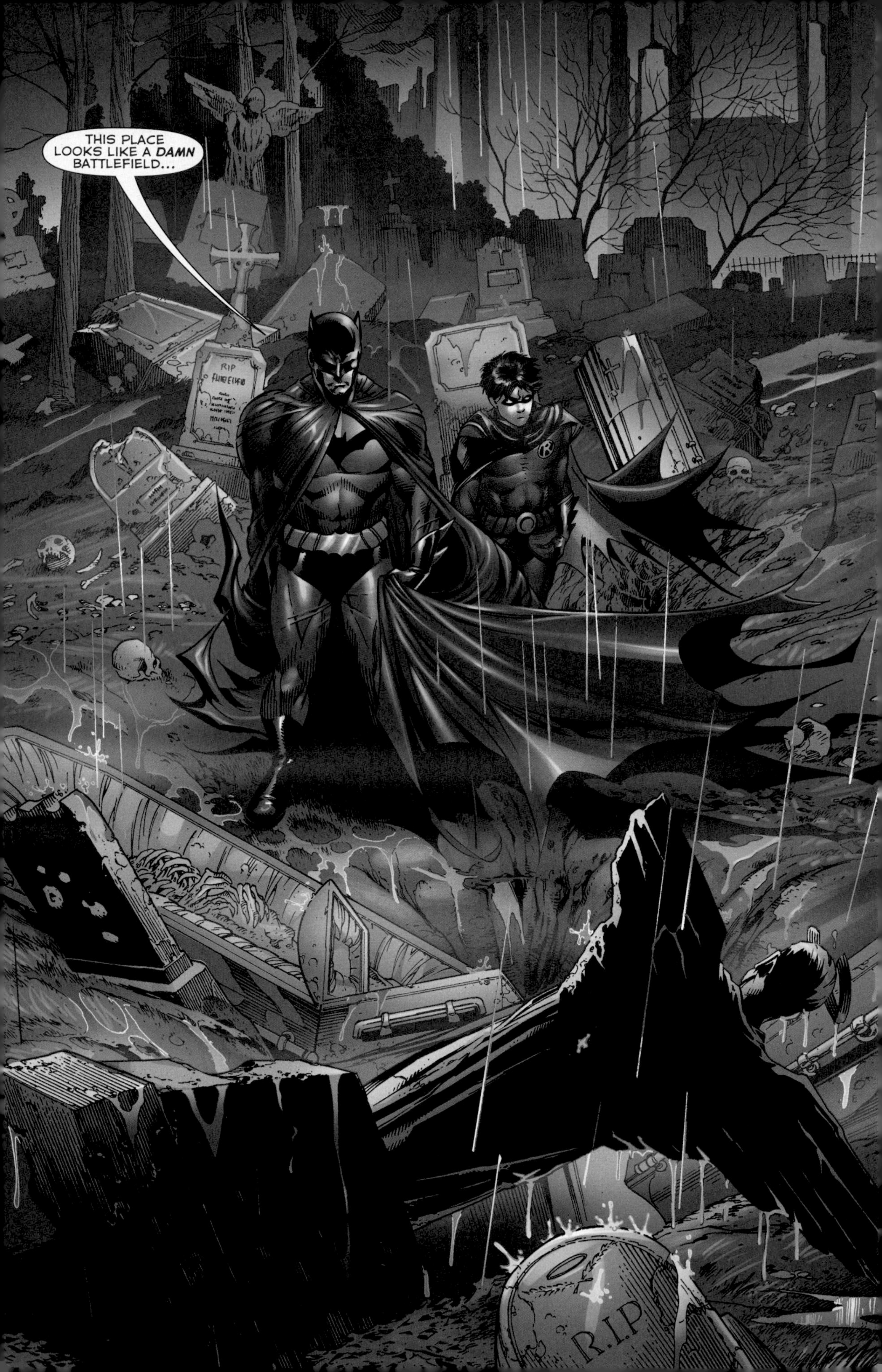
THIS PLACE LOOKS LIKE A *DAMN* BATTLEFIELD...

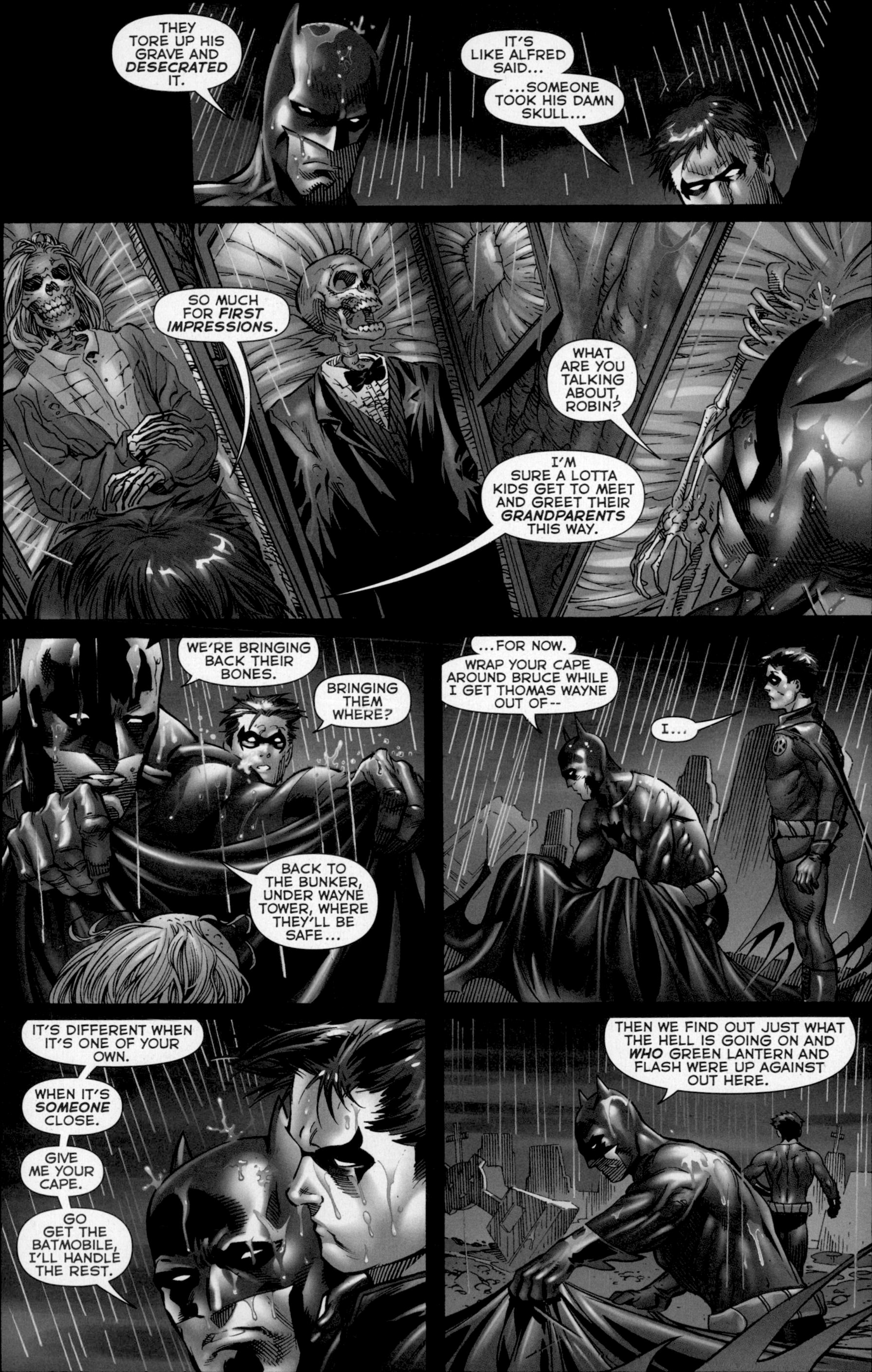
THEY TORE UP HIS GRAVE AND *DESECRATED* IT.
IT'S LIKE ALFRED SAID...
...SOMEONE TOOK HIS DAMN SKULL...
SO MUCH FOR *FIRST IMPRESSIONS*.
WHAT ARE YOU TALKING ABOUT, ROBIN?
I'M SURE A LOTTA KIDS GET TO MEET AND GREET THEIR *GRANDPARENTS* THIS WAY.
WE'RE BRINGING BACK THEIR BONES.
BRINGING THEM WHERE?
BACK TO THE BUNKER, UNDER WAYNE TOWER, WHERE THEY'LL BE SAFE...
...FOR NOW.
WRAP YOUR CAPE AROUND BRUCE WHILE I GET THOMAS WAYNE OUT OF--
I...
IT'S DIFFERENT WHEN IT'S ONE OF YOUR OWN.
WHEN IT'S *SOMEONE* CLOSE.
GIVE ME YOUR CAPE.
GO GET THE BATMOBILE, I'LL HANDLE THE REST.
THEN WE FIND OUT JUST WHAT THE HELL IS GOING ON AND *WHO* GREEN LANTERN AND FLASH WERE UP AGAINST OUT HERE.

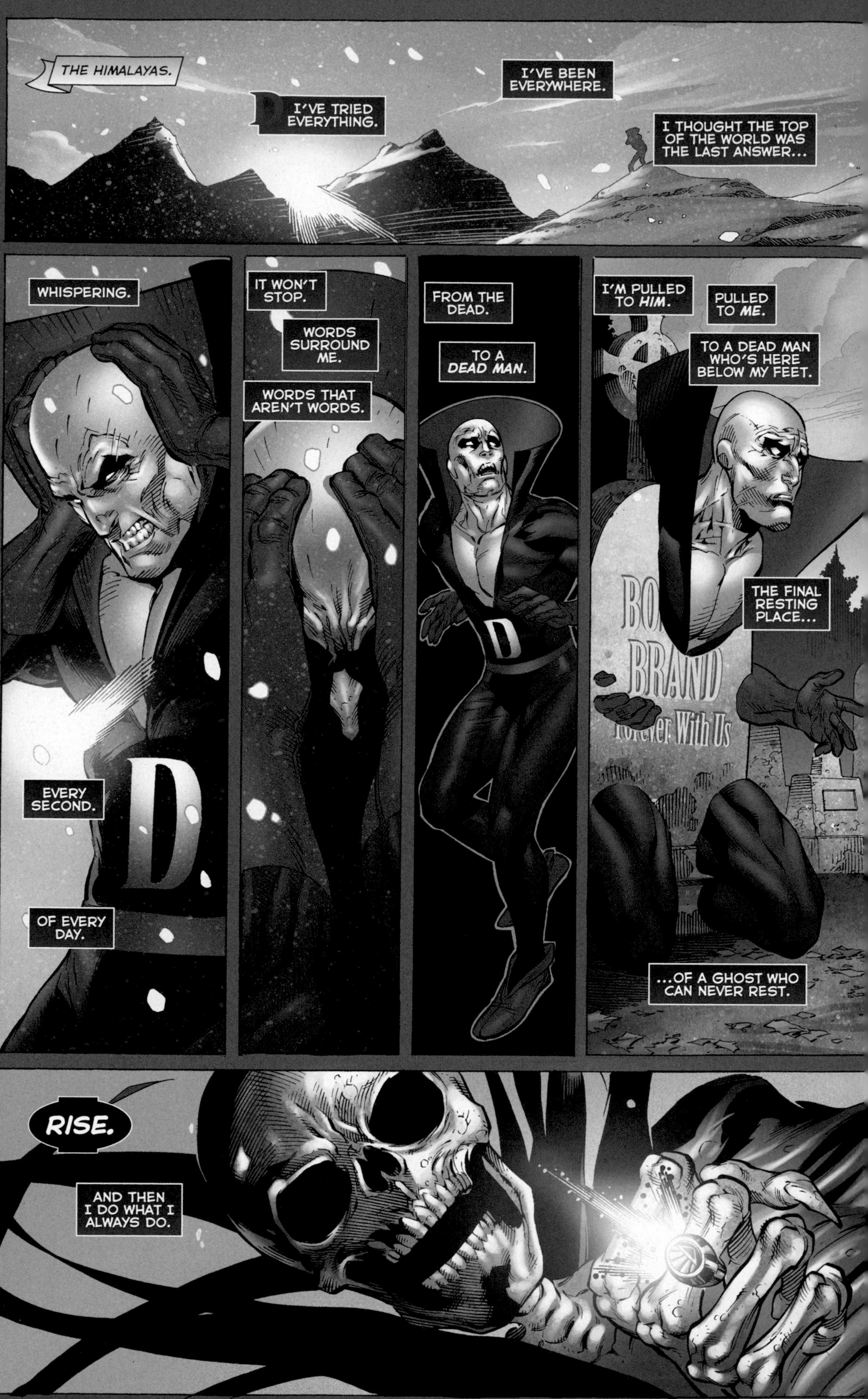
THE HIMALAYAS.
I'VE TRIED EVERYTHING.
I'VE BEEN EVERYWHERE.
I THOUGHT THE TOP OF THE WORLD WAS THE LAST ANSWER...
WHISPERING.
EVERY SECOND.
OF EVERY DAY.
IT WON'T STOP.
WORDS SURROUND ME.
WORDS THAT AREN'T WORDS.
FROM THE DEAD.
TO A *DEAD MAN*.
I'M PULLED TO *HIM*.
PULLED TO *ME*.
TO A DEAD MAN WHO'S HERE BELOW MY FEET.
BRAND
Forever With Us
THE FINAL RESTING PLACE...
...OF A GHOST WHO CAN NEVER REST.
RISE.
AND THEN I DO WHAT I ALWAYS DO.

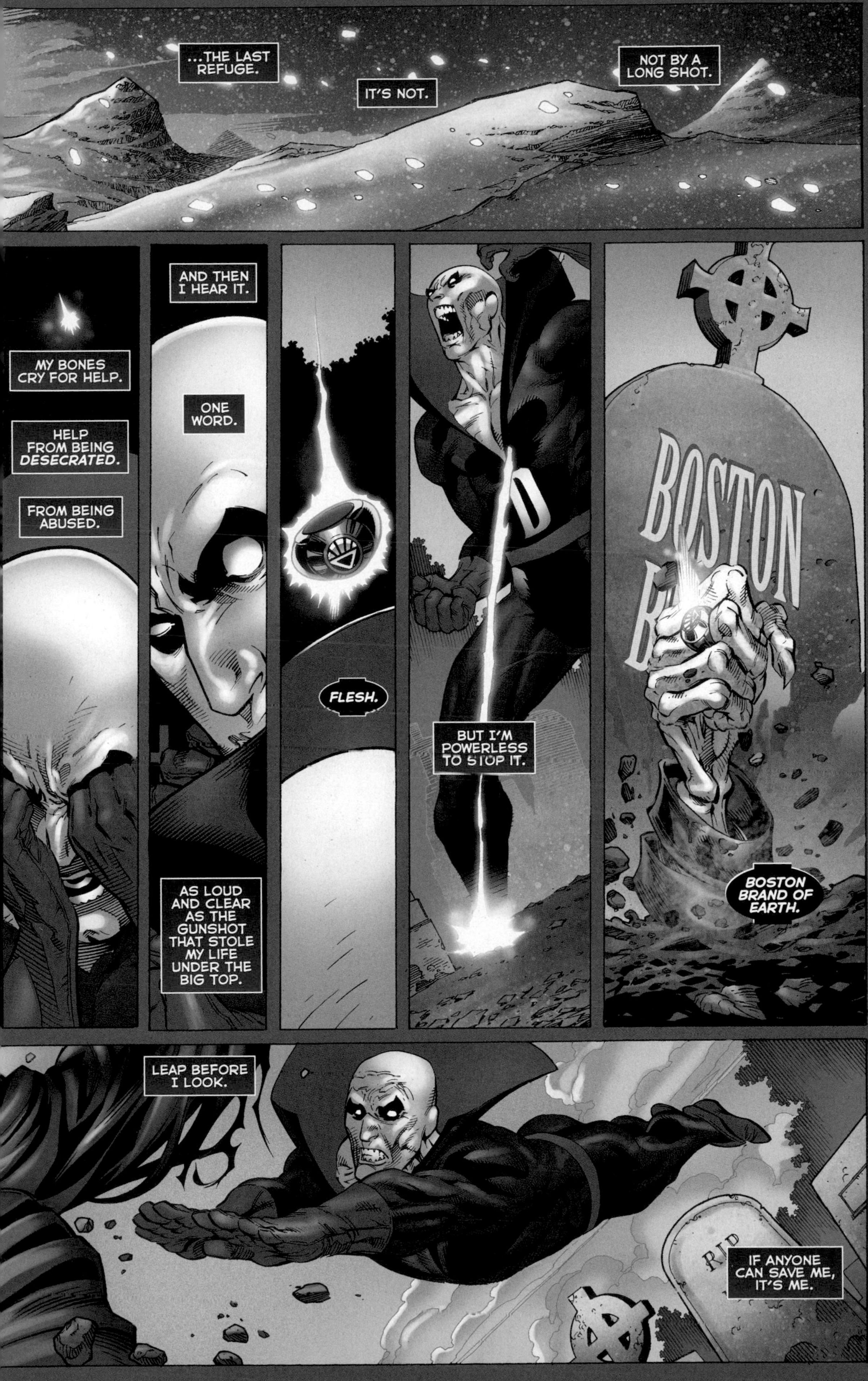
...THE LAST REFUGE.
IT'S NOT.
NOT BY A LONG SHOT.
MY BONES CRY FOR HELP.
HELP FROM BEING DESECRATED.
FROM BEING ABUSED.
AND THEN I HEAR IT.
ONE WORD.
AS LOUD AND CLEAR AS THE GUNSHOT THAT STOLE MY LIFE UNDER THE BIG TOP.
FLESH.
BUT I'M POWERLESS TO STOP IT.
BOSTON
BOSTON BRAND OF EARTH.
LEAP BEFORE I LOOK.
RIP
IF ANYONE CAN SAVE ME, IT'S ME.

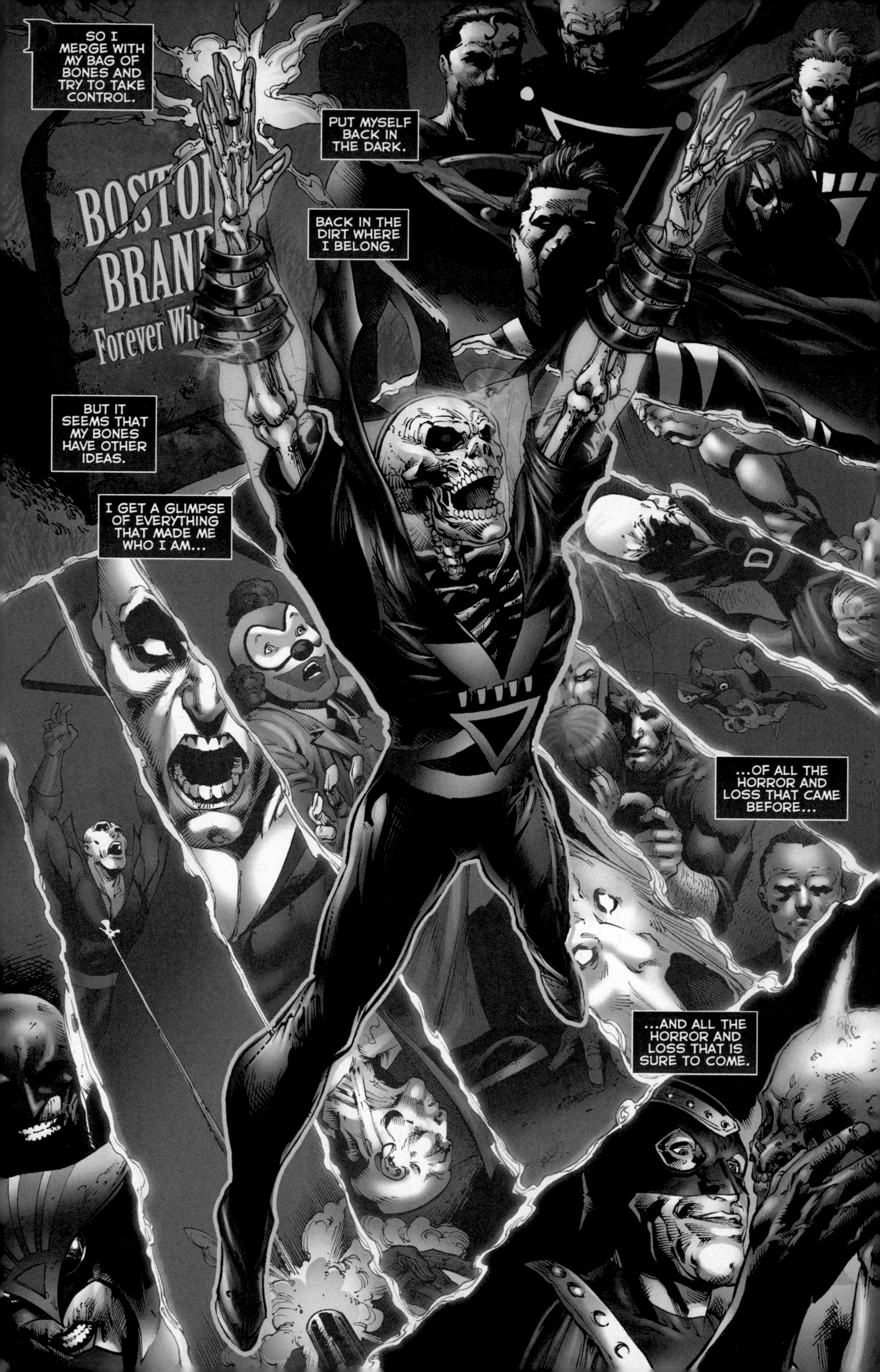
SO I MERGE WITH MY BAG OF BONES AND TRY TO TAKE CONTROL.
PUT MYSELF BACK IN THE DARK.
BACK IN THE DIRT WHERE I BELONG.
BOSTON BRAND
Forever Wi
BUT IT SEEMS THAT MY BONES HAVE OTHER IDEAS.
I GET A GLIMPSE OF EVERYTHING THAT MADE ME WHO I AM...
...OF ALL THE HORROR AND LOSS THAT CAME BEFORE...
...AND ALL THE HORROR AND LOSS THAT IS SURE TO COME.

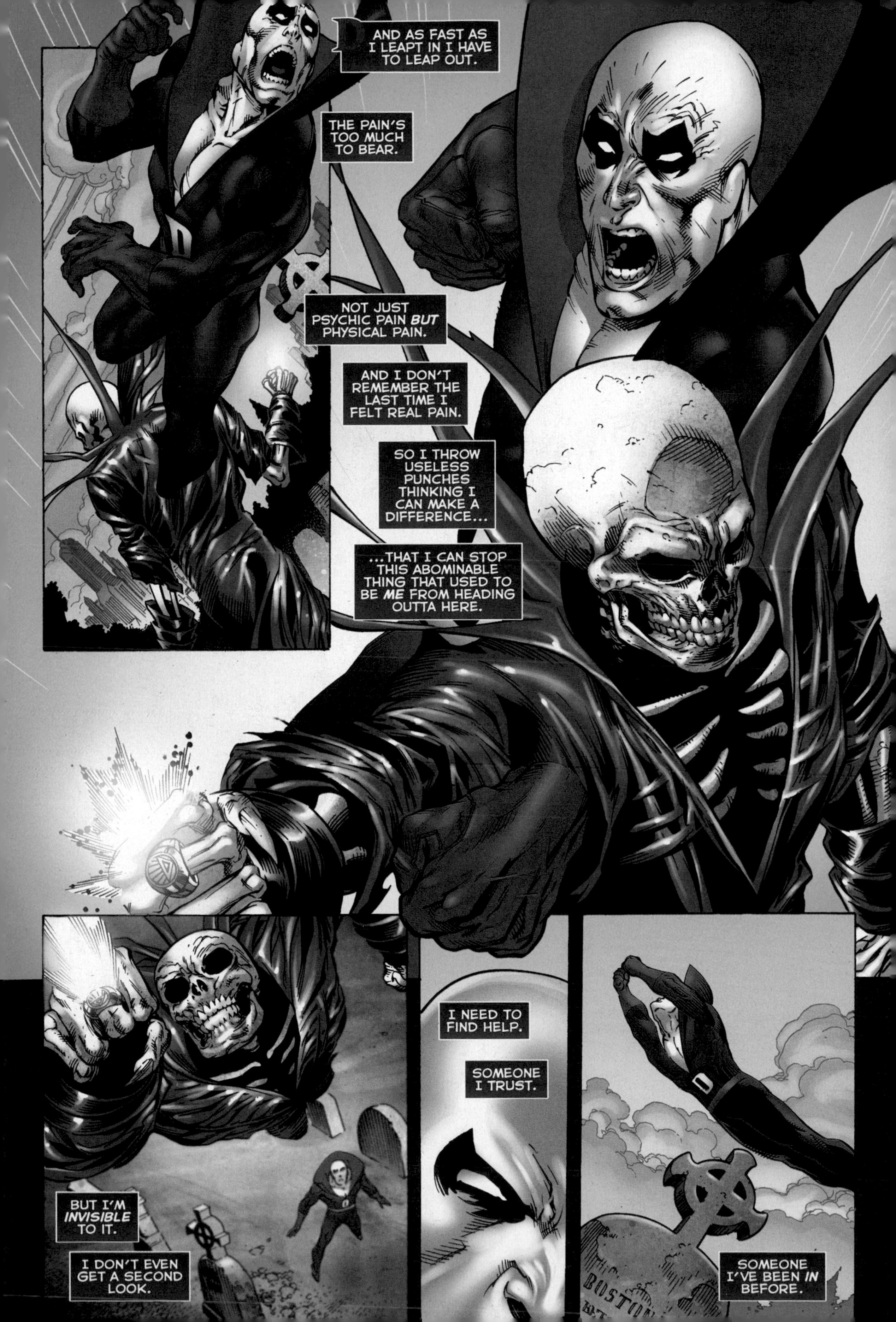
AND AS FAST AS I LEAPT IN I HAVE TO LEAP OUT.
THE PAIN'S TOO MUCH TO BEAR.
NOT JUST PSYCHIC PAIN *BUT* PHYSICAL PAIN.
AND I DON'T REMEMBER THE LAST TIME I FELT REAL PAIN.
SO I THROW USELESS PUNCHES THINKING I CAN MAKE A DIFFERENCE...
...THAT I CAN STOP THIS ABOMINABLE THING THAT USED TO BE *ME* FROM HEADING OUTTA HERE.
BUT I'M *INVISIBLE* TO IT.
I DON'T EVEN GET A SECOND LOOK.
I NEED TO FIND HELP.
SOMEONE I TRUST.
SOMEONE I'VE BEEN *IN* BEFORE.
BOSTON

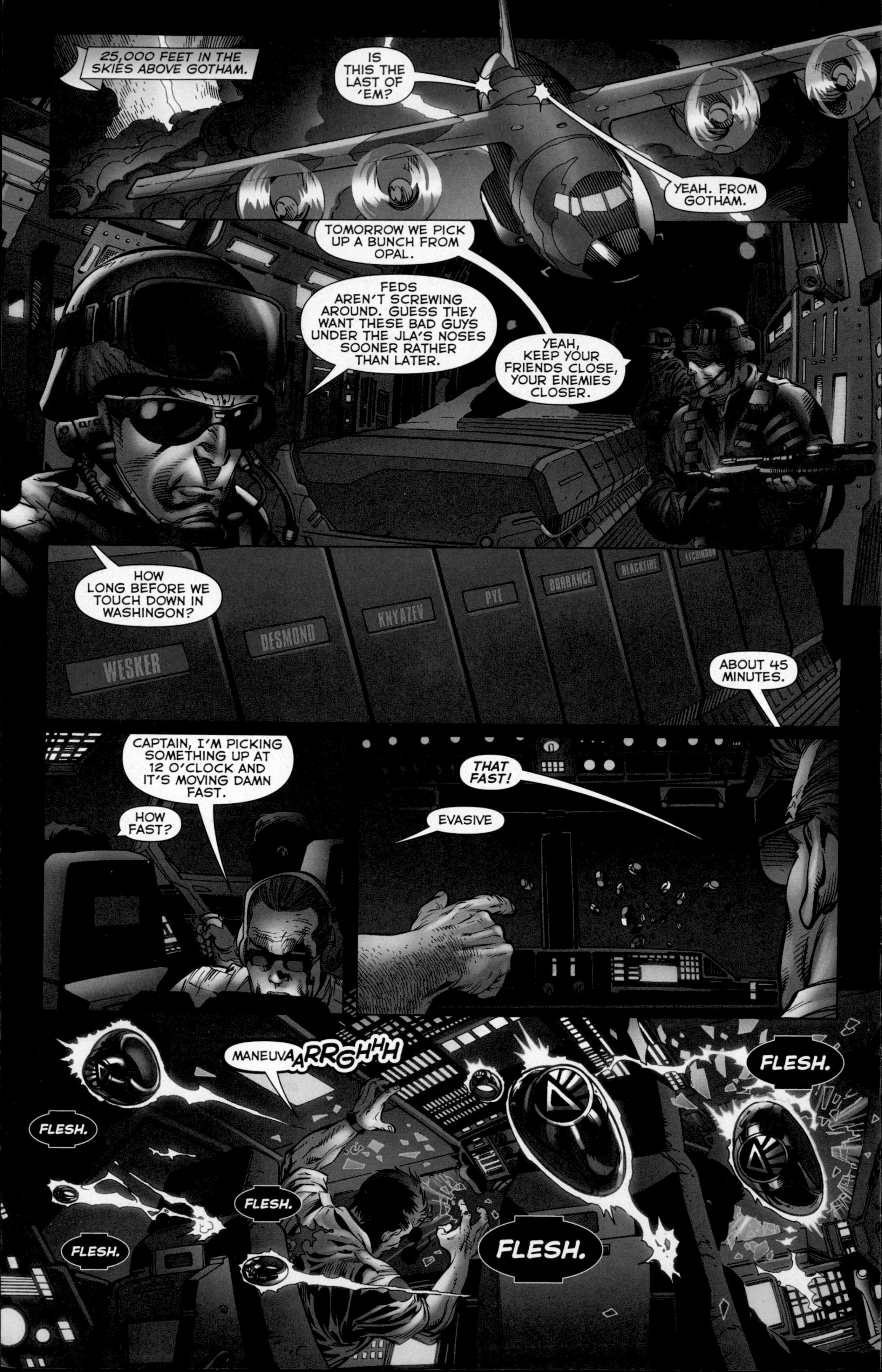
25,000 FEET IN THE SKIES ABOVE GOTHAM.
IS THIS THE LAST OF 'EM?
YEAH. FROM GOTHAM.
TOMORROW WE PICK UP A BUNCH FROM OPAL.
FEDS AREN'T SCREWING AROUND. GUESS THEY WANT THESE BAD GUYS UNDER THE JLA'S NOSES SOONER RATHER THAN LATER.
YEAH, KEEP YOUR FRIENDS CLOSE, YOUR ENEMIES CLOSER.
HOW LONG BEFORE WE TOUCH DOWN IN WASHINGON?
WESKER
DESMOND
KNYAZEV
PYE
DORRANCE
BLACKFIRE
ABOUT 45 MINUTES.
CAPTAIN, I'M PICKING SOMETHING UP AT 12 O'CLOCK AND IT'S MOVING DAMN FAST.
HOW FAST?
THAT FAST!
EVASIVE
MANEUVAARRRGHHH
FLESH.
FLESH.
FLESH.
FLESH.
FLESH.

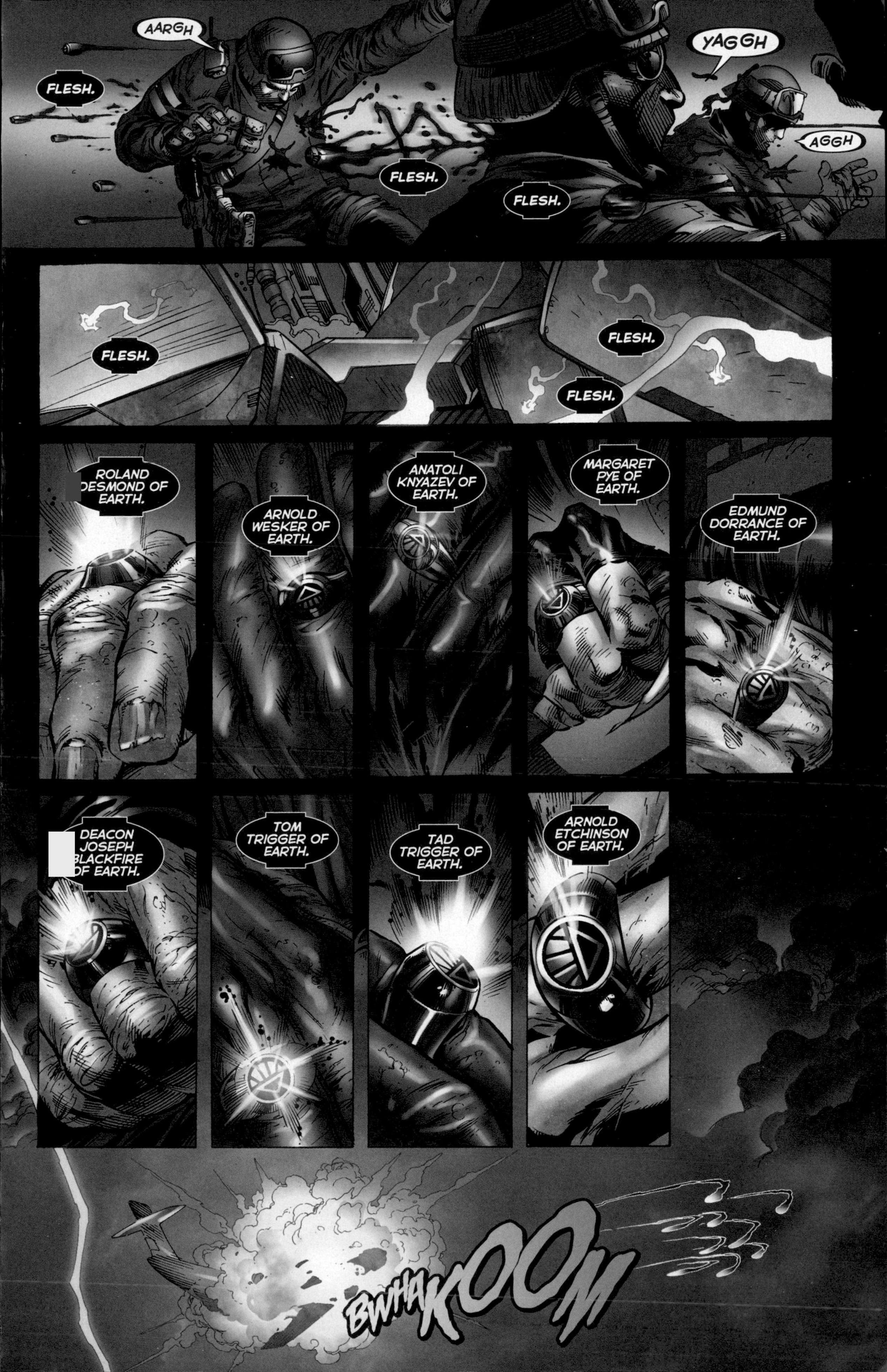
AARGH
FLESH.
YAGGH
AGGH
FLESH.
FLESH.
FLESH.
FLESH.
FLESH.
ROLAND [redacted]ESMOND OF EARTH.
ARNOLD WESKER OF EARTH.
ANATOLI KNYAZEV OF EARTH.
MARGARET PYE OF EARTH.
EDMUND DORRANCE OF EARTH.
DEACON JOSEPH BLACKFIRE OF EARTH.
TOM TRIGGER OF EARTH.
TAD TRIGGER OF EARTH.
ARNOLD ETCHINSON OF EARTH.
BWHAKOOM

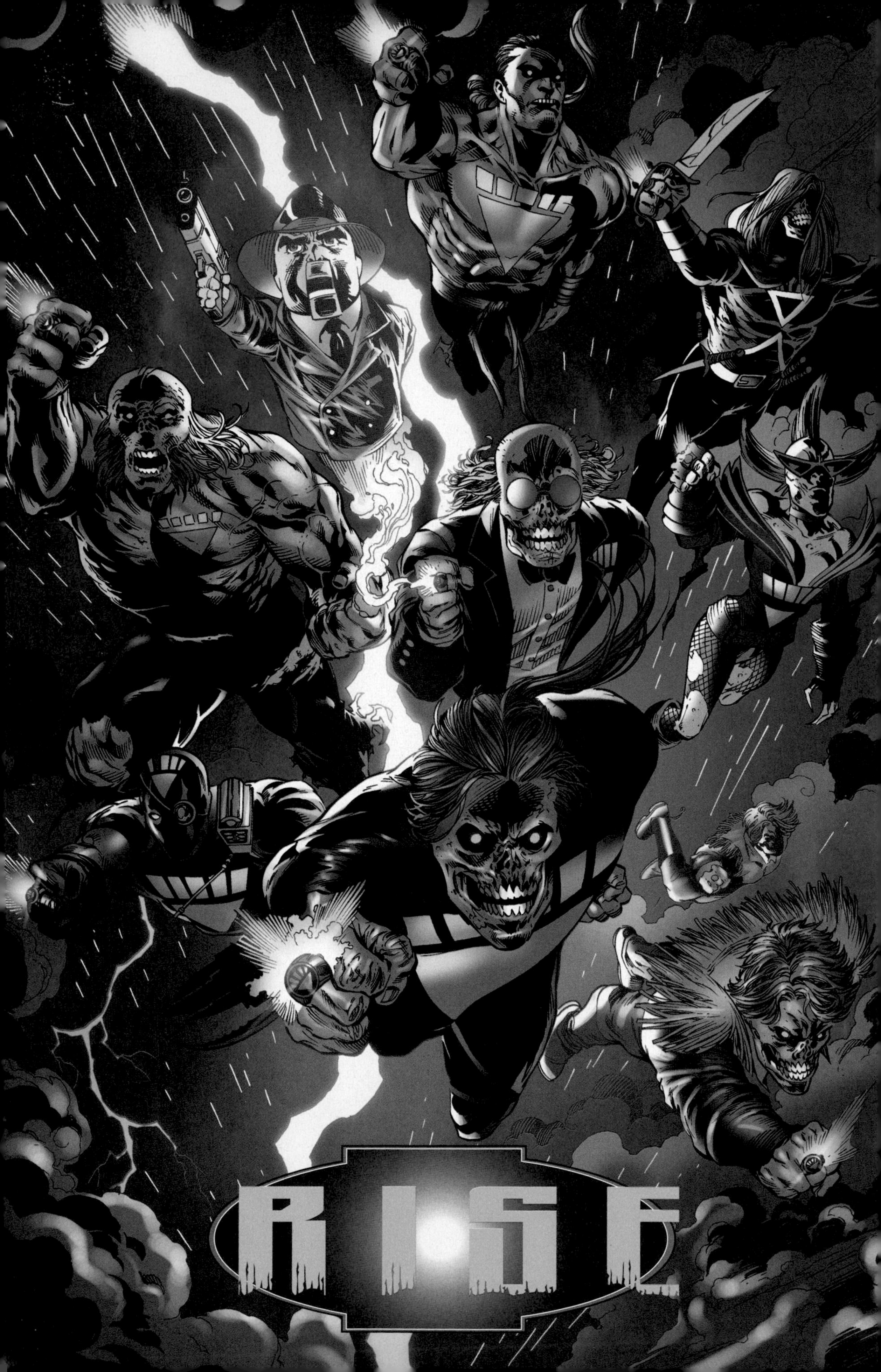
RISE

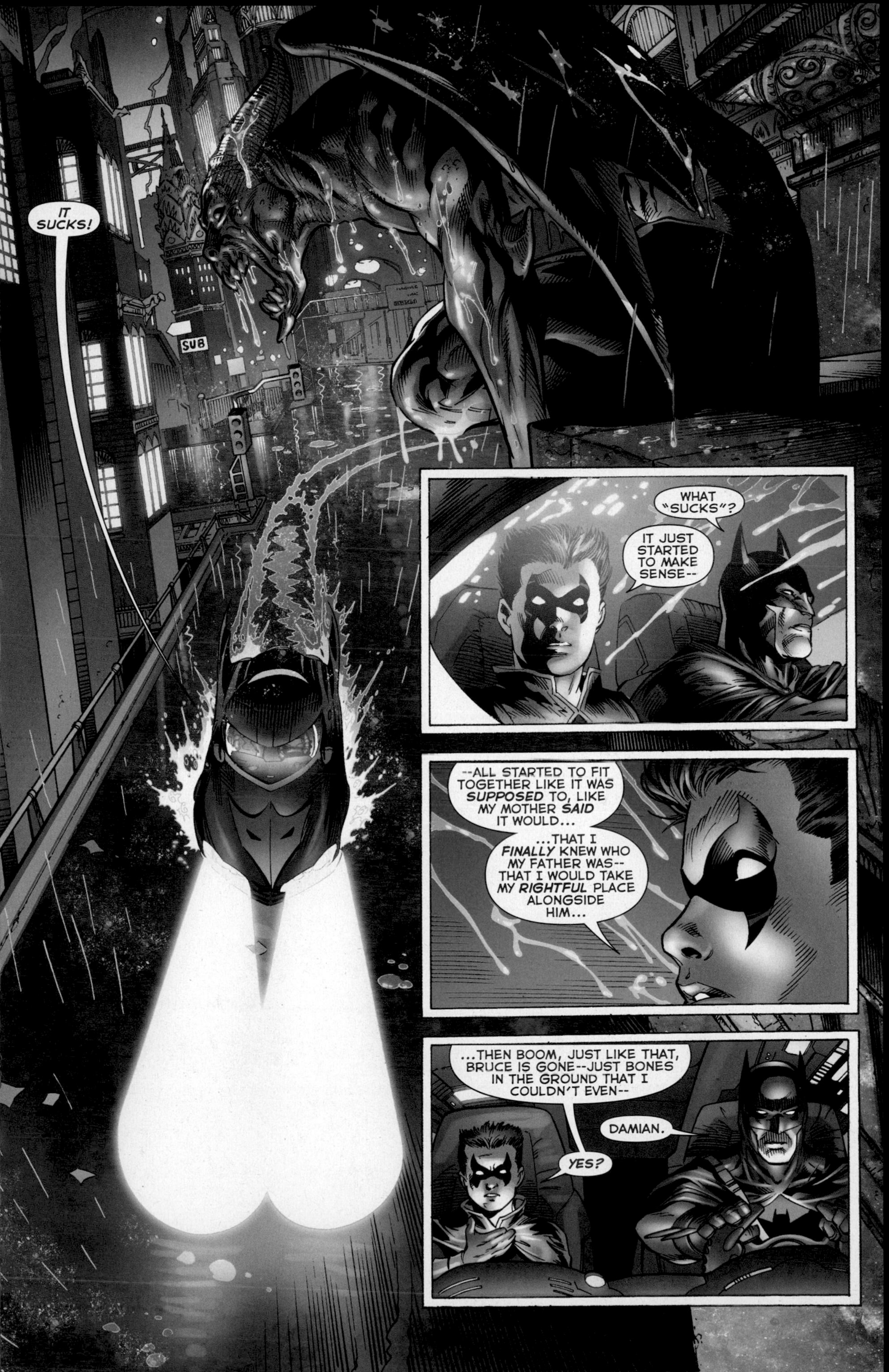
IT SUCKS!
WHAT "SUCKS"?
IT JUST STARTED TO MAKE SENSE--
--ALL STARTED TO FIT TOGETHER LIKE IT WAS SUPPOSED TO, LIKE MY MOTHER SAID IT WOULD...
...THAT I FINALLY KNEW WHO MY FATHER WAS--THAT I WOULD TAKE MY RIGHTFUL PLACE ALONGSIDE HIM...
...THEN BOOM, JUST LIKE THAT, BRUCE IS GONE--JUST BONES IN THE GROUND THAT I COULDN'T EVEN--
DAMIAN.
YES?

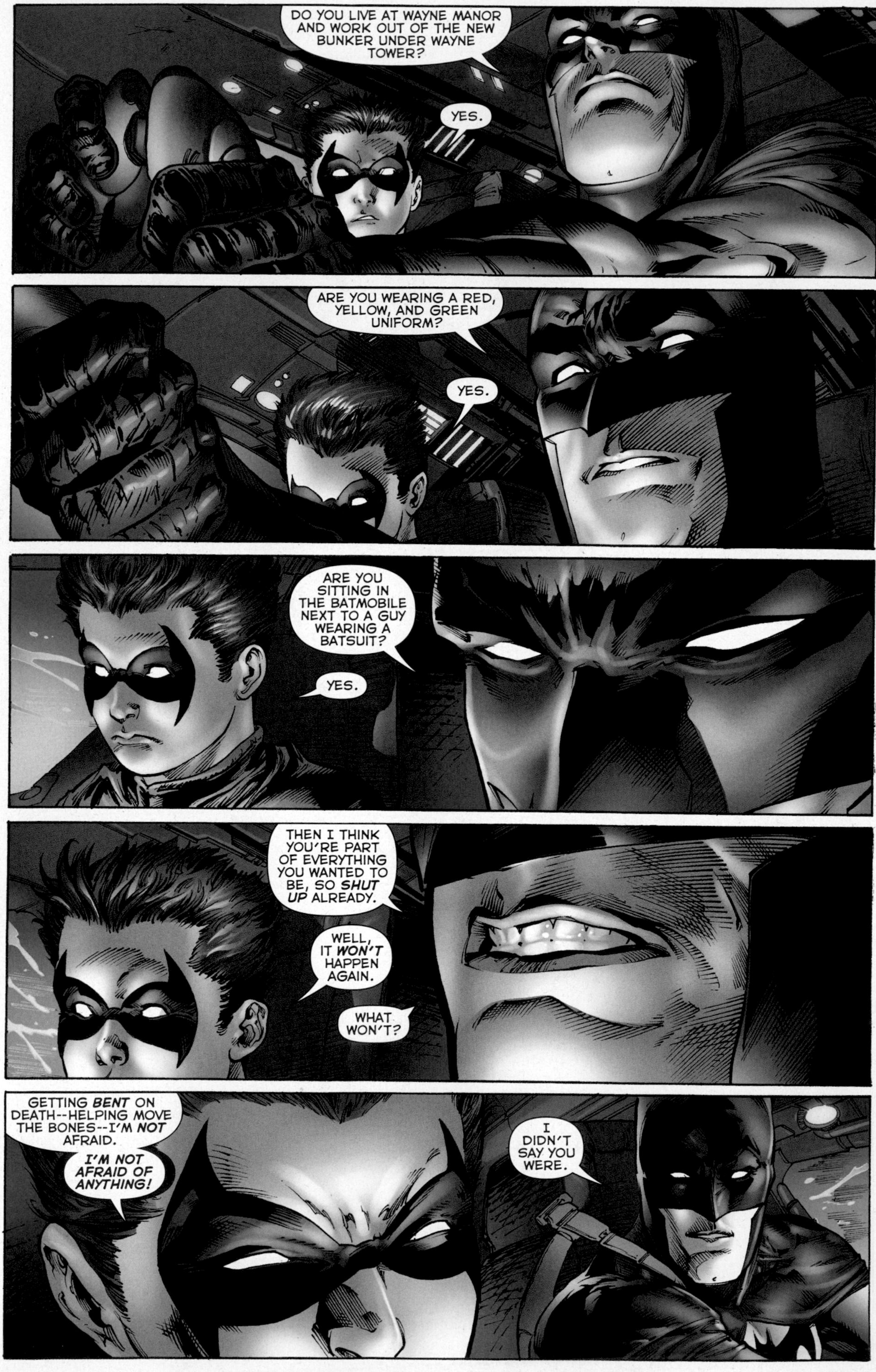
DO YOU LIVE AT WAYNE MANOR AND WORK OUT OF THE NEW BUNKER UNDER WAYNE TOWER?
YES.
ARE YOU WEARING A RED, YELLOW, AND GREEN UNIFORM?
YES.
ARE YOU SITTING IN THE BATMOBILE NEXT TO A GUY WEARING A BATSUIT?
YES.
THEN I THINK YOU'RE PART OF EVERYTHING YOU WANTED TO BE, SO SHUT UP ALREADY.
WELL, IT WON'T HAPPEN AGAIN.
WHAT WON'T?
GETTING BENT ON DEATH--HELPING MOVE THE BONES--I'M NOT AFRAID.
I'M NOT AFRAID OF ANYTHING!
I DIDN'T SAY YOU WERE.

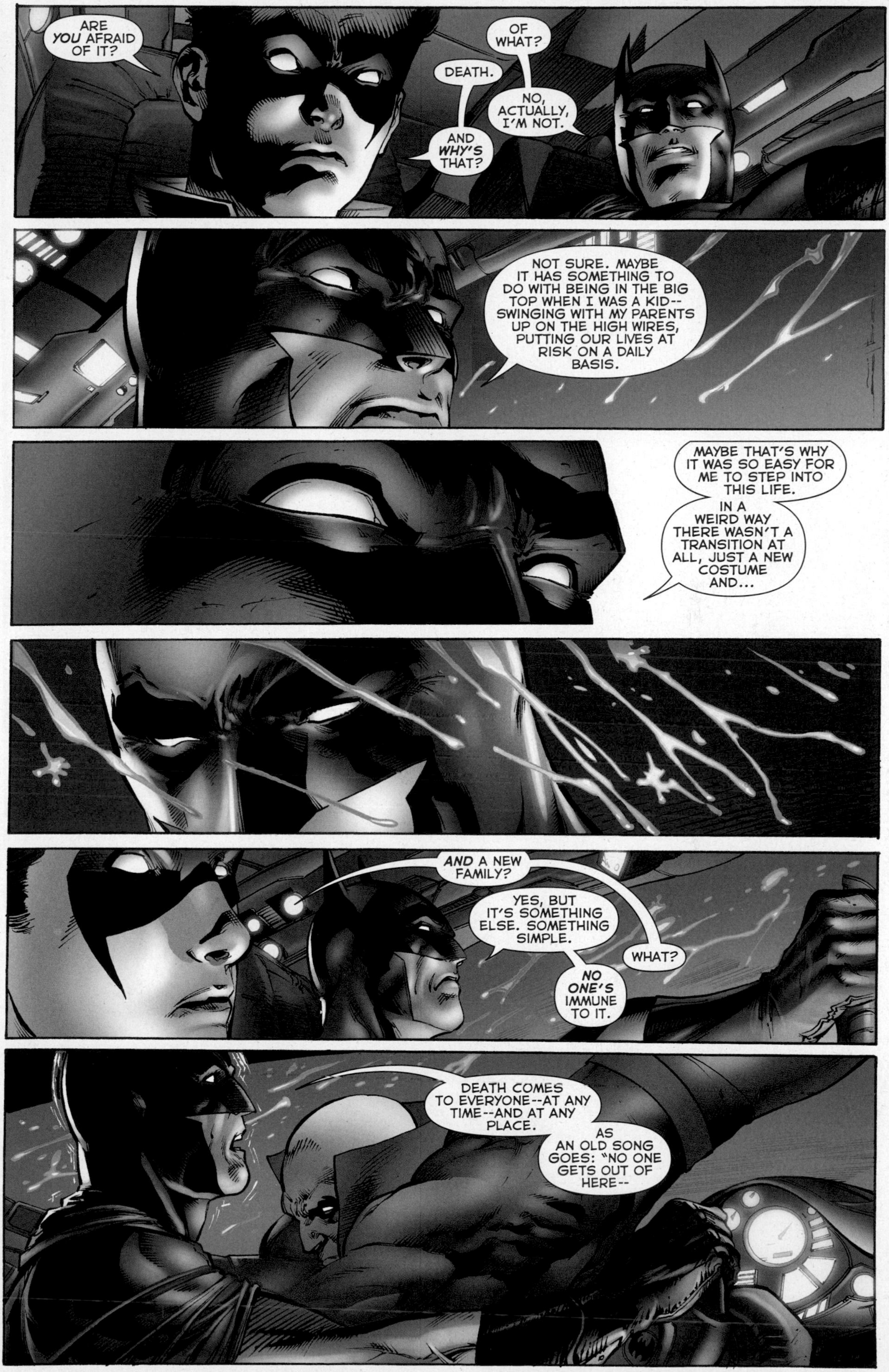
ARE YOU AFRAID OF IT?
OF WHAT?
DEATH.
NO, ACTUALLY, I'M NOT.
AND WHY'S THAT?
NOT SURE. MAYBE IT HAS SOMETHING TO DO WITH BEING IN THE BIG TOP WHEN I WAS A KID-- SWINGING WITH MY PARENTS UP ON THE HIGH WIRES, PUTTING OUR LIVES AT RISK ON A DAILY BASIS.
MAYBE THAT'S WHY IT WAS SO EASY FOR ME TO STEP INTO THIS LIFE.
IN A WEIRD WAY THERE WASN'T A TRANSITION AT ALL, JUST A NEW COSTUME AND...
AND A NEW FAMILY?
YES, BUT IT'S SOMETHING ELSE. SOMETHING SIMPLE.
WHAT?
NO ONE'S IMMUNE TO IT.
DEATH COMES TO EVERYONE--AT ANY TIME--AND AT ANY PLACE.
AS AN OLD SONG GOES: "NO ONE GETS OUT OF HERE--

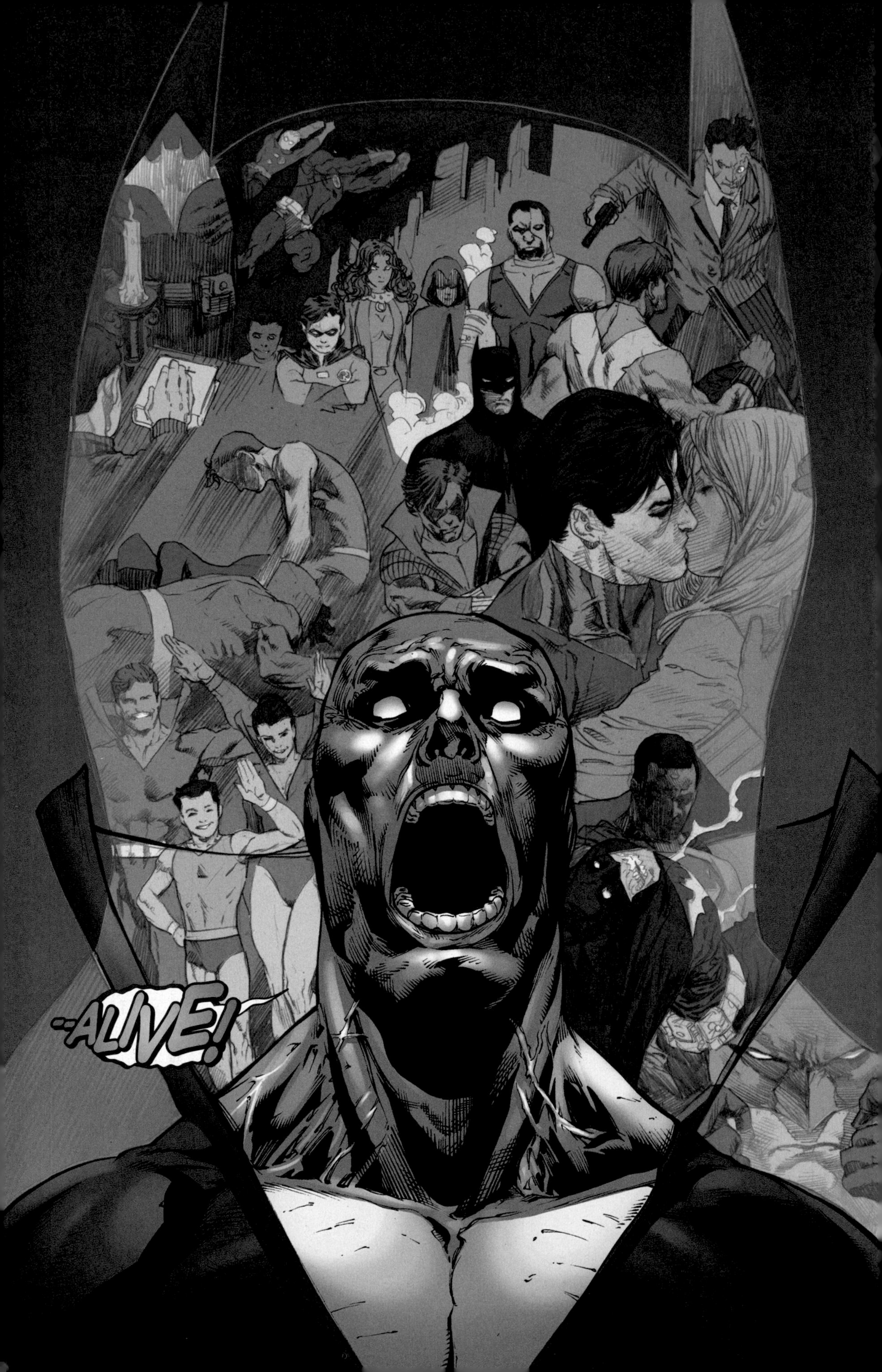
-ALIVE!

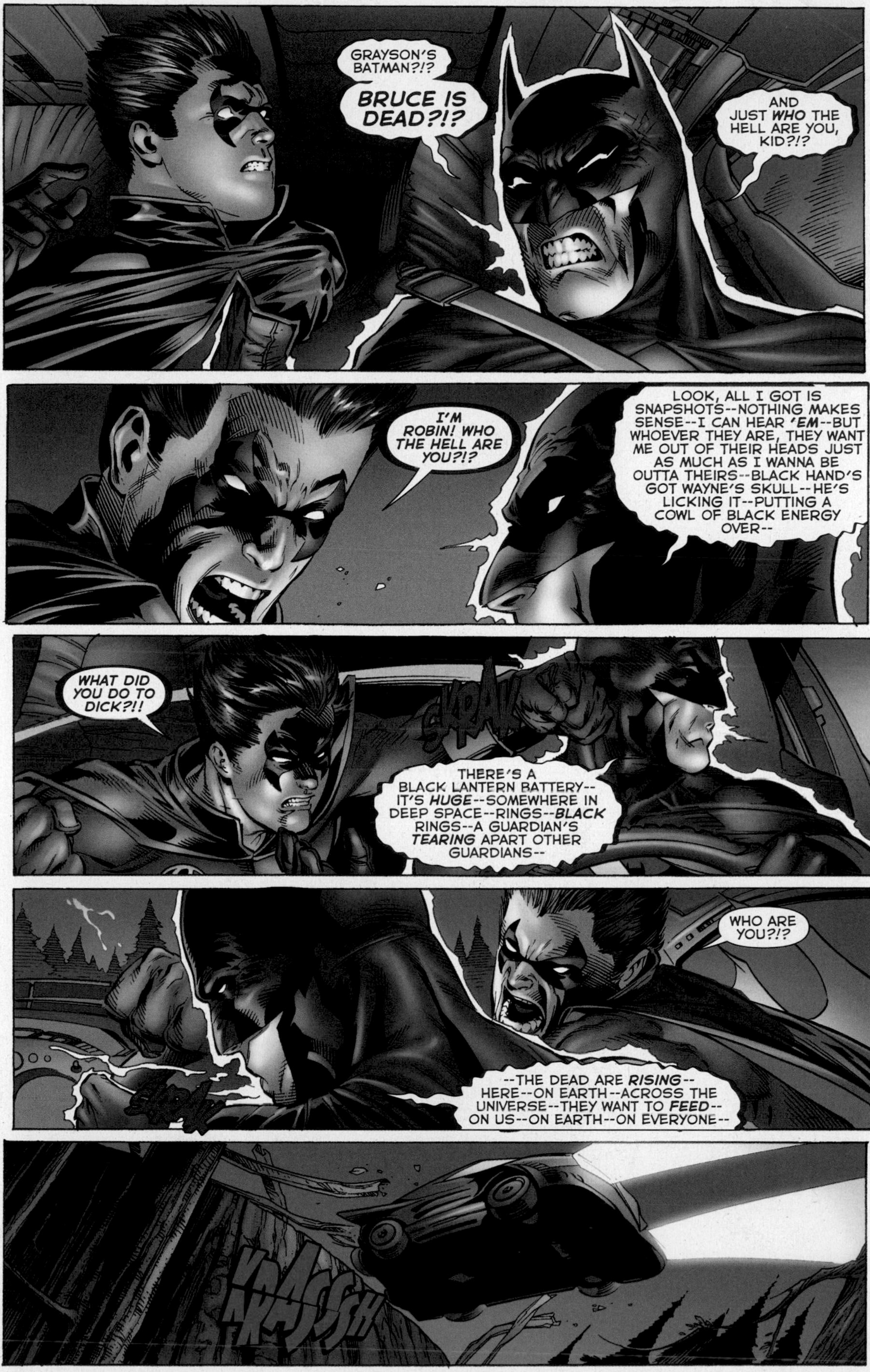
GRAYSON'S BATMAN?!?
BRUCE IS DEAD?!?
AND JUST WHO THE HELL ARE YOU, KID?!?
I'M ROBIN! WHO THE HELL ARE YOU?!?
LOOK, ALL I GOT IS SNAPSHOTS--NOTHING MAKES SENSE--I CAN HEAR 'EM--BUT WHOEVER THEY ARE, THEY WANT ME OUT OF THEIR HEADS JUST AS MUCH AS I WANNA BE OUTTA THEIRS--BLACK HAND'S GOT WAYNE'S SKULL--HE'S LICKING IT--PUTTING A COWL OF BLACK ENERGY OVER--
WHAT DID YOU DO TO DICK?!!
SKRAK
THERE'S A BLACK LANTERN BATTERY--IT'S HUGE--SOMEWHERE IN DEEP SPACE--RINGS--BLACK RINGS--A GUARDIAN'S TEARING APART OTHER GUARDIANS--
WHO ARE YOU?!?
--THE DEAD ARE RISING--HERE--ON EARTH--ACROSS THE UNIVERSE--THEY WANT TO FEED--ON US--ON EARTH--ON EVERYONE--
KRASSH

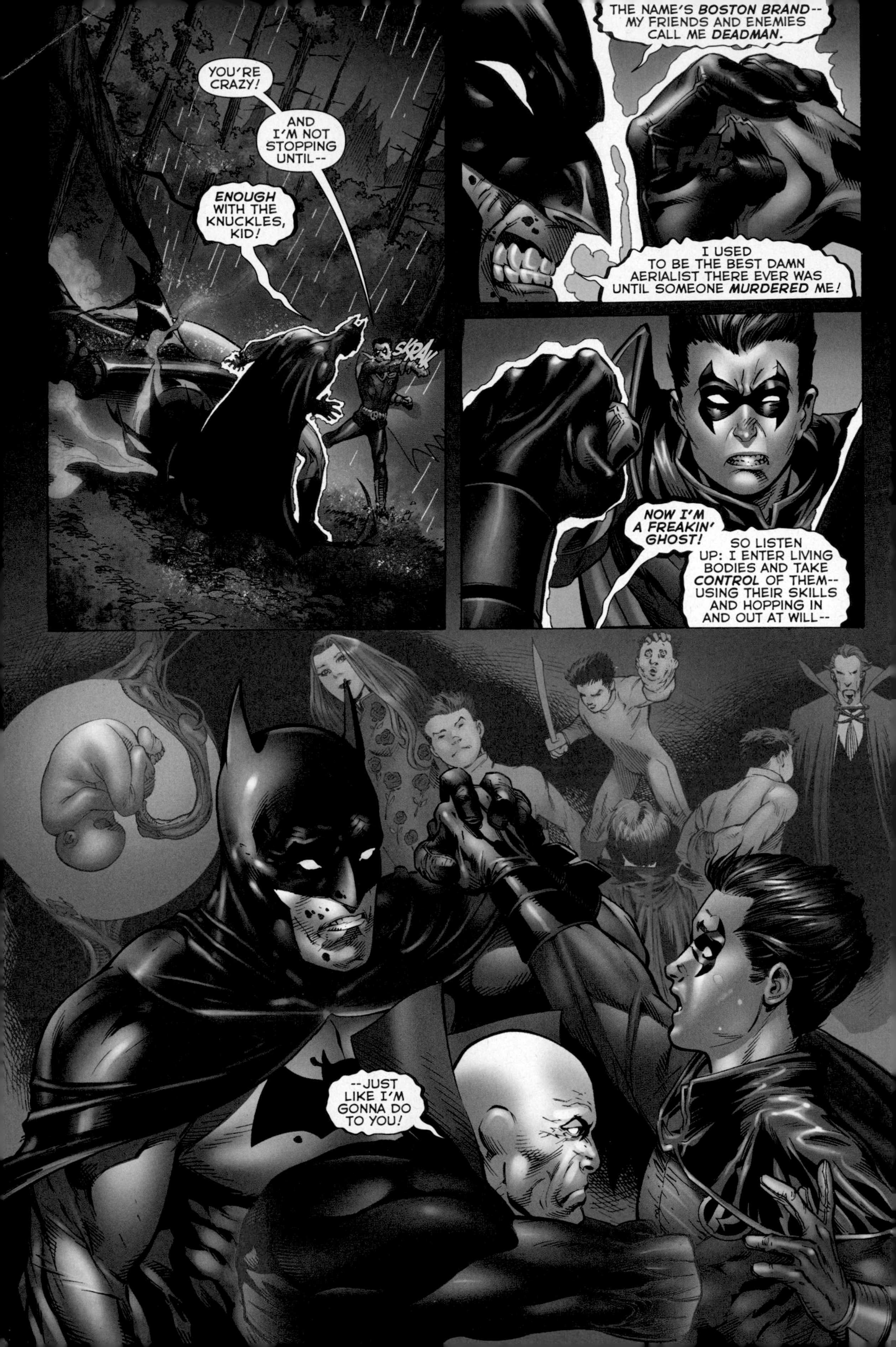
YOU'RE CRAZY!
AND I'M NOT STOPPING UNTIL--
ENOUGH WITH THE KNUCKLES, KID!
SKRAK
THE NAME'S BOSTON BRAND-- MY FRIENDS AND ENEMIES CALL ME DEADMAN.
FAP
I USED TO BE THE BEST DAMN AERIALIST THERE EVER WAS UNTIL SOMEONE MURDERED ME!
NOW I'M A FREAKIN' GHOST!
SO LISTEN UP: I ENTER LIVING BODIES AND TAKE CONTROL OF THEM-- USING THEIR SKILLS AND HOPPING IN AND OUT AT WILL--
--JUST LIKE I'M GONNA DO TO YOU!

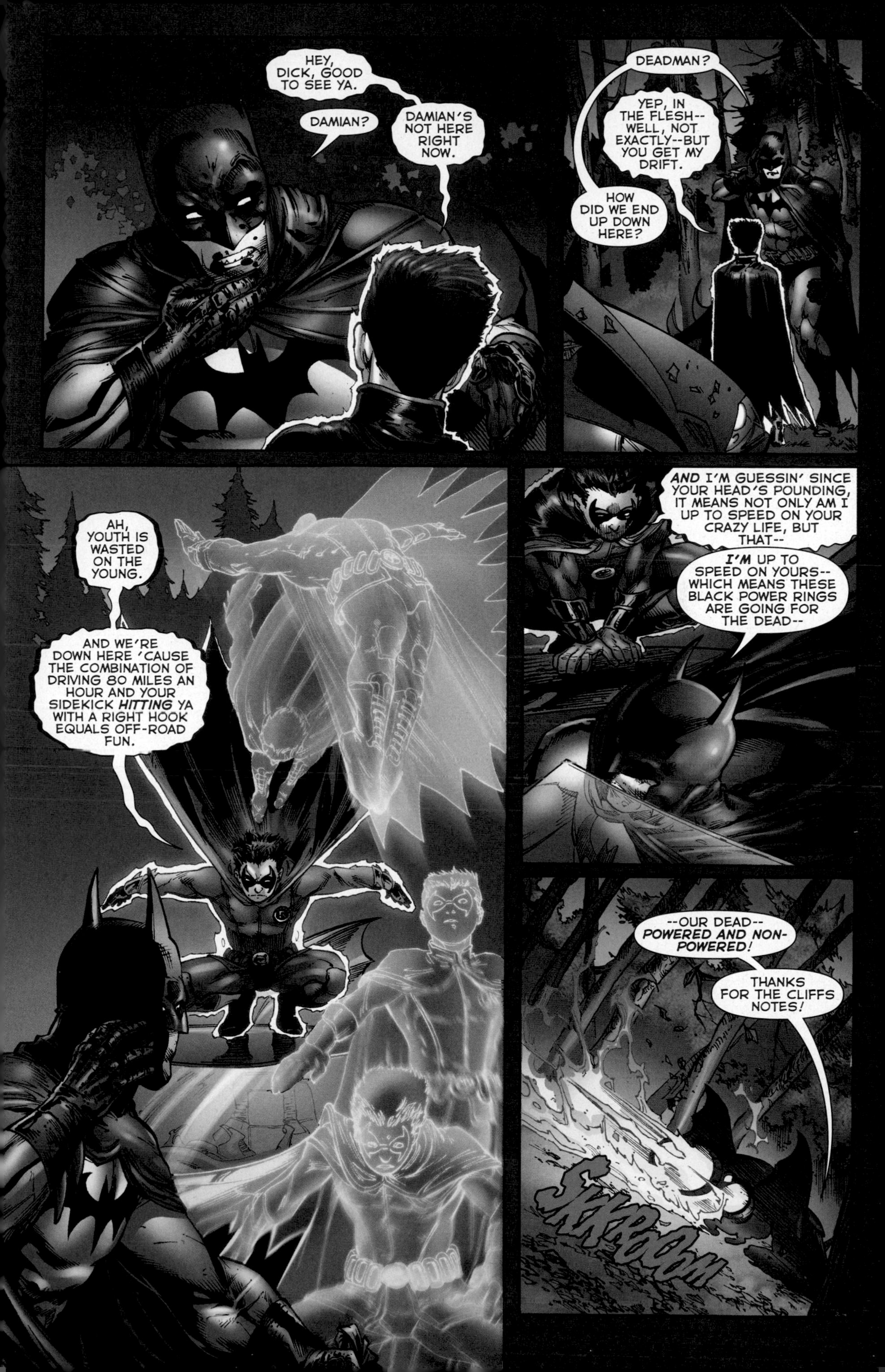
HEY, DICK, GOOD TO SEE YA.
DAMIAN?
DAMIAN'S NOT HERE RIGHT NOW.
DEADMAN?
YEP, IN THE FLESH-- WELL, NOT EXACTLY--BUT YOU GET MY DRIFT.
HOW DID WE END UP DOWN HERE?
AH, YOUTH IS WASTED ON THE YOUNG.
AND WE'RE DOWN HERE 'CAUSE THE COMBINATION OF DRIVING 80 MILES AN HOUR AND YOUR SIDEKICK HITTING YA WITH A RIGHT HOOK EQUALS OFF-ROAD FUN.
AND I'M GUESSIN' SINCE YOUR HEAD'S POUNDING, IT MEANS NOT ONLY AM I UP TO SPEED ON YOUR CRAZY LIFE, BUT THAT--
I'M UP TO SPEED ON YOURS-- WHICH MEANS THESE BLACK POWER RINGS ARE GOING FOR THE DEAD--
--OUR DEAD-- POWERED AND NON-POWERED!
THANKS FOR THE CLIFFS NOTES!
SKKROOOM

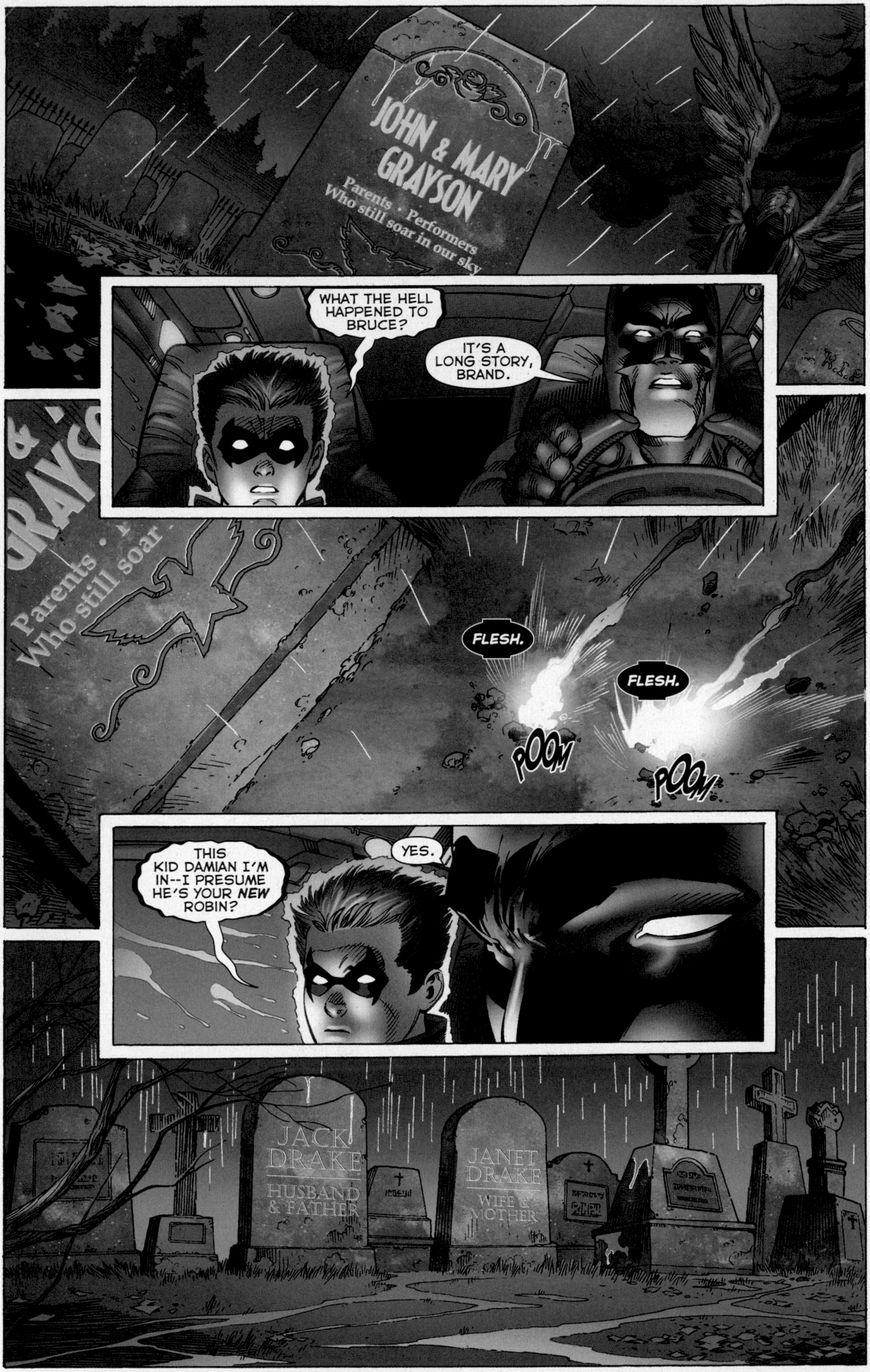
JOHN & MARY GRAYSON
Parents • Performers
Who still soar in our sky
WHAT THE HELL HAPPENED TO BRUCE?
IT'S A LONG STORY, BRAND.
FLESH.
FLESH.
POOM
POOM
THIS KID DAMIAN I'M IN--I PRESUME HE'S YOUR *NEW* ROBIN?
YES.
JACK DRAKE
HUSBAND & FATHER
JANET DRAKE
WIFE & MOTHER

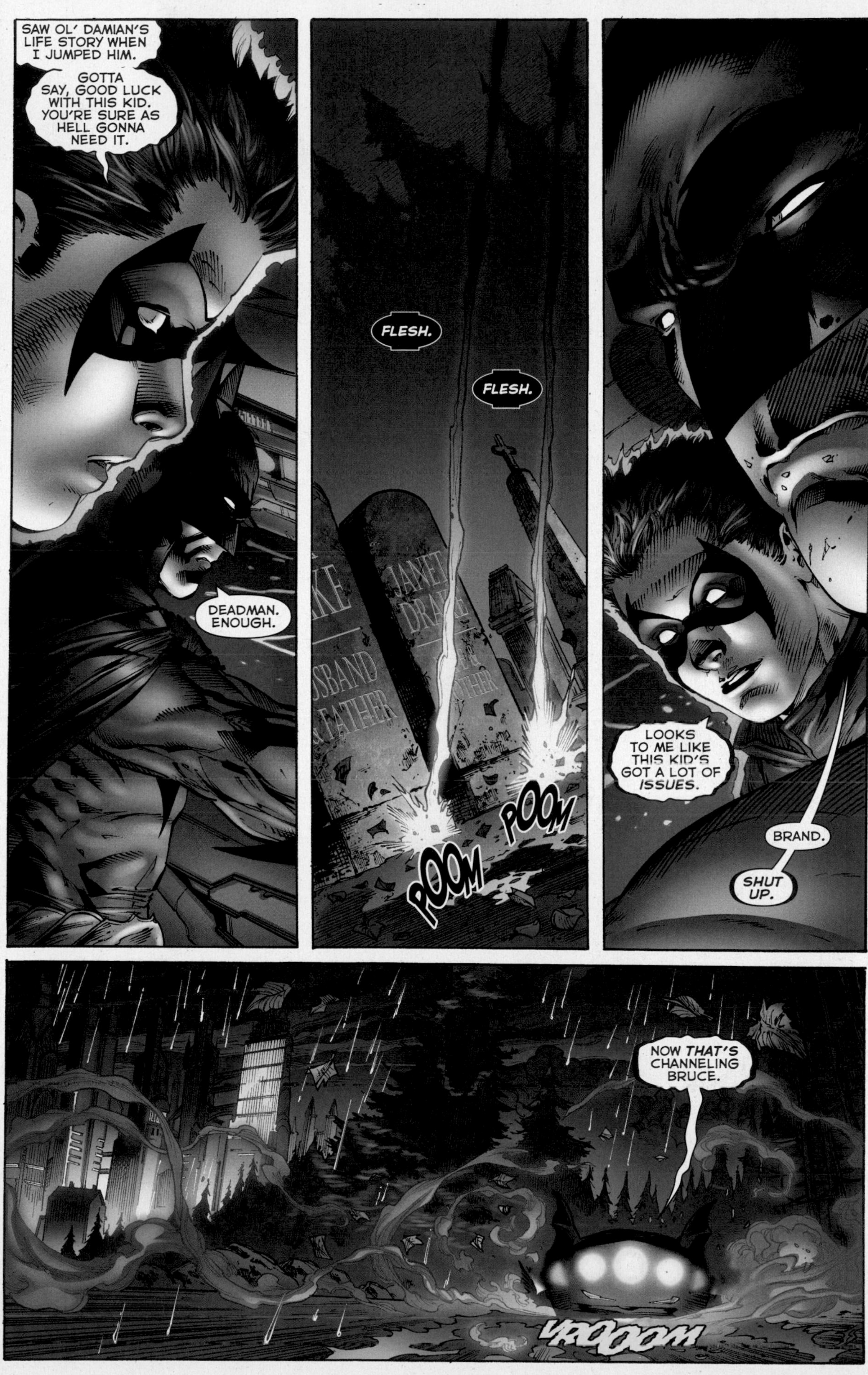
SAW OL' DAMIAN'S LIFE STORY WHEN I JUMPED HIM.
GOTTA SAY, GOOD LUCK WITH THIS KID. YOU'RE SURE AS HELL GONNA NEED IT.
DEADMAN. ENOUGH.
FLESH.
FLESH.
POOM
POOM
LOOKS TO ME LIKE THIS KID'S GOT A LOT OF ISSUES.
BRAND.
SHUT UP.
NOW THAT'S CHANNELING BRUCE.
VROOOOM

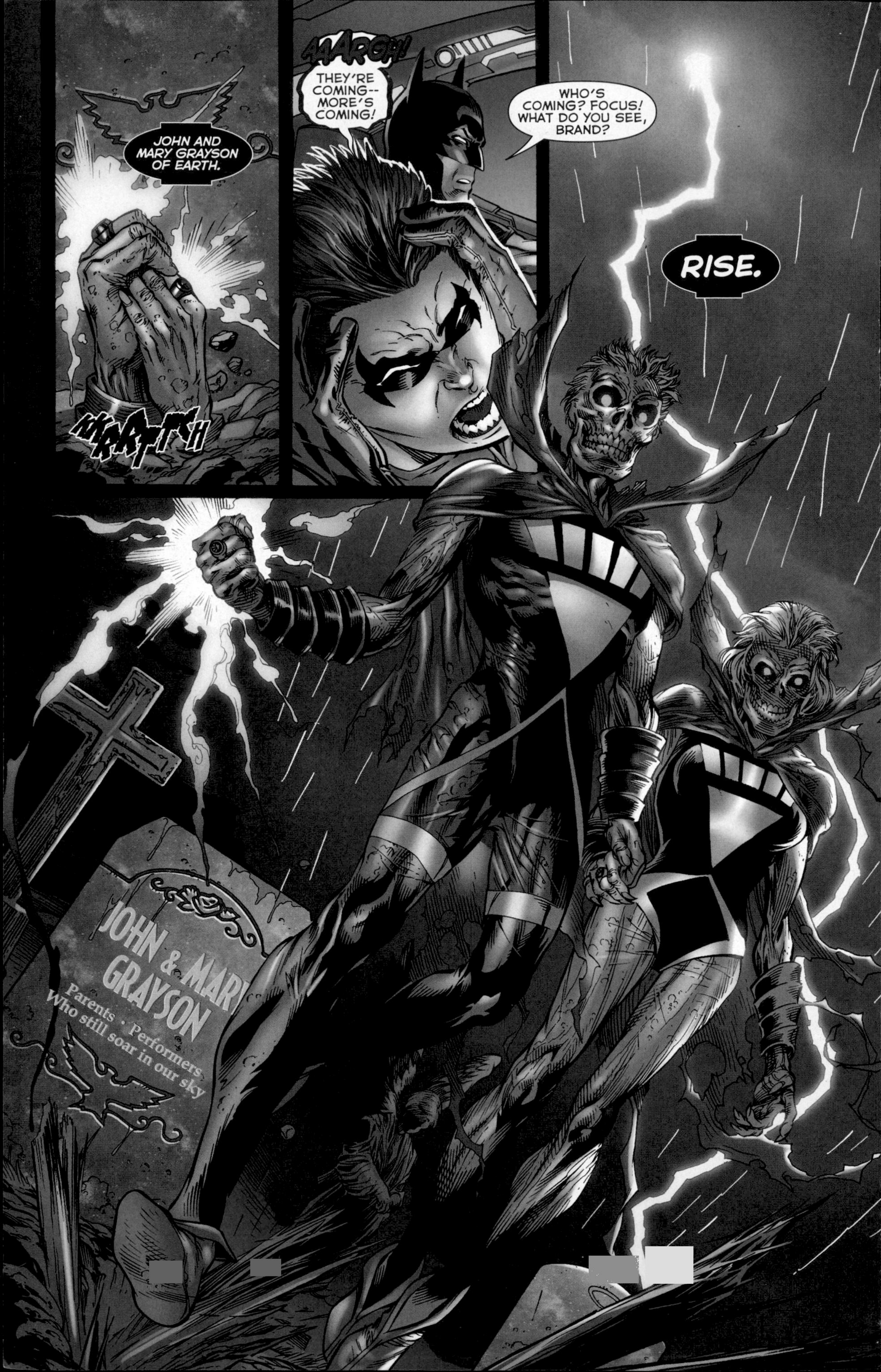
JOHN AND MARY GRAYSON OF EARTH.
AAARGH!
THEY'RE COMING-- MORE'S COMING!
WHO'S COMING? FOCUS! WHAT DO YOU SEE, BRAND?
RISE.
JOHN & MARY GRAYSON
Parents · Performers,
Who still soar in our sky

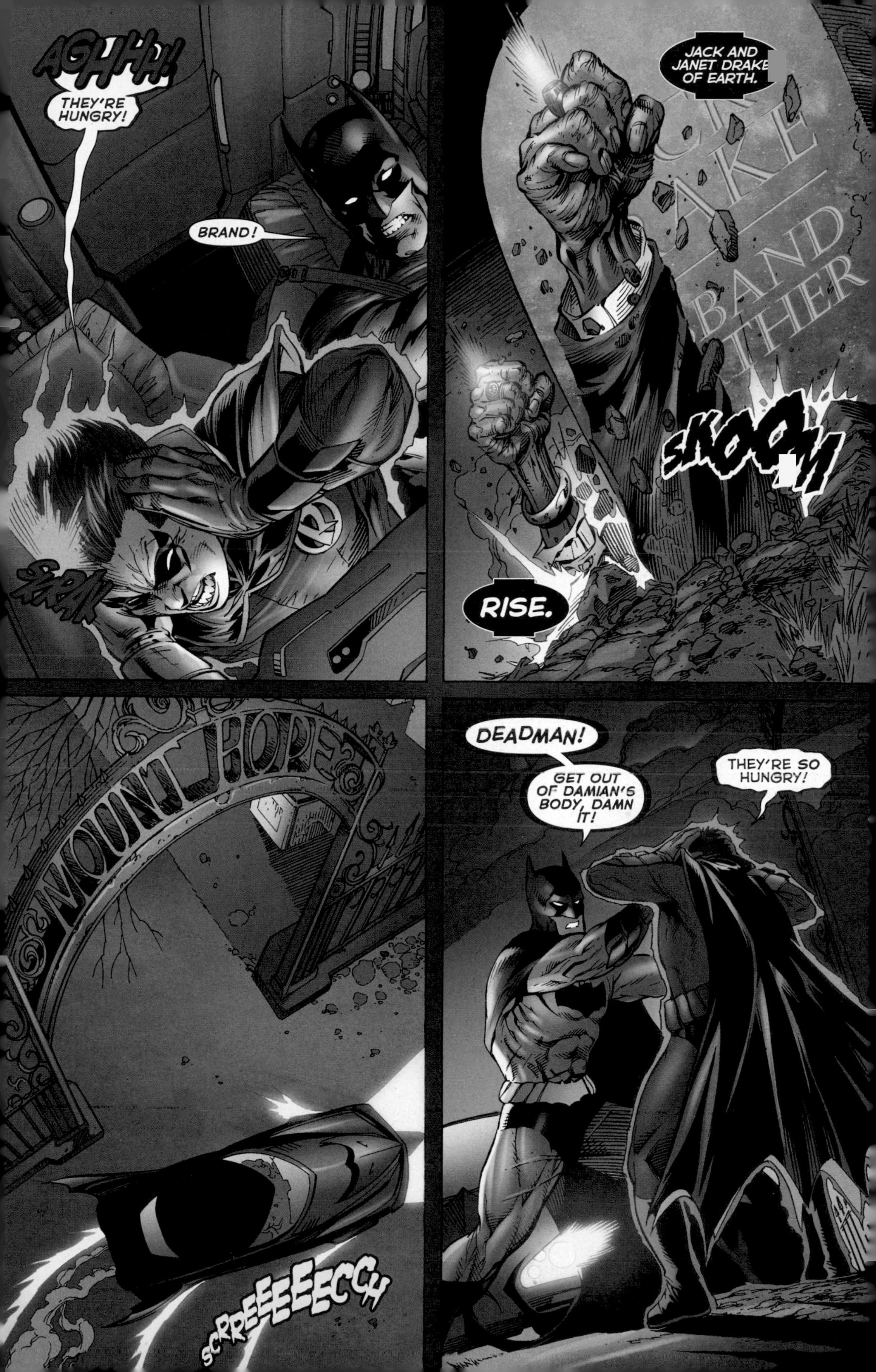
AGHHH!
THEY'RE HUNGRY!
BRAND!
SKRAK
JACK AND JANET DRAKE OF EARTH.
SKOOM
RISE.
MOUNT HOPE
SCREEEEEEECCH
DEADMAN!
GET OUT OF DAMIAN'S BODY, DAMN IT!
THEY'RE SO HUNGRY!

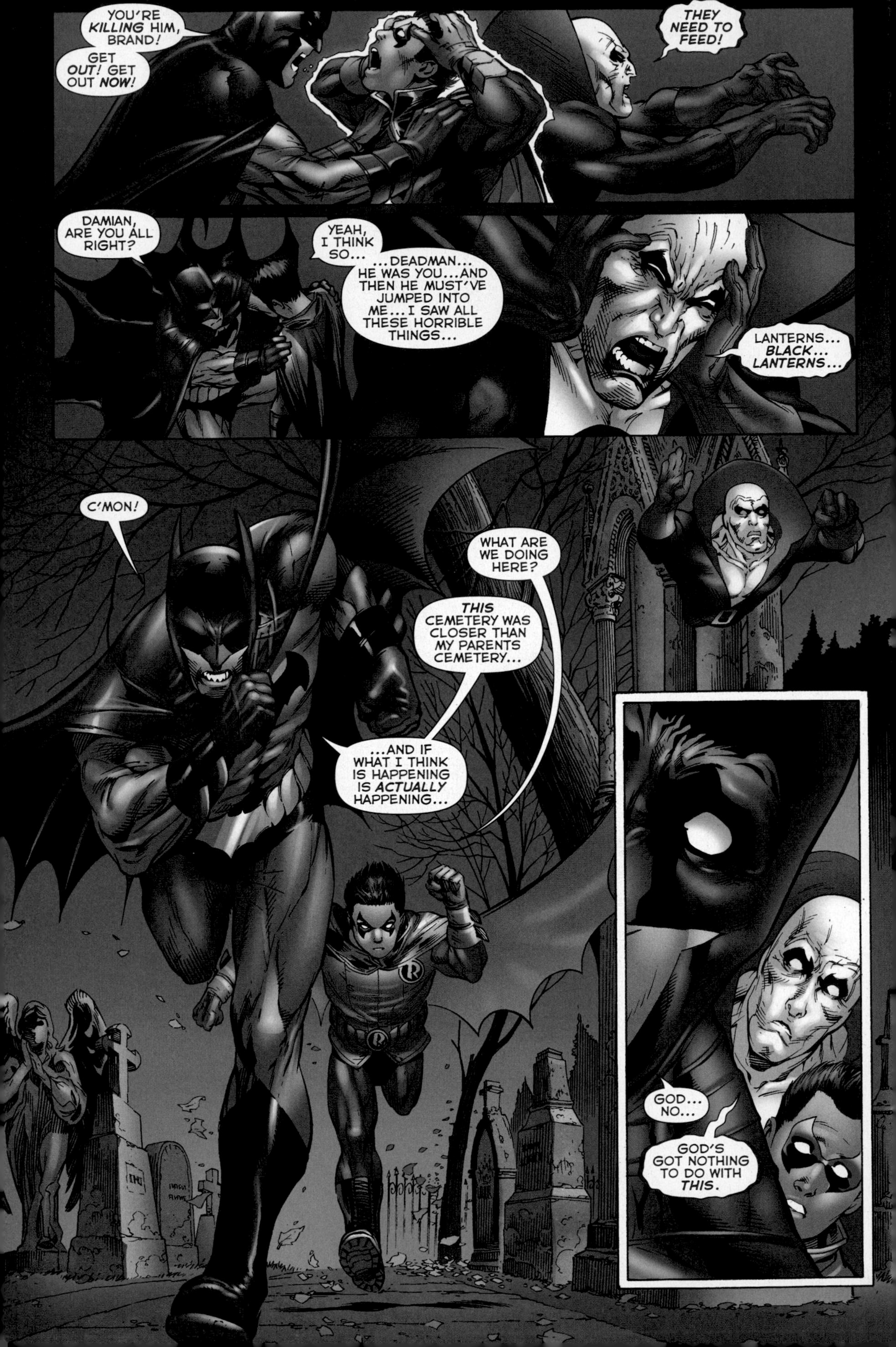

YOU'RE KILLING HIM, BRAND!
GET OUT! GET OUT NOW!
THEY NEED TO FEED!
DAMIAN, ARE YOU ALL RIGHT?
YEAH, I THINK SO...
...DEADMAN... HE WAS YOU...AND THEN HE MUST'VE JUMPED INTO ME...I SAW ALL THESE HORRIBLE THINGS...
LANTERNS... BLACK... LANTERNS...
C'MON!
WHAT ARE WE DOING HERE?
THIS CEMETERY WAS CLOSER THAN MY PARENTS CEMETERY...
...AND IF WHAT I THINK IS HAPPENING IS ACTUALLY HAPPENING...
GOD... NO...
GOD'S GOT NOTHING TO DO WITH THIS.

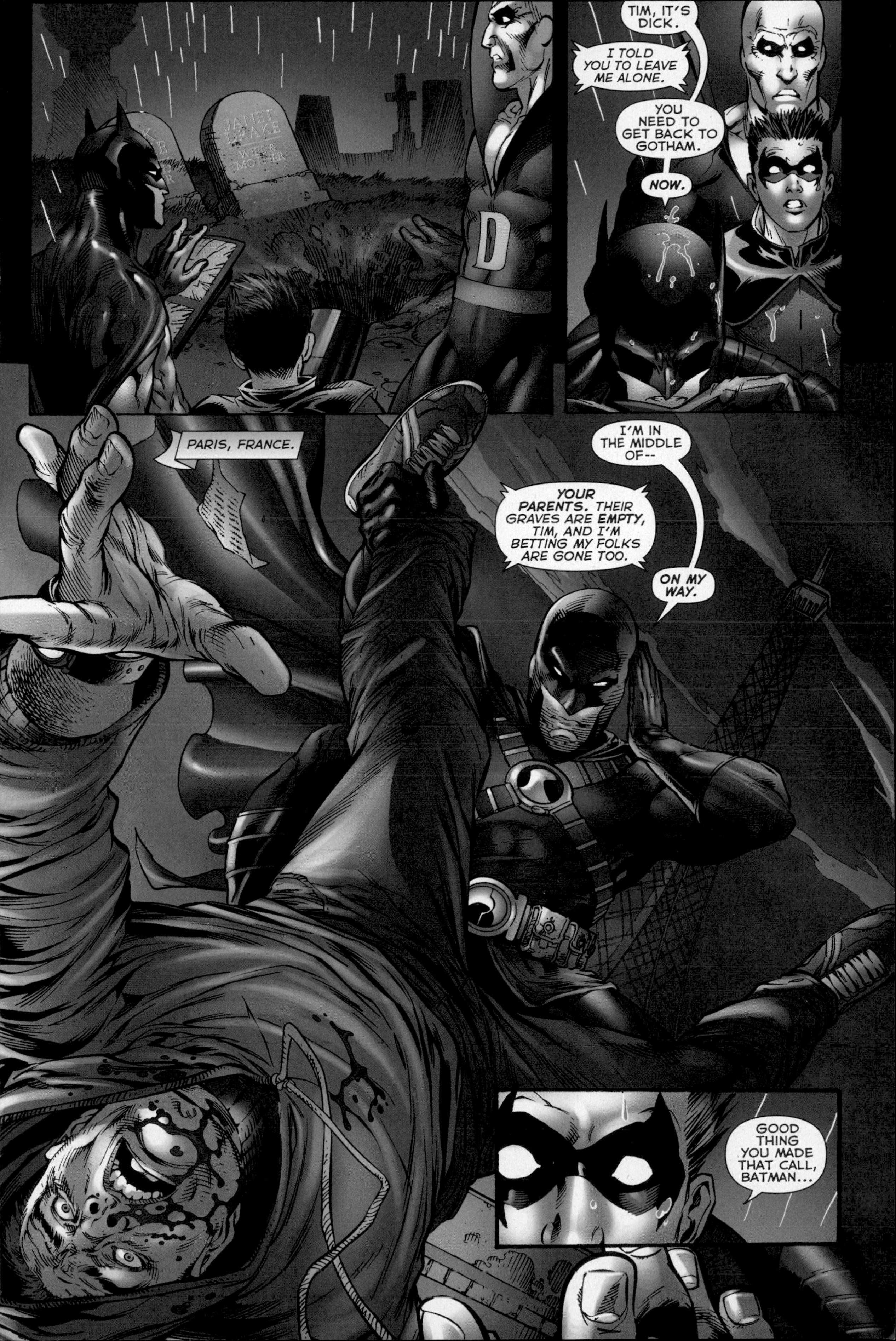
JANET DRAKE
WIFE & MOTHER
TIM, IT'S DICK.
I TOLD YOU TO LEAVE ME ALONE.
YOU NEED TO GET BACK TO GOTHAM.
NOW.
PARIS, FRANCE.
I'M IN THE MIDDLE OF--
YOUR PARENTS. THEIR GRAVES ARE EMPTY, TIM, AND I'M BETTING MY FOLKS ARE GONE TOO.
ON MY WAY.
GOOD THING YOU MADE THAT CALL, BATMAN...

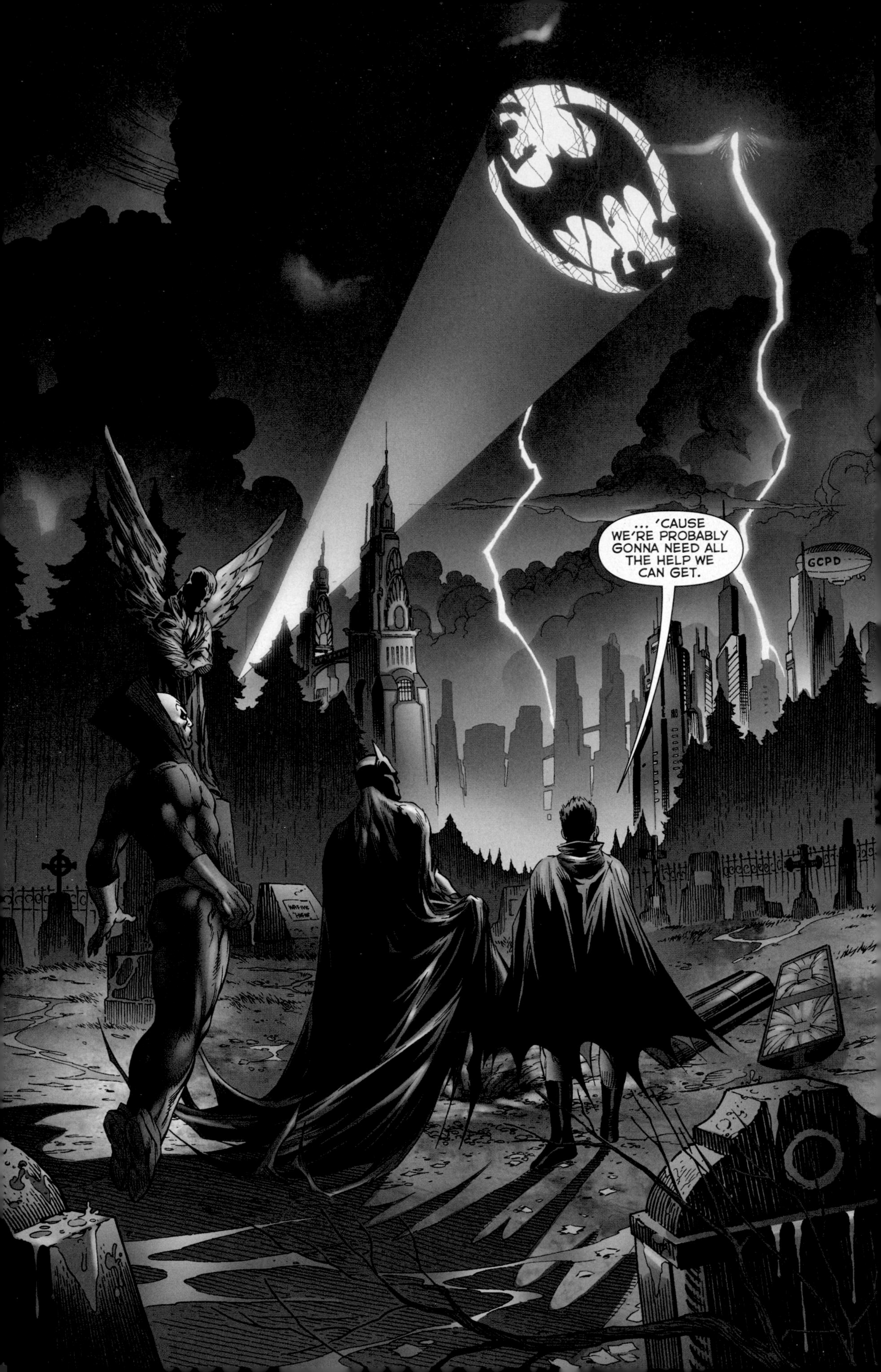
... 'CAUSE WE'RE PROBABLY GONNA NEED ALL THE HELP WE CAN GET.
GCPD

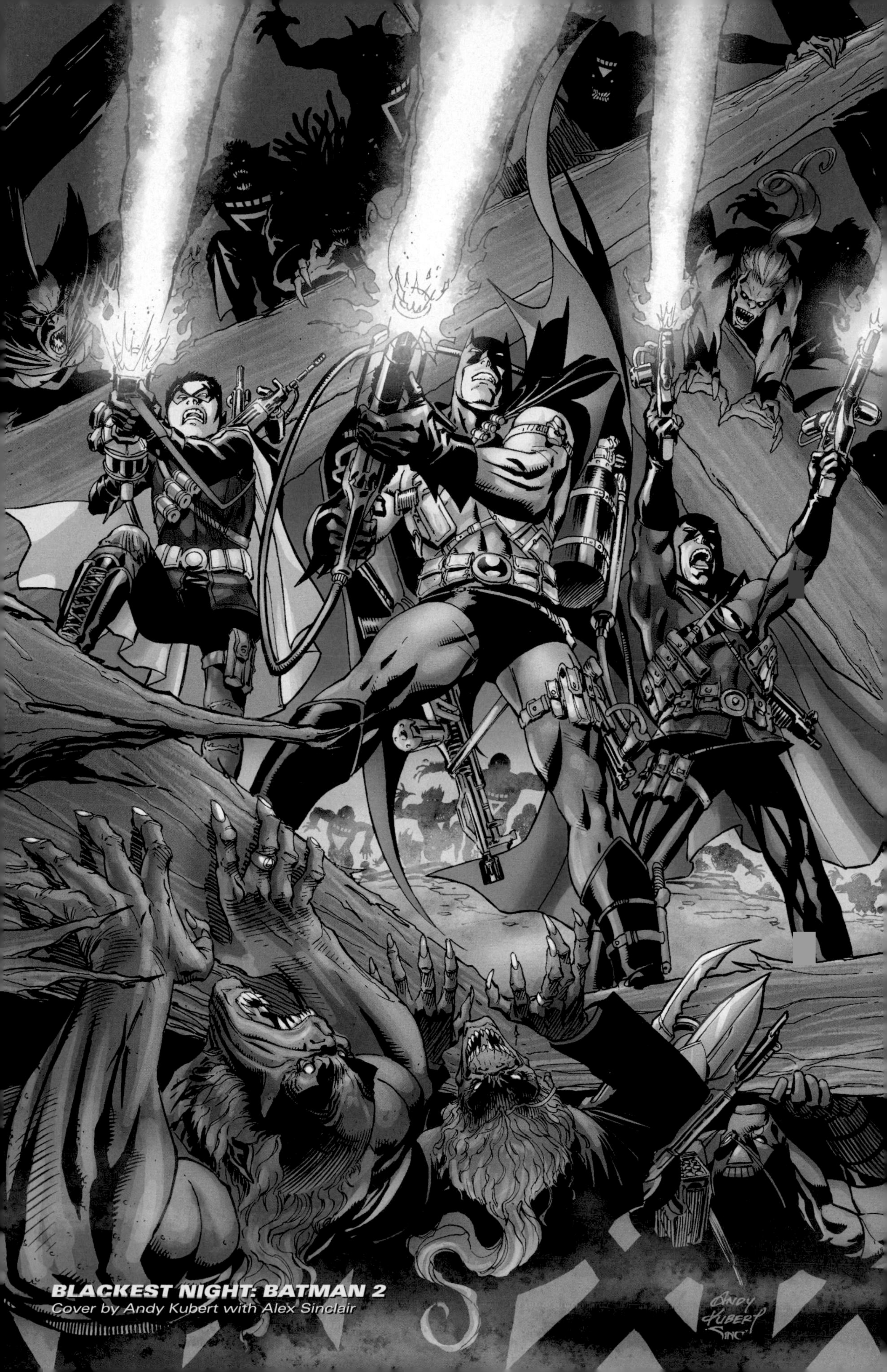
ANDY KUBERT SINC

BLACKEST NIGHT: BATMAN 2
Cover by Andy Kubert with Alex Sinclair

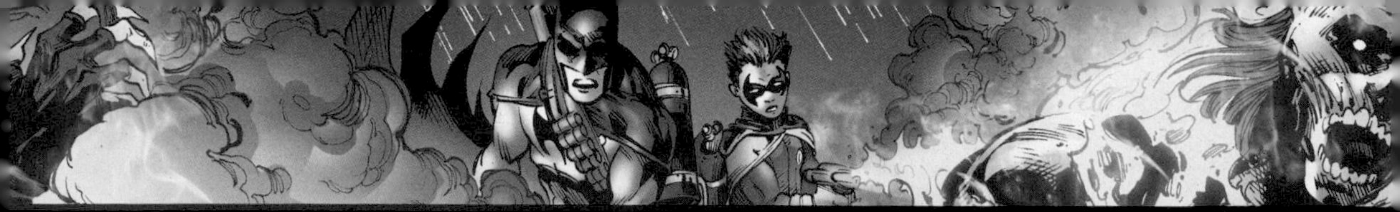

WHO BURNS WHO
PART TWO

PETER J. TOMASI
WRITER

ARDIAN SYAF
PENCILS

VICENTE CIFUENTES
INKS

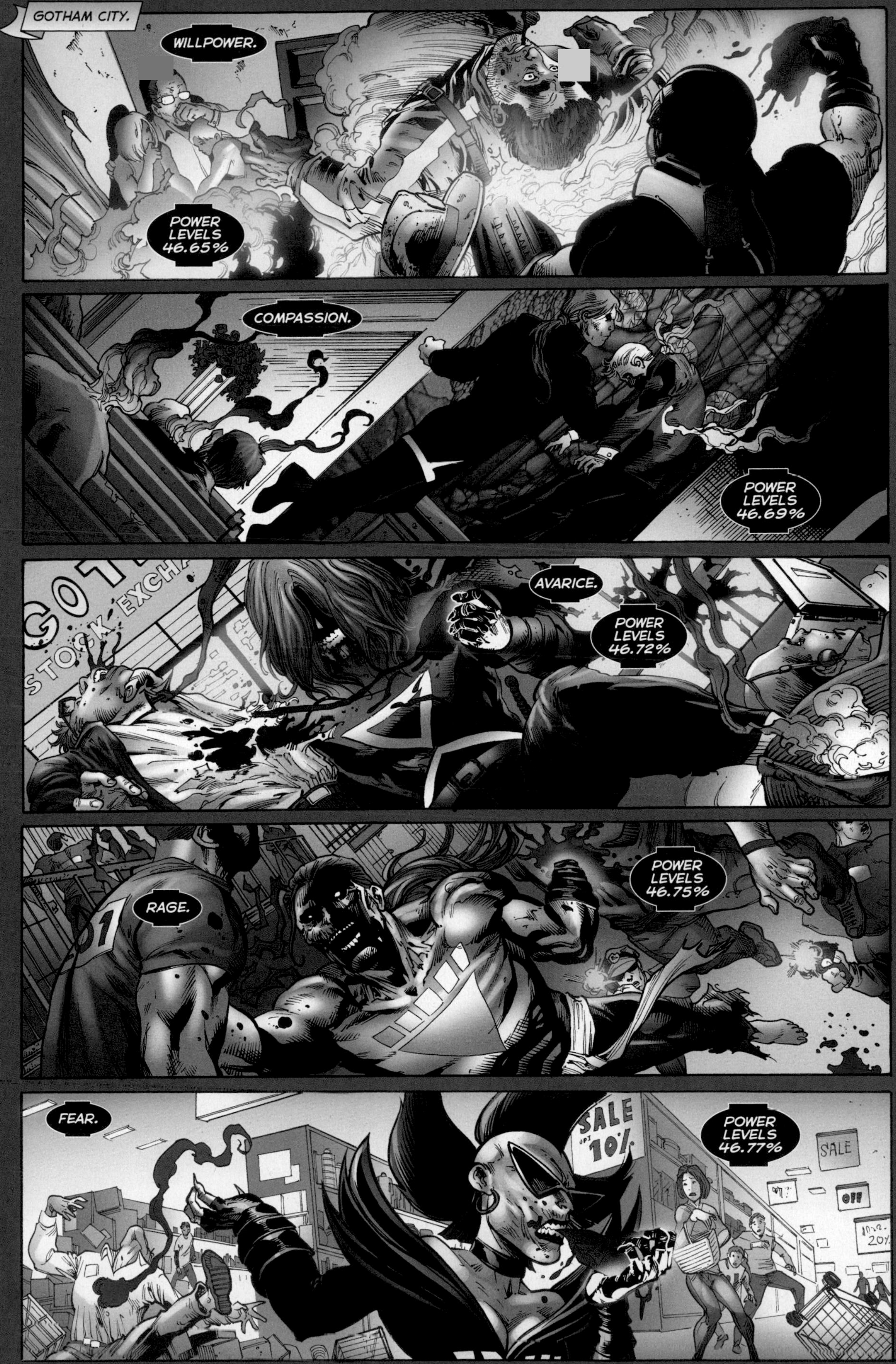
GOTHAM CITY.
WILLPOWER.
POWER LEVELS 46.65%
COMPASSION.
POWER LEVELS 46.69%
AVARICE.
POWER LEVELS 46.72%
RAGE.
POWER LEVELS 46.75%
FEAR.
POWER LEVELS 46.77%
SALE
SALE

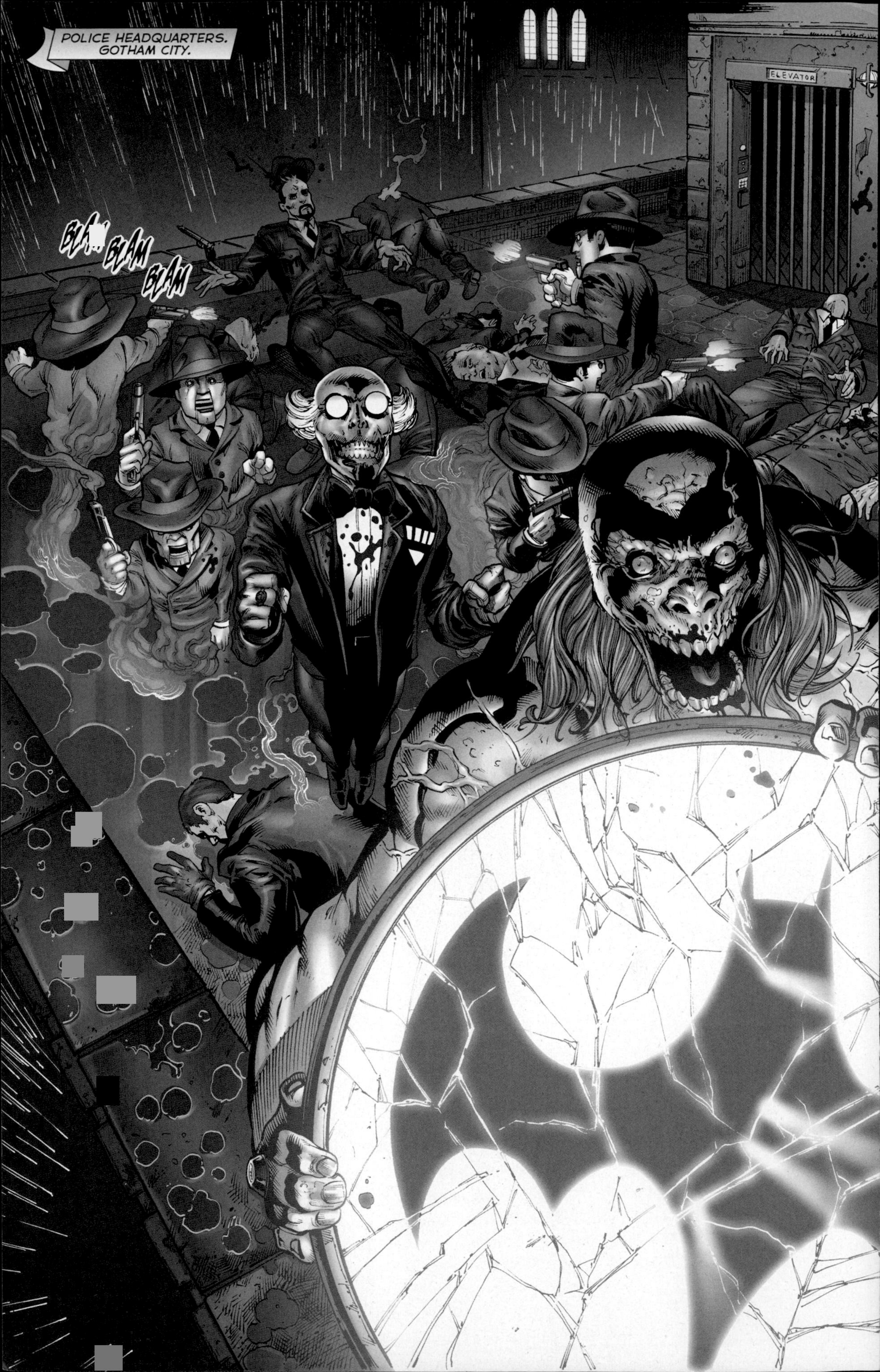
POLICE HEADQUARTERS.
GOTHAM CITY.
BLAM
BLAM

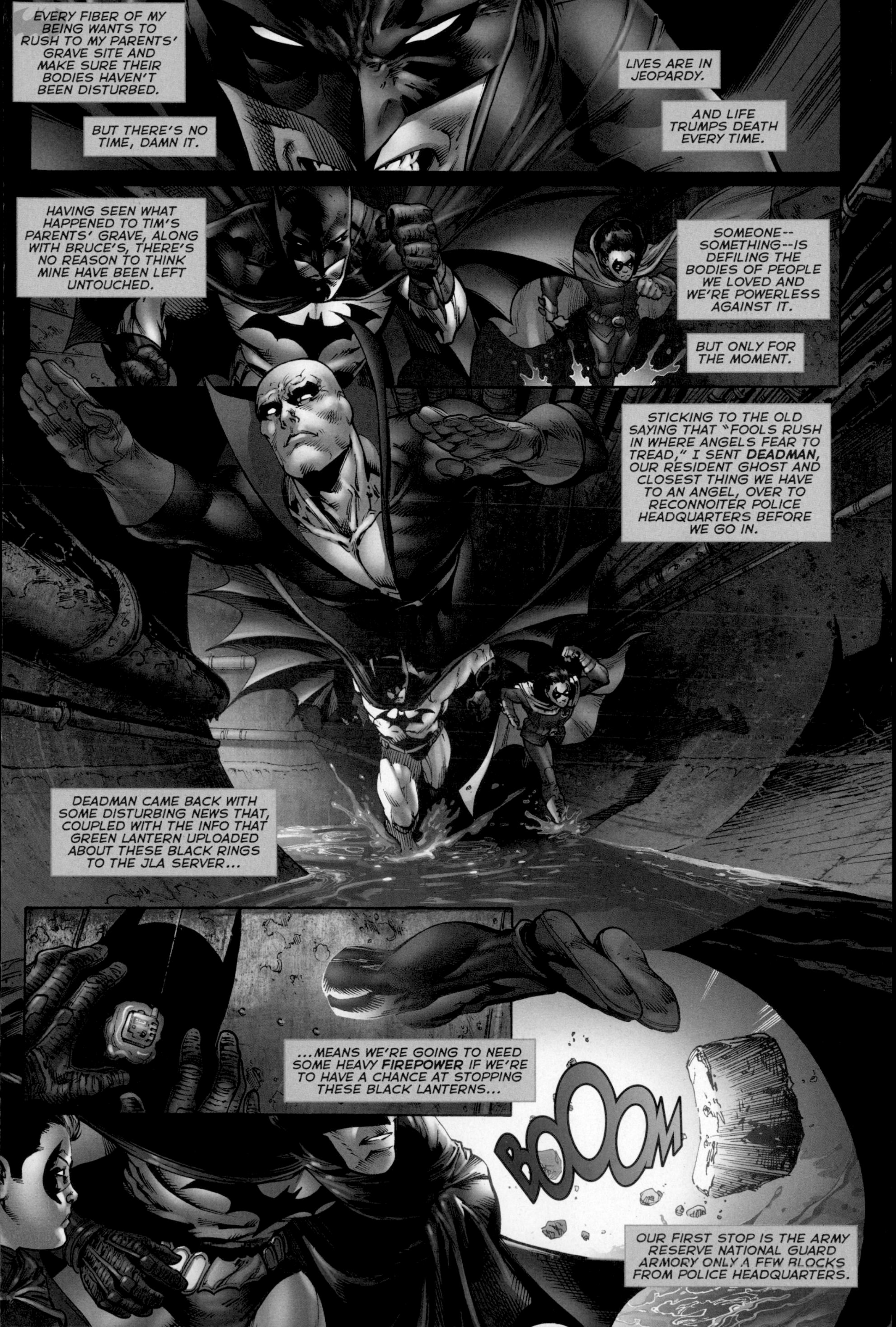
EVERY FIBER OF MY BEING WANTS TO RUSH TO MY PARENTS' GRAVE SITE AND MAKE SURE THEIR BODIES HAVEN'T BEEN DISTURBED.
BUT THERE'S NO TIME, DAMN IT.
LIVES ARE IN JEOPARDY.
AND LIFE TRUMPS DEATH EVERY TIME.
HAVING SEEN WHAT HAPPENED TO TIM'S PARENTS' GRAVE, ALONG WITH BRUCE'S, THERE'S NO REASON TO THINK MINE HAVE BEEN LEFT UNTOUCHED.
SOMEONE--SOMETHING--IS DEFILING THE BODIES OF PEOPLE WE LOVED AND WE'RE POWERLESS AGAINST IT.
BUT ONLY FOR THE MOMENT.
STICKING TO THE OLD SAYING THAT "FOOLS RUSH IN WHERE ANGELS FEAR TO TREAD," I SENT DEADMAN, OUR RESIDENT GHOST AND CLOSEST THING WE HAVE TO AN ANGEL, OVER TO RECONNOITER POLICE HEADQUARTERS BEFORE WE GO IN.
DEADMAN CAME BACK WITH SOME DISTURBING NEWS THAT, COUPLED WITH THE INFO THAT GREEN LANTERN UPLOADED ABOUT THESE BLACK RINGS TO THE JLA SERVER...
...MEANS WE'RE GOING TO NEED SOME HEAVY FIREPOWER IF WE'RE TO HAVE A CHANCE AT STOPPING THESE BLACK LANTERNS...
BOOOOM
OUR FIRST STOP IS THE ARMY RESERVE NATIONAL GUARD ARMORY ONLY A FEW BLOCKS FROM POLICE HEADQUARTERS.

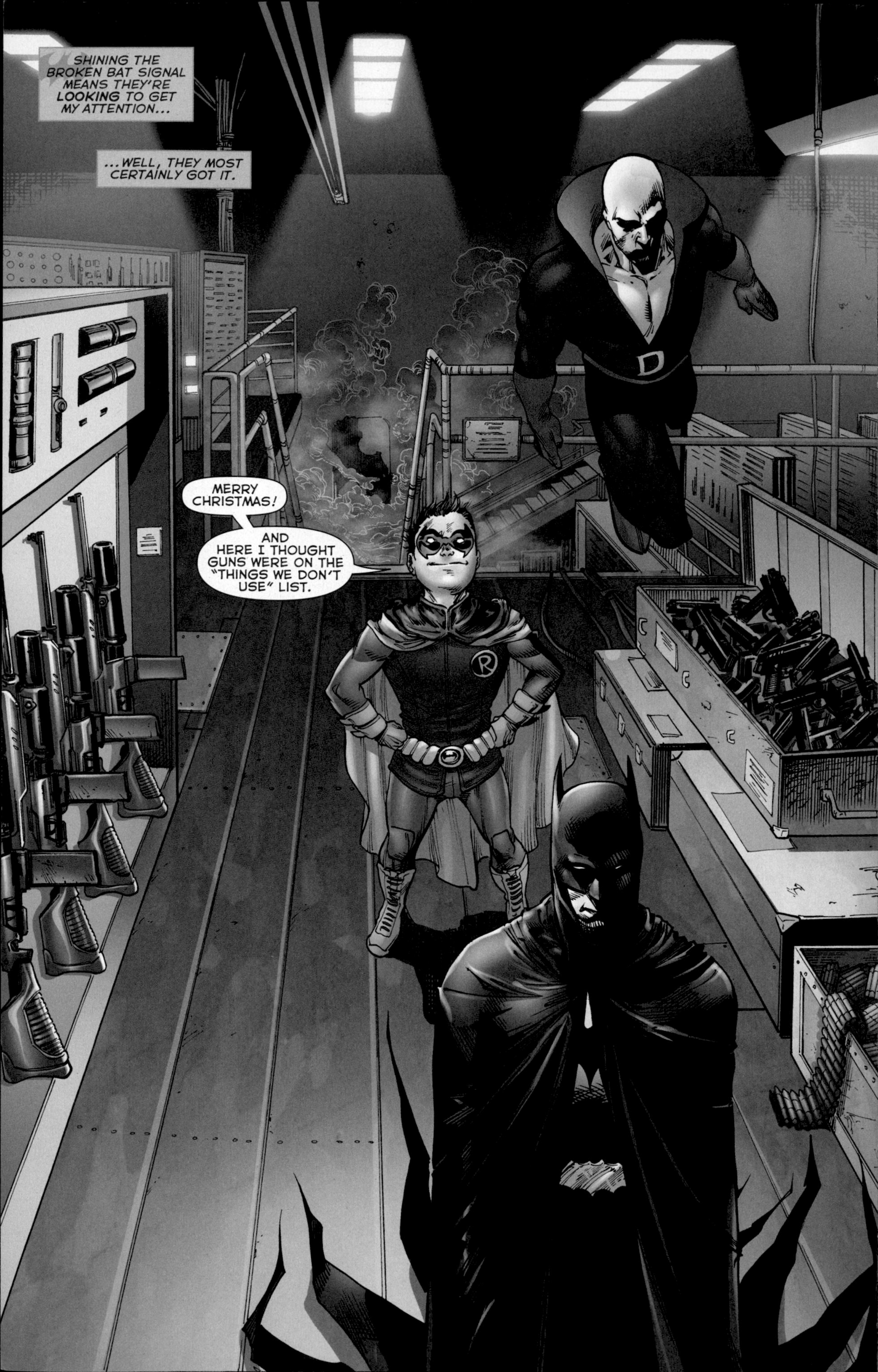
SHINING THE BROKEN BAT SIGNAL MEANS THEY'RE LOOKING TO GET MY ATTENTION...
...WELL, THEY MOST CERTAINLY GOT IT.
MERRY CHRISTMAS!
AND HERE I THOUGHT GUNS WERE ON THE "THINGS WE DON'T USE" LIST.

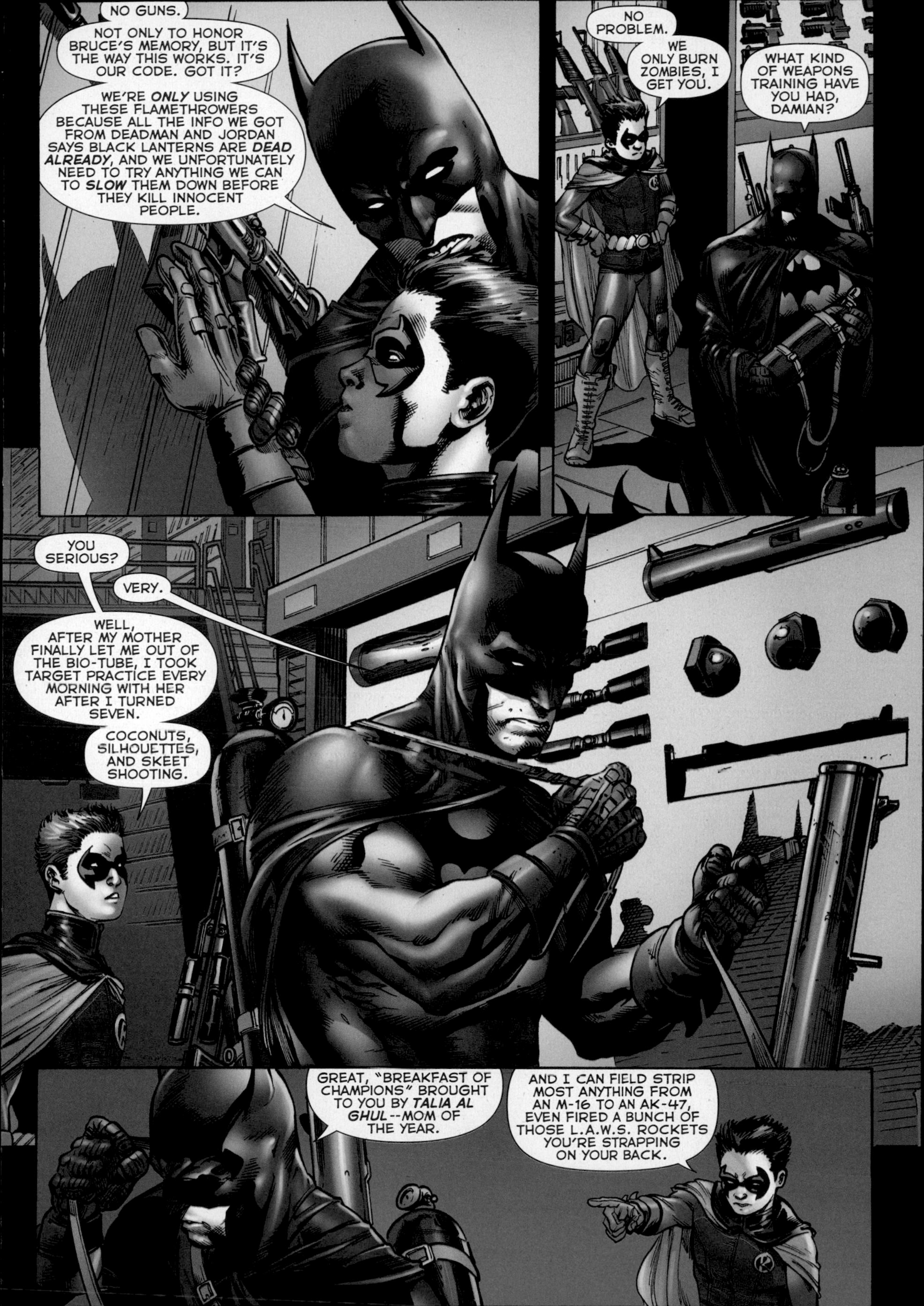
NO GUNS.
NOT ONLY TO HONOR BRUCE'S MEMORY, BUT IT'S THE WAY THIS WORKS. IT'S OUR CODE. GOT IT?
WE'RE ONLY USING THESE FLAMETHROWERS BECAUSE ALL THE INFO WE GOT FROM DEADMAN AND JORDAN SAYS BLACK LANTERNS ARE DEAD ALREADY, AND WE UNFORTUNATELY NEED TO TRY ANYTHING WE CAN TO SLOW THEM DOWN BEFORE THEY KILL INNOCENT PEOPLE.
NO PROBLEM.
WE ONLY BURN ZOMBIES, I GET YOU.
WHAT KIND OF WEAPONS TRAINING HAVE YOU HAD, DAMIAN?
YOU SERIOUS?
VERY.
WELL, AFTER MY MOTHER FINALLY LET ME OUT OF THE BIO-TUBE, I TOOK TARGET PRACTICE EVERY MORNING WITH HER AFTER I TURNED SEVEN.
COCONUTS, SILHOUETTES, AND SKEET SHOOTING.
GREAT, "BREAKFAST OF CHAMPIONS" BROUGHT TO YOU BY TALIA AL GHUL--MOM OF THE YEAR.
AND I CAN FIELD STRIP MOST ANYTHING FROM AN M-16 TO AN AK-47, EVEN FIRED A BUNCH OF THOSE L.A.W.S. ROCKETS YOU'RE STRAPPING ON YOUR BACK.

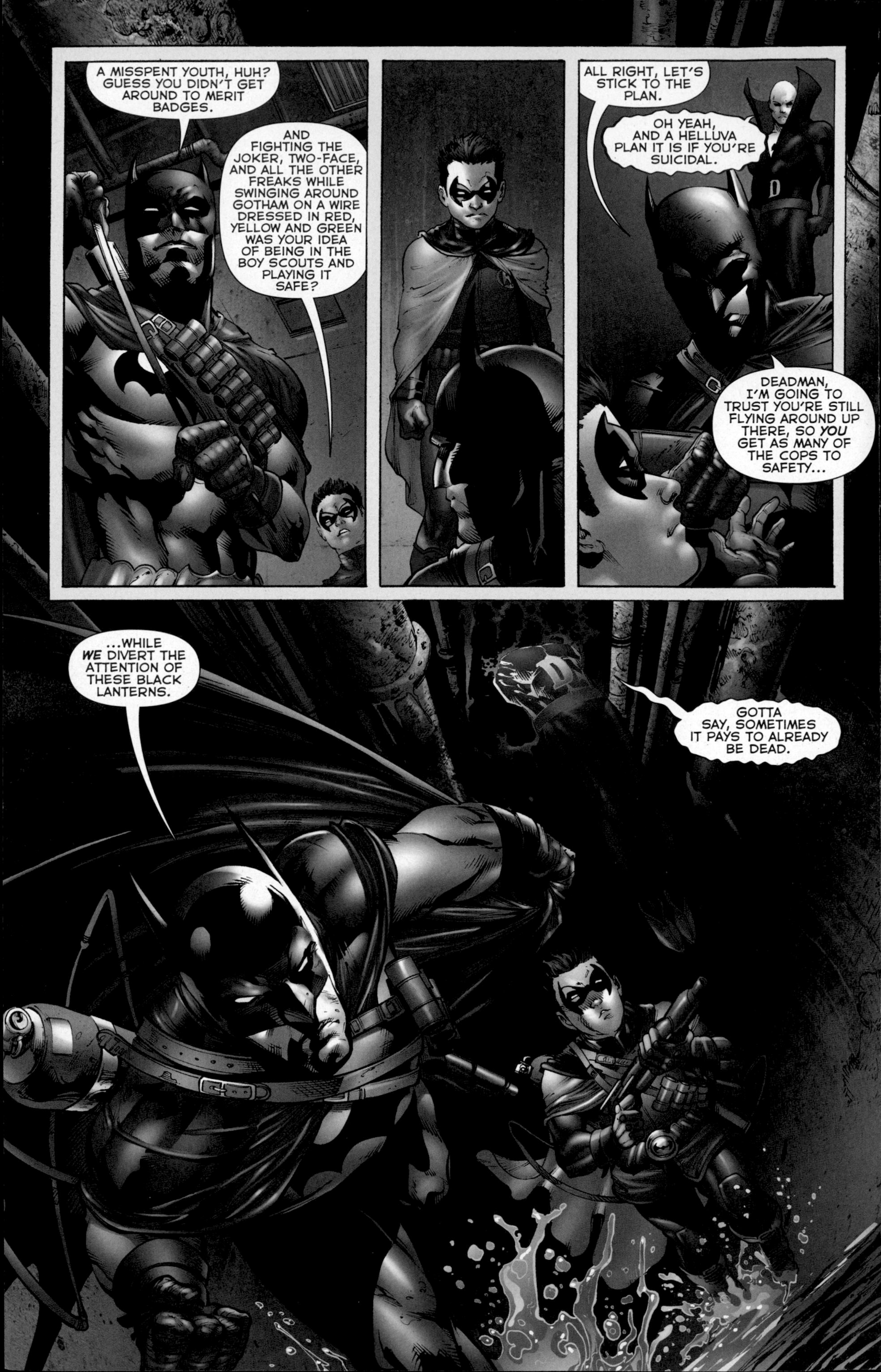

A MISSPENT YOUTH, HUH? GUESS YOU DIDN'T GET AROUND TO MERIT BADGES.
AND FIGHTING THE JOKER, TWO-FACE, AND ALL THE OTHER FREAKS WHILE SWINGING AROUND GOTHAM ON A WIRE DRESSED IN RED, YELLOW AND GREEN WAS YOUR IDEA OF BEING IN THE BOY SCOUTS AND PLAYING IT SAFE?
ALL RIGHT, LET'S STICK TO THE PLAN.
OH YEAH, AND A HELLUVA PLAN IT IS IF YOU'RE SUICIDAL.
DEADMAN, I'M GOING TO TRUST YOU'RE STILL FLYING AROUND UP THERE, SO *YOU* GET AS MANY OF THE COPS TO SAFETY...
...WHILE *WE* DIVERT THE ATTENTION OF THESE BLACK LANTERNS.
GOTTA SAY, SOMETIMES IT PAYS TO ALREADY BE DEAD.

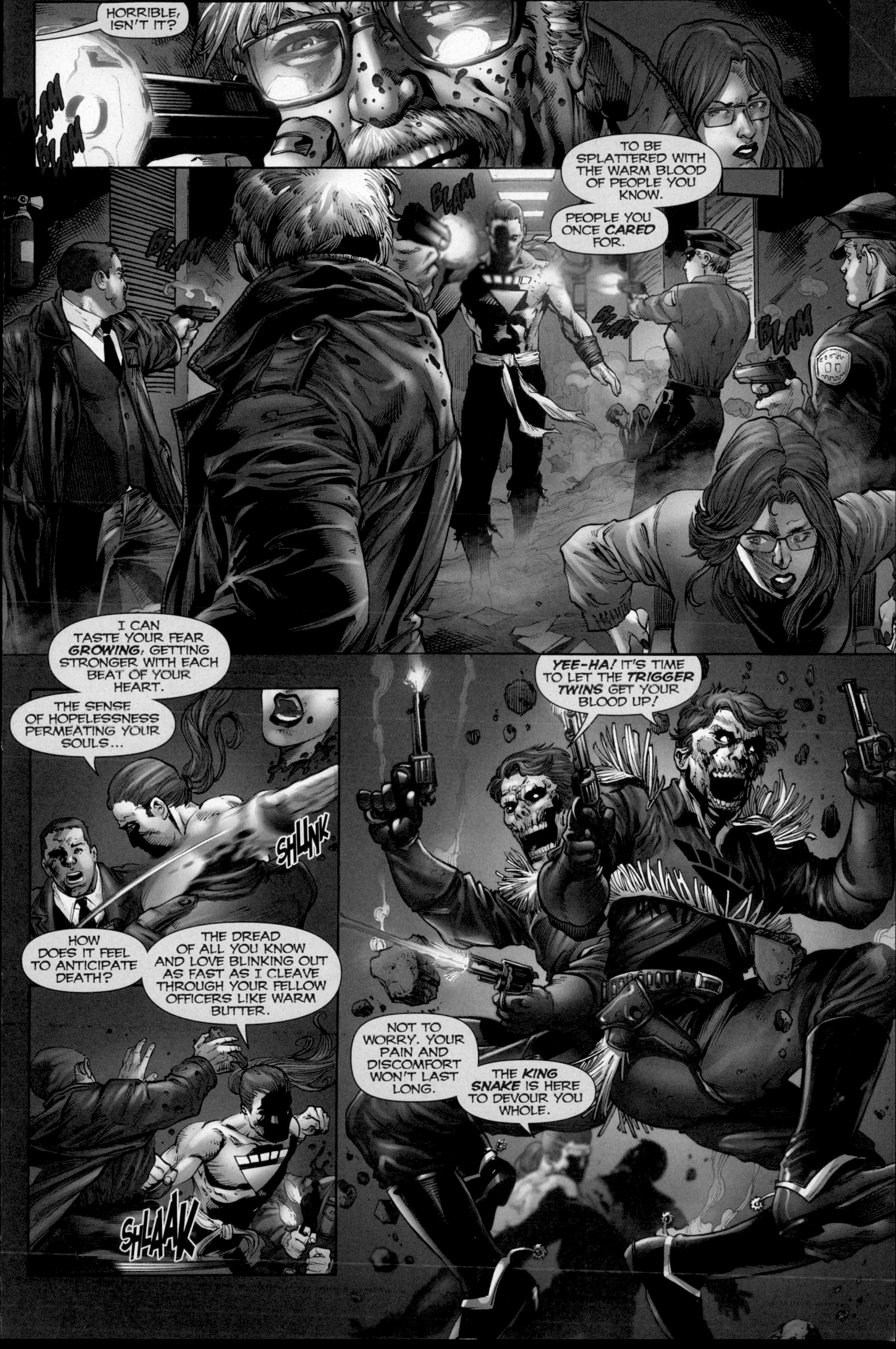
HORRIBLE, ISN'T IT?
BLAM
BLAM
TO BE SPLATTERED WITH THE WARM BLOOD OF PEOPLE YOU KNOW.
PEOPLE YOU ONCE CARED FOR.
BLAM
BLAM
BLAM
BLAM
I CAN TASTE YOUR FEAR GROWING, GETTING STRONGER WITH EACH BEAT OF YOUR HEART.
THE SENSE OF HOPELESSNESS PERMEATING YOUR SOULS...
SHUNK
HOW DOES IT FEEL TO ANTICIPATE DEATH?
THE DREAD OF ALL YOU KNOW AND LOVE BLINKING OUT AS FAST AS I CLEAVE THROUGH YOUR FELLOW OFFICERS LIKE WARM BUTTER.
SHLAAK
YEE-HA! IT'S TIME TO LET THE TRIGGER TWINS GET YOUR BLOOD UP!
NOT TO WORRY. YOUR PAIN AND DISCOMFORT WON'T LAST LONG.
THE KING SNAKE IS HERE TO DEVOUR YOU WHOLE.

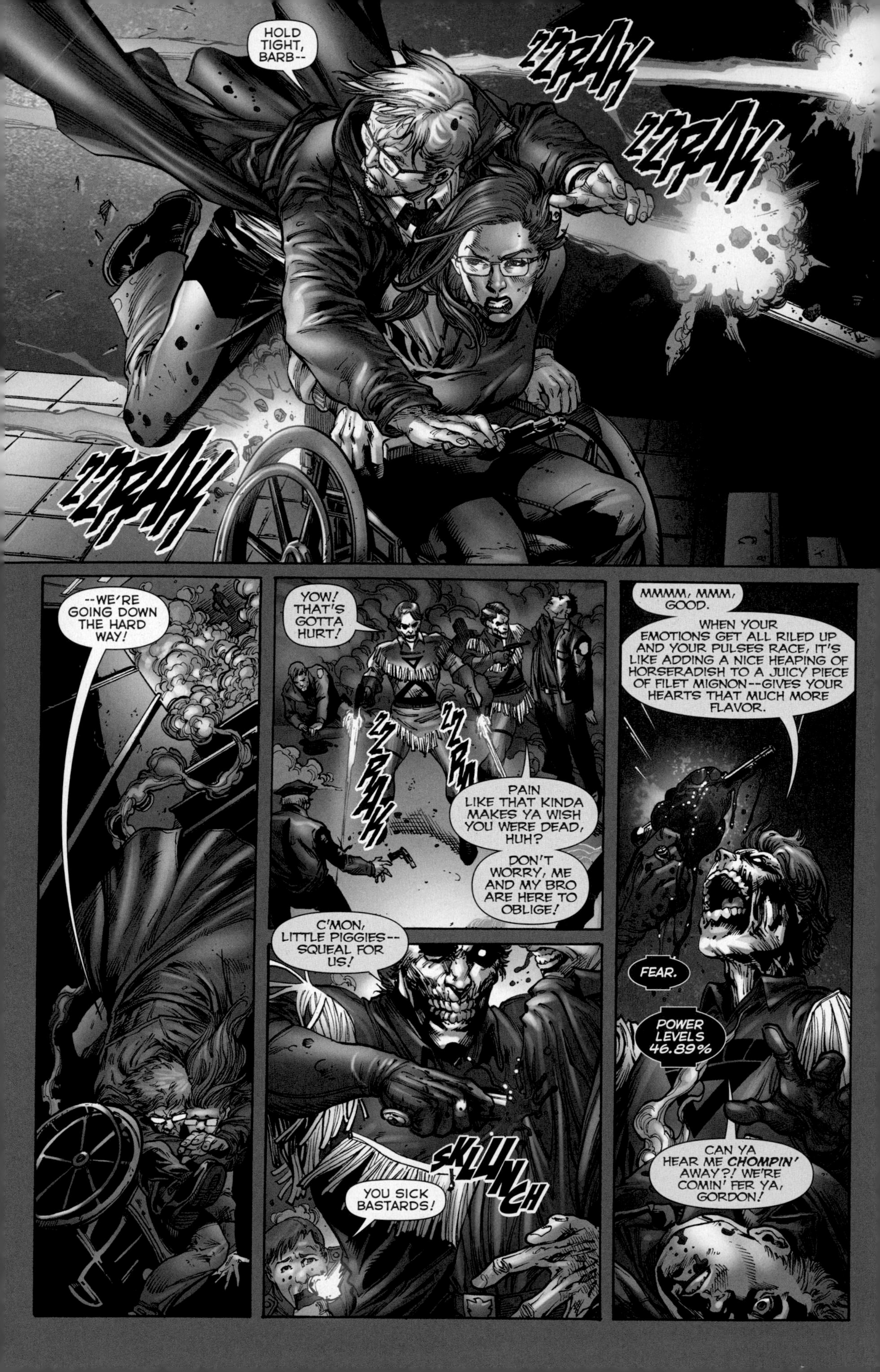
HOLD TIGHT, BARB--
ZZRAK
ZZRAK
ZZRAK
--WE'RE GOING DOWN THE HARD WAY!
YOW! THAT'S GOTTA HURT!
ZZRAK
ZZRAK
PAIN LIKE THAT KINDA MAKES YA WISH YOU WERE DEAD, HUH?
DON'T WORRY, ME AND MY BRO ARE HERE TO OBLIGE!
C'MON, LITTLE PIGGIES-- SQUEAL FOR US!
SKLUNCH
YOU SICK BASTARDS!
MMMM, MMM, GOOD.
WHEN YOUR EMOTIONS GET ALL RILED UP AND YOUR PULSES RACE, IT'S LIKE ADDING A NICE HEAPING OF HORSERADISH TO A JUICY PIECE OF FILET MIGNON--GIVES YOUR HEARTS THAT MUCH MORE FLAVOR.
FEAR.
POWER LEVELS 46.89%
CAN YA HEAR ME CHOMPIN' AWAY?! WE'RE COMIN' FER YA, GORDON!

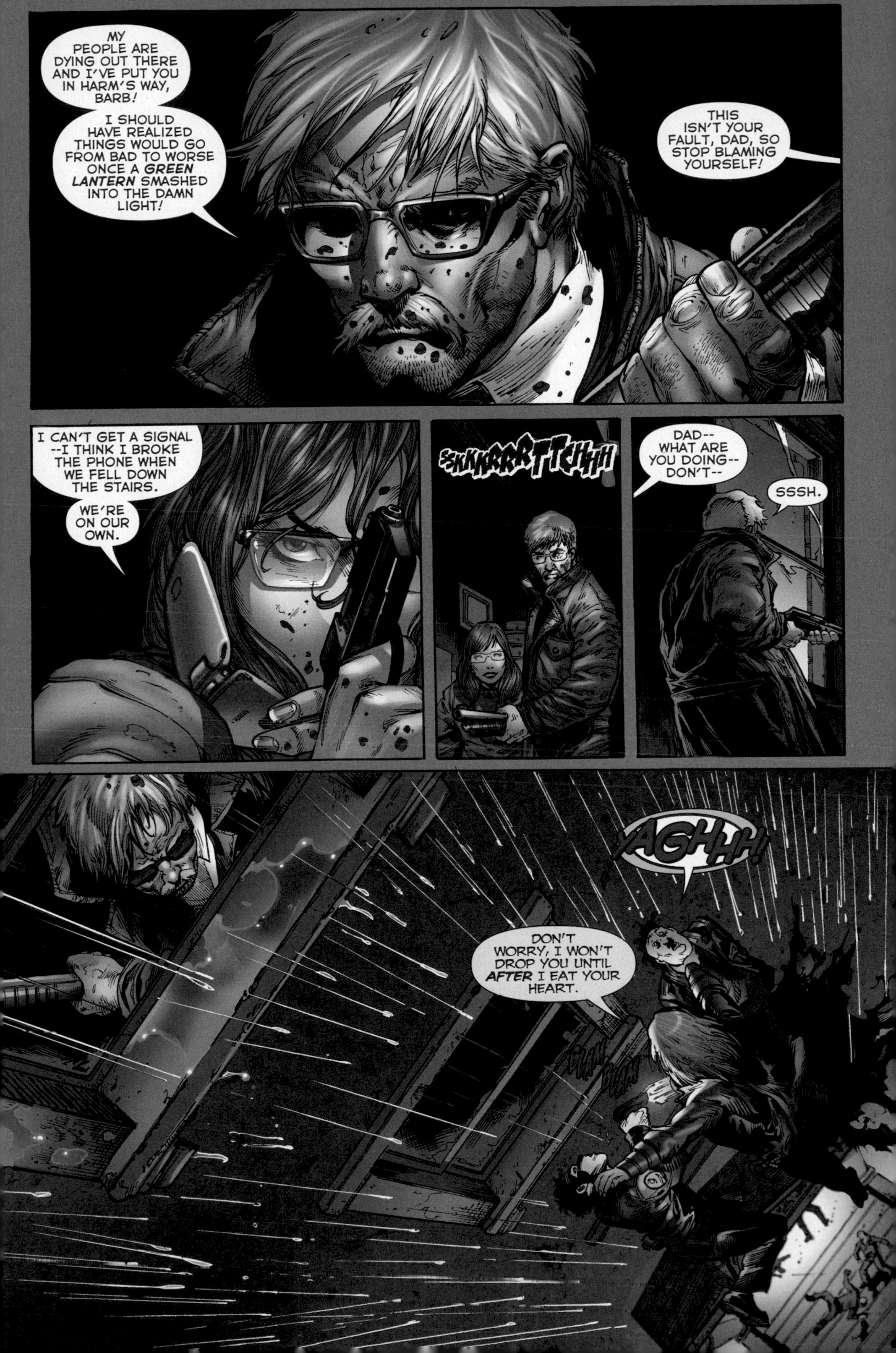
MY PEOPLE ARE DYING OUT THERE AND I'VE PUT YOU IN HARM'S WAY, BARB!
I SHOULD HAVE REALIZED THINGS WOULD GO FROM BAD TO WORSE ONCE A GREEN LANTERN SMASHED INTO THE DAMN LIGHT!
THIS ISN'T YOUR FAULT, DAD, SO STOP BLAMING YOURSELF!
I CAN'T GET A SIGNAL --I THINK I BROKE THE PHONE WHEN WE FELL DOWN THE STAIRS.
WE'RE ON OUR OWN.
SKKKRRRRTTCHHH
DAD-- WHAT ARE YOU DOING-- DON'T--
SSSH.
YAGHHH!
DON'T WORRY, I WON'T DROP YOU UNTIL AFTER I EAT YOUR HEART.

FEAR.

POWER LEVELS 47.01%

CHOMP
SKKRR
SHLRRP RLL

KNOCK KNOCK, IS ANYBODY--

PEEK-A-BOO, I SEE YOU.

YAGHHH!

BOOM

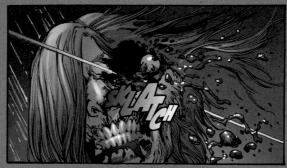

SKLATCH

...UM, I THINK WE SHOULD BE LEAVING, DAD.

I COMPLETELY AGREE--

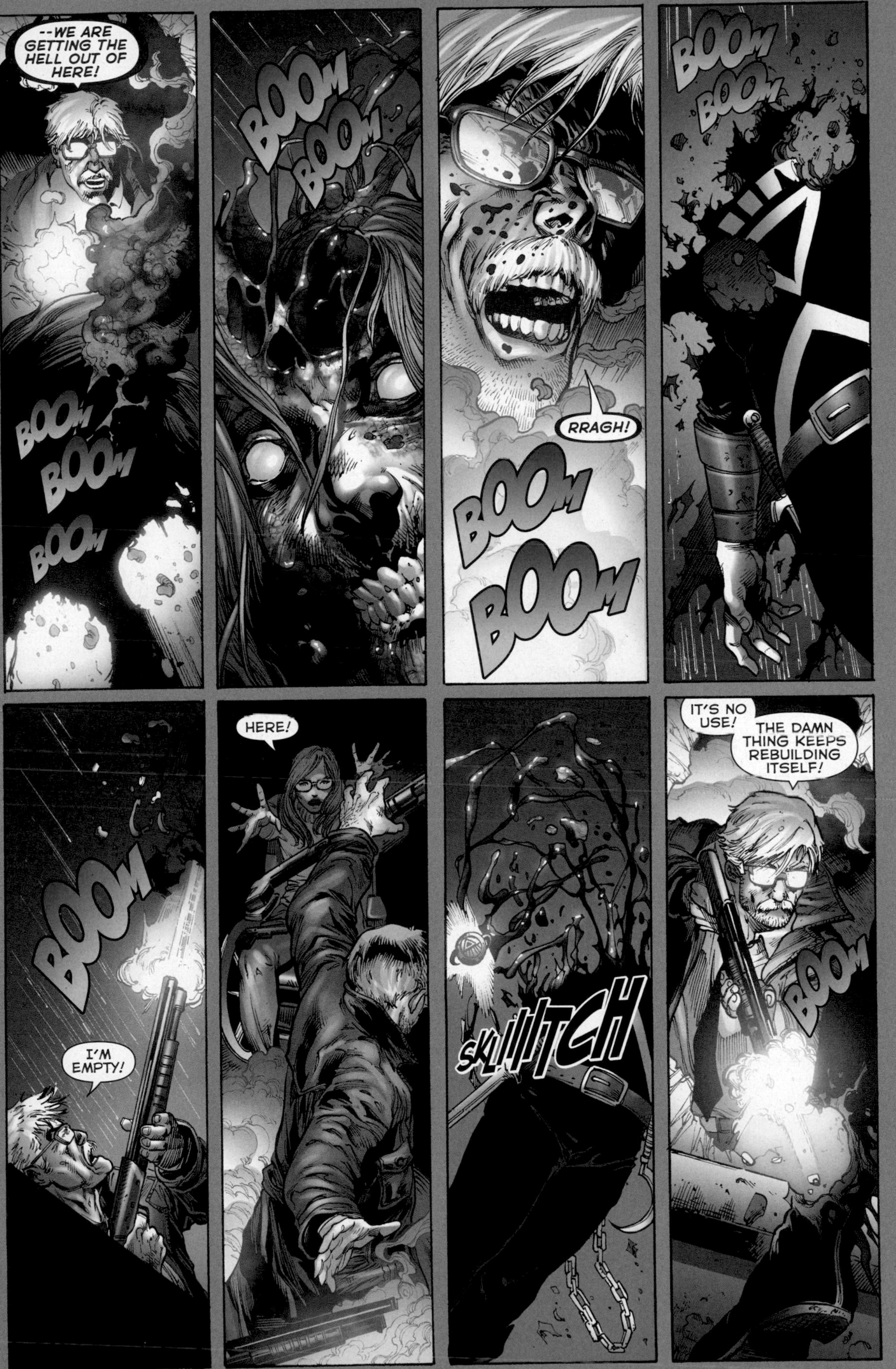
--WE ARE GETTING THE HELL OUT OF HERE!
BOOM BOOM BOOM
BOOM BOOM
RRAGH!
BOOM BOOM
BOOM BOOM
BOOM
I'M EMPTY!
HERE!
SKLIIIITCH
IT'S NO USE!
THE DAMN THING KEEPS REBUILDING ITSELF!
BOOM

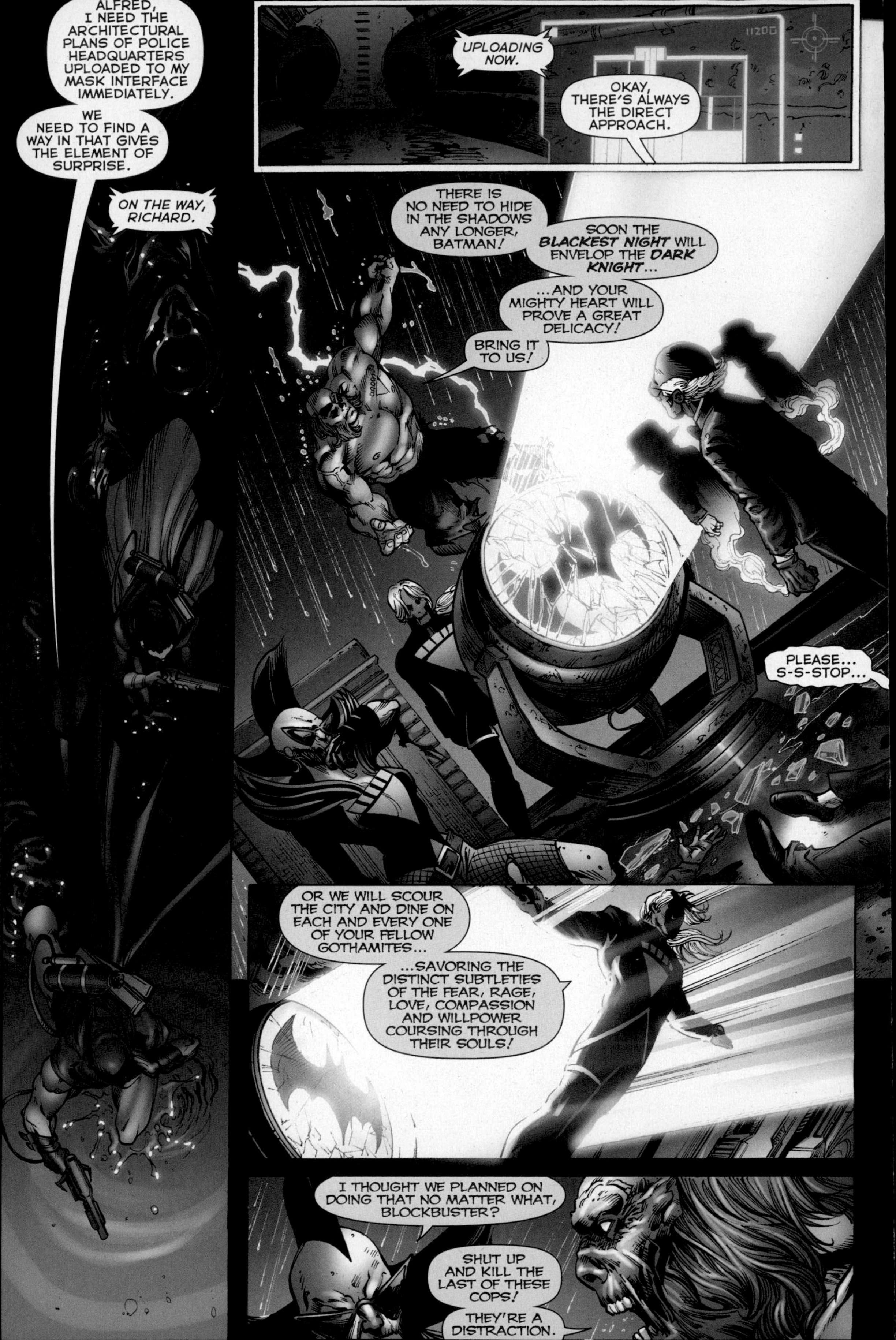
ALFRED, I NEED THE ARCHITECTURAL PLANS OF POLICE HEADQUARTERS UPLOADED TO MY MASK INTERFACE IMMEDIATELY.
WE NEED TO FIND A WAY IN THAT GIVES THE ELEMENT OF SURPRISE.
ON THE WAY, RICHARD.
UPLOADING NOW.
11200
OKAY, THERE'S ALWAYS THE DIRECT APPROACH.
THERE IS NO NEED TO HIDE IN THE SHADOWS ANY LONGER, BATMAN!
SOON THE BLACKEST NIGHT WILL ENVELOP THE DARK KNIGHT...
...AND YOUR MIGHTY HEART WILL PROVE A GREAT DELICACY!
BRING IT TO US!
PLEASE... S-S-STOP...
OR WE WILL SCOUR THE CITY AND DINE ON EACH AND EVERY ONE OF YOUR FELLOW GOTHAMITES...
...SAVORING THE DISTINCT SUBTLETIES OF THE FEAR, RAGE, LOVE, COMPASSION AND WILLPOWER COURSING THROUGH THEIR SOULS!
I THOUGHT WE PLANNED ON DOING THAT NO MATTER WHAT, BLOCKBUSTER?
SHUT UP AND KILL THE LAST OF THESE COPS!
THEY'RE A DISTRACTION.

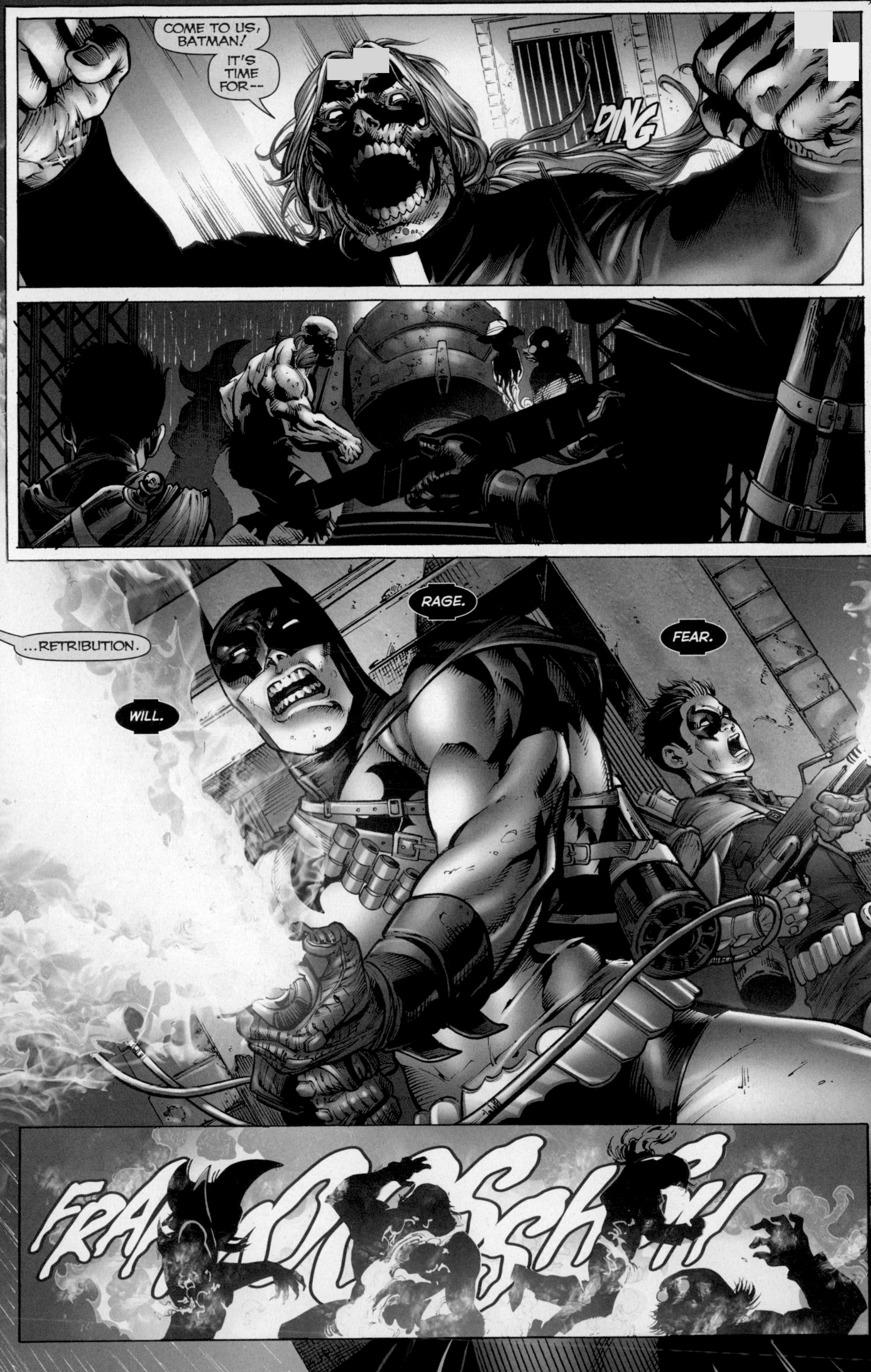
COME TO US, BATMAN!
IT'S TIME FOR--
DING
...RETRIBUTION.
RAGE.
FEAR.
WILL.

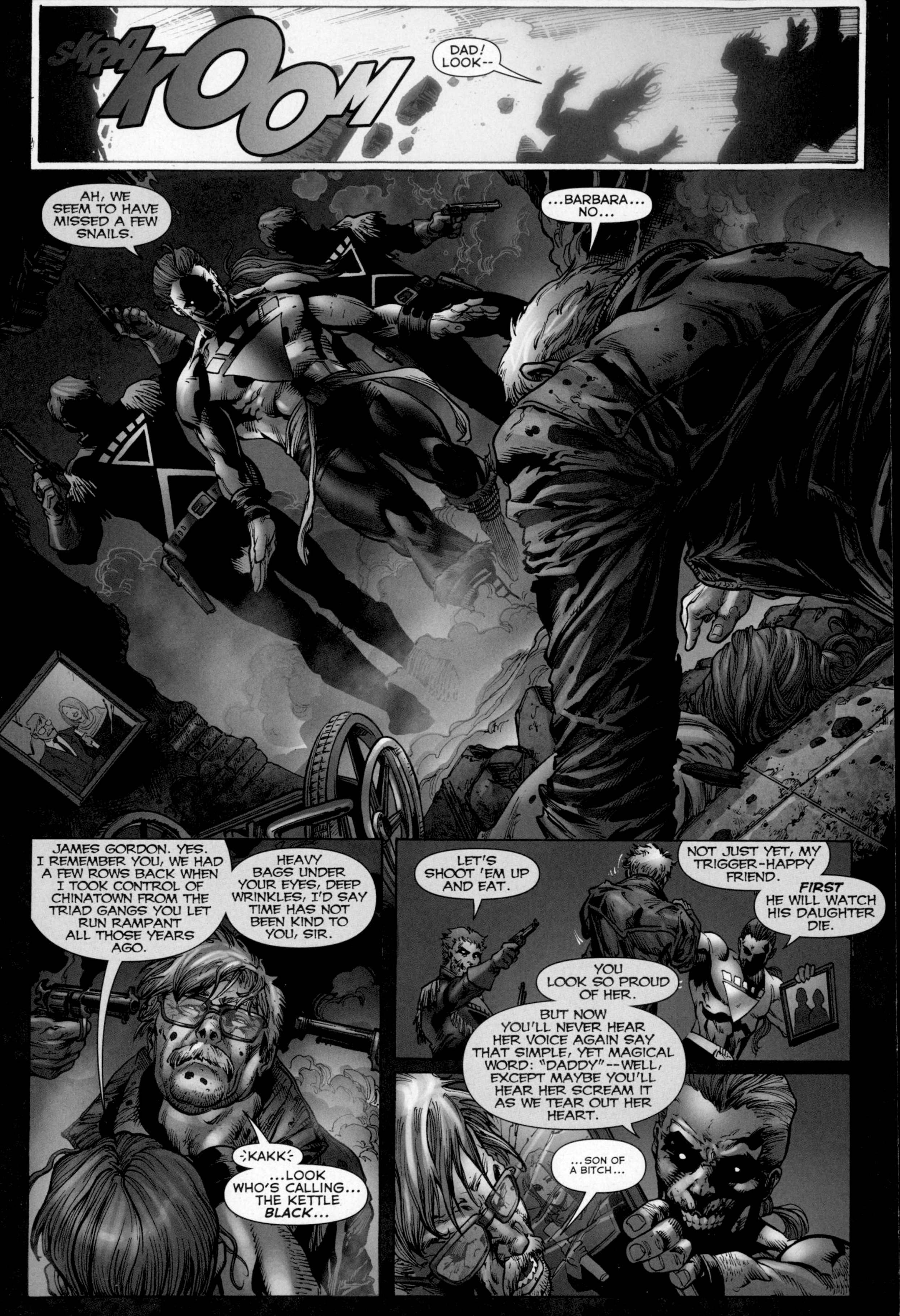
SKRAKOOM
DAD! LOOK--
AH, WE SEEM TO HAVE MISSED A FEW SNAILS.
...BARBARA... NO...
JAMES GORDON. YES. I REMEMBER YOU, WE HAD A FEW ROWS BACK WHEN I TOOK CONTROL OF CHINATOWN FROM THE TRIAD GANGS YOU LET RUN RAMPANT ALL THOSE YEARS AGO.
HEAVY BAGS UNDER YOUR EYES, DEEP WRINKLES, I'D SAY TIME HAS NOT BEEN KIND TO YOU, SIR.
KAKK
...LOOK WHO'S CALLING... THE KETTLE BLACK...
LET'S SHOOT 'EM UP AND EAT.
NOT JUST YET, MY TRIGGER-HAPPY FRIEND. FIRST HE WILL WATCH HIS DAUGHTER DIE.
YOU LOOK SO PROUD OF HER.
BUT NOW YOU'LL NEVER HEAR HER VOICE AGAIN SAY THAT SIMPLE, YET MAGICAL WORD: "DADDY"--WELL, EXCEPT MAYBE YOU'LL HEAR HER SCREAM IT AS WE TEAR OUT HER HEART.
...SON OF A BITCH...

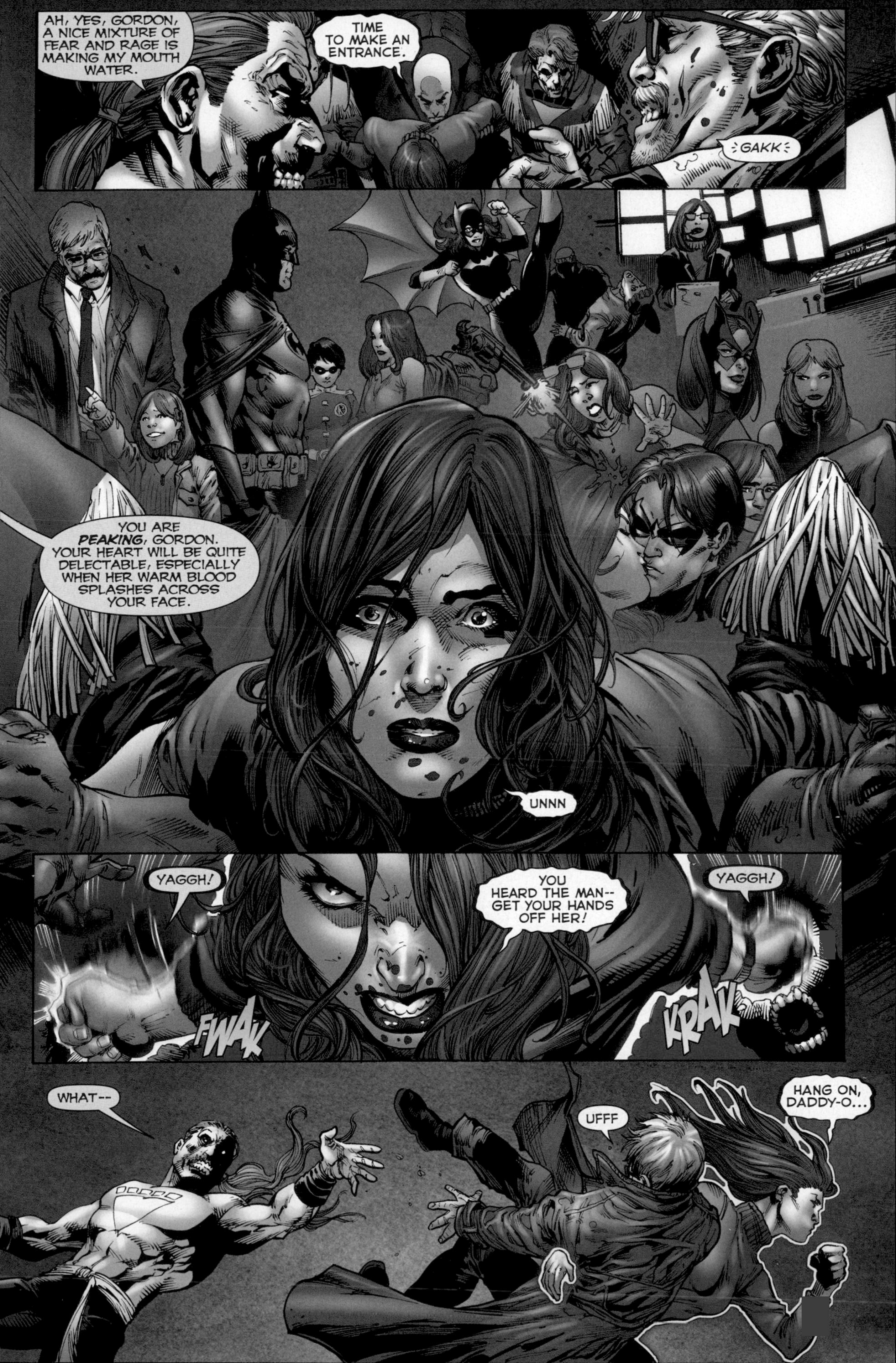
AH, YES, GORDON, A NICE MIXTURE OF FEAR AND RAGE IS MAKING MY MOUTH WATER.
TIME TO MAKE AN ENTRANCE.
GAKK
YOU ARE PEAKING, GORDON. YOUR HEART WILL BE QUITE DELECTABLE, ESPECIALLY WHEN HER WARM BLOOD SPLASHES ACROSS YOUR FACE.
UNNN
YAGGH!
YOU HEARD THE MAN-- GET YOUR HANDS OFF HER!
YAGGH!
FWAK
KRAK
WHAT--
UFFF
HANG ON, DADDY-O...

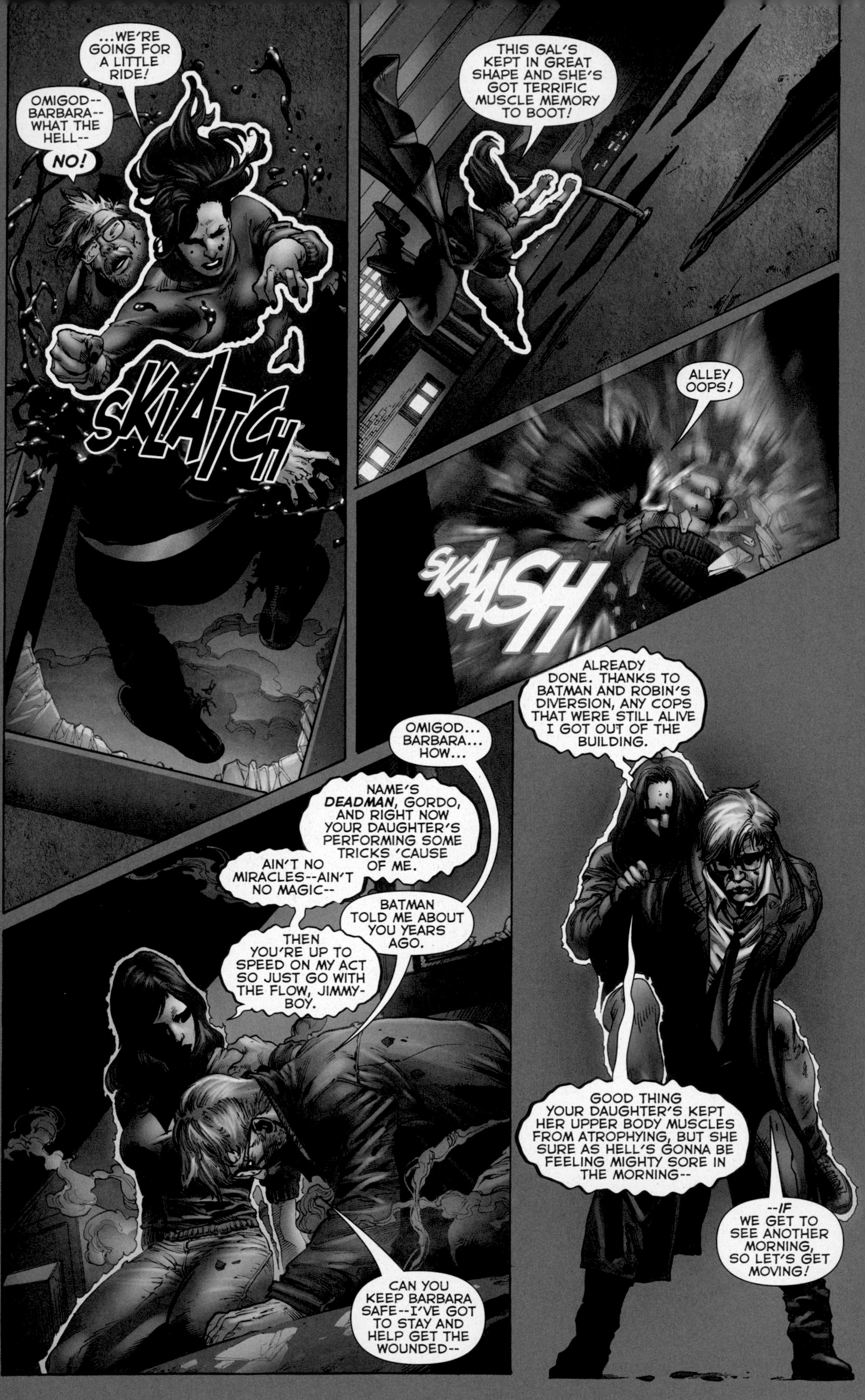
...WE'RE GOING FOR A LITTLE RIDE!
OMIGOD-- BARBARA-- WHAT THE HELL-- NO!
SKLATCH
THIS GAL'S KEPT IN GREAT SHAPE AND SHE'S GOT TERRIFIC MUSCLE MEMORY TO BOOT!
ALLEY OOPS!
SKAASH
OMIGOD... BARBARA... HOW...
NAME'S DEADMAN, GORDO, AND RIGHT NOW YOUR DAUGHTER'S PERFORMING SOME TRICKS 'CAUSE OF ME.
AIN'T NO MIRACLES--AIN'T NO MAGIC--
BATMAN TOLD ME ABOUT YOU YEARS AGO.
THEN YOU'RE UP TO SPEED ON MY ACT SO JUST GO WITH THE FLOW, JIMMY-BOY.
CAN YOU KEEP BARBARA SAFE--I'VE GOT TO STAY AND HELP GET THE WOUNDED--
ALREADY DONE. THANKS TO BATMAN AND ROBIN'S DIVERSION, ANY COPS THAT WERE STILL ALIVE I GOT OUT OF THE BUILDING.
GOOD THING YOUR DAUGHTER'S KEPT HER UPPER BODY MUSCLES FROM ATROPHYING, BUT SHE SURE AS HELL'S GONNA BE FEELING MIGHTY SORE IN THE MORNING--
--IF WE GET TO SEE ANOTHER MORNING, SO LET'S GET MOVING!

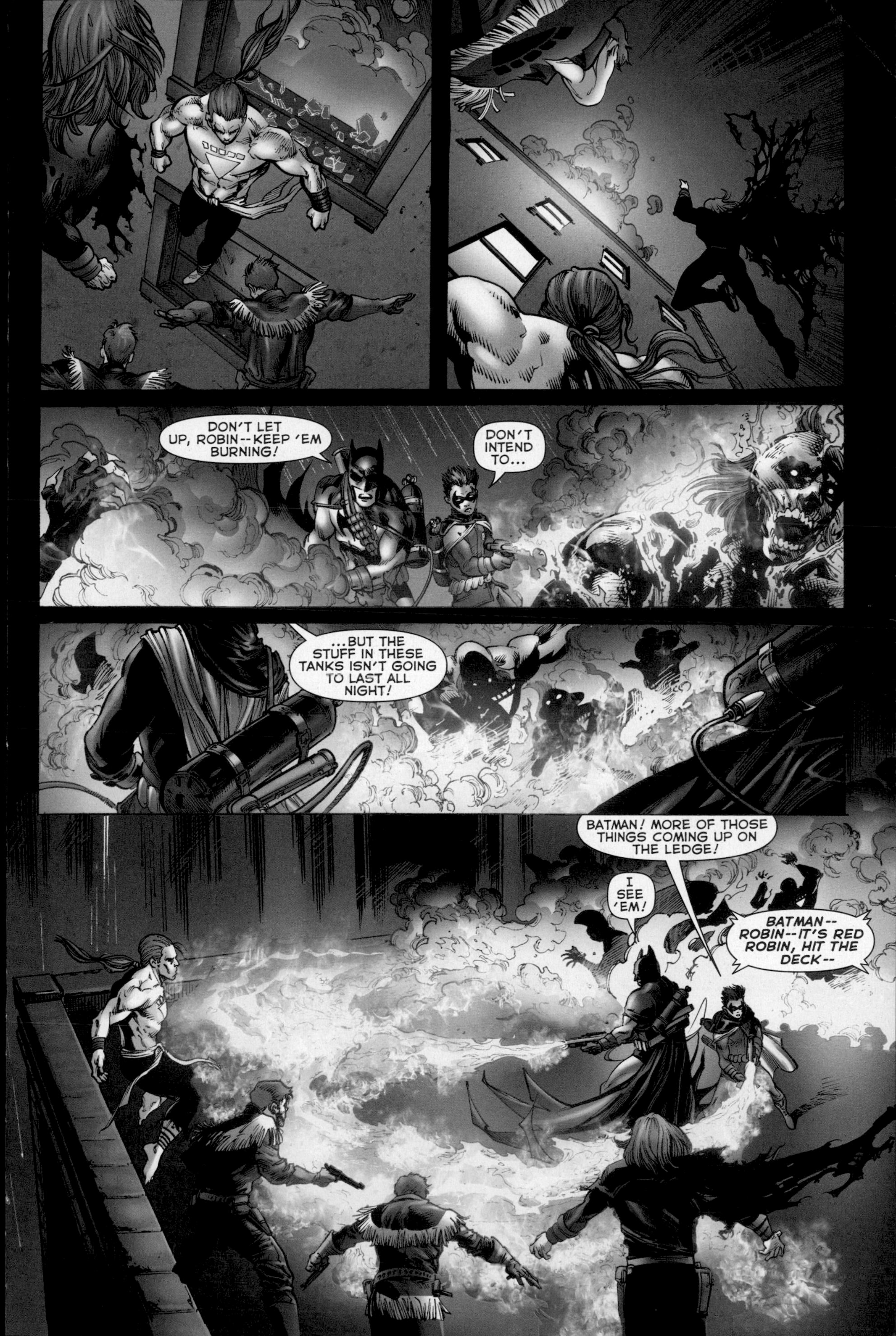
DON'T LET UP, ROBIN--KEEP 'EM BURNING!
DON'T INTEND TO...
...BUT THE STUFF IN THESE TANKS ISN'T GOING TO LAST ALL NIGHT!
BATMAN! MORE OF THOSE THINGS COMING UP ON THE LEDGE!
I SEE 'EM!
BATMAN--ROBIN--IT'S RED ROBIN, HIT THE DECK--

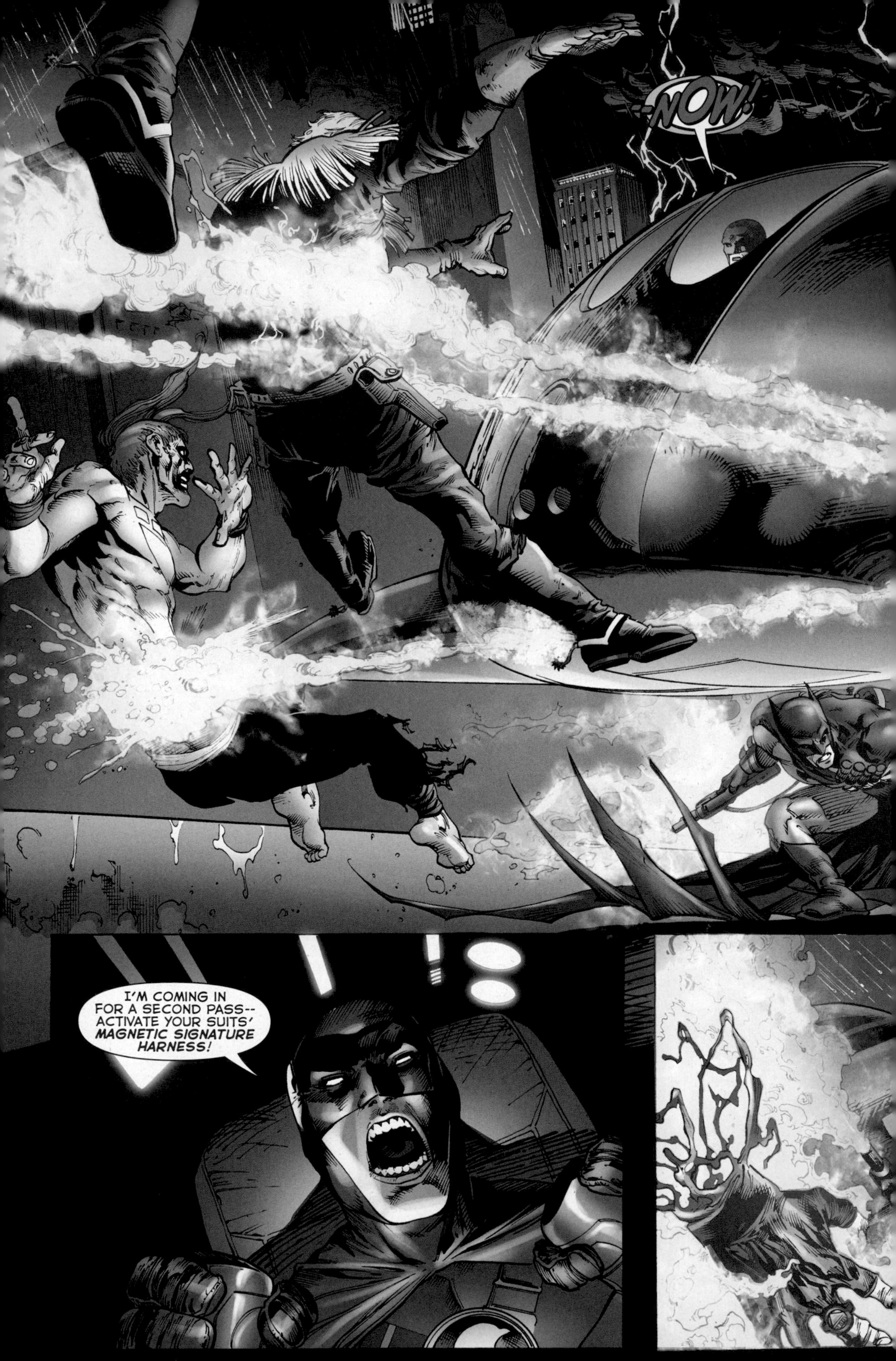
--NOW!
I'M COMING IN FOR A SECOND PASS-- ACTIVATE YOUR SUITS' MAGNETIC SIGNATURE HARNESS!

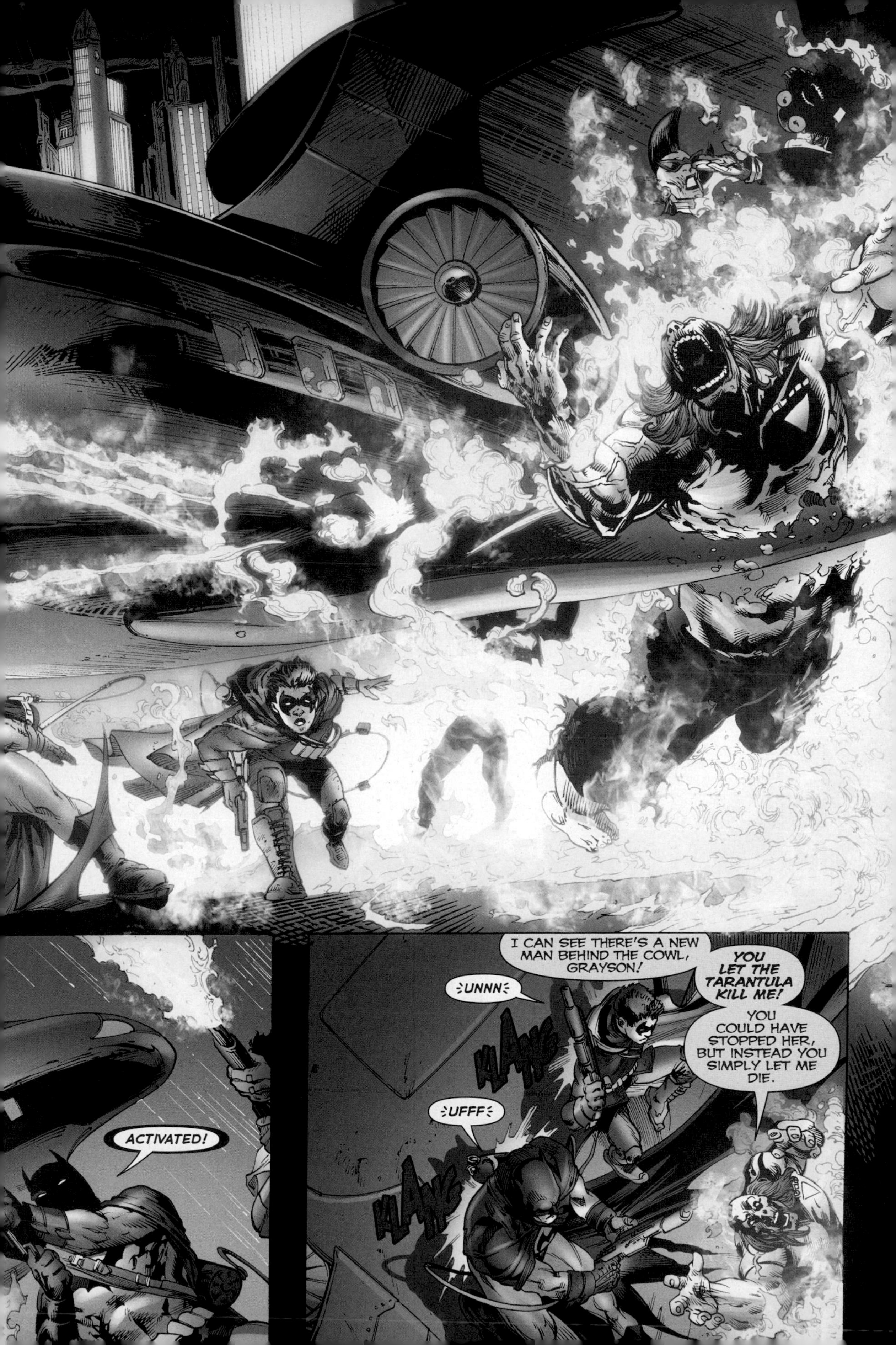
ACTIVATED!
I CAN SEE THERE'S A NEW MAN BEHIND THE COWL, GRAYSON!
UNNN
YOU LET THE TARANTULA KILL ME!
YOU COULD HAVE STOPPED HER, BUT INSTEAD YOU SIMPLY LET ME DIE.
UFFF

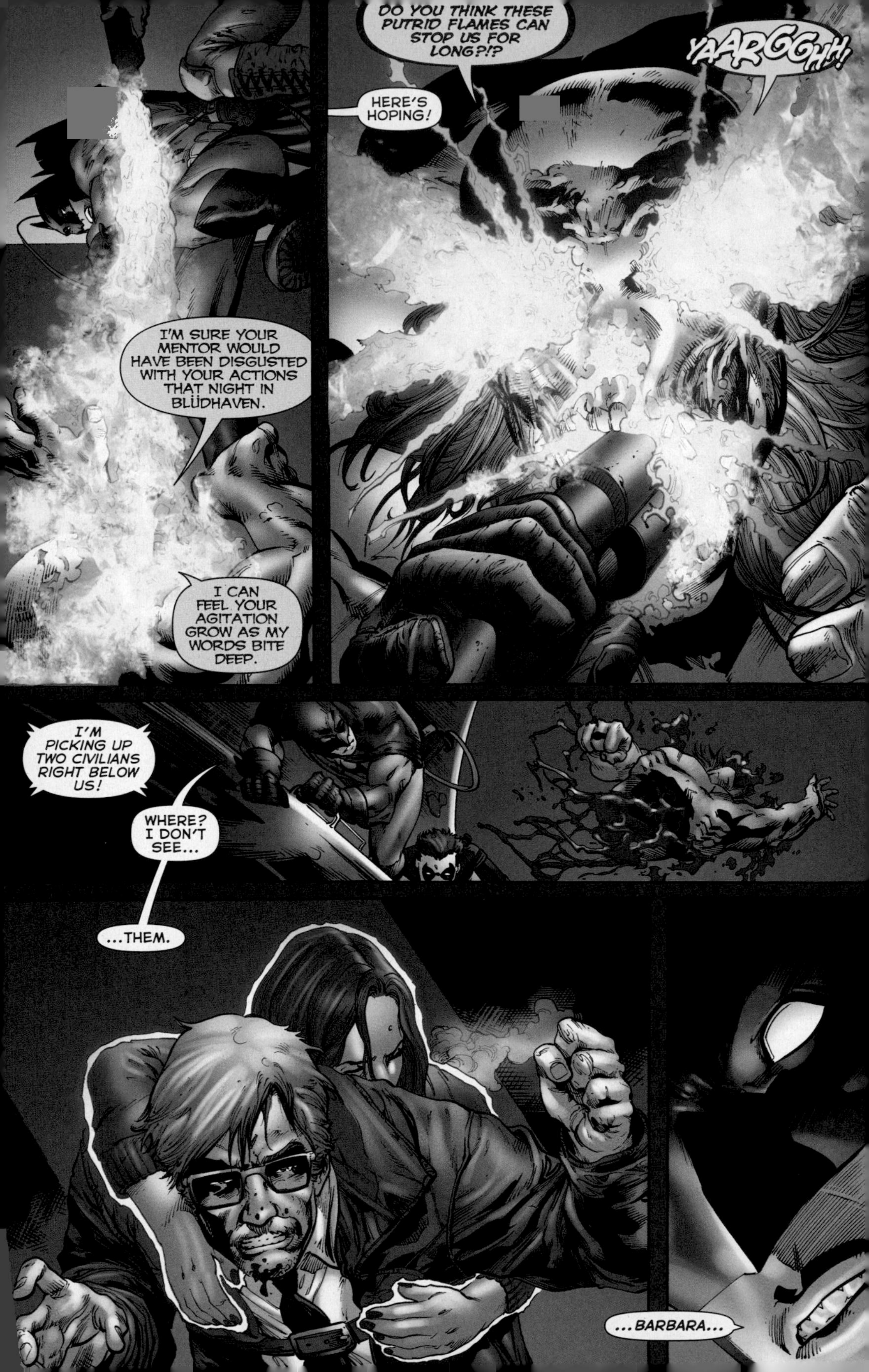
I'M SURE YOUR MENTOR WOULD HAVE BEEN DISGUSTED WITH YOUR ACTIONS THAT NIGHT IN BLÜDHAVEN.
I CAN FEEL YOUR AGITATION GROW AS MY WORDS BITE DEEP.
DO YOU THINK THESE PUTRID FLAMES CAN STOP US FOR LONG?!?
HERE'S HOPING!
YAARGGHH!
I'M PICKING UP TWO CIVILIANS RIGHT BELOW US!
WHERE? I DON'T SEE...
...THEM.
...BARBARA...

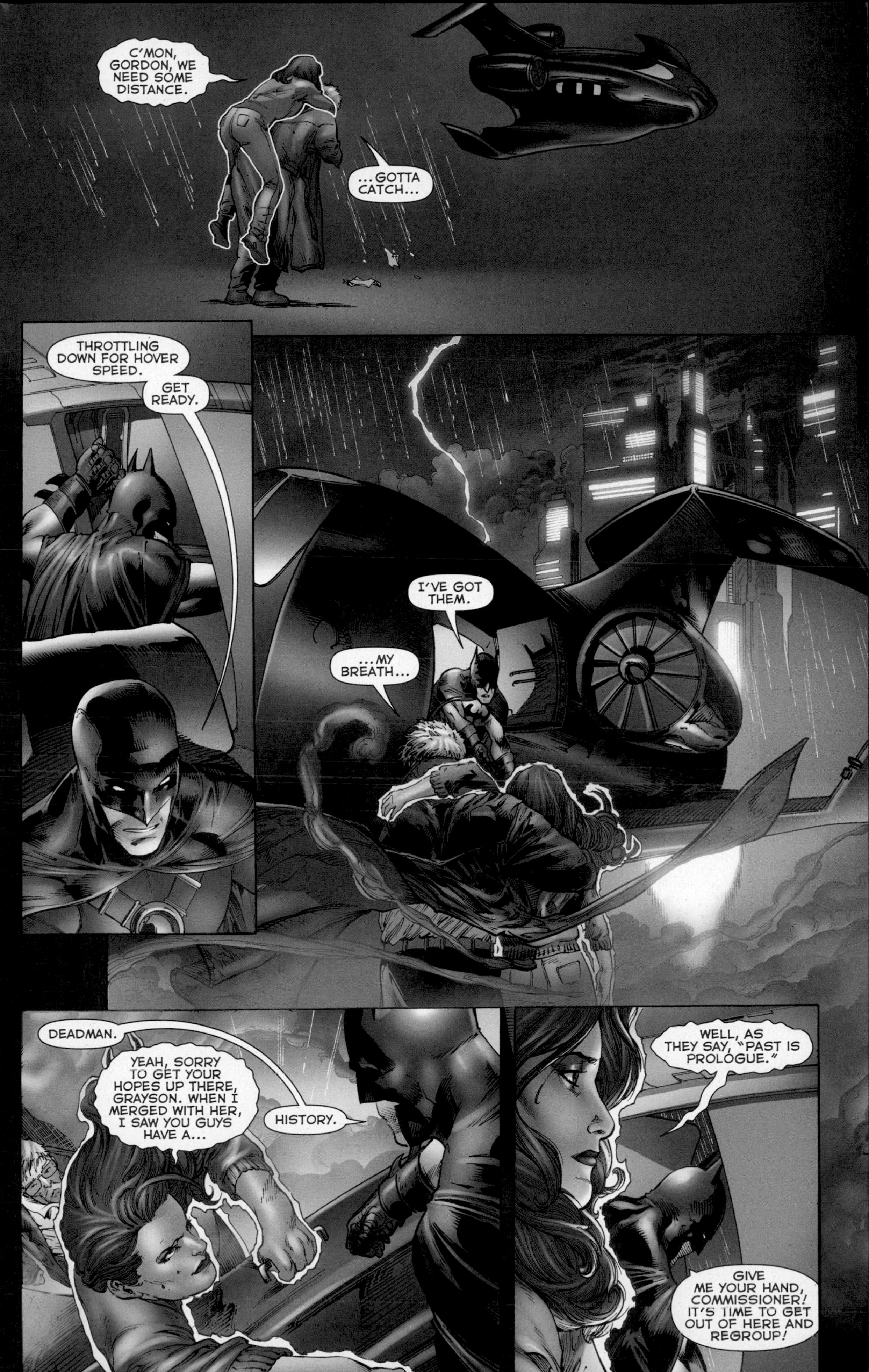
C'MON, GORDON, WE NEED SOME DISTANCE.
...GOTTA CATCH...
THROTTLING DOWN FOR HOVER SPEED.
GET READY.
I'VE GOT THEM.
...MY BREATH...
DEADMAN.
YEAH, SORRY TO GET YOUR HOPES UP THERE, GRAYSON. WHEN I MERGED WITH HER, I SAW YOU GUYS HAVE A...
HISTORY.
WELL, AS THEY SAY, "PAST IS PROLOGUE."
GIVE ME YOUR HAND, COMMISSIONER! IT'S TIME TO GET OUT OF HERE AND REGROUP!

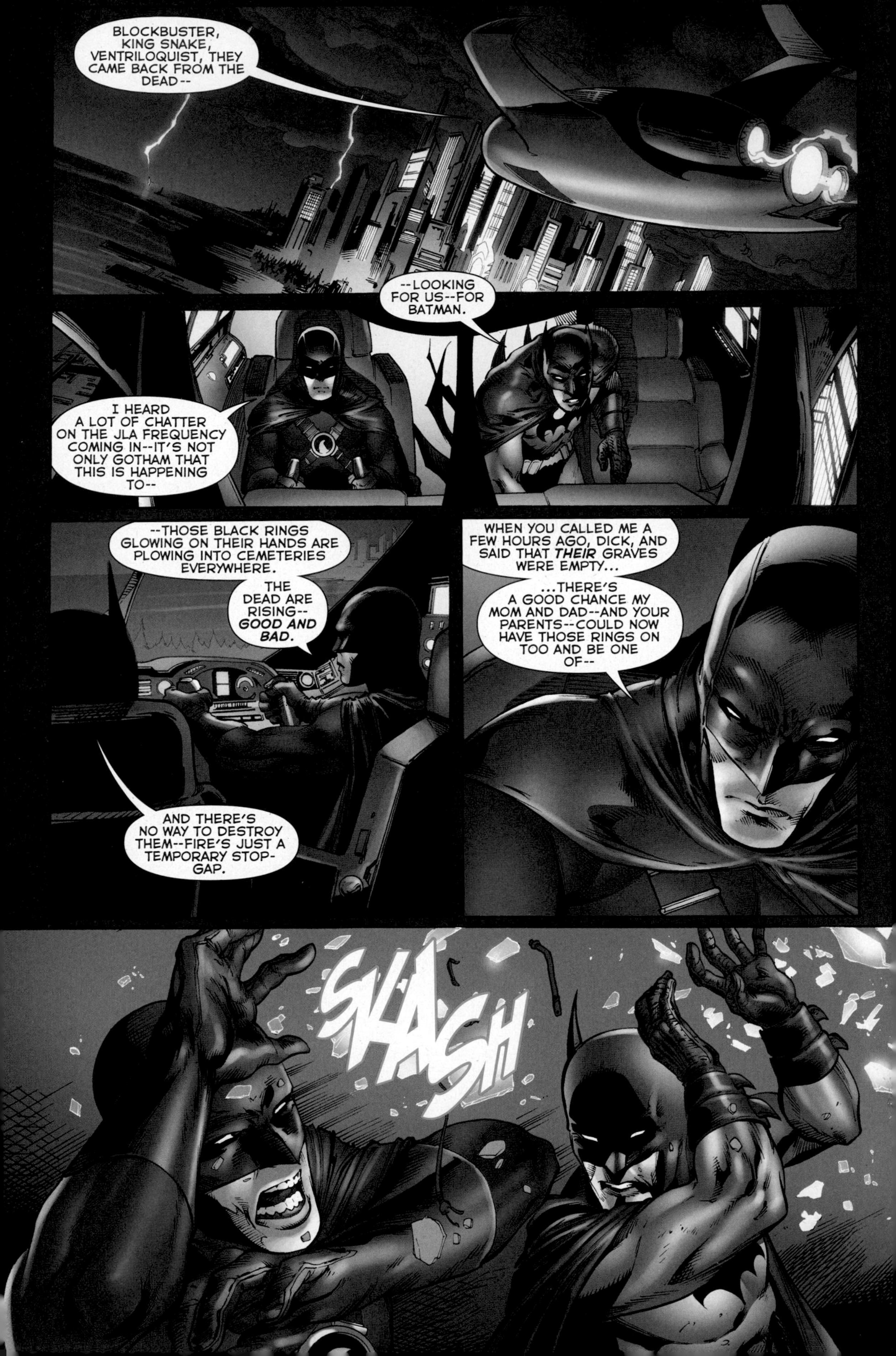

BLOCKBUSTER, KING SNAKE, VENTRILOQUIST, THEY CAME BACK FROM THE DEAD--
--LOOKING FOR US--FOR BATMAN.
I HEARD A LOT OF CHATTER ON THE JLA FREQUENCY COMING IN--IT'S NOT ONLY GOTHAM THAT THIS IS HAPPENING TO--
--THOSE BLACK RINGS GLOWING ON THEIR HANDS ARE PLOWING INTO CEMETERIES EVERYWHERE.
THE DEAD ARE RISING--*GOOD AND BAD.*
AND THERE'S NO WAY TO DESTROY THEM--FIRE'S JUST A TEMPORARY STOP-GAP.
WHEN YOU CALLED ME A FEW HOURS AGO, DICK, AND SAID THAT *THEIR* GRAVES WERE EMPTY...
...THERE'S A GOOD CHANCE MY MOM AND DAD--AND YOUR PARENTS--COULD NOW HAVE THOSE RINGS ON TOO AND BE ONE OF--
SKASH

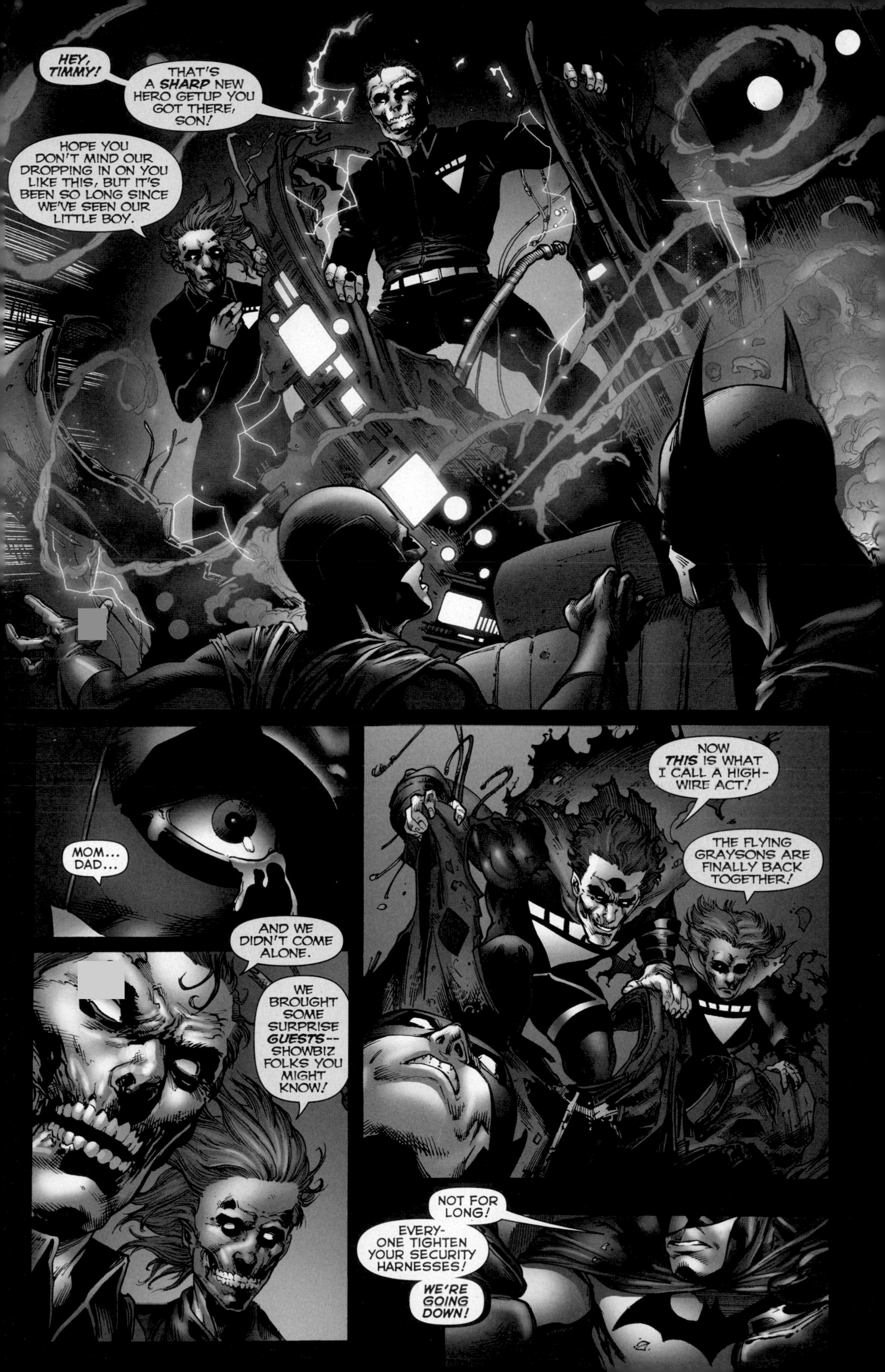
HEY, TIMMY!
THAT'S A SHARP NEW HERO GETUP YOU GOT THERE, SON!
HOPE YOU DON'T MIND OUR DROPPING IN ON YOU LIKE THIS, BUT IT'S BEEN SO LONG SINCE WE'VE SEEN OUR LITTLE BOY.
MOM... DAD...
AND WE DIDN'T COME ALONE.
WE BROUGHT SOME SURPRISE GUESTS-- SHOWBIZ FOLKS YOU MIGHT KNOW!
NOW THIS IS WHAT I CALL A HIGH-WIRE ACT!
THE FLYING GRAYSONS ARE FINALLY BACK TOGETHER!
NOT FOR LONG!
EVERY-ONE TIGHTEN YOUR SECURITY HARNESSES!
WE'RE GOING DOWN!

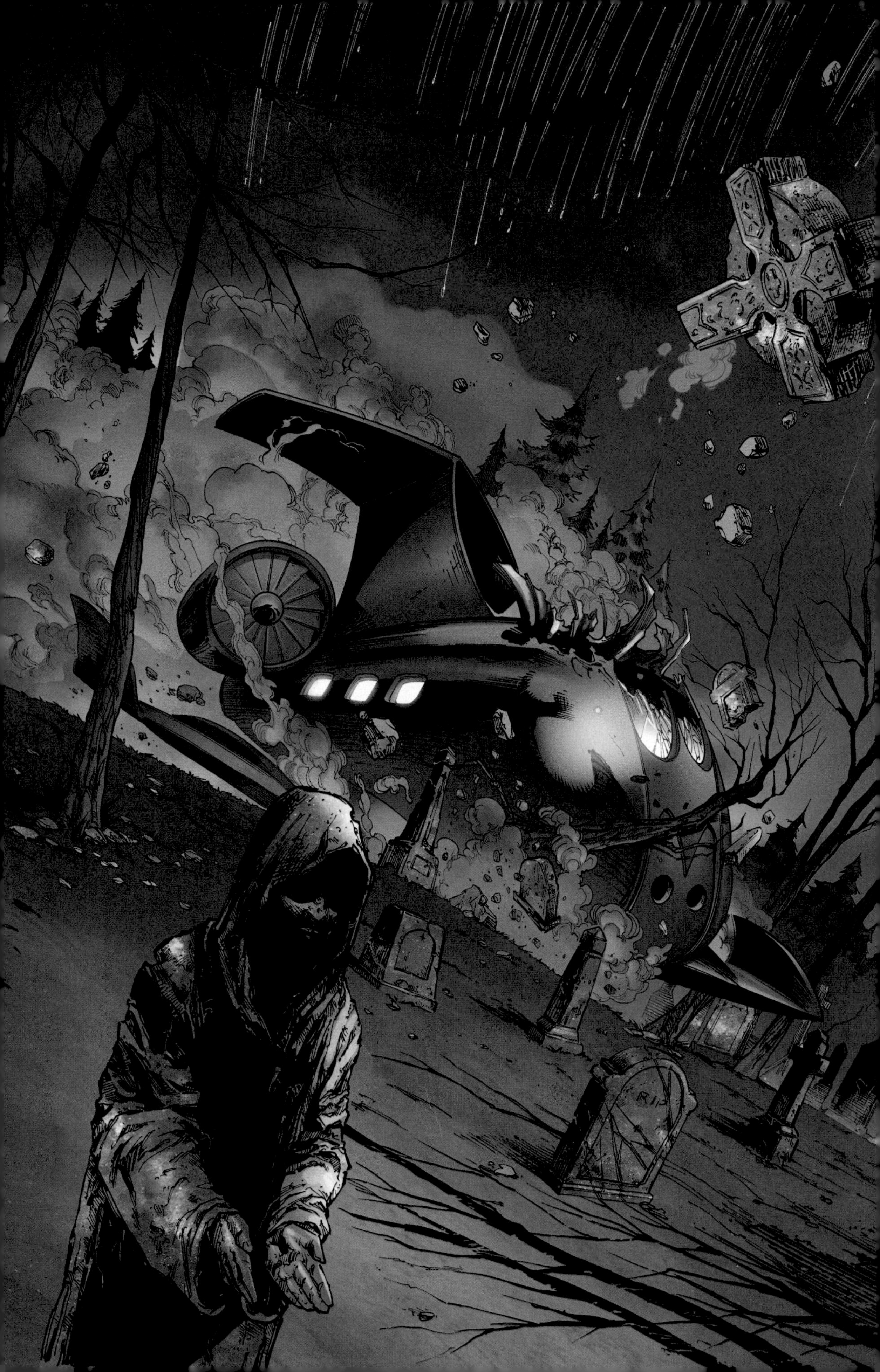

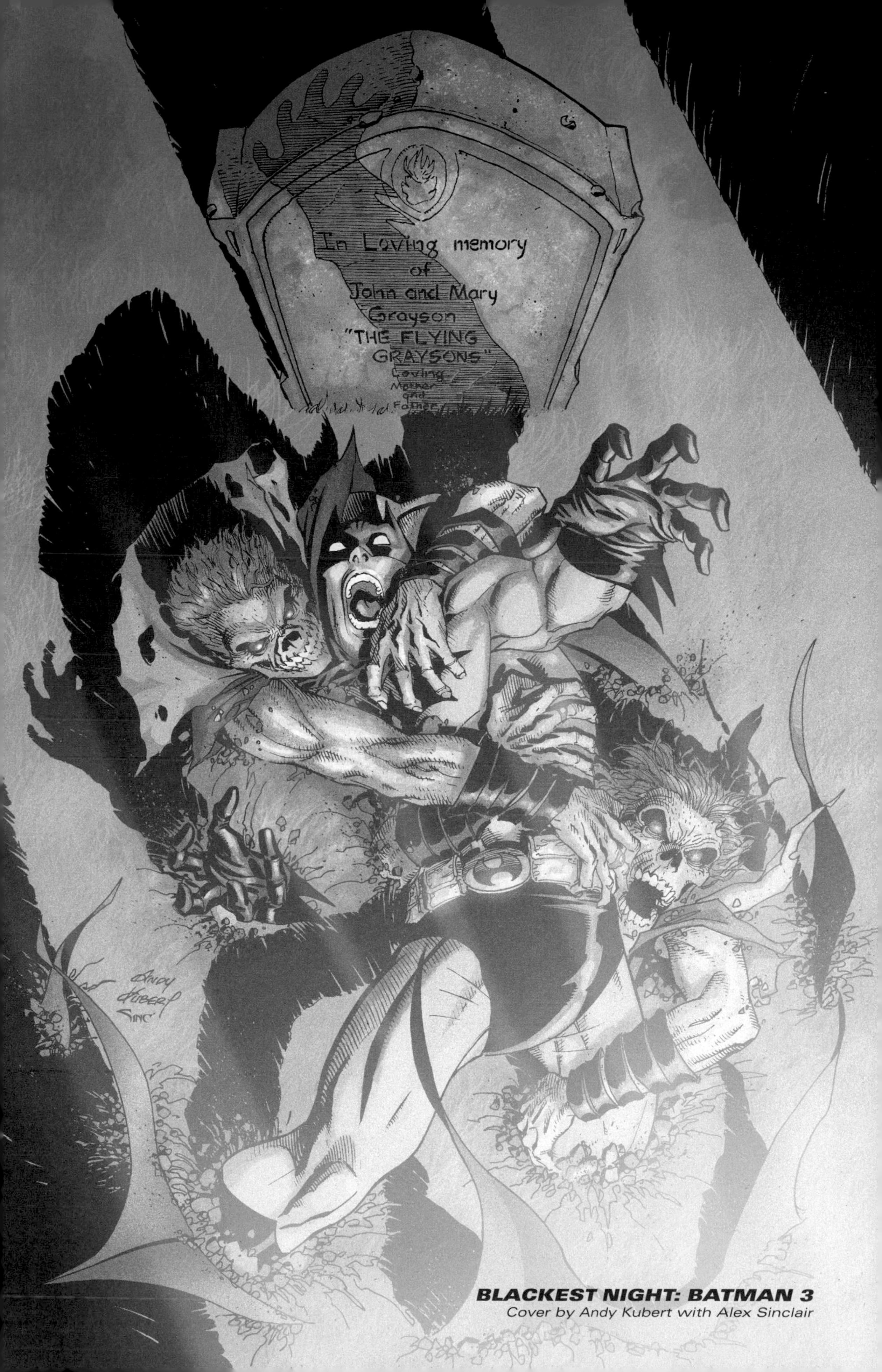
In Loving memory
of
John and Mary
Grayson
"THE FLYING
GRAYSONS"
Loving
Mother
and
Father
ANDY
KUBERT
SINC

BLACKEST NIGHT: BATMAN 3
Cover by Andy Kubert with Alex Sinclair

WHO BURNS WHO
CONCLUSION

PETER J. TOMASI
WRITER

ARDIAN SYAF
PENCILS

VICENTE CIFUENTES
INKS

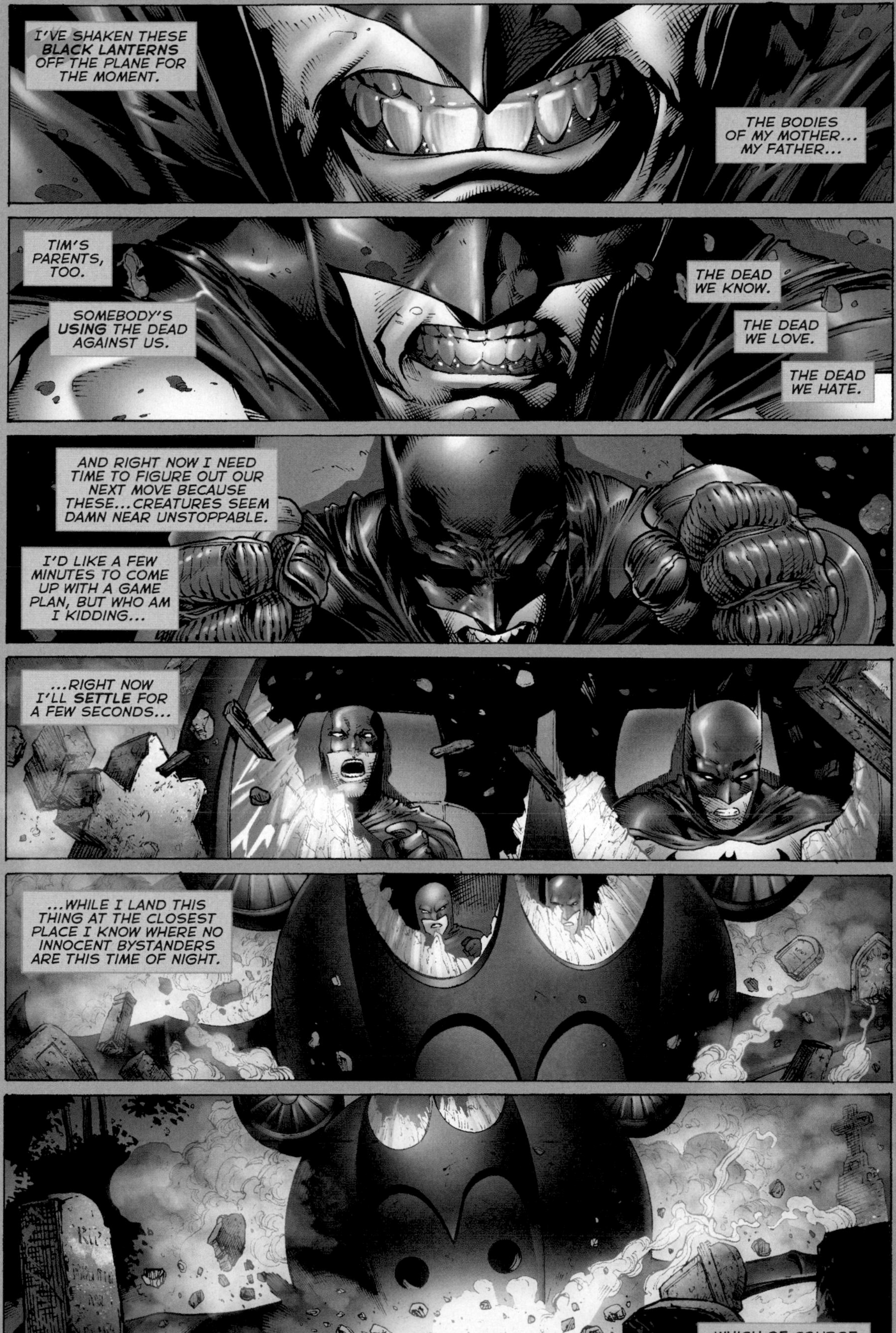
I'VE SHAKEN THESE BLACK LANTERNS OFF THE PLANE FOR THE MOMENT.
THE BODIES OF MY MOTHER... MY FATHER...
TIM'S PARENTS, TOO.
SOMEBODY'S USING THE DEAD AGAINST US.
THE DEAD WE KNOW.
THE DEAD WE LOVE.
THE DEAD WE HATE.
AND RIGHT NOW I NEED TIME TO FIGURE OUT OUR NEXT MOVE BECAUSE THESE...CREATURES SEEM DAMN NEAR UNSTOPPABLE.
I'D LIKE A FEW MINUTES TO COME UP WITH A GAME PLAN, BUT WHO AM I KIDDING...
...RIGHT NOW I'LL SETTLE FOR A FEW SECONDS...
...WHILE I LAND THIS THING AT THE CLOSEST PLACE I KNOW WHERE NO INNOCENT BYSTANDERS ARE THIS TIME OF NIGHT.
WHICH OF COURSE HAPPENS TO BE A...

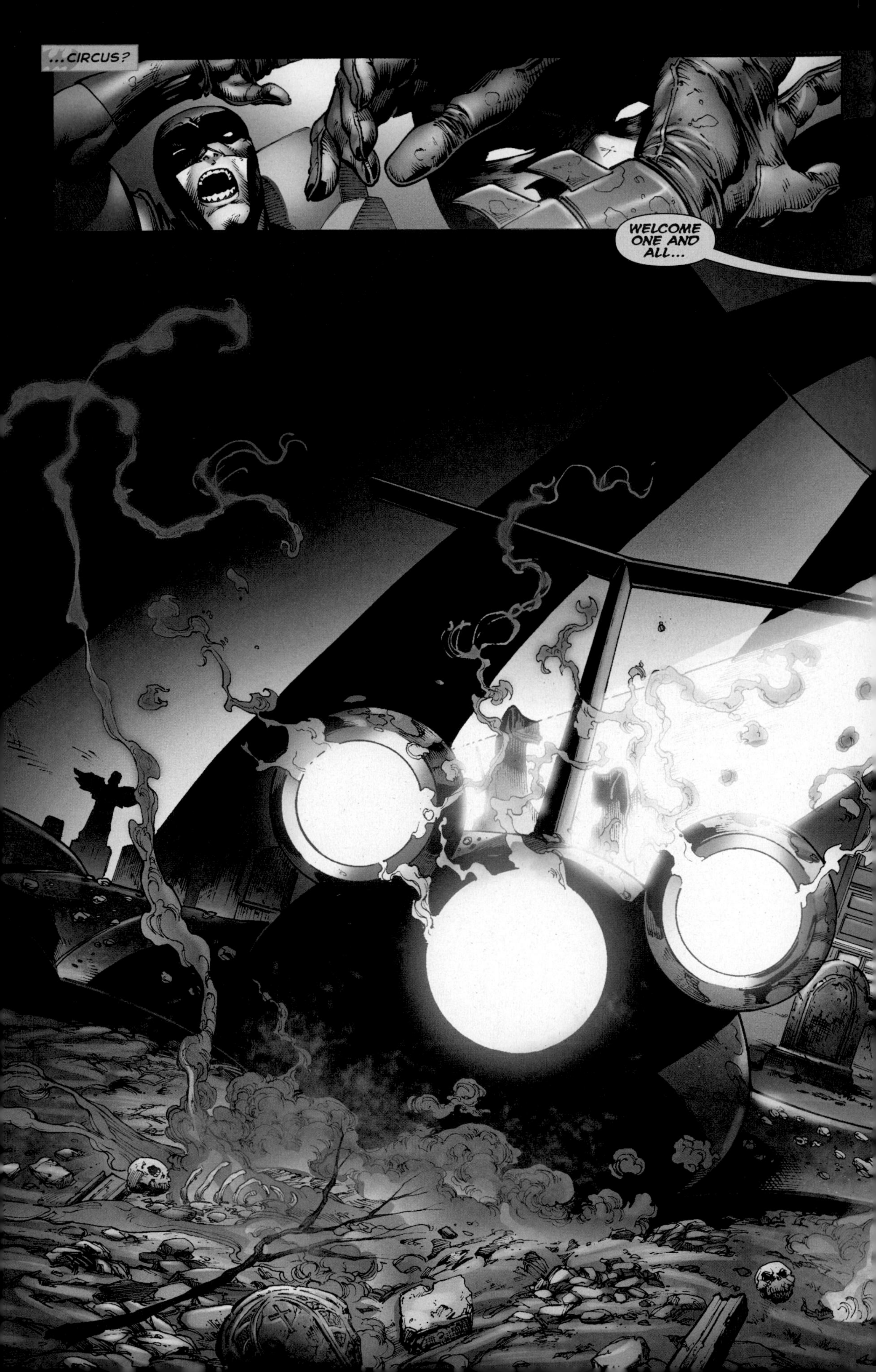
...CIRCUS?
WELCOME ONE AND ALL...

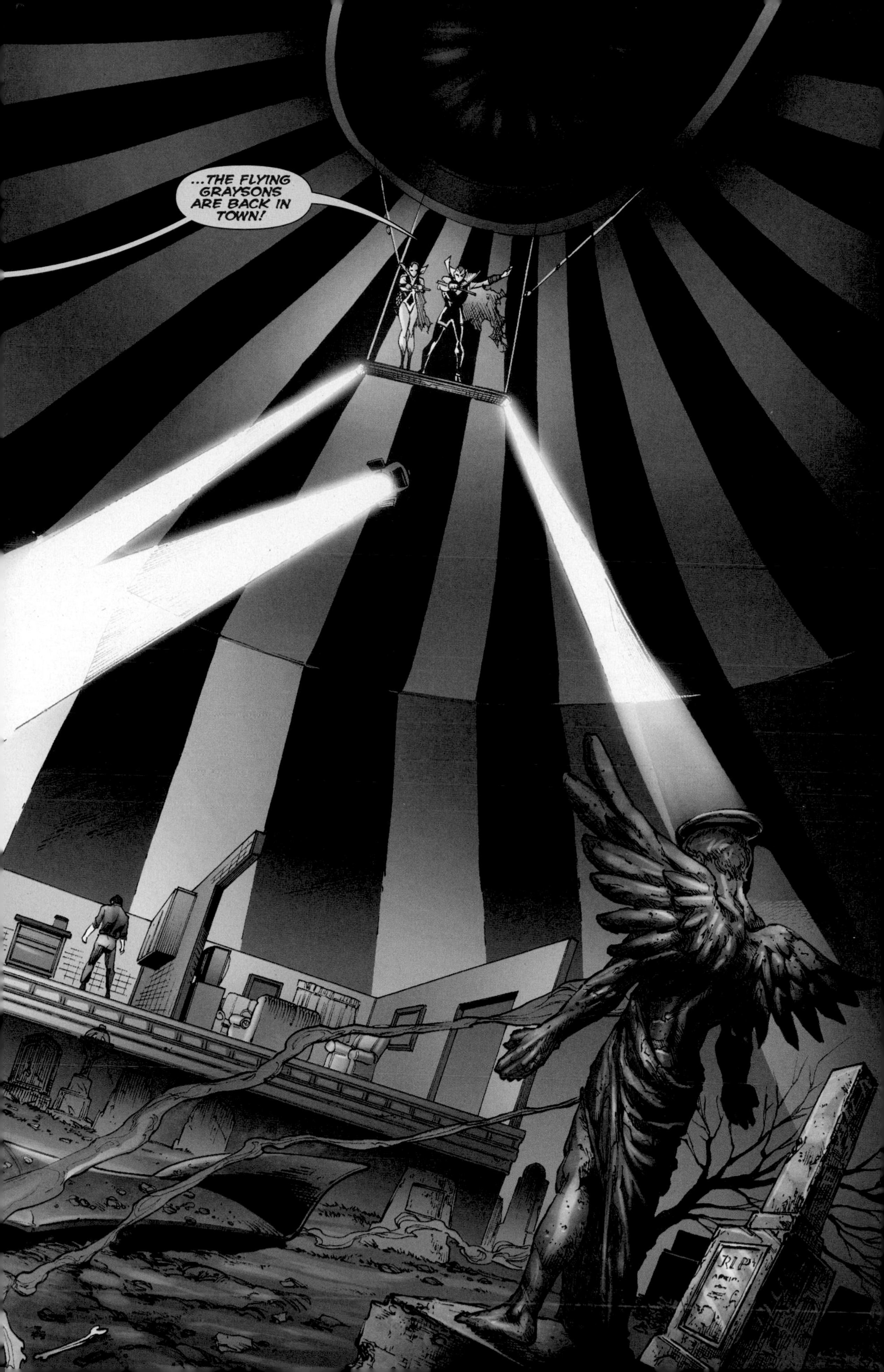
...THE FLYING GRAYSONS ARE BACK IN TOWN!
RIP

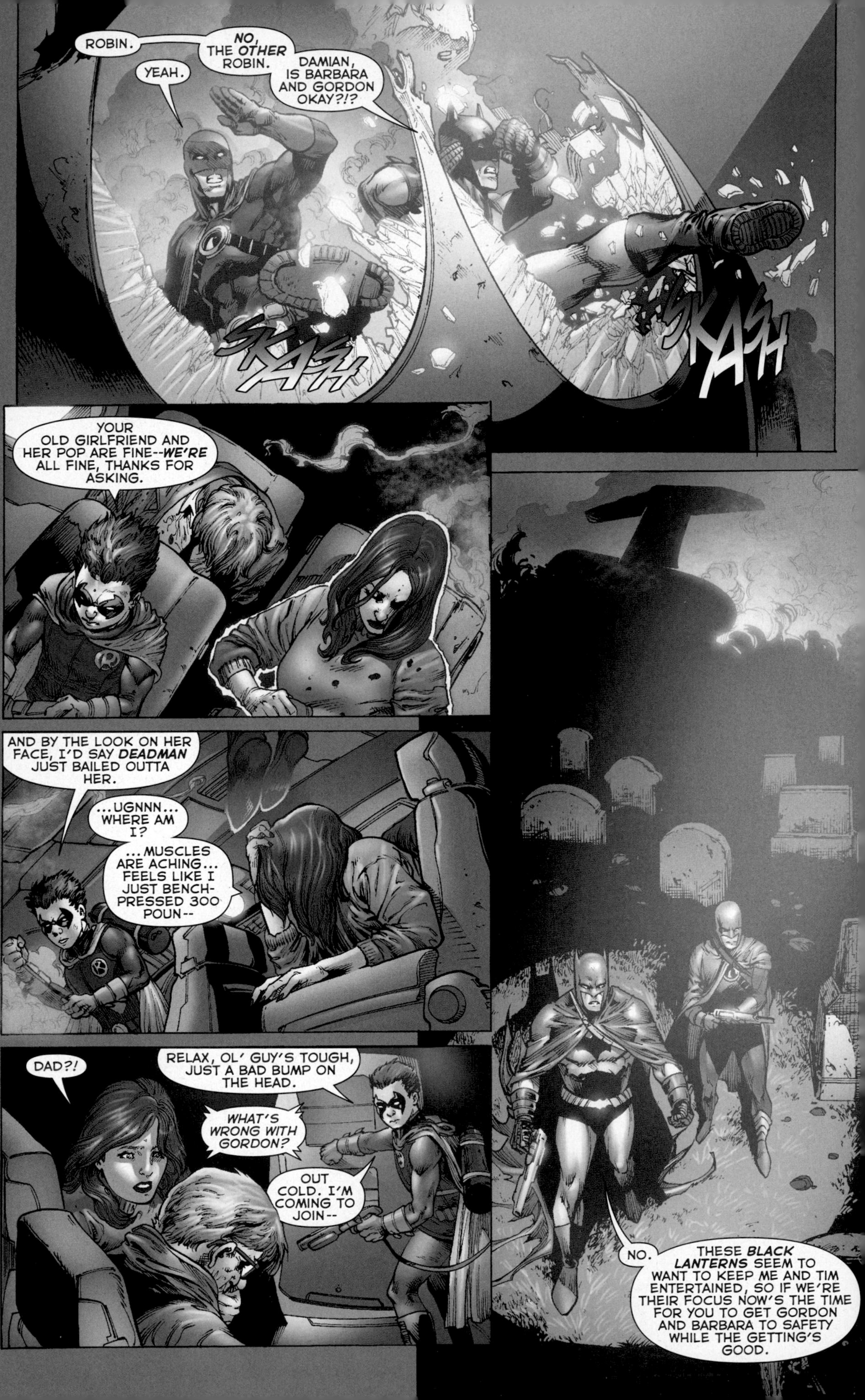
ROBIN.
NO, THE OTHER ROBIN.
YEAH.
DAMIAN, IS BARBARA AND GORDON OKAY?!?
SKASH
SKASH
YOUR OLD GIRLFRIEND AND HER POP ARE FINE--WE'RE ALL FINE, THANKS FOR ASKING.
AND BY THE LOOK ON HER FACE, I'D SAY DEADMAN JUST BAILED OUTTA HER.
...UGNNN... WHERE AM I?
...MUSCLES ARE ACHING... FEELS LIKE I JUST BENCH-PRESSED 300 POUN--
DAD?!
RELAX, OL' GUY'S TOUGH, JUST A BAD BUMP ON THE HEAD.
WHAT'S WRONG WITH GORDON?
OUT COLD. I'M COMING TO JOIN--
NO.
THESE BLACK LANTERNS SEEM TO WANT TO KEEP ME AND TIM ENTERTAINED, SO IF WE'RE THEIR FOCUS NOW'S THE TIME FOR YOU TO GET GORDON AND BARBARA TO SAFETY WHILE THE GETTING'S GOOD.

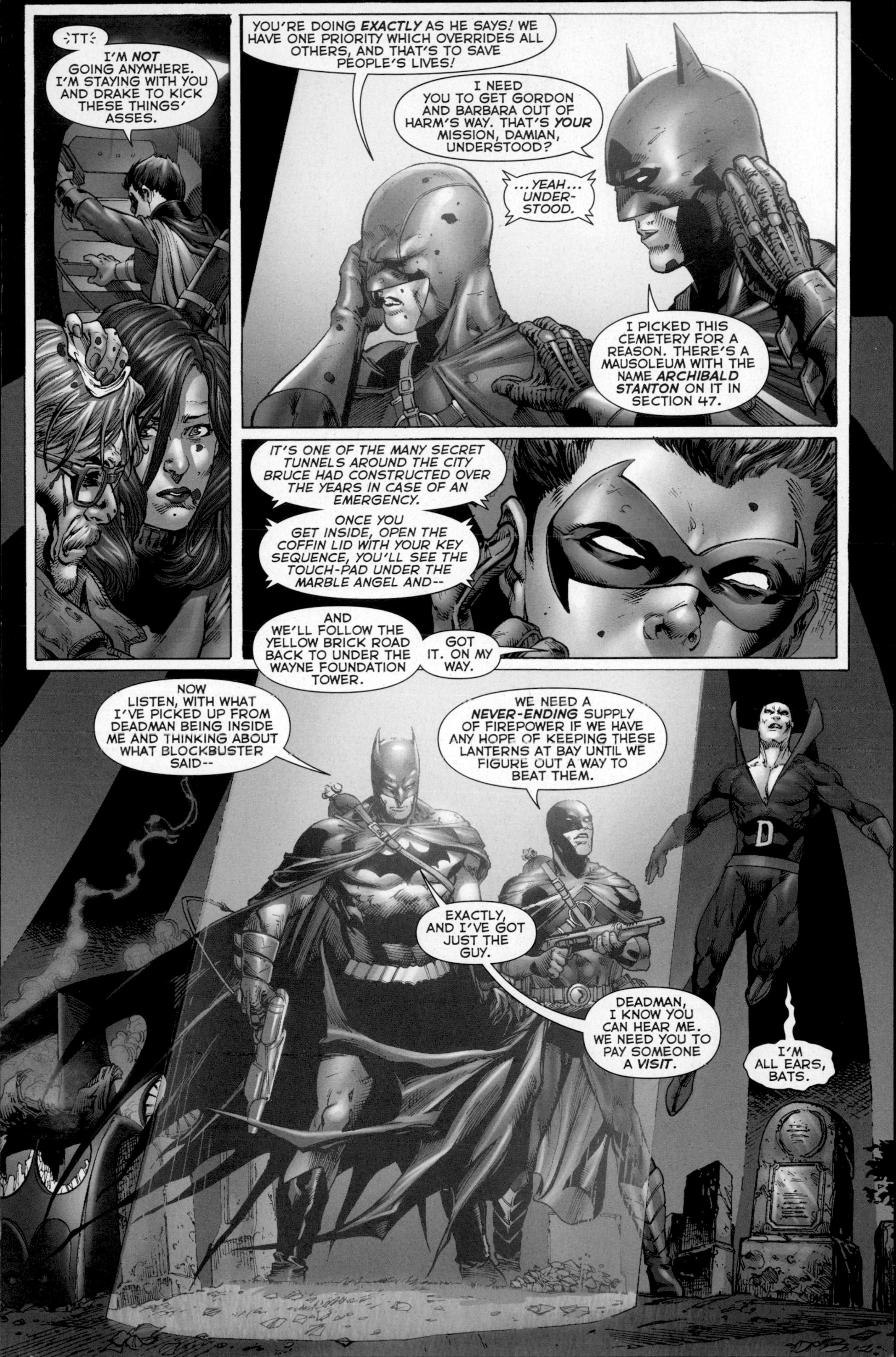
TT
I'M NOT GOING ANYWHERE. I'M STAYING WITH YOU AND DRAKE TO KICK THESE THINGS' ASSES.
YOU'RE DOING EXACTLY AS HE SAYS! WE HAVE ONE PRIORITY WHICH OVERRIDES ALL OTHERS, AND THAT'S TO SAVE PEOPLE'S LIVES!
I NEED YOU TO GET GORDON AND BARBARA OUT OF HARM'S WAY. THAT'S YOUR MISSION, DAMIAN, UNDERSTOOD?
...YEAH... UNDERSTOOD.
I PICKED THIS CEMETERY FOR A REASON. THERE'S A MAUSOLEUM WITH THE NAME ARCHIBALD STANTON ON IT IN SECTION 47.
IT'S ONE OF THE MANY SECRET TUNNELS AROUND THE CITY BRUCE HAD CONSTRUCTED OVER THE YEARS IN CASE OF AN EMERGENCY.
ONCE YOU GET INSIDE, OPEN THE COFFIN LID WITH YOUR KEY SEQUENCE, YOU'LL SEE THE TOUCH-PAD UNDER THE MARBLE ANGEL AND--
AND WE'LL FOLLOW THE YELLOW BRICK ROAD BACK TO UNDER THE WAYNE FOUNDATION TOWER.
GOT IT. ON MY WAY.
NOW LISTEN, WITH WHAT I'VE PICKED UP FROM DEADMAN BEING INSIDE ME AND THINKING ABOUT WHAT BLOCKBUSTER SAID--
WE NEED A NEVER-ENDING SUPPLY OF FIREPOWER IF WE HAVE ANY HOPE OF KEEPING THESE LANTERNS AT BAY UNTIL WE FIGURE OUT A WAY TO BEAT THEM.
EXACTLY, AND I'VE GOT JUST THE GUY.
DEADMAN, I KNOW YOU CAN HEAR ME. WE NEED YOU TO PAY SOMEONE A VISIT.
I'M ALL EARS, BATS.

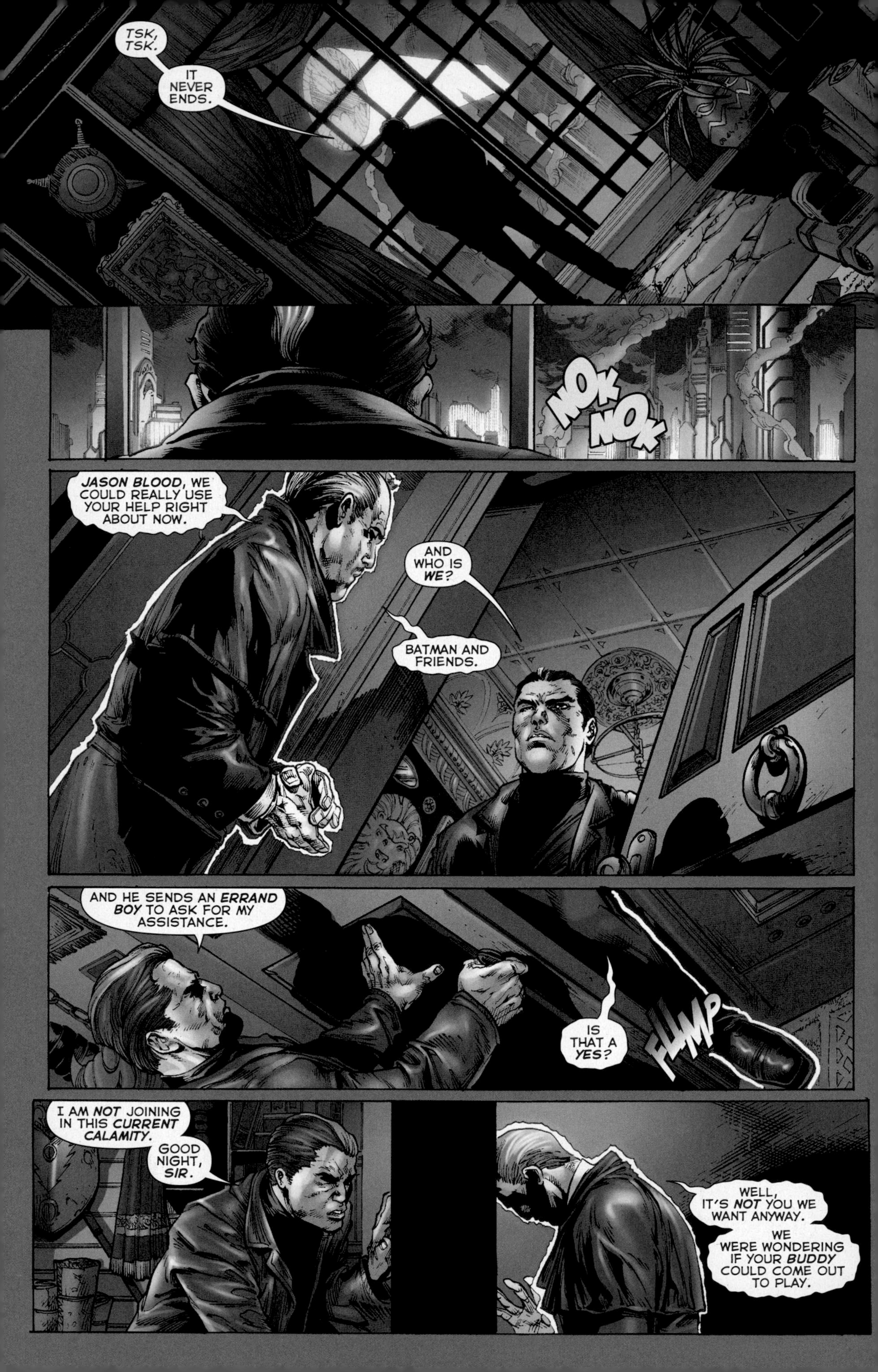
TSK, TSK.
IT NEVER ENDS.
NOK NOK
JASON BLOOD, WE COULD REALLY USE YOUR HELP RIGHT ABOUT NOW.
AND WHO IS WE?
BATMAN AND FRIENDS.
AND HE SENDS AN ERRAND BOY TO ASK FOR MY ASSISTANCE.
IS THAT A YES?
FLMP
I AM NOT JOINING IN THIS CURRENT CALAMITY.
GOOD NIGHT, SIR.
WELL, IT'S NOT YOU WE WANT ANYWAY.
WE WERE WONDERING IF YOUR BUDDY COULD COME OUT TO PLAY.

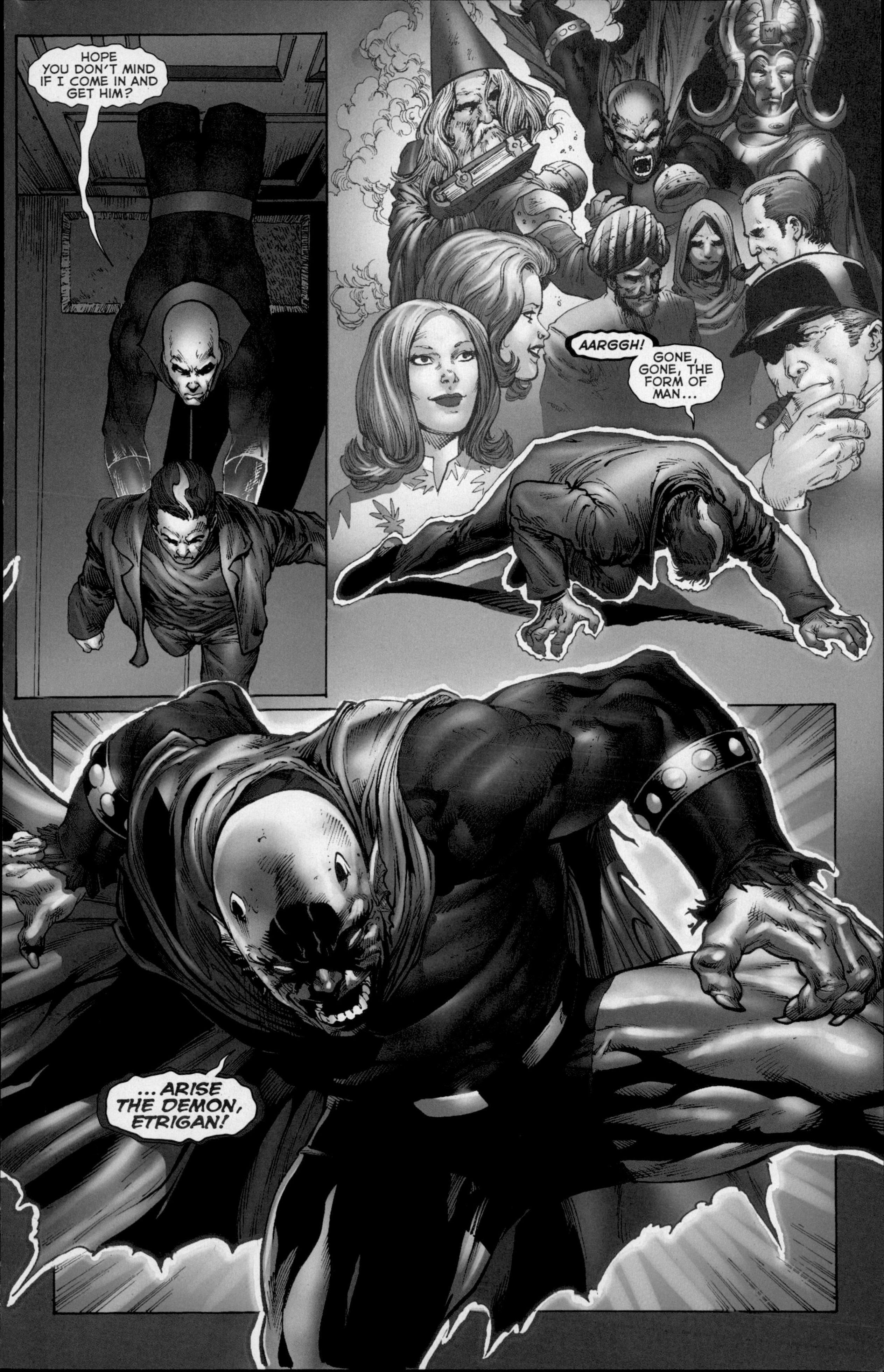
HOPE YOU DON'T MIND IF I COME IN AND GET HIM?
AARGGH! GONE, GONE, THE FORM OF MAN...
...ARISE THE DEMON, ETRIGAN!

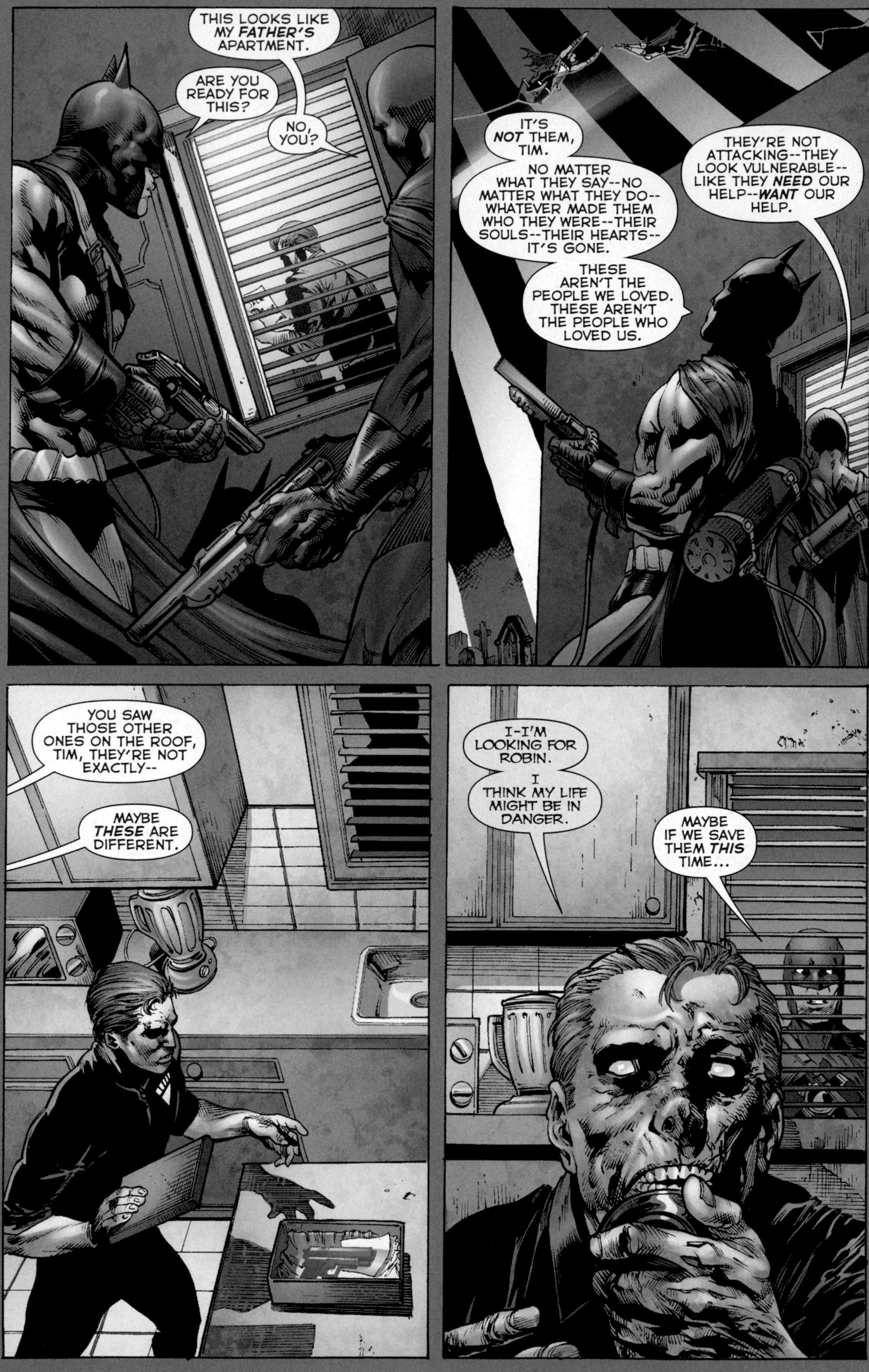
THIS LOOKS LIKE MY *FATHER'S* APARTMENT.
ARE YOU READY FOR THIS?
NO, YOU?
IT'S *NOT* THEM, TIM.
NO MATTER WHAT THEY SAY--NO MATTER WHAT THEY DO--WHATEVER MADE THEM WHO THEY WERE--THEIR SOULS--THEIR HEARTS--IT'S GONE.
THESE AREN'T THE PEOPLE WE LOVED. THESE AREN'T THE PEOPLE WHO LOVED US.
THEY'RE NOT ATTACKING--THEY LOOK VULNERABLE--LIKE THEY *NEED* OUR HELP--*WANT* OUR HELP.
YOU SAW THOSE OTHER ONES ON THE ROOF, TIM, THEY'RE NOT EXACTLY--
MAYBE *THESE* ARE DIFFERENT.
I-I'M LOOKING FOR ROBIN.
I THINK MY LIFE MIGHT BE IN DANGER.
MAYBE IF WE SAVE THEM *THIS* TIME...

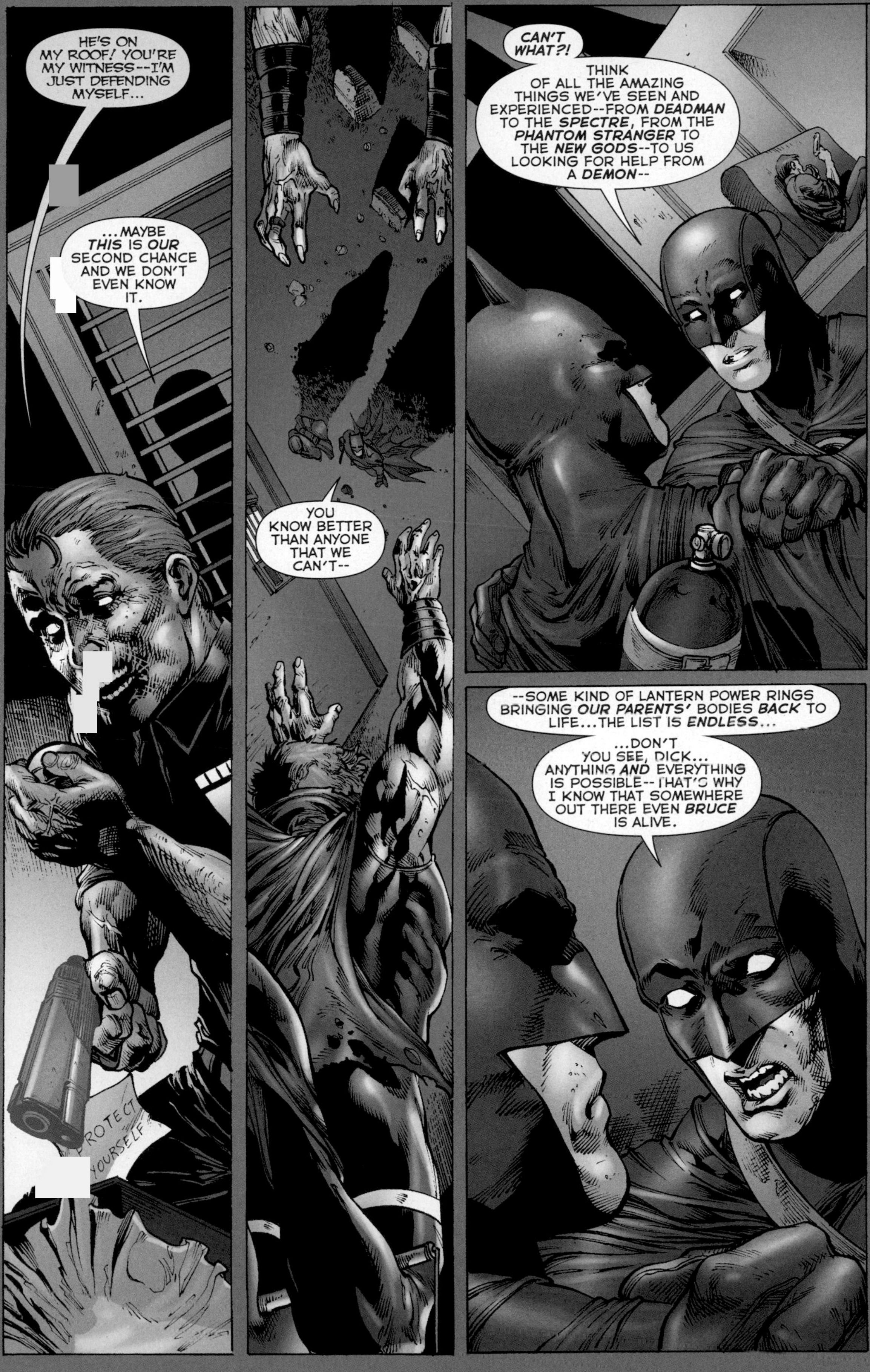
HE'S ON MY ROOF! YOU'RE MY WITNESS--I'M JUST DEFENDING MYSELF...
...MAYBE THIS IS OUR SECOND CHANCE AND WE DON'T EVEN KNOW IT.
PROTECT YOURSELF
YOU KNOW BETTER THAN ANYONE THAT WE CAN'T--
CAN'T WHAT?!
THINK OF ALL THE AMAZING THINGS WE'VE SEEN AND EXPERIENCED--FROM DEADMAN TO THE SPECTRE, FROM THE PHANTOM STRANGER TO THE NEW GODS--TO US LOOKING FOR HELP FROM A DEMON--
--SOME KIND OF LANTERN POWER RINGS BRINGING OUR PARENTS' BODIES BACK TO LIFE...THE LIST IS ENDLESS...
...DON'T YOU SEE, DICK... ANYTHING AND EVERYTHING IS POSSIBLE--THAT'S WHY I KNOW THAT SOMEWHERE OUT THERE EVEN BRUCE IS ALIVE.

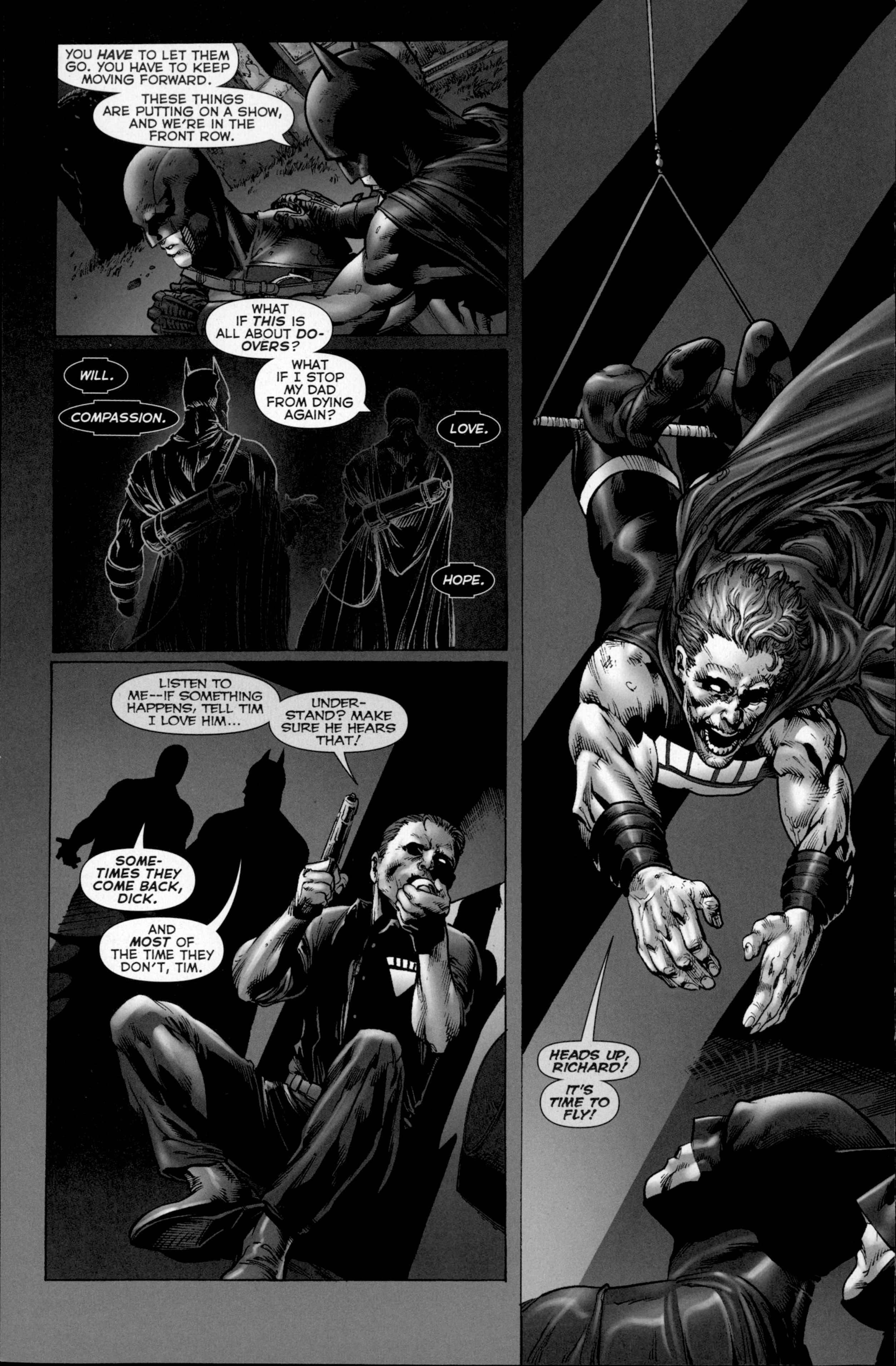
YOU HAVE TO LET THEM GO. YOU HAVE TO KEEP MOVING FORWARD.
THESE THINGS ARE PUTTING ON A SHOW, AND WE'RE IN THE FRONT ROW.
WHAT IF THIS IS ALL ABOUT DO-OVERS?
WHAT IF I STOP MY DAD FROM DYING AGAIN?
WILL.
COMPASSION.
LOVE.
HOPE.
LISTEN TO ME--IF SOMETHING HAPPENS, TELL TIM I LOVE HIM...
UNDER-STAND? MAKE SURE HE HEARS THAT!
SOME-TIMES THEY COME BACK, DICK.
AND MOST OF THE TIME THEY DON'T, TIM.
HEADS UP, RICHARD!
IT'S TIME TO FLY!

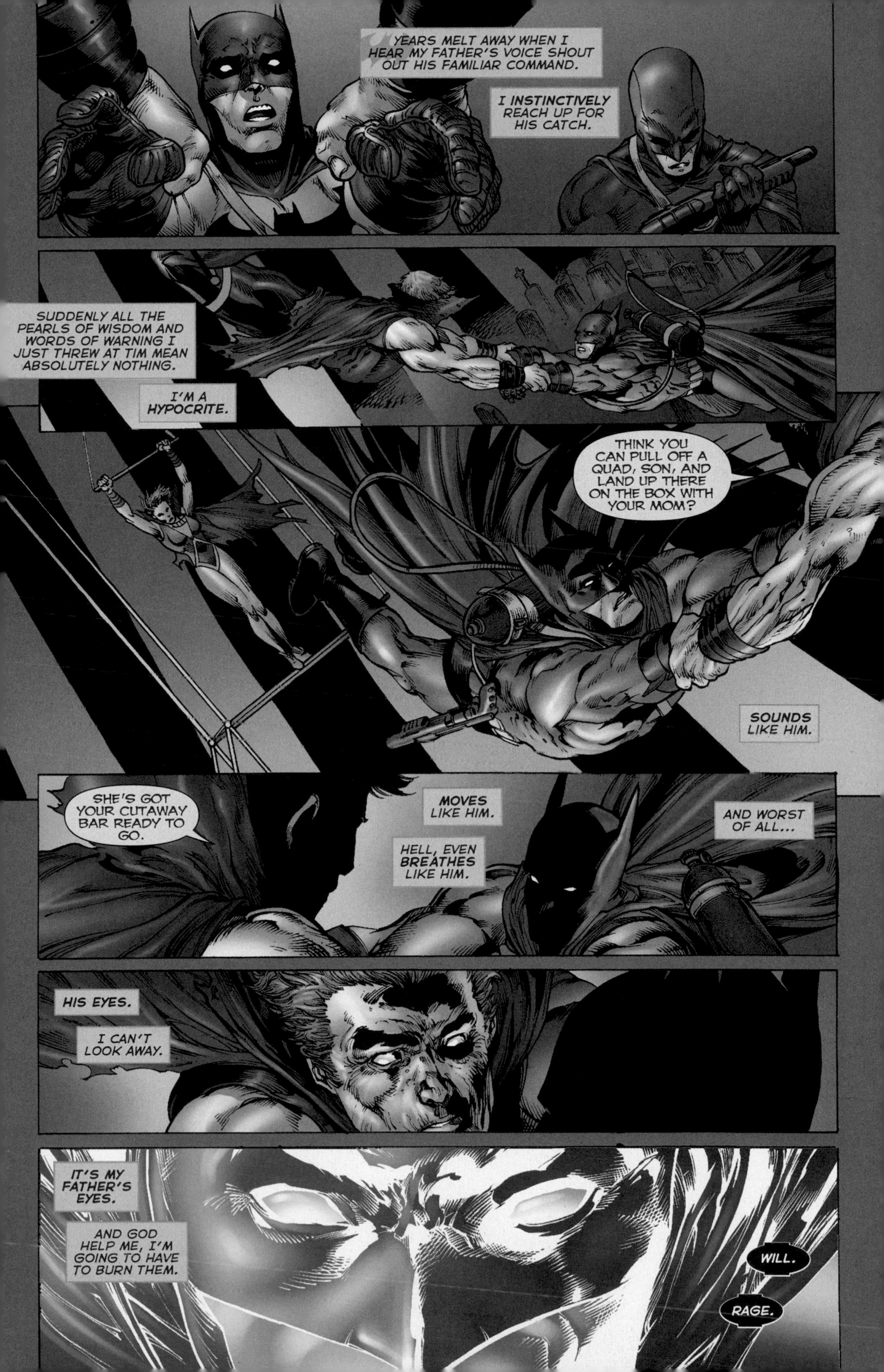
YEARS MELT AWAY WHEN I HEAR MY FATHER'S VOICE SHOUT OUT HIS FAMILIAR COMMAND.
I INSTINCTIVELY REACH UP FOR HIS CATCH.
SUDDENLY ALL THE PEARLS OF WISDOM AND WORDS OF WARNING I JUST THREW AT TIM MEAN ABSOLUTELY NOTHING.
I'M A HYPOCRITE.
THINK YOU CAN PULL OFF A QUAD, SON, AND LAND UP THERE ON THE BOX WITH YOUR MOM?
SOUNDS LIKE HIM.
SHE'S GOT YOUR CUTAWAY BAR READY TO GO.
MOVES LIKE HIM.
HELL, EVEN BREATHES LIKE HIM.
AND WORST OF ALL...
HIS EYES.
I CAN'T LOOK AWAY.
IT'S MY FATHER'S EYES.
AND GOD HELP ME, I'M GOING TO HAVE TO BURN THEM.
WILL.
RAGE.

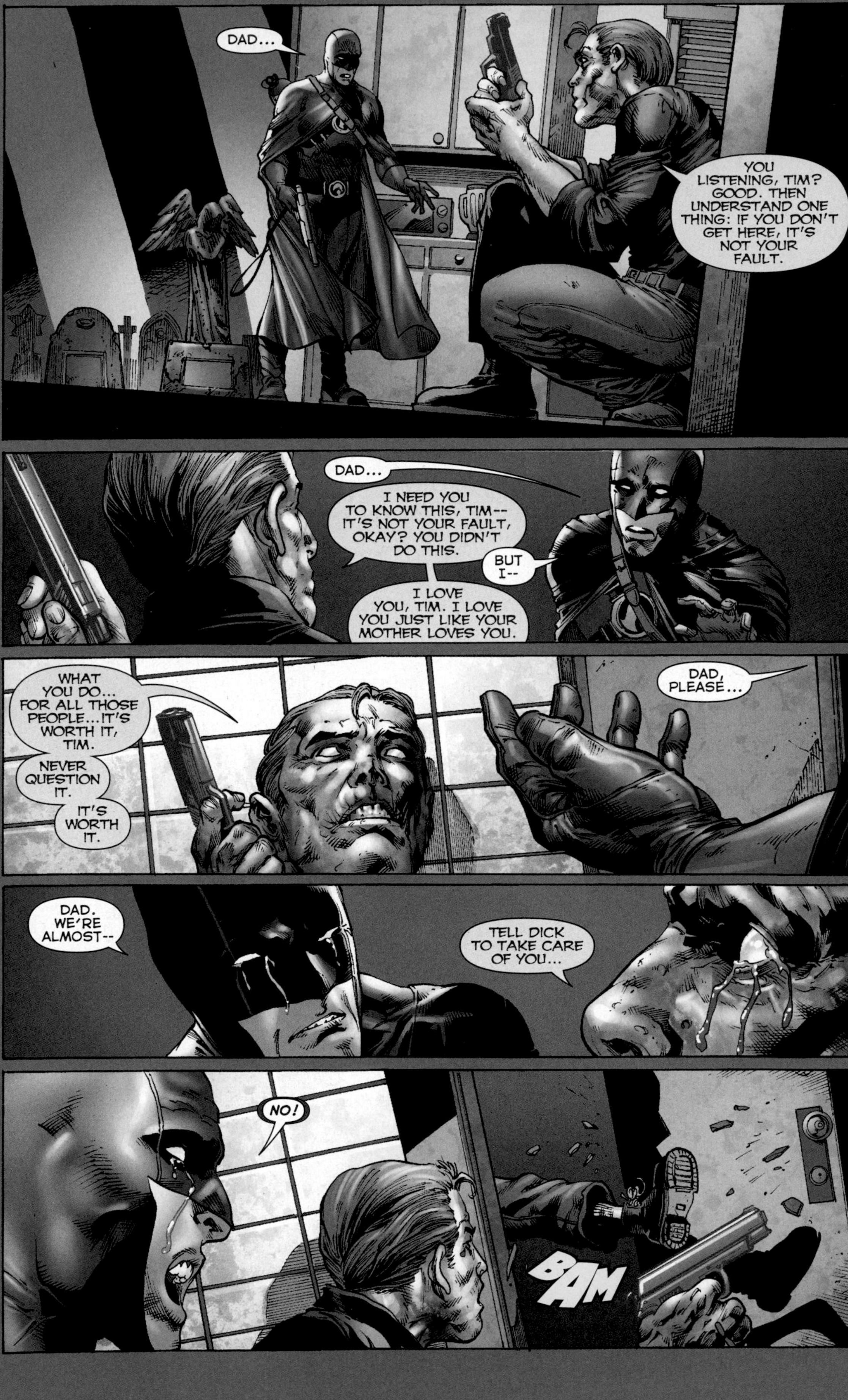
DAD...
YOU LISTENING, TIM? GOOD. THEN UNDERSTAND ONE THING: IF YOU DON'T GET HERE, IT'S NOT YOUR FAULT.
DAD...
I NEED YOU TO KNOW THIS, TIM-- IT'S NOT YOUR FAULT, OKAY? YOU DIDN'T DO THIS.
BUT I--
I LOVE YOU, TIM. I LOVE YOU JUST LIKE YOUR MOTHER LOVES YOU.
WHAT YOU DO... FOR ALL THOSE PEOPLE...IT'S WORTH IT, TIM.
NEVER QUESTION IT.
IT'S WORTH IT.
DAD, PLEASE...
DAD. WE'RE ALMOST--
TELL DICK TO TAKE CARE OF YOU...
NO!
BAM

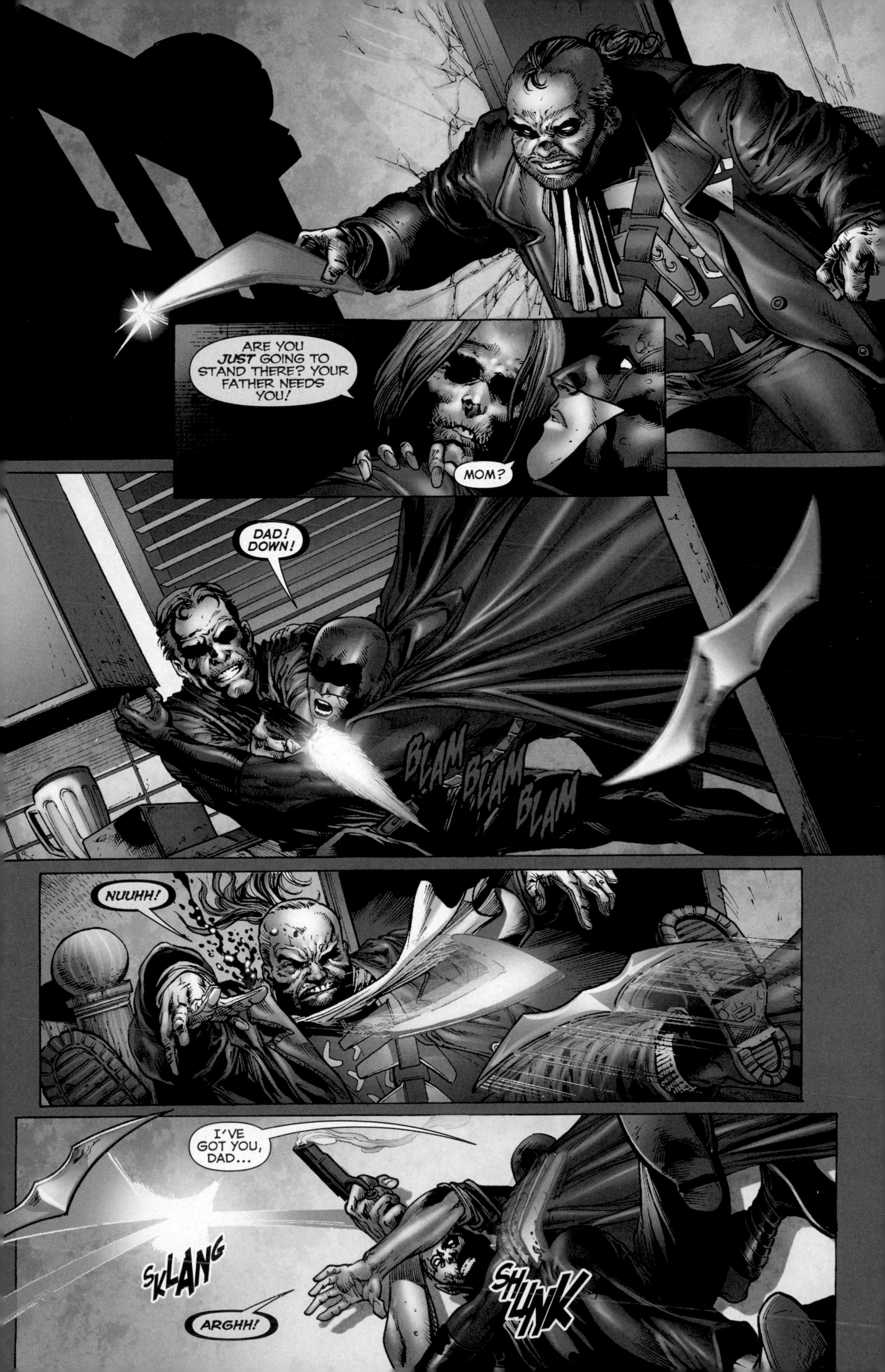
ARE YOU JUST GOING TO STAND THERE? YOUR FATHER NEEDS YOU!
MOM?
DAD! DOWN!
BLAM BLAM BLAM
NUUHH!
I'VE GOT YOU, DAD...
SKLANG
SHUNK
ARGHH!

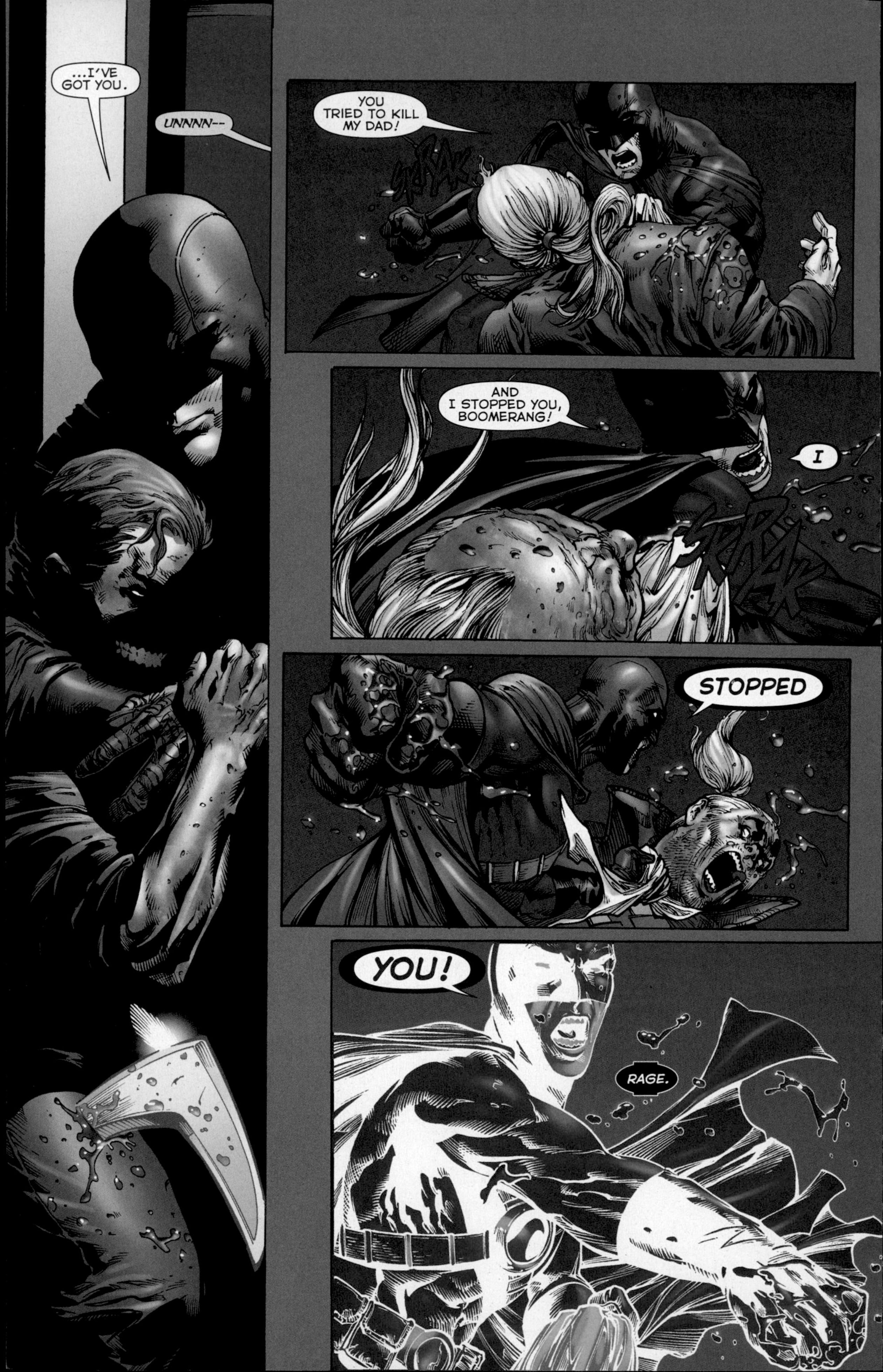
...I'VE GOT YOU.
UNNNN--
YOU TRIED TO KILL MY DAD!
AND I STOPPED YOU, BOOMERANG!
I
STOPPED
YOU!
RAGE.

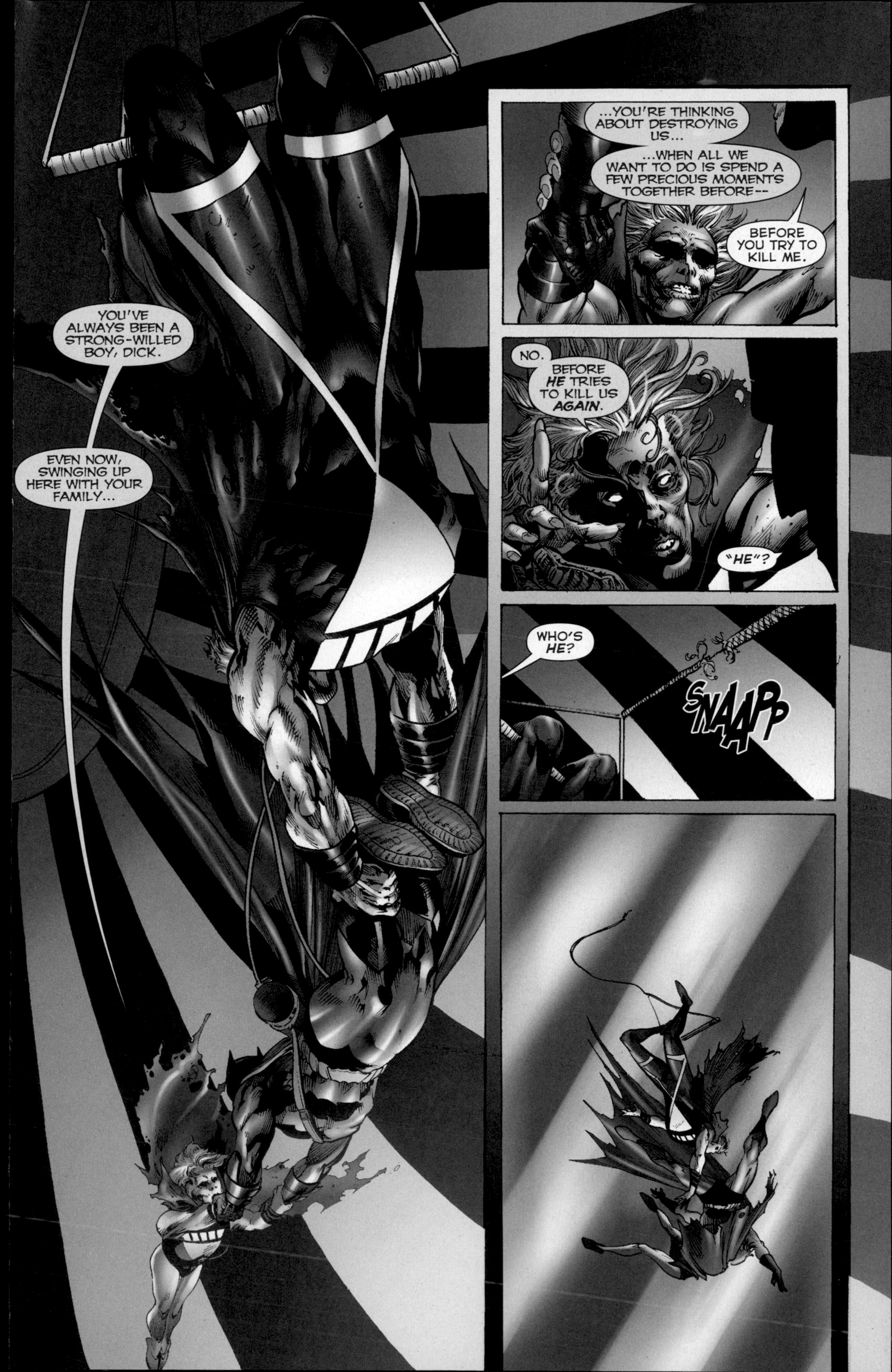
YOU'VE ALWAYS BEEN A STRONG-WILLED BOY, DICK.
EVEN NOW, SWINGING UP HERE WITH YOUR FAMILY...
...YOU'RE THINKING ABOUT DESTROYING US...
...WHEN ALL WE WANT TO DO IS SPEND A FEW PRECIOUS MOMENTS TOGETHER BEFORE--
BEFORE YOU TRY TO KILL ME.
NO.
BEFORE HE TRIES TO KILL US AGAIN.
"HE"?
WHO'S HE?
SNAAPP

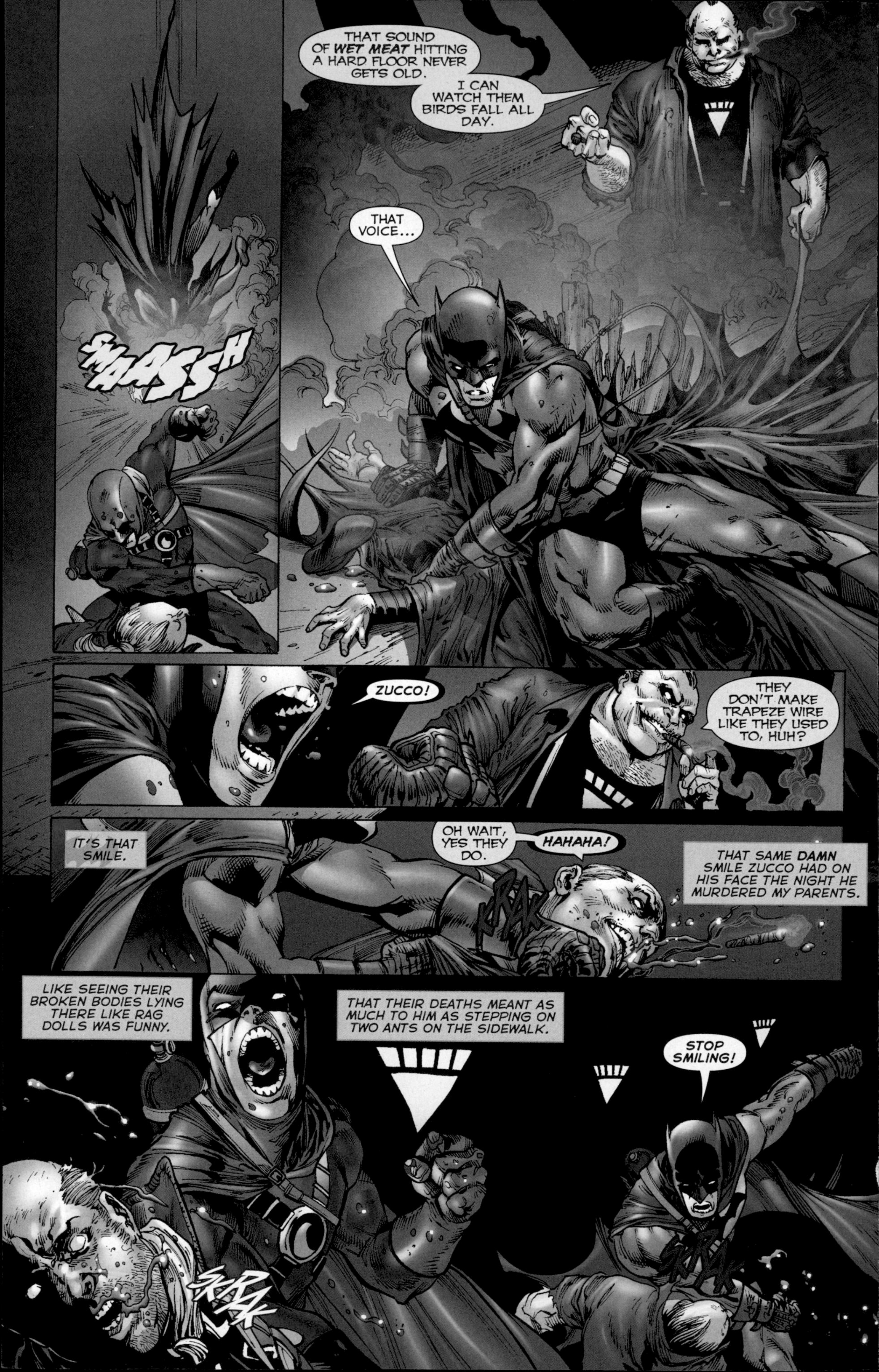
SMAASSH
THAT SOUND OF WET MEAT HITTING A HARD FLOOR NEVER GETS OLD.
I CAN WATCH THEM BIRDS FALL ALL DAY.
THAT VOICE...
ZUCCO!
THEY DON'T MAKE TRAPEZE WIRE LIKE THEY USED TO, HUH?
IT'S THAT SMILE.
OH WAIT, YES THEY DO.
HAHAHA!
THAT SAME DAMN SMILE ZUCCO HAD ON HIS FACE THE NIGHT HE MURDERED MY PARENTS.
KRAK
LIKE SEEING THEIR BROKEN BODIES LYING THERE LIKE RAG DOLLS WAS FUNNY.
THAT THEIR DEATHS MEANT AS MUCH TO HIM AS STEPPING ON TWO ANTS ON THE SIDEWALK.
STOP SMILING!
SKRAK
SKRAK

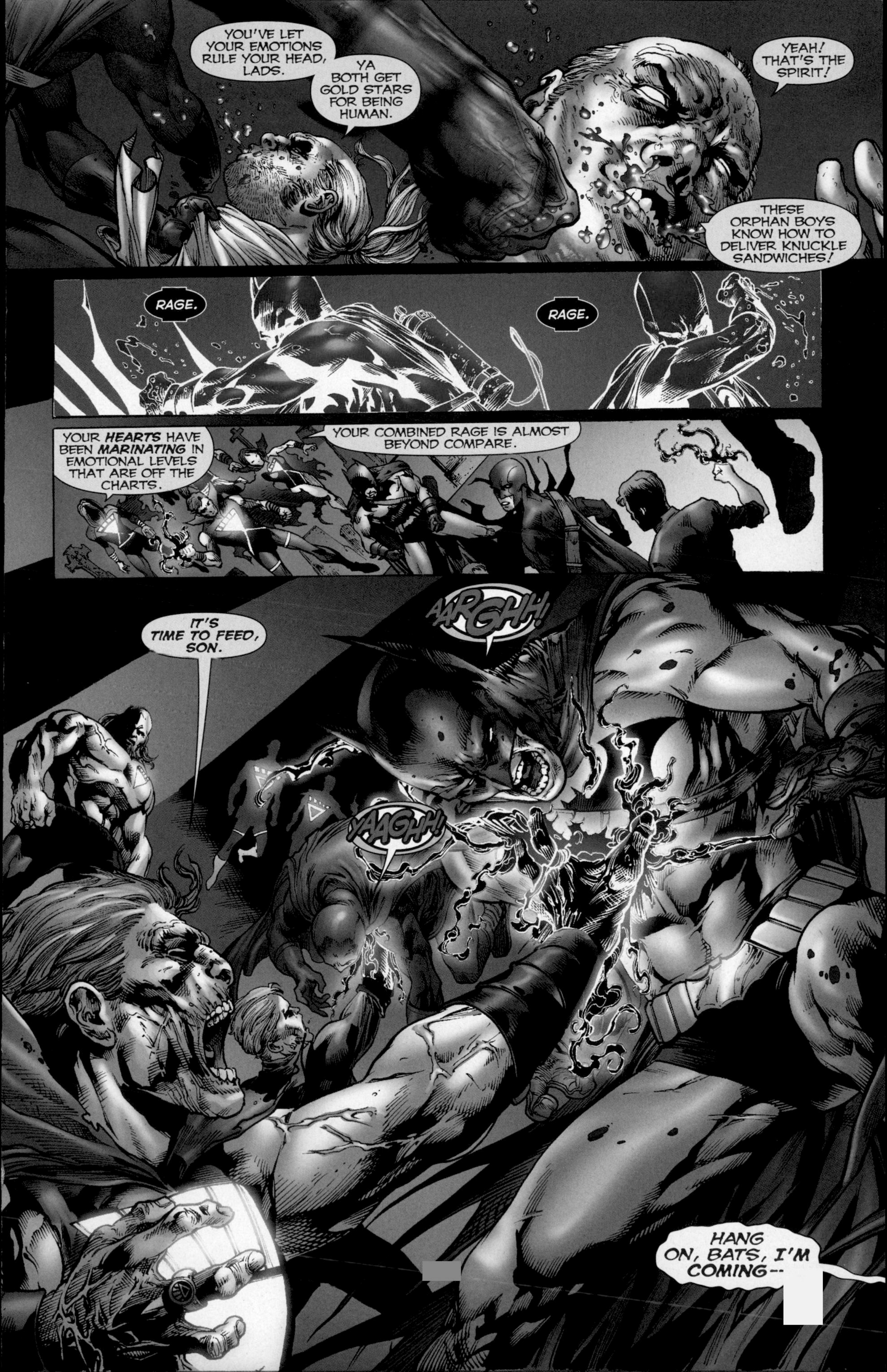
YOU'VE LET YOUR EMOTIONS RULE YOUR HEAD, LADS.
YA BOTH GET GOLD STARS FOR BEING HUMAN.
YEAH! THAT'S THE SPIRIT!
THESE ORPHAN BOYS KNOW HOW TO DELIVER KNUCKLE SANDWICHES!
RAGE.
RAGE.
YOUR HEARTS HAVE BEEN MARINATING IN EMOTIONAL LEVELS THAT ARE OFF THE CHARTS.
YOUR COMBINED RAGE IS ALMOST BEYOND COMPARE.
IT'S TIME TO FEED, SON.
AARGHH!
YAAGHH!
HANG ON, BATS, I'M COMING--

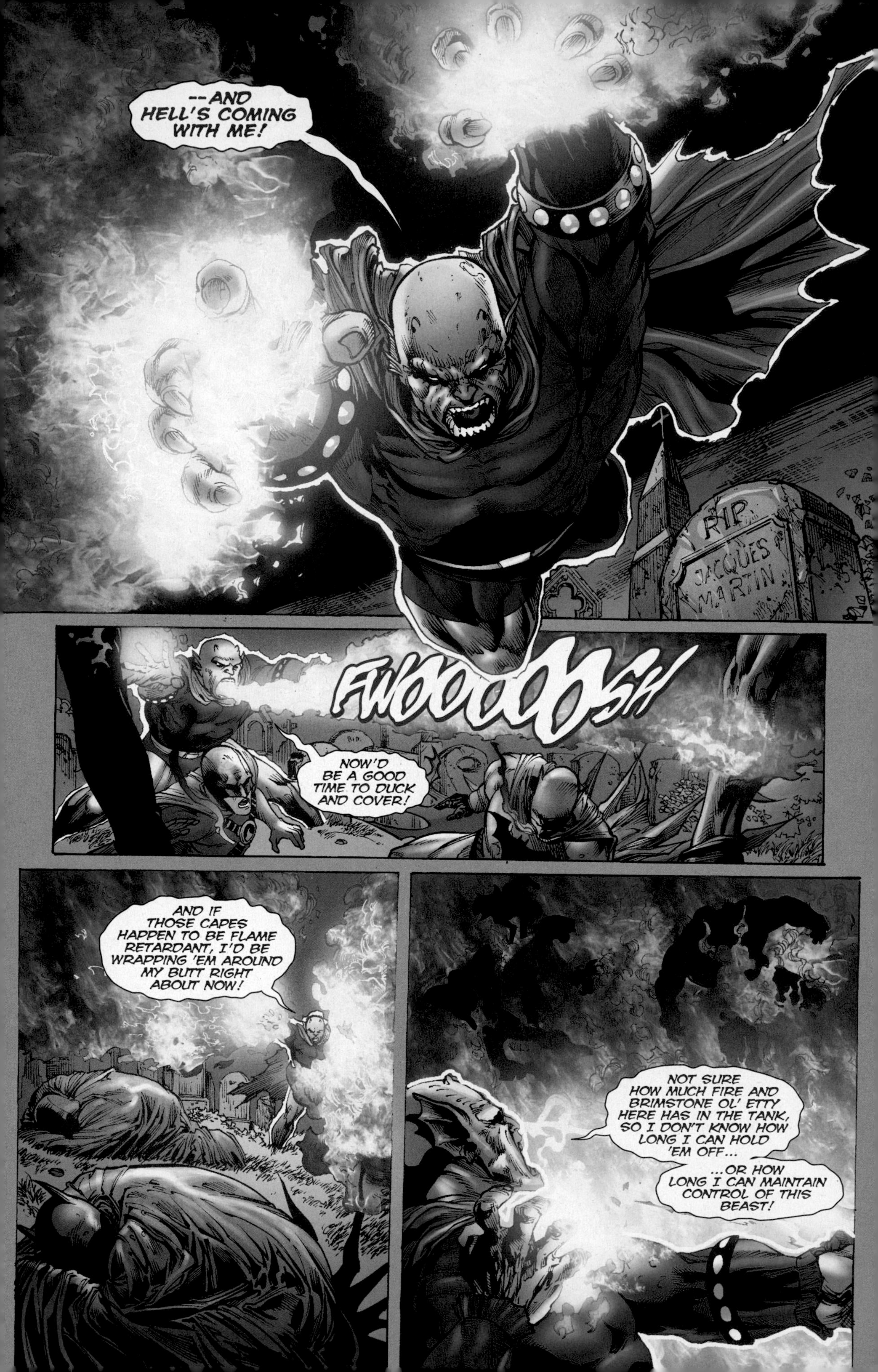
--AND HELL'S COMING WITH ME!
RIP JACQUES MARTIN
FWOOOOOSH
NOW'D BE A GOOD TIME TO DUCK AND COVER!
AND IF THOSE CAPES HAPPEN TO BE FLAME RETARDANT, I'D BE WRAPPING 'EM AROUND MY BUTT RIGHT ABOUT NOW!
NOT SURE HOW MUCH FIRE AND BRIMSTONE OL' ETTY HERE HAS IN THE TANK, SO I DON'T KNOW HOW LONG I CAN HOLD 'EM OFF...
...OR HOW LONG I CAN MAINTAIN CONTROL OF THIS BEAST!

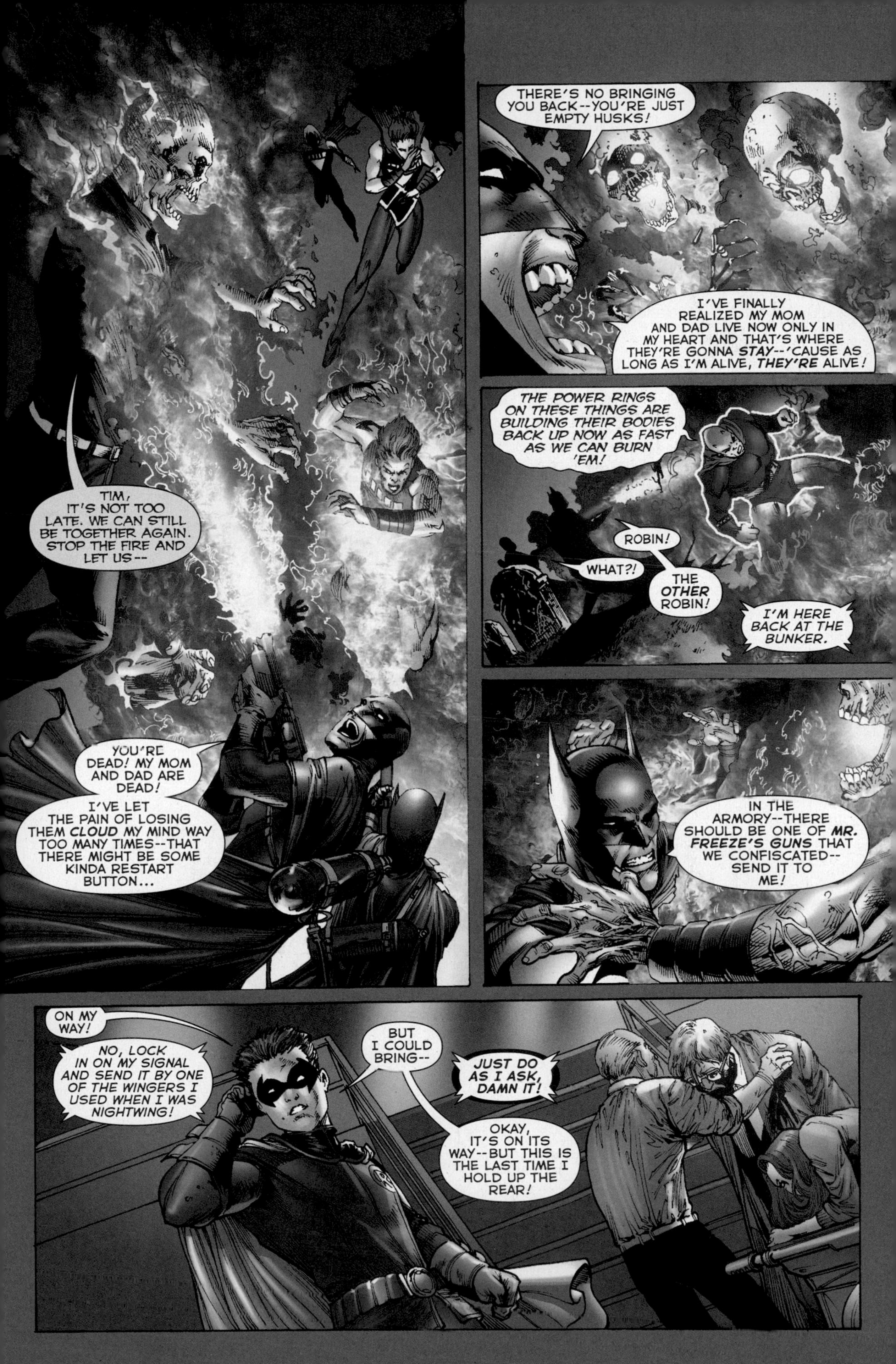
TIM, IT'S NOT TOO LATE. WE CAN STILL BE TOGETHER AGAIN. STOP THE FIRE AND LET US--
YOU'RE DEAD! MY MOM AND DAD ARE DEAD!
I'VE LET THE PAIN OF LOSING THEM CLOUD MY MIND WAY TOO MANY TIMES--THAT THERE MIGHT BE SOME KINDA RESTART BUTTON...
THERE'S NO BRINGING YOU BACK--YOU'RE JUST EMPTY HUSKS!
I'VE FINALLY REALIZED MY MOM AND DAD LIVE NOW ONLY IN MY HEART AND THAT'S WHERE THEY'RE GONNA STAY--'CAUSE AS LONG AS I'M ALIVE, THEY'RE ALIVE!
THE POWER RINGS ON THESE THINGS ARE BUILDING THEIR BODIES BACK UP NOW AS FAST AS WE CAN BURN 'EM!
ROBIN!
WHAT?!
THE OTHER ROBIN!
I'M HERE BACK AT THE BUNKER.
IN THE ARMORY--THERE SHOULD BE ONE OF MR. FREEZE'S GUNS THAT WE CONFISCATED--SEND IT TO ME!
ON MY WAY!
NO, LOCK IN ON MY SIGNAL AND SEND IT BY ONE OF THE WINGERS I USED WHEN I WAS NIGHTWING!
BUT I COULD BRING--
JUST DO AS I ASK, DAMN IT!
OKAY, IT'S ON ITS WAY--BUT THIS IS THE LAST TIME I HOLD UP THE REAR!

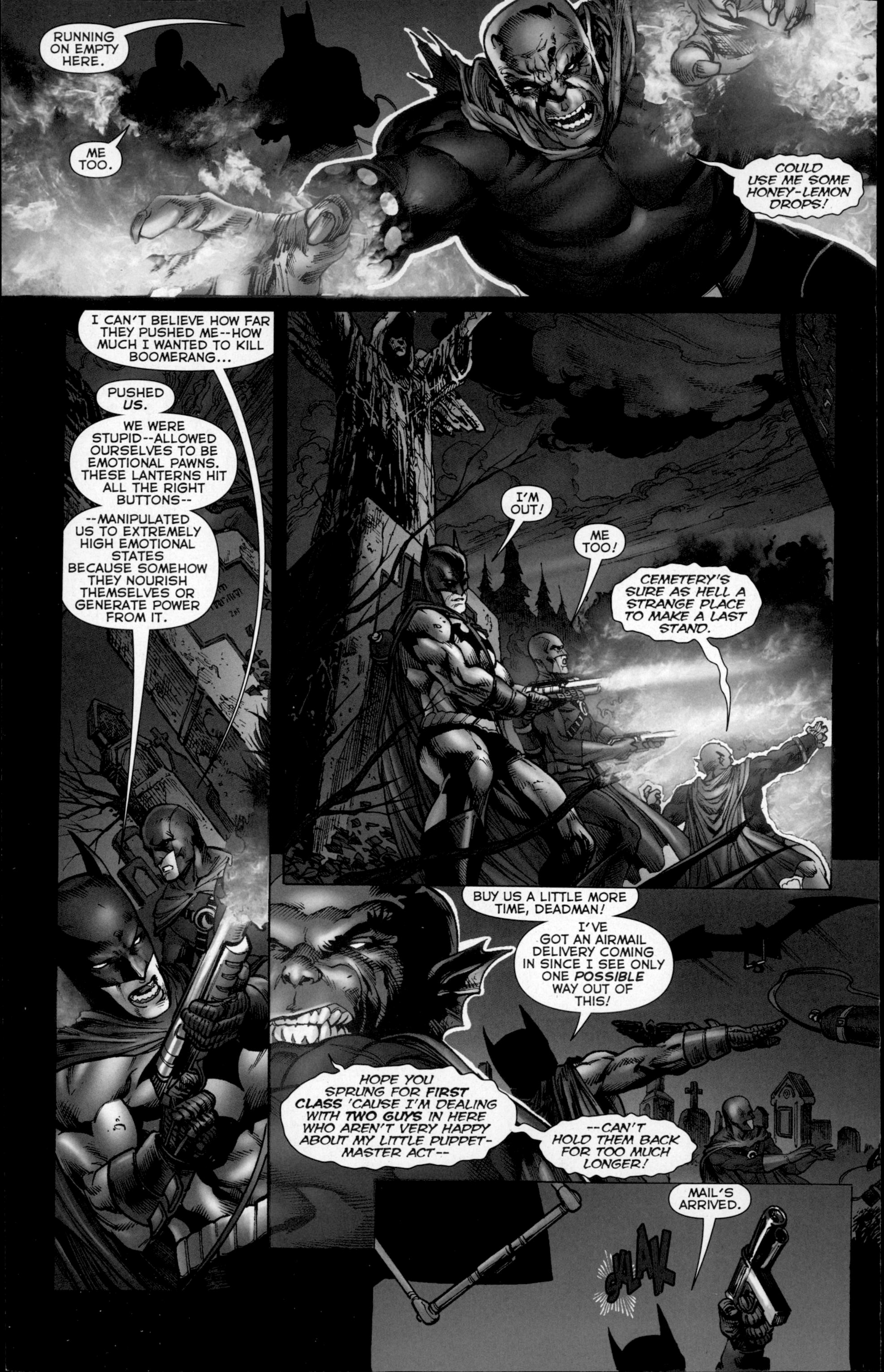
RUNNING ON EMPTY HERE.
ME TOO.
COULD USE ME SOME HONEY-LEMON DROPS!
I CAN'T BELIEVE HOW FAR THEY PUSHED ME--HOW MUCH I WANTED TO KILL BOOMERANG...
PUSHED *US.*
WE WERE STUPID--ALLOWED OURSELVES TO BE EMOTIONAL PAWNS. THESE LANTERNS HIT ALL THE RIGHT BUTTONS--
--MANIPULATED US TO EXTREMELY HIGH EMOTIONAL STATES BECAUSE SOMEHOW THEY NOURISH THEMSELVES OR GENERATE POWER FROM IT.
I'M OUT!
ME TOO!
CEMETERY'S SURE AS HELL A STRANGE PLACE TO MAKE A LAST STAND.
BUY US A LITTLE MORE TIME, DEADMAN!
I'VE GOT AN AIRMAIL DELIVERY COMING IN SINCE I SEE ONLY ONE *POSSIBLE* WAY OUT OF THIS!
HOPE YOU SPRUNG FOR **FIRST CLASS** 'CAUSE I'M DEALING WITH **TWO GUYS** IN HERE WHO AREN'T VERY HAPPY ABOUT MY LITTLE PUPPET-MASTER ACT--
--CAN'T HOLD THEM BACK FOR TOO MUCH LONGER!
MAIL'S ARRIVED.
SHLAK

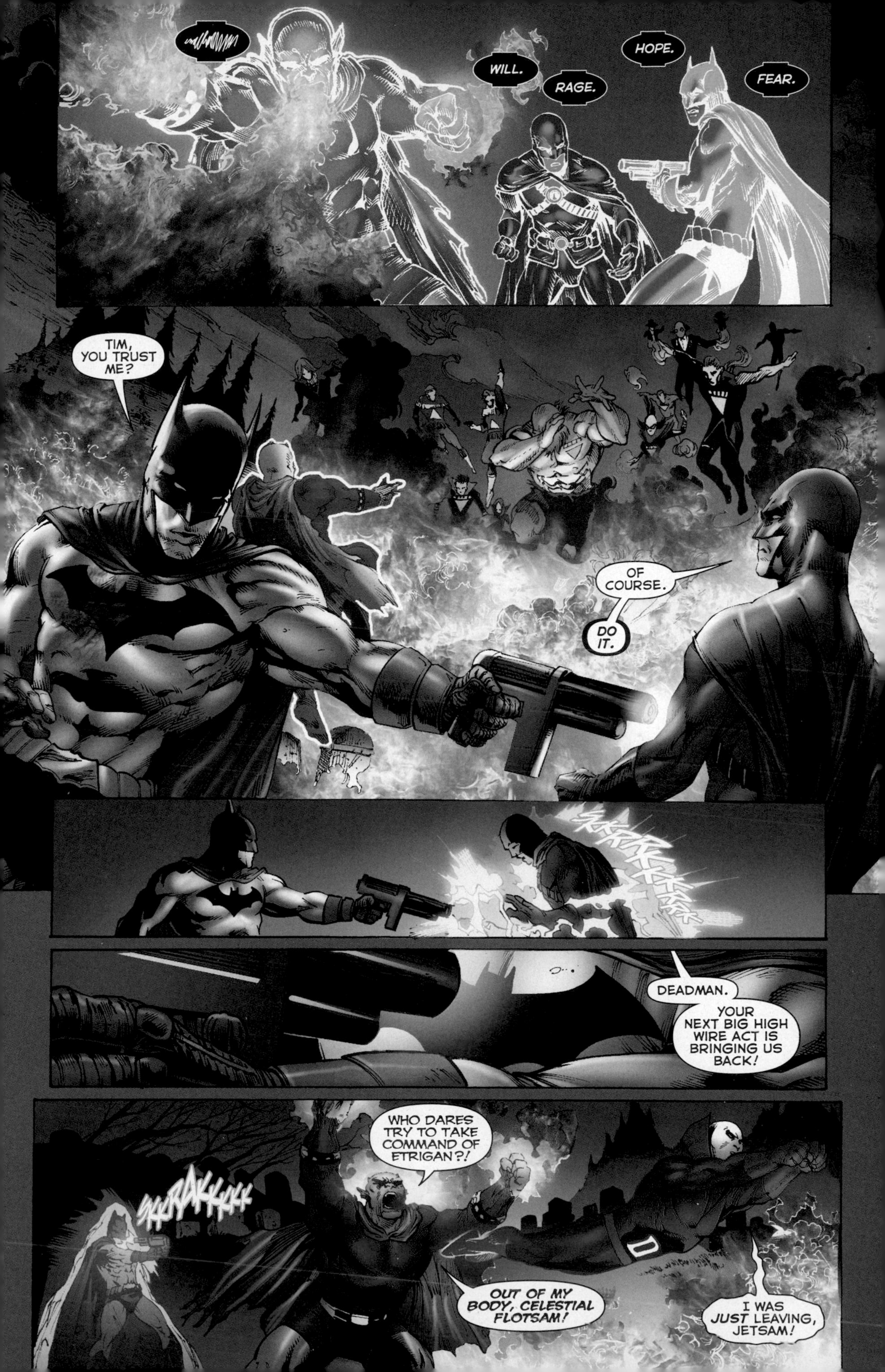
WILL.
RAGE.
HOPE.
FEAR.
TIM, YOU TRUST ME?
OF COURSE.
DO IT.
SKKRRKKKKKK
...
DEADMAN.
YOUR NEXT BIG HIGH WIRE ACT IS BRINGING US BACK!
WHO DARES TRY TO TAKE COMMAND OF ETRIGAN?!
SKKRAKKKKK
OUT OF MY BODY, CELESTIAL FLOTSAM!
I WAS JUST LEAVING, JETSAM!

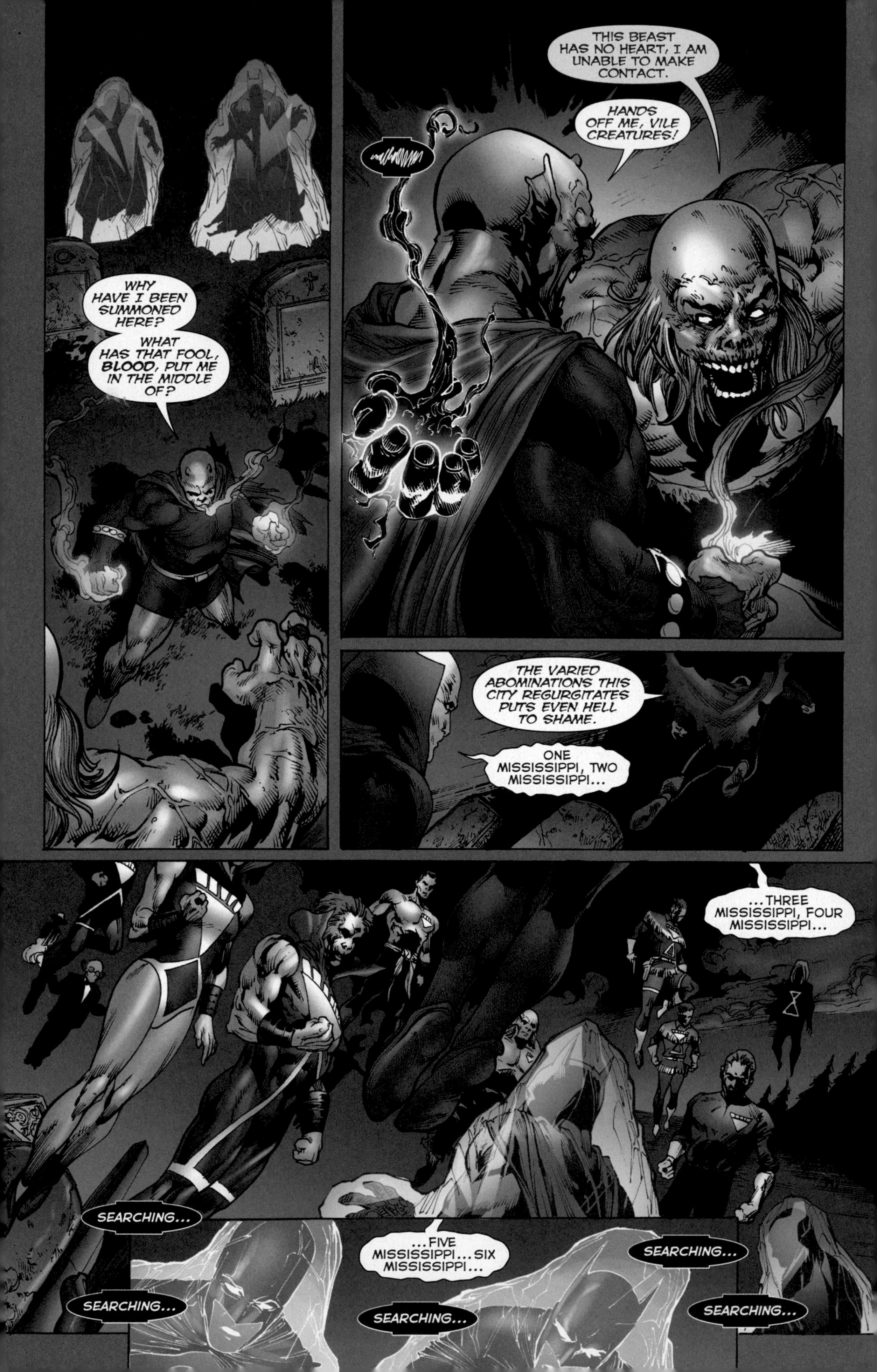
WHY HAVE I BEEN SUMMONED HERE?
WHAT HAS THAT FOOL, BLOOD, PUT ME IN THE MIDDLE OF?
THIS BEAST HAS NO HEART, I AM UNABLE TO MAKE CONTACT.
HANDS OFF ME, VILE CREATURES!
THE VARIED ABOMINATIONS THIS CITY REGURGITATES PUTS EVEN HELL TO SHAME.
ONE MISSISSIPPI, TWO MISSISSIPPI...
...THREE MISSISSIPPI, FOUR MISSISSIPPI...
SEARCHING...
...FIVE MISSISSIPPI... SIX MISSISSIPPI...
SEARCHING...
SEARCHING...
SEARCHING...
SEARCHING...

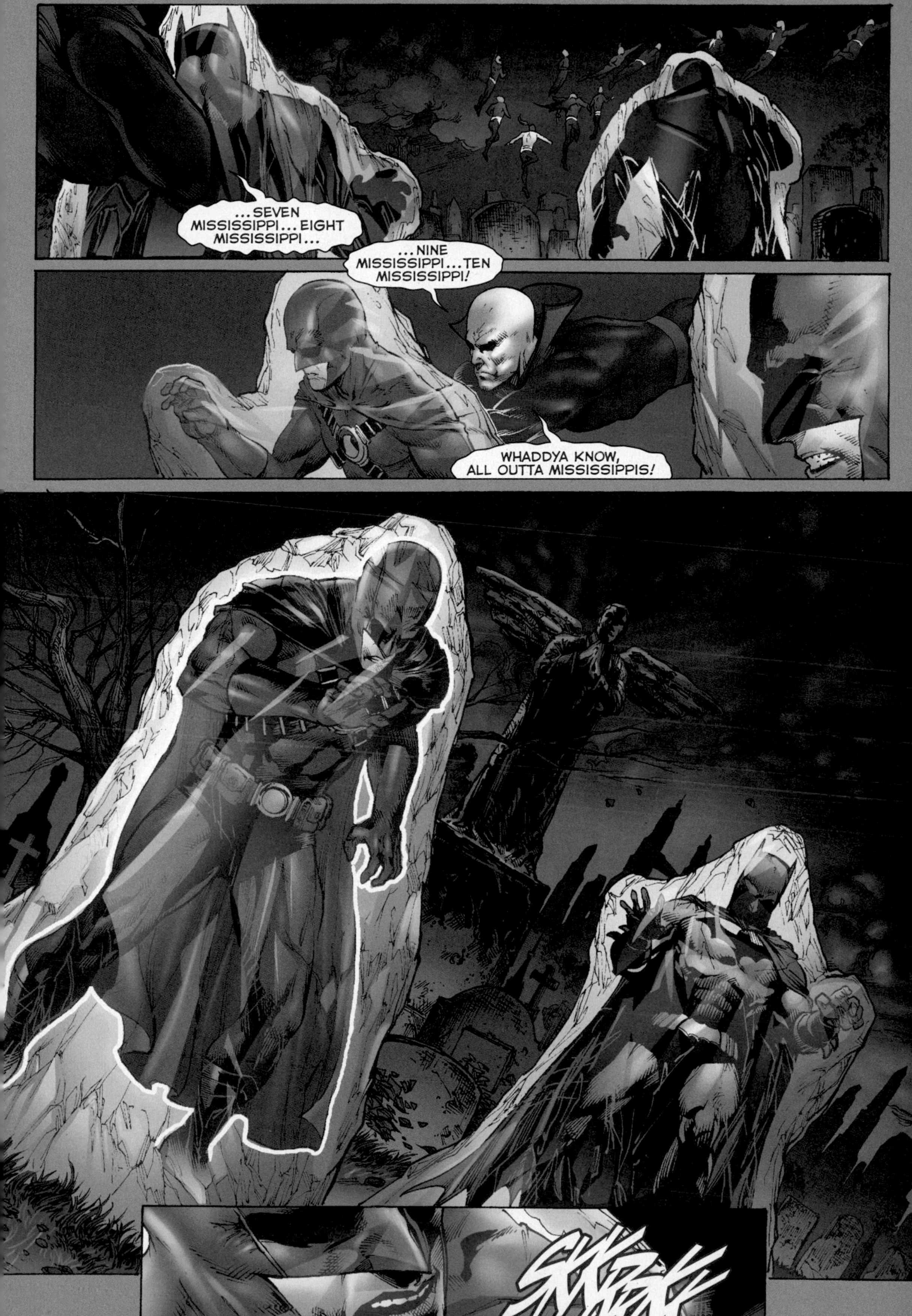
...SEVEN MISSISSIPPI... EIGHT MISSISSIPPI...
...NINE MISSISSIPPI...TEN MISSISSIPPI!
WHADDYA KNOW, ALL OUTTA MISSISSIPPIS!

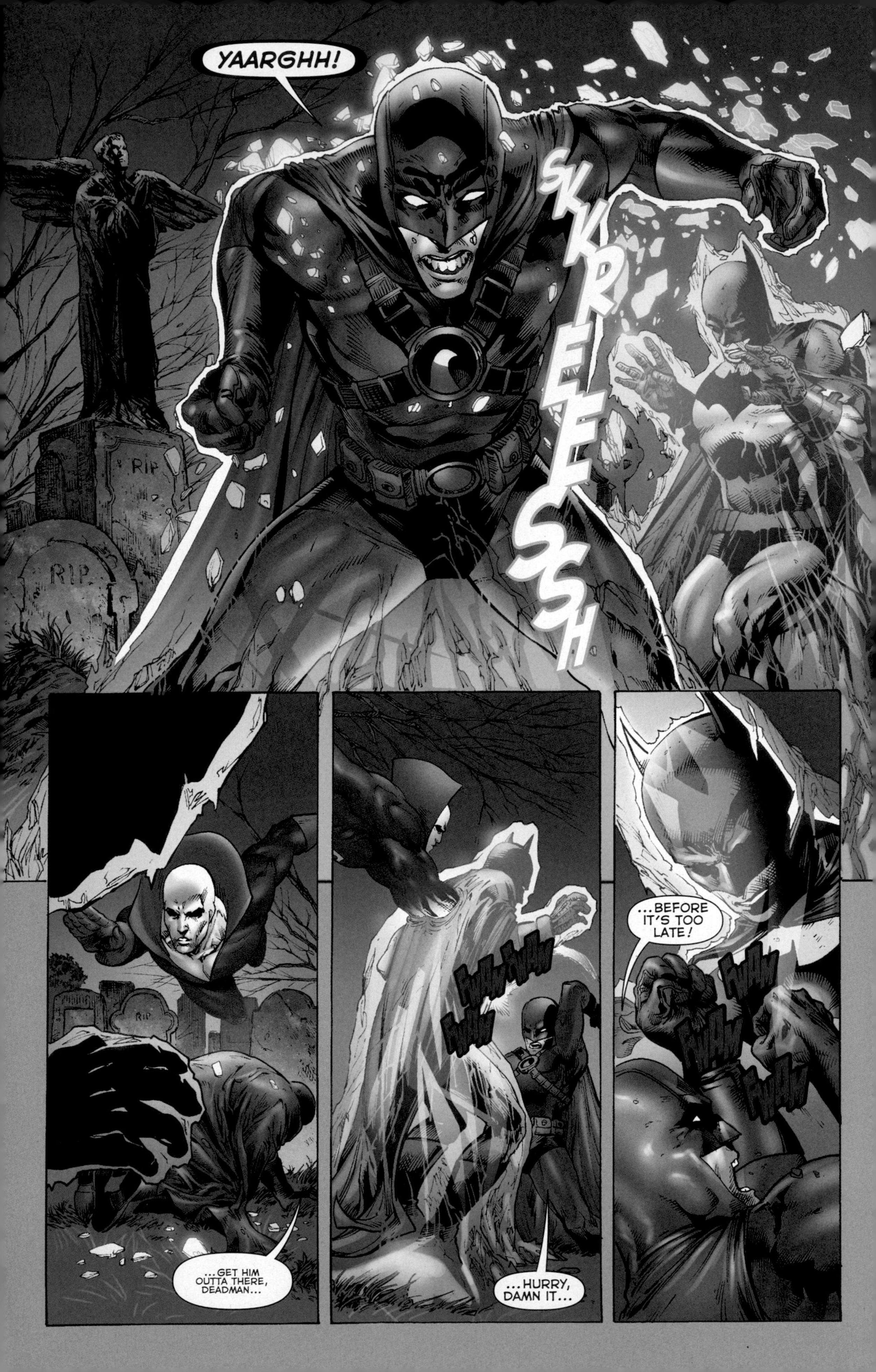
YAARGHH!
SKKREEESSSH
...GET HIM OUTTA THERE, DEADMAN...
FWAM FWAM FWAM FWAM
...HURRY, DAMN IT...
...BEFORE IT'S TOO LATE!
FWAM FWAM FWAM FWAM

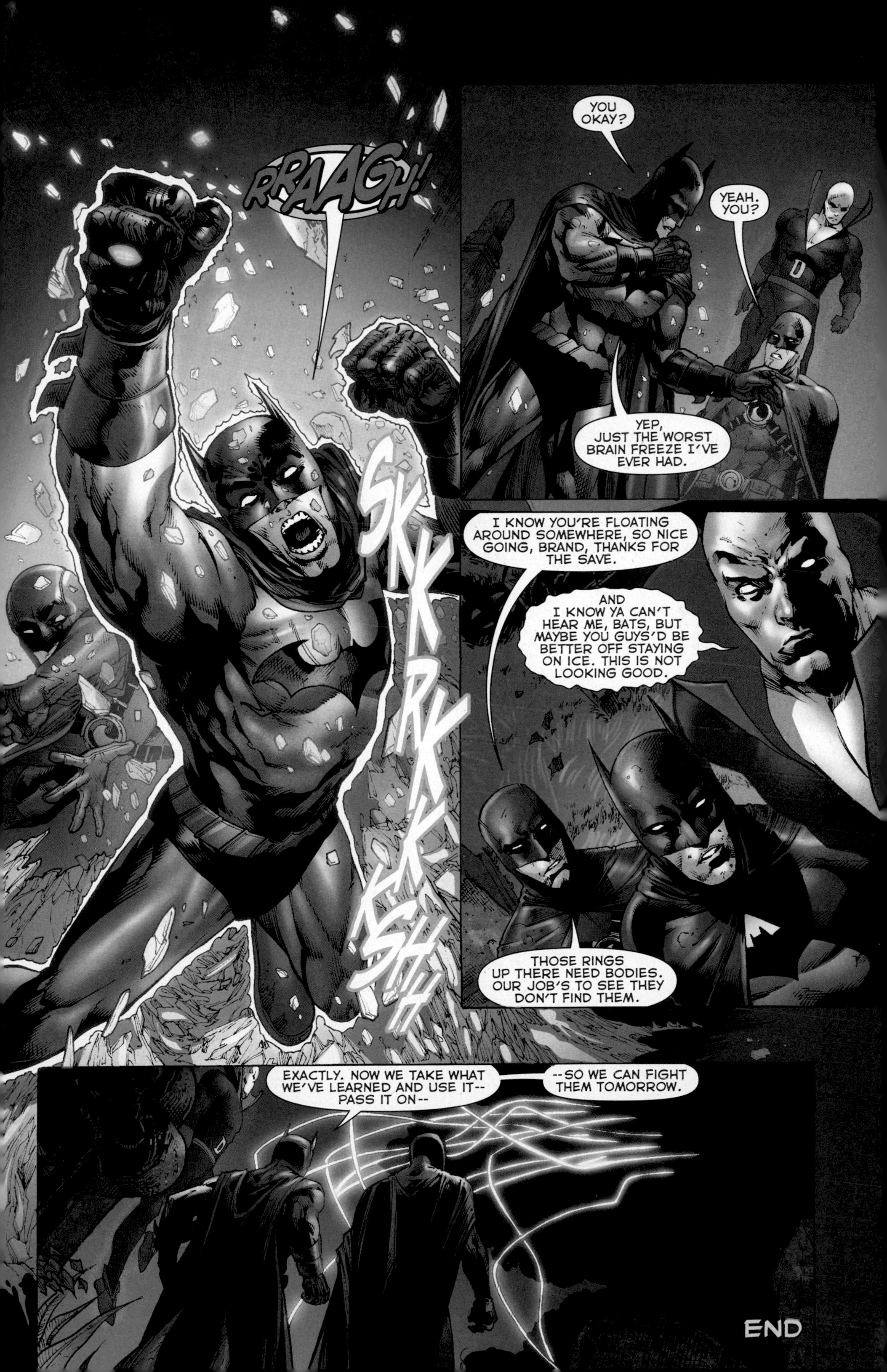
RRAAGH!
SKKRKKKSHH
YOU OKAY?
YEAH. YOU?
YEP, JUST THE WORST BRAIN FREEZE I'VE EVER HAD.
I KNOW YOU'RE FLOATING AROUND SOMEWHERE, SO NICE GOING, BRAND, THANKS FOR THE SAVE.
AND I KNOW YA CAN'T HEAR ME, BATS, BUT MAYBE YOU GUYS'D BE BETTER OFF STAYING ON ICE. THIS IS NOT LOOKING GOOD.
THOSE RINGS UP THERE NEED BODIES. OUR JOB'S TO SEE THEY DON'T FIND THEM.
EXACTLY. NOW WE TAKE WHAT WE'VE LEARNED AND USE IT-- PASS IT ON--
--SO WE CAN FIGHT THEM TOMORROW.
END

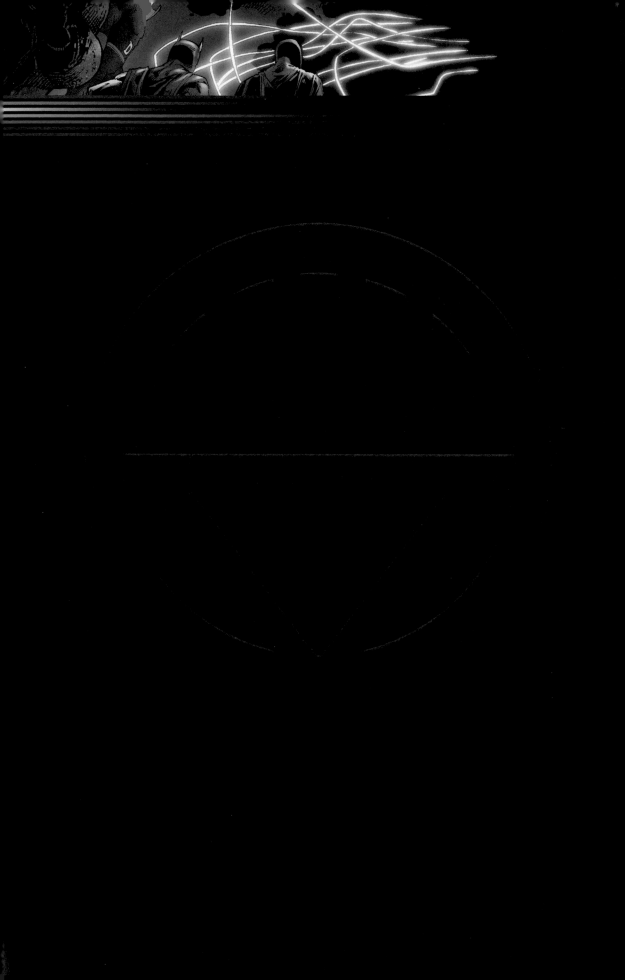

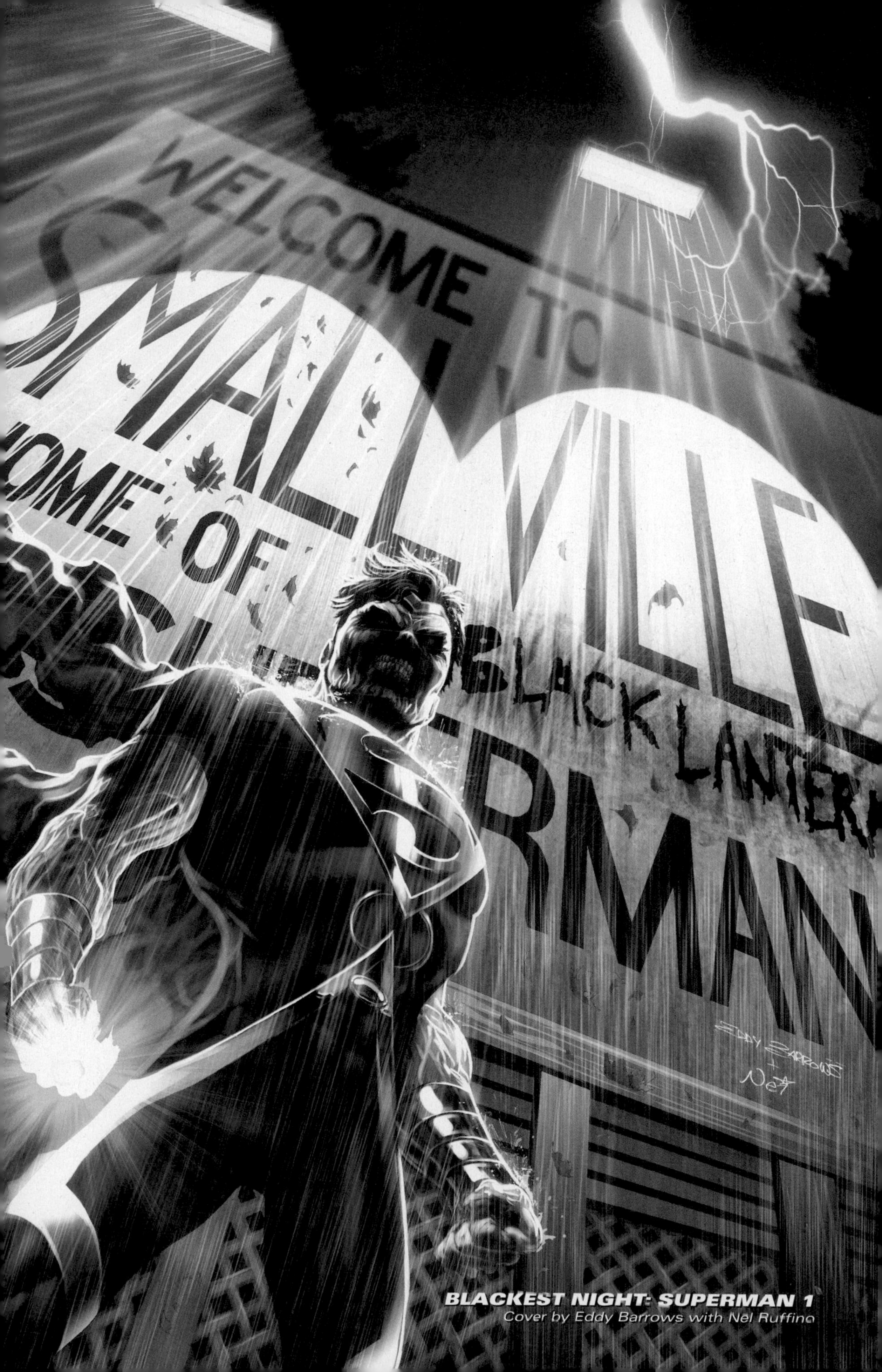
WELCOME TO
MALLVILLE
HOME OF
RMAN
BLACK LANTER

BLACKEST NIGHT: SUPERMAN 1
Cover by Eddy Barrows with Nel Ruffino

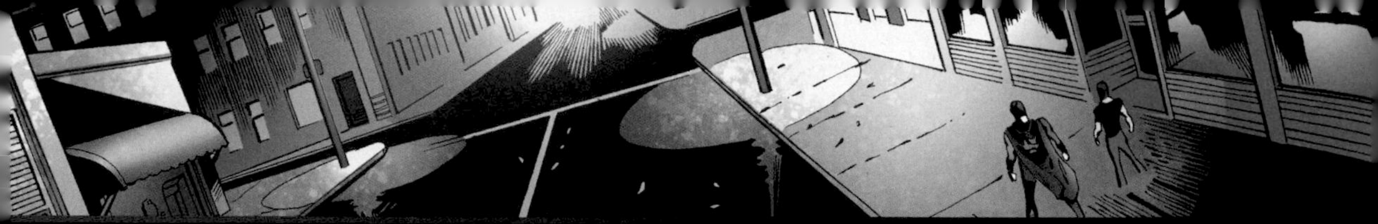

A SLEEPY LITTLE TOWN

JAMES ROBINSON
WRITER

EDDY BARROWS
PENCILS

RUY JOSÉ
JULIO FERREIRA
INKS

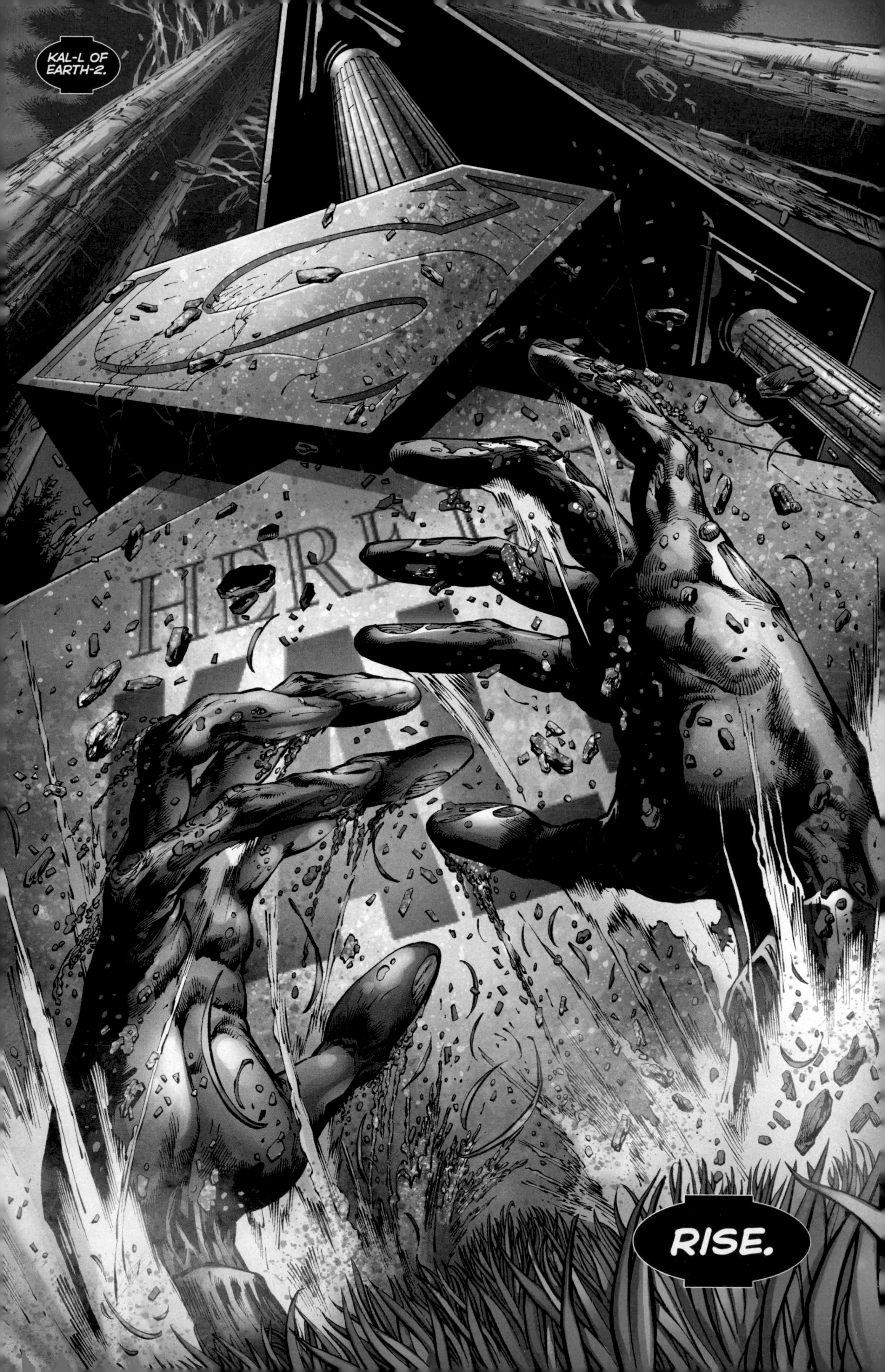
KAL-L OF
EARTH-2.
RISE.

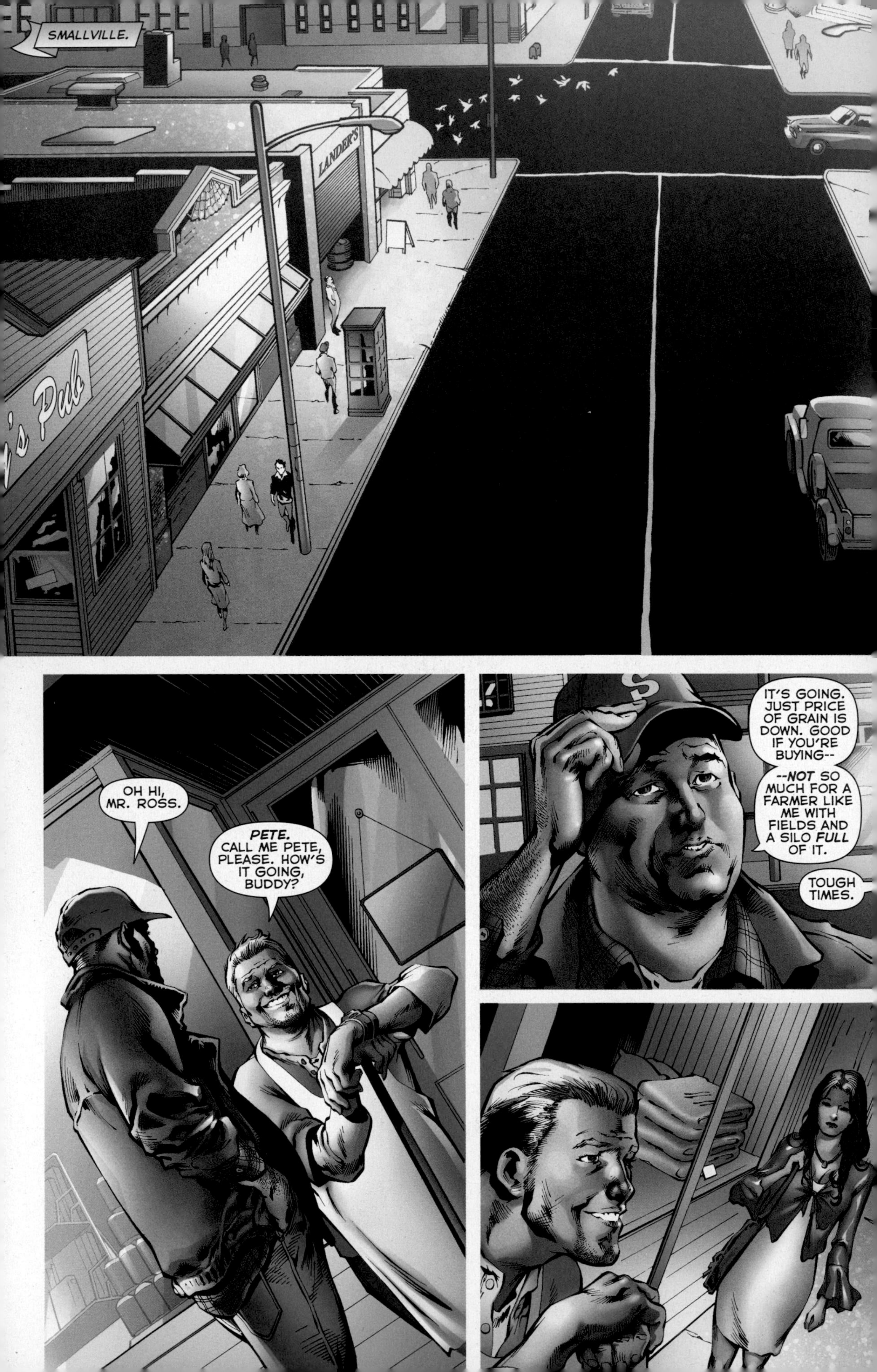
SMALLVILLE.
LANDER'S
'S PUB
OH HI, MR. ROSS.
PETE. CALL ME PETE, PLEASE. HOW'S IT GOING, BUDDY?
IT'S GOING. JUST PRICE OF GRAIN IS DOWN. GOOD IF YOU'RE BUYING--
--NOT SO MUCH FOR A FARMER LIKE ME WITH FIELDS AND A SILO FULL OF IT.
TOUGH TIMES.

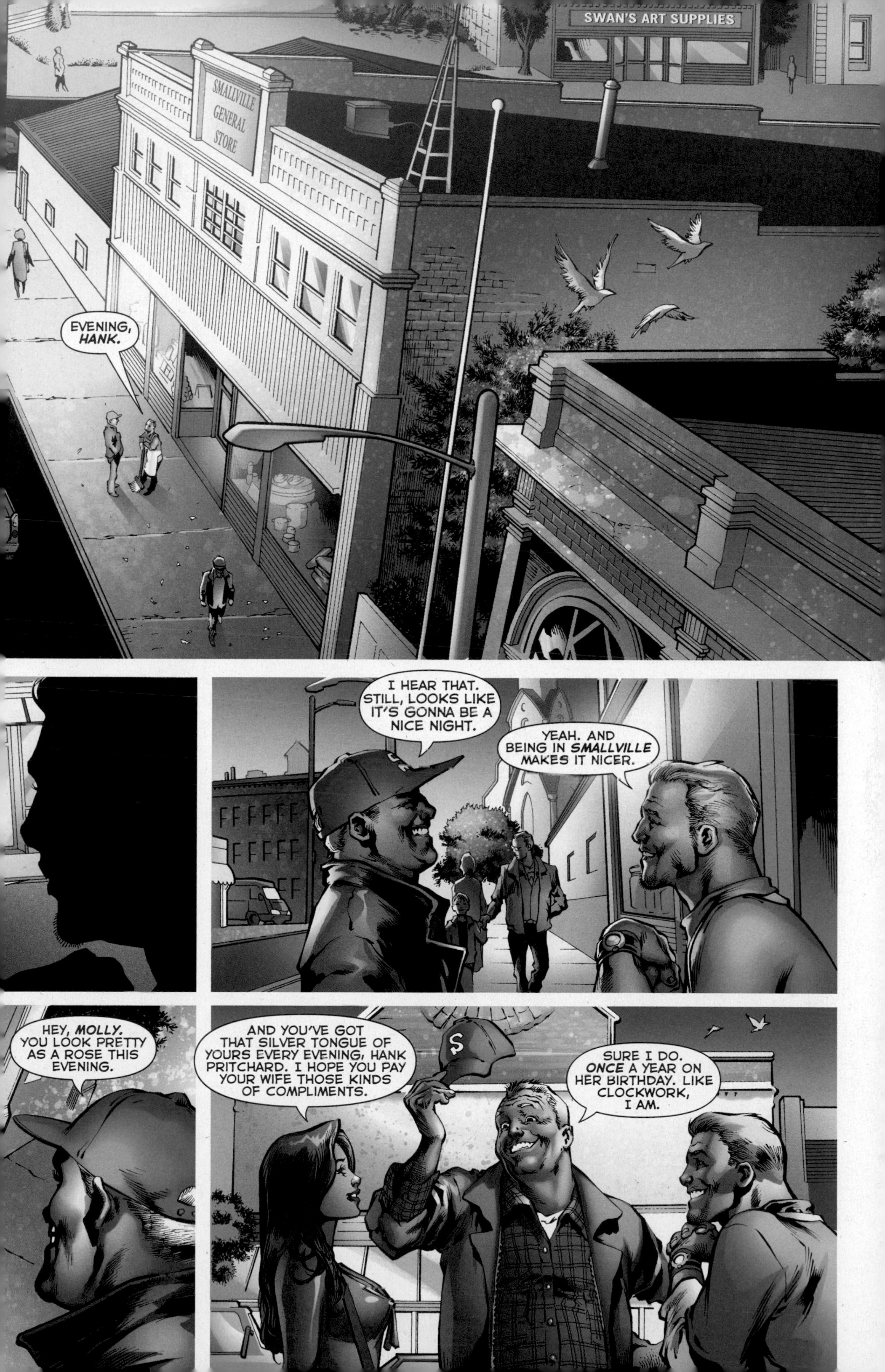
SWAN'S ART SUPPLIES
SMALLVILLE GENERAL STORE
EVENING, HANK.
I HEAR THAT. STILL, LOOKS LIKE IT'S GONNA BE A NICE NIGHT.
YEAH. AND BEING IN SMALLVILLE MAKES IT NICER.
HEY, MOLLY. YOU LOOK PRETTY AS A ROSE THIS EVENING.
AND YOU'VE GOT THAT SILVER TONGUE OF YOURS EVERY EVENING, HANK PRITCHARD. I HOPE YOU PAY YOUR WIFE THOSE KINDS OF COMPLIMENTS.
SURE I DO. ONCE A YEAR ON HER BIRTHDAY. LIKE CLOCKWORK, I AM.

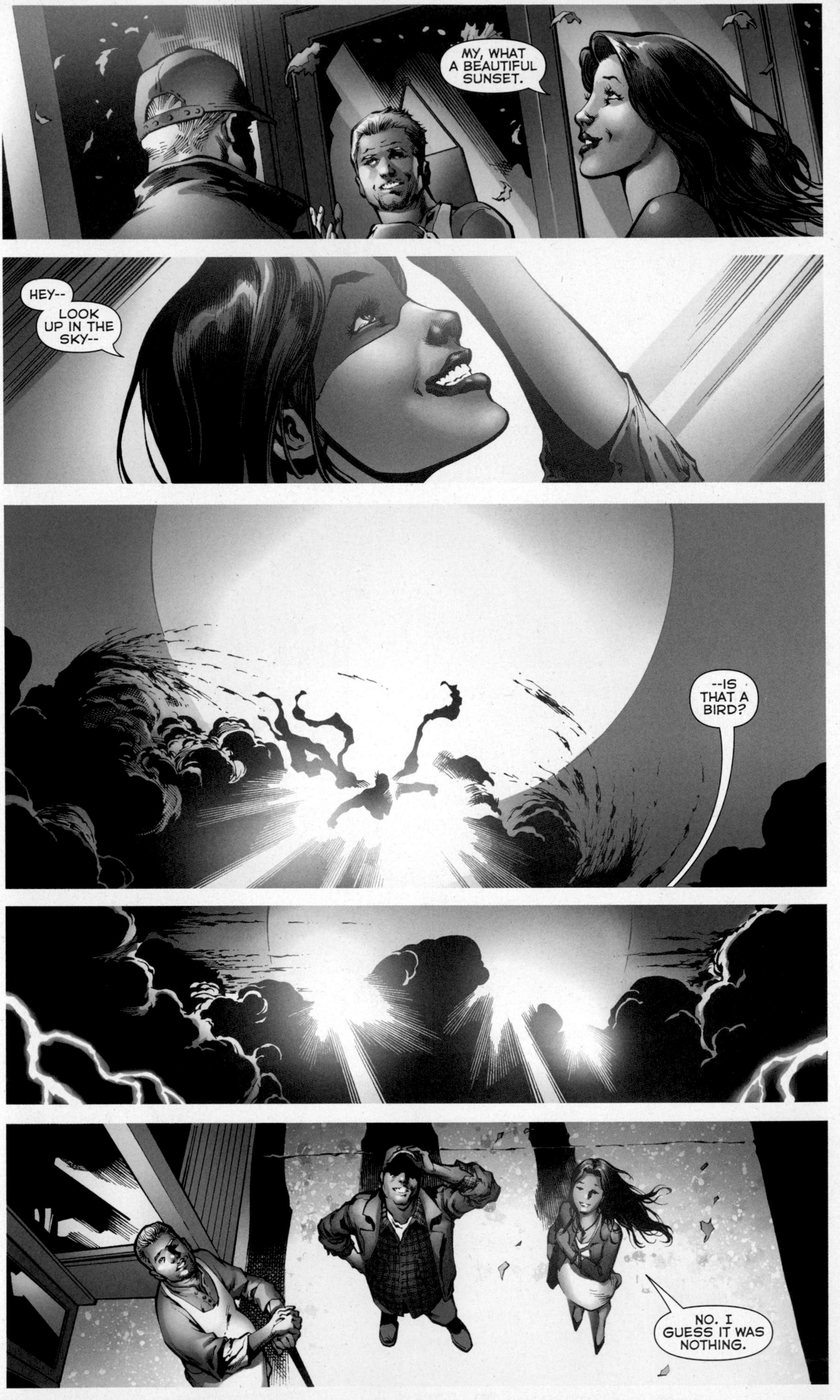
MY, WHAT A BEAUTIFUL SUNSET.
HEY--
LOOK UP IN THE SKY--
--IS THAT A BIRD?
NO. I GUESS IT WAS NOTHING.

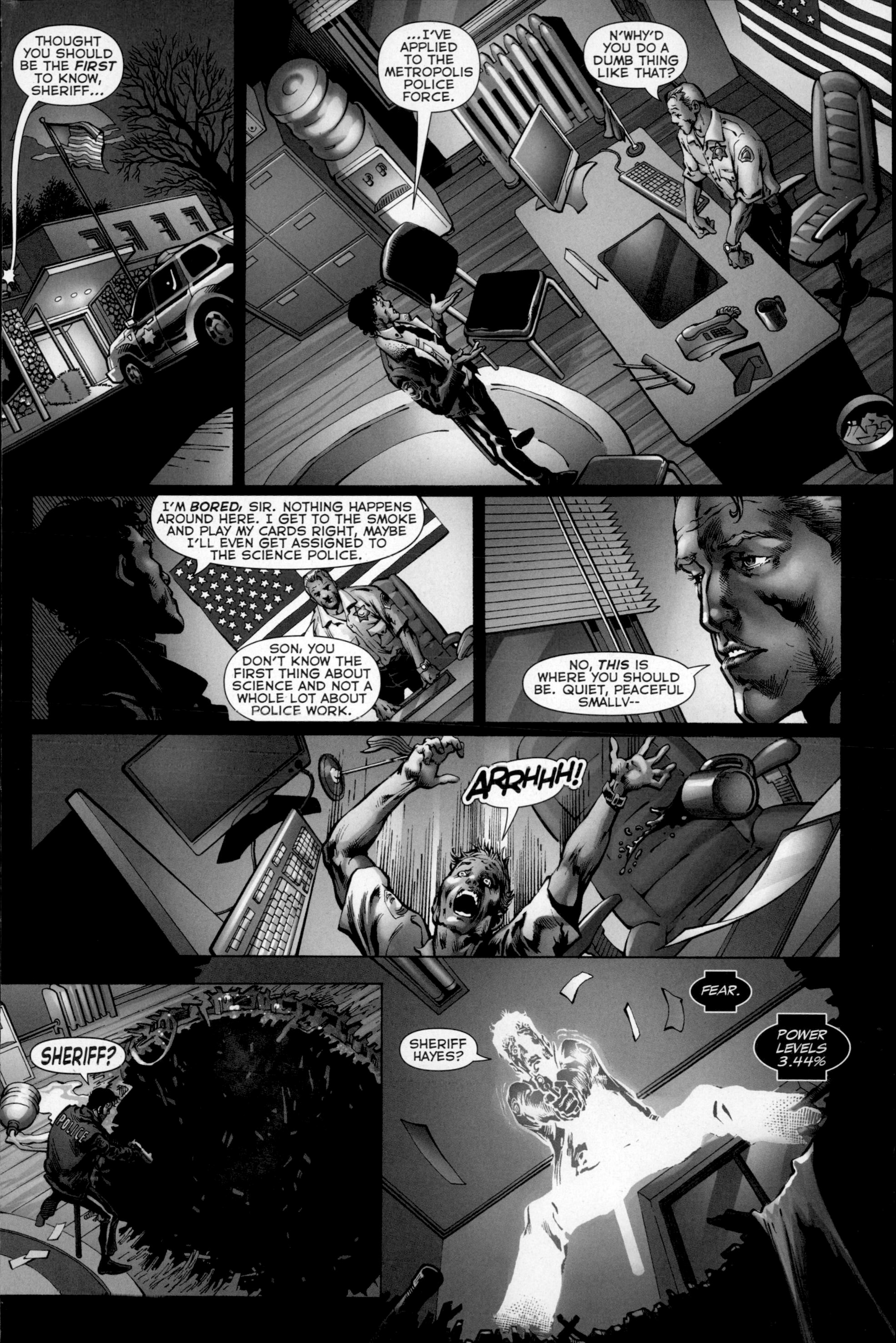
THOUGHT YOU SHOULD BE THE *FIRST* TO KNOW, SHERIFF...
...I'VE APPLIED TO THE METROPOLIS POLICE FORCE.
N'WHY'D YOU DO A DUMB THING LIKE THAT?
I'M *BORED,* SIR. NOTHING HAPPENS AROUND HERE. I GET TO THE SMOKE AND PLAY MY CARDS RIGHT, MAYBE I'LL EVEN GET ASSIGNED TO THE SCIENCE POLICE.
SON, YOU DON'T KNOW THE FIRST THING ABOUT SCIENCE AND NOT A WHOLE LOT ABOUT POLICE WORK.
NO, *THIS* IS WHERE YOU SHOULD BE. QUIET, PEACEFUL SMALLV--
ARRHHH!
SHERIFF?
SHERIFF HAYES?
FEAR.
POWER LEVELS 3.44%

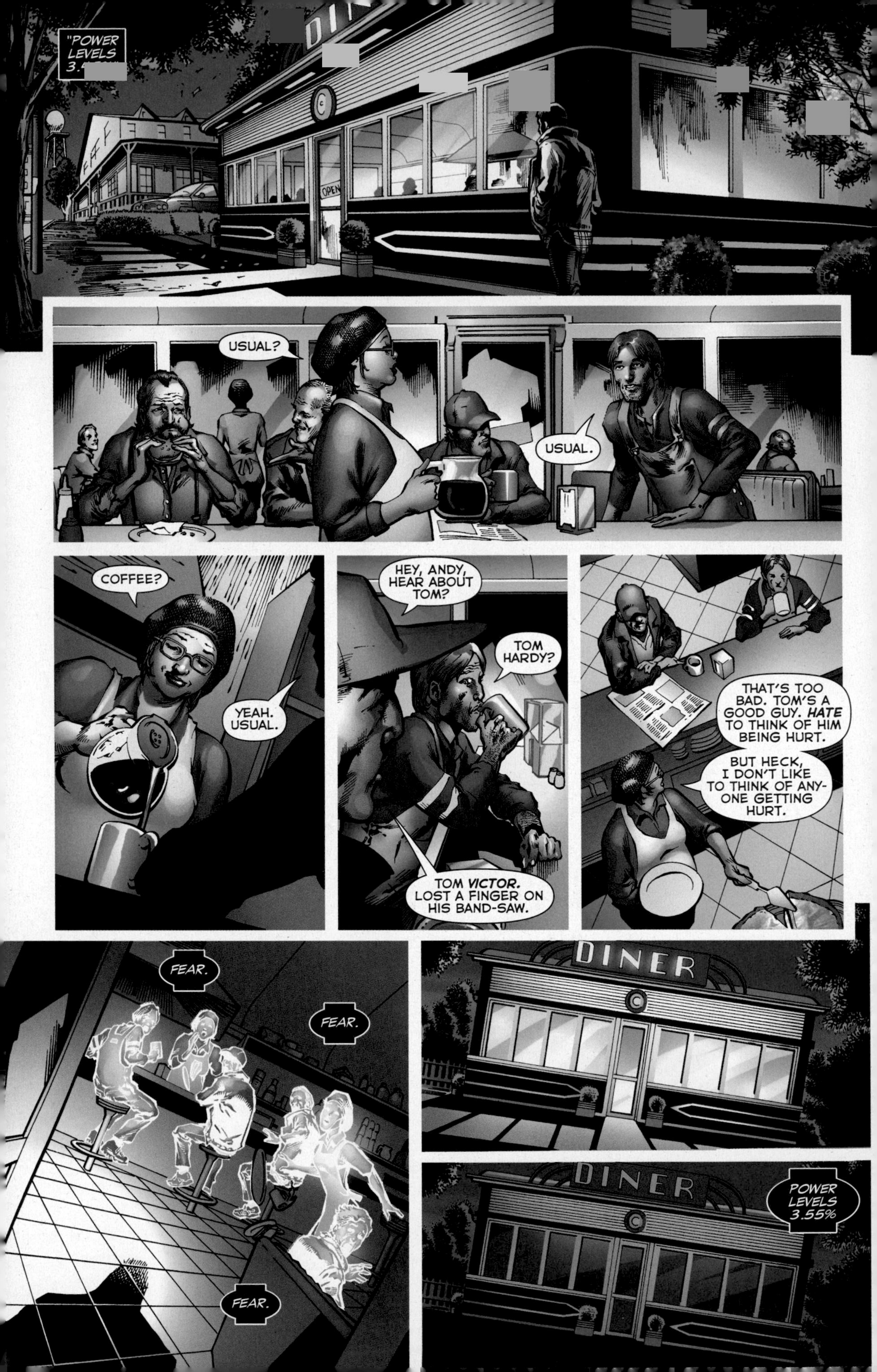
"POWER LEVELS 3.4
DINER
OPEN
USUAL?
USUAL.
COFFEE?
YEAH. USUAL.
HEY, ANDY, HEAR ABOUT TOM?
TOM HARDY?
TOM VICTOR. LOST A FINGER ON HIS BAND-SAW.
THAT'S TOO BAD. TOM'S A GOOD GUY. HATE TO THINK OF HIM BEING HURT.
BUT HECK, I DON'T LIKE TO THINK OF ANY-ONE GETTING HURT.
FEAR.
FEAR.
FEAR.
DINER
DINER
POWER LEVELS 3.55%

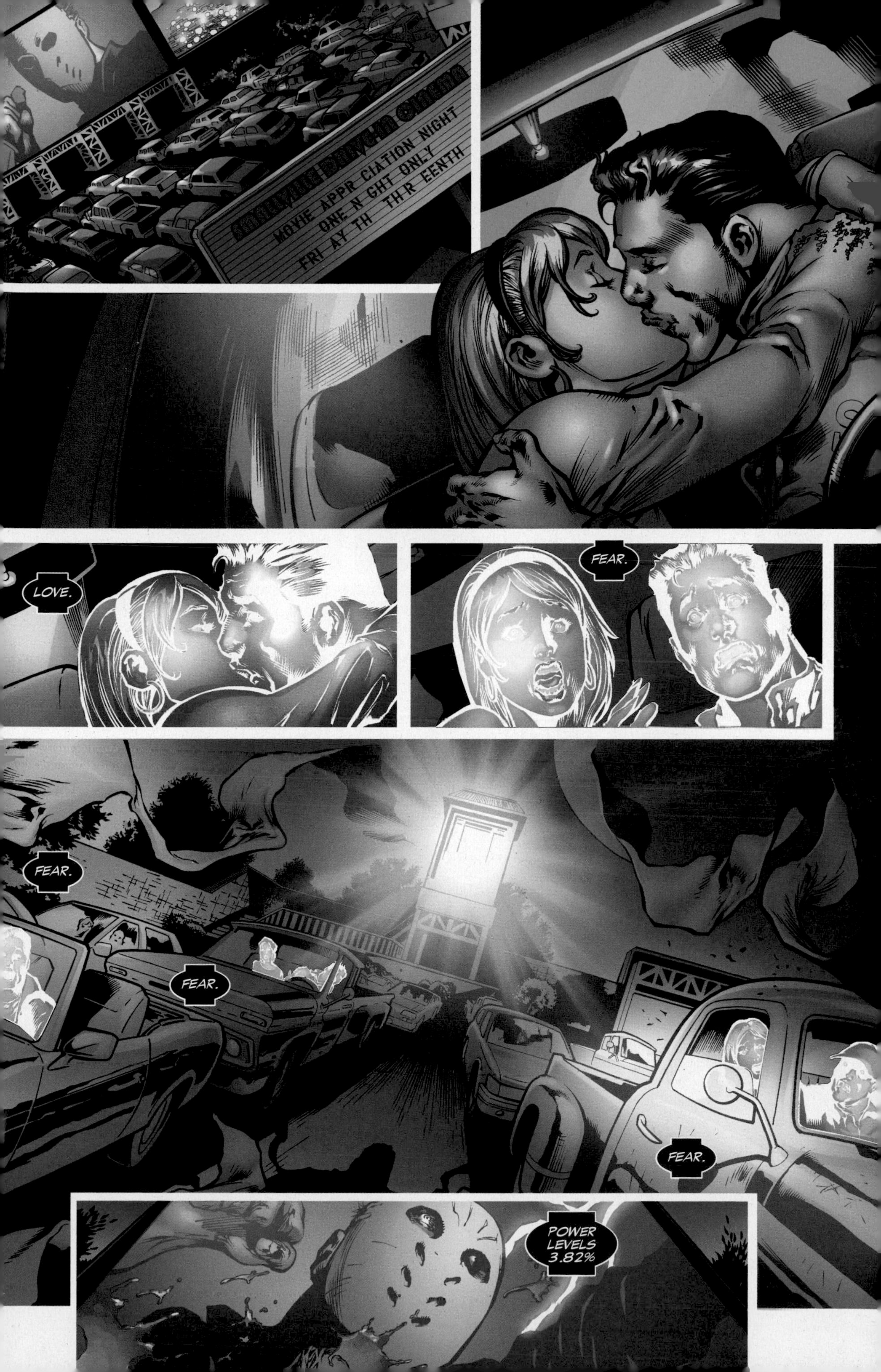
MOVIE APPR CIATION NIGHT
ONE N GHT ONLY
FRI AY TH THR EENTH
LOVE.
FEAR.
FEAR.
FEAR.
FEAR.
POWER LEVELS 3.82%

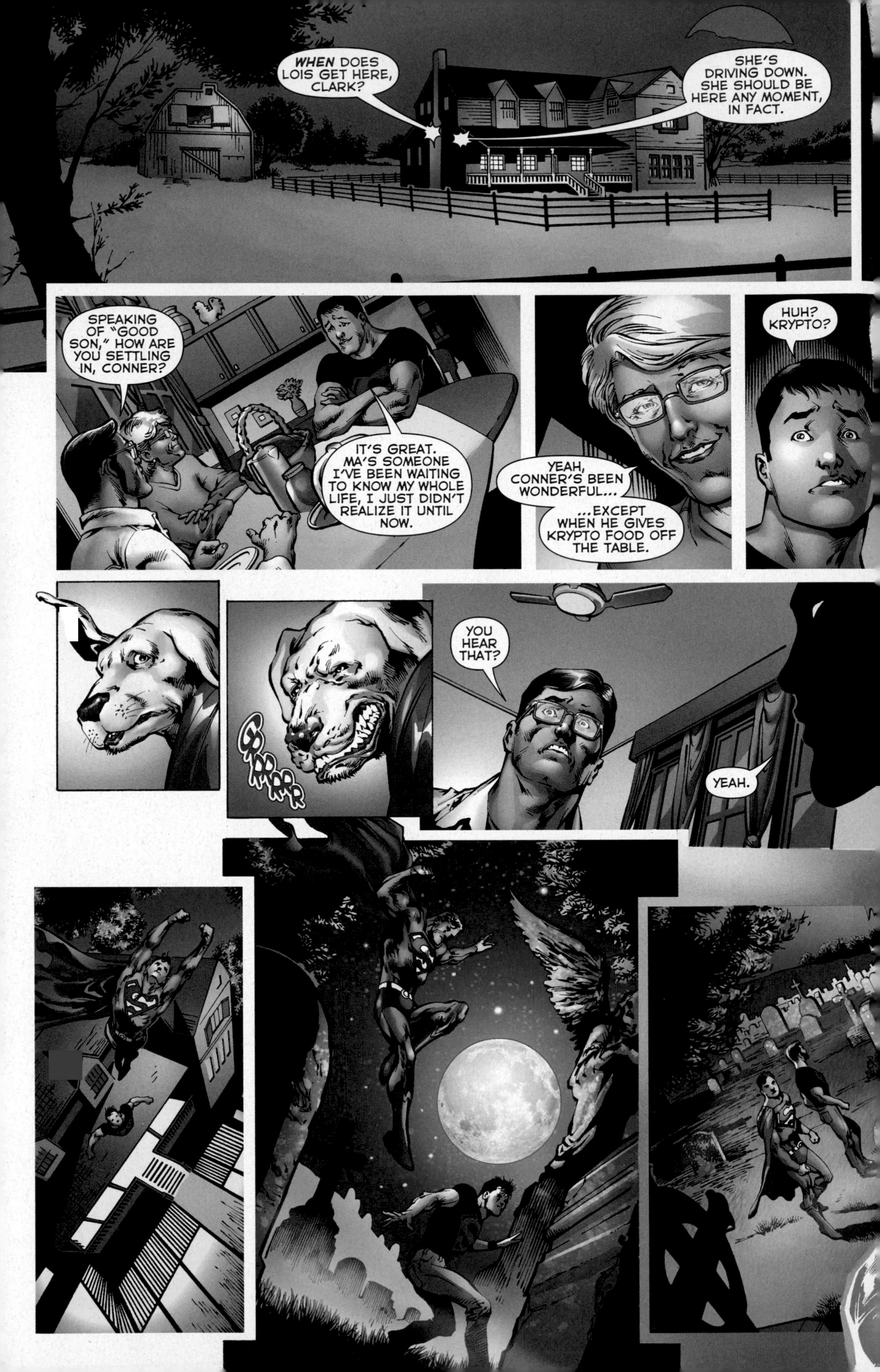

WHEN DOES LOIS GET HERE, CLARK?
SHE'S DRIVING DOWN. SHE SHOULD BE HERE ANY MOMENT, IN FACT.
SPEAKING OF "GOOD SON," HOW ARE YOU SETTLING IN, CONNER?
IT'S GREAT. MA'S SOMEONE I'VE BEEN WAITING TO KNOW MY WHOLE LIFE, I JUST DIDN'T REALIZE IT UNTIL NOW.
YEAH, CONNER'S BEEN WONDERFUL...
...EXCEPT WHEN HE GIVES KRYPTO FOOD OFF THE TABLE.
HUH? KRYPTO?
GRRRRRR
YOU HEAR THAT?
YEAH.

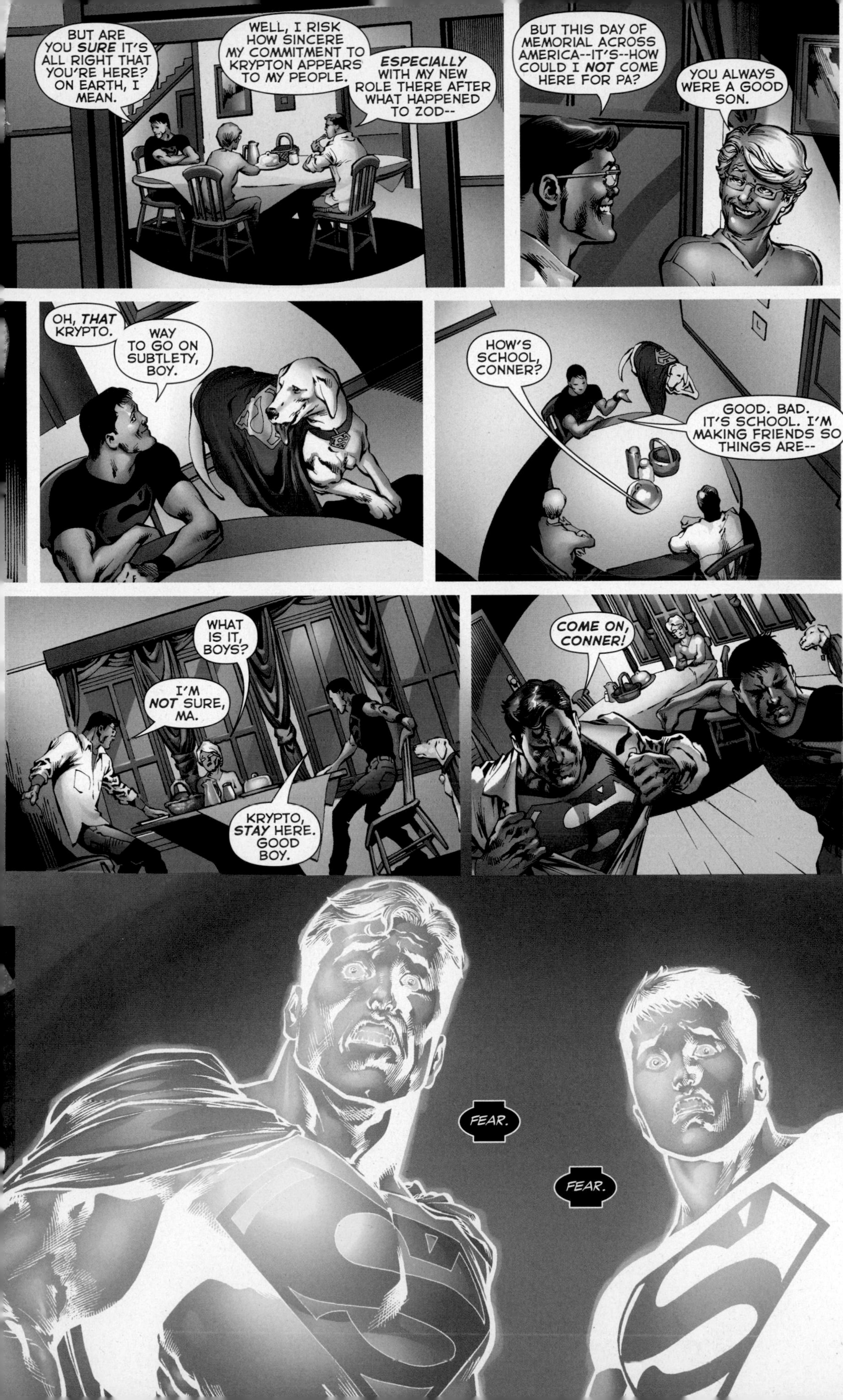
BUT ARE YOU SURE IT'S ALL RIGHT THAT YOU'RE HERE? ON EARTH, I MEAN.
WELL, I RISK HOW SINCERE MY COMMITMENT TO KRYPTON APPEARS TO MY PEOPLE.
ESPECIALLY WITH MY NEW ROLE THERE AFTER WHAT HAPPENED TO ZOD--
BUT THIS DAY OF MEMORIAL ACROSS AMERICA--IT'S--HOW COULD I NOT COME HERE FOR PA?
YOU ALWAYS WERE A GOOD SON.
OH, THAT KRYPTO.
WAY TO GO ON SUBTLETY, BOY.
HOW'S SCHOOL, CONNER?
GOOD. BAD. IT'S SCHOOL. I'M MAKING FRIENDS SO THINGS ARE--
WHAT IS IT, BOYS?
I'M NOT SURE, MA.
KRYPTO, STAY HERE. GOOD BOY.
COME ON, CONNER!
FEAR.
FEAR.

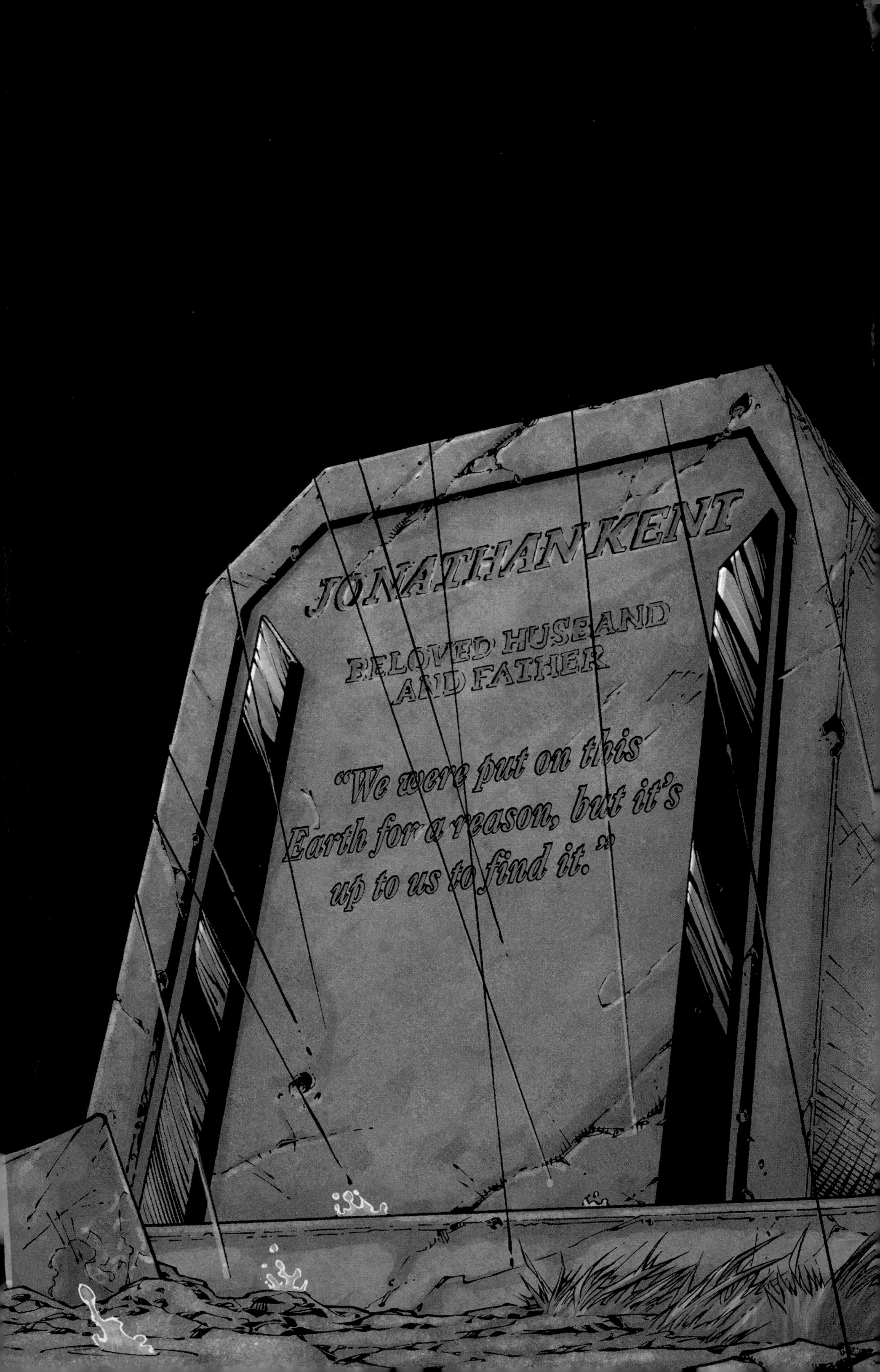

JONATHAN KENT
BELOVED HUSBAND AND FATHER
"We were put on this Earth for a reason, but it's up to us to find it."

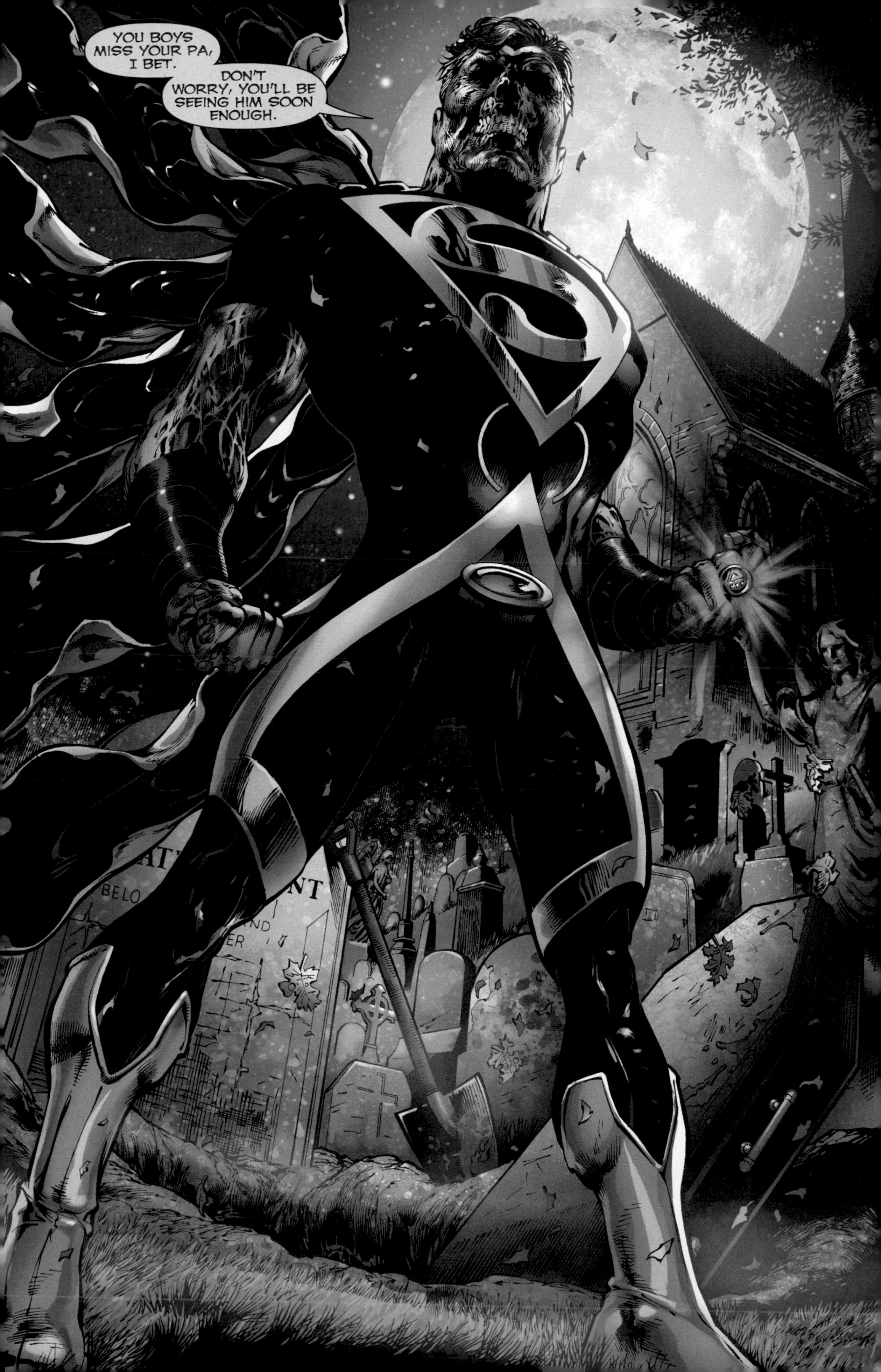
YOU BOYS MISS YOUR PA, I BET.
DON'T WORRY, YOU'LL BE SEEING HIM SOON ENOUGH.

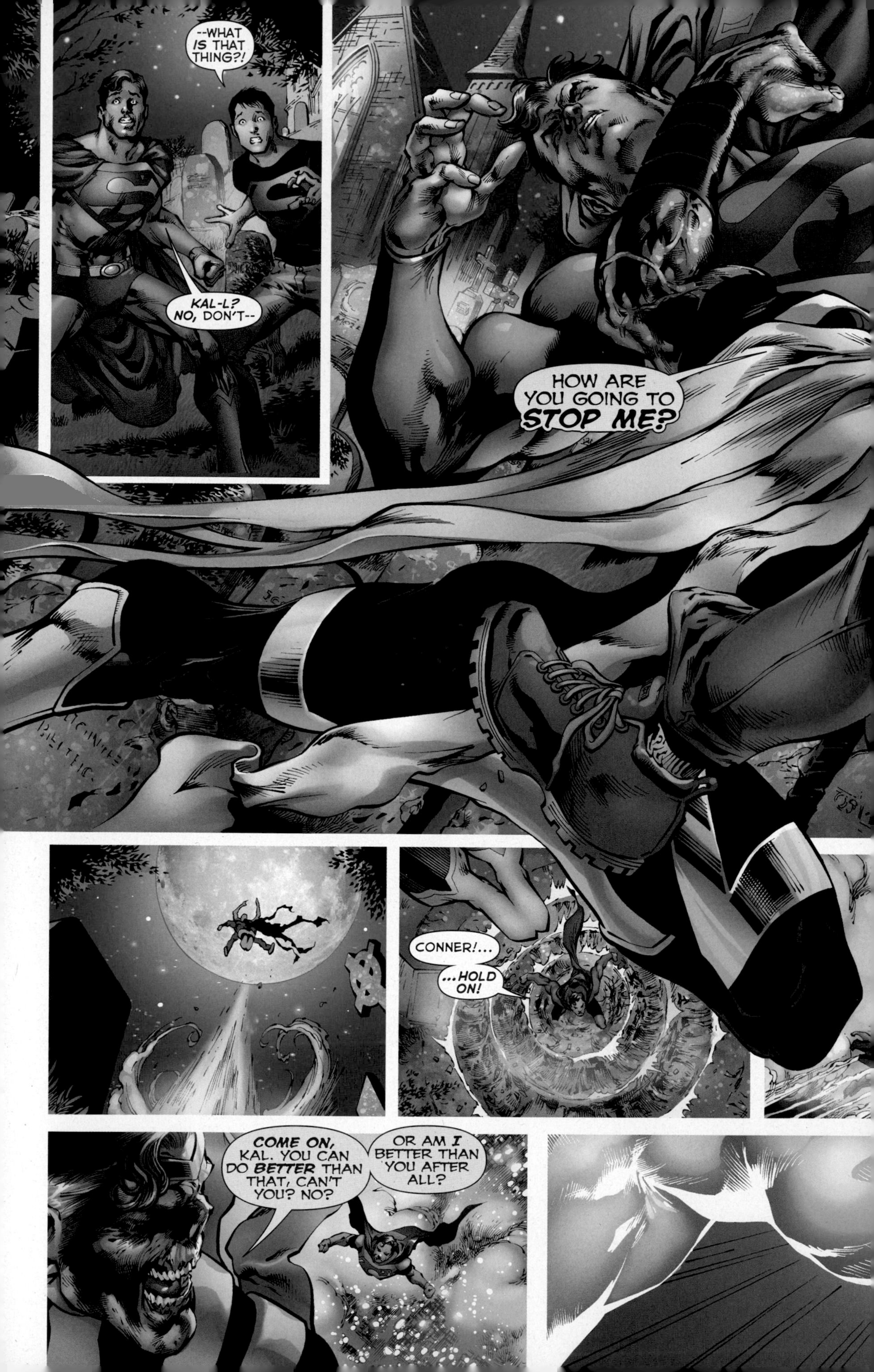
--WHAT IS THAT THING?!
KAL-L? NO, DON'T--
HOW ARE YOU GOING TO STOP ME?
CONNER!...
...HOLD ON!
COME ON, KAL. YOU CAN DO BETTER THAN THAT, CAN'T YOU? NO?
OR AM I BETTER THAN YOU AFTER ALL?

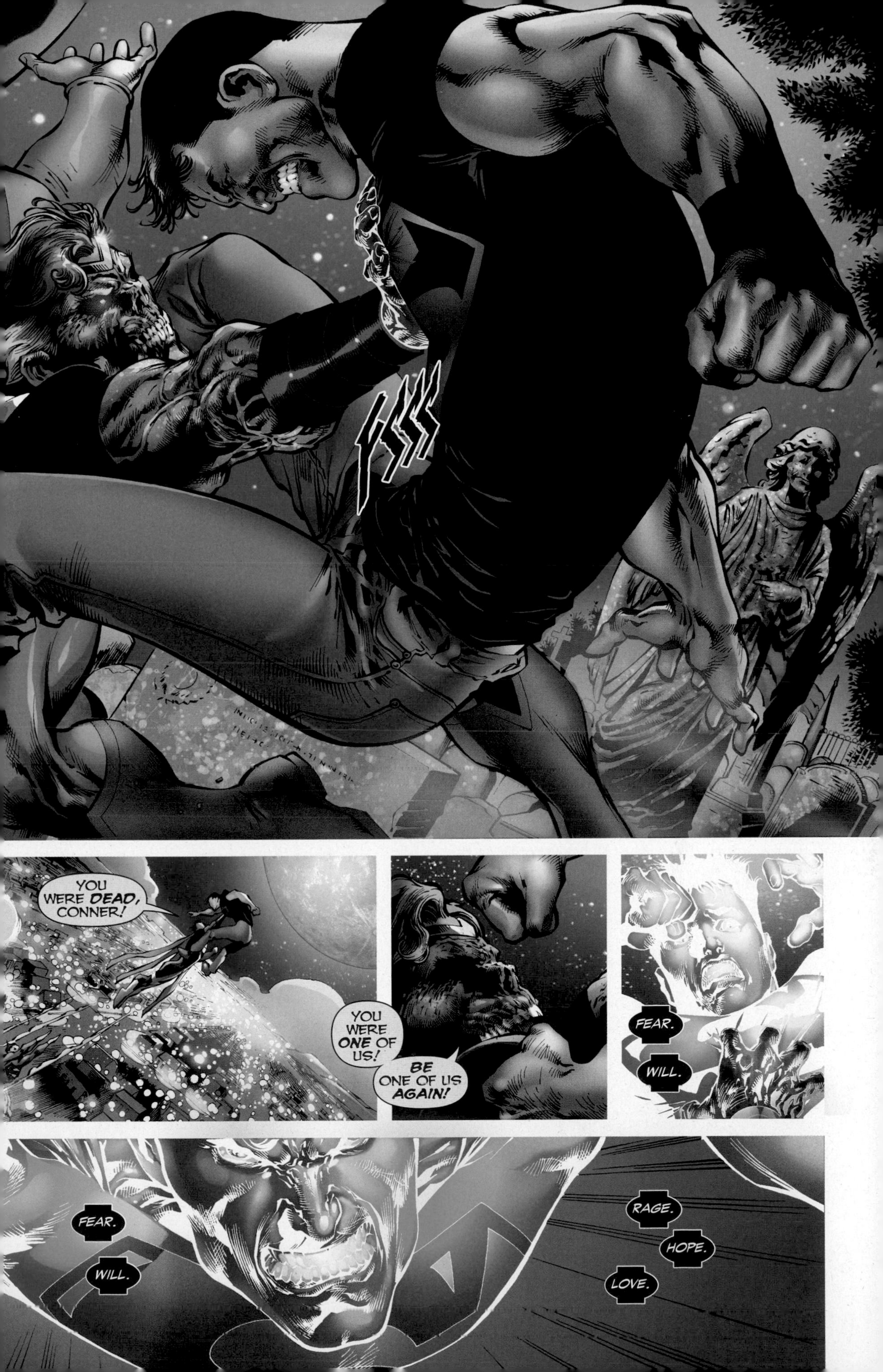
YOU WERE DEAD, CONNER!
YOU WERE ONE OF US!
BE ONE OF US AGAIN!
FEAR.
WILL.
FEAR.
WILL.
RAGE.
HOPE.
LOVE.

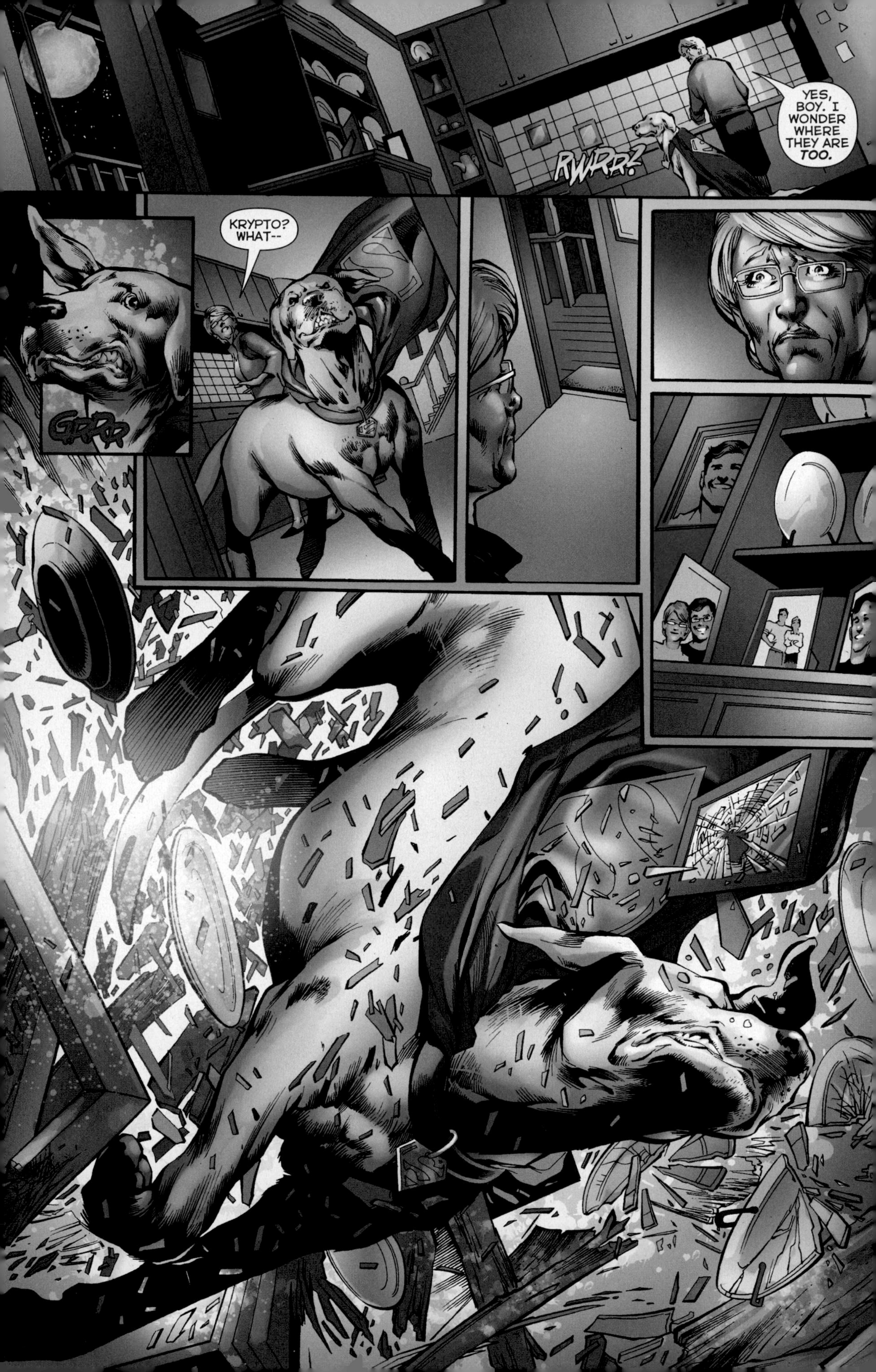
RWRRR?
YES, BOY. I WONDER WHERE THEY ARE TOO.
GRRRR
KRYPTO? WHAT--

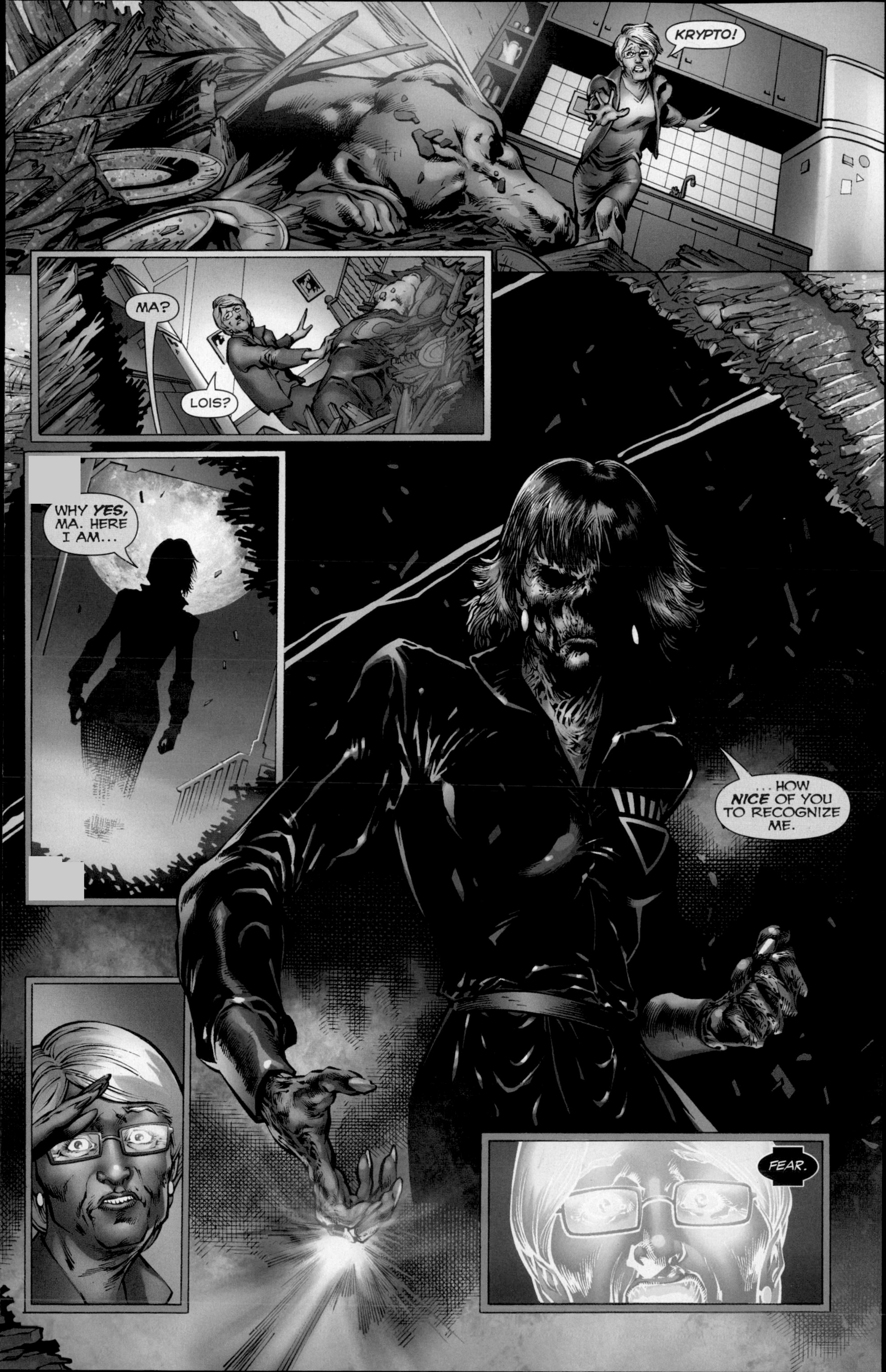
KRYPTO!
MA?
LOIS?
WHY YES, MA. HERE I AM...
...HOW NICE OF YOU TO RECOGNIZE ME.
FEAR.

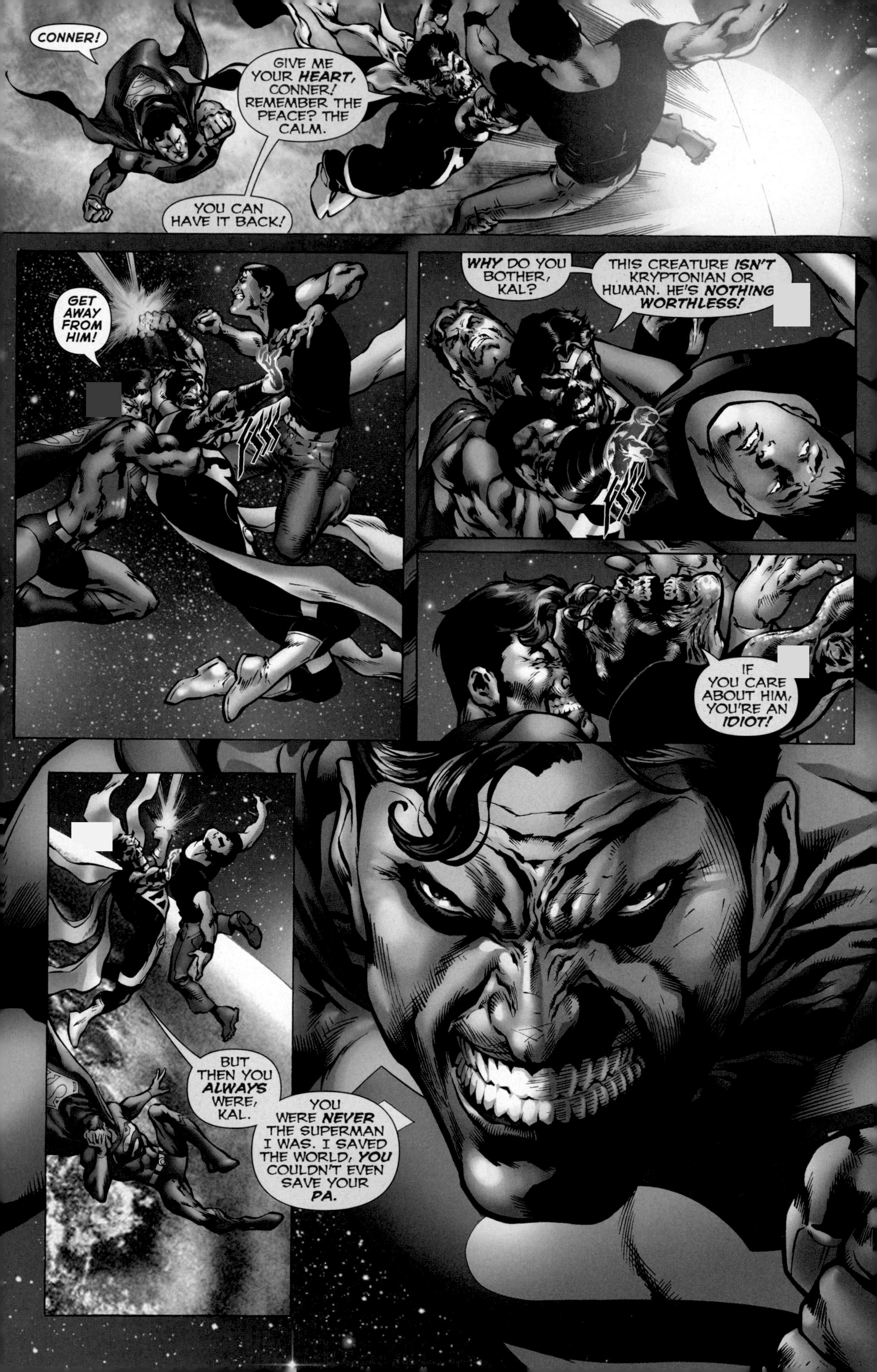
CONNER!
GIVE ME YOUR **HEART,** CONNER! REMEMBER THE PEACE? THE CALM.
YOU CAN HAVE IT BACK!
GET AWAY FROM HIM!
WHY DO YOU BOTHER, KAL?
THIS CREATURE **ISN'T** KRYPTONIAN OR HUMAN. HE'S **NOTHING WORTHLESS!**
IF YOU CARE ABOUT HIM, YOU'RE AN **IDIOT!**
BUT THEN YOU **ALWAYS** WERE, KAL.
YOU WERE **NEVER** THE SUPERMAN I WAS. I SAVED THE WORLD, **YOU** COULDN'T EVEN SAVE YOUR **PA.**

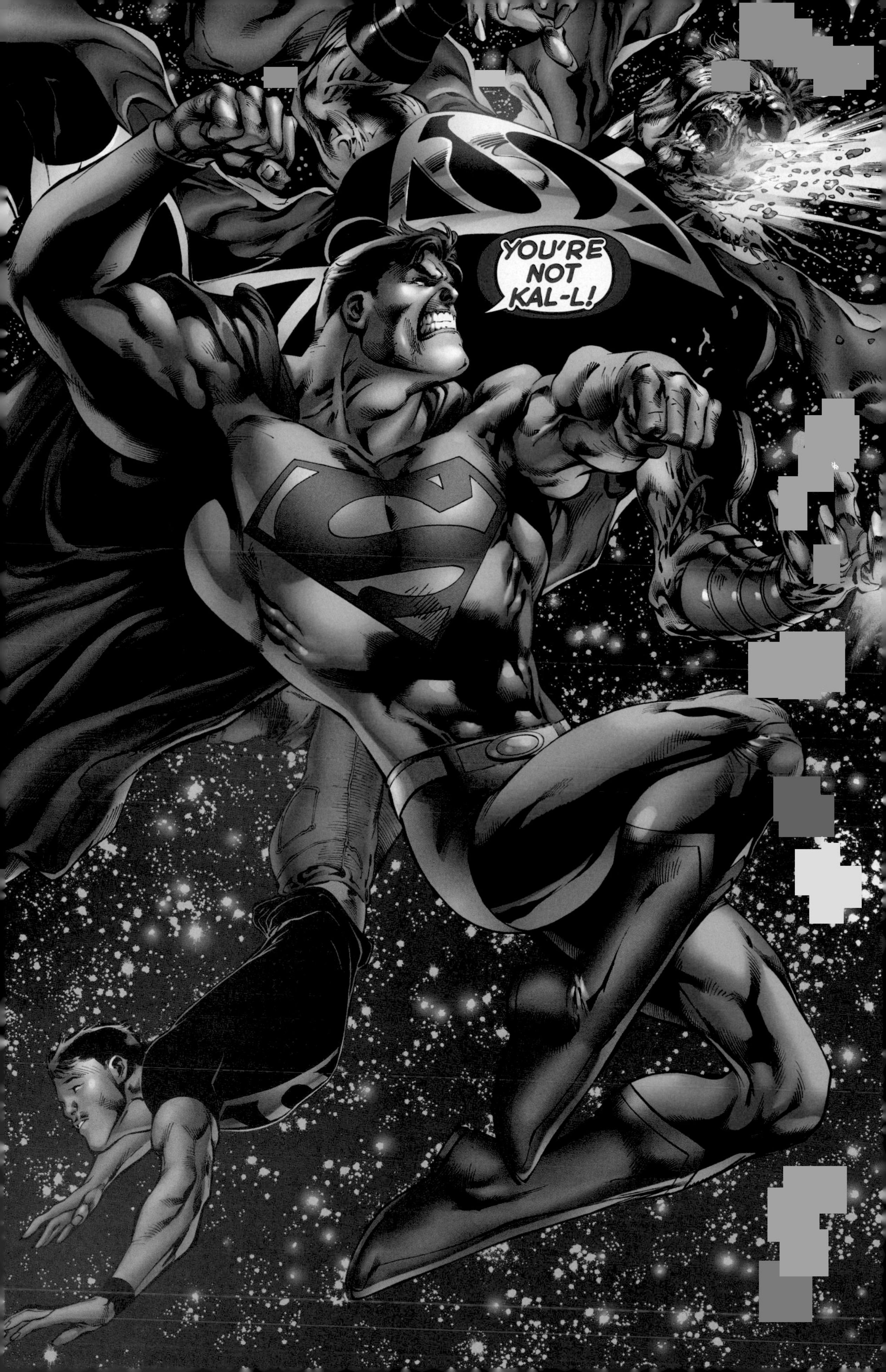
YOU'RE NOT KAL-L!

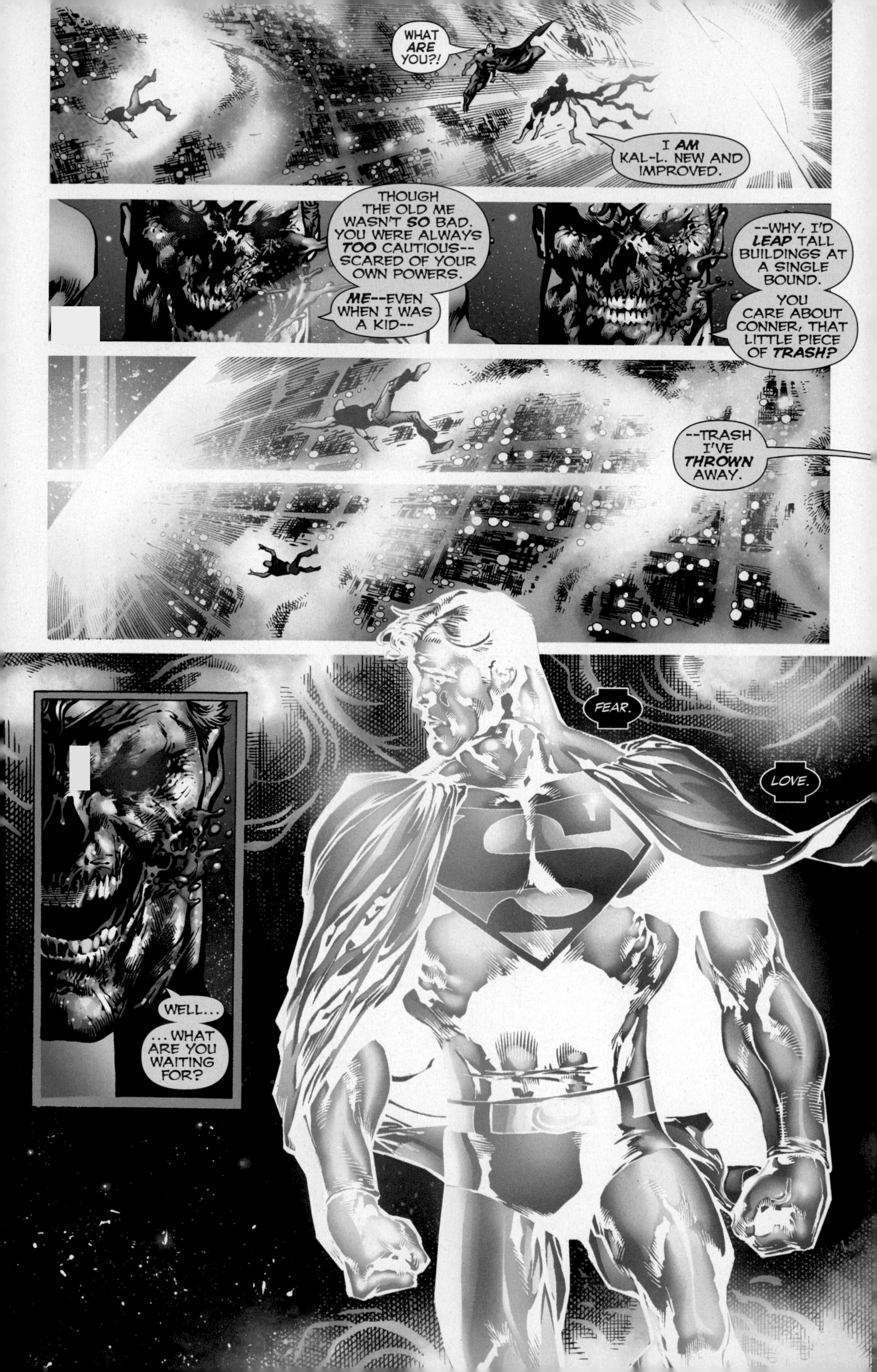

WHAT ARE YOU?!
I AM KAL-L. NEW AND IMPROVED.
THOUGH THE OLD ME WASN'T SO BAD. YOU WERE ALWAYS TOO CAUTIOUS-- SCARED OF YOUR OWN POWERS.
ME--EVEN WHEN I WAS A KID--
--WHY, I'D LEAP TALL BUILDINGS AT A SINGLE BOUND.
YOU CARE ABOUT CONNER, THAT LITTLE PIECE OF TRASH?
--TRASH I'VE THROWN AWAY.
FEAR.
LOVE.
WELL...
...WHAT ARE YOU WAITING FOR?

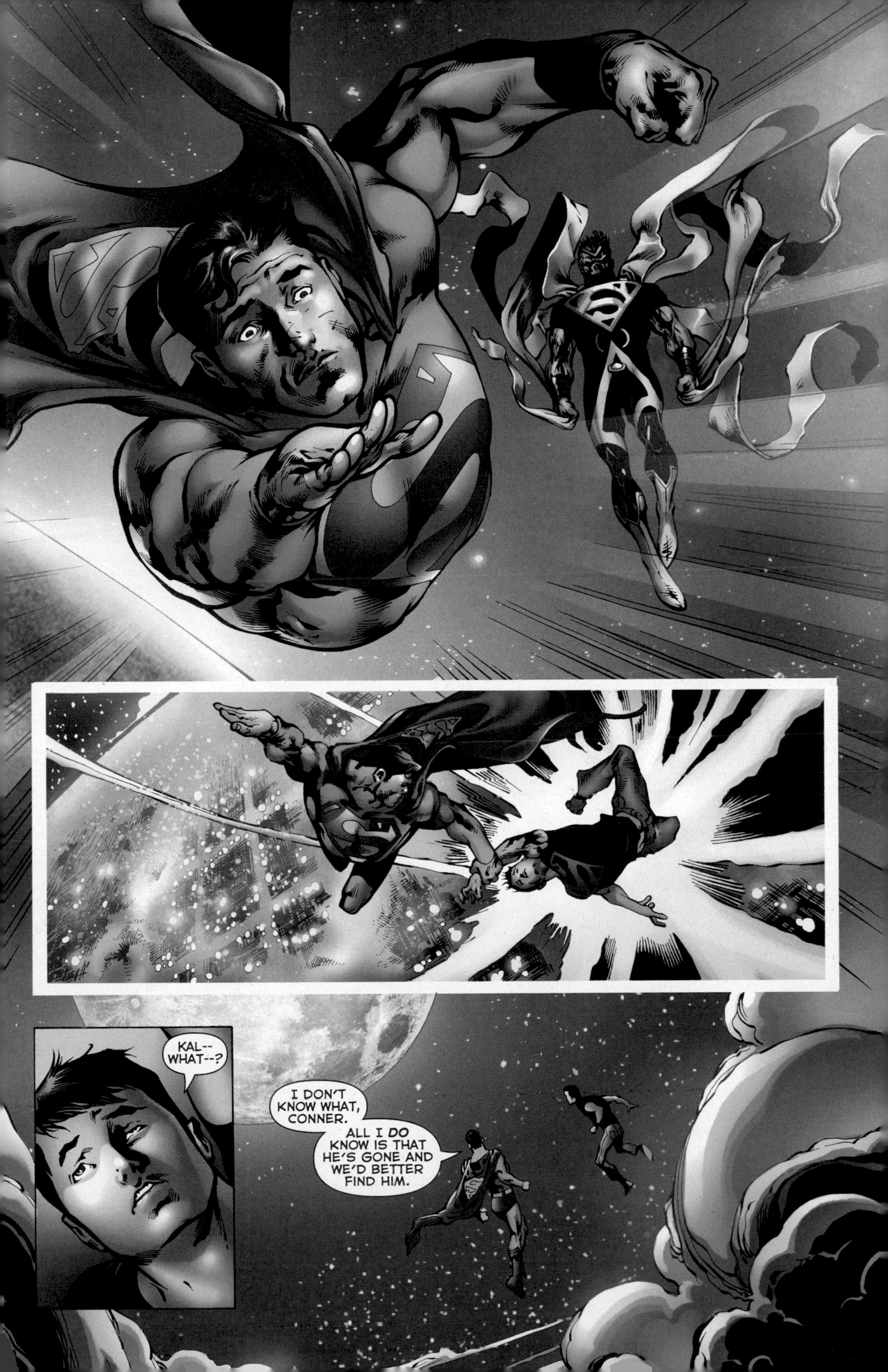
KAL-- WHAT--?
I DON'T KNOW WHAT, CONNER.
ALL I DO KNOW IS THAT HE'S GONE AND WE'D BETTER FIND HIM.

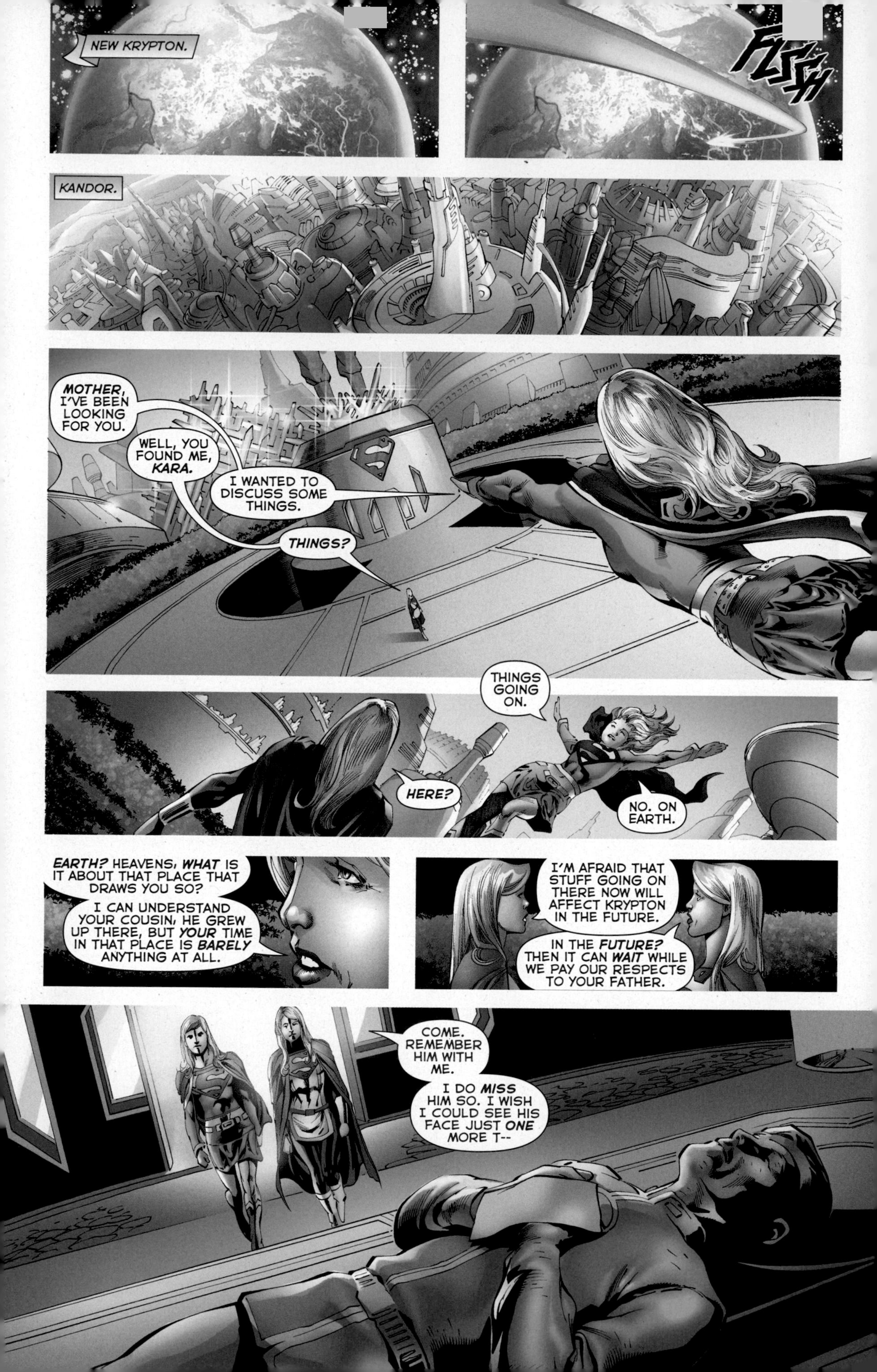
NEW KRYPTON.
FLSSH
KANDOR.
MOTHER, I'VE BEEN LOOKING FOR YOU.
WELL, YOU FOUND ME, KARA.
I WANTED TO DISCUSS SOME THINGS.
THINGS?
THINGS GOING ON.
HERE?
NO. ON EARTH.
EARTH? HEAVENS, WHAT IS IT ABOUT THAT PLACE THAT DRAWS YOU SO?
I CAN UNDERSTAND YOUR COUSIN, HE GREW UP THERE, BUT YOUR TIME IN THAT PLACE IS BARELY ANYTHING AT ALL.
I'M AFRAID THAT STUFF GOING ON THERE NOW WILL AFFECT KRYPTON IN THE FUTURE.
IN THE FUTURE? THEN IT CAN WAIT WHILE WE PAY OUR RESPECTS TO YOUR FATHER.
COME. REMEMBER HIM WITH ME.
I DO MISS HIM SO. I WISH I COULD SEE HIS FACE JUST ONE MORE T--

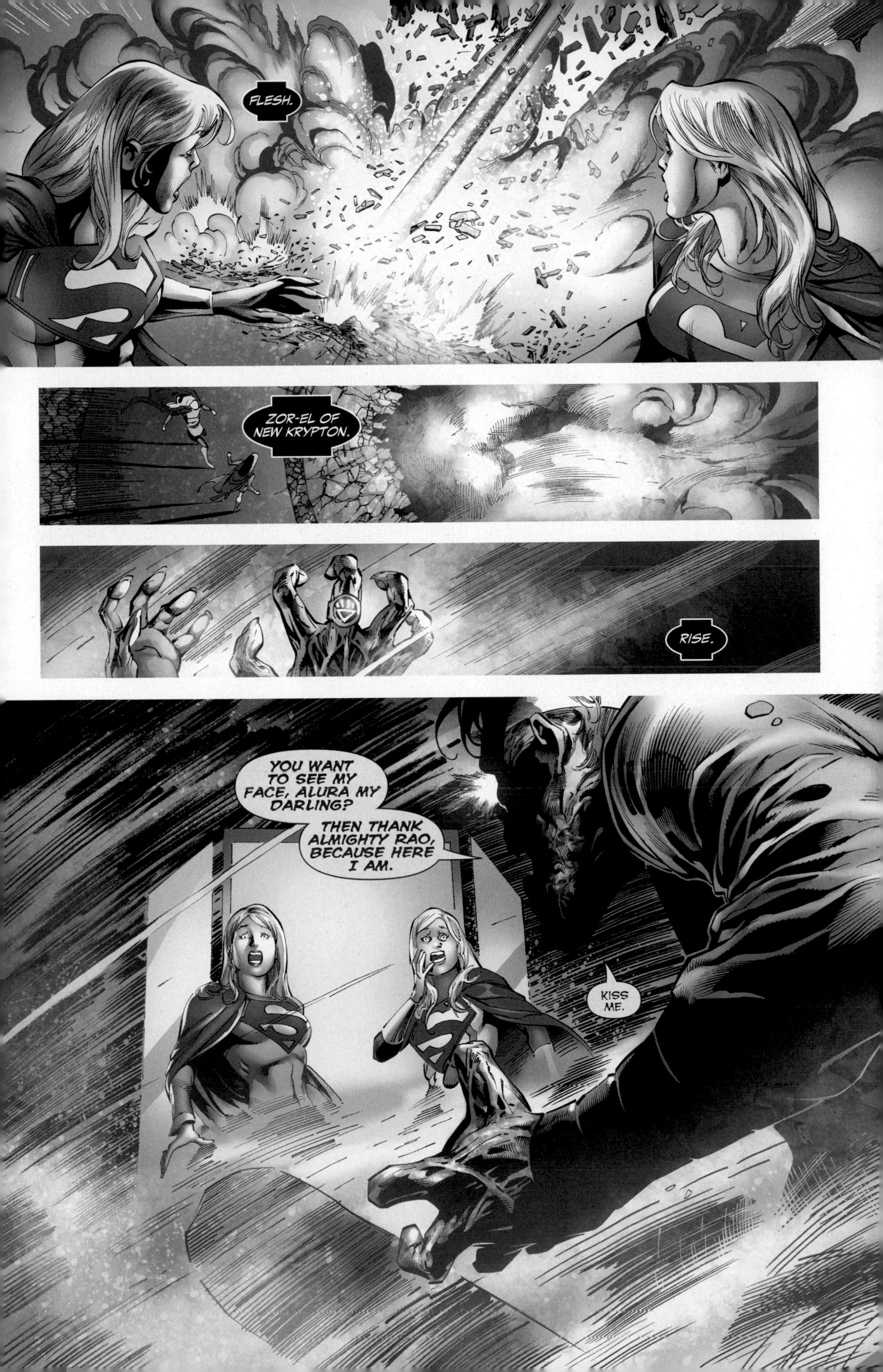
FLESH.
ZOR-EL OF NEW KRYPTON.
RISE.
YOU WANT TO SEE MY FACE, ALURA MY DARLING?
THEN THANK ALMIGHTY RAO, BECAUSE HERE I AM.
KISS ME.

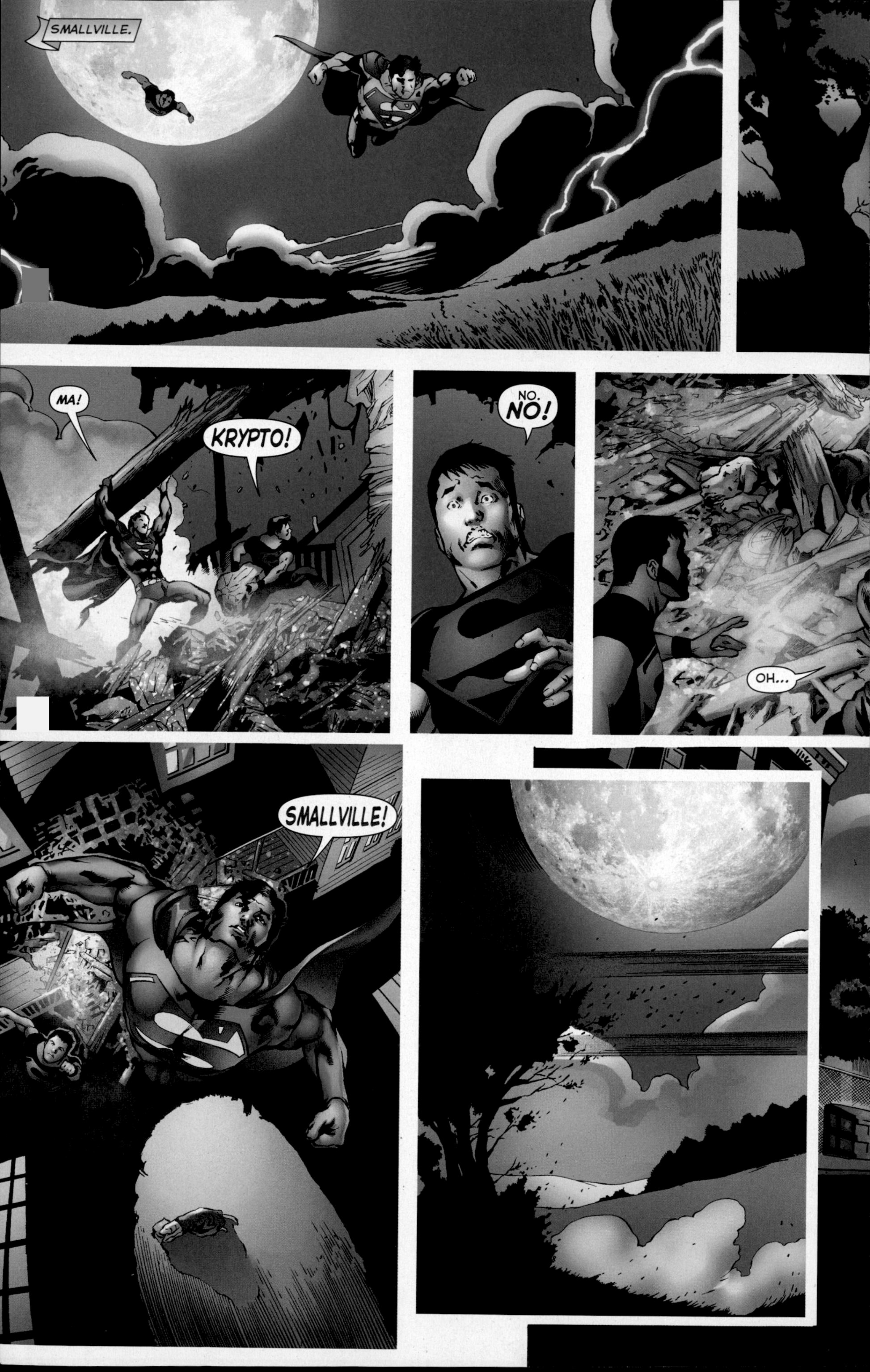
SMALLVILLE.
MA!
KRYPTO!
NO. NO!
OH...
SMALLVILLE!

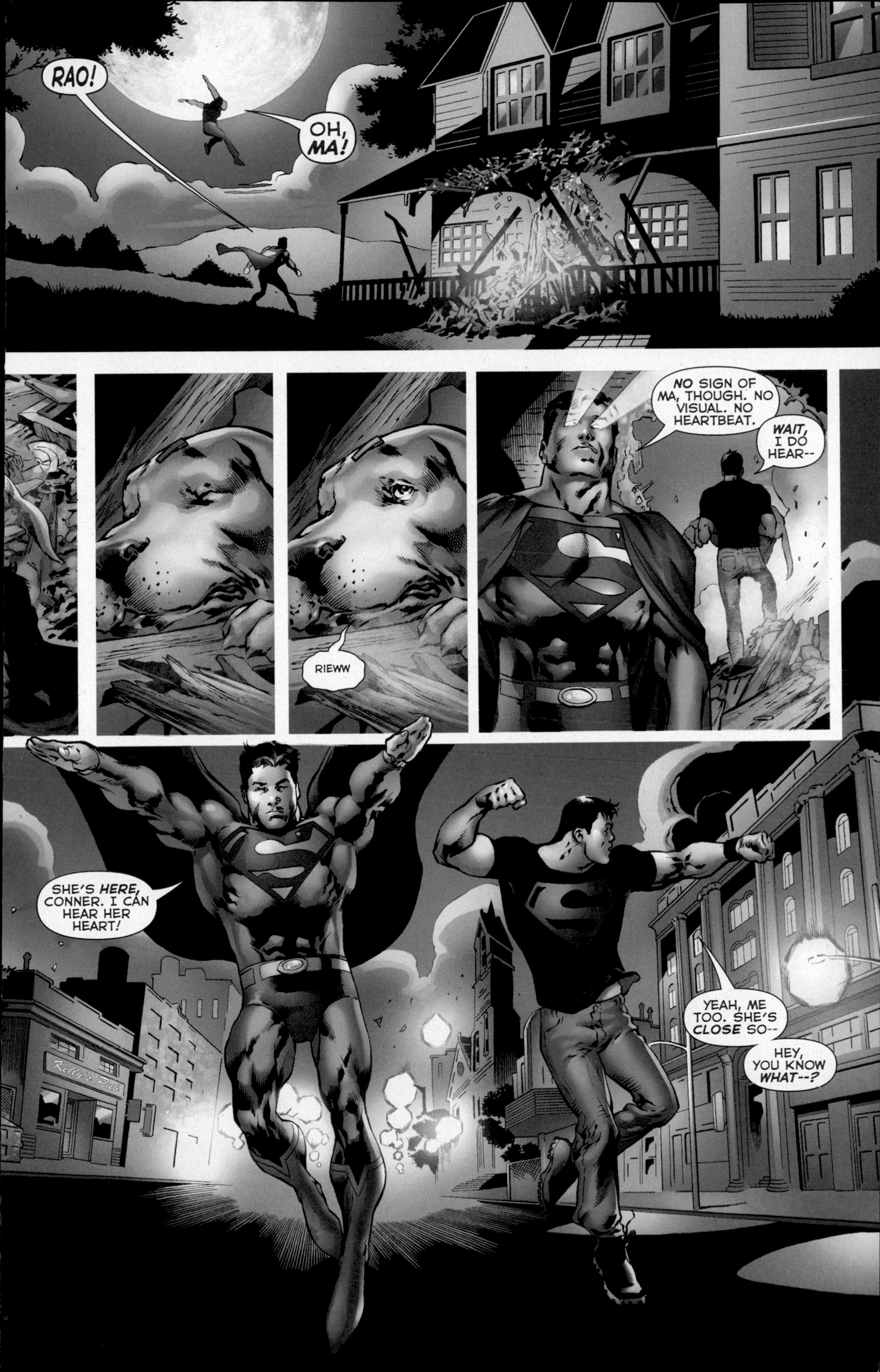
RAO!
OH, MA!
RIEWW
NO SIGN OF MA, THOUGH. NO VISUAL. NO HEARTBEAT.
WAIT, I DO HEAR--
SHE'S HERE, CONNER. I CAN HEAR HER HEART!
Kelly's Pub
YEAH, ME TOO. SHE'S CLOSE SO--
HEY, YOU KNOW WHAT--?

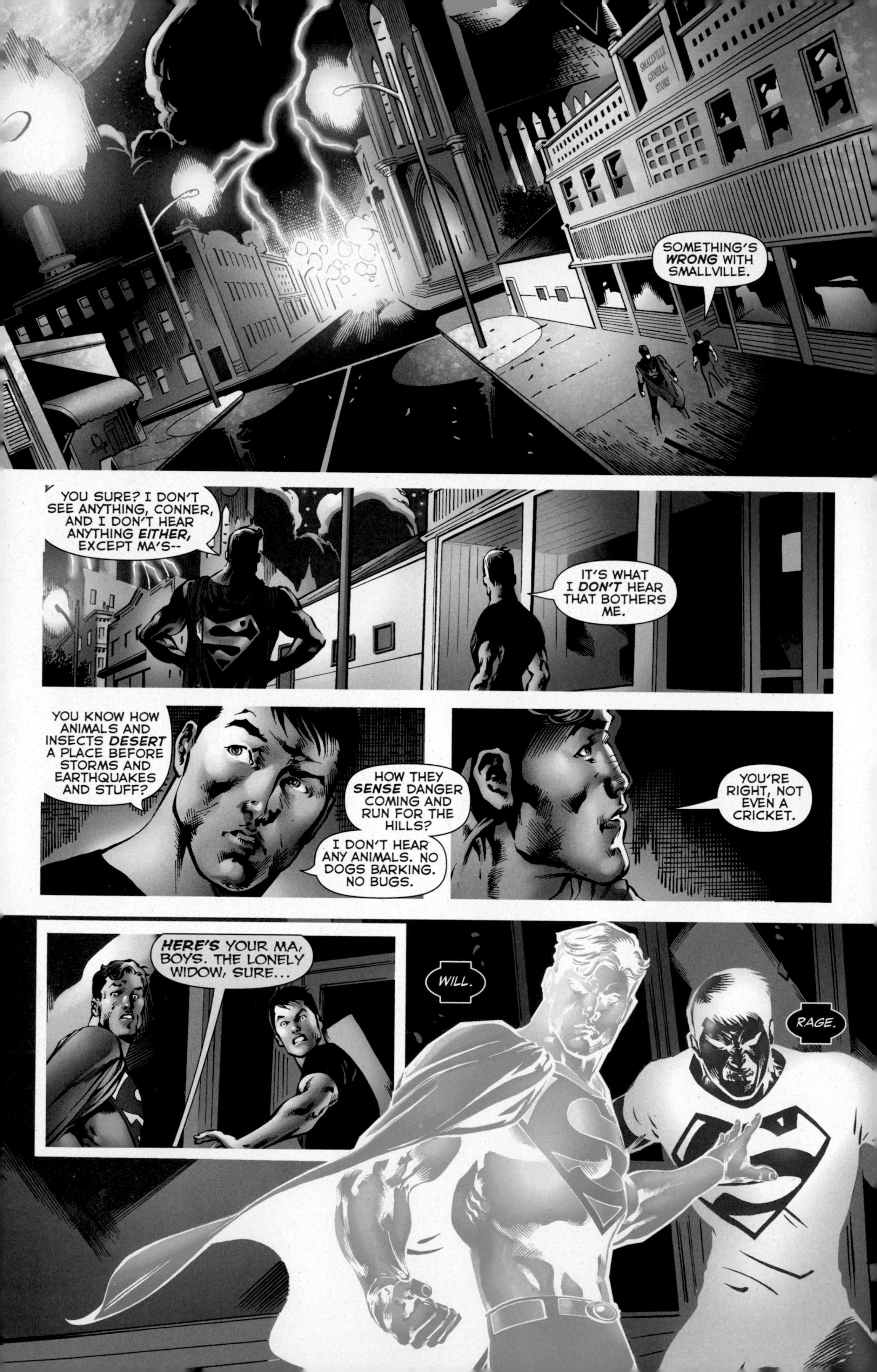
SMALLVILLE GENERAL STORE
SOMETHING'S WRONG WITH SMALLVILLE.
YOU SURE? I DON'T SEE ANYTHING, CONNER, AND I DON'T HEAR ANYTHING EITHER, EXCEPT MA'S--
IT'S WHAT I DON'T HEAR THAT BOTHERS ME.
YOU KNOW HOW ANIMALS AND INSECTS DESERT A PLACE BEFORE STORMS AND EARTHQUAKES AND STUFF?
HOW THEY SENSE DANGER COMING AND RUN FOR THE HILLS?
I DON'T HEAR ANY ANIMALS. NO DOGS BARKING. NO BUGS.
YOU'RE RIGHT, NOT EVEN A CRICKET.
HERE'S YOUR MA, BOYS. THE LONELY WIDOW, SURE...
WILL.
RAGE.

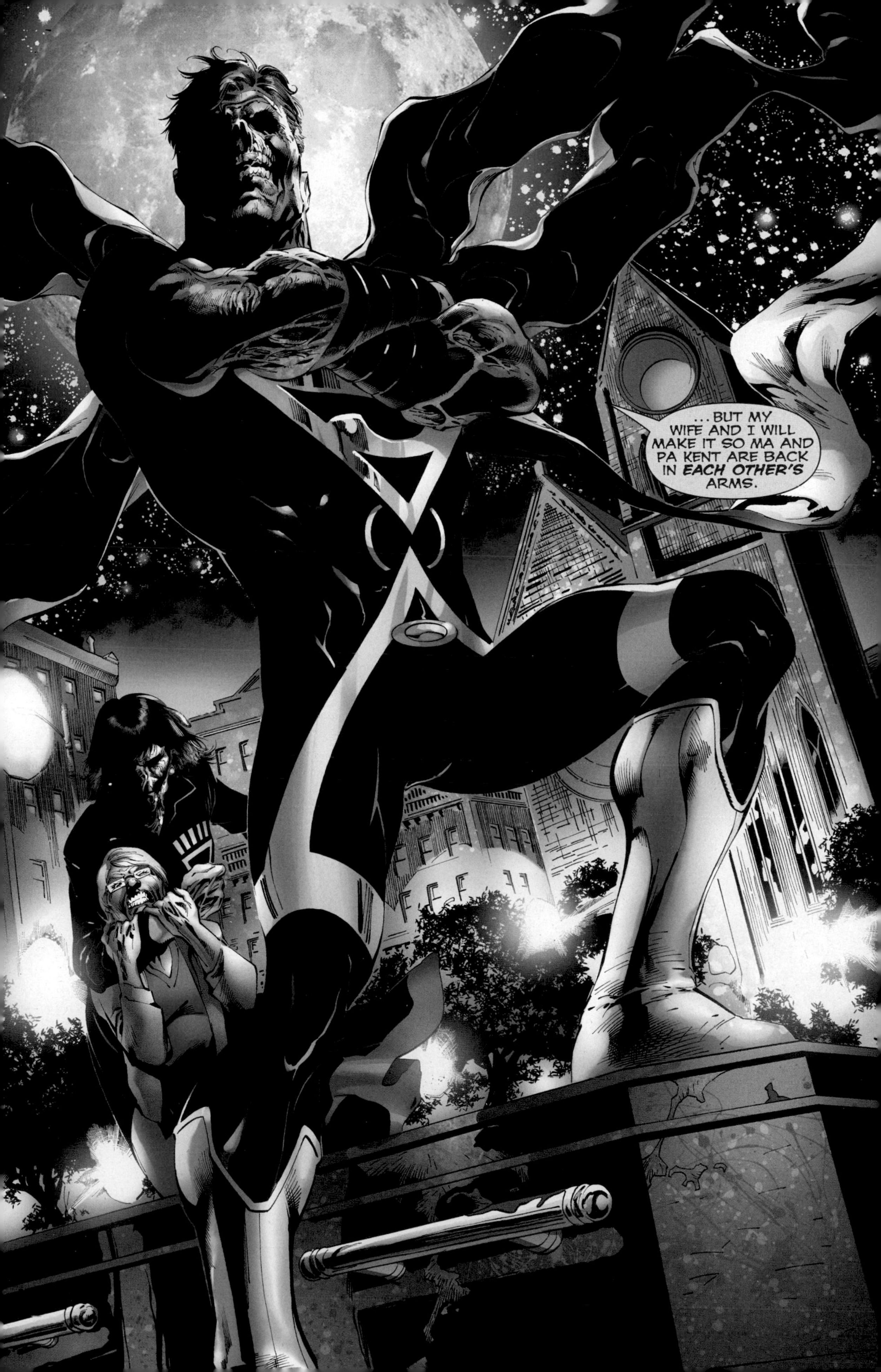
...BUT MY WIFE AND I WILL MAKE IT SO MA AND PA KENT ARE BACK IN EACH OTHER'S ARMS.

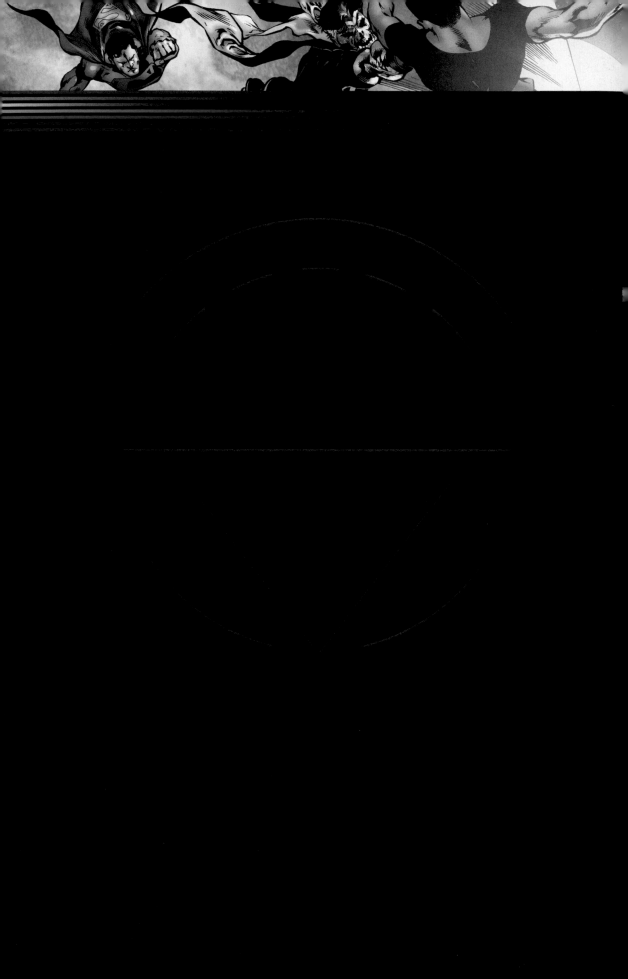

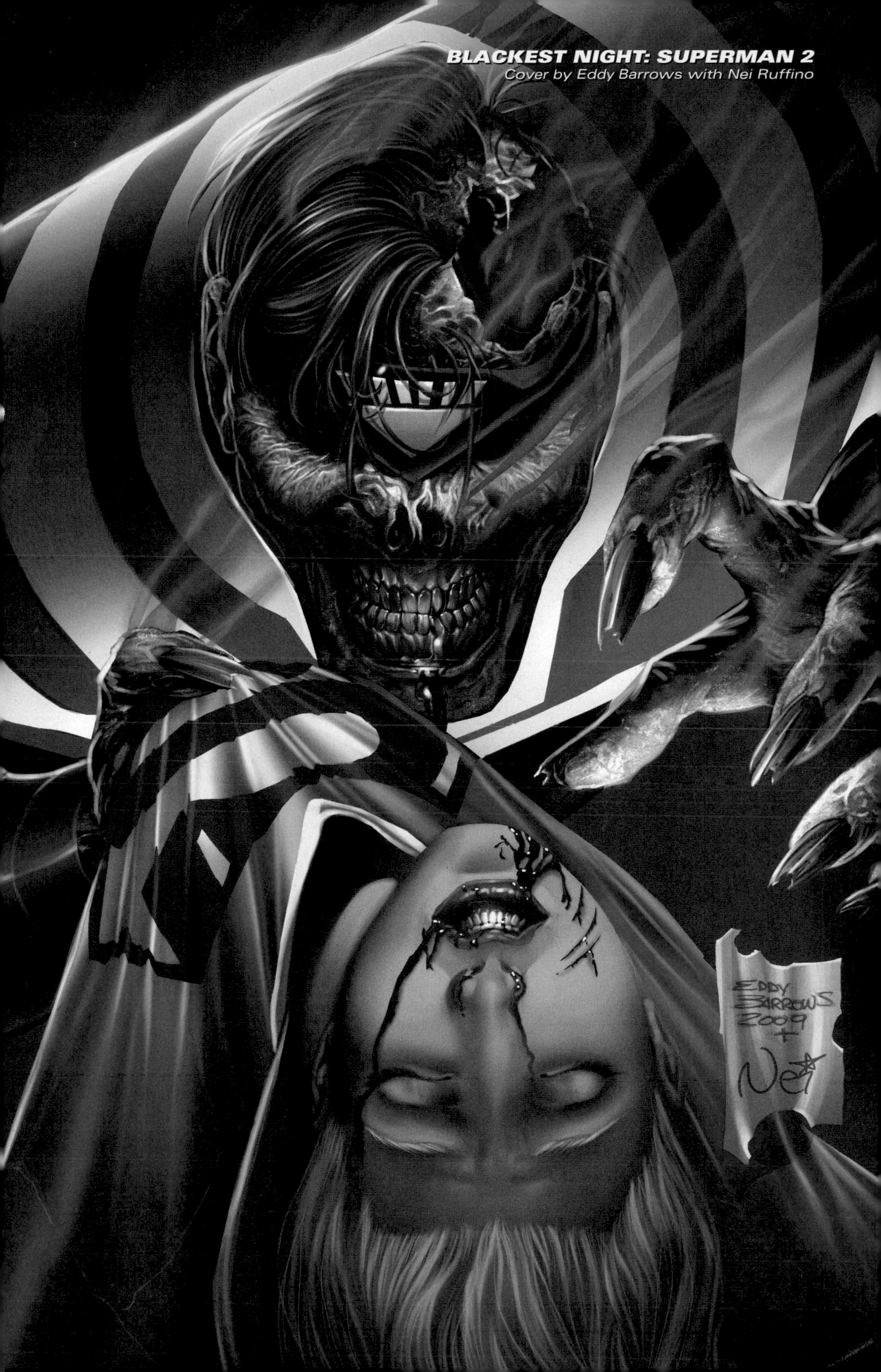
EDDY BARROWS 2009 + Nei

BLACKEST NIGHT: SUPERMAN 2
Cover by Eddy Barrows with Nei Ruffino

PSYCHO PIRACY!

JAMES ROBINSON
WRITER

EDDY BARROWS
PENCILS

RUY JOSÉ
JULIO FERREIRA
INKS

SMALLVILLE.

THIS MORNING.

THANKS FOR STAYING OPEN, DAVEY. IT'S JUST I'VE BEEN SO *BUSY* LATELY AND--

YOU KIDDING? *RELAX,* I'D RATHER KEEP MY DOOR OPEN *ALL* NIGHT THAN HAVE MY CUSTOMERS WALKING AROUND LOOKING LIKE HIPPIES.

NOW SETTLE BACK.

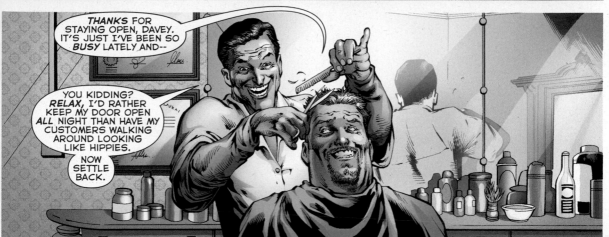

SIMON, COME DOWNSTAIRS. DINNER'S READY.

NOT HUNGRY, MOM. GOTTA GET THIS DISPLAY *DONE* FOR THE SCIENCE FAIR TOMORROW...

...AND I'M ALREADY DISAPPOINTED THAT IT'S GOING TO BE SO *UNIMPRESSIVE.*

YEAH, I *KNOW* GRACE IS RODDY'S GIRLFRIEND.

N'YEAH, *SHE* WANTED THE BAG, SURE I KNOW THAT TOO.

LOOK, WHEN I ASKED HIM, I DIDN'T THINK RODDY WOULD *ACTUALLY* SPEND HIS MONEY ON ME *INSTEAD* OF HER...SO IT'S *NOT* MY FAULT.

IT'S *ON* THE HOUSE, SOLDIER. YOUR MONEY'S NO GOOD HERE.

THANKS, I DON'T KNOW WHAT TO SAY.

YOU JUST GOT *BACK* FROM OVER THERE, RIGHT? I KNOW WHAT TO SAY... *THANK YOU.*

SMALLVILLE THAT NIGHT!

KEEP ON HIM, CONNER! THIS MONSTROSITY CAN'T BE THE REAL KAL-L. I KNOW WE CAN BEAT IT!

WHO'RE THEY FIGHTING? CAN YOU MAKE IT OUT?

CAN'T QUITE--

LOOKS KINDA LIKE ANOTHER SUPERMAN, YOU ASK ME.

YOU CRAZY, LOOKS NOTHING LIKE H--

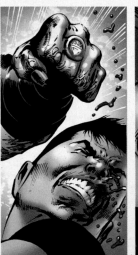

OH MY GOD!!

SUPERBOY GOT PUNCHED CLEAN THROUGH--

YOU SEE HIM GETTING UP?

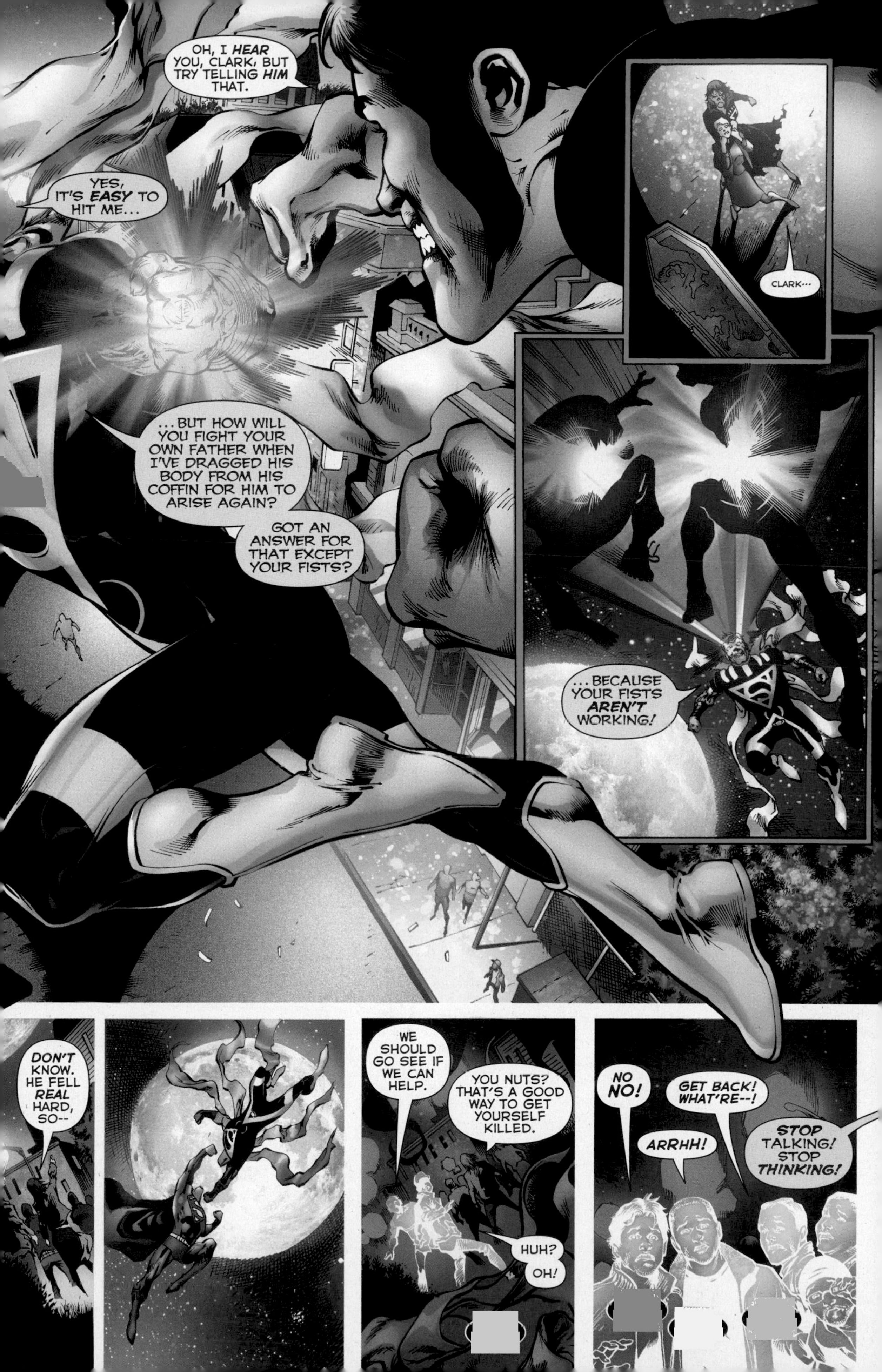
OH, I HEAR YOU, CLARK, BUT TRY TELLING HIM THAT.
YES, IT'S EASY TO HIT ME...
CLARK...
...BUT HOW WILL YOU FIGHT YOUR OWN FATHER WHEN I'VE DRAGGED HIS BODY FROM HIS COFFIN FOR HIM TO ARISE AGAIN?
GOT AN ANSWER FOR THAT EXCEPT YOUR FISTS?
...BECAUSE YOUR FISTS AREN'T WORKING!
DON'T KNOW. HE FELL REAL HARD, SO--
WE SHOULD GO SEE IF WE CAN HELP.
YOU NUTS? THAT'S A GOOD WAY TO GET YOURSELF KILLED.
HUH?
OH!
NO NO!
GET BACK! WHAT'RE--!
ARRHH!
STOP TALKING! STOP THINKING!

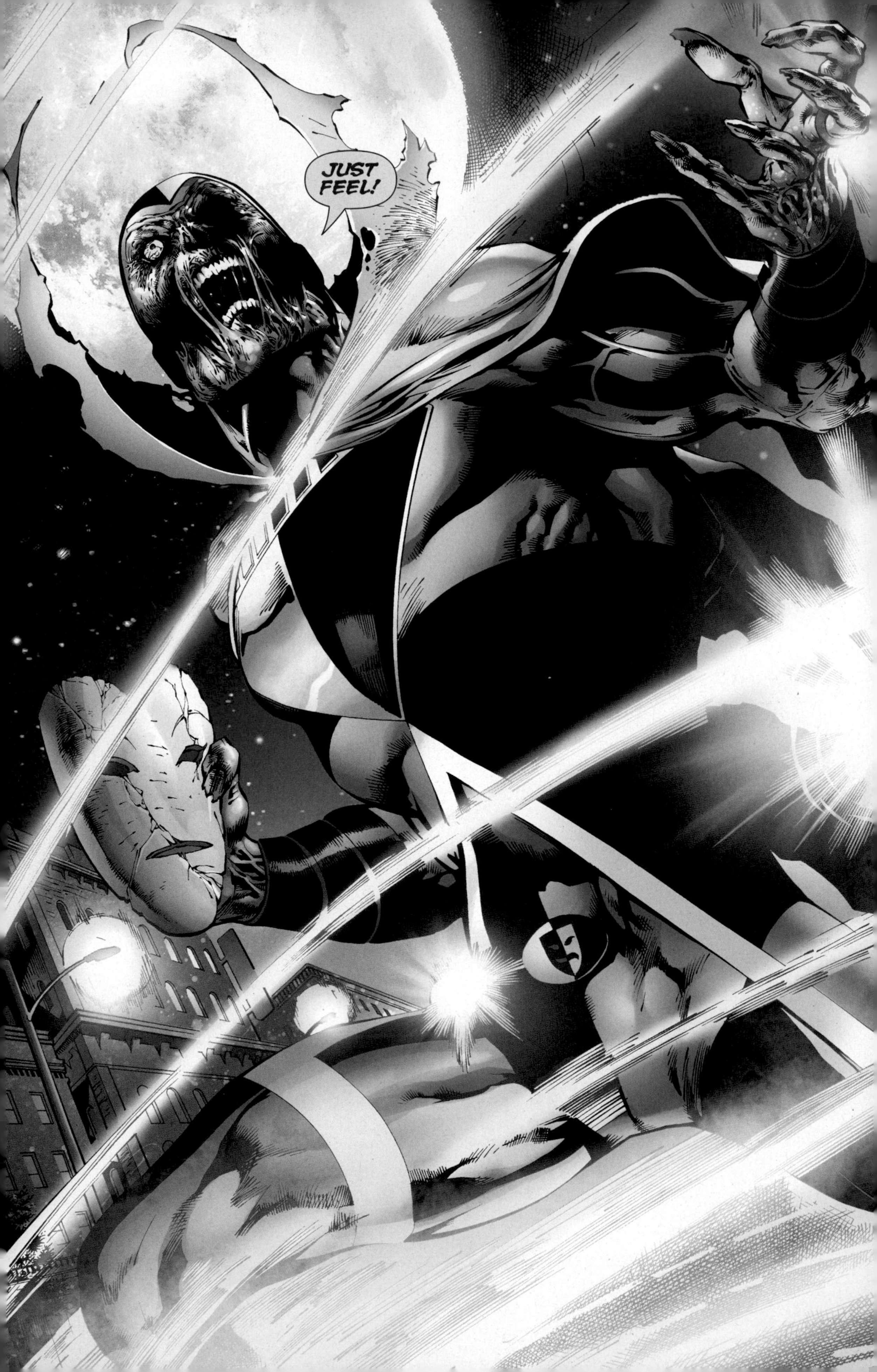
JUST FEEL!

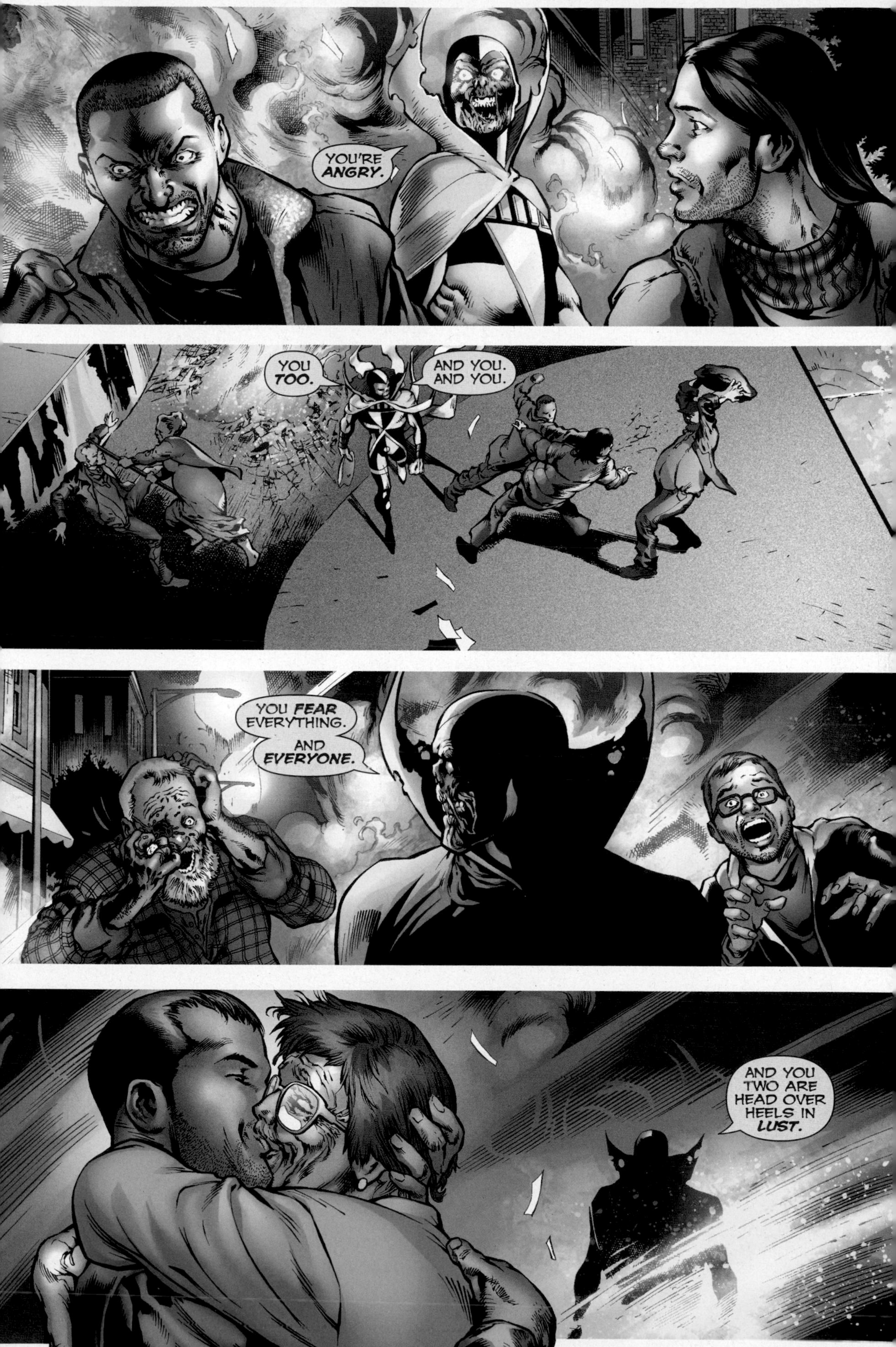
YOU'RE ANGRY.
YOU TOO.
AND YOU. AND YOU.
YOU FEAR EVERYTHING.
AND EVERYONE.
AND YOU TWO ARE HEAD OVER HEELS IN LUST.

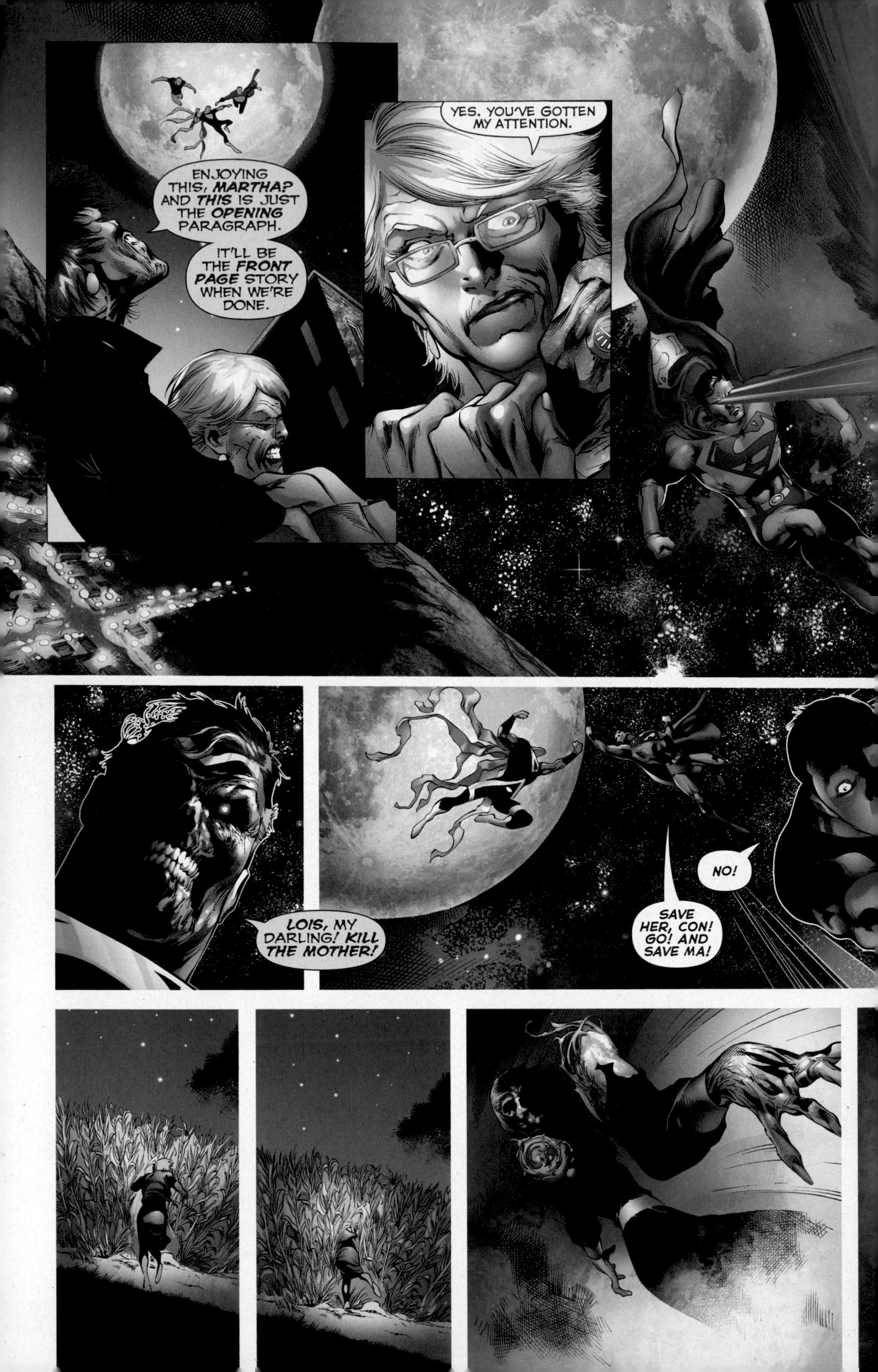
ENJOYING THIS, MARTHA? AND THIS IS JUST THE OPENING PARAGRAPH.
IT'LL BE THE FRONT PAGE STORY WHEN WE'RE DONE.
YES. YOU'VE GOTTEN MY ATTENTION.
LOIS, MY DARLING! KILL THE MOTHER!
SAVE HER, CON! GO! AND SAVE MA!
NO!

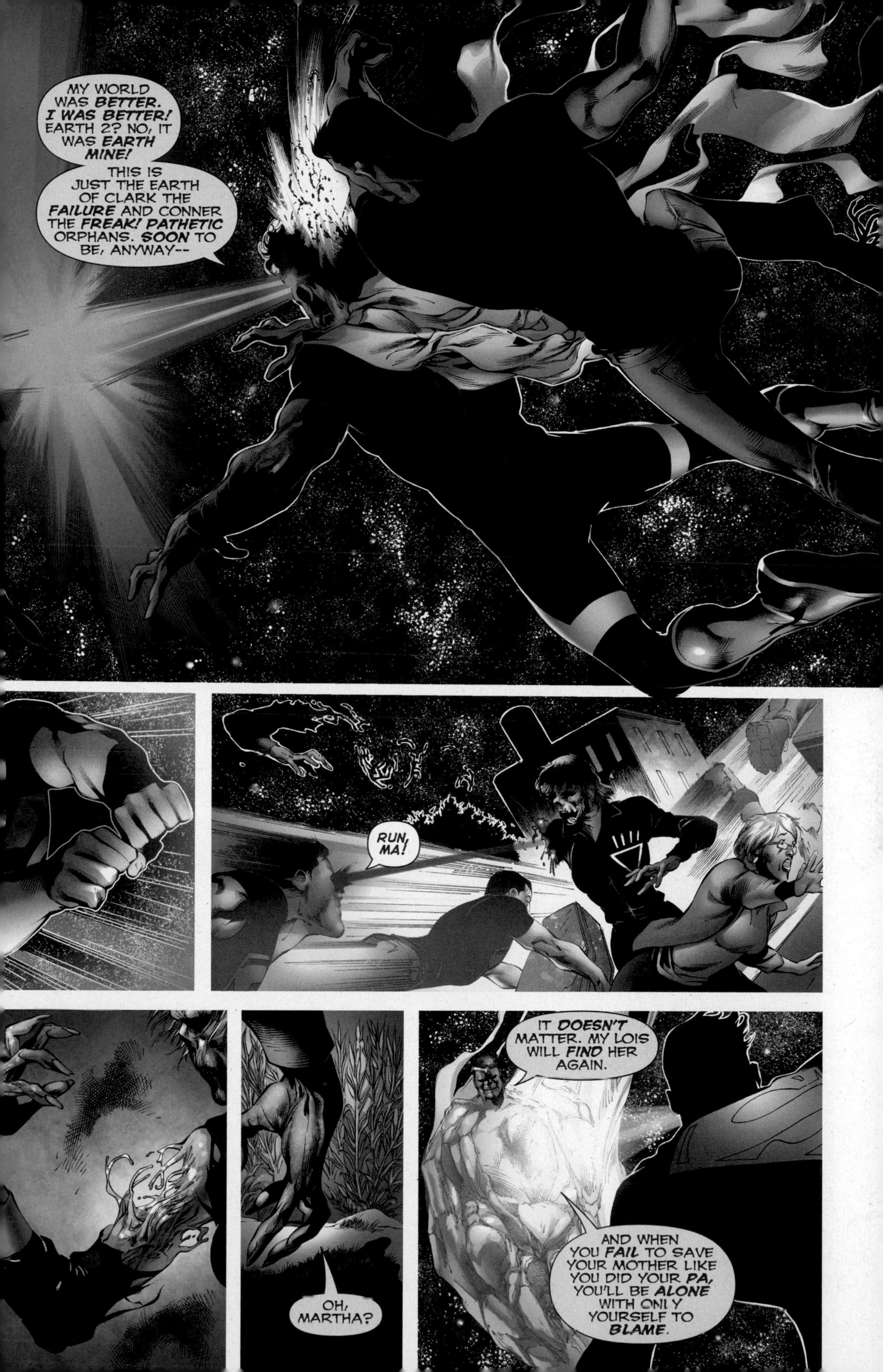

MY WORLD WAS BETTER. I WAS BETTER! EARTH 2? NO, IT WAS EARTH MINE!
THIS IS JUST THE EARTH OF CLARK THE FAILURE AND CONNER THE FREAK! PATHETIC ORPHANS. SOON TO BE, ANYWAY--
RUN, MA!
OH, MARTHA?
IT DOESN'T MATTER. MY LOIS WILL FIND HER AGAIN.
AND WHEN YOU FAIL TO SAVE YOUR MOTHER LIKE YOU DID YOUR PA, YOU'LL BE ALONE WITH ONLY YOURSELF TO BLAME.

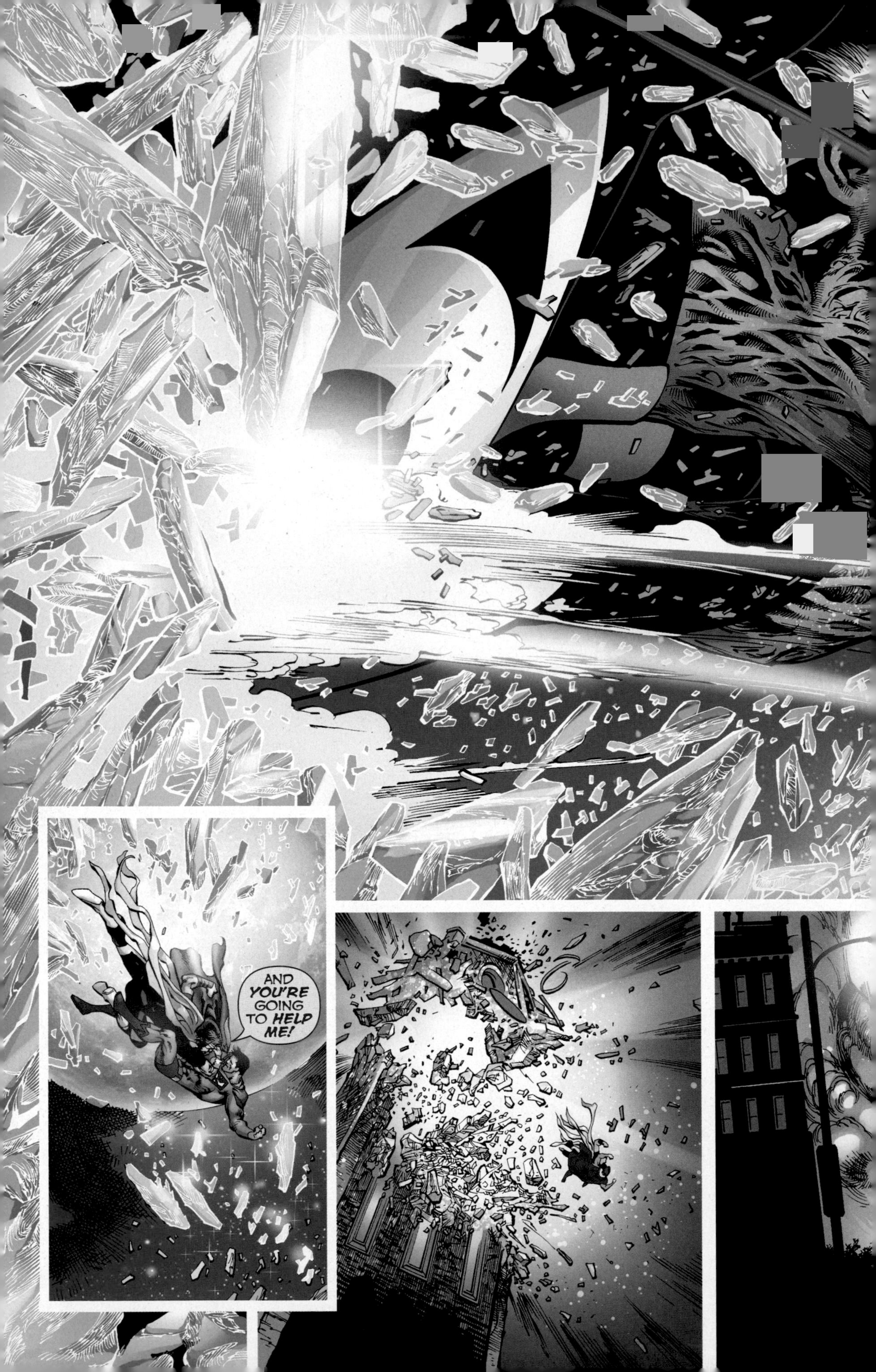
AND YOU'RE GOING TO HELP ME!

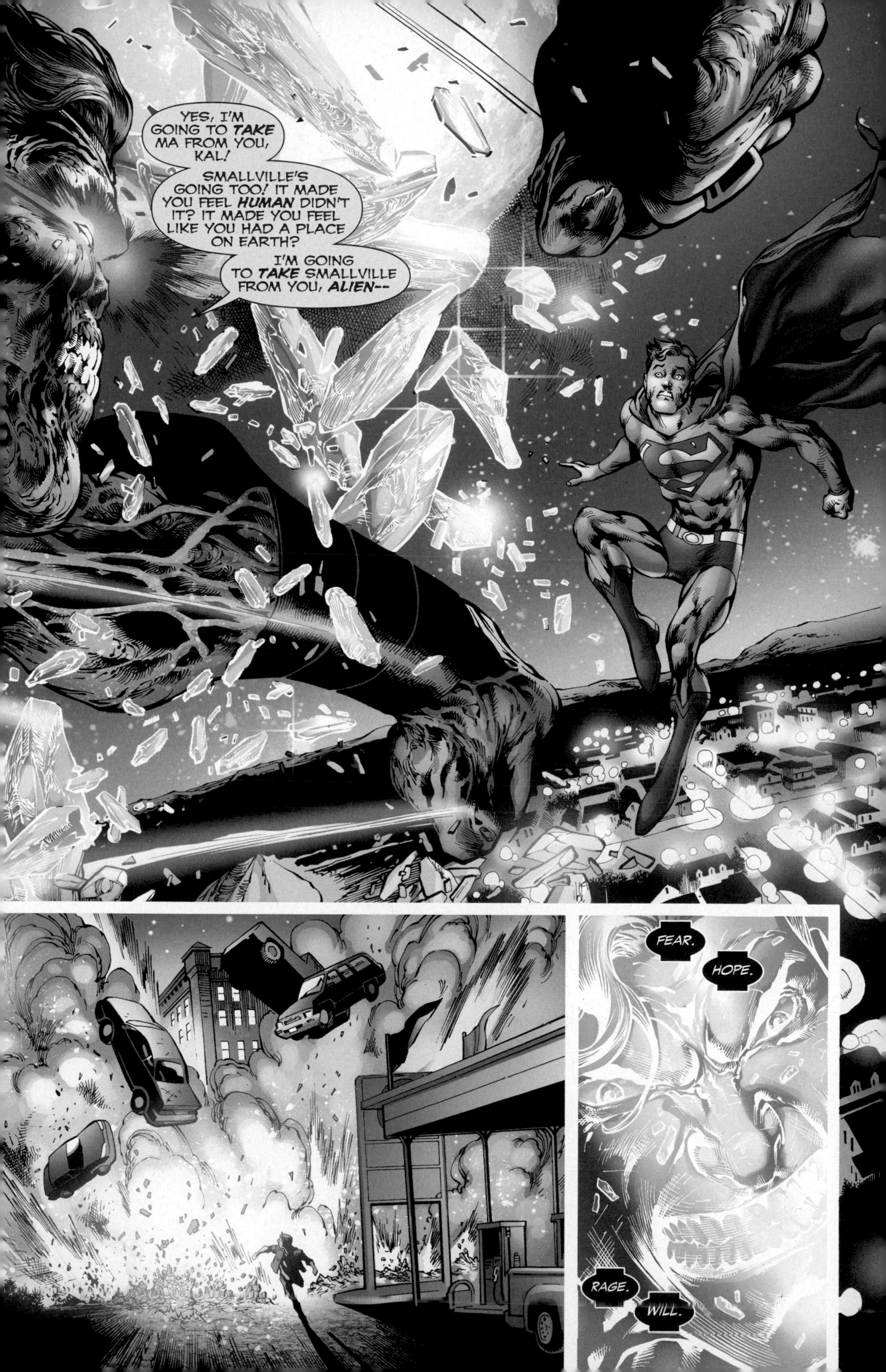
YES, I'M GOING TO TAKE MA FROM YOU, KAL!
SMALLVILLE'S GOING TOO! IT MADE YOU FEEL HUMAN DIDN'T IT? IT MADE YOU FEEL LIKE YOU HAD A PLACE ON EARTH?
I'M GOING TO TAKE SMALLVILLE FROM YOU, ALIEN--
FEAR.
HOPE.
RAGE.
WILL.

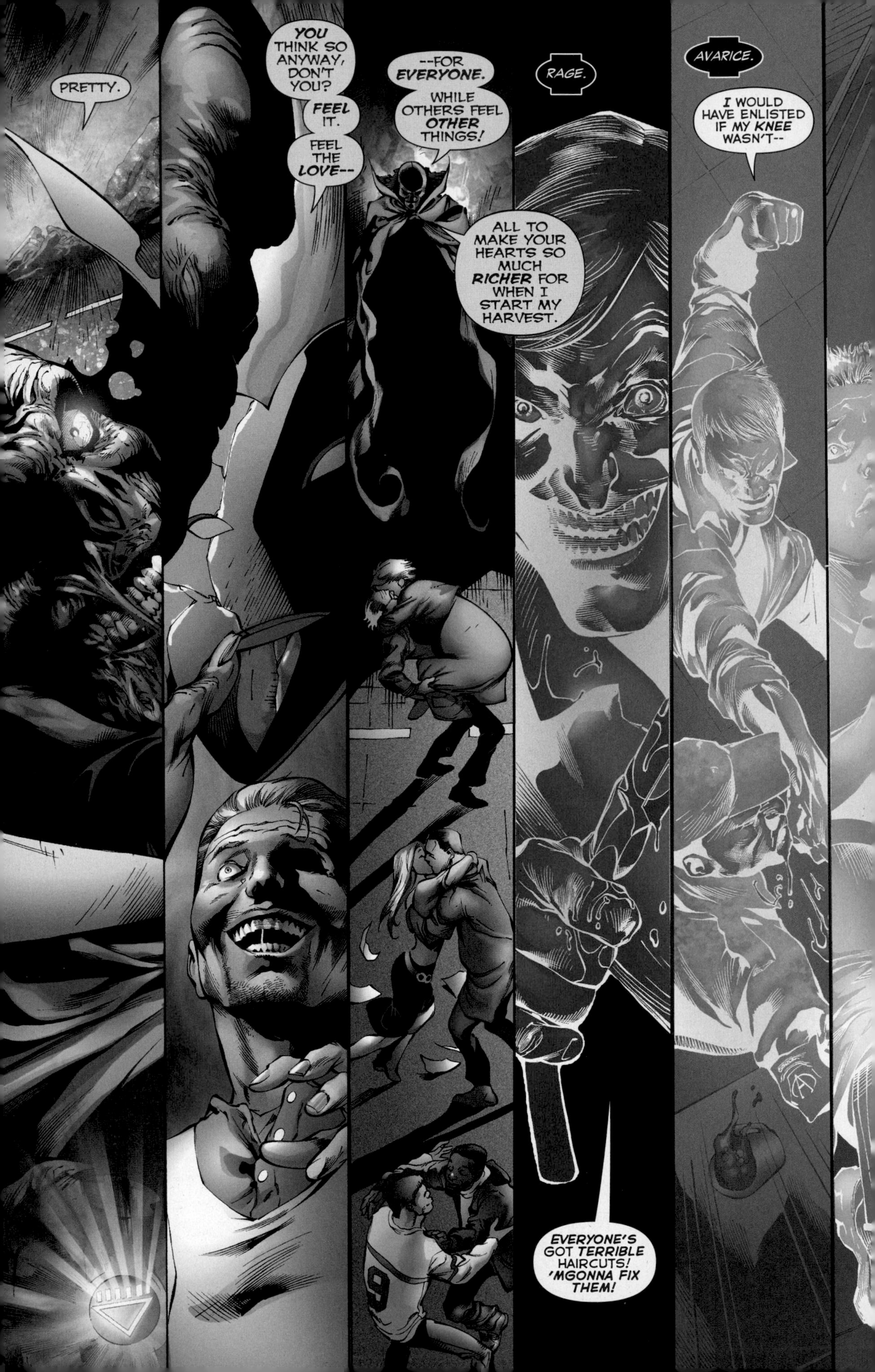
PRETTY.
YOU THINK SO ANYWAY, DON'T YOU?
FEEL IT.
FEEL THE LOVE--
--FOR EVERYONE.
WHILE OTHERS FEEL OTHER THINGS!
ALL TO MAKE YOUR HEARTS SO MUCH RICHER FOR WHEN I START MY HARVEST.
RAGE.
EVERYONE'S GOT TERRIBLE HAIRCUTS! 'MGONNA FIX THEM!
AVARICE.
I WOULD HAVE ENLISTED IF MY KNEE WASN'T--

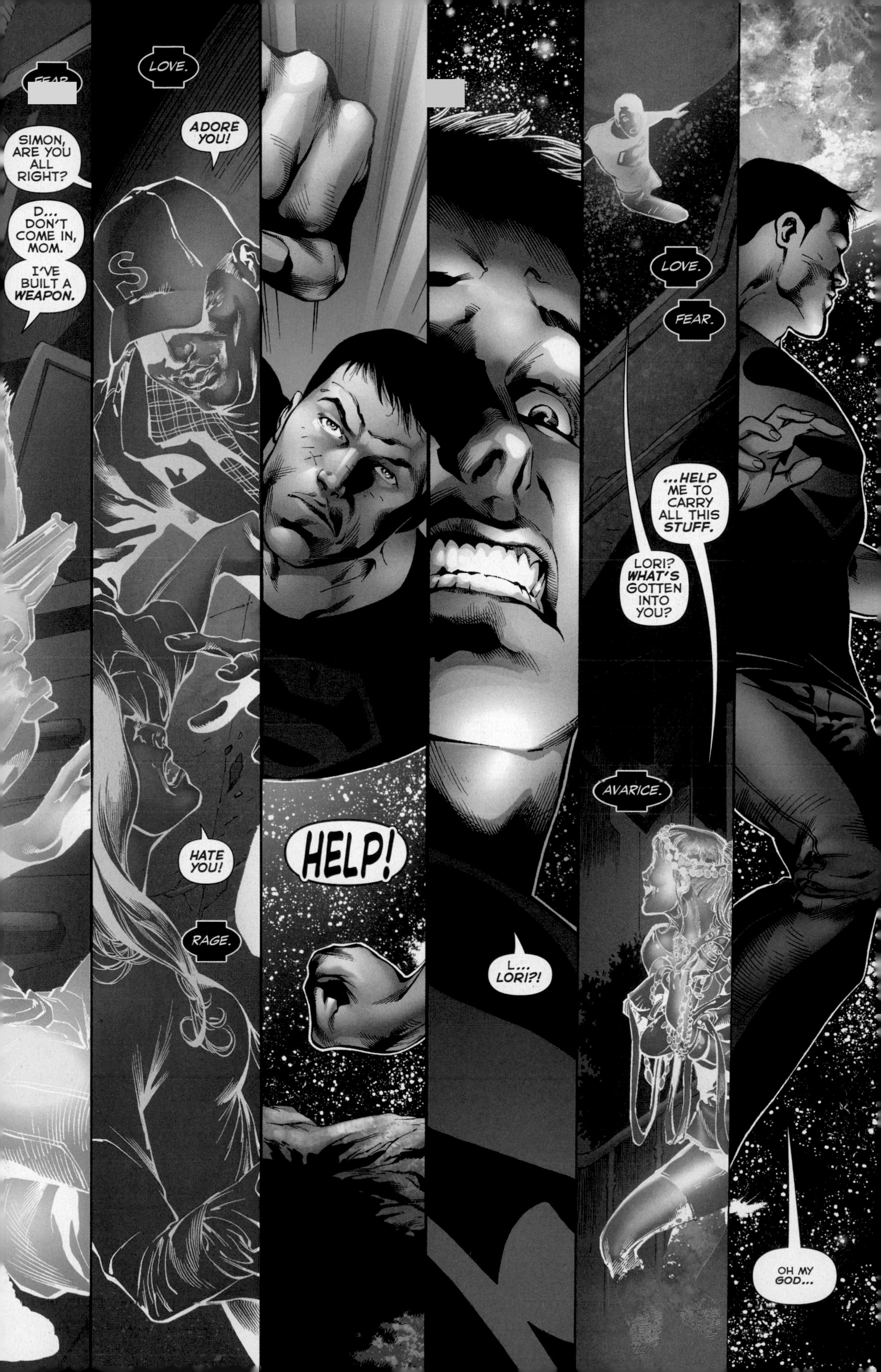
SIMON, ARE YOU ALL RIGHT?
D... DON'T COME IN, MOM.
I'VE BUILT A WEAPON.
LOVE.
ADORE YOU!
HATE YOU!
RAGE.
HELP!
L... LORI?!
LOVE.
FEAR.
...HELP ME TO CARRY ALL THIS STUFF.
LORI? WHAT'S GOTTEN INTO YOU?
AVARICE.
OH MY GOD...

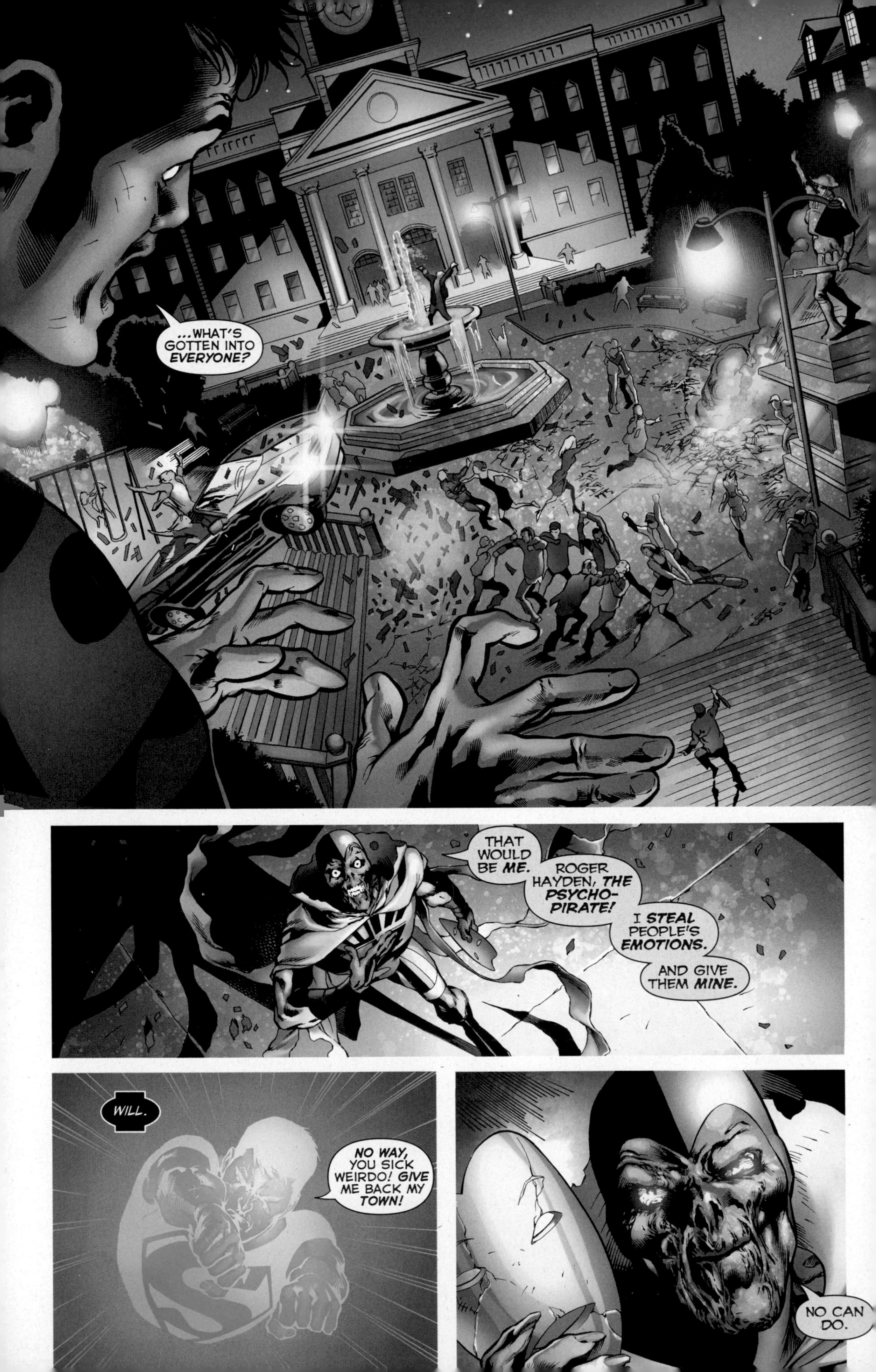
...WHAT'S GOTTEN INTO EVERYONE?
THAT WOULD BE ME.
ROGER HAYDEN, THE PSYCHO-PIRATE!
I STEAL PEOPLE'S EMOTIONS.
AND GIVE THEM MINE.
WILL.
NO WAY, YOU SICK WEIRDO! GIVE ME BACK MY TOWN!
NO CAN DO.

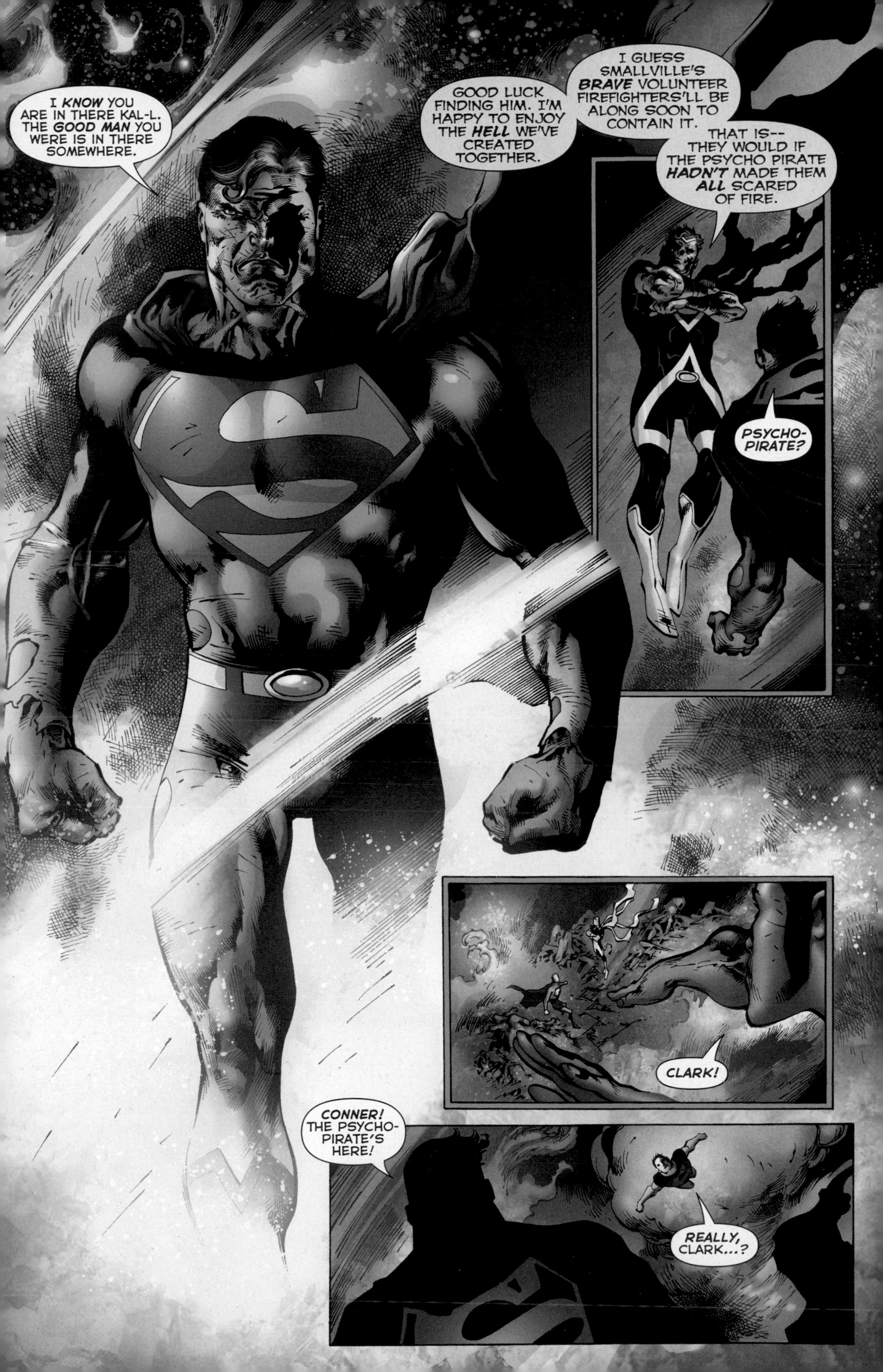
I KNOW YOU ARE IN THERE KAL-L. THE GOOD MAN YOU WERE IS IN THERE SOMEWHERE.
GOOD LUCK FINDING HIM. I'M HAPPY TO ENJOY THE HELL WE'VE CREATED TOGETHER.
I GUESS SMALLVILLE'S BRAVE VOLUNTEER FIREFIGHTERS'LL BE ALONG SOON TO CONTAIN IT.
THAT IS-- THEY WOULD IF THE PSYCHO PIRATE HADN'T MADE THEM ALL SCARED OF FIRE.
PSYCHO-PIRATE?
CLARK!
CONNER! THE PSYCHO-PIRATE'S HERE!
REALLY, CLARK...?

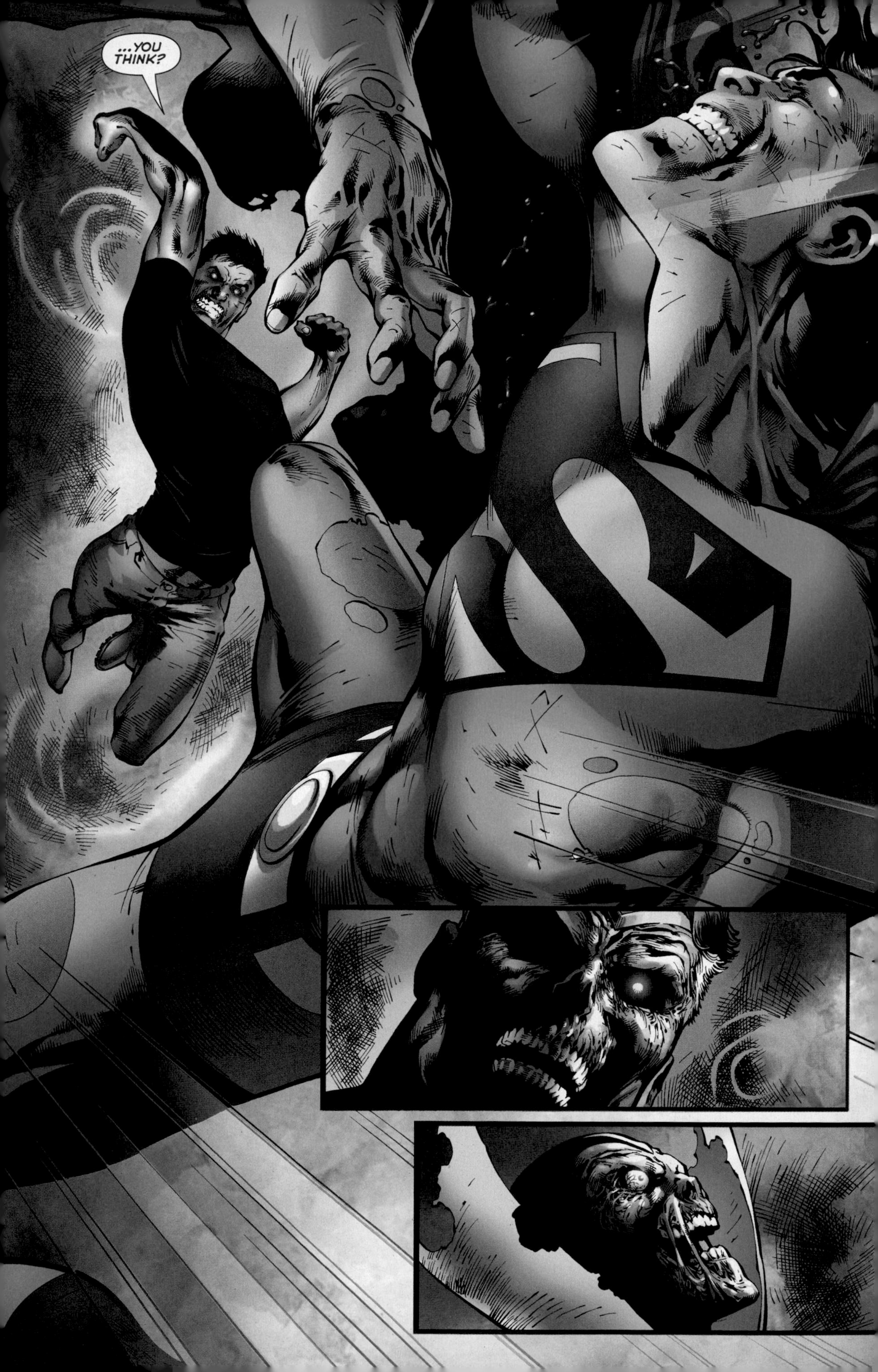
...YOU THINK?

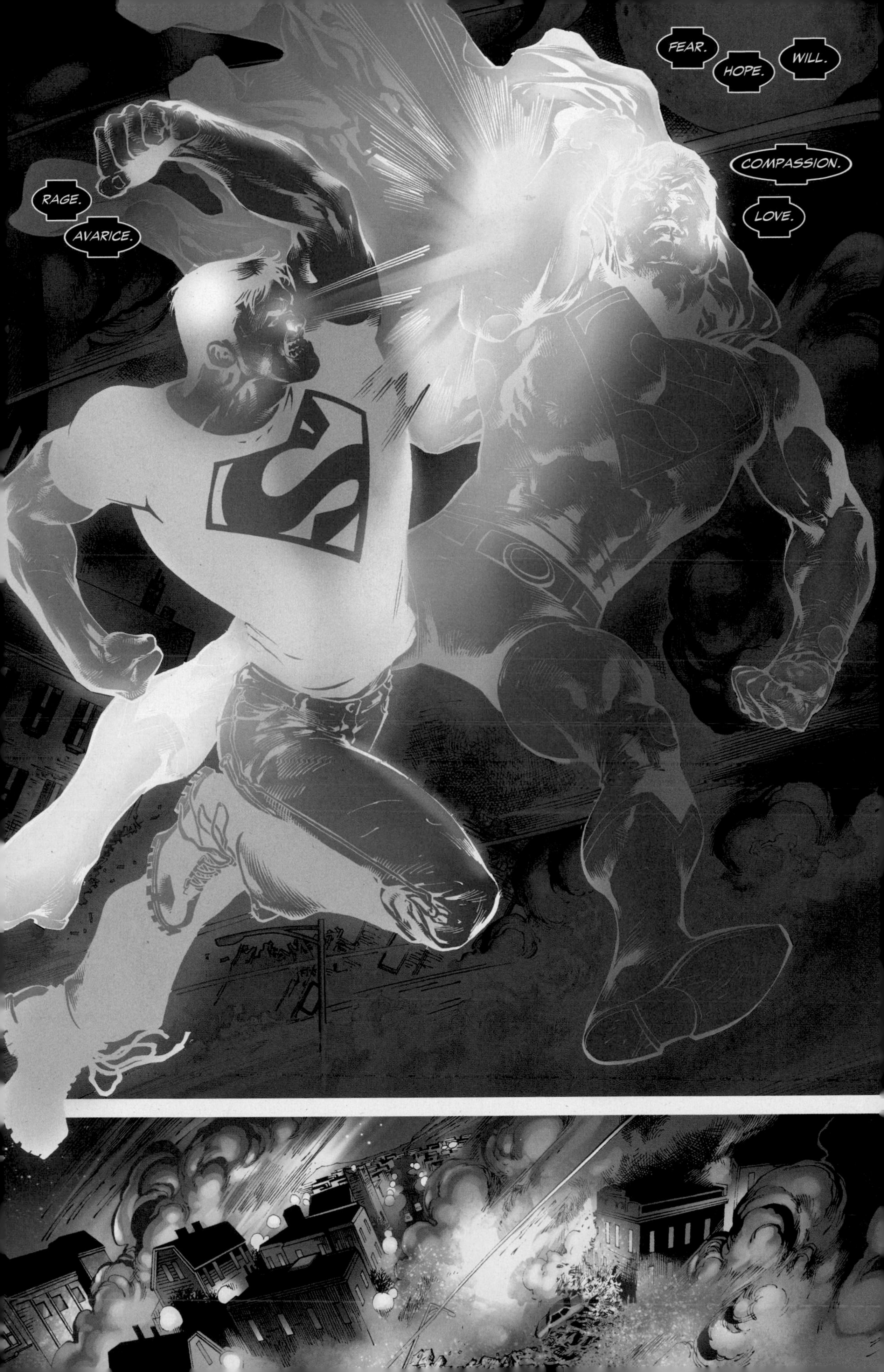
FEAR.
HOPE.
WILL.
COMPASSION.
LOVE.
RAGE.
AVARICE.

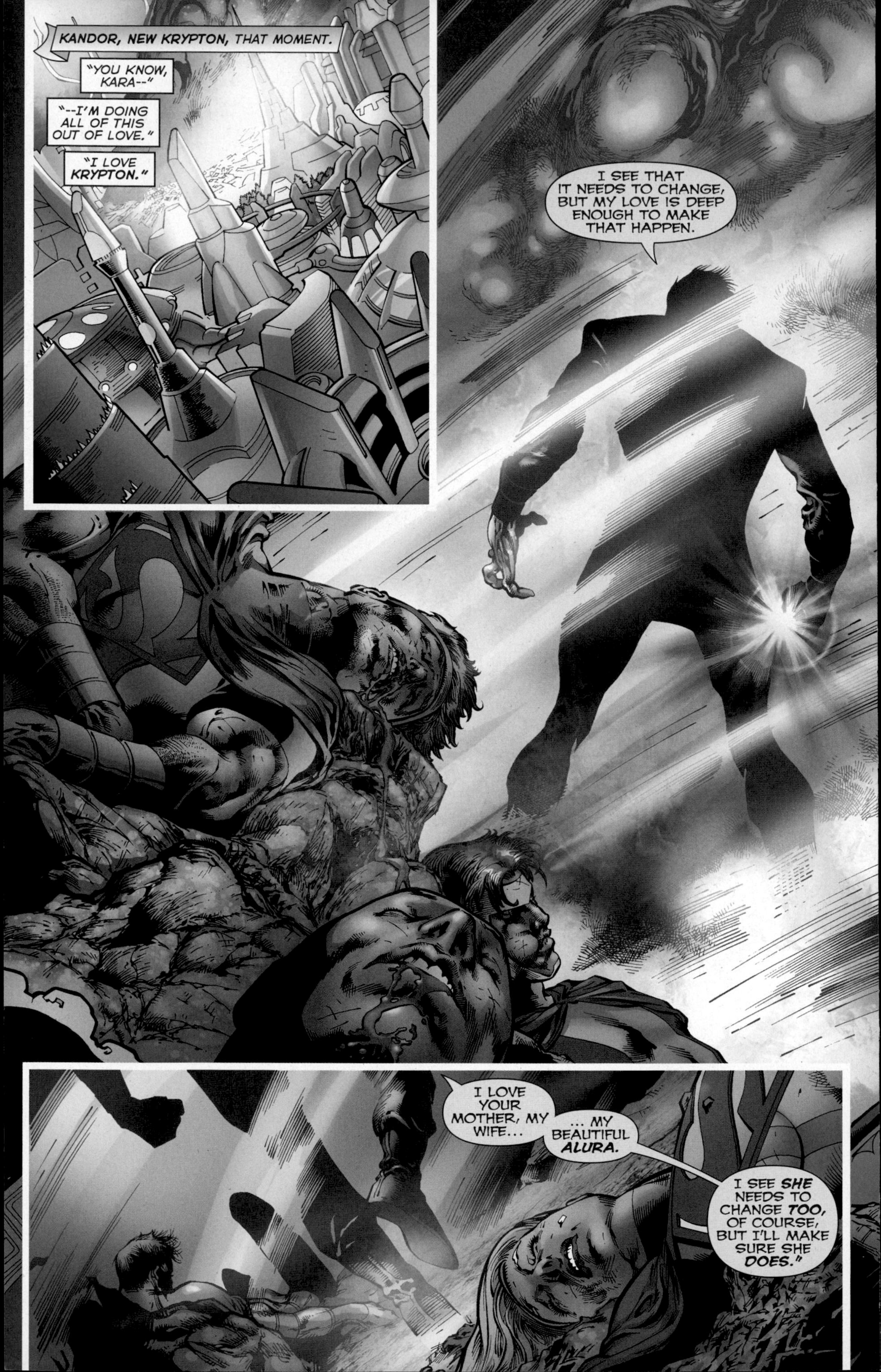
KANDOR, NEW KRYPTON, THAT MOMENT.
"YOU KNOW, KARA--"
"--I'M DOING ALL OF THIS OUT OF LOVE."
"I LOVE KRYPTON."
I SEE THAT IT NEEDS TO CHANGE, BUT MY LOVE IS DEEP ENOUGH TO MAKE THAT HAPPEN.
I LOVE YOUR MOTHER, MY WIFE...
... MY BEAUTIFUL ALURA.
I SEE SHE NEEDS TO CHANGE TOO, OF COURSE, BUT I'LL MAKE SURE SHE DOES."

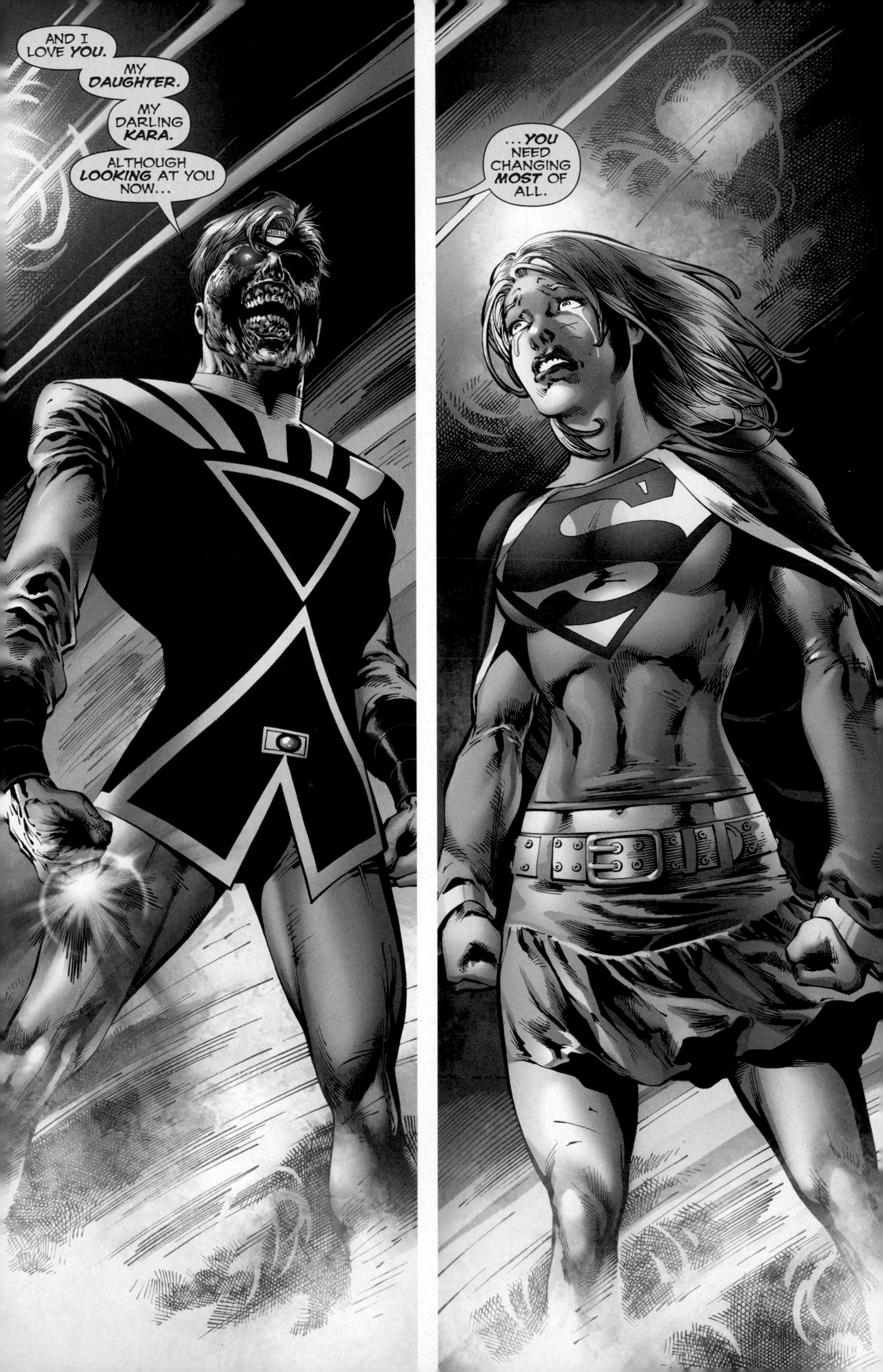
AND I LOVE YOU.
MY DAUGHTER.
MY DARLING KARA.
ALTHOUGH LOOKING AT YOU NOW...
...YOU NEED CHANGING MOST OF ALL.

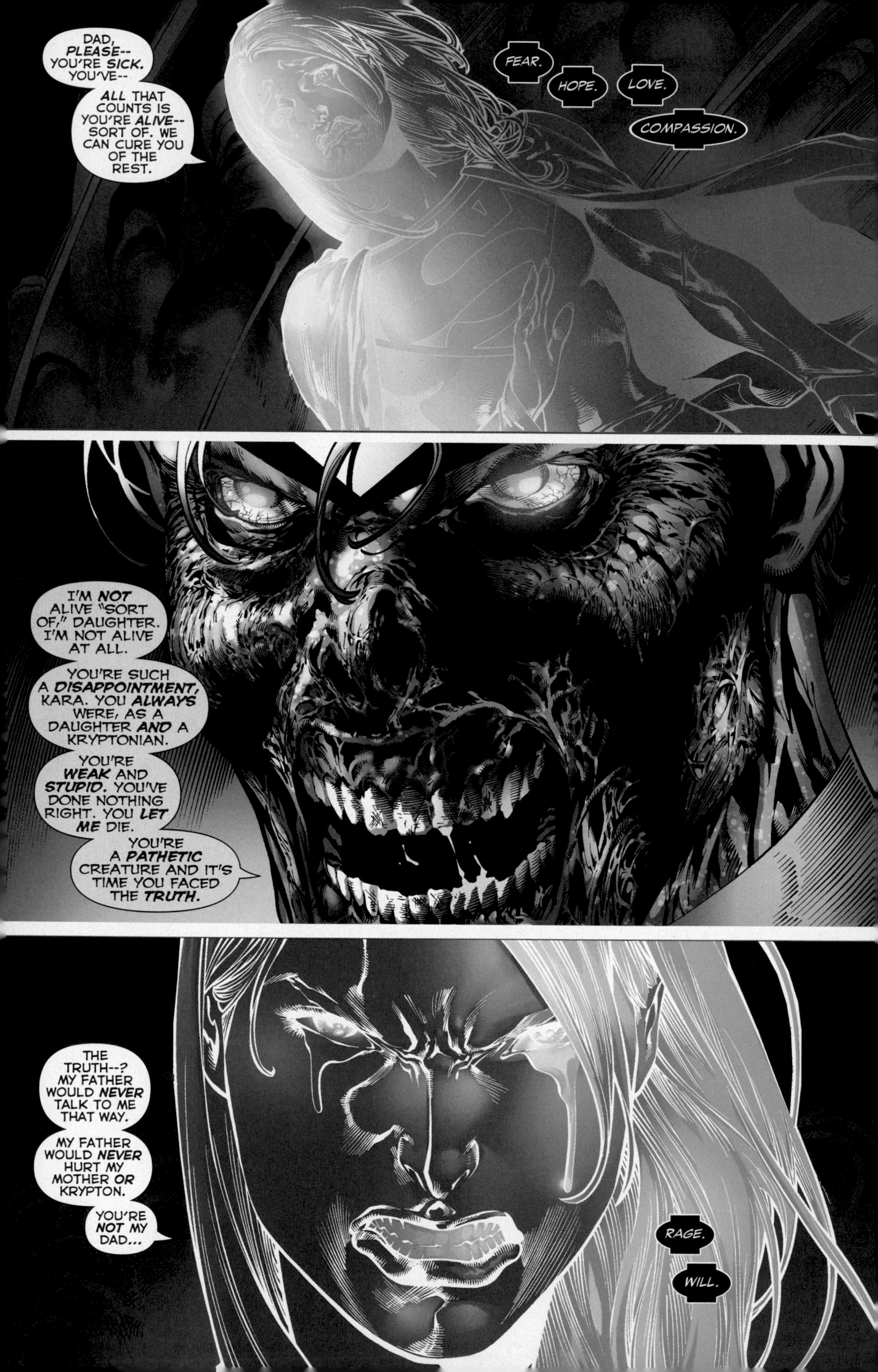

DAD, PLEASE-- YOU'RE SICK. YOU'VE--
ALL THAT COUNTS IS YOU'RE ALIVE-- SORT OF. WE CAN CURE YOU OF THE REST.
FEAR.
HOPE.
LOVE.
COMPASSION.
I'M NOT ALIVE "SORT OF," DAUGHTER. I'M NOT ALIVE AT ALL.
YOU'RE SUCH A DISAPPOINTMENT, KARA. YOU ALWAYS WERE, AS A DAUGHTER AND A KRYPTONIAN.
YOU'RE WEAK AND STUPID. YOU'VE DONE NOTHING RIGHT. YOU LET ME DIE.
YOU'RE A PATHETIC CREATURE AND IT'S TIME YOU FACED THE TRUTH.
THE TRUTH--? MY FATHER WOULD NEVER TALK TO ME THAT WAY.
MY FATHER WOULD NEVER HURT MY MOTHER OR KRYPTON.
YOU'RE NOT MY DAD...
RAGE.
WILL.

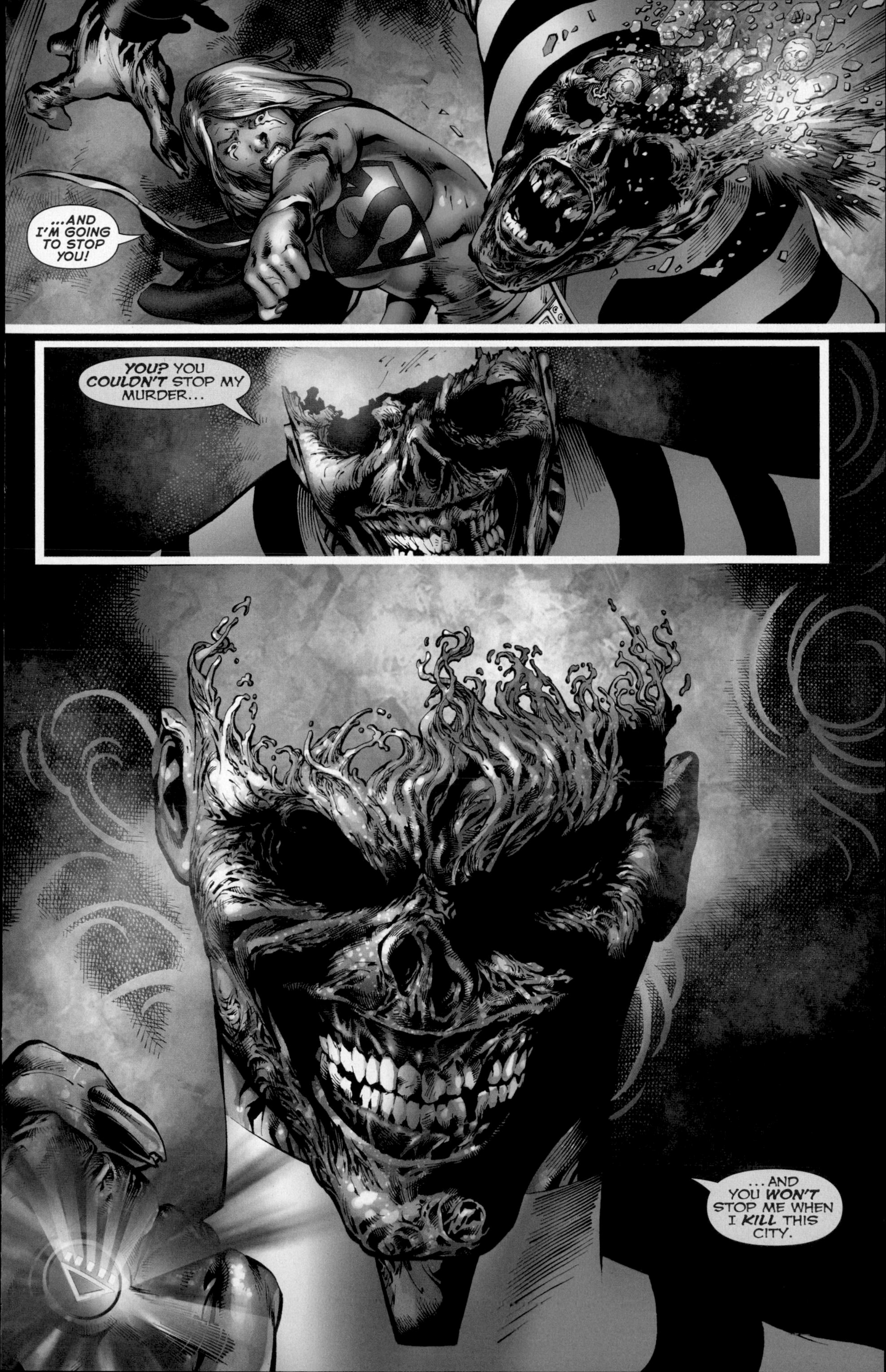
...AND I'M GOING TO STOP YOU!
YOU? YOU COULDN'T STOP MY MURDER...
...AND YOU WON'T STOP ME WHEN I KILL THIS CITY.

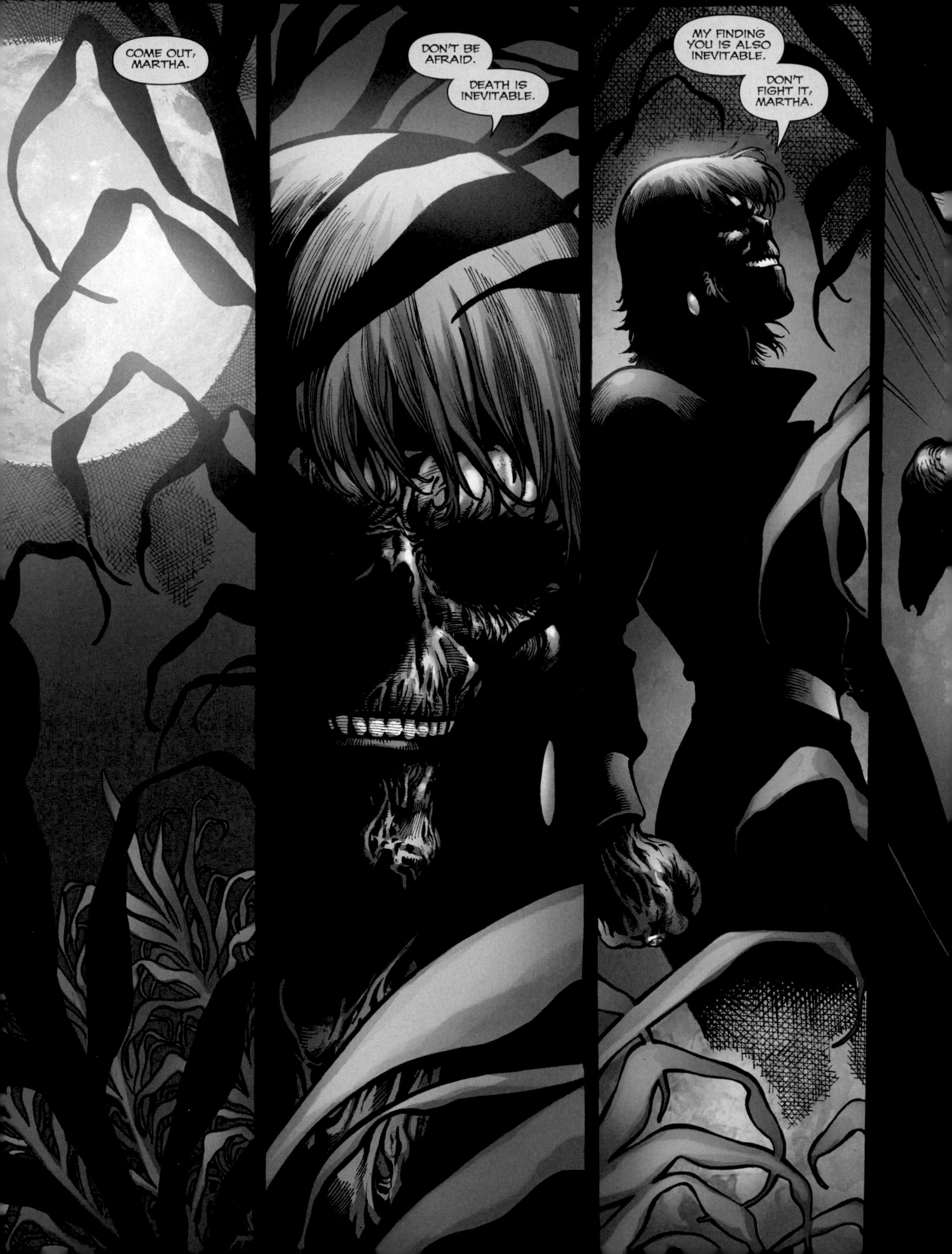
COME OUT, MARTHA.
DON'T BE AFRAID.
DEATH IS INEVITABLE.
MY FINDING YOU IS ALSO INEVITABLE.
DON'T FIGHT IT, MARTHA.

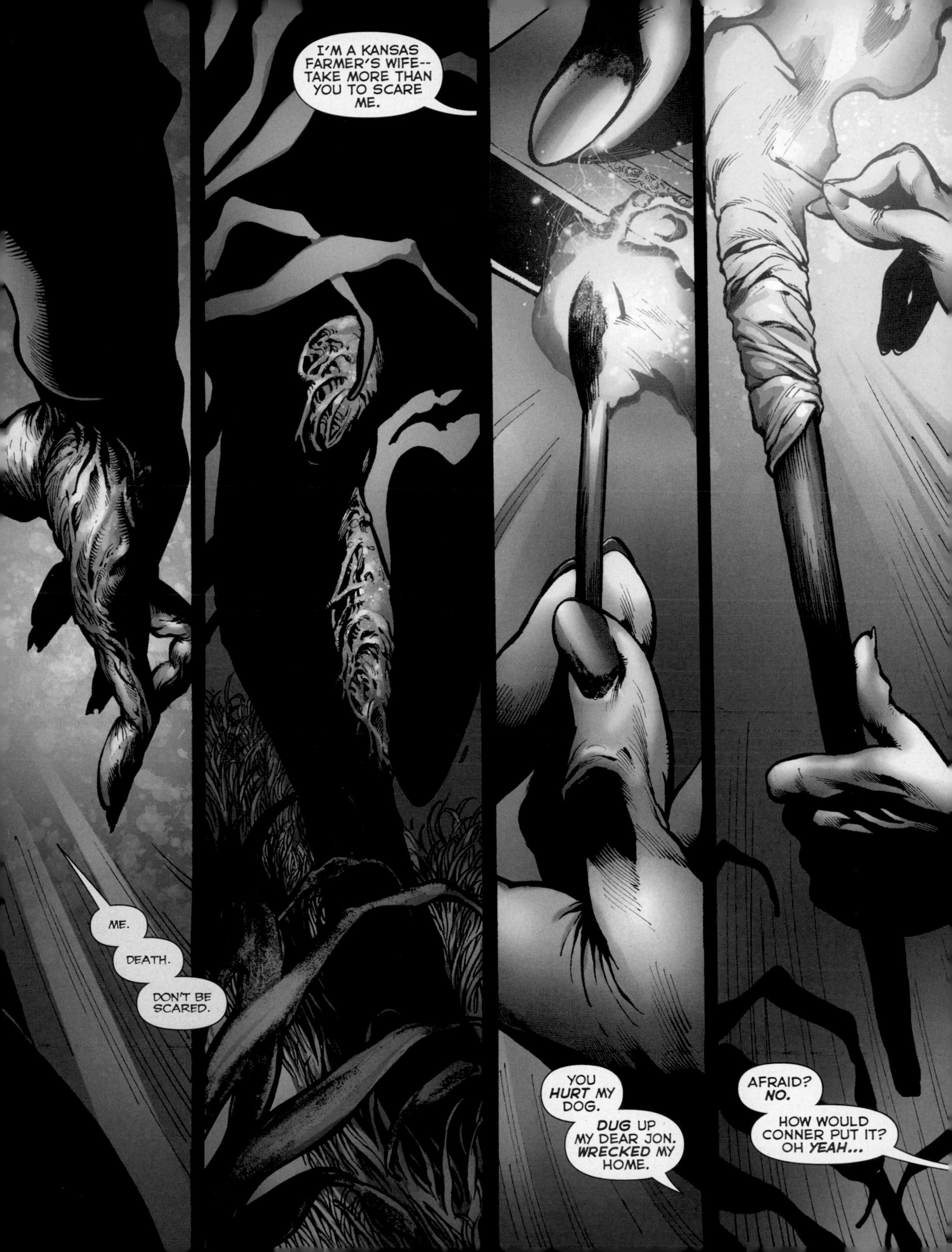
I'M A KANSAS FARMER'S WIFE-- TAKE MORE THAN YOU TO SCARE ME.
ME.
DEATH.
DON'T BE SCARED.
YOU HURT MY DOG.
DUG UP MY DEAR JON. WRECKED MY HOME.
AFRAID? NO.
HOW WOULD CONNER PUT IT? OH YEAH...

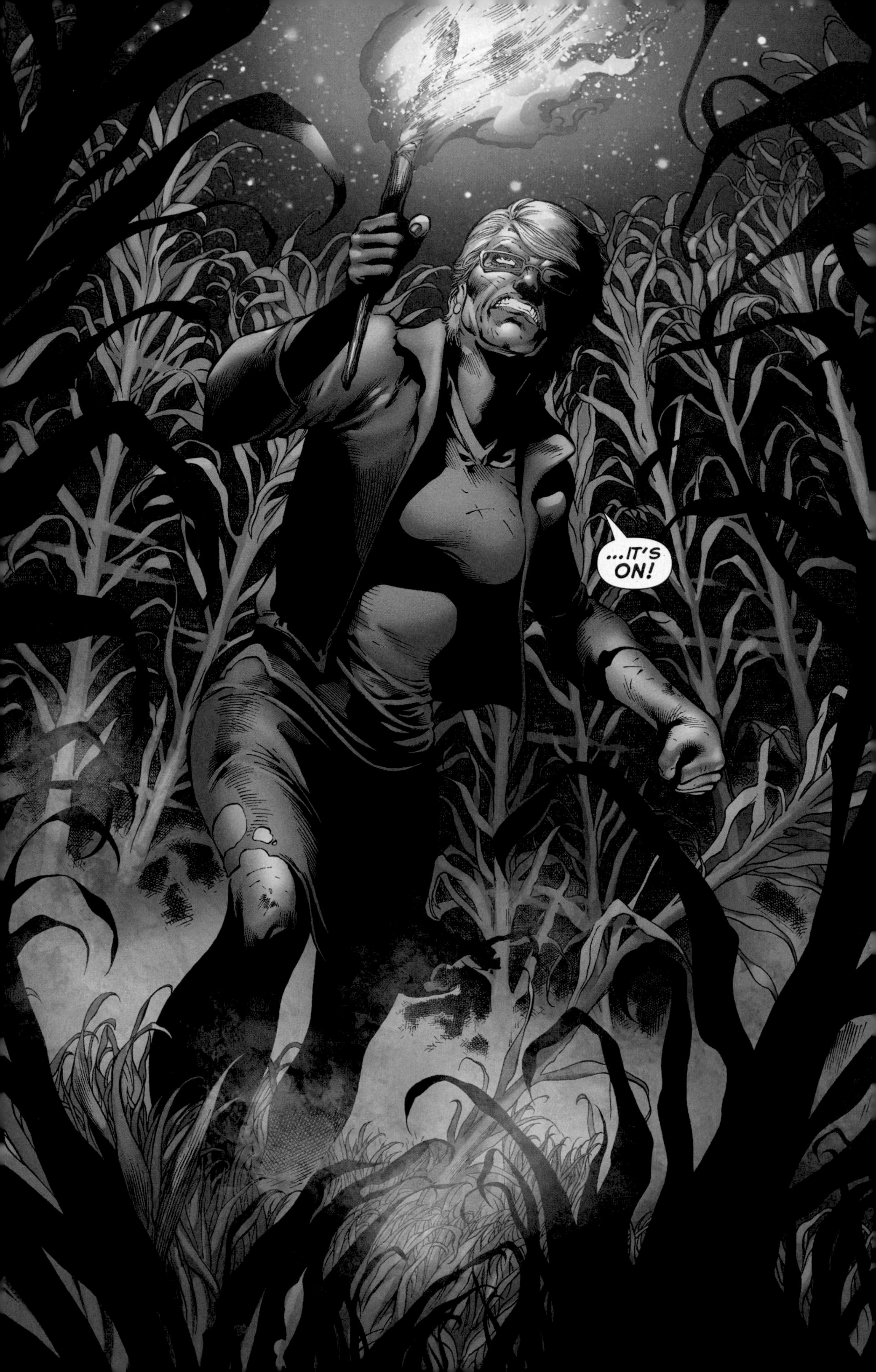
...IT'S ON!

BLACKEST NIGHT: SUPERMAN 3
Cover by Eddy Barrows with Nei Ruffino

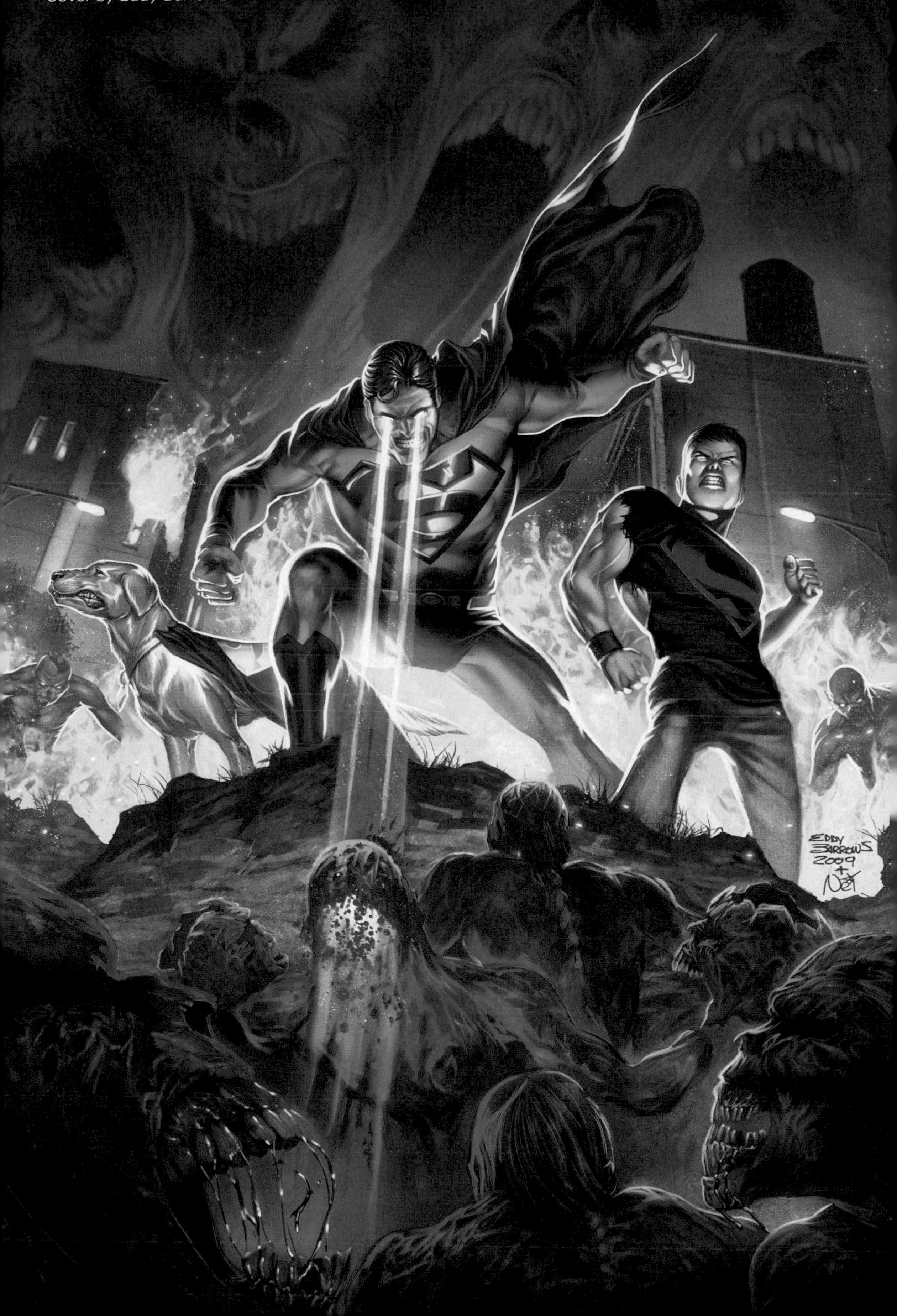
EDDY BARROWS 2009 + NEI

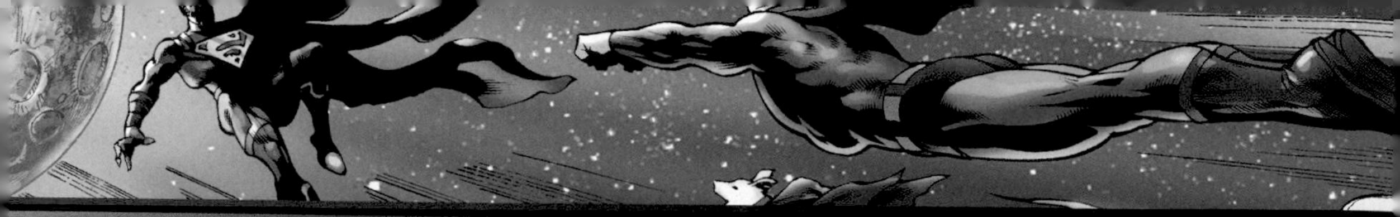

THE LONG DARK NIGHT

JAMES ROBINSON
WRITER

EDDY BARROWS
ALLAN GOLDMAN
PENCILS

RUY JOSÉ
EBER FERREIRA
INKS

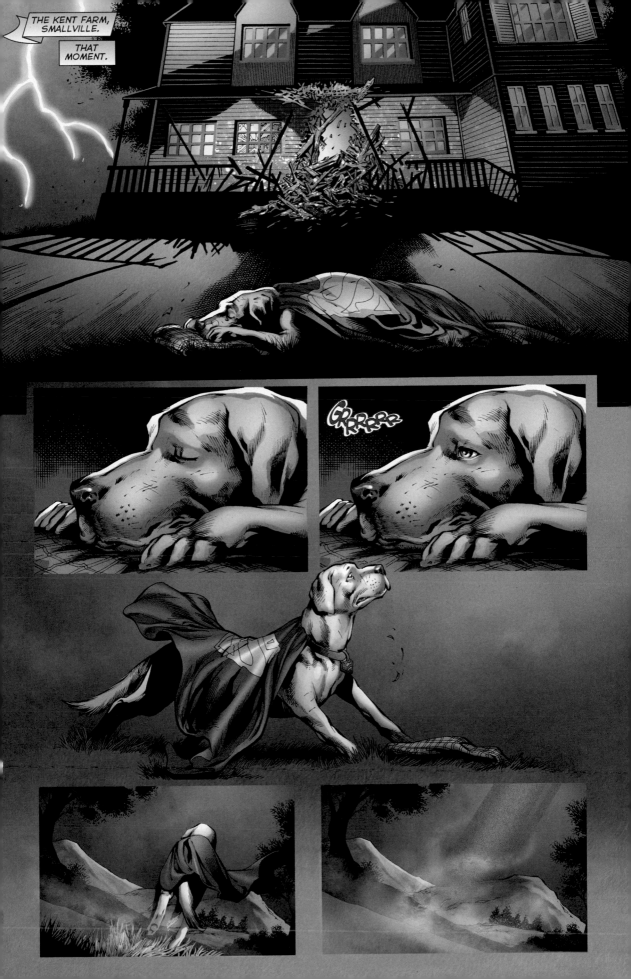

THE KENT FARM, SMALLVILLE.

THAT MOMENT.

GRRRRR

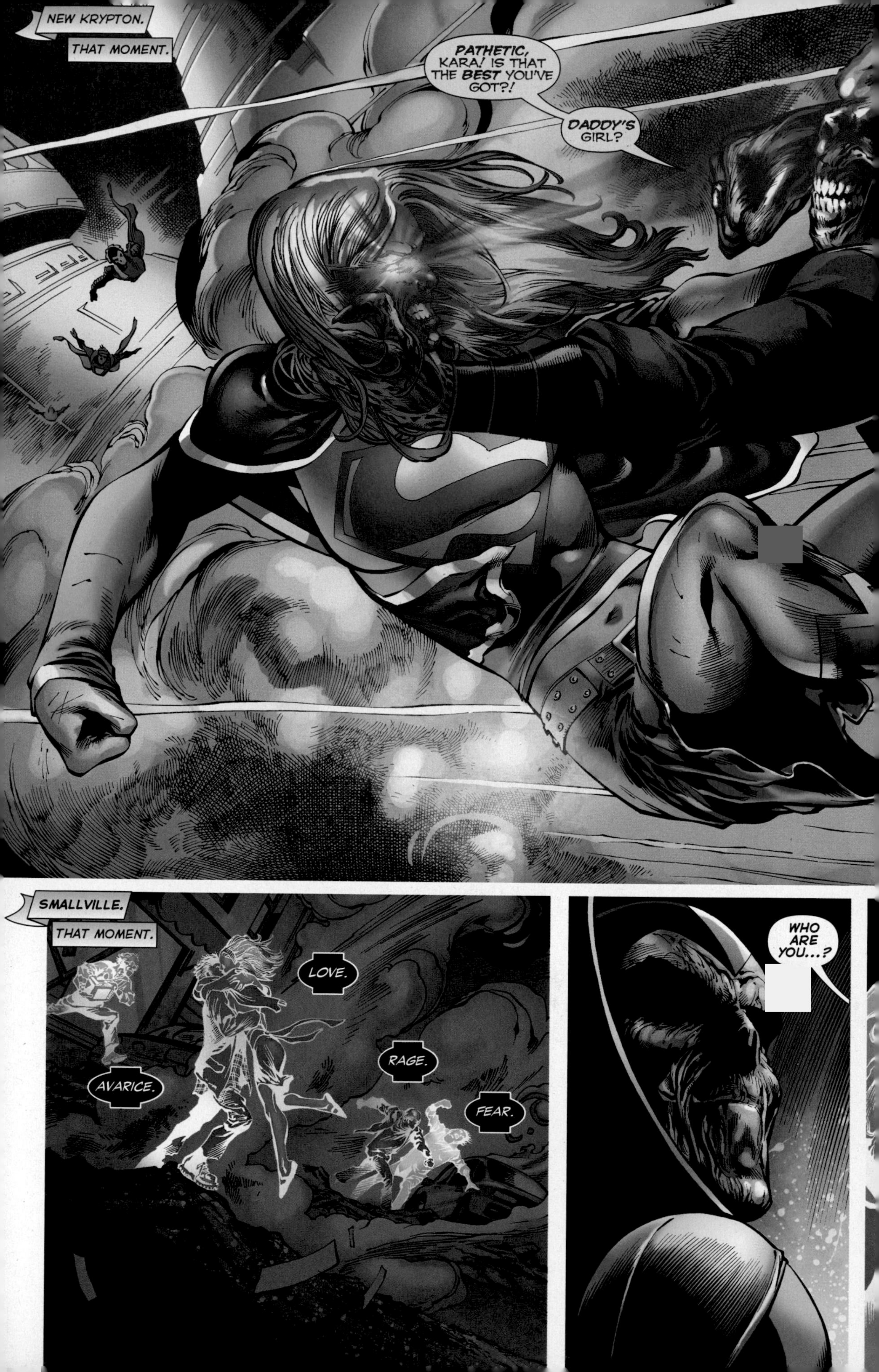
NEW KRYPTON.
THAT MOMENT.
PATHETIC, KARA! IS THAT THE BEST YOU'VE GOT?!
DADDY'S GIRL?
SMALLVILLE.
THAT MOMENT.
LOVE.
AVARICE.
RAGE.
FEAR.
WHO ARE YOU...?

WILL.

YOU'RE DADDY'S EMBAR-RASSMENT!

WILL.

DADDY'S WEAKLING! DADDY'S BANE!

WILL.

RAGE.

AND IF YOU WERE MY FATHER SAYING THAT--

--I'D GIVE A DAMN!

...AND WHY ARE YOU DOING THIS?

FEAR.

FEAR.

BECAUSE I CAN. BECAUSE SMALLVILLE IS THE HOME OF SUPERMAN AND SUPERBOY.

WHO AM I?

--THE PSYCHO-PIRATE! NOW STOP TALKING AND HATE.

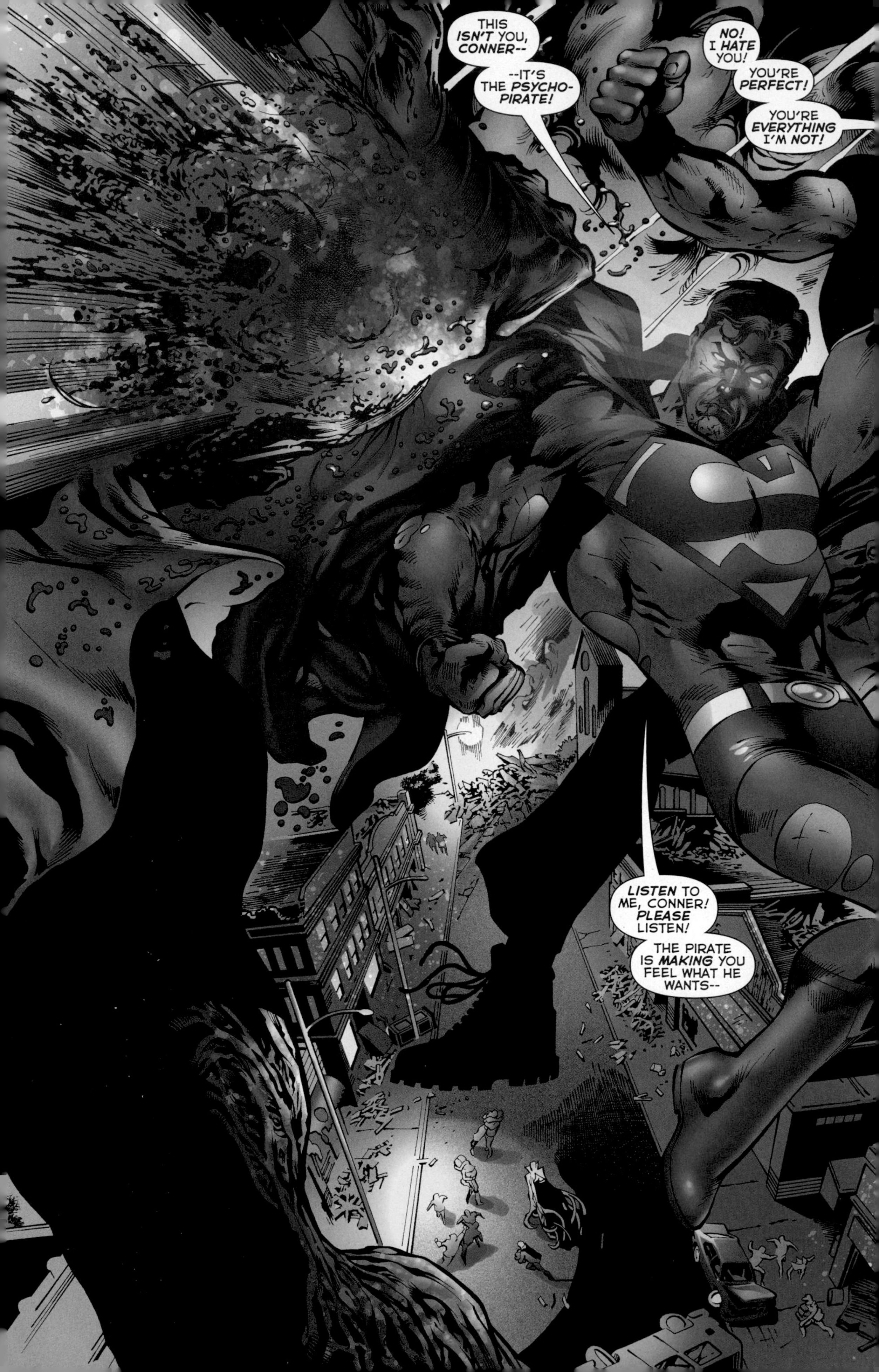
THIS ISN'T YOU, CONNER--
--IT'S THE PSYCHO-PIRATE!
NO! I HATE YOU!
YOU'RE PERFECT!
YOU'RE EVERYTHING I'M NOT!
LISTEN TO ME, CONNER! PLEASE LISTEN!
THE PIRATE IS MAKING YOU FEEL WHAT HE WANTS--

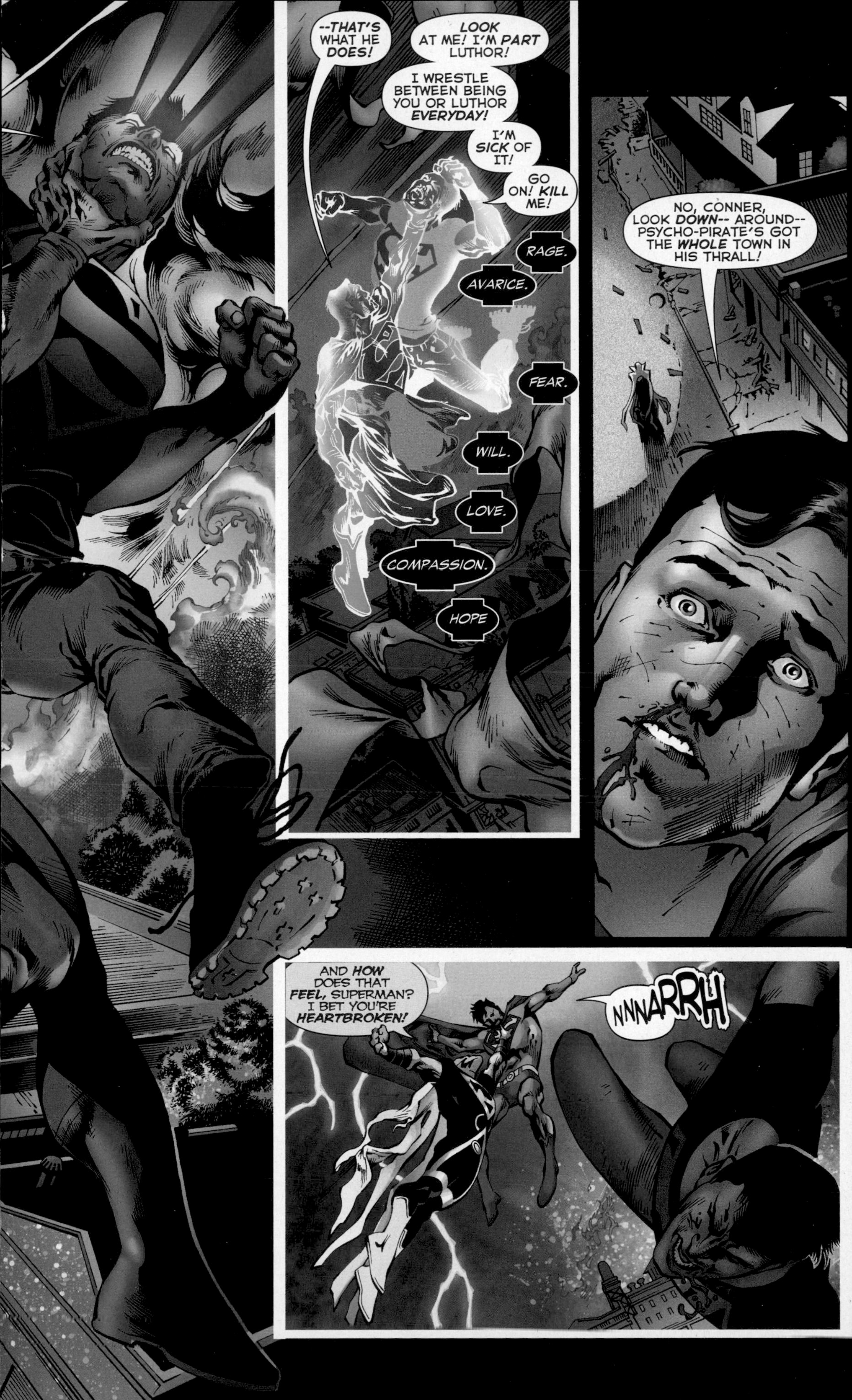

--THAT'S WHAT HE DOES!
LOOK AT ME! I'M PART LUTHOR!
I WRESTLE BETWEEN BEING YOU OR LUTHOR EVERYDAY!
I'M SICK OF IT!
GO ON! KILL ME!
RAGE.
AVARICE.
FEAR.
WILL.
LOVE.
COMPASSION.
HOPE
NO, CONNER, LOOK DOWN-- AROUND-- PSYCHO-PIRATE'S GOT THE WHOLE TOWN IN HIS THRALL!
AND HOW DOES THAT FEEL, SUPERMAN? I BET YOU'RE HEARTBROKEN!
NNNARRRH

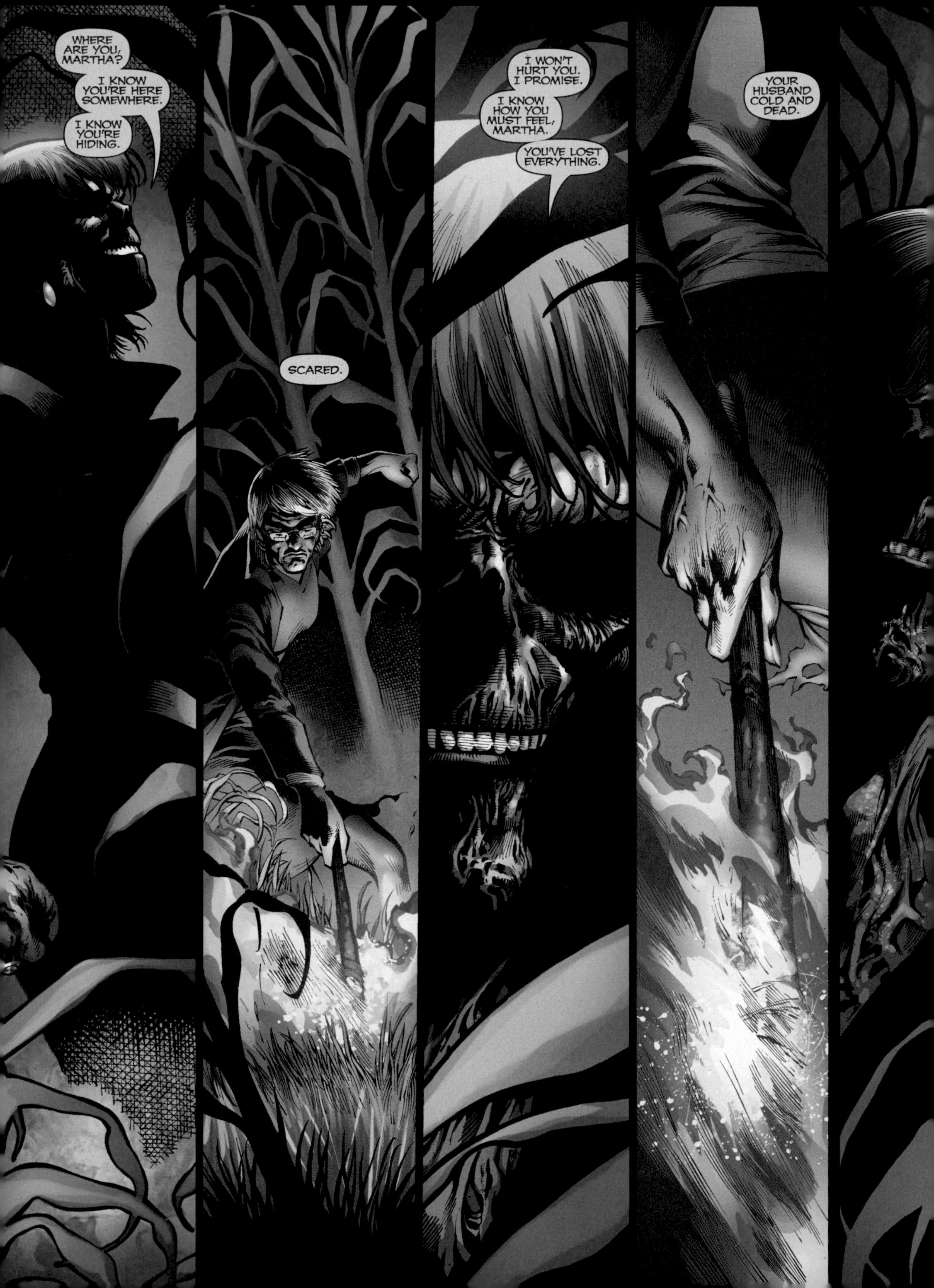
WHERE ARE YOU, MARTHA?
I KNOW YOU'RE HERE SOMEWHERE.
I KNOW YOU'RE HIDING.
SCARED.
I WON'T HURT YOU. I PROMISE.
I KNOW HOW YOU MUST FEEL, MARTHA.
YOU'VE LOST EVERYTHING.
YOUR HUSBAND COLD AND DEAD.

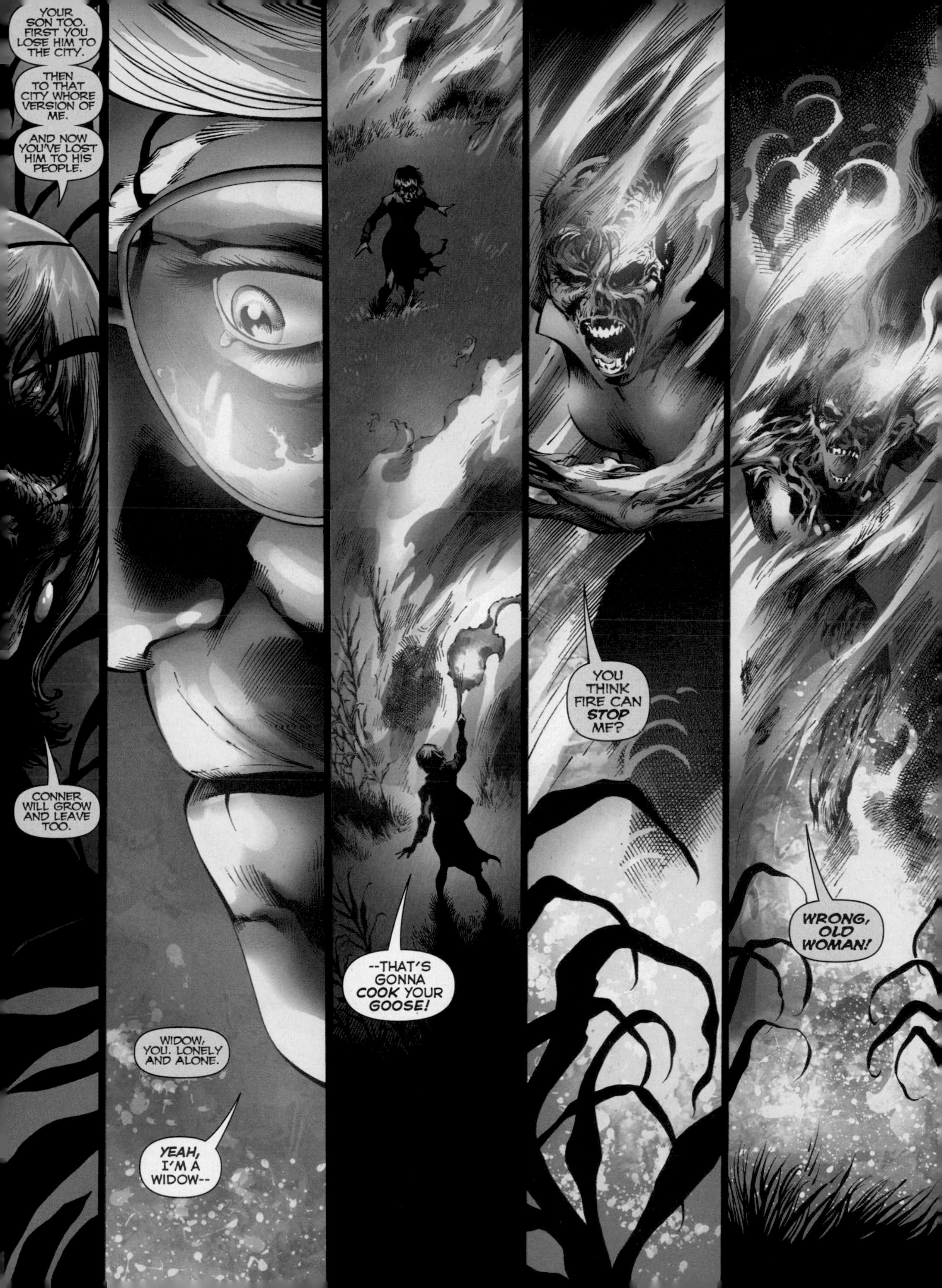
YOUR SON TOO. FIRST YOU LOSE HIM TO THE CITY.
THEN TO THAT CITY WHORE VERSION OF ME.
AND NOW YOU'VE LOST HIM TO HIS PEOPLE.
CONNER WILL GROW AND LEAVE TOO.
WIDOW, YOU. LONELY AND ALONE.
YEAH, I'M A WIDOW--
--THAT'S GONNA COOK YOUR GOOSE!
YOU THINK FIRE CAN STOP ME?
WRONG, OLD WOMAN!

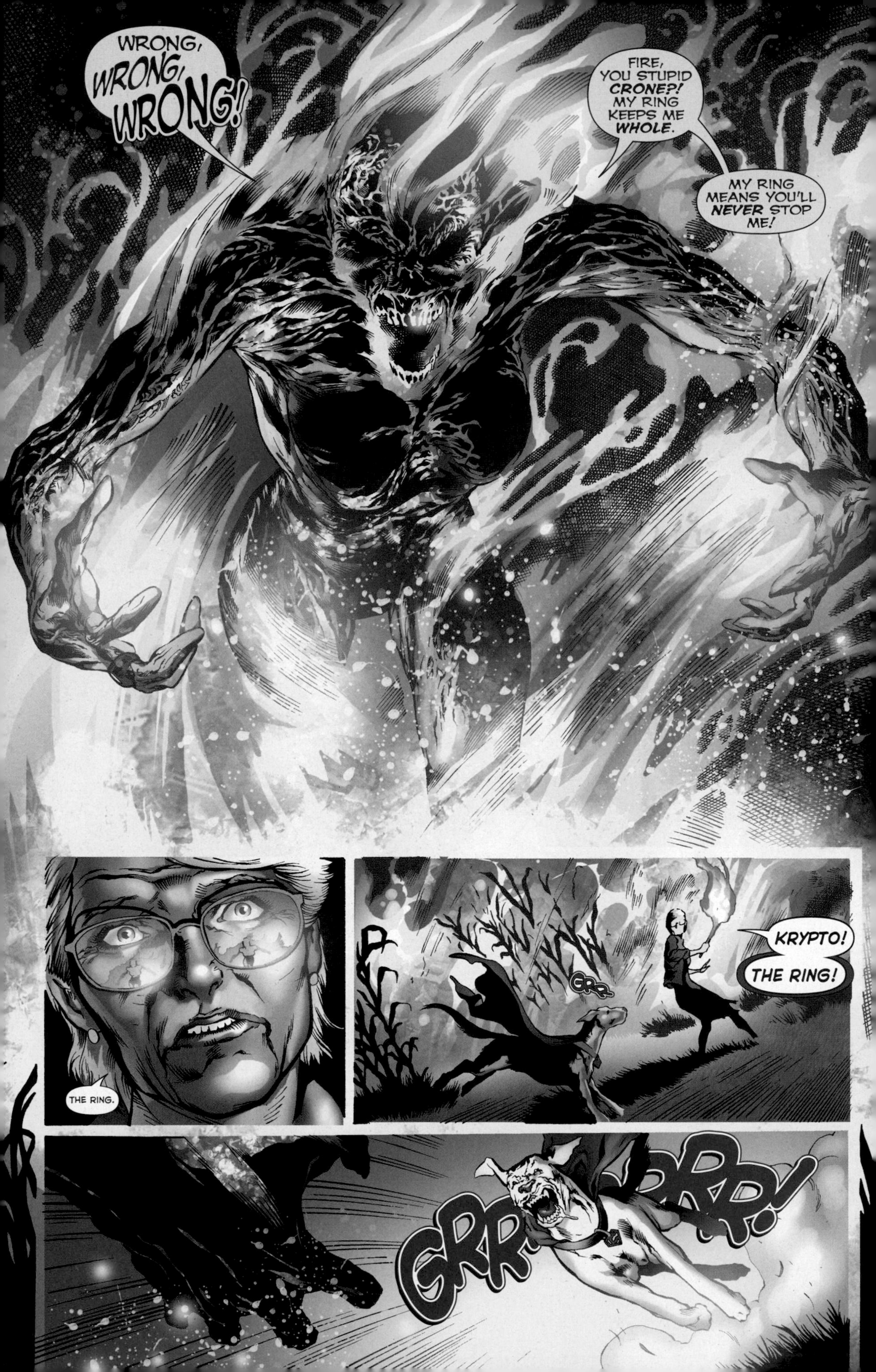
WRONG, WRONG, WRONG!
FIRE, YOU STUPID CRONE?! MY RING KEEPS ME WHOLE.
MY RING MEANS YOU'LL NEVER STOP ME!
THE RING.
GRR
KRYPTO!
THE RING!

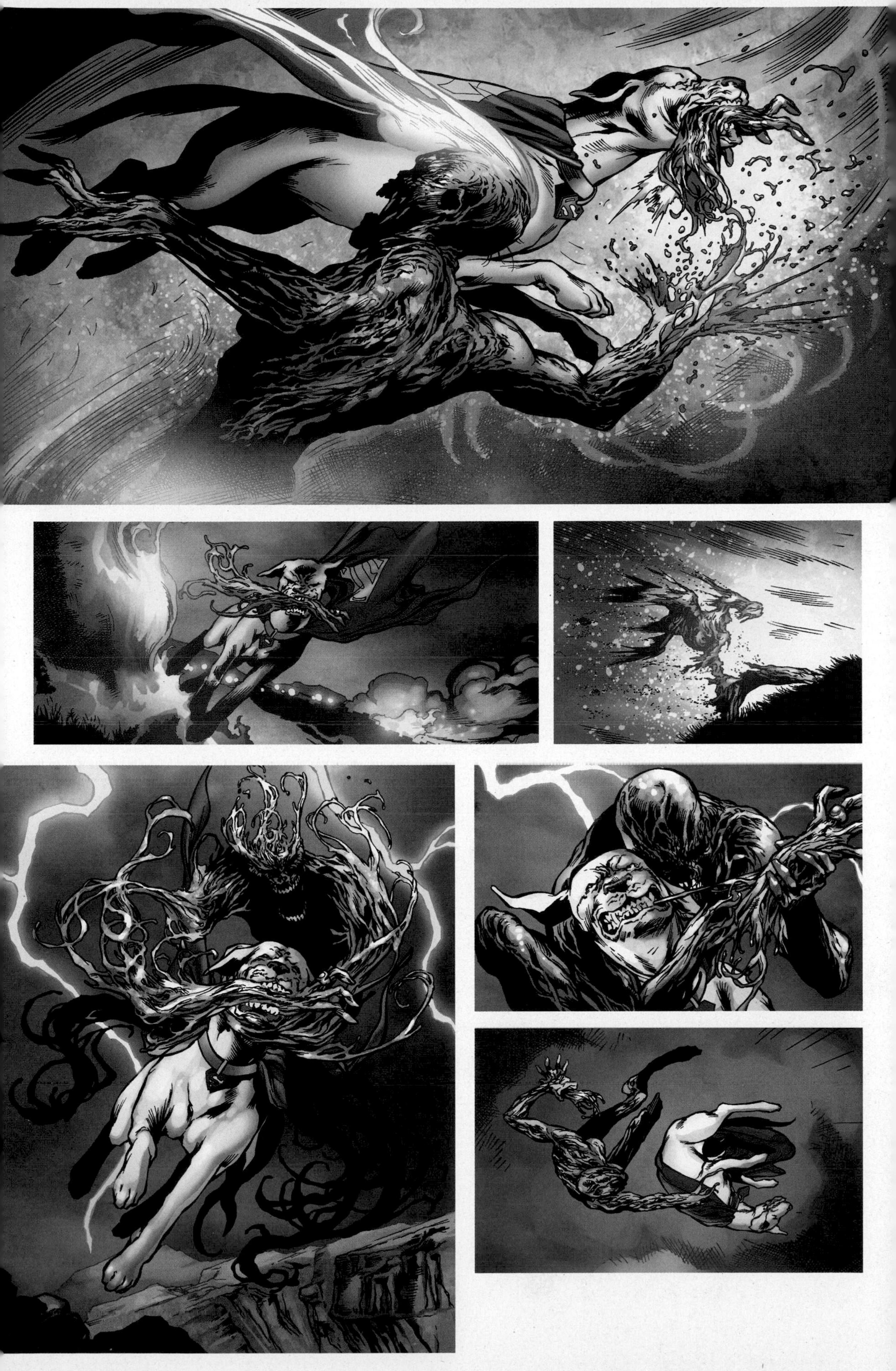

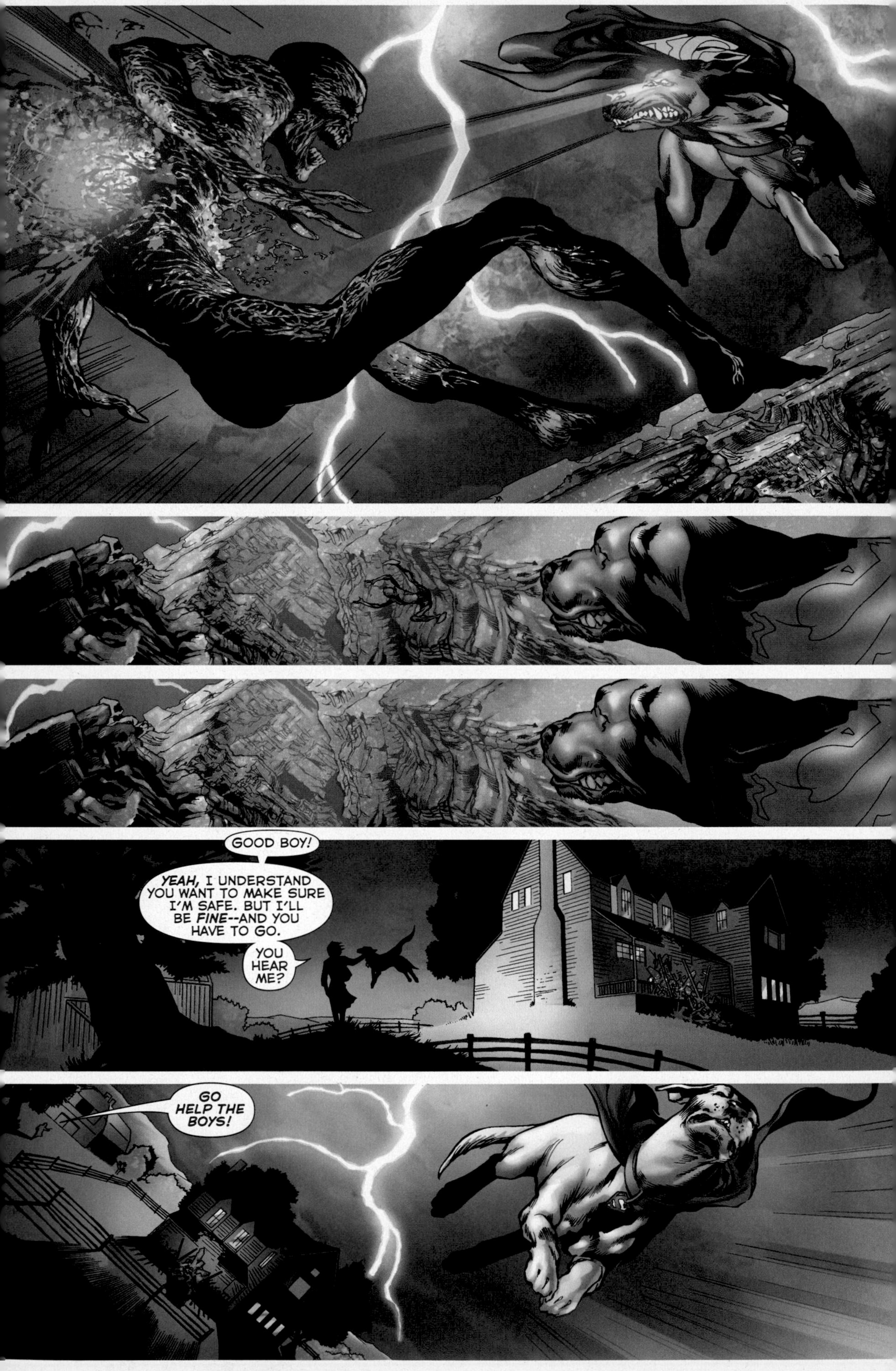
GOOD BOY!
YEAH, I UNDERSTAND YOU WANT TO MAKE SURE I'M SAFE. BUT I'LL BE FINE--AND YOU HAVE TO GO.
YOU HEAR ME?
GO HELP THE BOYS!

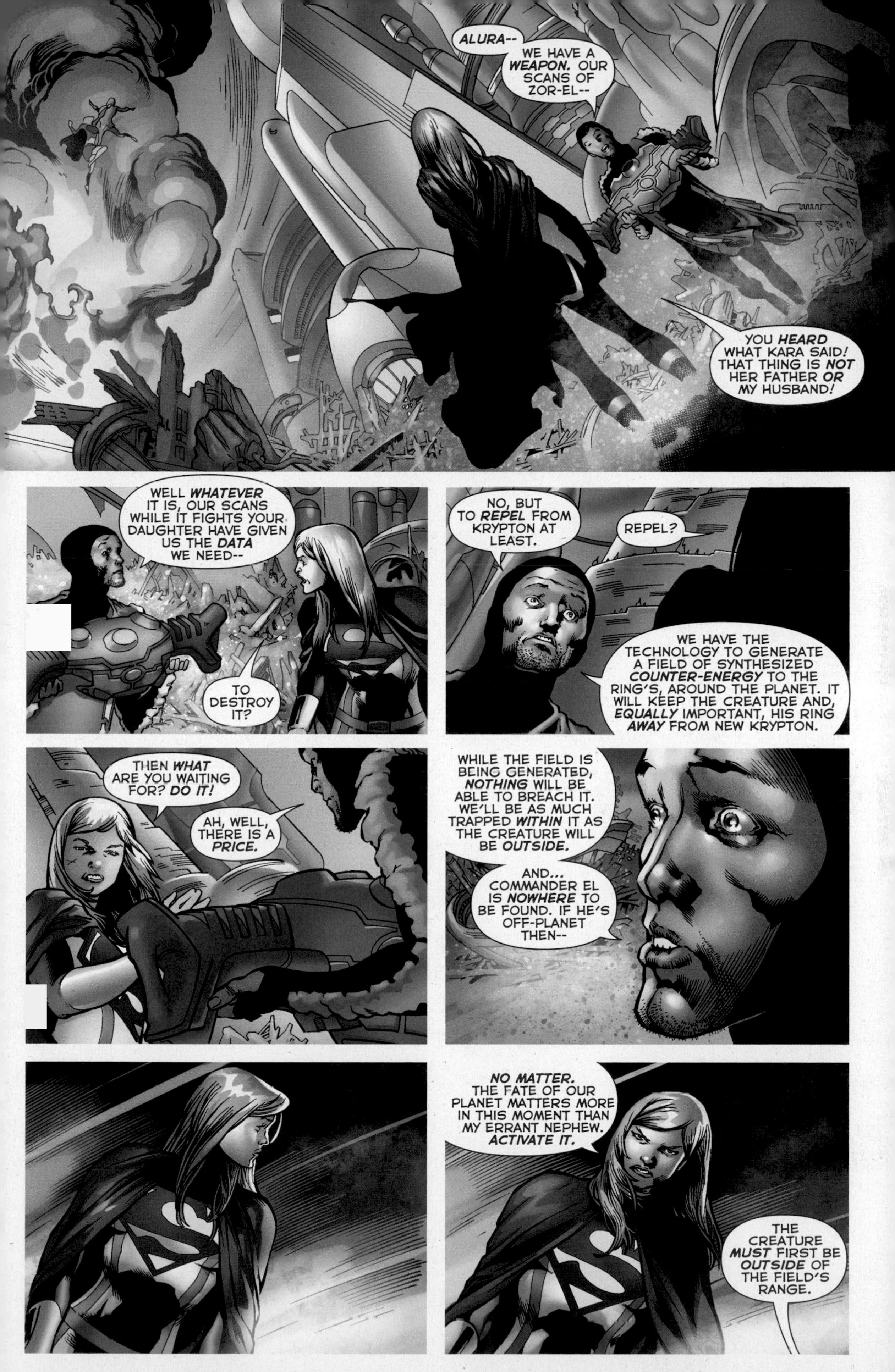
ALURA--
WE HAVE A WEAPON. OUR SCANS OF ZOR-EL--
YOU HEARD WHAT KARA SAID! THAT THING IS NOT HER FATHER OR MY HUSBAND!
WELL WHATEVER IT IS, OUR SCANS WHILE IT FIGHTS YOUR DAUGHTER HAVE GIVEN US THE DATA WE NEED--
TO DESTROY IT?
NO, BUT TO REPEL FROM KRYPTON AT LEAST.
REPEL?
WE HAVE THE TECHNOLOGY TO GENERATE A FIELD OF SYNTHESIZED COUNTER-ENERGY TO THE RING'S, AROUND THE PLANET. IT WILL KEEP THE CREATURE AND, EQUALLY IMPORTANT, HIS RING AWAY FROM NEW KRYPTON.
THEN WHAT ARE YOU WAITING FOR? DO IT!
AH, WELL, THERE IS A PRICE.
WHILE THE FIELD IS BEING GENERATED, NOTHING WILL BE ABLE TO BREACH IT. WE'LL BE AS MUCH TRAPPED WITHIN IT AS THE CREATURE WILL BE OUTSIDE.
AND... COMMANDER EL IS NOWHERE TO BE FOUND. IF HE'S OFF-PLANET THEN--
NO MATTER. THE FATE OF OUR PLANET MATTERS MORE IN THIS MOMENT THAN MY ERRANT NEPHEW. ACTIVATE IT.
THE CREATURE MUST FIRST BE OUTSIDE OF THE FIELD'S RANGE.

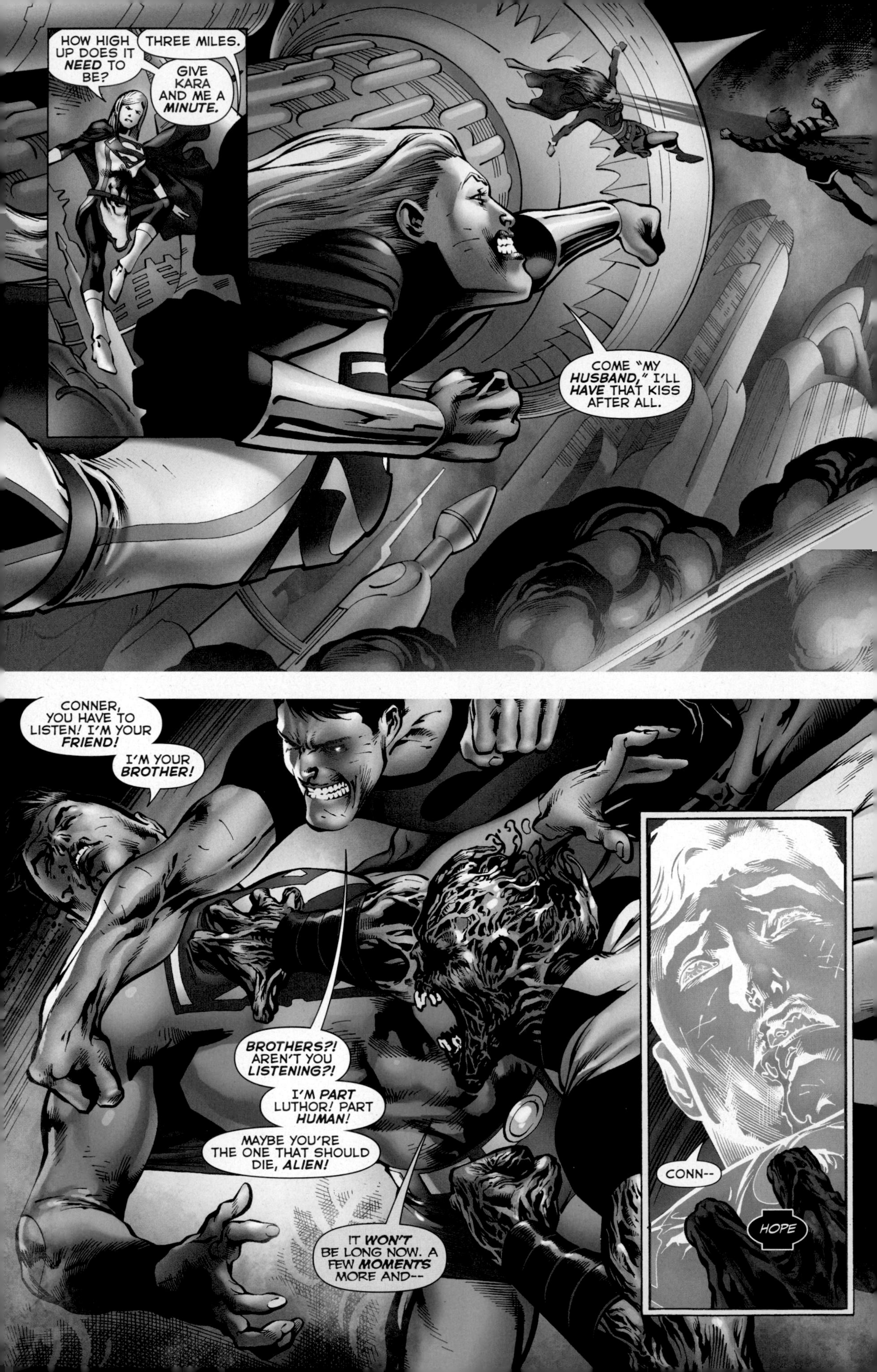
HOW HIGH UP DOES IT NEED TO BE?
THREE MILES.
GIVE KARA AND ME A MINUTE.
COME "MY HUSBAND," I'LL HAVE THAT KISS AFTER ALL.
CONNER, YOU HAVE TO LISTEN! I'M YOUR FRIEND!
I'M YOUR BROTHER!
BROTHERS?! AREN'T YOU LISTENING?!
I'M PART LUTHOR! PART HUMAN!
MAYBE YOU'RE THE ONE THAT SHOULD DIE, ALIEN!
IT WON'T BE LONG NOW. A FEW MOMENTS MORE AND--
CONN--
HOPE

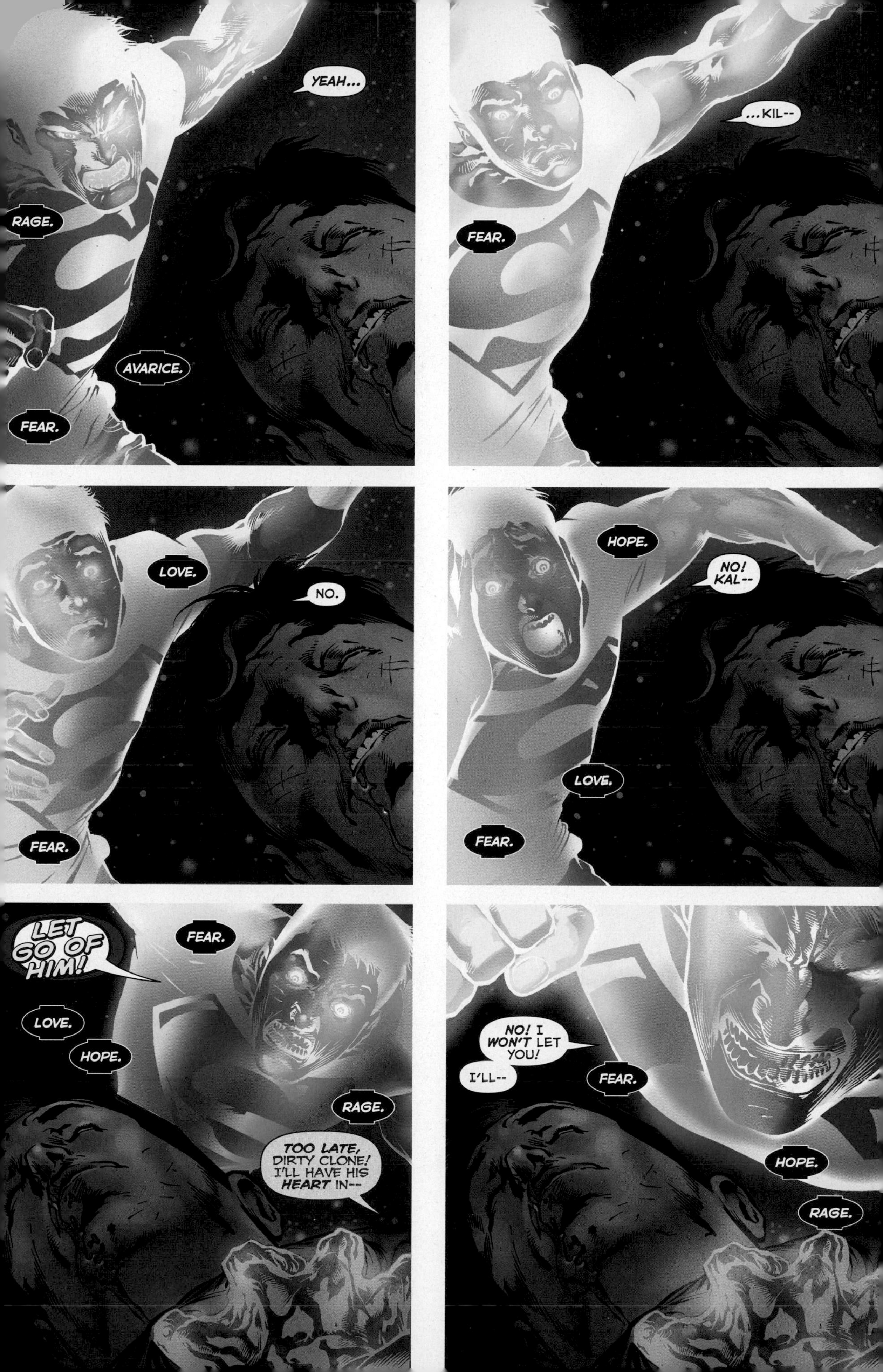

YEAH...
RAGE.
AVARICE.
FEAR.
...KIL--
FEAR.
LOVE.
NO.
FEAR.
HOPE.
NO! KAL--
LOVE.
FEAR.
LET GO OF HIM!
FEAR.
LOVE.
HOPE.
RAGE.
TOO LATE, DIRTY CLONE! I'LL HAVE HIS HEART IN--
NO! I WON'T LET YOU!
I'LL--
FEAR.
HOPE.
RAGE.

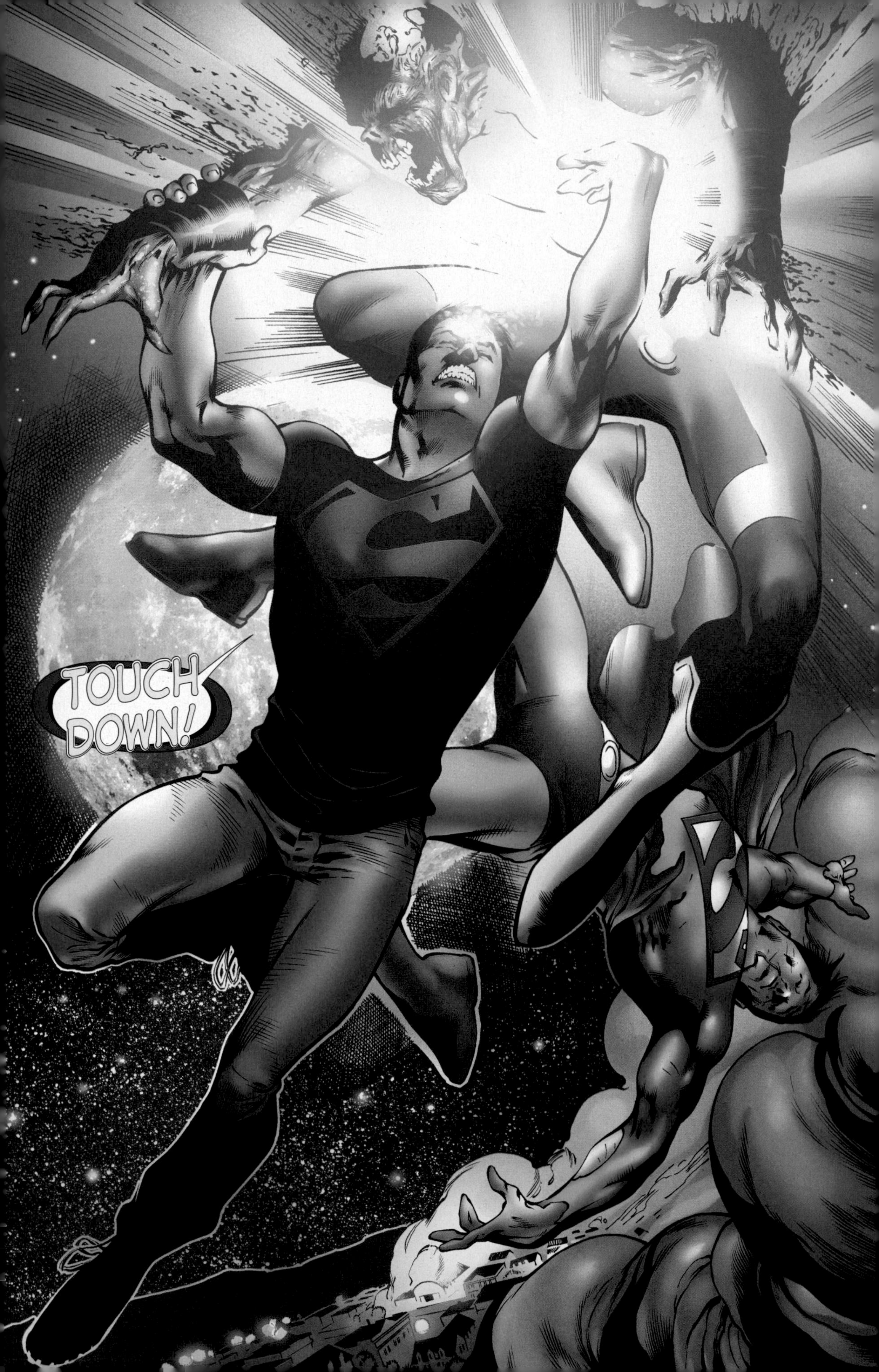
TOUCH DOWN!

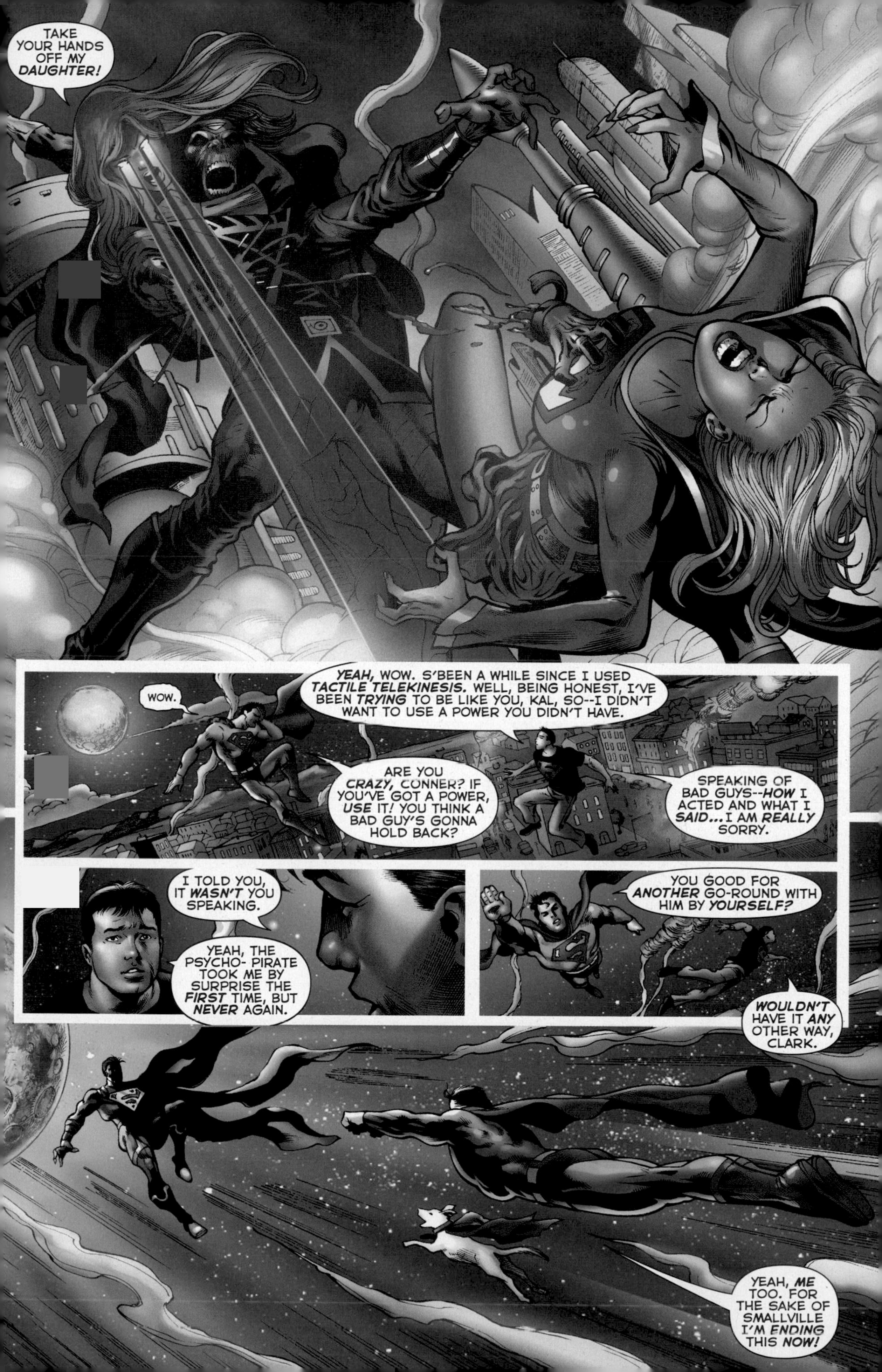
TAKE YOUR HANDS OFF MY DAUGHTER!
WOW.
YEAH, WOW. S'BEEN A WHILE SINCE I USED TACTILE TELEKINESIS. WELL, BEING HONEST, I'VE BEEN TRYING TO BE LIKE YOU, KAL, SO--I DIDN'T WANT TO USE A POWER YOU DIDN'T HAVE.
ARE YOU CRAZY, CONNER? IF YOU'VE GOT A POWER, USE IT! YOU THINK A BAD GUY'S GONNA HOLD BACK?
SPEAKING OF BAD GUYS--HOW I ACTED AND WHAT I SAID... I AM REALLY SORRY.
I TOLD YOU, IT WASN'T YOU SPEAKING.
YEAH, THE PSYCHO- PIRATE TOOK ME BY SURPRISE THE FIRST TIME, BUT NEVER AGAIN.
YOU GOOD FOR ANOTHER GO-ROUND WITH HIM BY YOURSELF?
WOULDN'T HAVE IT ANY OTHER WAY, CLARK.
YEAH, ME TOO. FOR THE SAKE OF SMALLVILLE I'M ENDING THIS NOW!

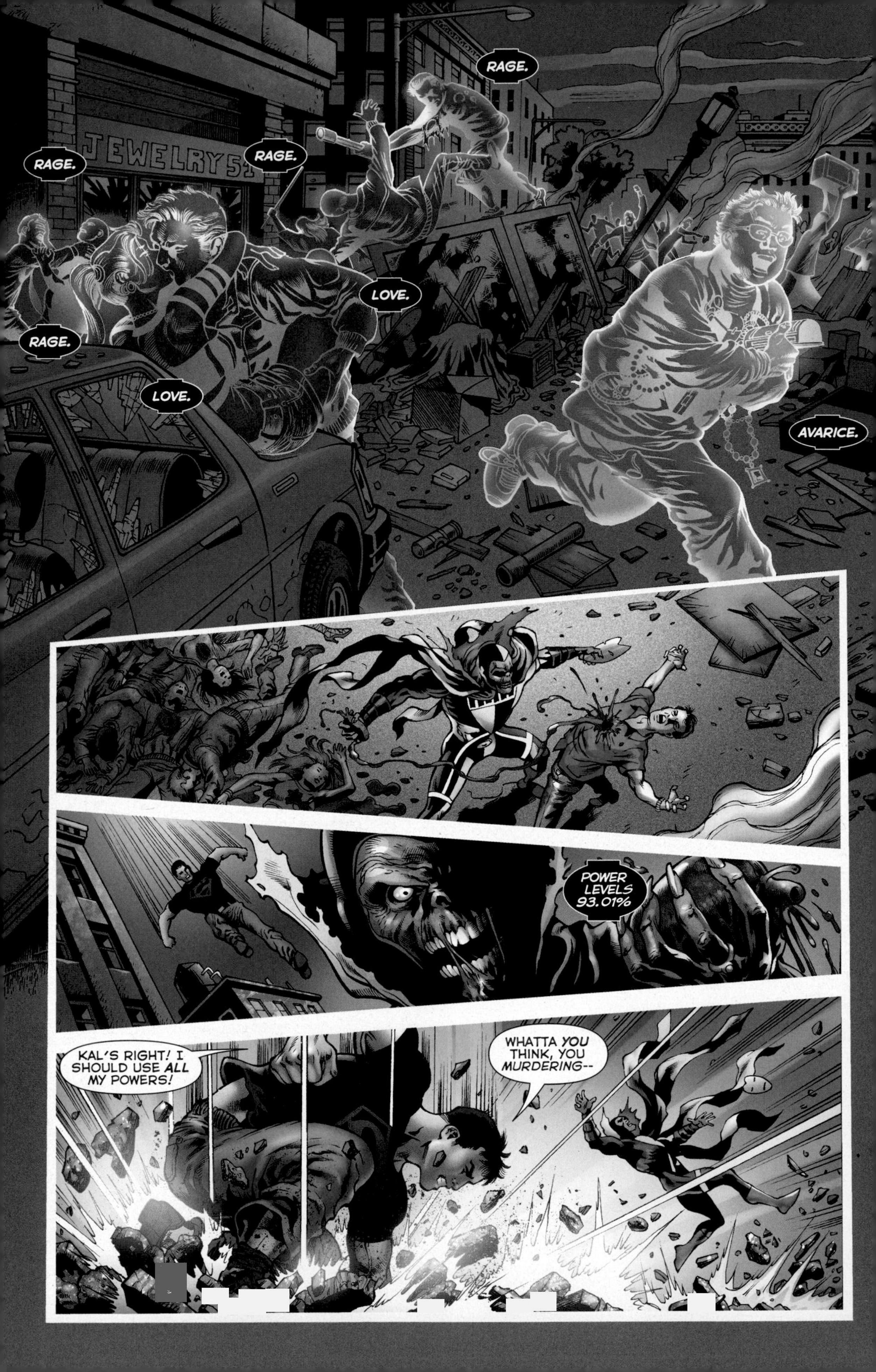
RAGE.
RAGE.
RAGE.
RAGE.
LOVE.
LOVE.
AVARICE.
JEWELRY 51
POWER LEVELS 93.01%
KAL'S RIGHT! I SHOULD USE *ALL* MY POWERS!
WHATTA *YOU* THINK, YOU *MURDERING*--

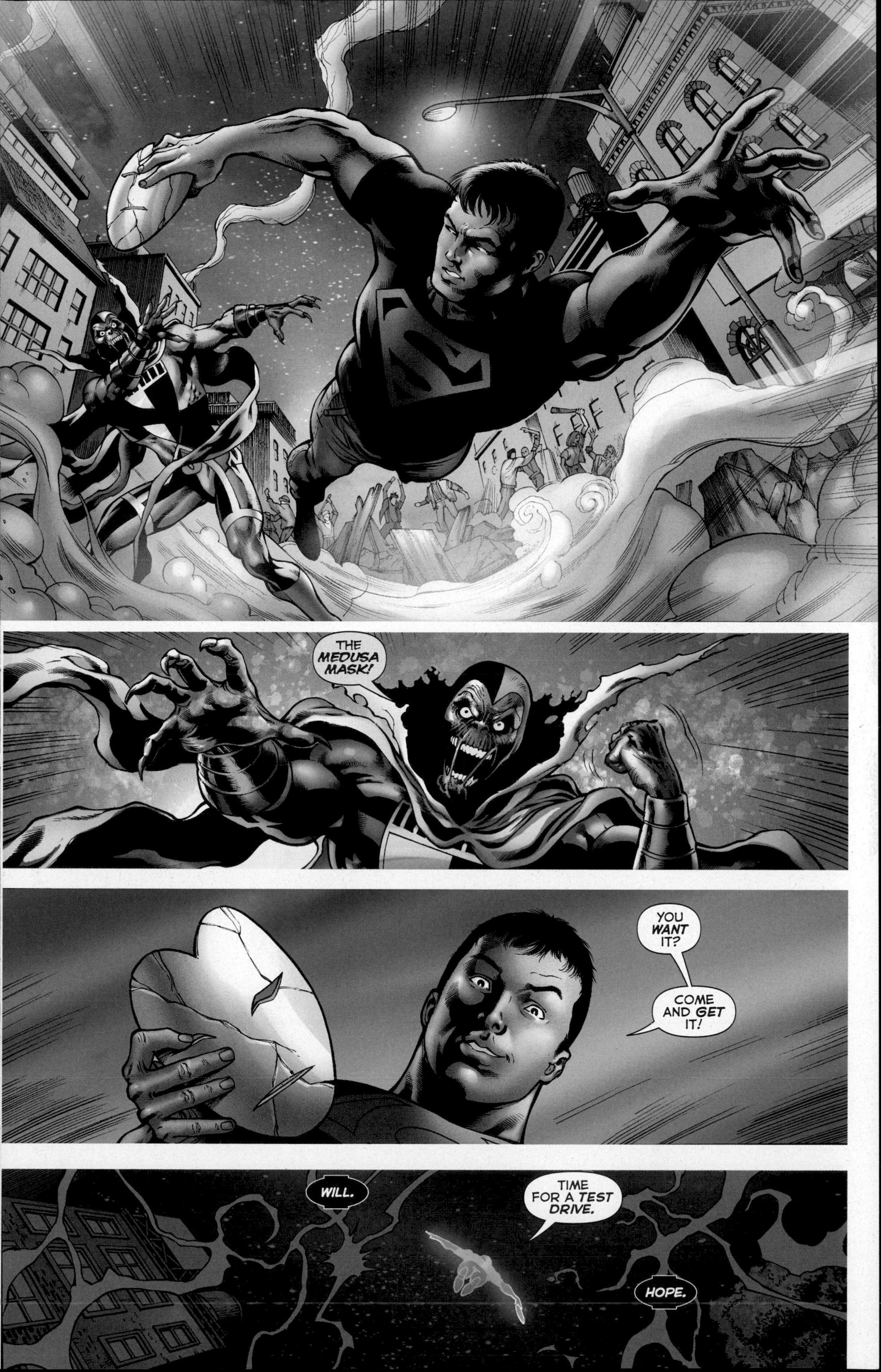
THE MEDUSA MASK!
YOU WANT IT?
COME AND GET IT!
WILL.
TIME FOR A TEST DRIVE.
HOPE.

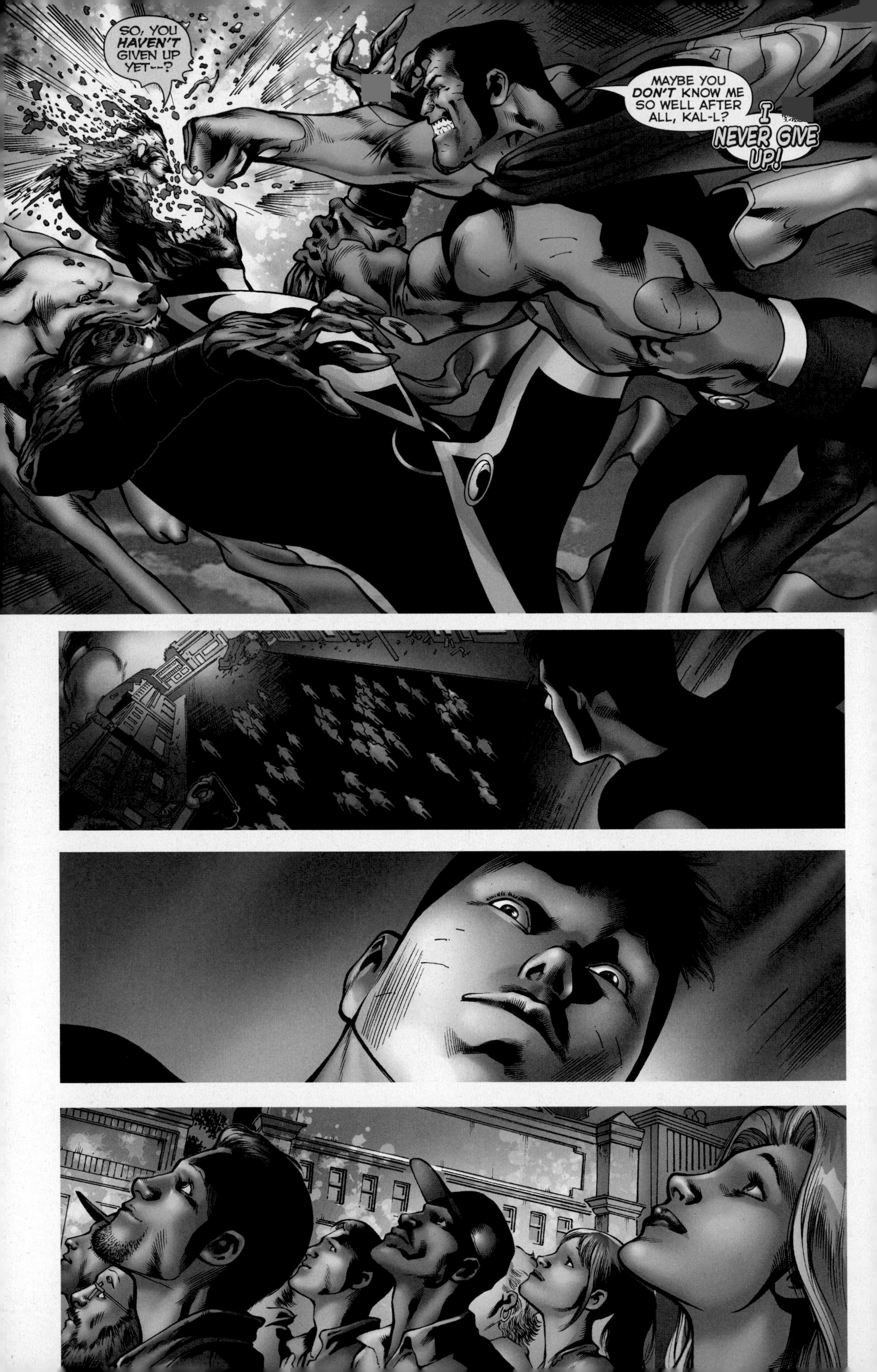
SO, YOU **HAVEN'T** GIVEN UP YET--?
MAYBE YOU **DON'T** KNOW ME SO WELL AFTER ALL, KAL-L?
I NEVER GIVE UP!

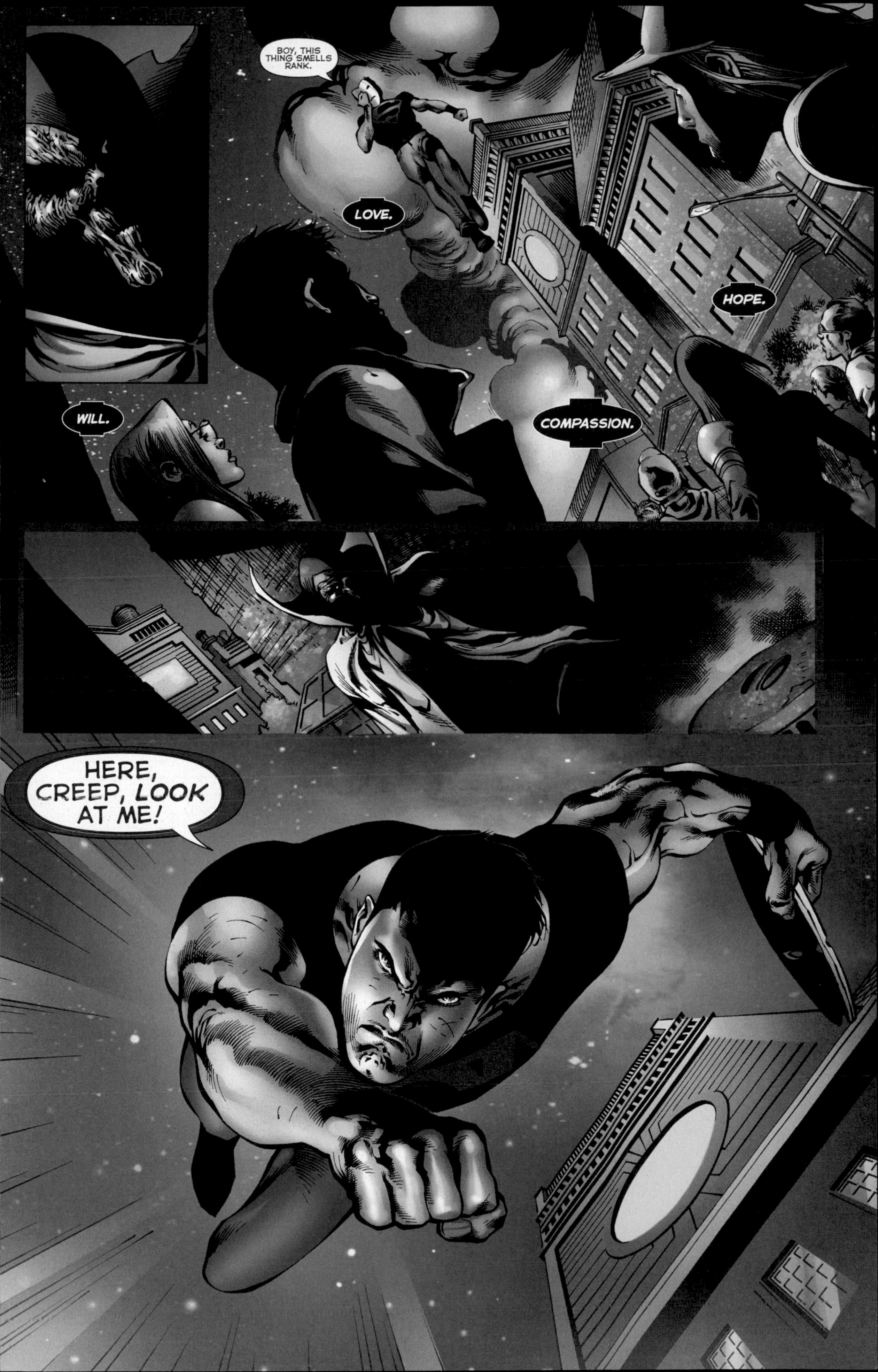
BOY, THIS THING SMELLS RANK.
LOVE.
HOPE.
WILL.
COMPASSION.
HERE, CREEP, LOOK AT ME!

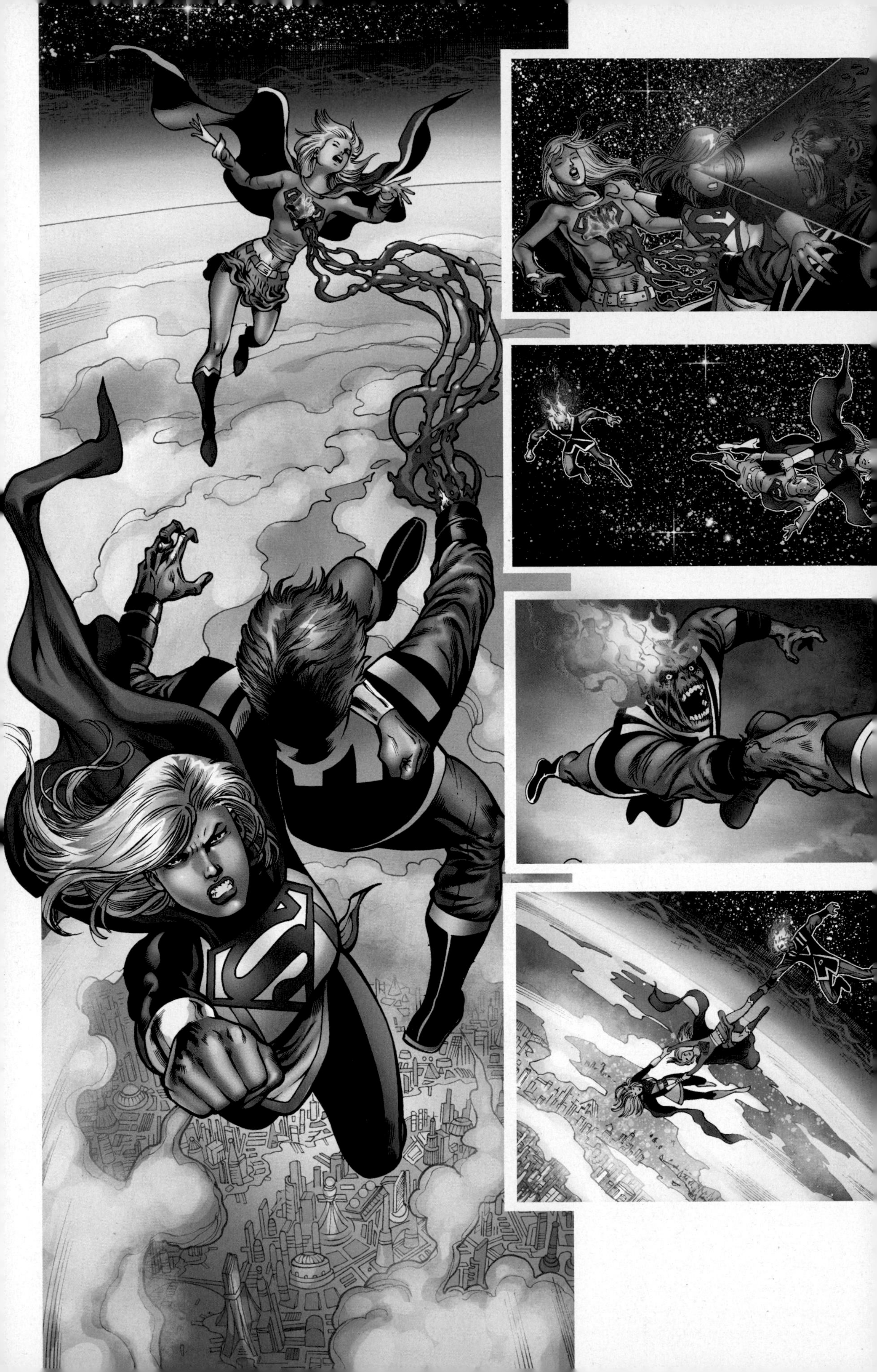

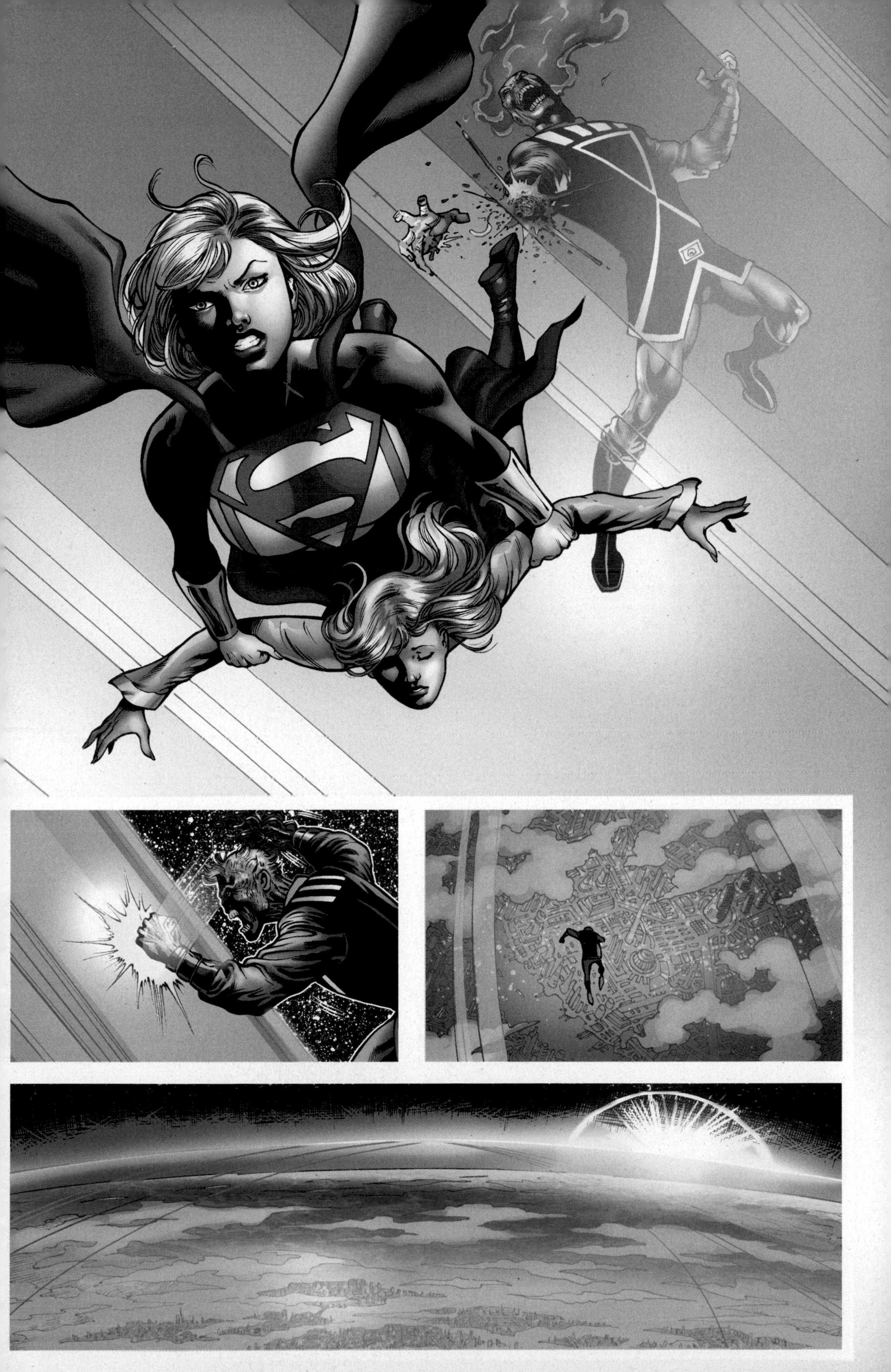

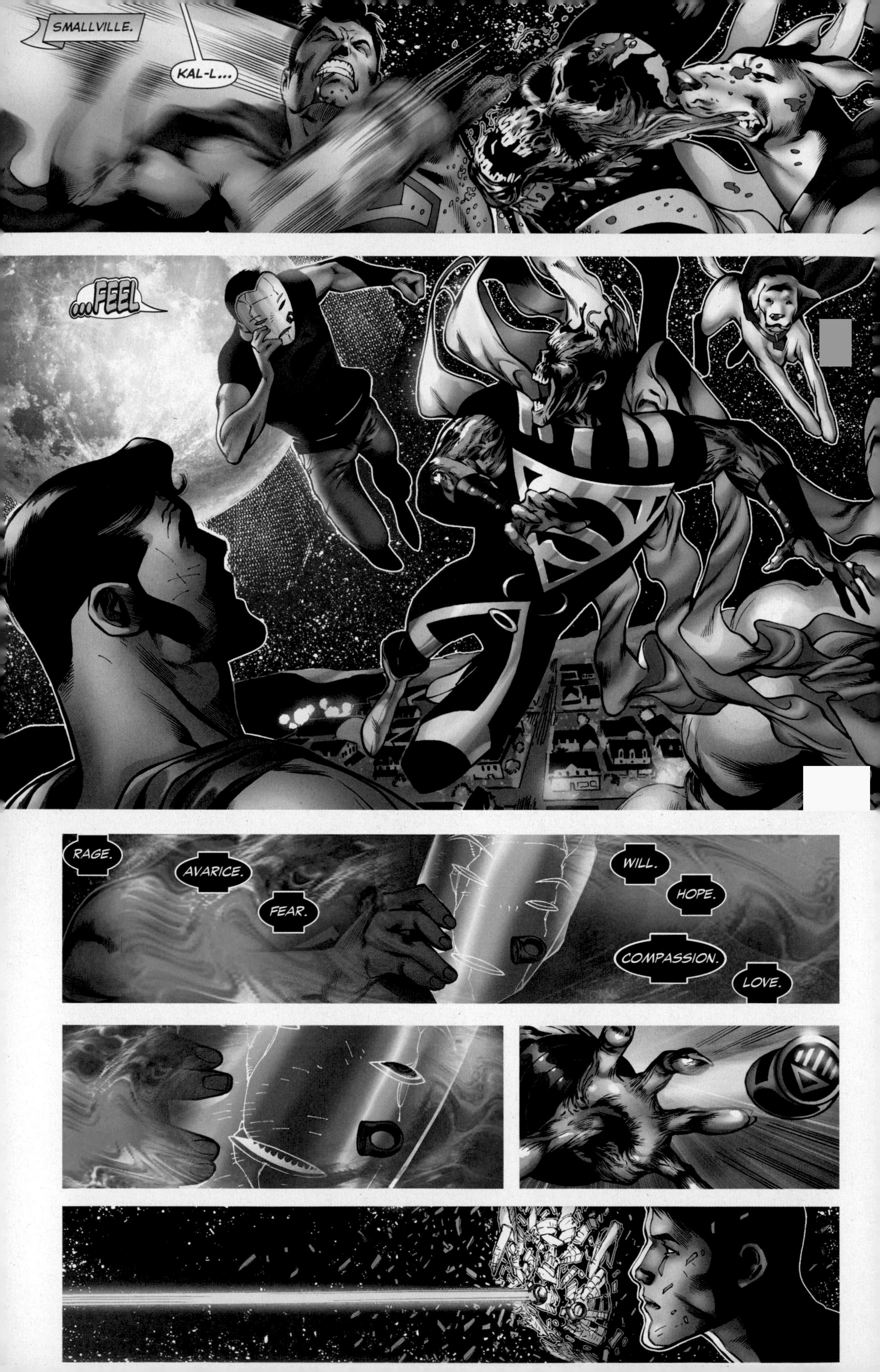
SMALLVILLE.
KAL-L...
...FEEL
RAGE.
AVARICE.
FEAR.
WILL.
HOPE.
COMPASSION.
LOVE.

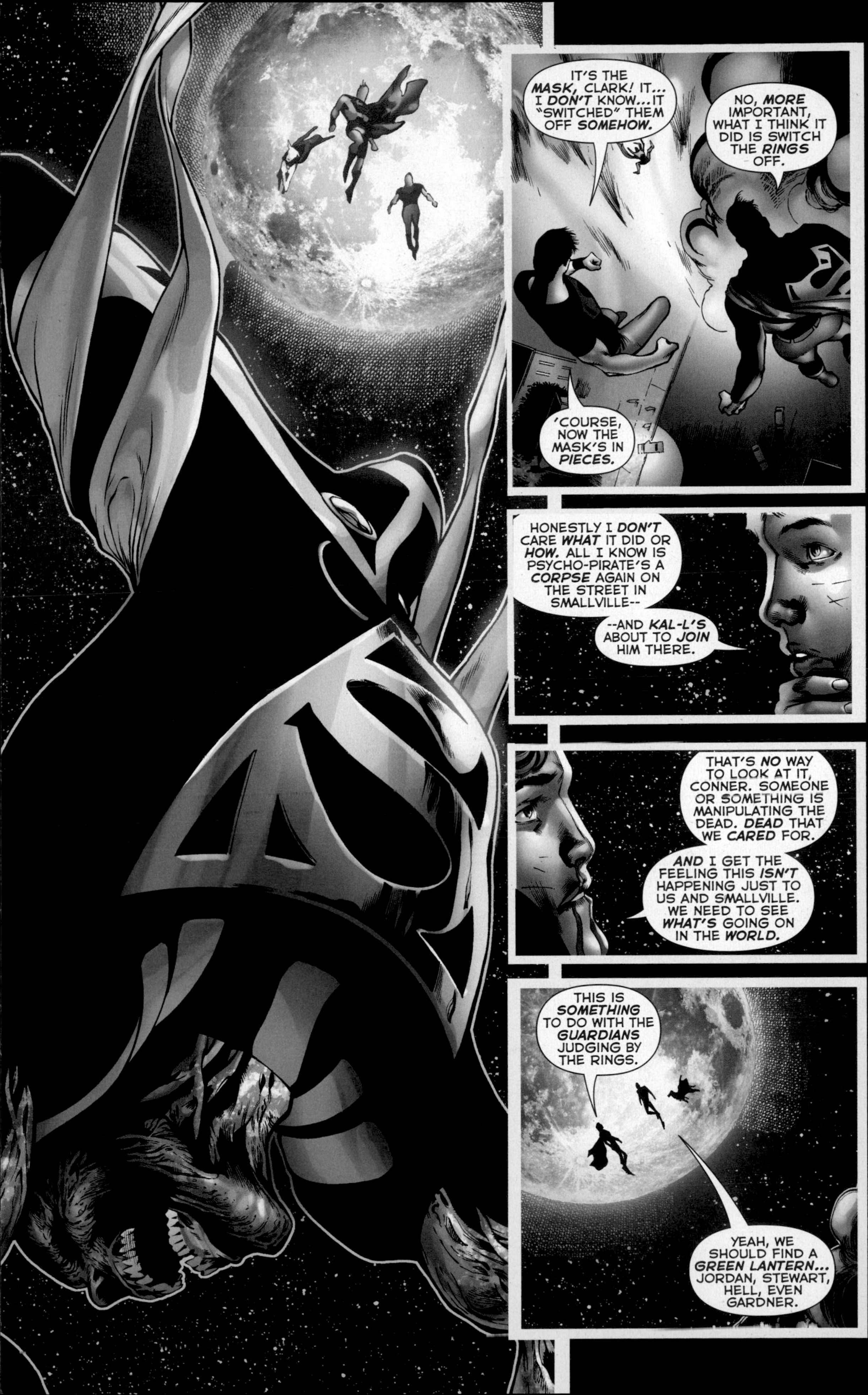

IT'S THE MASK, CLARK! IT... I DON'T KNOW...IT "SWITCHED" THEM OFF SOMEHOW.
NO, MORE IMPORTANT, WHAT I THINK IT DID IS SWITCH THE RINGS OFF.
'COURSE, NOW THE MASK'S IN PIECES.
HONESTLY I DON'T CARE WHAT IT DID OR HOW. ALL I KNOW IS PSYCHO-PIRATE'S A CORPSE AGAIN ON THE STREET IN SMALLVILLE--
--AND KAL-L'S ABOUT TO JOIN HIM THERE.
THAT'S NO WAY TO LOOK AT IT, CONNER. SOMEONE OR SOMETHING IS MANIPULATING THE DEAD. DEAD THAT WE CARED FOR.
AND I GET THE FEELING THIS ISN'T HAPPENING JUST TO US AND SMALLVILLE. WE NEED TO SEE WHAT'S GOING ON IN THE WORLD.
THIS IS SOMETHING TO DO WITH THE GUARDIANS JUDGING BY THE RINGS.
YEAH, WE SHOULD FIND A GREEN LANTERN... JORDAN, STEWART, HELL, EVEN GARDNER.

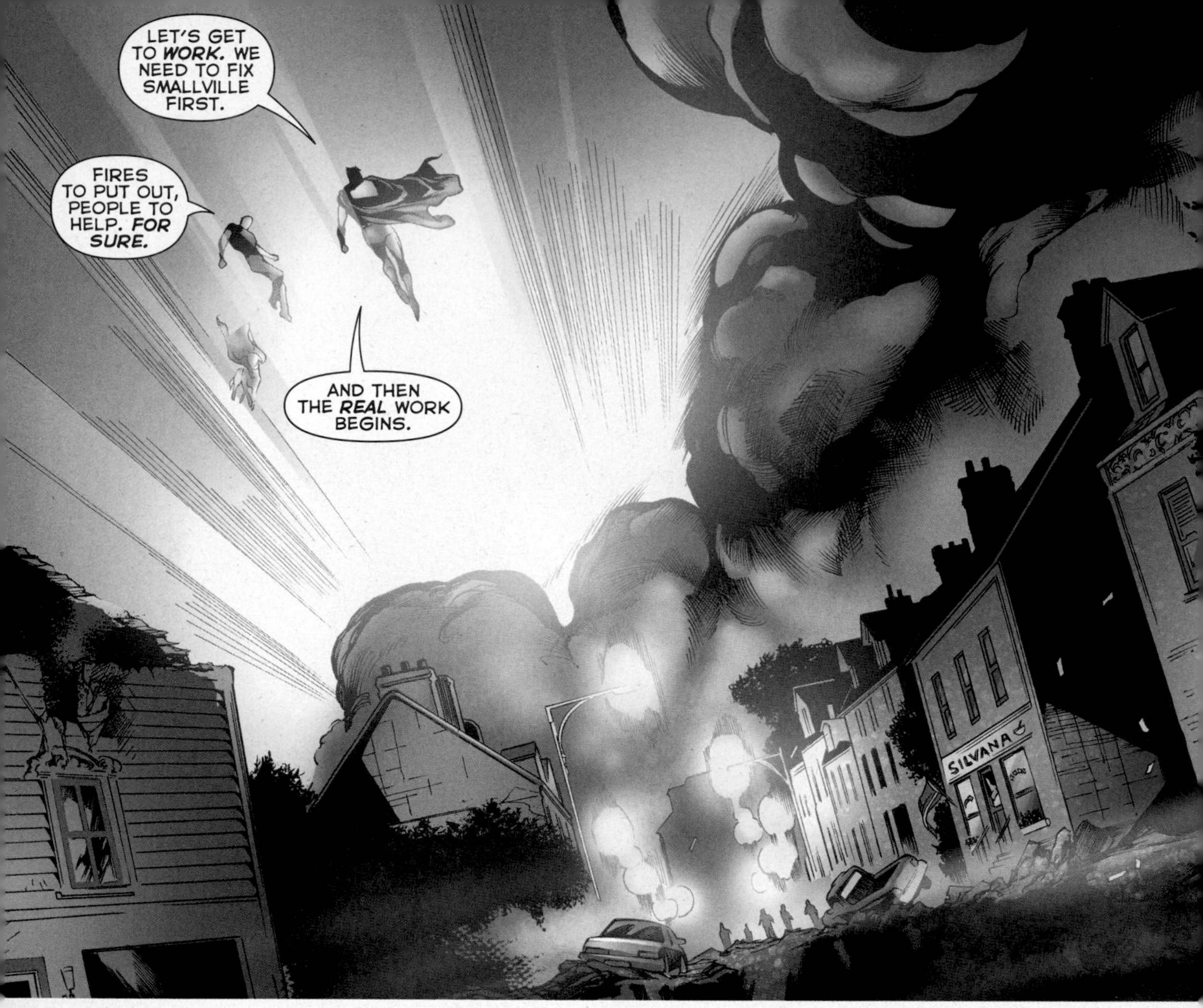
LET'S GET TO WORK. WE NEED TO FIX SMALLVILLE FIRST.
FIRES TO PUT OUT, PEOPLE TO HELP. FOR SURE.
AND THEN THE REAL WORK BEGINS.
SILVANA
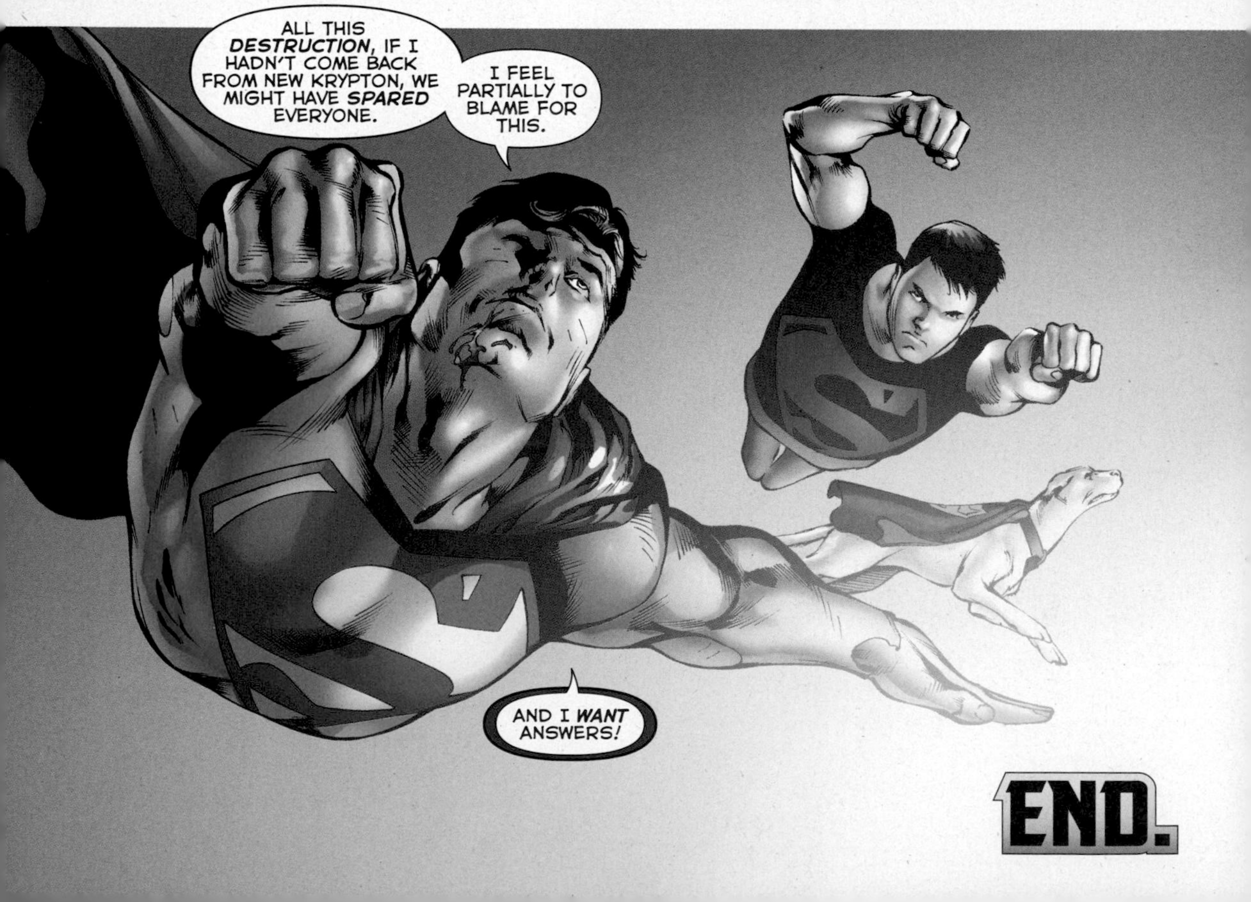
ALL THIS DESTRUCTION, IF I HADN'T COME BACK FROM NEW KRYPTON, WE MIGHT HAVE SPARED EVERYONE.
I FEEL PARTIALLY TO BLAME FOR THIS.
AND I WANT ANSWERS!
END.

BLACKEST NIGHT: TITANS 1
Cover by Ed Benes and
Rob Hunter with Rod Reis

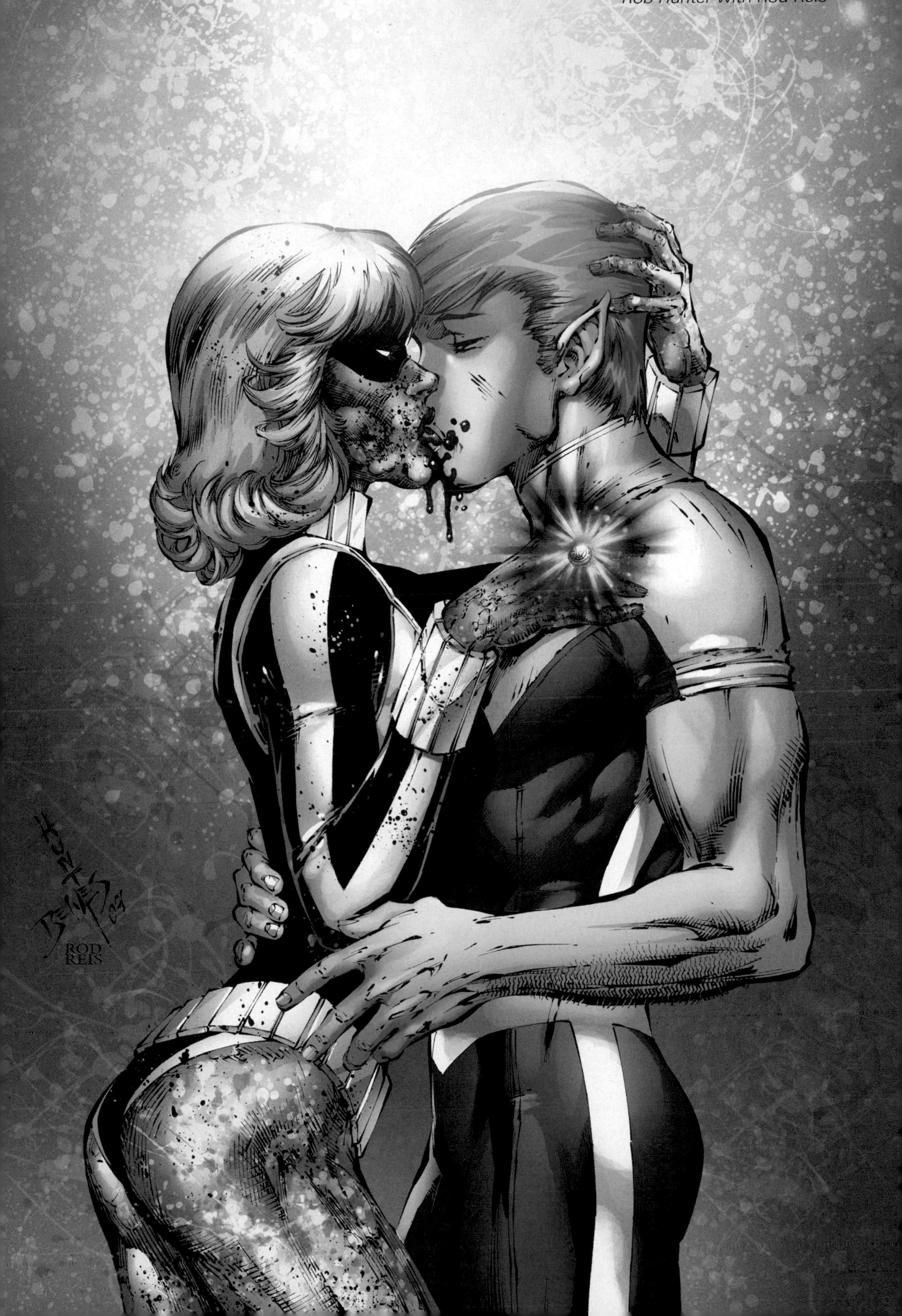
HUNTER
BENES 09
ROD REIS

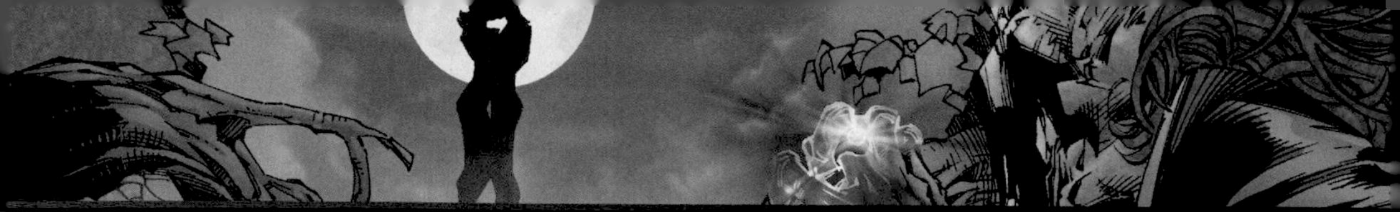

WHEN DEATH COMES KNOCKING

J.T. KRUL
WRITER

ED BENES
PENCILS

ROB HUNTER
JON SIBAL
JP MAYER
INKS

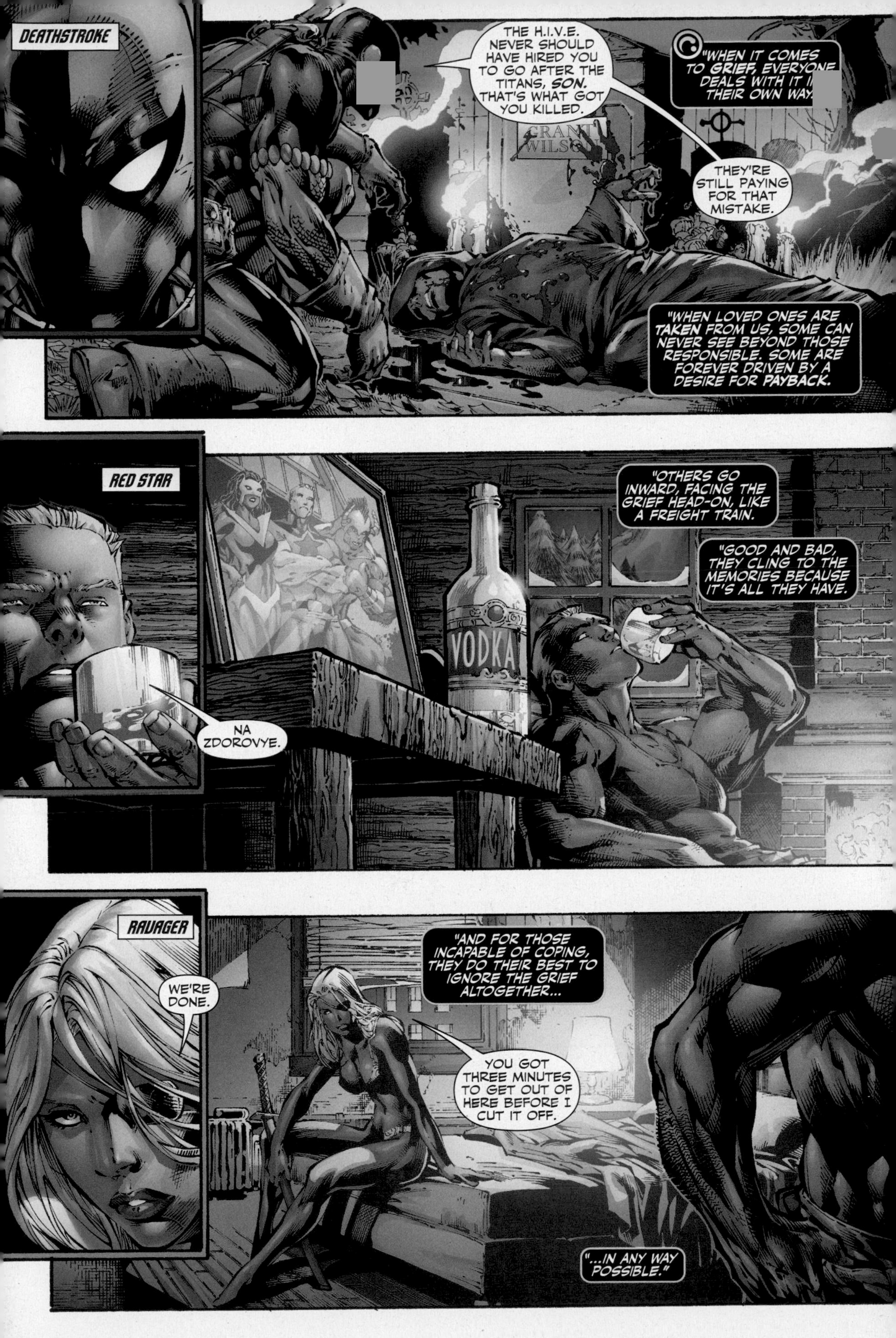
DEATHSTROKE
THE H.I.V.E. NEVER SHOULD HAVE HIRED YOU TO GO AFTER THE TITANS, SON. THAT'S WHAT GOT YOU KILLED.
"WHEN IT COMES TO GRIEF, EVERYONE DEALS WITH IT IN THEIR OWN WAY.
GRANT WILSON
THEY'RE STILL PAYING FOR THAT MISTAKE.
"WHEN LOVED ONES ARE TAKEN FROM US, SOME CAN NEVER SEE BEYOND THOSE RESPONSIBLE. SOME ARE FOREVER DRIVEN BY A DESIRE FOR PAYBACK.
RED STAR
"OTHERS GO INWARD, FACING THE GRIEF HEAD-ON, LIKE A FREIGHT TRAIN.
"GOOD AND BAD, THEY CLING TO THE MEMORIES BECAUSE IT'S ALL THEY HAVE.
VODKA
NA ZDOROVYE.
RAVAGER
"AND FOR THOSE INCAPABLE OF COPING, THEY DO THEIR BEST TO IGNORE THE GRIEF ALTOGETHER...
WE'RE DONE.
YOU GOT THREE MINUTES TO GET OUT OF HERE BEFORE I CUT IT OFF.
"...IN ANY WAY POSSIBLE."

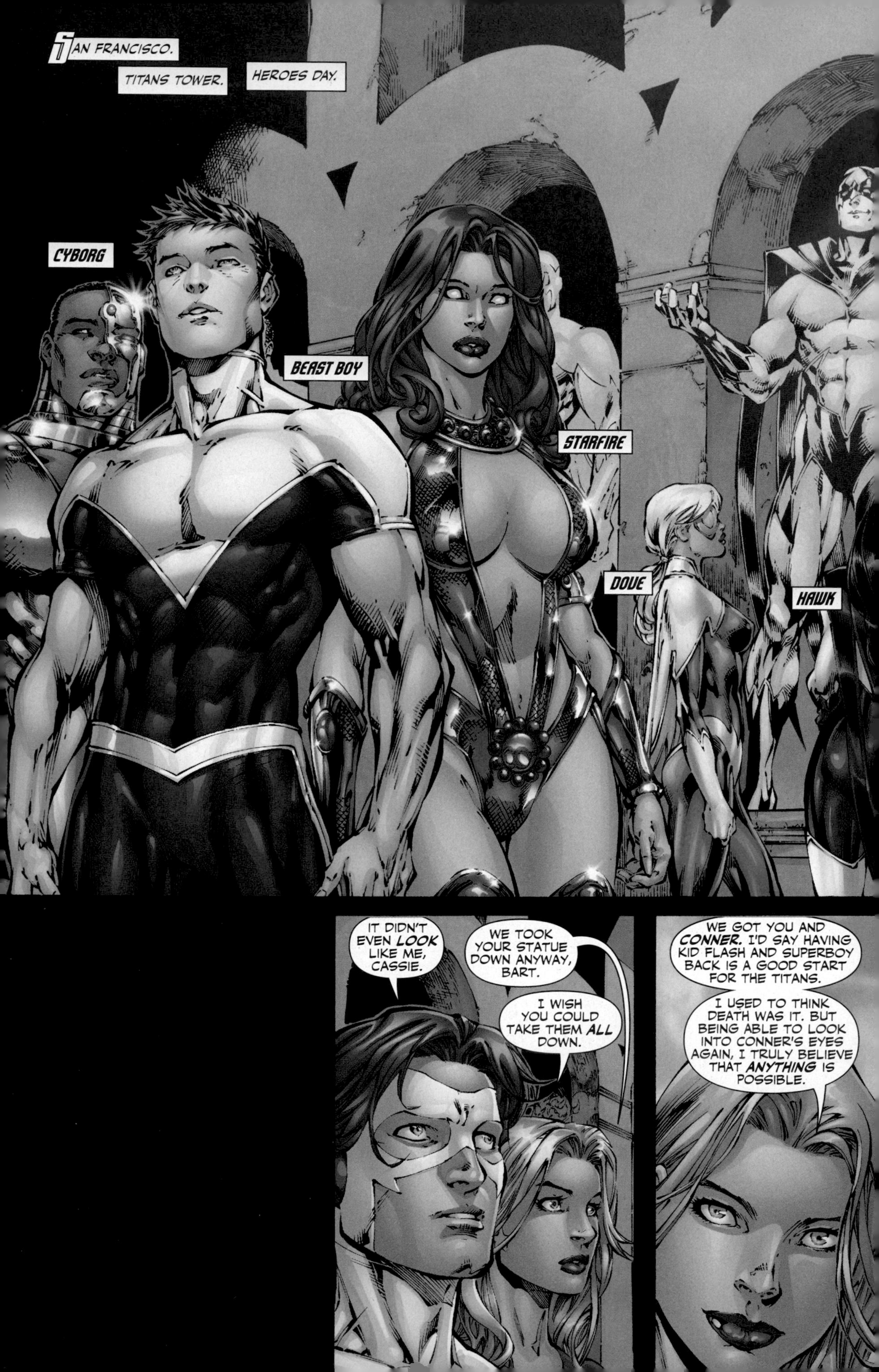
SAN FRANCISCO.
TITANS TOWER.
HEROES DAY.
CYBORG
BEAST BOY
STARFIRE
DOVE
HAWK
IT DIDN'T EVEN LOOK LIKE ME, CASSIE.
WE TOOK YOUR STATUE DOWN ANYWAY, BART.
I WISH YOU COULD TAKE THEM ALL DOWN.
WE GOT YOU AND CONNER. I'D SAY HAVING KID FLASH AND SUPERBOY BACK IS A GOOD START FOR THE TITANS.
I USED TO THINK DEATH WAS IT. BUT BEING ABLE TO LOOK INTO CONNER'S EYES AGAIN, I TRULY BELIEVE THAT ANYTHING IS POSSIBLE.

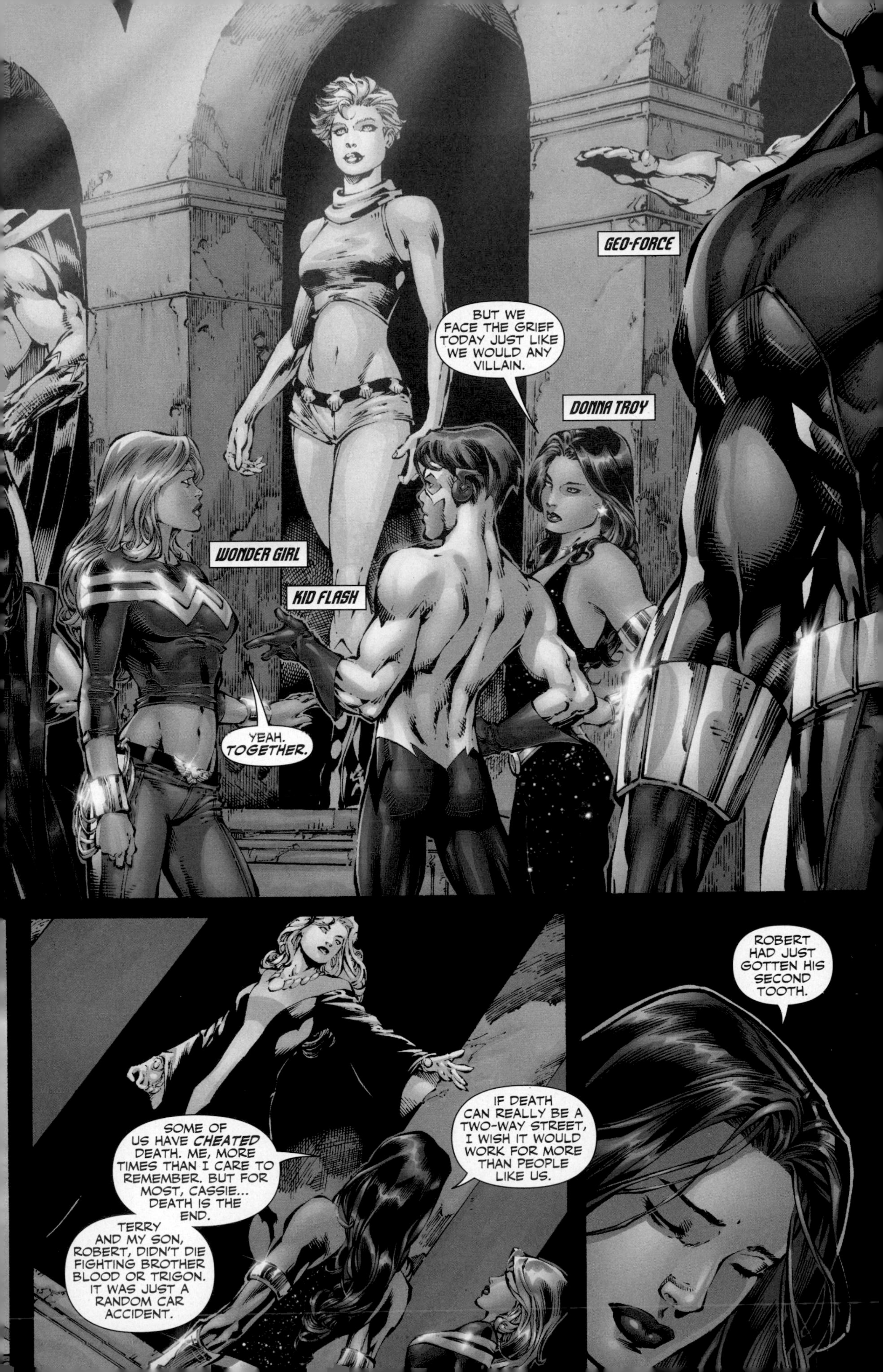
GEO-FORCE
BUT WE FACE THE GRIEF TODAY JUST LIKE WE WOULD ANY VILLAIN.
DONNA TROY
WONDER GIRL
KID FLASH
YEAH. *TOGETHER.*
SOME OF US HAVE *CHEATED* DEATH. ME, MORE TIMES THAN I CARE TO REMEMBER. BUT FOR MOST, CASSIE... DEATH IS THE END.
TERRY AND MY SON, ROBERT, DIDN'T DIE FIGHTING BROTHER BLOOD OR TRIGON. IT WAS JUST A RANDOM CAR ACCIDENT.
IF DEATH CAN REALLY BE A TWO-WAY STREET, I WISH IT WOULD WORK FOR MORE THAN PEOPLE LIKE US.
ROBERT HAD JUST GOTTEN HIS SECOND TOOTH.

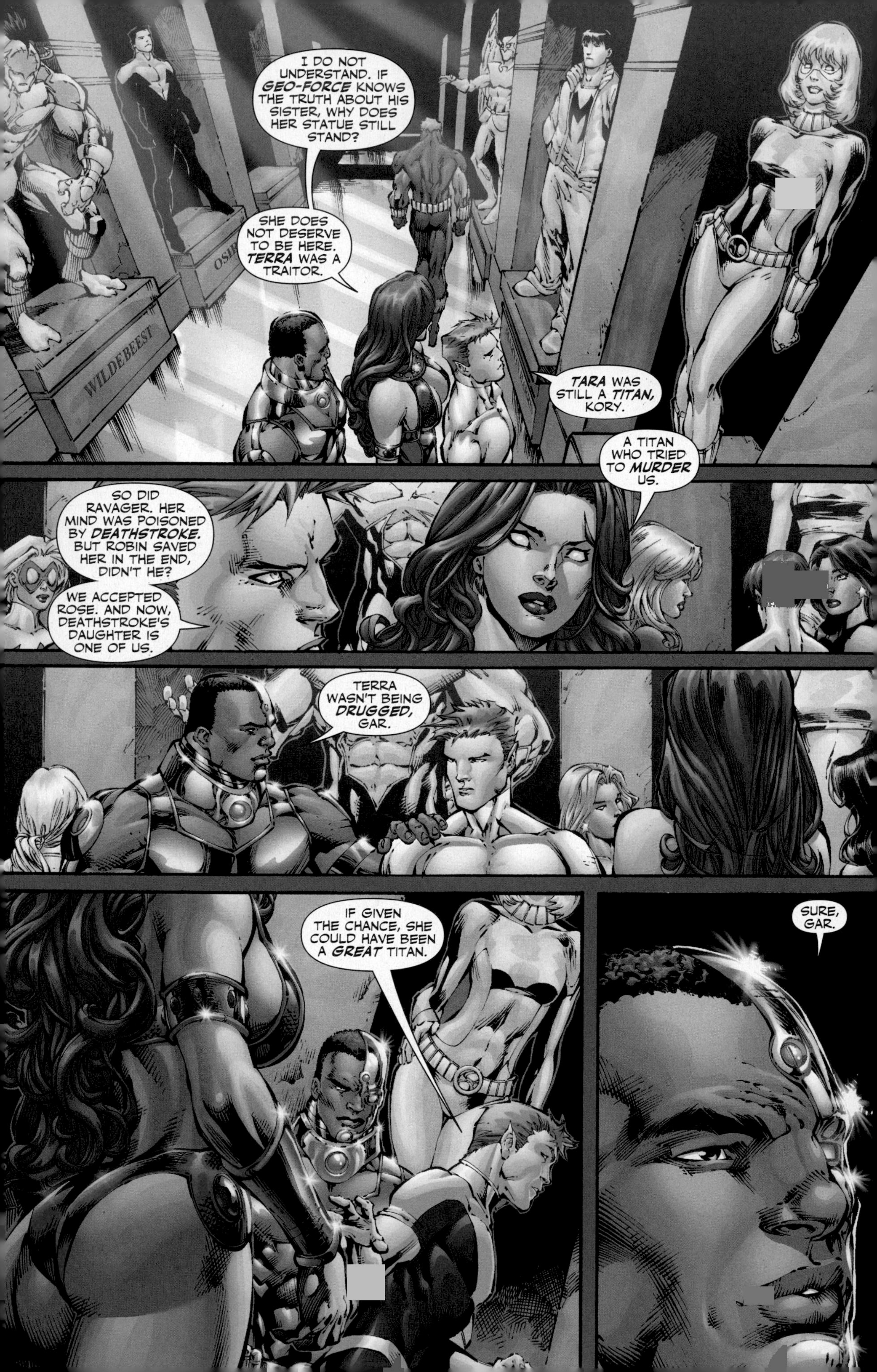
I DO NOT UNDERSTAND. IF GEO-FORCE KNOWS THE TRUTH ABOUT HIS SISTER, WHY DOES HER STATUE STILL STAND?
SHE DOES NOT DESERVE TO BE HERE. TERRA WAS A TRAITOR.
WILDEBEEST
TARA WAS STILL A TITAN, KORY.
A TITAN WHO TRIED TO MURDER US.
SO DID RAVAGER. HER MIND WAS POISONED BY DEATHSTROKE. BUT ROBIN SAVED HER IN THE END, DIDN'T HE?
WE ACCEPTED ROSE. AND NOW, DEATHSTROKE'S DAUGHTER IS ONE OF US.
TERRA WASN'T BEING DRUGGED, GAR.
IF GIVEN THE CHANCE, SHE COULD HAVE BEEN A GREAT TITAN.
SURE, GAR.

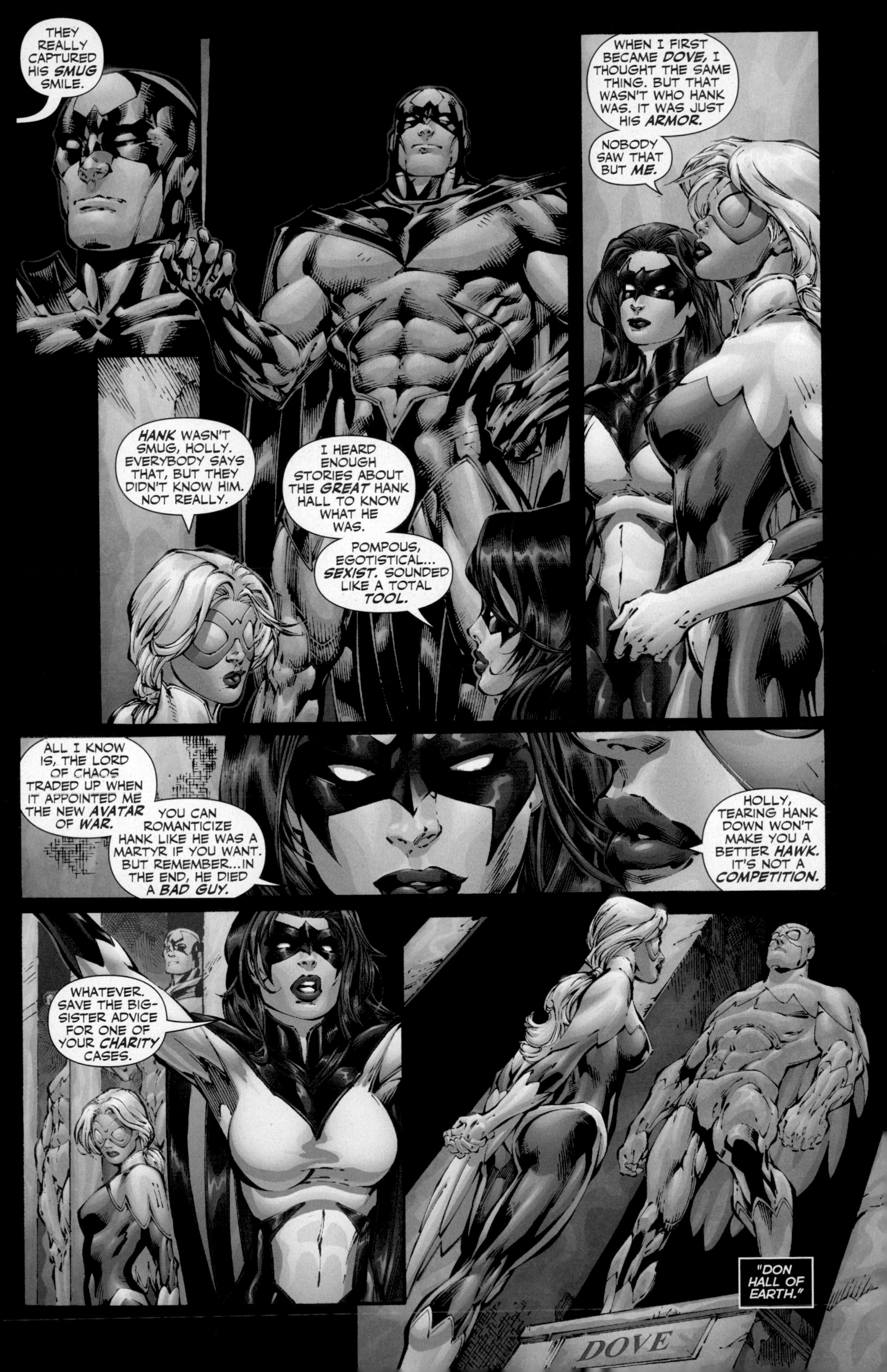
THEY REALLY CAPTURED HIS SMUG SMILE.
WHEN I FIRST BECAME DOVE, I THOUGHT THE SAME THING. BUT THAT WASN'T WHO HANK WAS. IT WAS JUST HIS ARMOR.
NOBODY SAW THAT BUT ME.
HANK WASN'T SMUG, HOLLY. EVERYBODY SAYS THAT, BUT THEY DIDN'T KNOW HIM. NOT REALLY.
I HEARD ENOUGH STORIES ABOUT THE GREAT HANK HALL TO KNOW WHAT HE WAS.
POMPOUS, EGOTISTICAL... SEXIST. SOUNDED LIKE A TOTAL TOOL.
ALL I KNOW IS, THE LORD OF CHAOS TRADED UP WHEN IT APPOINTED ME THE NEW AVATAR OF WAR.
YOU CAN ROMANTICIZE HANK LIKE HE WAS A MARTYR IF YOU WANT. BUT REMEMBER...IN THE END, HE DIED A BAD GUY.
HOLLY, TEARING HANK DOWN WON'T MAKE YOU A BETTER HAWK. IT'S NOT A COMPETITION.
WHATEVER. SAVE THE BIG-SISTER ADVICE FOR ONE OF YOUR CHARITY CASES.
"DON HALL OF EARTH."
DOVE

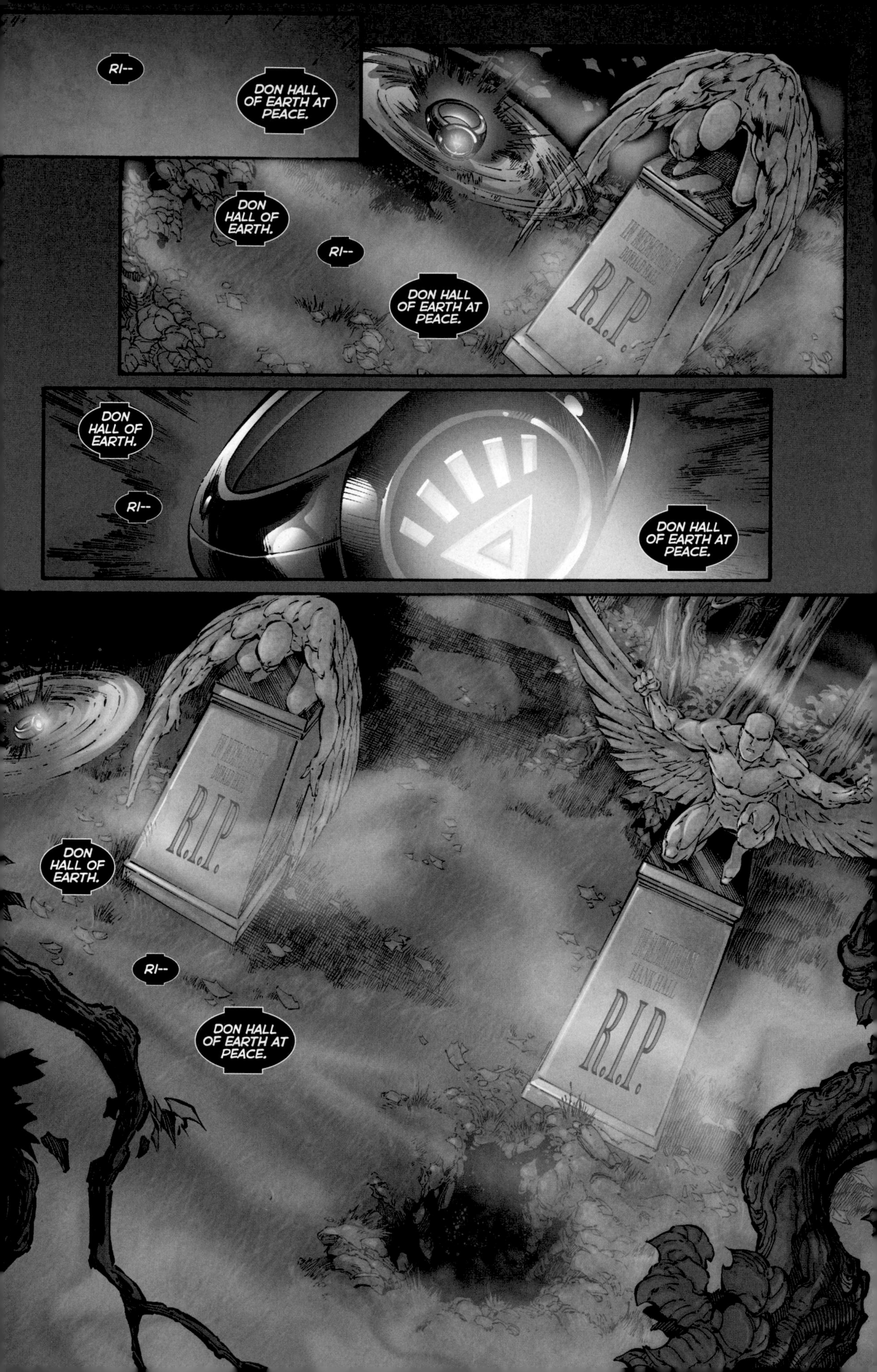
RI--
DON HALL OF EARTH AT PEACE.
DON HALL OF EARTH.
RI--
DON HALL OF EARTH AT PEACE.
DON HALL OF EARTH.
RI--
DON HALL OF EARTH AT PEACE.
DON HALL OF EARTH.
RI--
DON HALL OF EARTH AT PEACE.

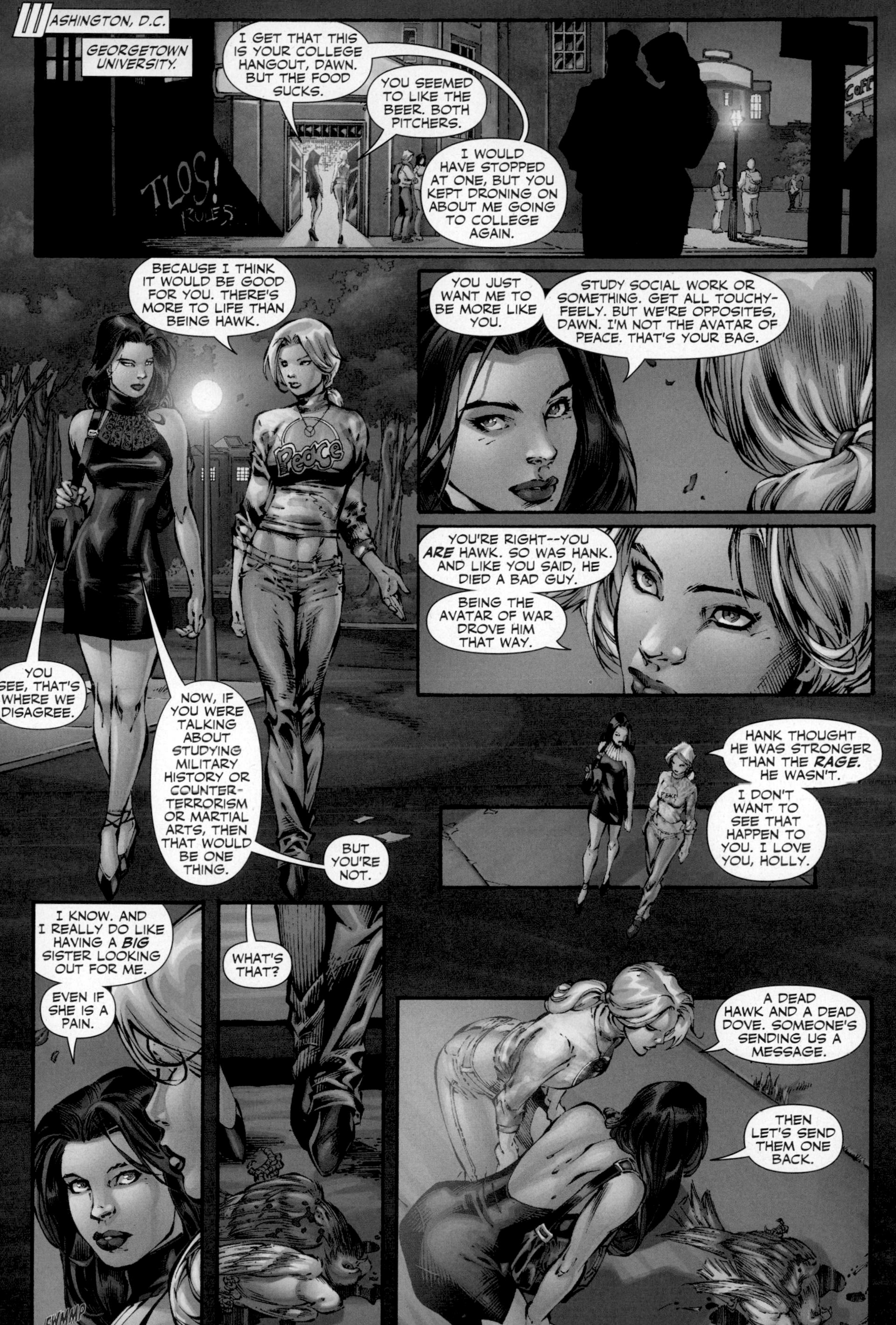
WASHINGTON, D.C.
GEORGETOWN UNIVERSITY.
I GET THAT THIS IS YOUR COLLEGE HANGOUT, DAWN. BUT THE FOOD SUCKS.
YOU SEEMED TO LIKE THE BEER. BOTH PITCHERS.
I WOULD HAVE STOPPED AT ONE, BUT YOU KEPT DRONING ON ABOUT ME GOING TO COLLEGE AGAIN.
TLOS! RULES
BECAUSE I THINK IT WOULD BE GOOD FOR YOU. THERE'S MORE TO LIFE THAN BEING HAWK.
YOU SEE, THAT'S WHERE WE DISAGREE.
NOW, IF YOU WERE TALKING ABOUT STUDYING MILITARY HISTORY OR COUNTER-TERRORISM OR MARTIAL ARTS, THEN THAT WOULD BE ONE THING.
BUT YOU'RE NOT.
PEACE
YOU JUST WANT ME TO BE MORE LIKE YOU.
STUDY SOCIAL WORK OR SOMETHING. GET ALL TOUCHY-FEELY. BUT WE'RE OPPOSITES, DAWN. I'M NOT THE AVATAR OF PEACE. THAT'S YOUR BAG.
YOU'RE RIGHT--YOU ARE HAWK. SO WAS HANK. AND LIKE YOU SAID, HE DIED A BAD GUY.
BEING THE AVATAR OF WAR DROVE HIM THAT WAY.
HANK THOUGHT HE WAS STRONGER THAN THE RAGE. HE WASN'T.
I DON'T WANT TO SEE THAT HAPPEN TO YOU. I LOVE YOU, HOLLY.
I KNOW. AND I REALLY DO LIKE HAVING A BIG SISTER LOOKING OUT FOR ME.
EVEN IF SHE IS A PAIN.
FWMMP
WHAT'S THAT?
A DEAD HAWK AND A DEAD DOVE. SOMEONE'S SENDING US A MESSAGE.
THEN LET'S SEND THEM ONE BACK.

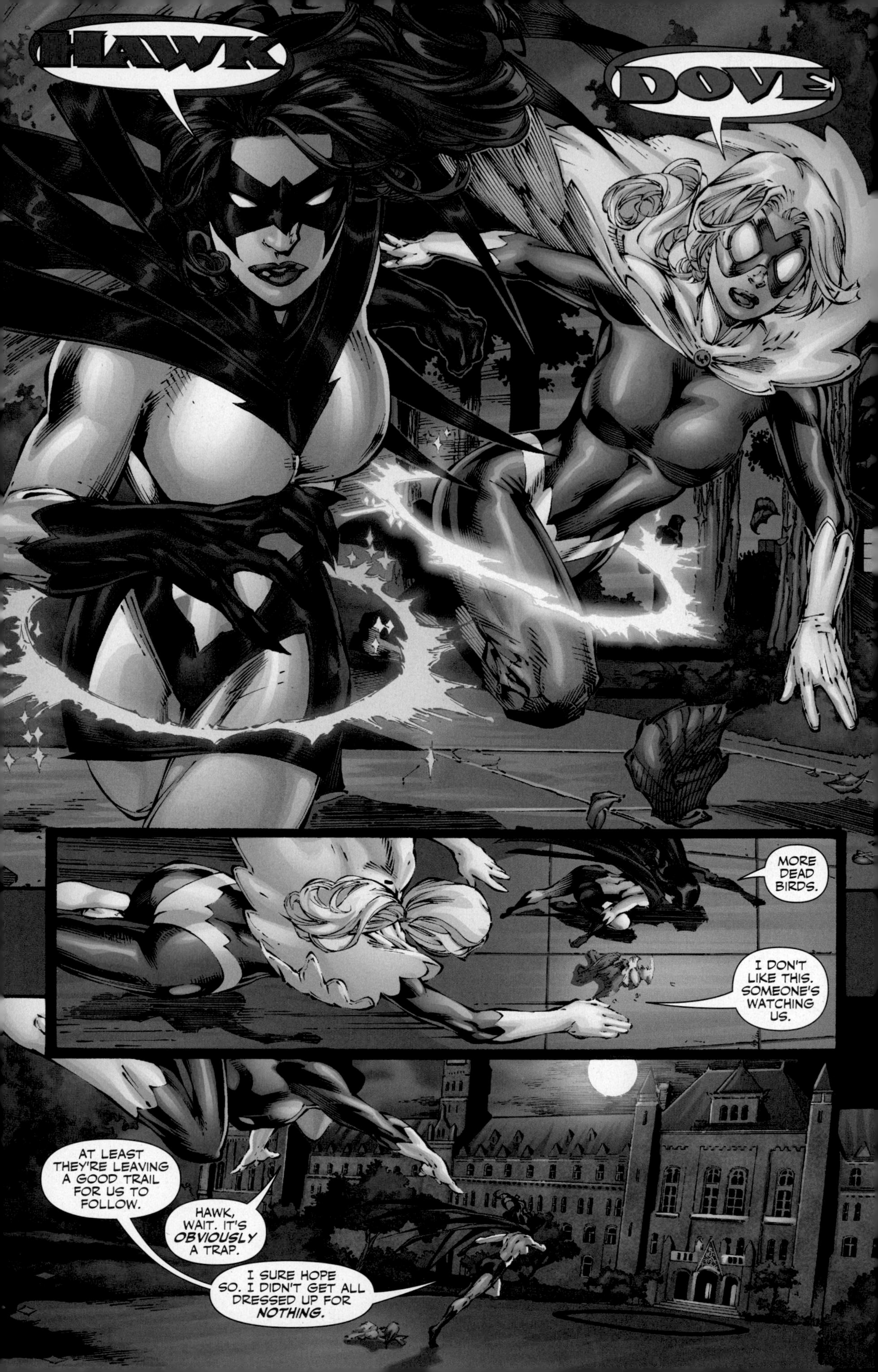
HAWK
DOVE
MORE DEAD BIRDS.
I DON'T LIKE THIS. SOMEONE'S WATCHING US.
AT LEAST THEY'RE LEAVING A GOOD TRAIL FOR US TO FOLLOW.
HAWK, WAIT. IT'S *OBVIOUSLY* A TRAP.
I SURE HOPE SO. I DIDN'T GET ALL DRESSED UP FOR *NOTHING.*

OKAY, PSYCHO-STALKER! YOU GOT OUR ATTENTION. COME OUT, COME OUT WHEREVER YOU ARE.

DO YOU HAVE TO SHOUT?

RAGE.

WHAT? THE LIBRARY'S CLOSED. I DON'T THINK THE RULE ABOUT SILENCE APPLIES.

WHOEVER IS OUT THERE, YOU DON'T NEED TO PROVOKE HIM.

THEY STARTED IT. I'M JUST GOING TO FINISH IT.

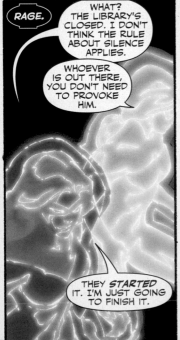

YOU CAN'T PUNCH YOUR WAY THROUGH EVERY CONFLICT.

YOU'RE RIGHT, MAYBE YOU COULD KUMBAYA THEM INTO SUBMISSION.

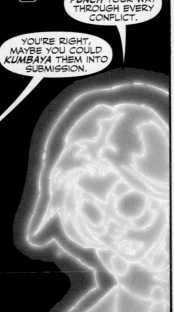

WELL, WELL, WELL. GUESS IT'S LADIES' NIGHT.

HANK?!?

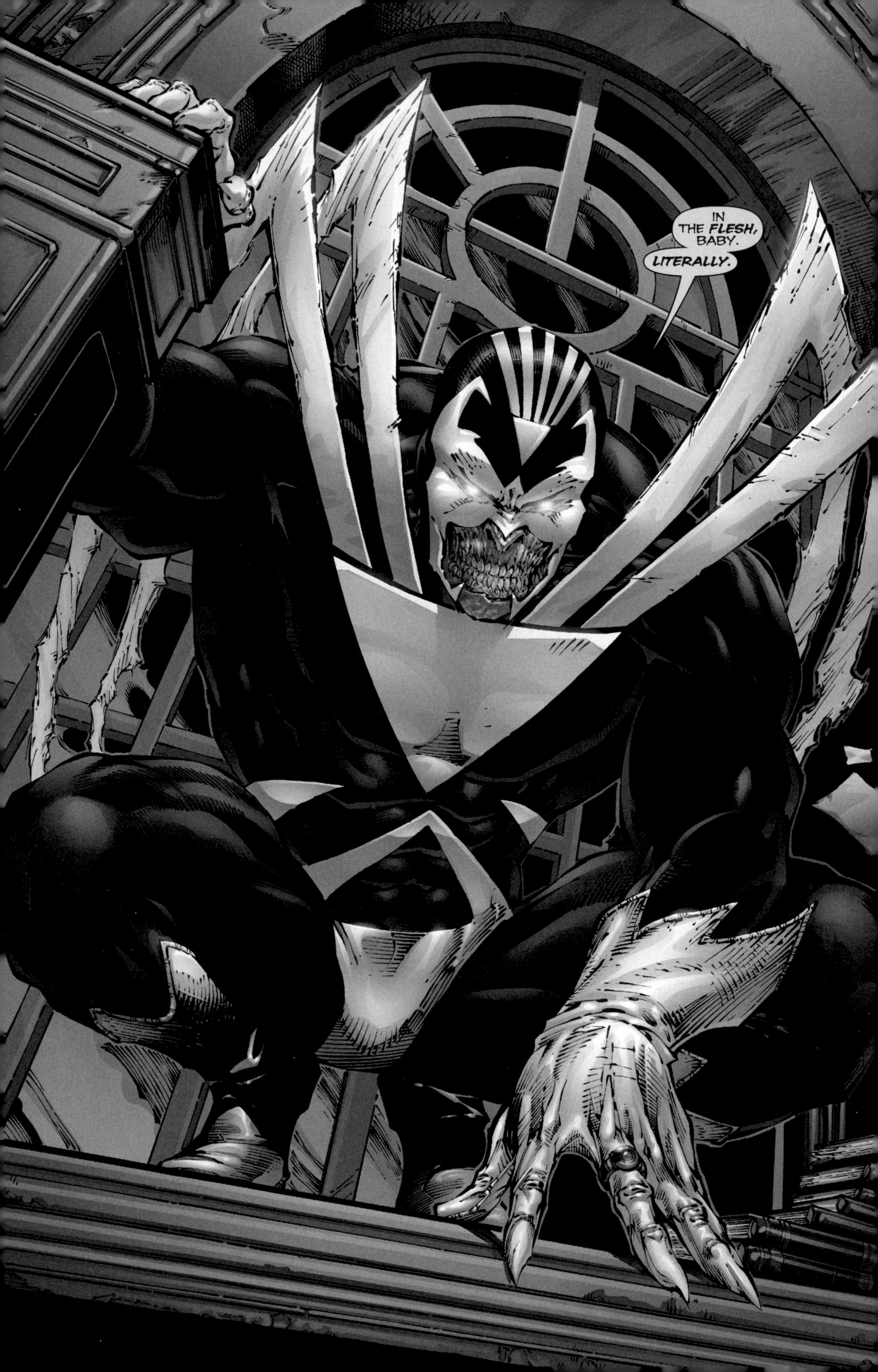
IN THE *FLESH*, BABY.
LITERALLY.

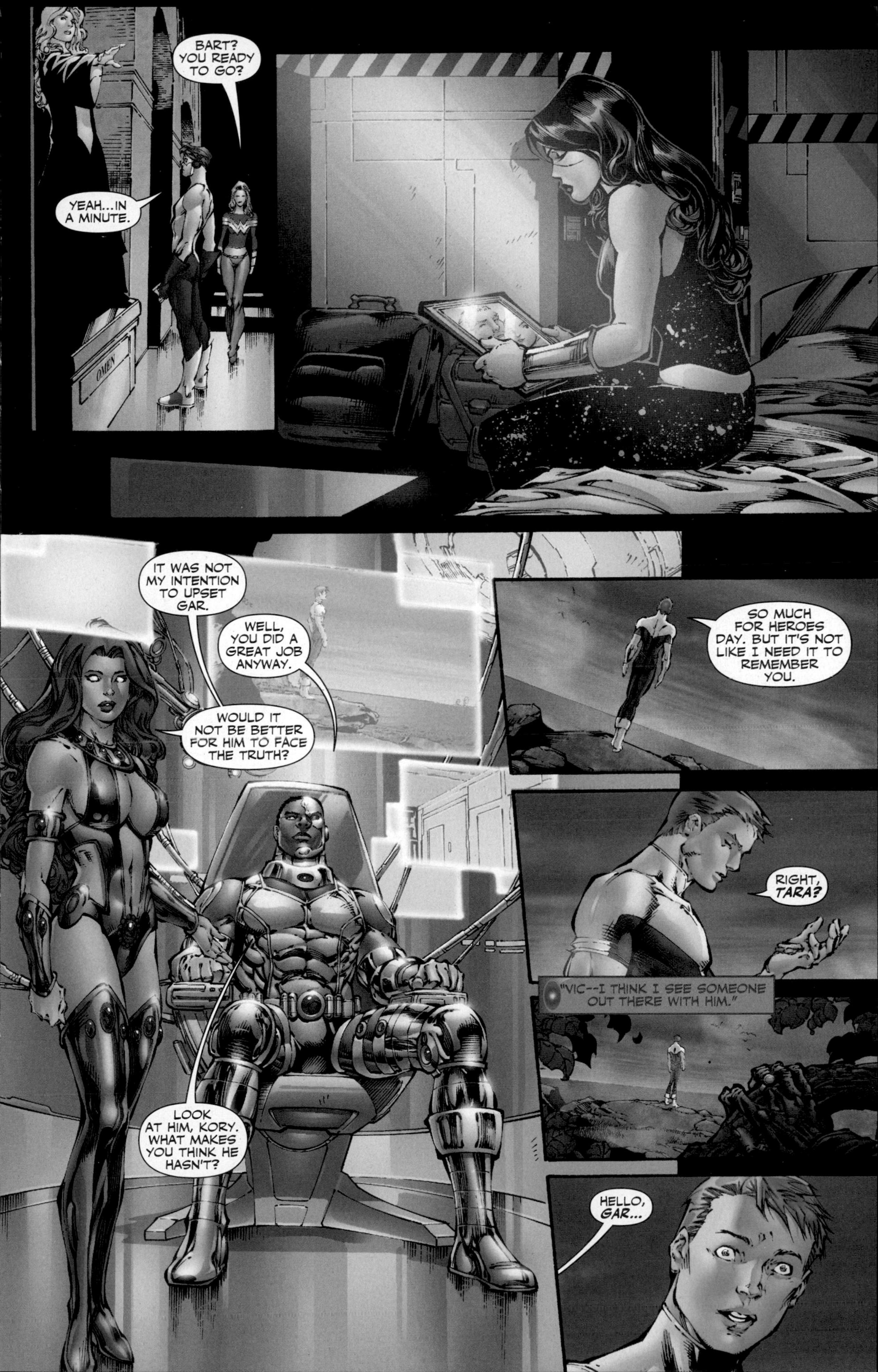
BART? YOU READY TO GO?
YEAH...IN A MINUTE.
IT WAS NOT MY INTENTION TO UPSET GAR.
WELL, YOU DID A GREAT JOB ANYWAY.
WOULD IT NOT BE BETTER FOR HIM TO FACE THE TRUTH?
LOOK AT HIM, KORY. WHAT MAKES YOU THINK HE HASN'T?
SO MUCH FOR HEROES DAY. BUT IT'S NOT LIKE I NEED IT TO REMEMBER YOU.
RIGHT, TARA?
"VIC--I THINK I SEE SOMEONE OUT THERE WITH HIM."
HELLO, GAR...

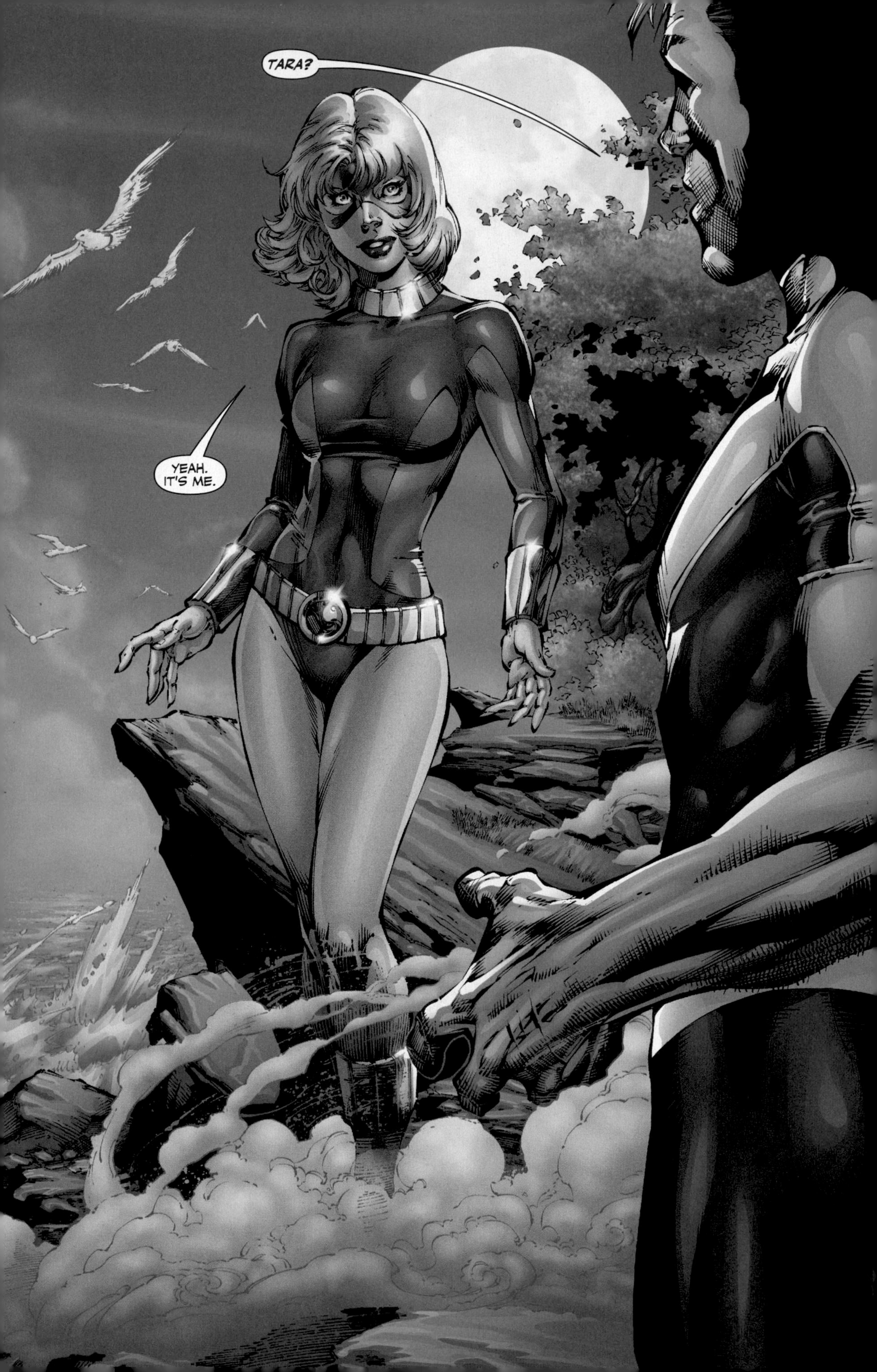
TARA?
YEAH. IT'S ME.

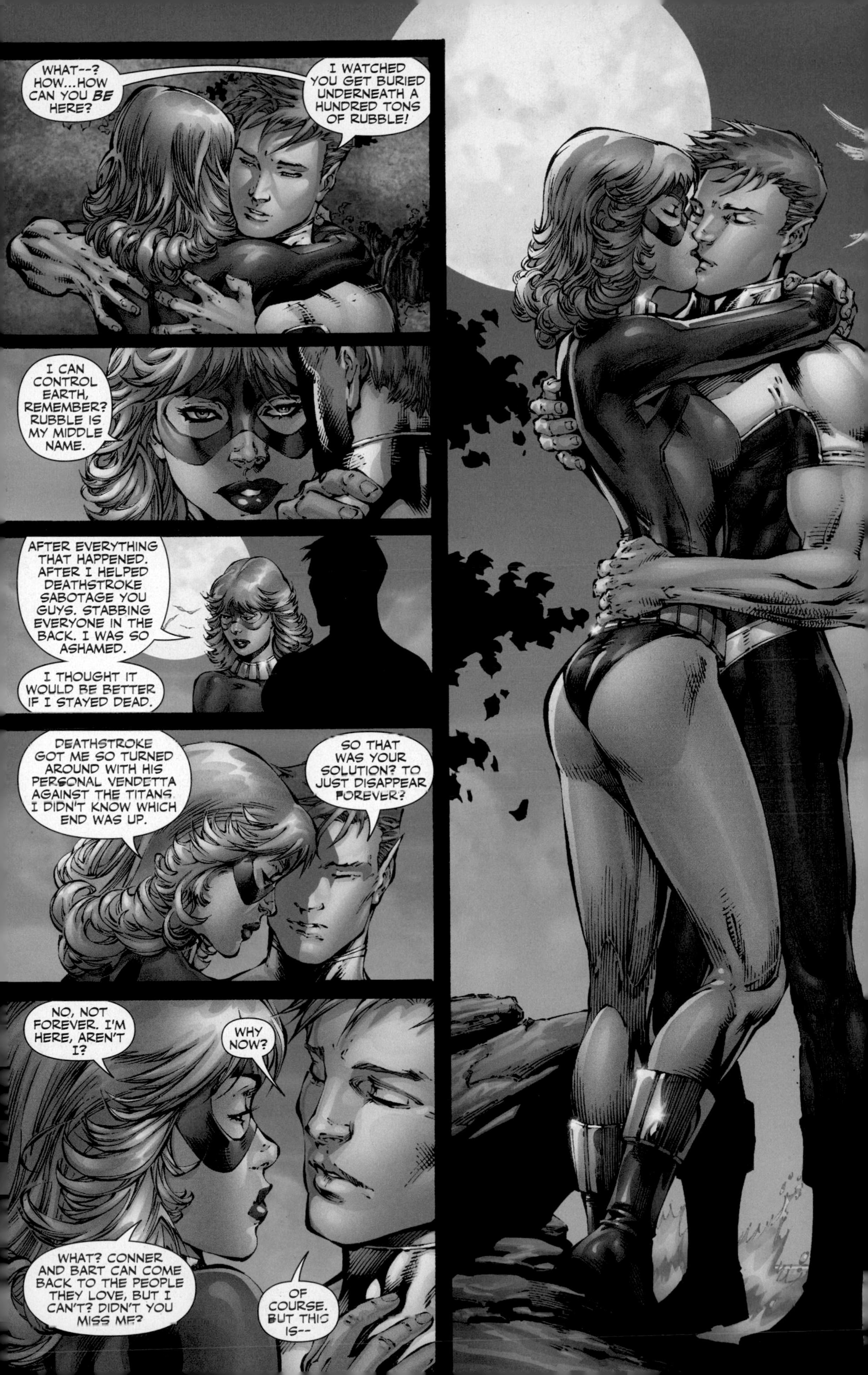
WHAT--? HOW...HOW CAN YOU BE HERE?
I WATCHED YOU GET BURIED UNDERNEATH A HUNDRED TONS OF RUBBLE!
I CAN CONTROL EARTH, REMEMBER? RUBBLE IS MY MIDDLE NAME.
AFTER EVERYTHING THAT HAPPENED. AFTER I HELPED DEATHSTROKE SABOTAGE YOU GUYS. STABBING EVERYONE IN THE BACK. I WAS SO ASHAMED.
I THOUGHT IT WOULD BE BETTER IF I STAYED DEAD.
DEATHSTROKE GOT ME SO TURNED AROUND WITH HIS PERSONAL VENDETTA AGAINST THE TITANS I DIDN'T KNOW WHICH END WAS UP.
SO THAT WAS YOUR SOLUTION? TO JUST DISAPPEAR FOREVER?
NO, NOT FOREVER. I'M HERE, AREN'T I?
WHY NOW?
WHAT? CONNER AND BART CAN COME BACK TO THE PEOPLE THEY LOVE, BUT I CAN'T? DIDN'T YOU MISS ME?
OF COURSE. BUT THIS IS--

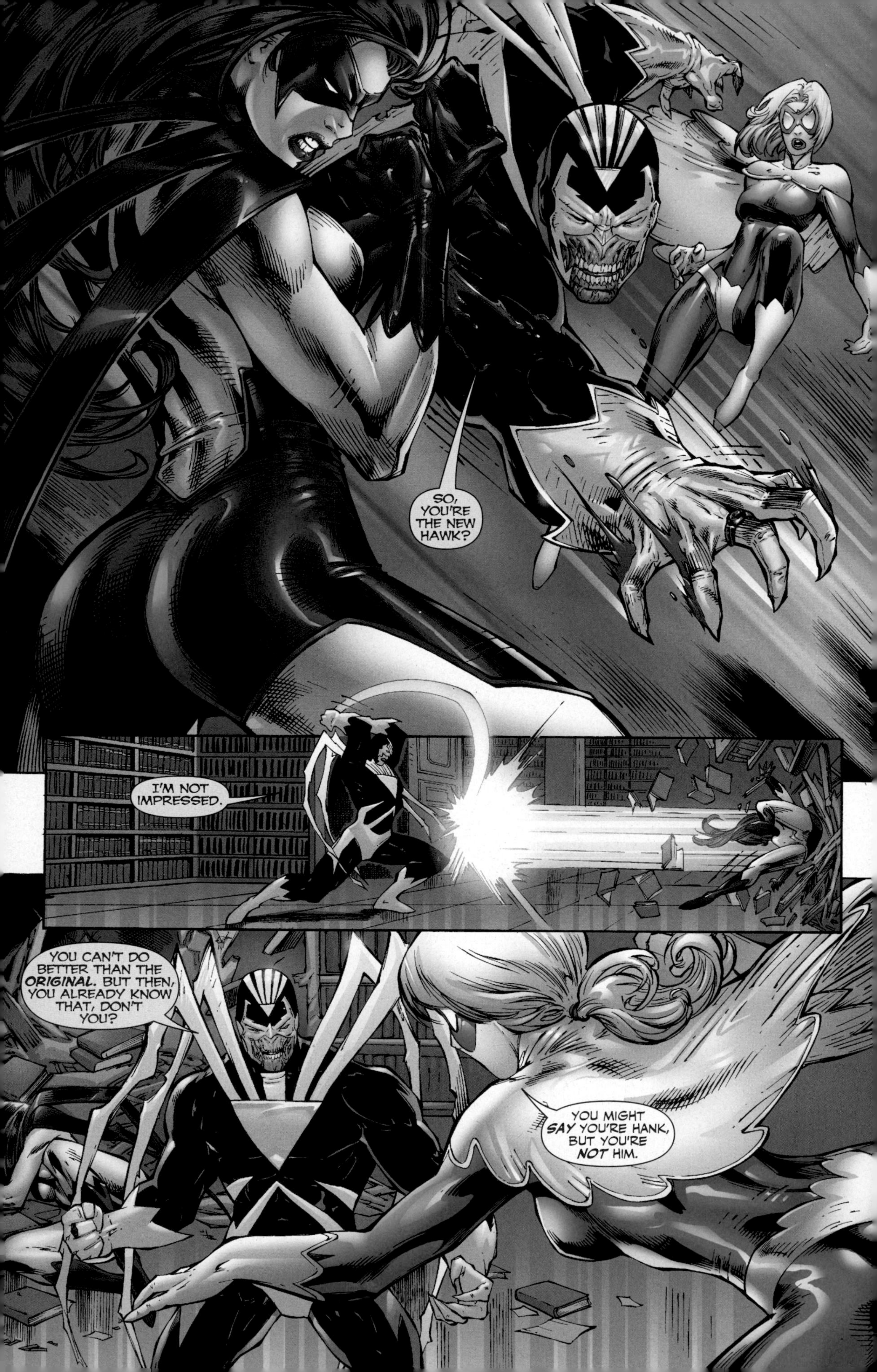
SO, YOU'RE THE NEW HAWK?
I'M NOT IMPRESSED.
YOU CAN'T DO BETTER THAN THE ORIGINAL. BUT THEN, YOU ALREADY KNOW THAT, DON'T YOU?
YOU MIGHT SAY YOU'RE HANK, BUT YOU'RE NOT HIM.

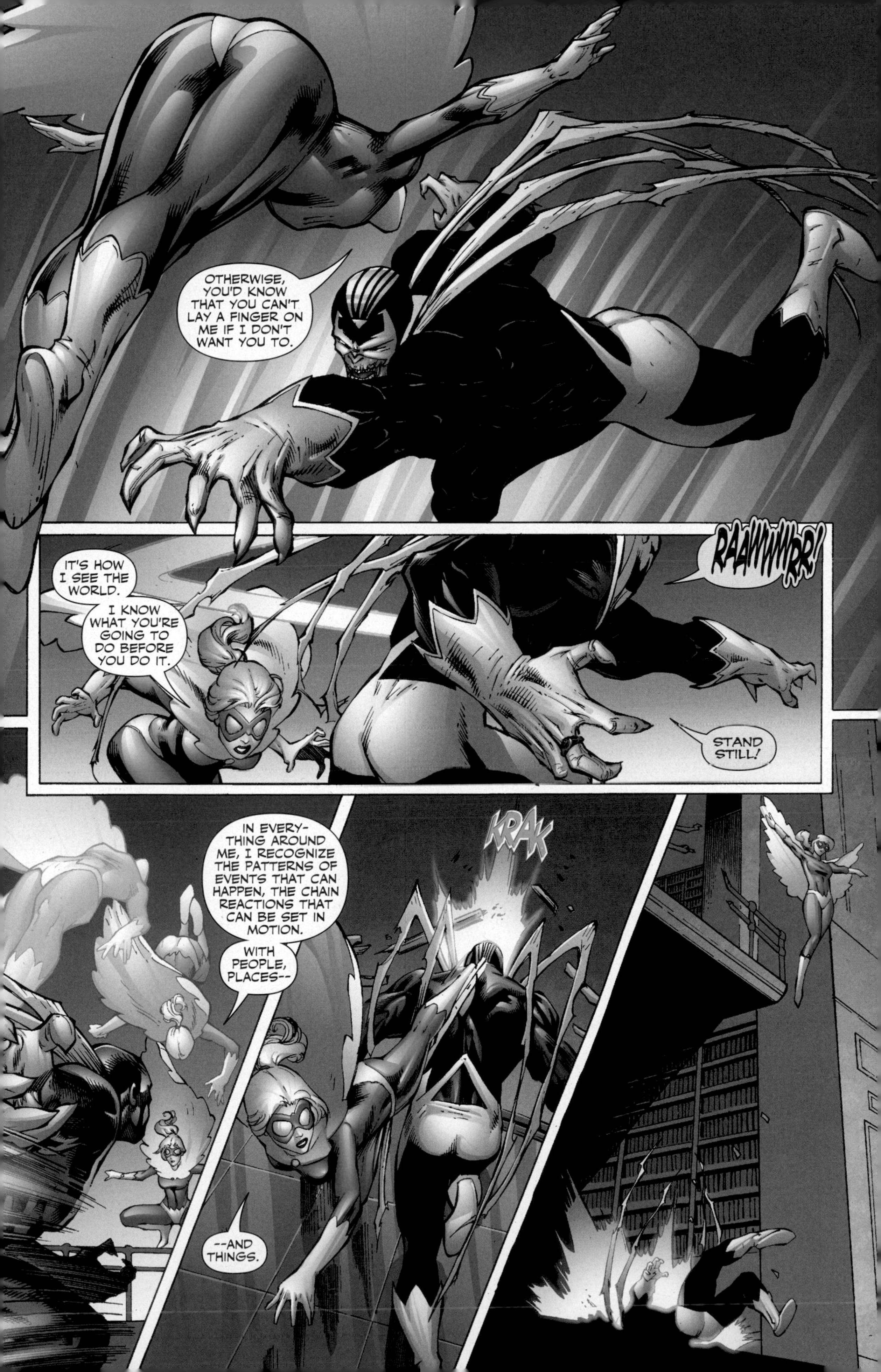
OTHERWISE, YOU'D KNOW THAT YOU CAN'T LAY A FINGER ON ME IF I DON'T WANT YOU TO.
IT'S HOW I SEE THE WORLD.
I KNOW WHAT YOU'RE GOING TO DO BEFORE YOU DO IT.
RAAWWWRR!
STAND STILL!
IN EVERY-THING AROUND ME, I RECOGNIZE THE PATTERNS OF EVENTS THAT CAN HAPPEN, THE CHAIN REACTIONS THAT CAN BE SET IN MOTION.
WITH PEOPLE, PLACES--
KRAK
--AND THINGS.

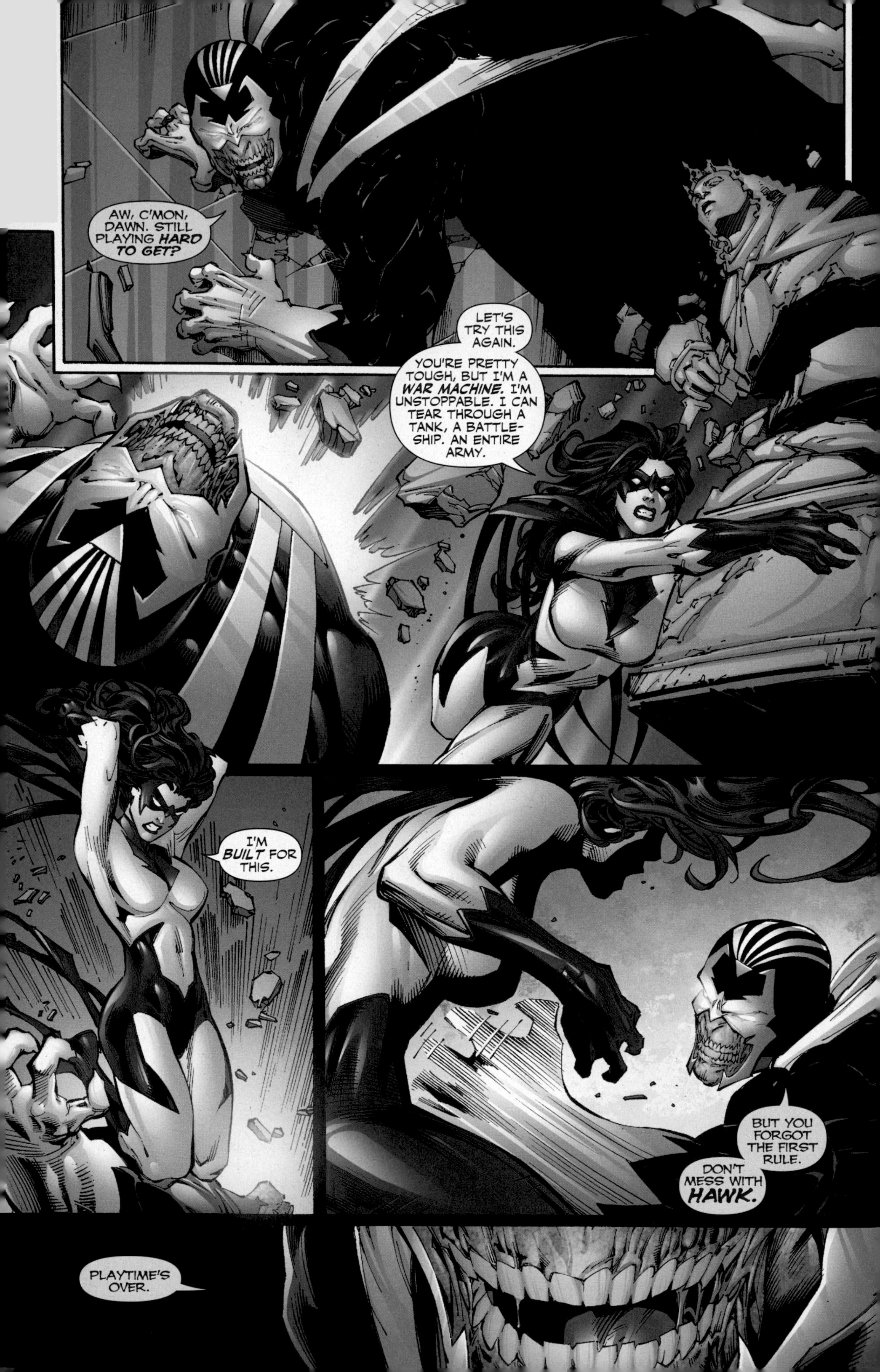
AW, C'MON, DAWN. STILL PLAYING HARD TO GET?
LET'S TRY THIS AGAIN.
YOU'RE PRETTY TOUGH, BUT I'M A WAR MACHINE. I'M UNSTOPPABLE. I CAN TEAR THROUGH A TANK, A BATTLE-SHIP. AN ENTIRE ARMY.
I'M BUILT FOR THIS.
BUT YOU FORGOT THE FIRST RULE.
DON'T MESS WITH HAWK.
PLAYTIME'S OVER.

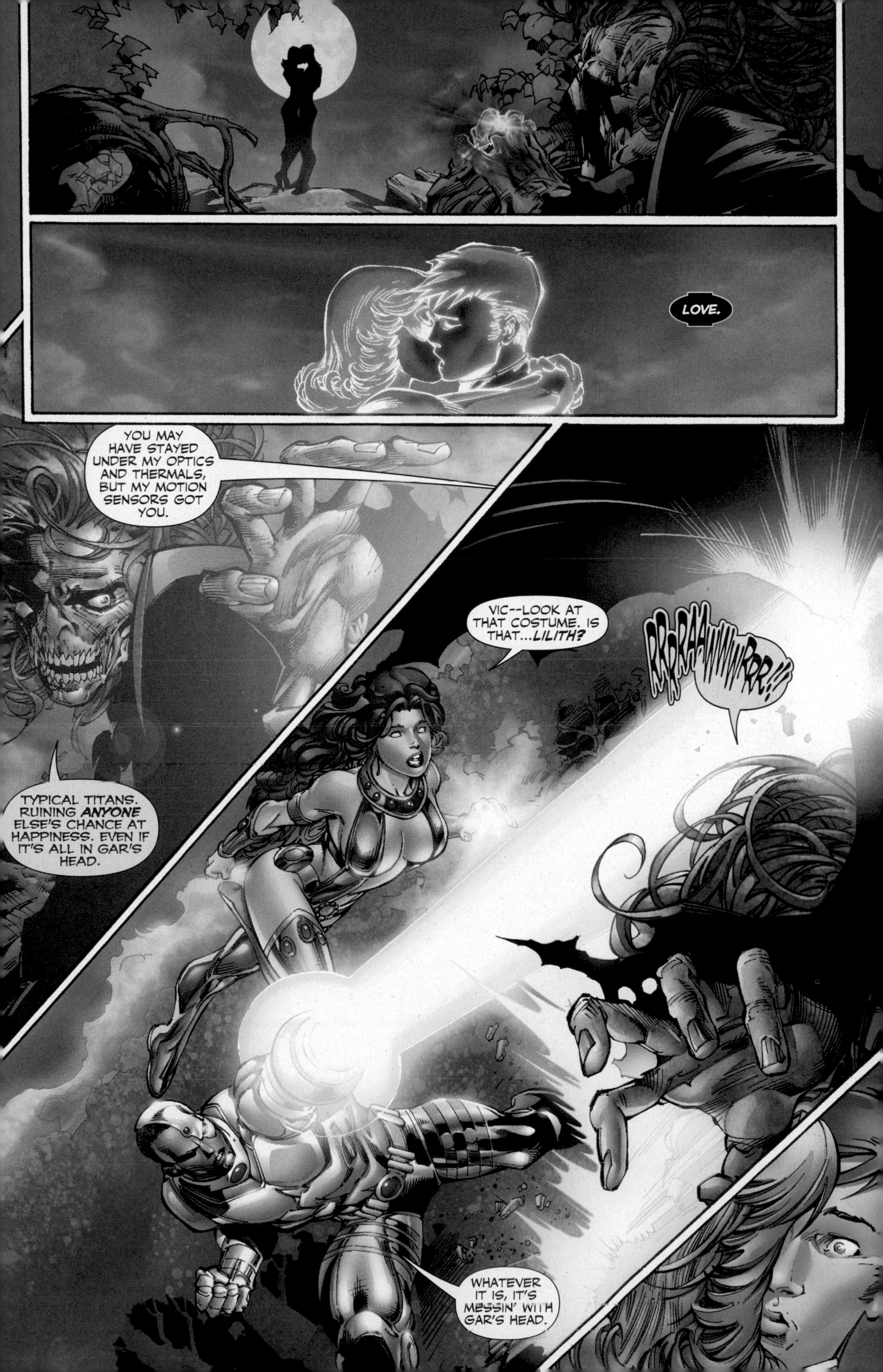
LOVE.
YOU MAY HAVE STAYED UNDER MY OPTICS AND THERMALS, BUT MY MOTION SENSORS GOT YOU.
TYPICAL TITANS. RUINING ANYONE ELSE'S CHANCE AT HAPPINESS. EVEN IF IT'S ALL IN GAR'S HEAD.
VIC--LOOK AT THAT COSTUME. IS THAT...LILITH?
RRRRAAWWWRRR!!
WHATEVER IT IS, IT'S MESSIN' WITH GAR'S HEAD.

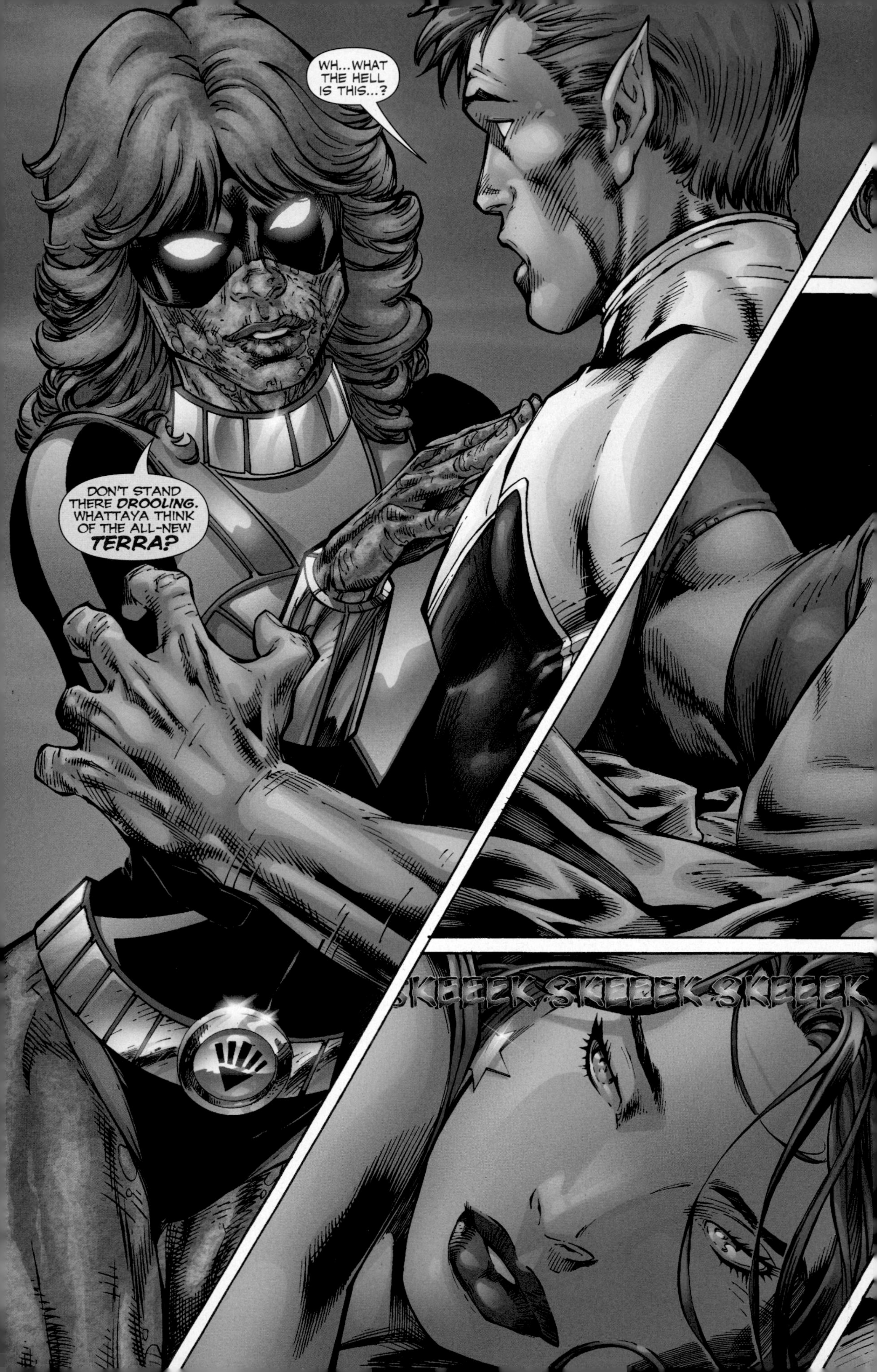
WH...WHAT THE HELL IS THIS...?
DON'T STAND THERE DROOLING. WHATTAYA THINK OF THE ALL-NEW TERRA?
SKEEEK SKEEEK SKEEEK

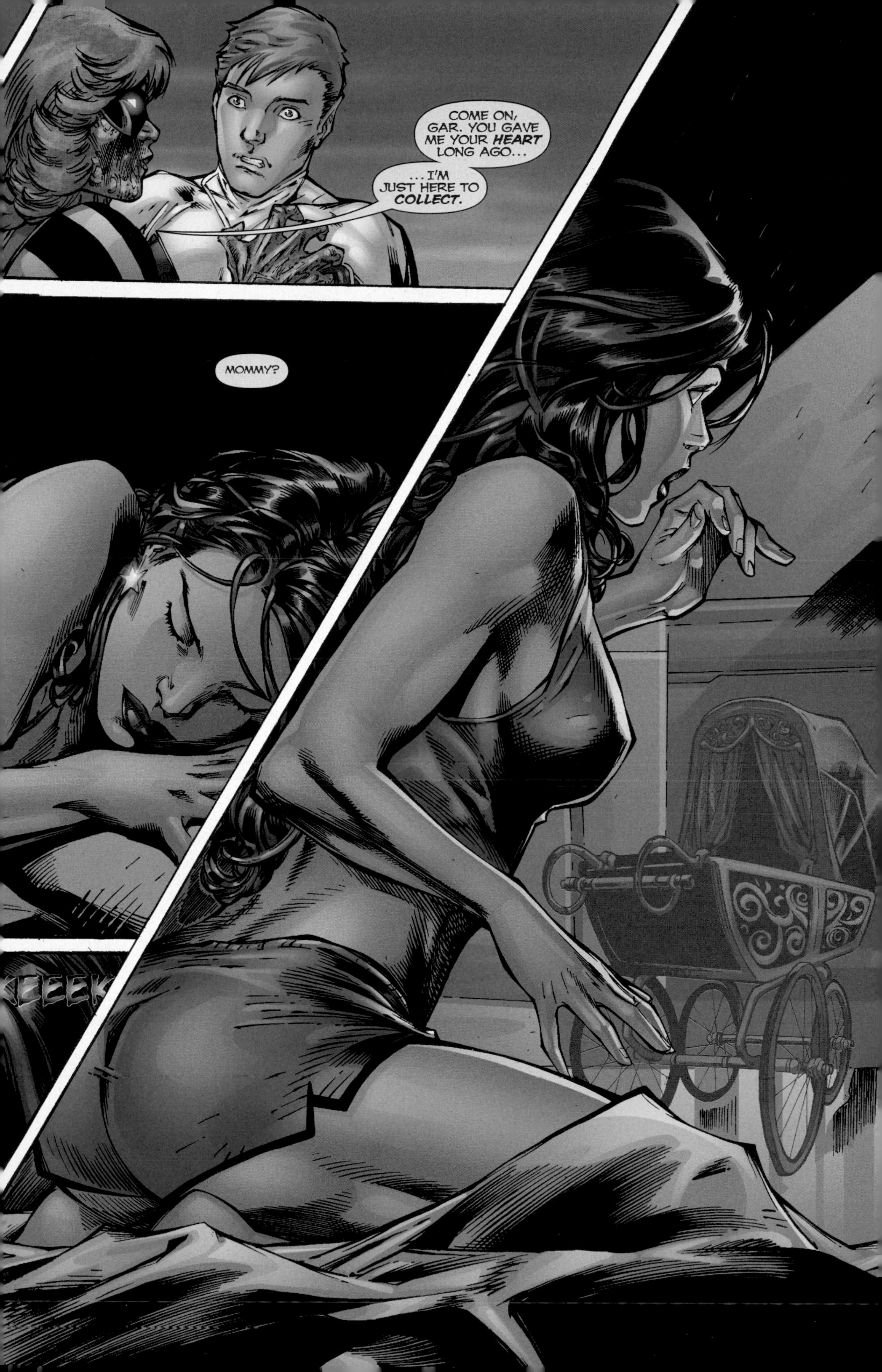
COME ON, GAR. YOU GAVE ME YOUR HEART LONG AGO...
...I'M JUST HERE TO COLLECT.
MOMMY?
KEEEK

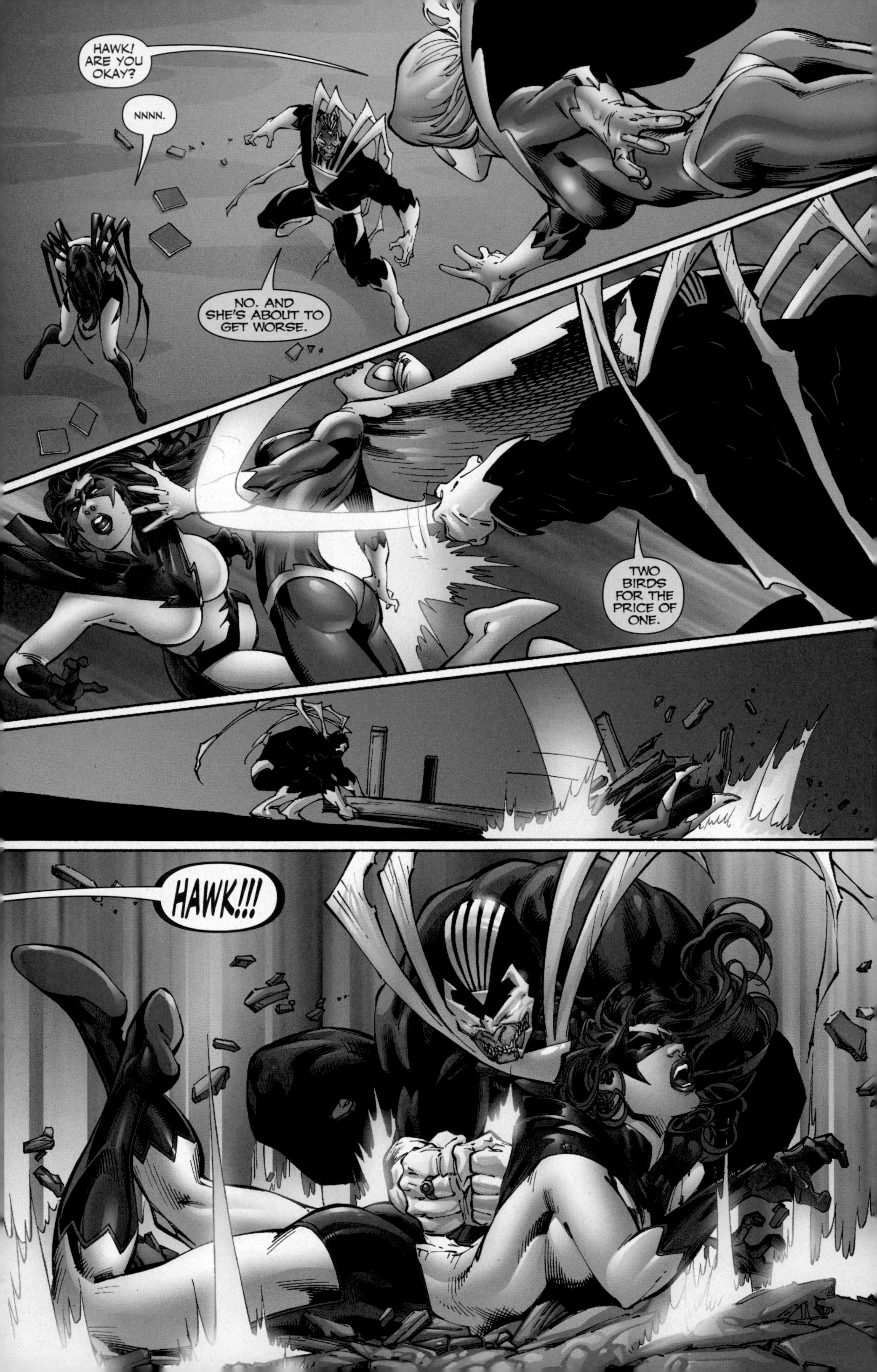
HAWK! ARE YOU OKAY?
NNNN.
NO. AND SHE'S ABOUT TO GET WORSE.
TWO BIRDS FOR THE PRICE OF ONE.
HAWK!!!

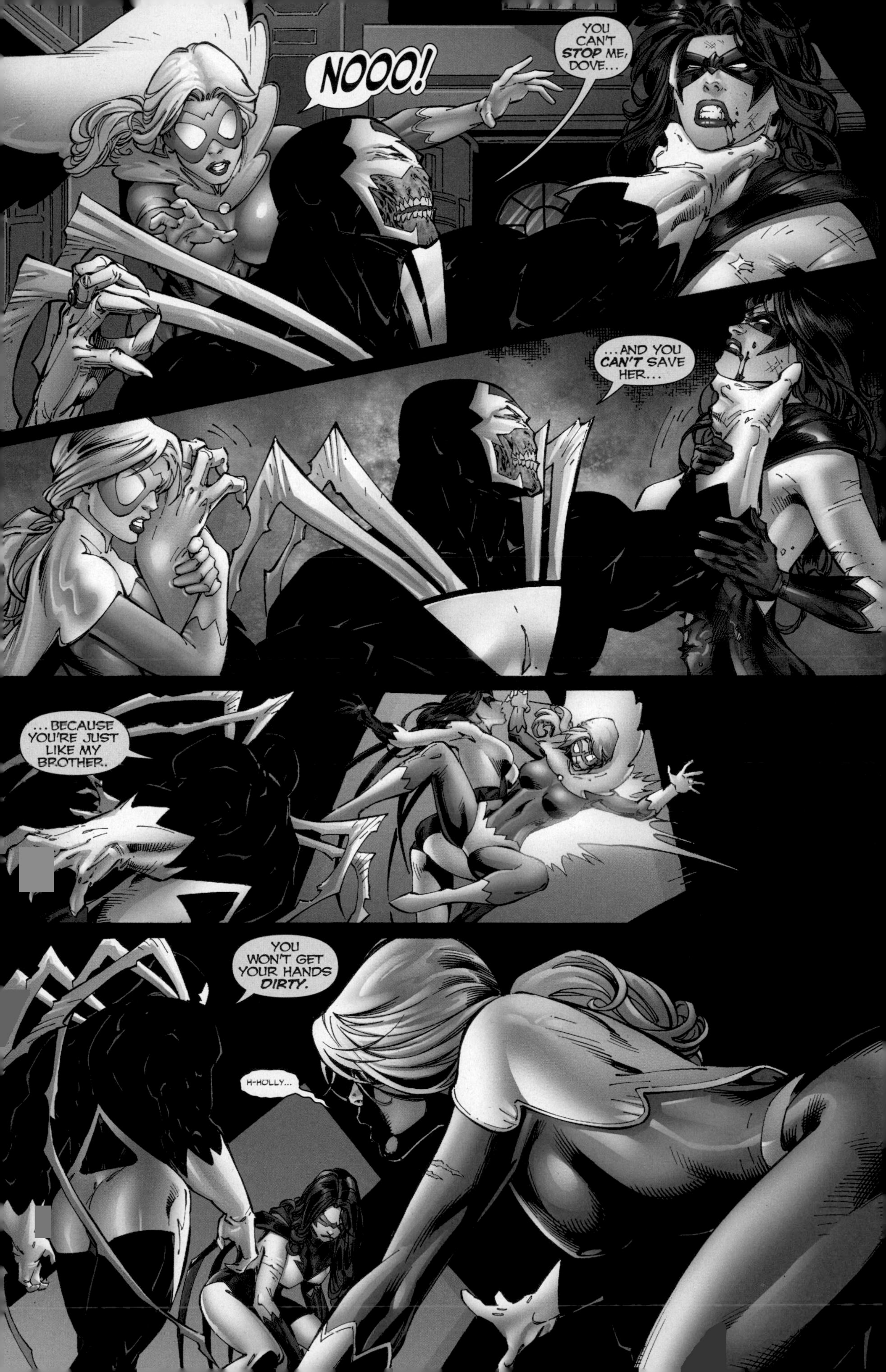
NOOO!
YOU CAN'T STOP ME, DOVE...
...AND YOU CAN'T SAVE HER...
...BECAUSE YOU'RE JUST LIKE MY BROTHER.
YOU WON'T GET YOUR HANDS DIRTY.
H-HOLLY...

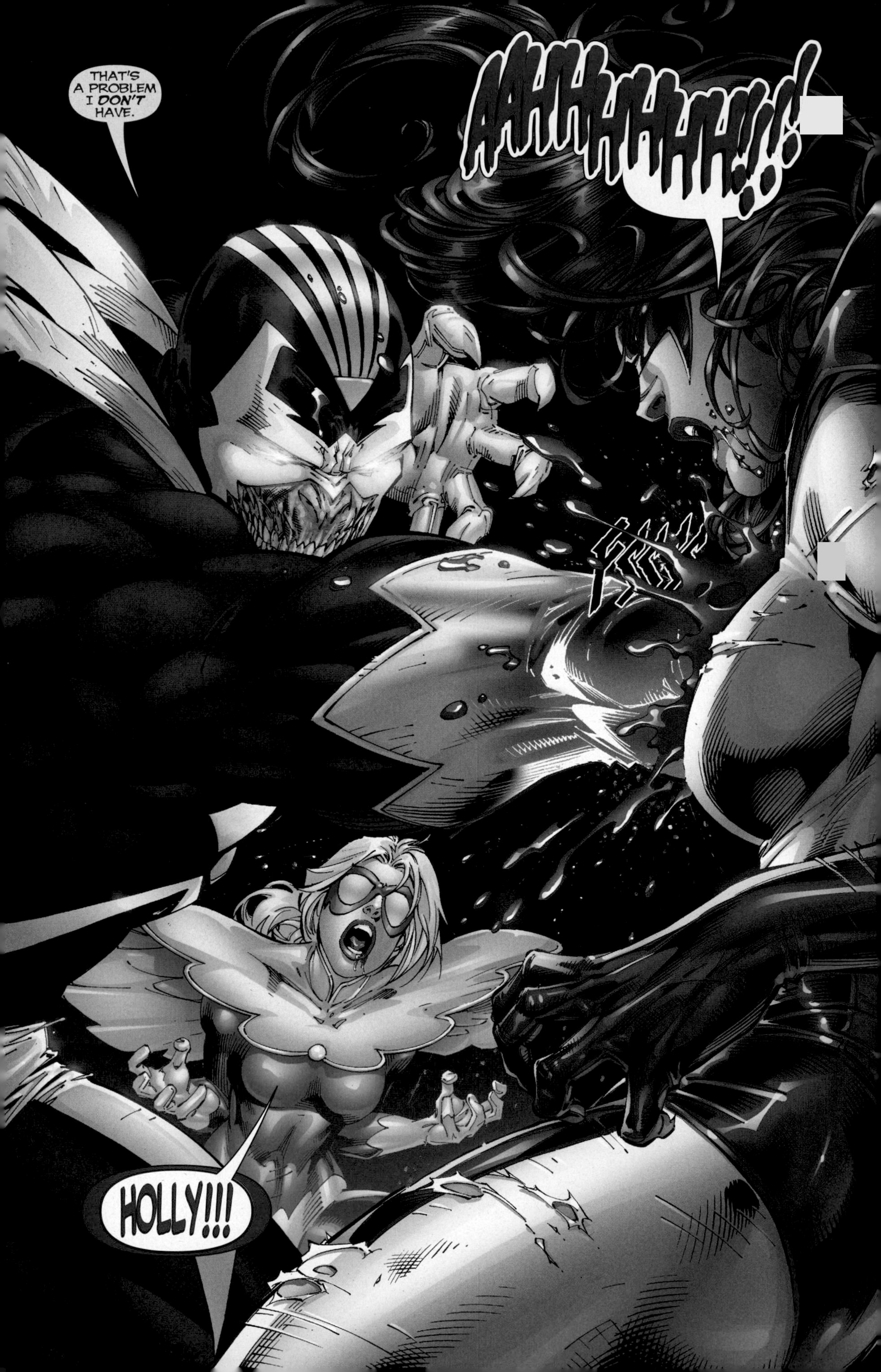
THAT'S A PROBLEM I DON'T HAVE.
AAHHHHHHH!!!
HOLLY!!!

BLACKEST NIGHT: TITANS 2
Cover by Ed Benes and
Rob Hunter with Pete Pantazis

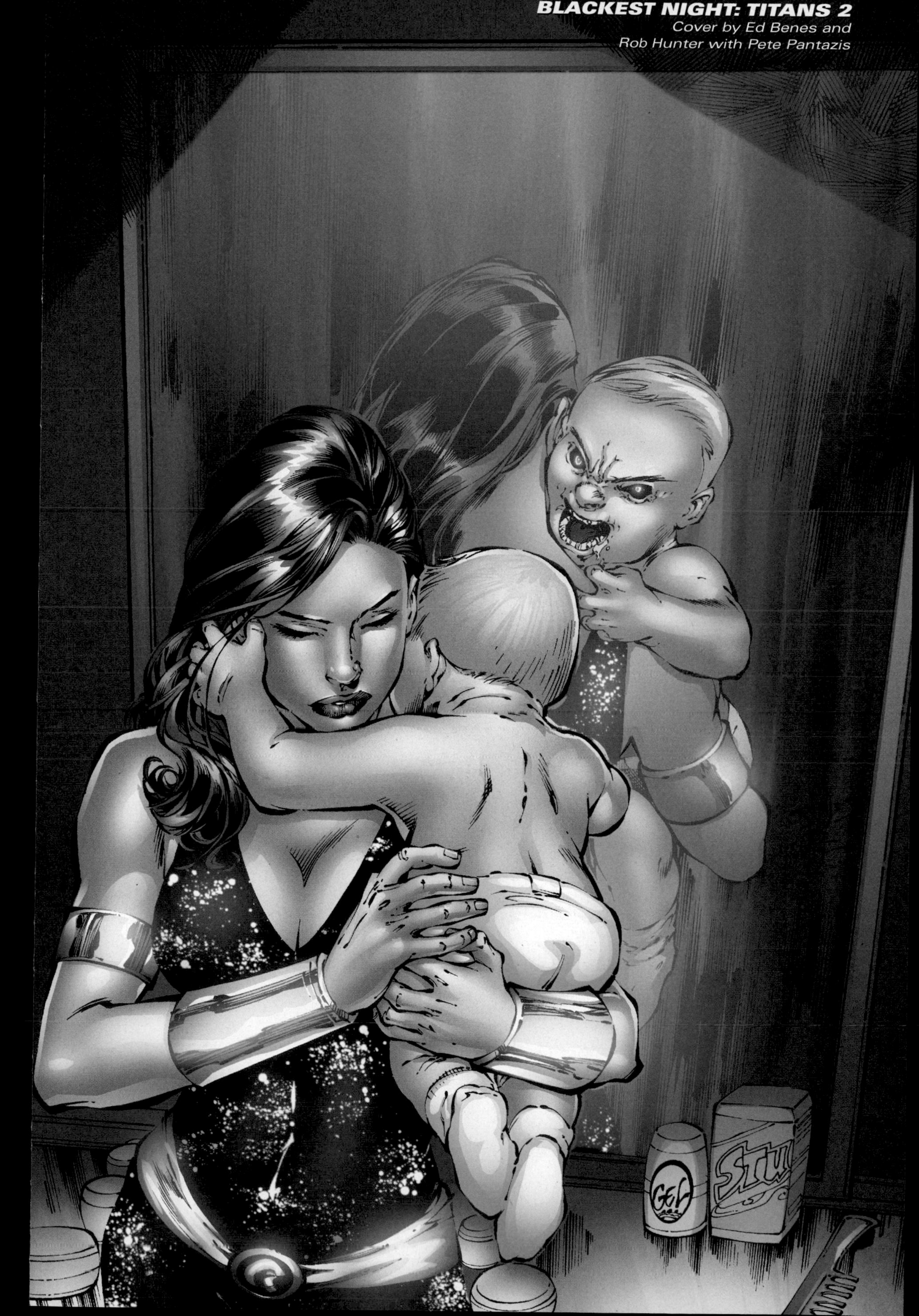
GEL

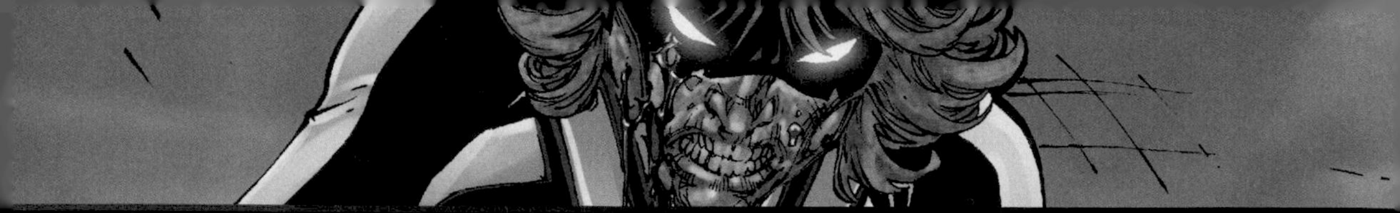

BITE THE HAND THAT FEEDS

J.T. KRUL
WRITER

ED BENES
PENCILS

SCOTT WILLIAMS
ED BENES
INKS

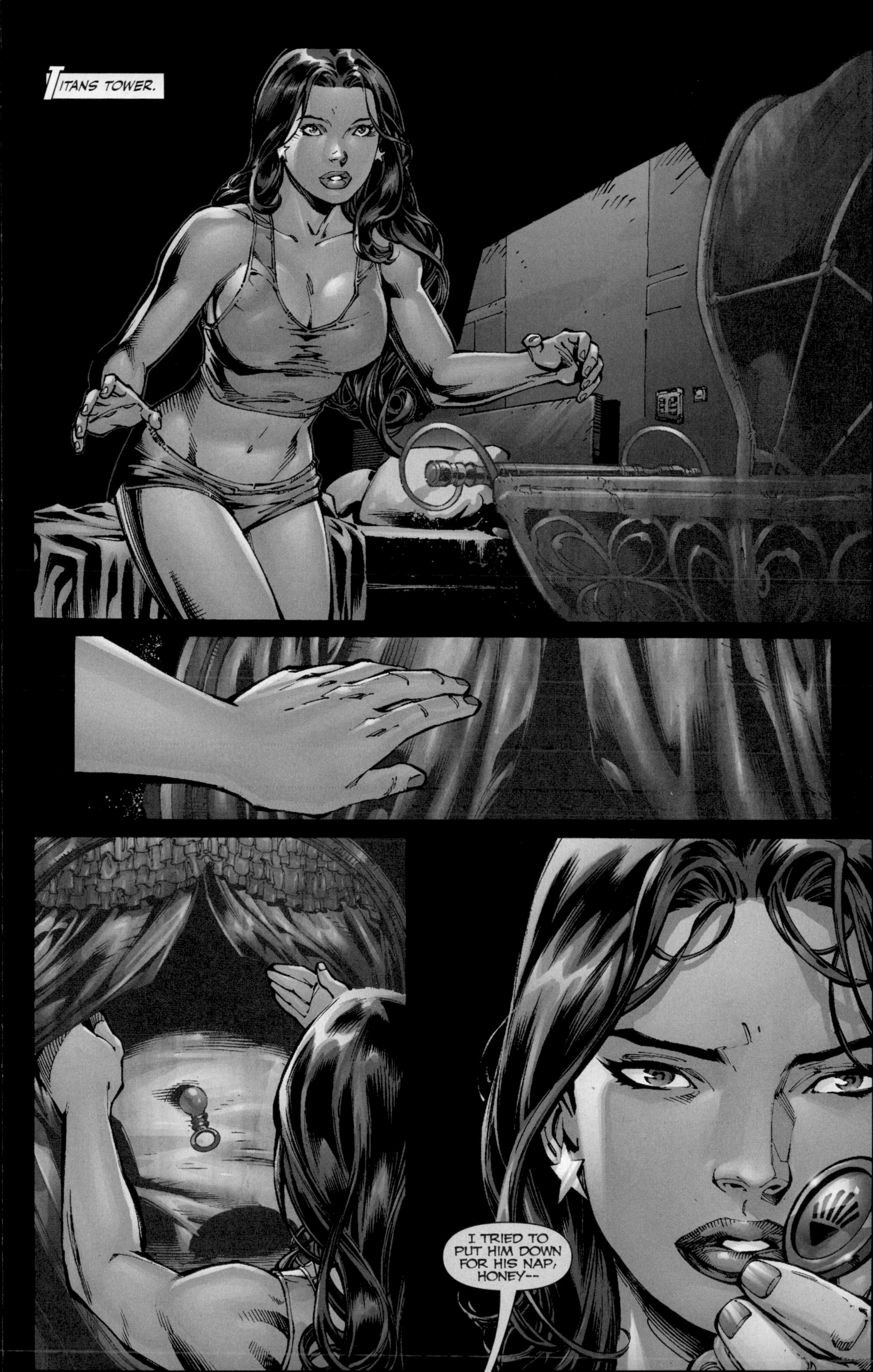
TITANS TOWER.
I TRIED TO PUT HIM DOWN FOR HIS NAP, HONEY--

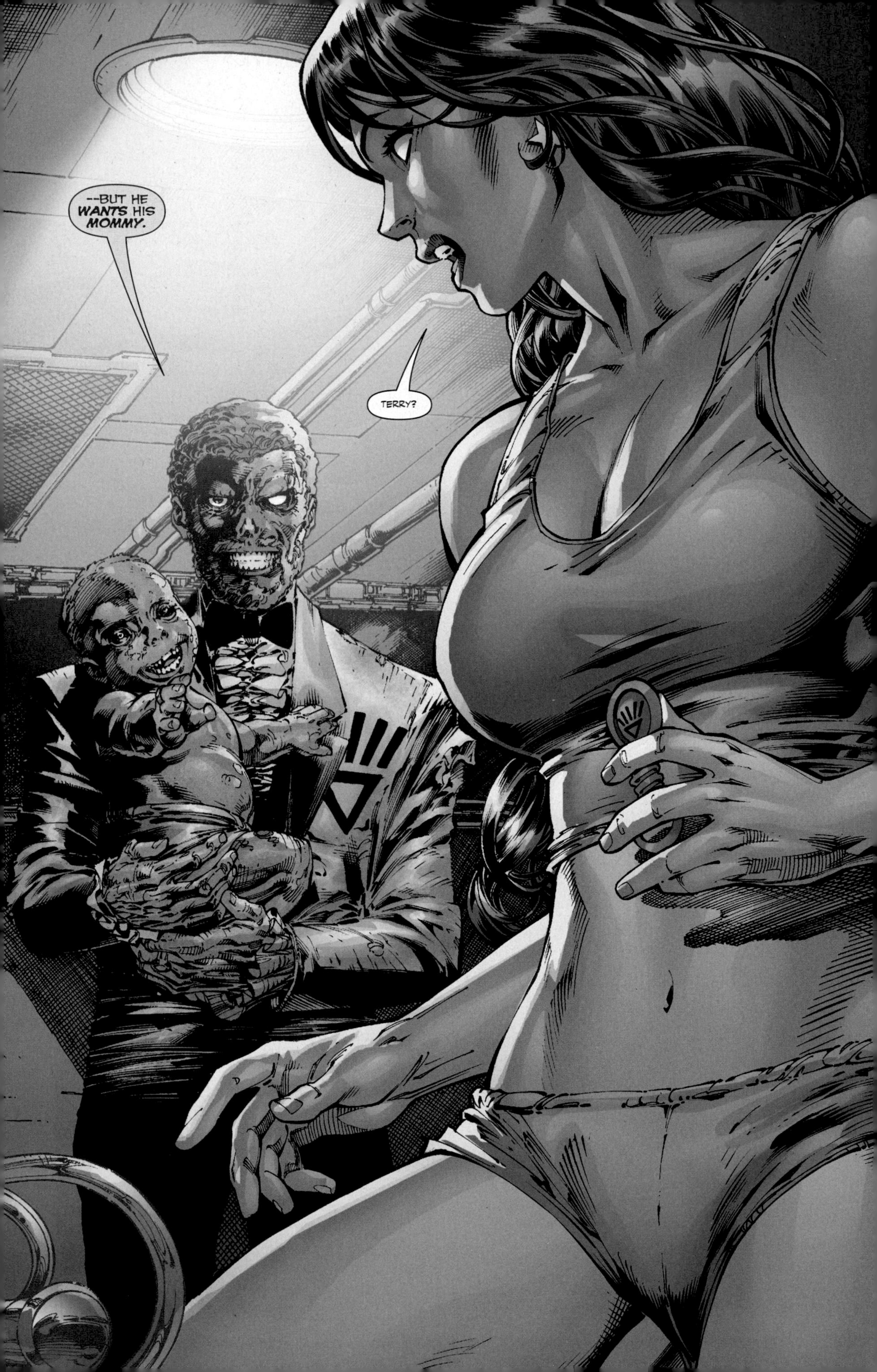
--BUT HE WANTS HIS MOMMY.
TERRY?

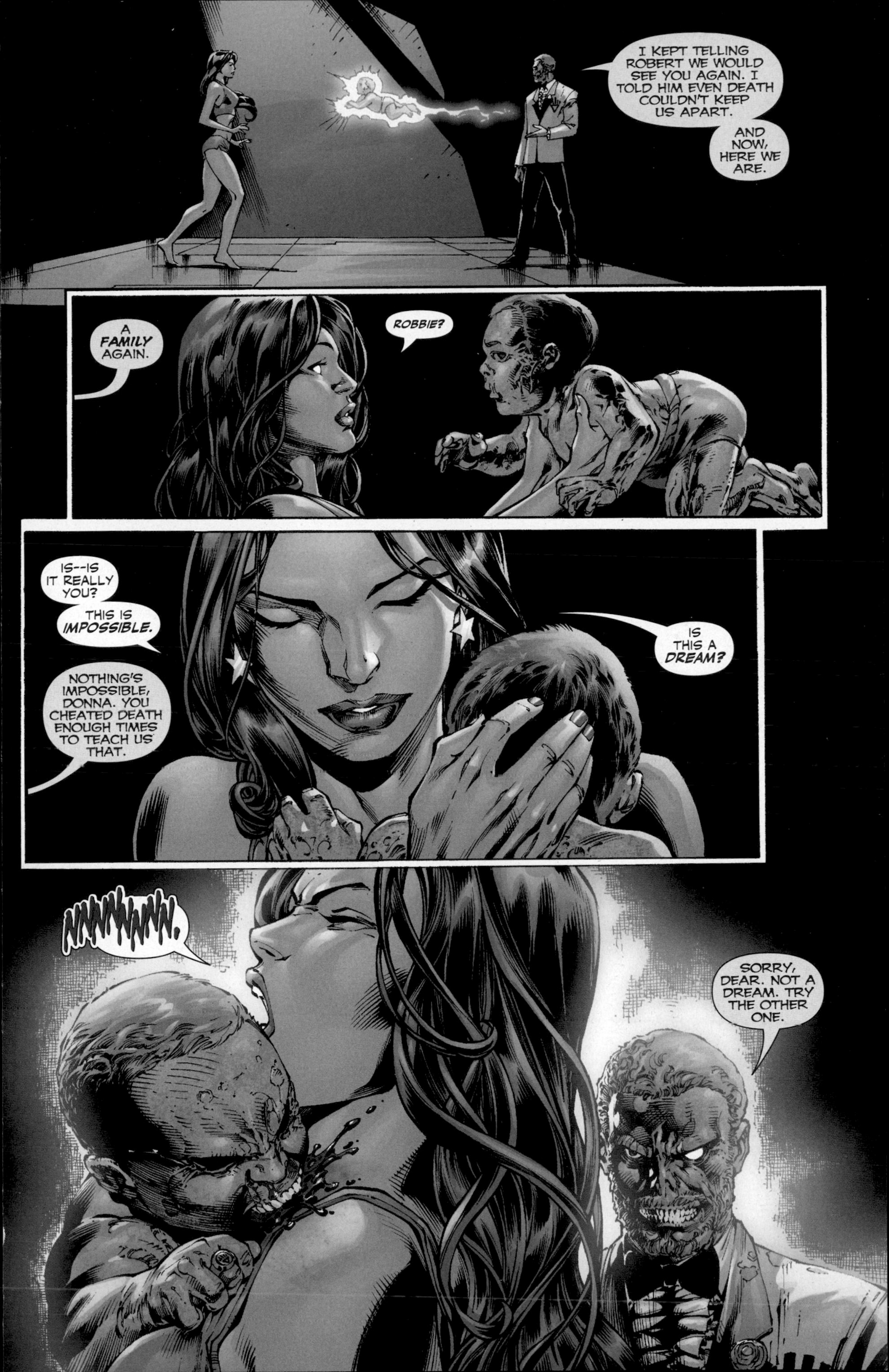
I KEPT TELLING ROBERT WE WOULD SEE YOU AGAIN. I TOLD HIM EVEN DEATH COULDN'T KEEP US APART.
AND NOW, HERE WE ARE.
A *FAMILY* AGAIN.
ROBBIE?
IS--IS IT REALLY YOU?
THIS IS *IMPOSSIBLE.*
NOTHING'S IMPOSSIBLE, DONNA. YOU CHEATED DEATH ENOUGH TIMES TO TEACH US THAT.
IS THIS A *DREAM?*
NNNNNNN.
SORRY, DEAR. NOT A DREAM. TRY THE OTHER ONE.

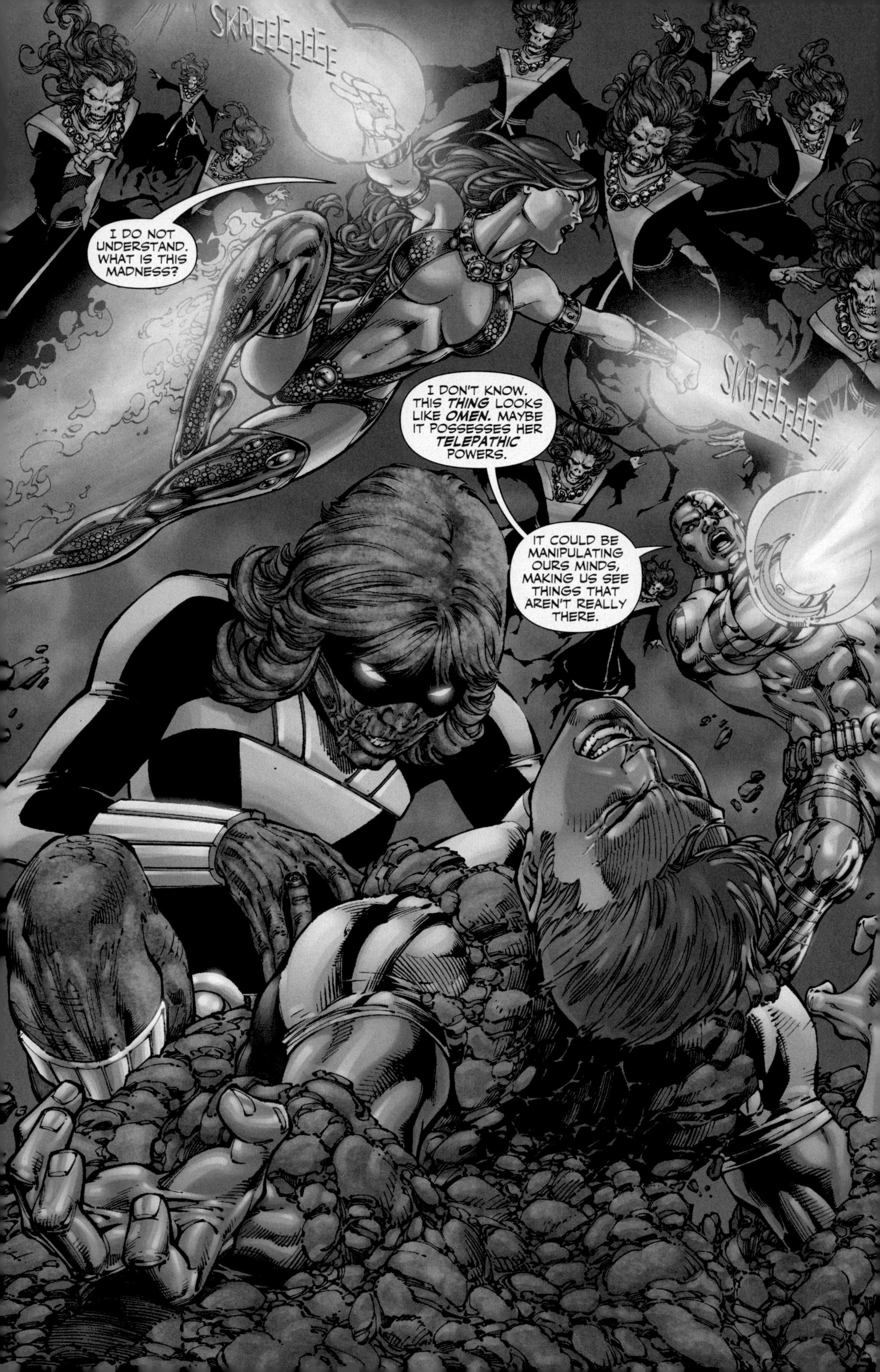
SKREEEEEEEE
I DO NOT UNDERSTAND. WHAT IS THIS MADNESS?
I DON'T KNOW. THIS *THING* LOOKS LIKE *OMEN.* MAYBE IT POSSESSES HER *TELEPATHIC* POWERS.
IT COULD BE MANIPULATING OURS MINDS, MAKING US SEE THINGS THAT AREN'T REALLY THERE.
SKREEEEEEEE

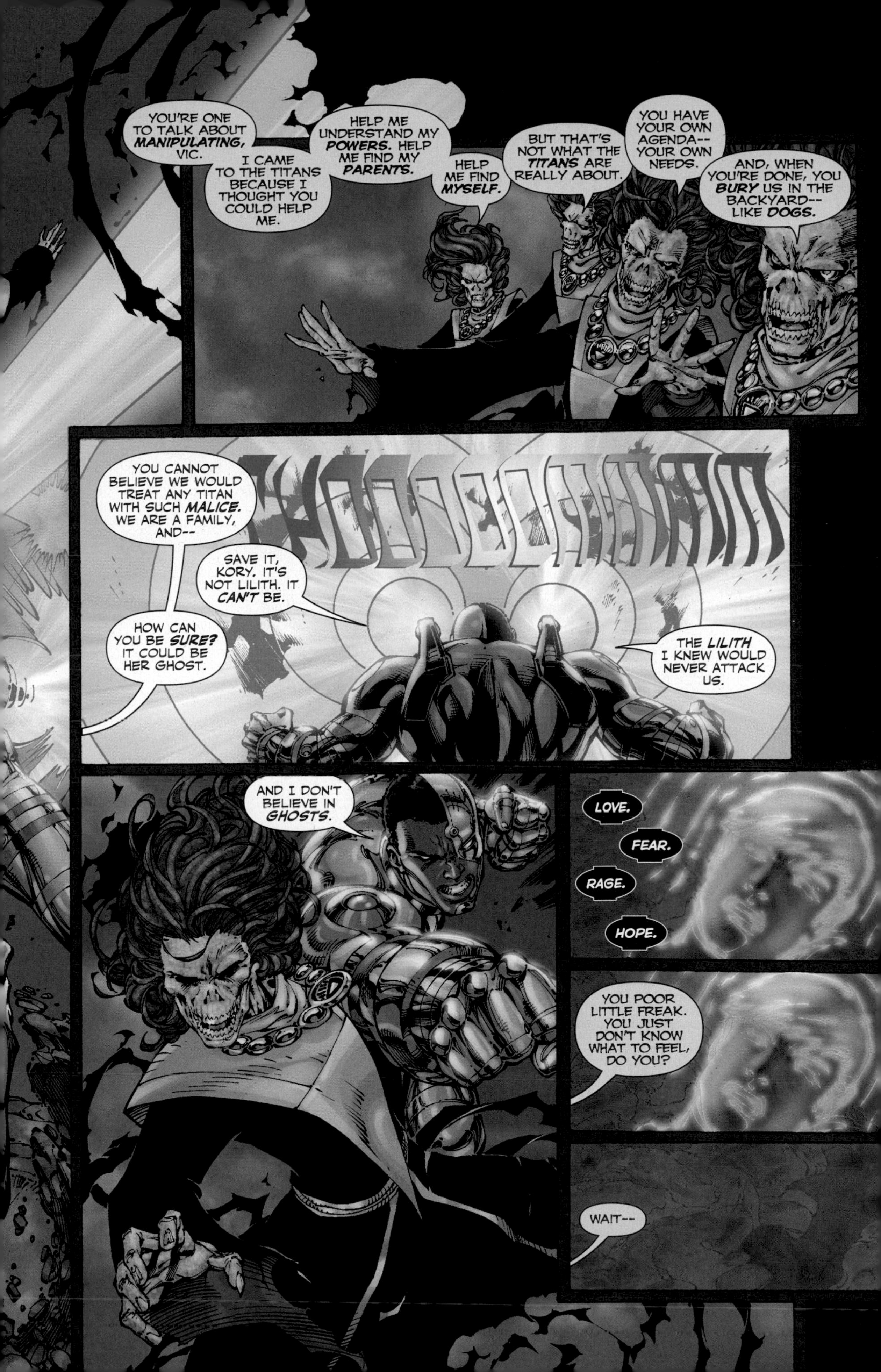
YOU'RE ONE TO TALK ABOUT MANIPULATING, VIC.
I CAME TO THE TITANS BECAUSE I THOUGHT YOU COULD HELP ME.
HELP ME UNDERSTAND MY POWERS. HELP ME FIND MY PARENTS.
HELP ME FIND MYSELF.
BUT THAT'S NOT WHAT THE TITANS ARE REALLY ABOUT.
YOU HAVE YOUR OWN AGENDA-- YOUR OWN NEEDS.
AND, WHEN YOU'RE DONE, YOU BURY US IN THE BACKYARD-- LIKE DOGS.
YOU CANNOT BELIEVE WE WOULD TREAT ANY TITAN WITH SUCH MALICE. WE ARE A FAMILY, AND--
CHOOOOOMMMMM
SAVE IT, KORY. IT'S NOT LILITH. IT CAN'T BE.
HOW CAN YOU BE SURE? IT COULD BE HER GHOST.
THE LILITH I KNEW WOULD NEVER ATTACK US.
AND I DON'T BELIEVE IN GHOSTS.
LOVE.
FEAR.
RAGE.
HOPE.
YOU POOR LITTLE FREAK. YOU JUST DON'T KNOW WHAT TO FEEL, DO YOU?
WAIT--

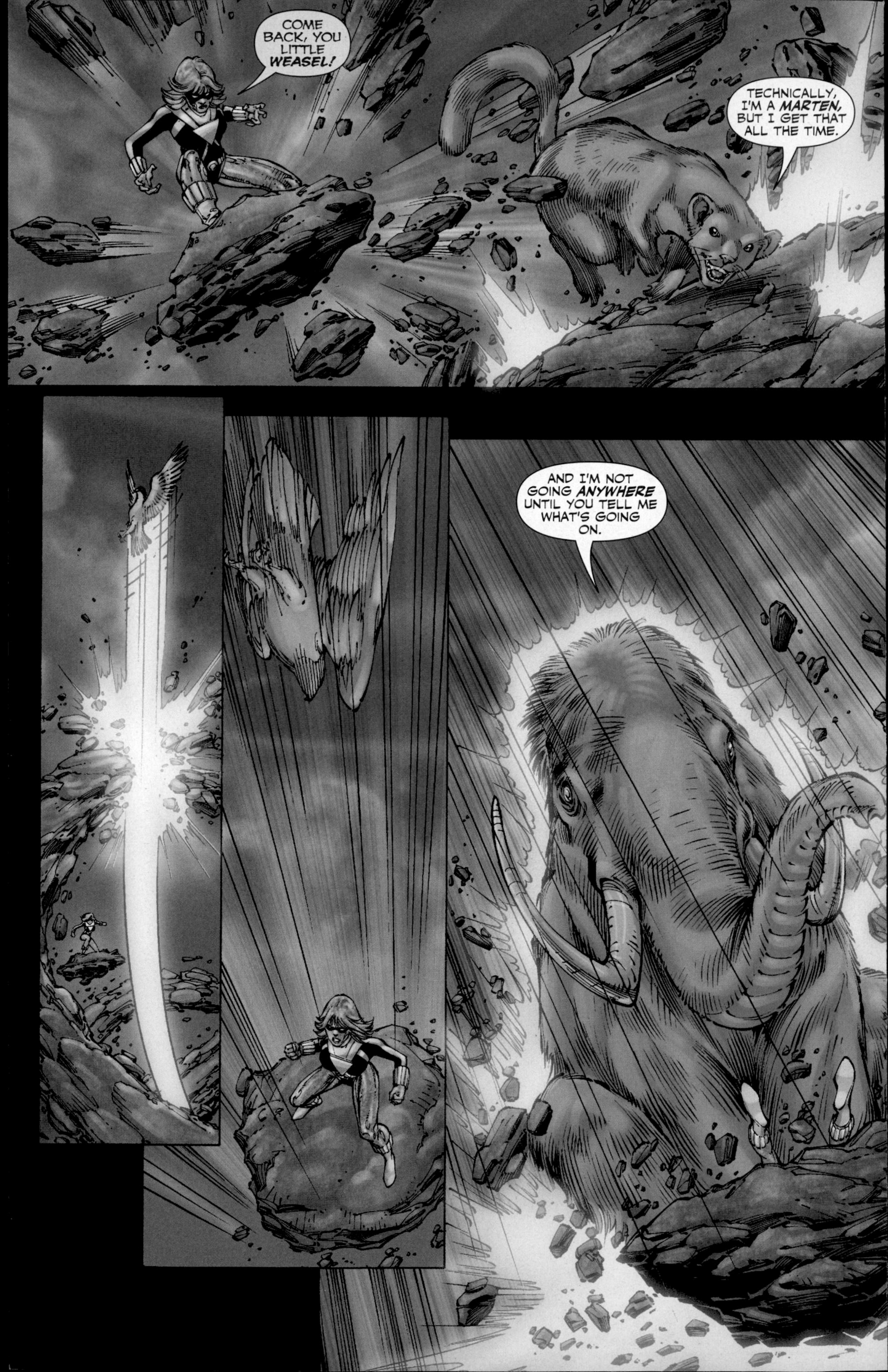
COME BACK, YOU LITTLE WEASEL!
TECHNICALLY, I'M A MARTEN, BUT I GET THAT ALL THE TIME.
AND I'M NOT GOING ANYWHERE UNTIL YOU TELL ME WHAT'S GOING ON.

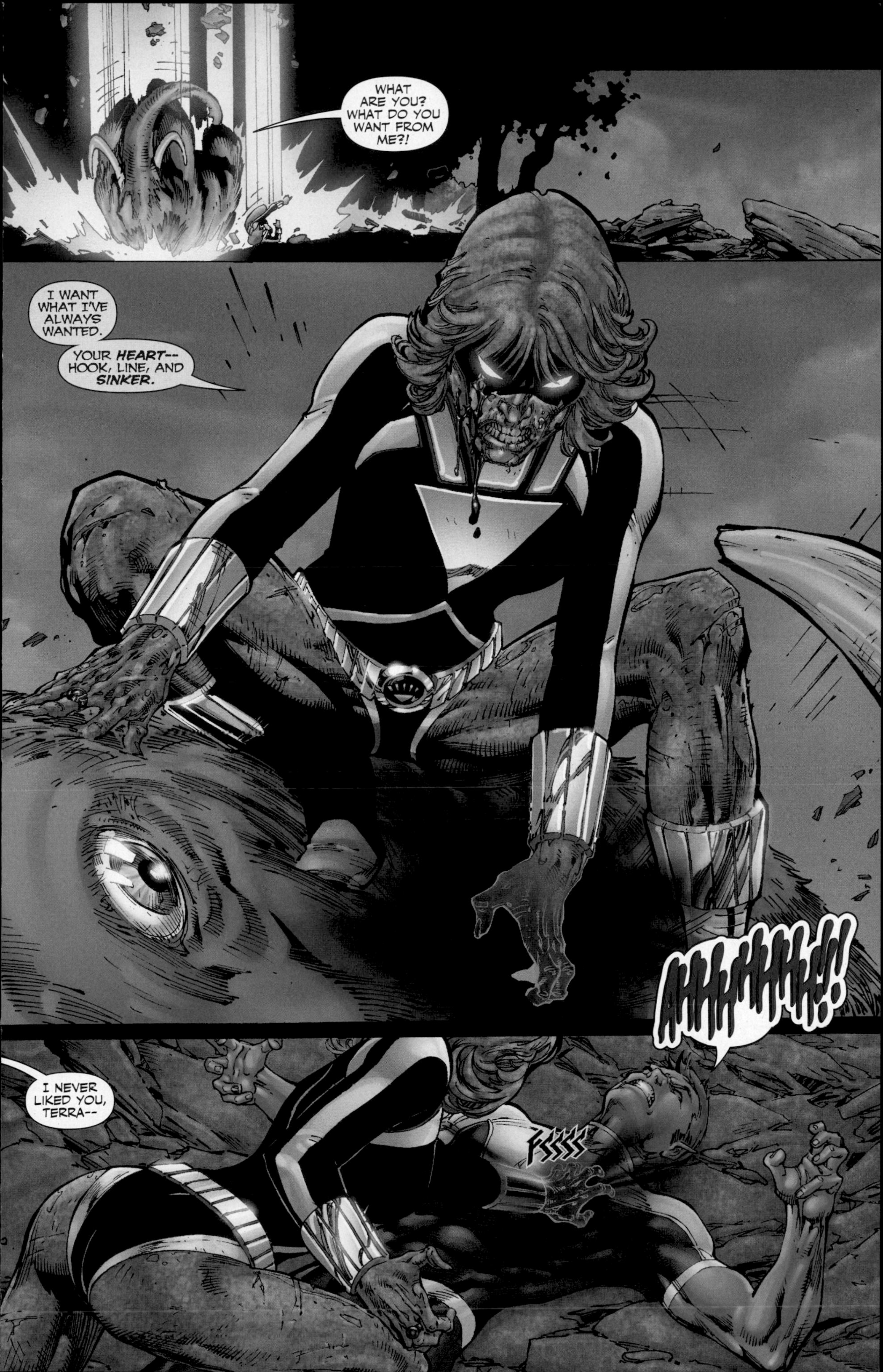
WHAT ARE YOU? WHAT DO YOU WANT FROM ME?!
I WANT WHAT I'VE ALWAYS WANTED.
YOUR HEART-- HOOK, LINE, AND SINKER.
AHHHHHHH!!
I NEVER LIKED YOU, TERRA--
FSSSS

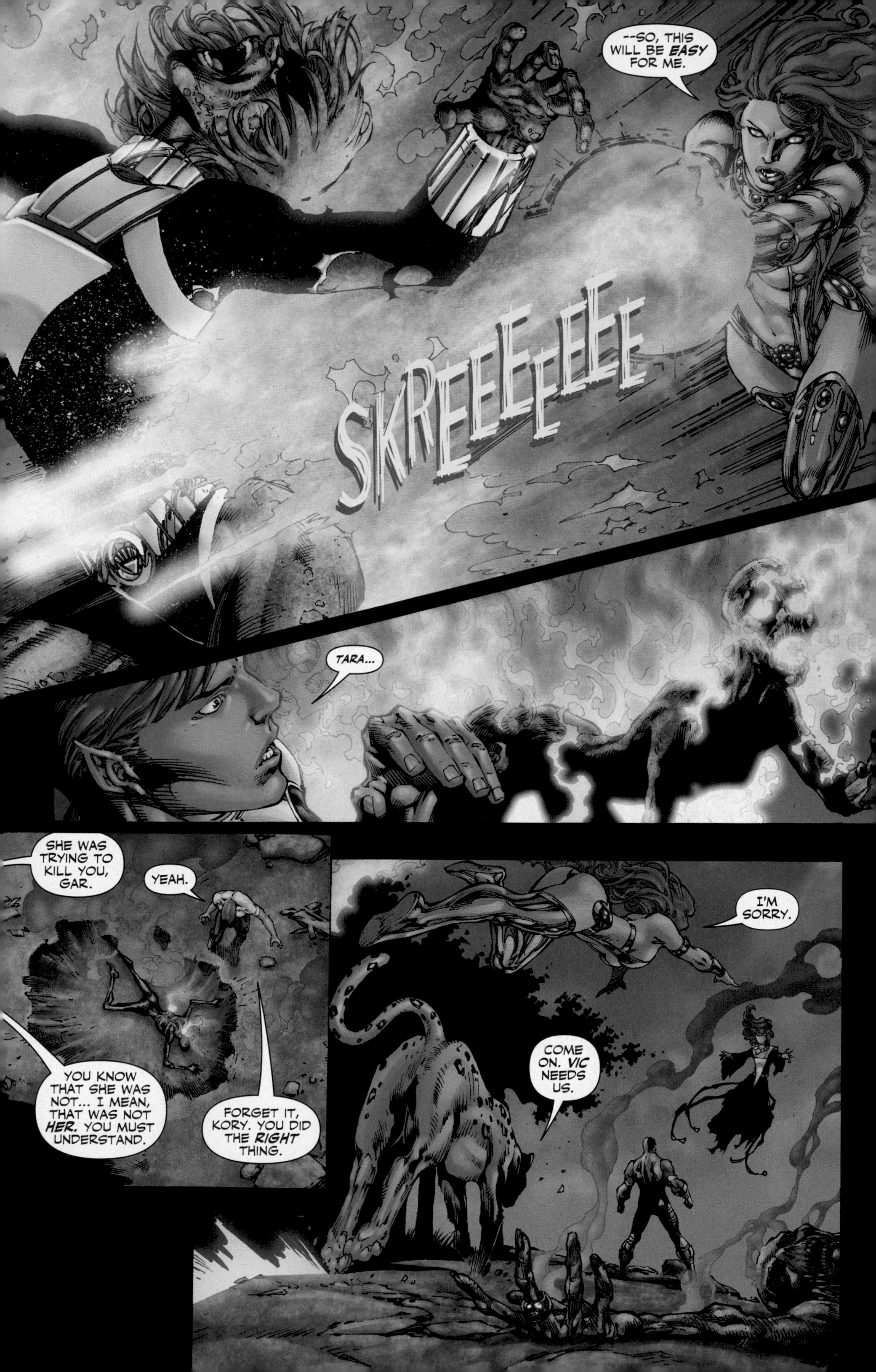
--SO, THIS WILL BE *EASY* FOR ME.
SKREEEEEEE
TARA...
SHE WAS TRYING TO KILL YOU, GAR.
YEAH.
YOU KNOW THAT SHE WAS NOT... I MEAN, THAT WAS NOT *HER*. YOU MUST UNDERSTAND.
FORGET IT, KORY. YOU DID THE *RIGHT* THING.
I'M SORRY.
COME ON. *VIC* NEEDS US.

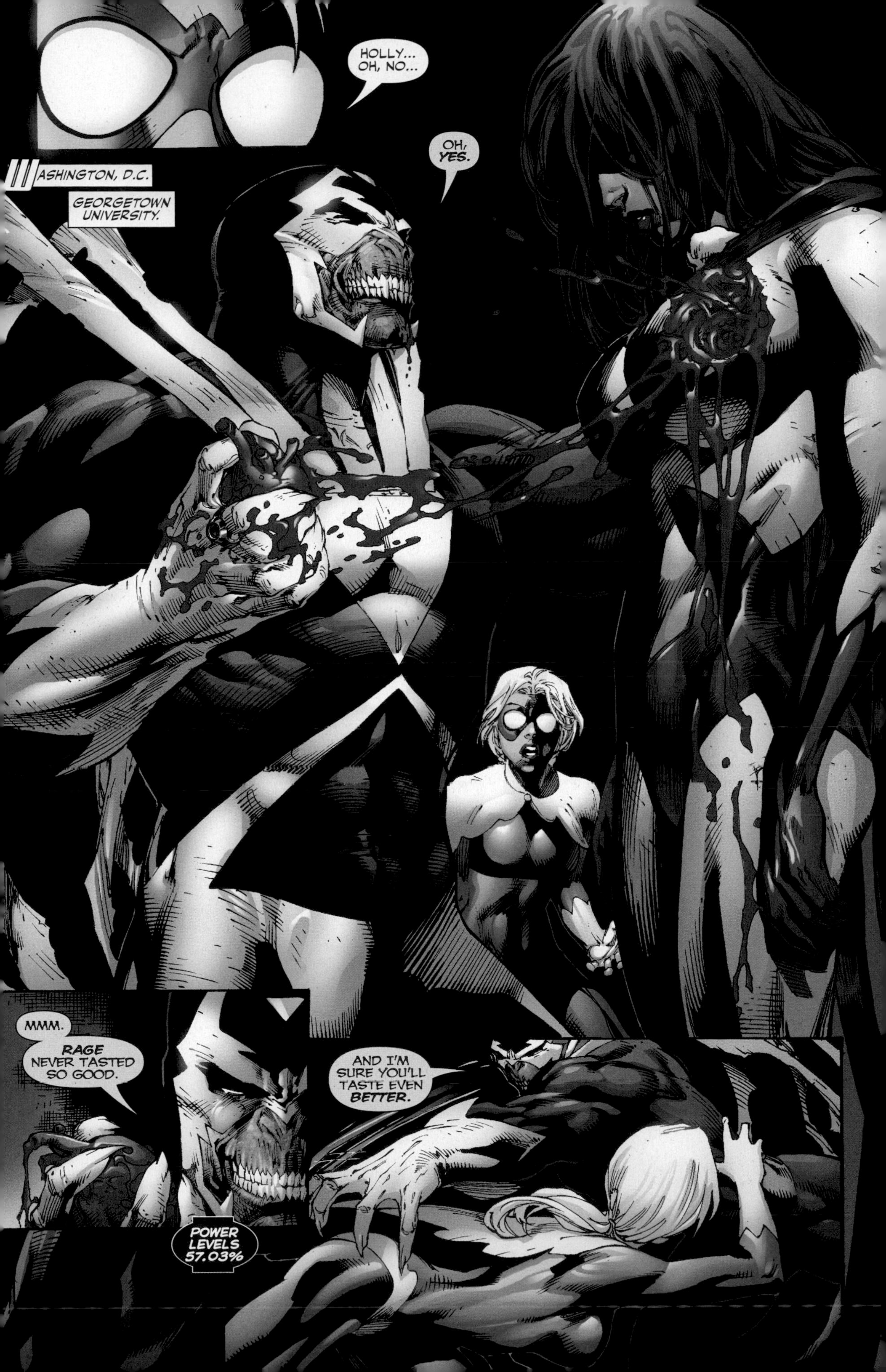
HOLLY... OH, NO...
OH, YES.
WASHINGTON, D.C.
GEORGETOWN UNIVERSITY.
MMM. RAGE NEVER TASTED SO GOOD.
AND I'M SURE YOU'LL TASTE EVEN BETTER.
POWER LEVELS 57.03%

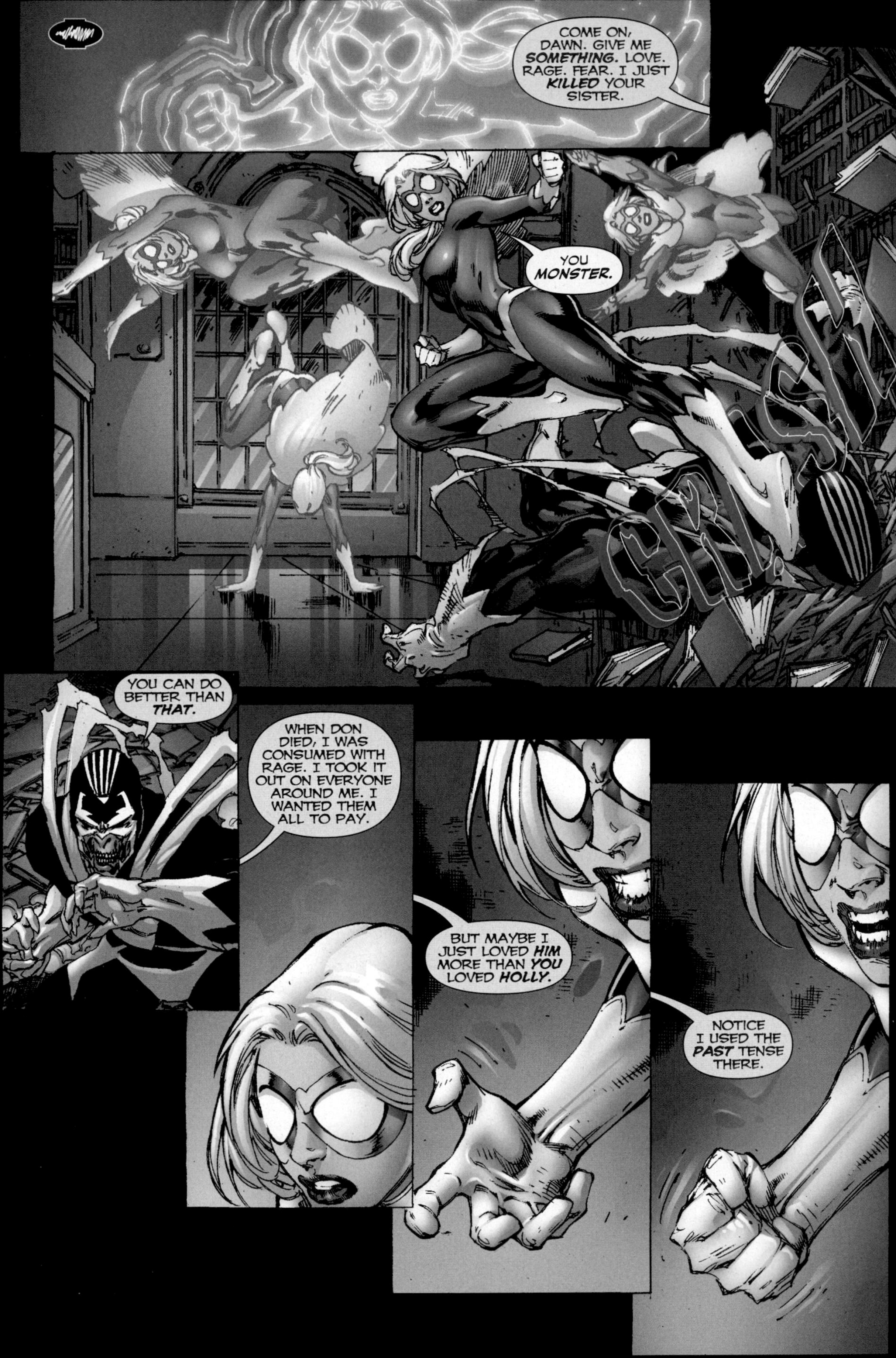
COME ON, DAWN. GIVE ME SOMETHING. LOVE. RAGE. FEAR. I JUST KILLED YOUR SISTER.
YOU MONSTER.
YOU CAN DO BETTER THAN THAT.
WHEN DON DIED, I WAS CONSUMED WITH RAGE. I TOOK IT OUT ON EVERYONE AROUND ME. I WANTED THEM ALL TO PAY.
BUT MAYBE I JUST LOVED HIM MORE THAN YOU LOVED HOLLY.
NOTICE I USED THE PAST TENSE THERE.

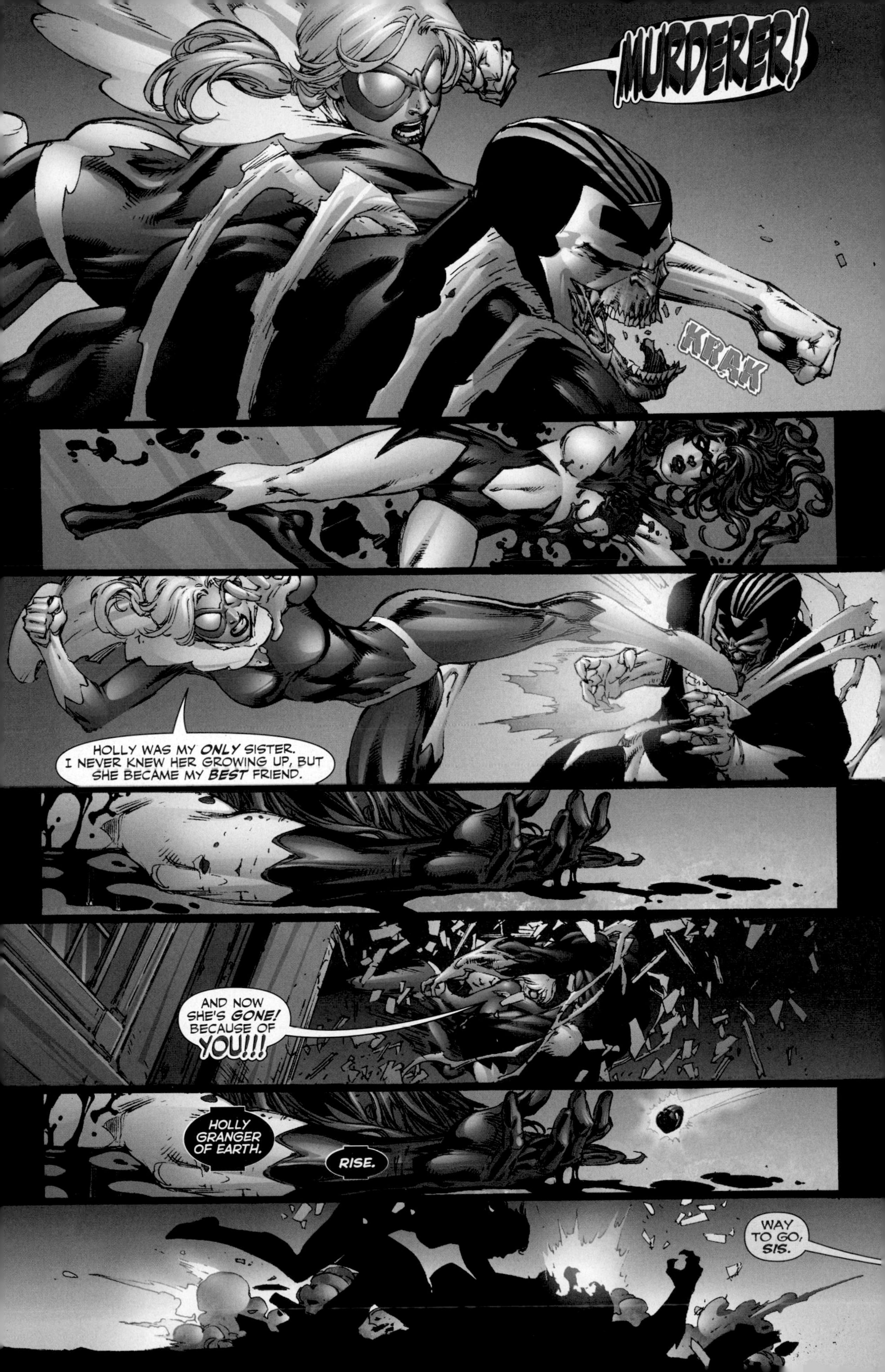
MURDERER!
KRAK
HOLLY WAS MY *ONLY* SISTER. I NEVER KNEW HER GROWING UP, BUT SHE BECAME MY *BEST* FRIEND.
AND NOW SHE'S *GONE!* BECAUSE OF YOU!!!
HOLLY GRANGER OF EARTH.
RISE.
WAY TO GO, SIS.

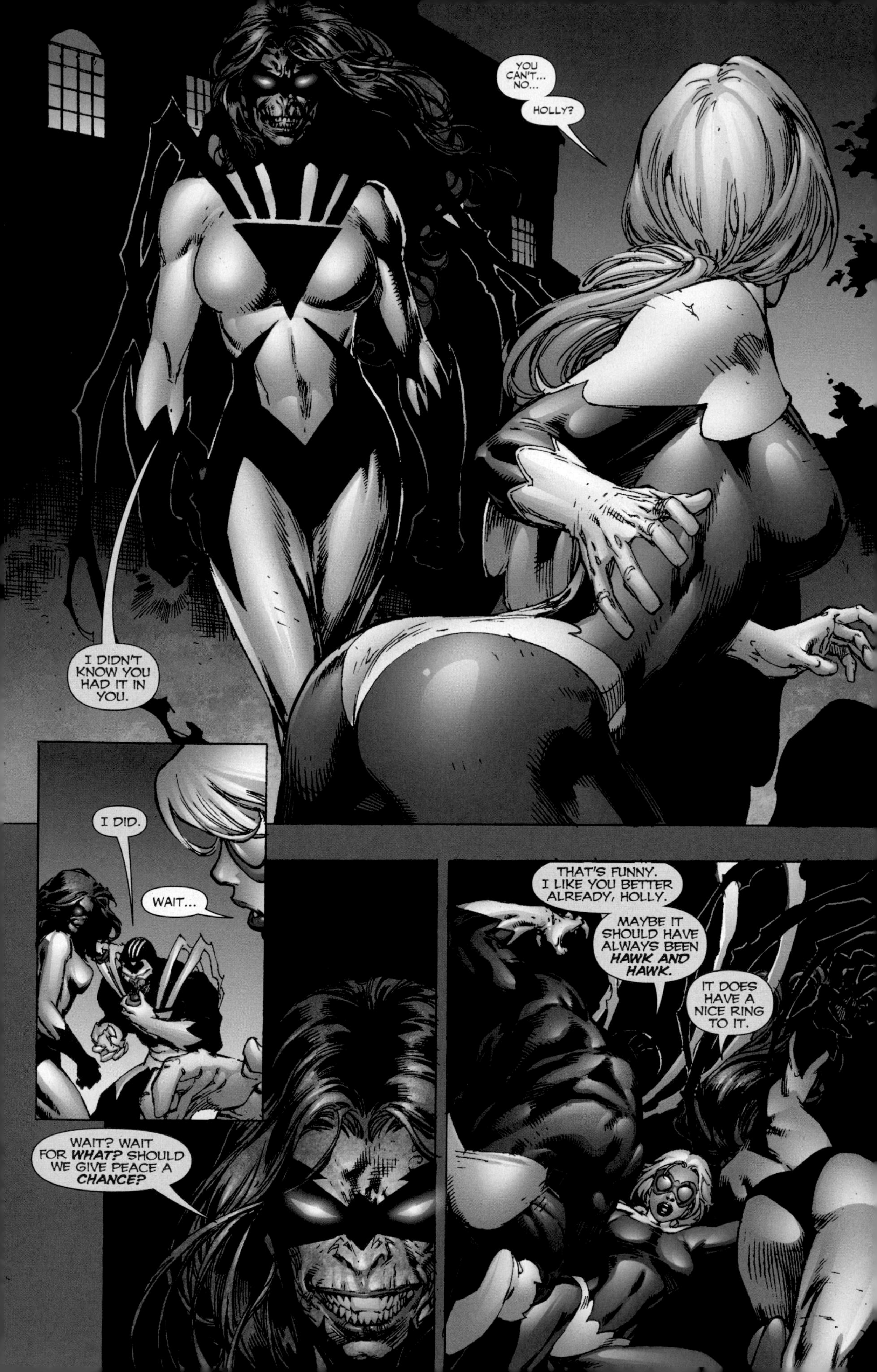
YOU CAN'T... NO...
HOLLY?
I DIDN'T KNOW YOU HAD IT IN YOU.
I DID.
WAIT...
WAIT? WAIT FOR *WHAT?* SHOULD WE GIVE PEACE A *CHANCE?*
THAT'S FUNNY. I LIKE YOU BETTER ALREADY, HOLLY.
MAYBE IT SHOULD HAVE ALWAYS BEEN *HAWK AND HAWK.*
IT DOES HAVE A NICE RING TO IT.

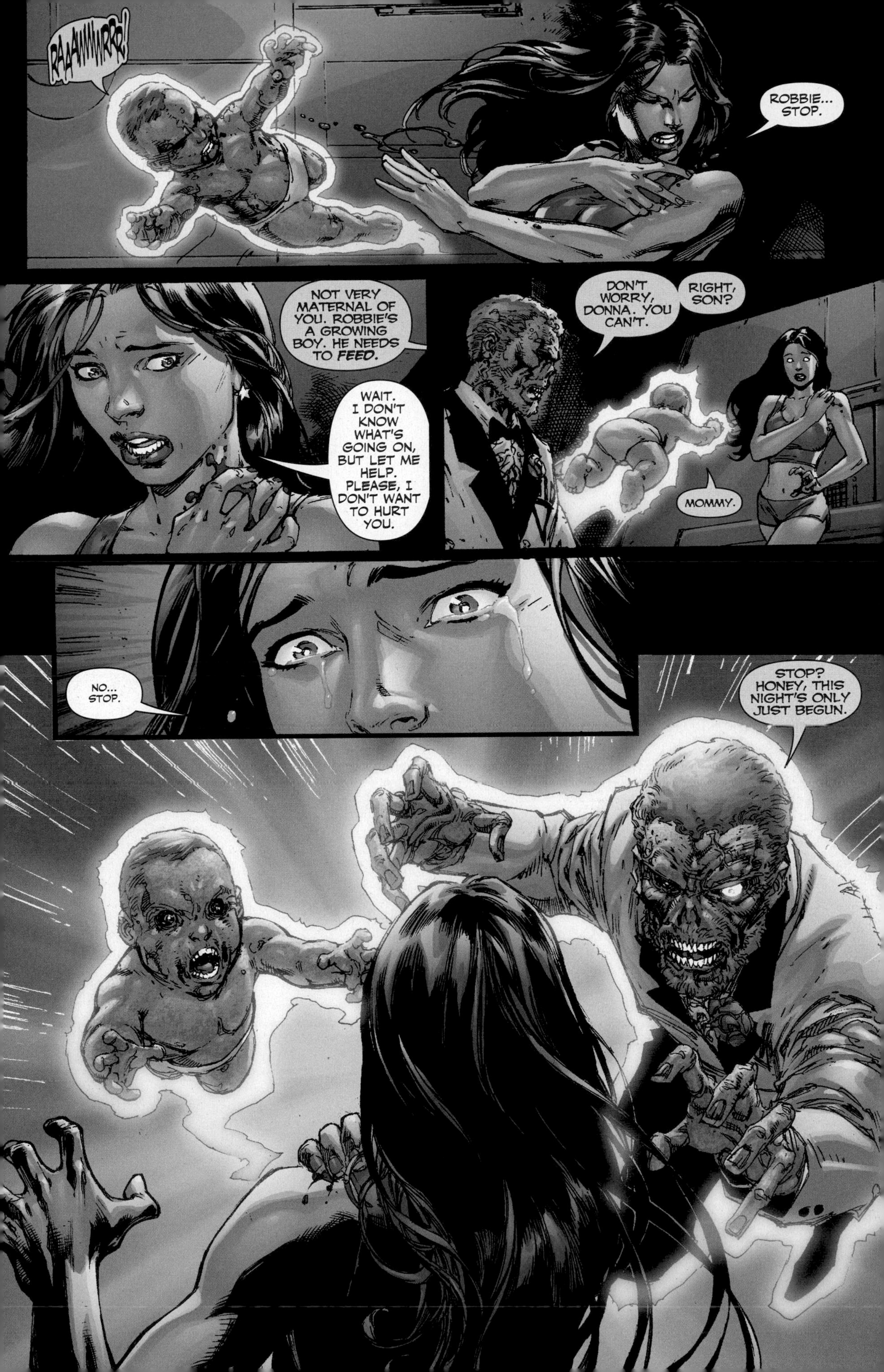
RAAAWWWRRR!
ROBBIE... STOP.
NOT VERY MATERNAL OF YOU. ROBBIE'S A GROWING BOY. HE NEEDS TO **FEED**.
WAIT. I DON'T KNOW WHAT'S GOING ON, BUT LET ME HELP. PLEASE, I DON'T WANT TO HURT YOU.
DON'T WORRY, DONNA. YOU CAN'T.
RIGHT, SON?
MOMMY.
NO... STOP.
STOP? HONEY, THIS NIGHT'S ONLY JUST BEGUN.

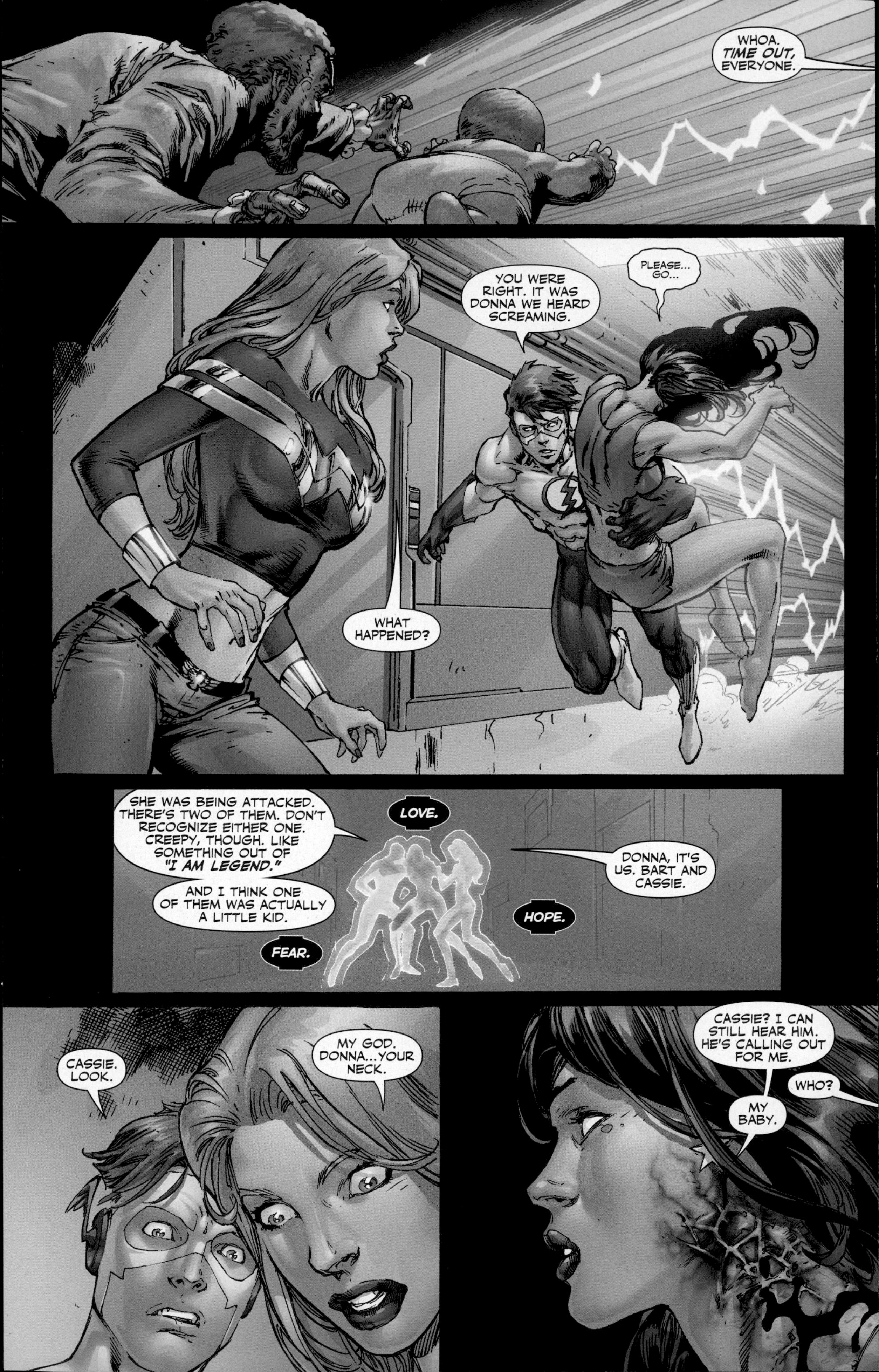
WHOA. *TIME OUT*, EVERYONE.
YOU WERE RIGHT. IT WAS DONNA WE HEARD SCREAMING.
PLEASE... GO...
WHAT HAPPENED?
SHE WAS BEING ATTACKED. THERE'S TWO OF THEM. DON'T RECOGNIZE EITHER ONE. CREEPY, THOUGH. LIKE SOMETHING OUT OF *"I AM LEGEND."*
AND I THINK ONE OF THEM WAS ACTUALLY A LITTLE KID.
LOVE.
FEAR.
HOPE.
DONNA, IT'S US. BART AND CASSIE.
CASSIE. LOOK.
MY GOD. DONNA...YOUR NECK.
CASSIE? I CAN STILL HEAR HIM. HE'S CALLING OUT FOR ME.
WHO?
MY BABY.

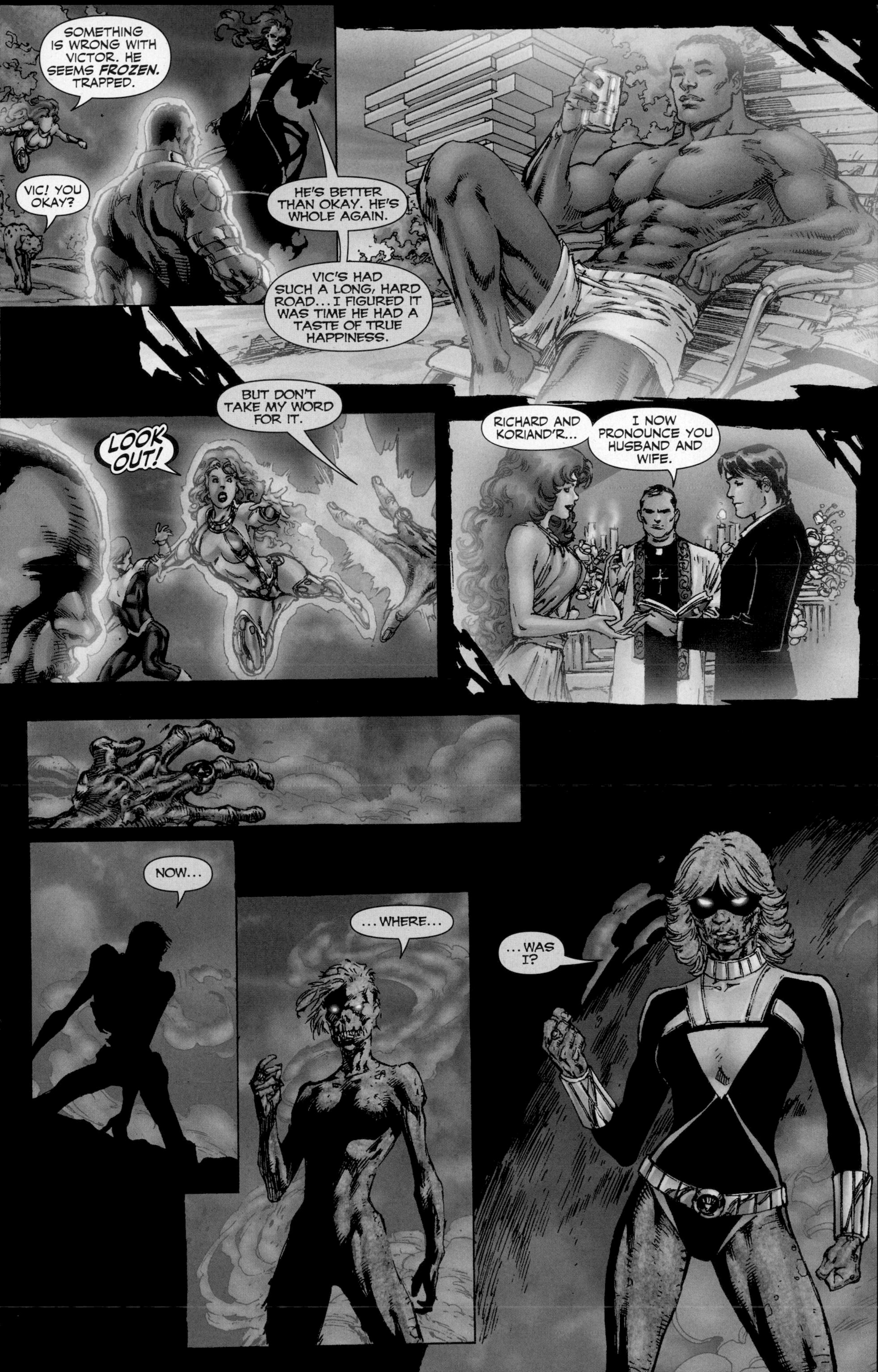
SOMETHING IS WRONG WITH VICTOR. HE SEEMS FROZEN. TRAPPED.
VIC! YOU OKAY?
HE'S BETTER THAN OKAY. HE'S WHOLE AGAIN.
VIC'S HAD SUCH A LONG, HARD ROAD... I FIGURED IT WAS TIME HE HAD A TASTE OF TRUE HAPPINESS.
BUT DON'T TAKE MY WORD FOR IT.
LOOK OUT!
RICHARD AND KORIAND'R...
I NOW PRONOUNCE YOU HUSBAND AND WIFE.
NOW...
...WHERE...
...WAS I?

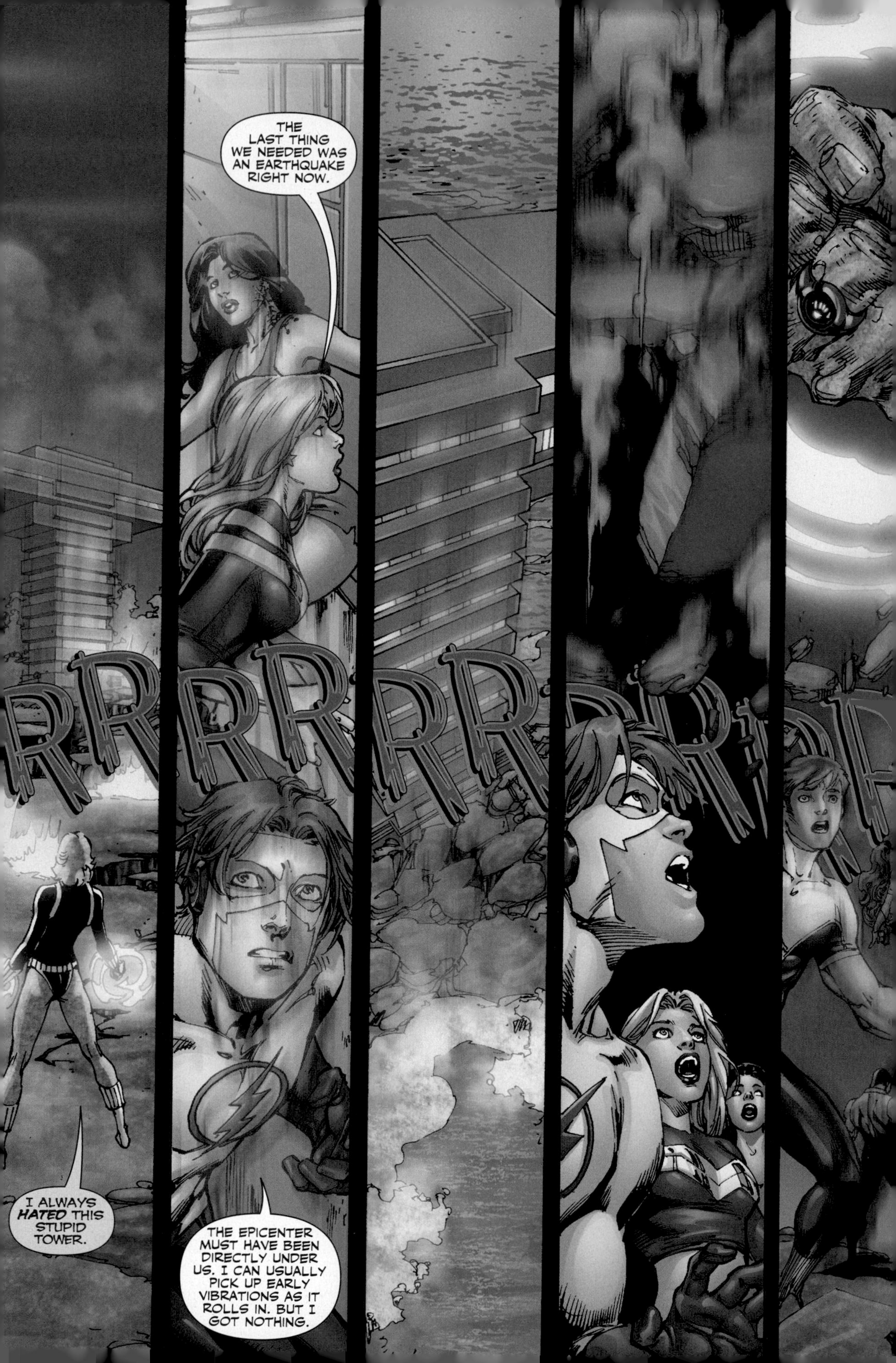
THE LAST THING WE NEEDED WAS AN EARTHQUAKE RIGHT NOW.
RRRRRRRRR
I ALWAYS *HATED* THIS STUPID TOWER.
THE EPICENTER MUST HAVE BEEN DIRECTLY UNDER US. I CAN USUALLY PICK UP EARLY VIBRATIONS AS IT ROLLS IN. BUT I GOT NOTHING.

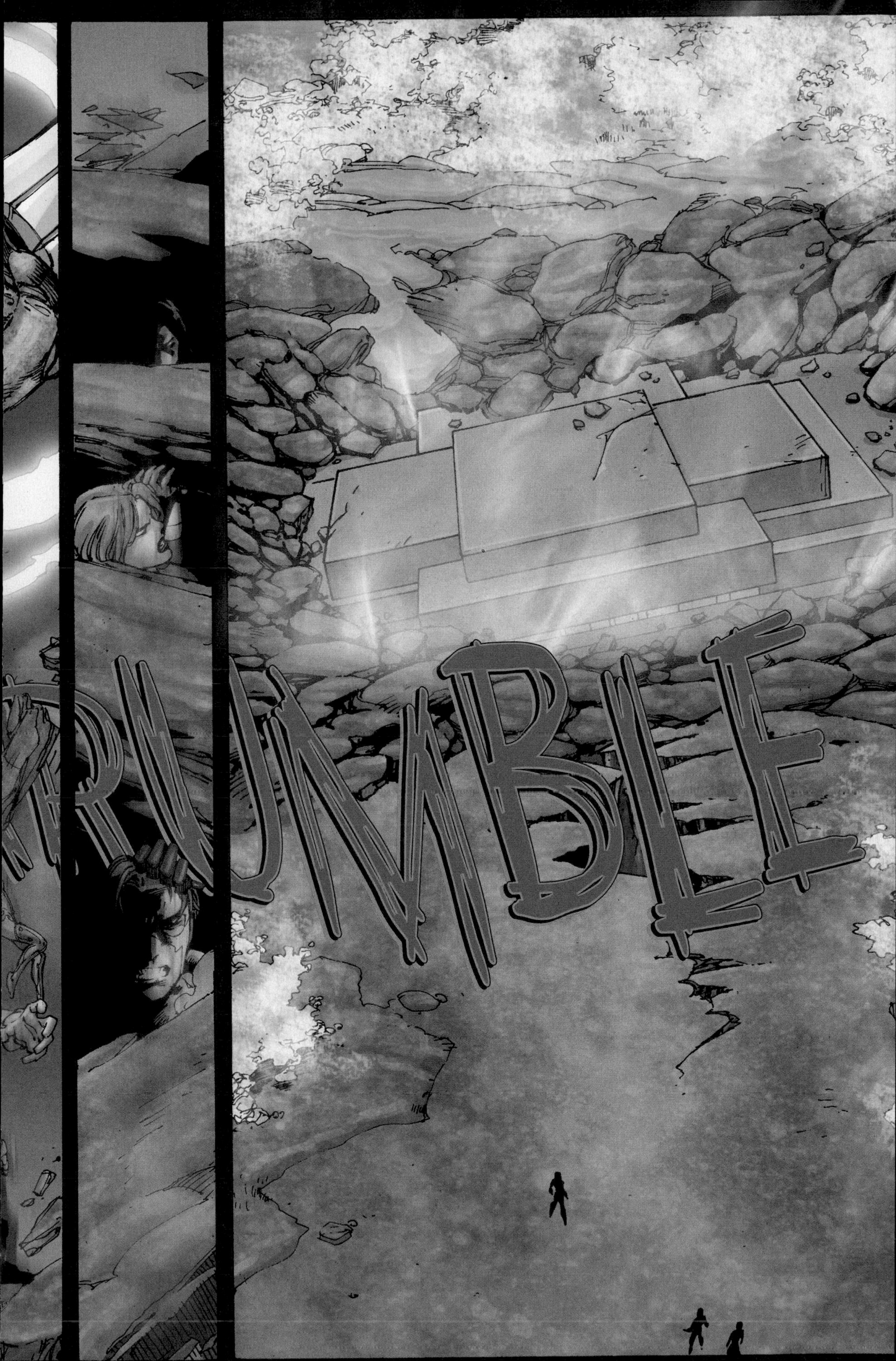
RUMBLE

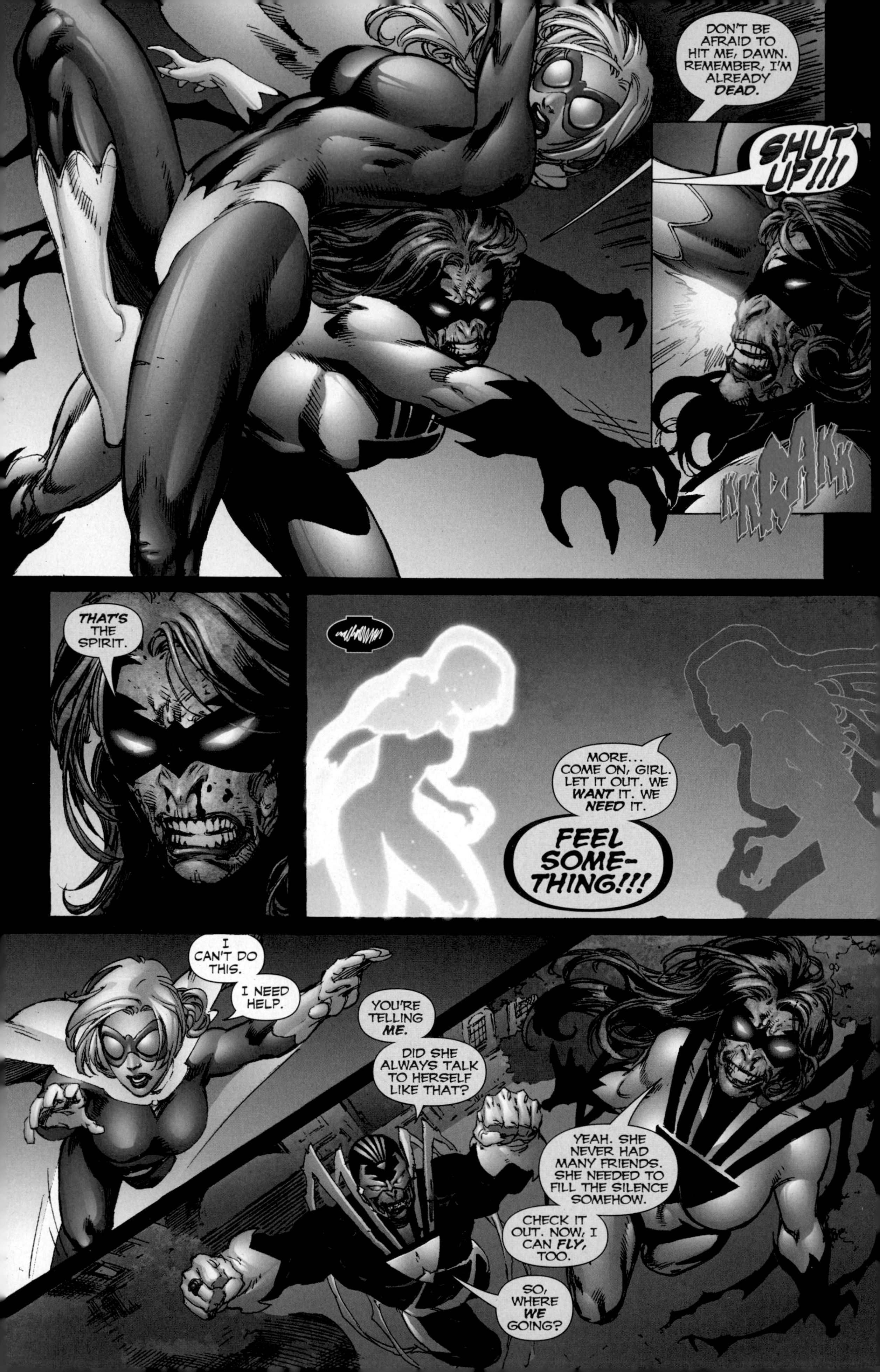

DON'T BE AFRAID TO HIT ME, DAWN. REMEMBER, I'M ALREADY DEAD.
SHUT UP!!!
KKRAKK
THAT'S THE SPIRIT.
MORE... COME ON, GIRL. LET IT OUT. WE WANT IT. WE NEED IT.
FEEL SOMETHING!!!
I CAN'T DO THIS.
I NEED HELP.
YOU'RE TELLING ME.
DID SHE ALWAYS TALK TO HERSELF LIKE THAT?
YEAH. SHE NEVER HAD MANY FRIENDS. SHE NEEDED TO FILL THE SILENCE SOMEHOW.
CHECK IT OUT. NOW, I CAN FLY, TOO.
SO, WHERE WE GOING?

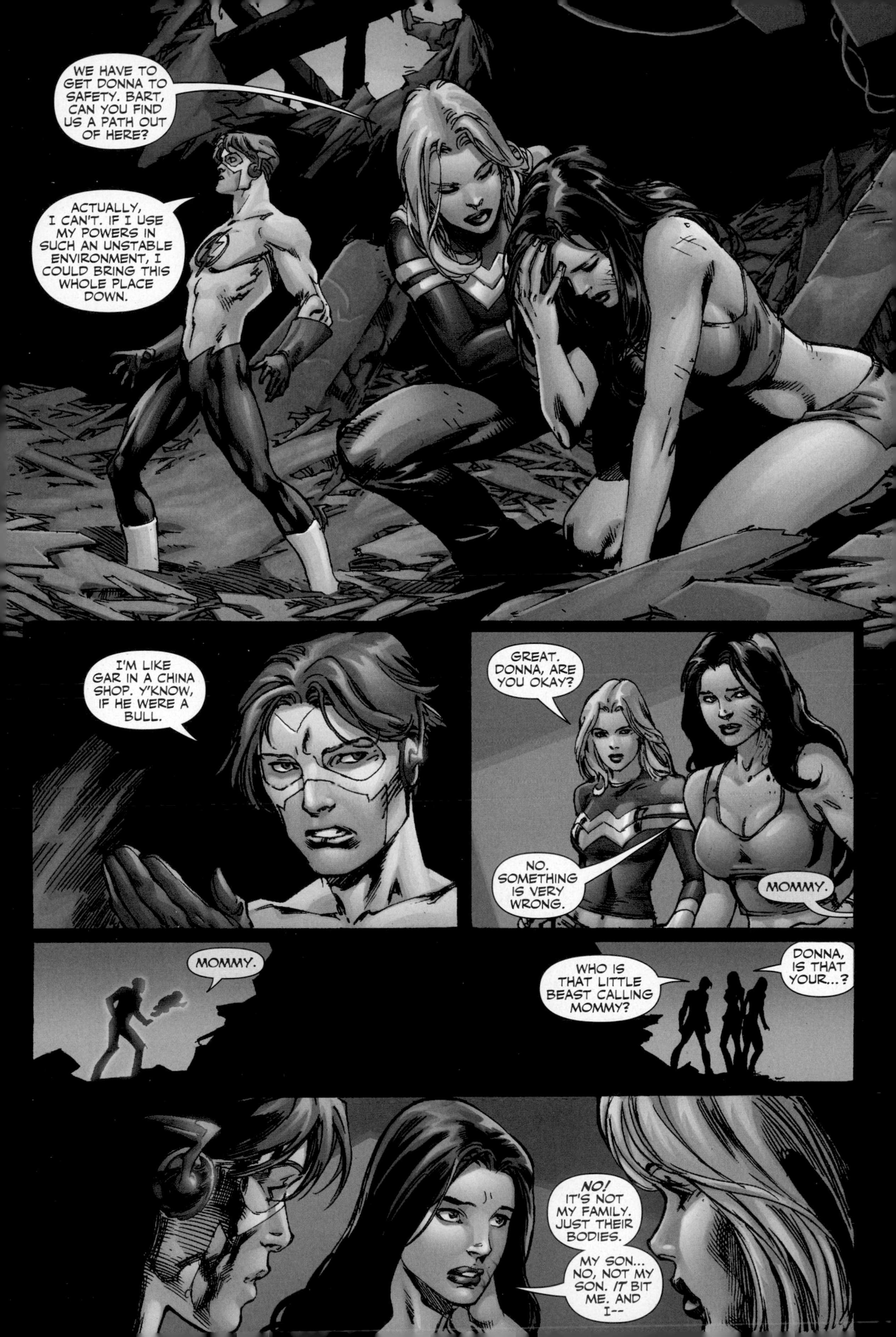
WE HAVE TO GET DONNA TO SAFETY. BART, CAN YOU FIND US A PATH OUT OF HERE?
ACTUALLY, I CAN'T. IF I USE MY POWERS IN SUCH AN UNSTABLE ENVIRONMENT, I COULD BRING THIS WHOLE PLACE DOWN.
I'M LIKE GAR IN A CHINA SHOP. Y'KNOW, IF HE WERE A BULL.
GREAT. DONNA, ARE YOU OKAY?
NO. SOMETHING IS VERY WRONG.
MOMMY.
MOMMY.
WHO IS THAT LITTLE BEAST CALLING MOMMY?
DONNA, IS THAT YOUR...?
NO! IT'S NOT MY FAMILY. JUST THEIR BODIES.
MY SON... NO, NOT MY SON. IT BIT ME. AND I--

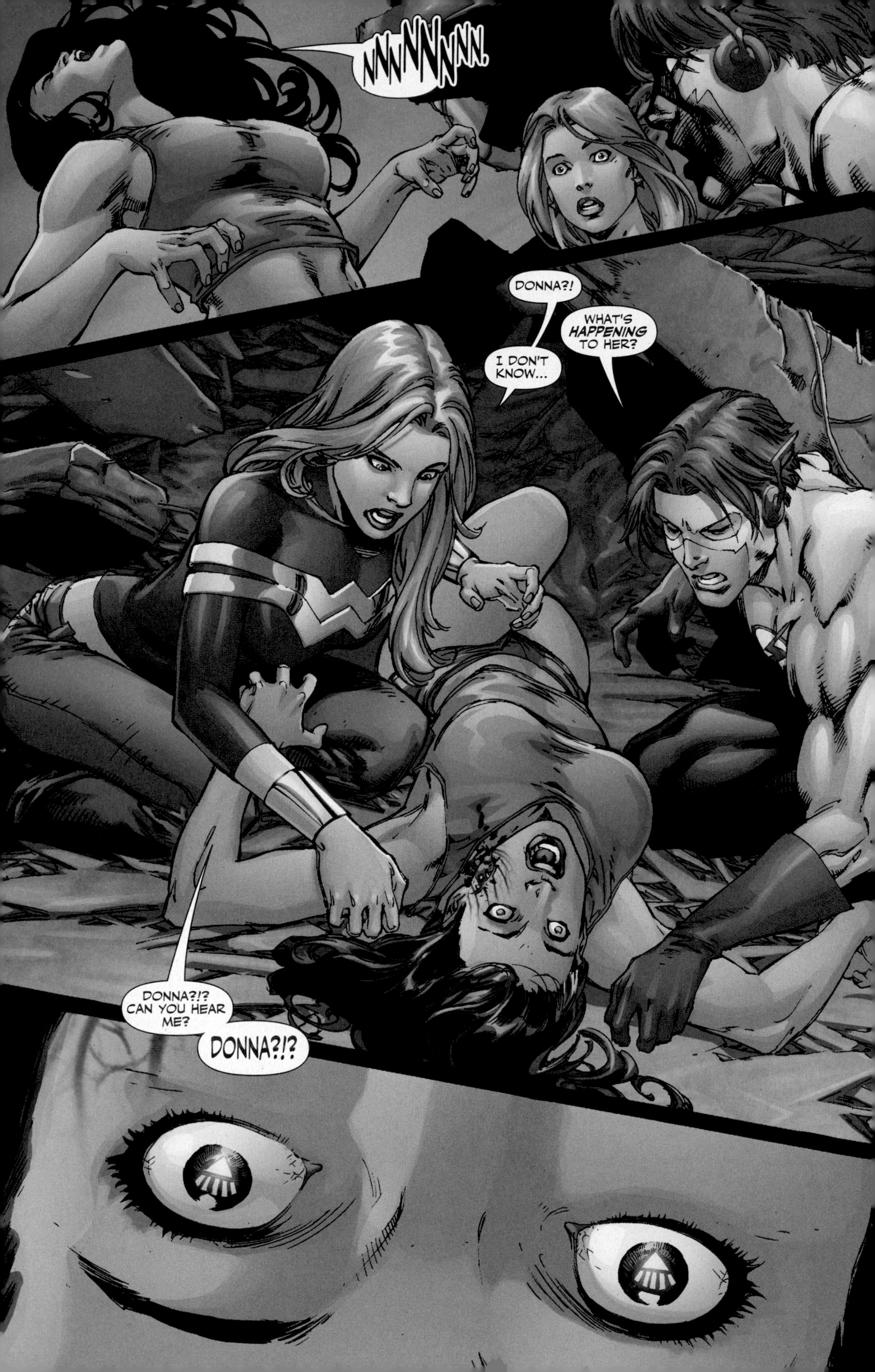
NNNNNNNN.
DONNA?!
WHAT'S *HAPPENING* TO HER?
I DON'T KNOW...
DONNA?!? CAN YOU HEAR ME?
DONNA?!?

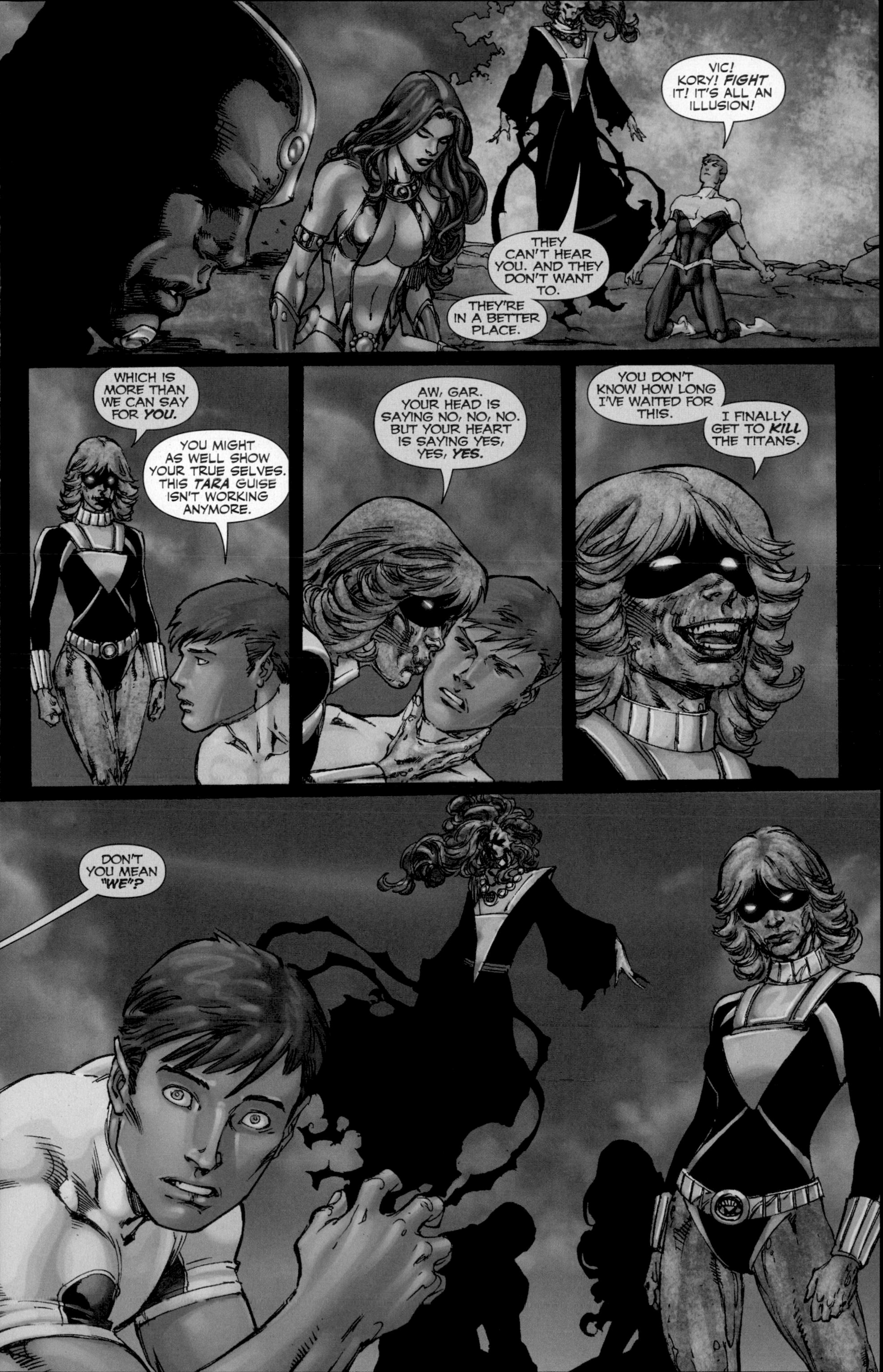
VIC! KORY! FIGHT IT! IT'S ALL AN ILLUSION!
THEY CAN'T HEAR YOU. AND THEY DON'T WANT TO.
THEY'RE IN A BETTER PLACE.
WHICH IS MORE THAN WE CAN SAY FOR YOU.
YOU MIGHT AS WELL SHOW YOUR TRUE SELVES. THIS TARA GUISE ISN'T WORKING ANYMORE.
AW, GAR. YOUR HEAD IS SAYING NO, NO, NO. BUT YOUR HEART IS SAYING YES, YES, YES.
YOU DON'T KNOW HOW LONG I'VE WAITED FOR THIS.
I FINALLY GET TO KILL THE TITANS.
DON'T YOU MEAN "WE"?

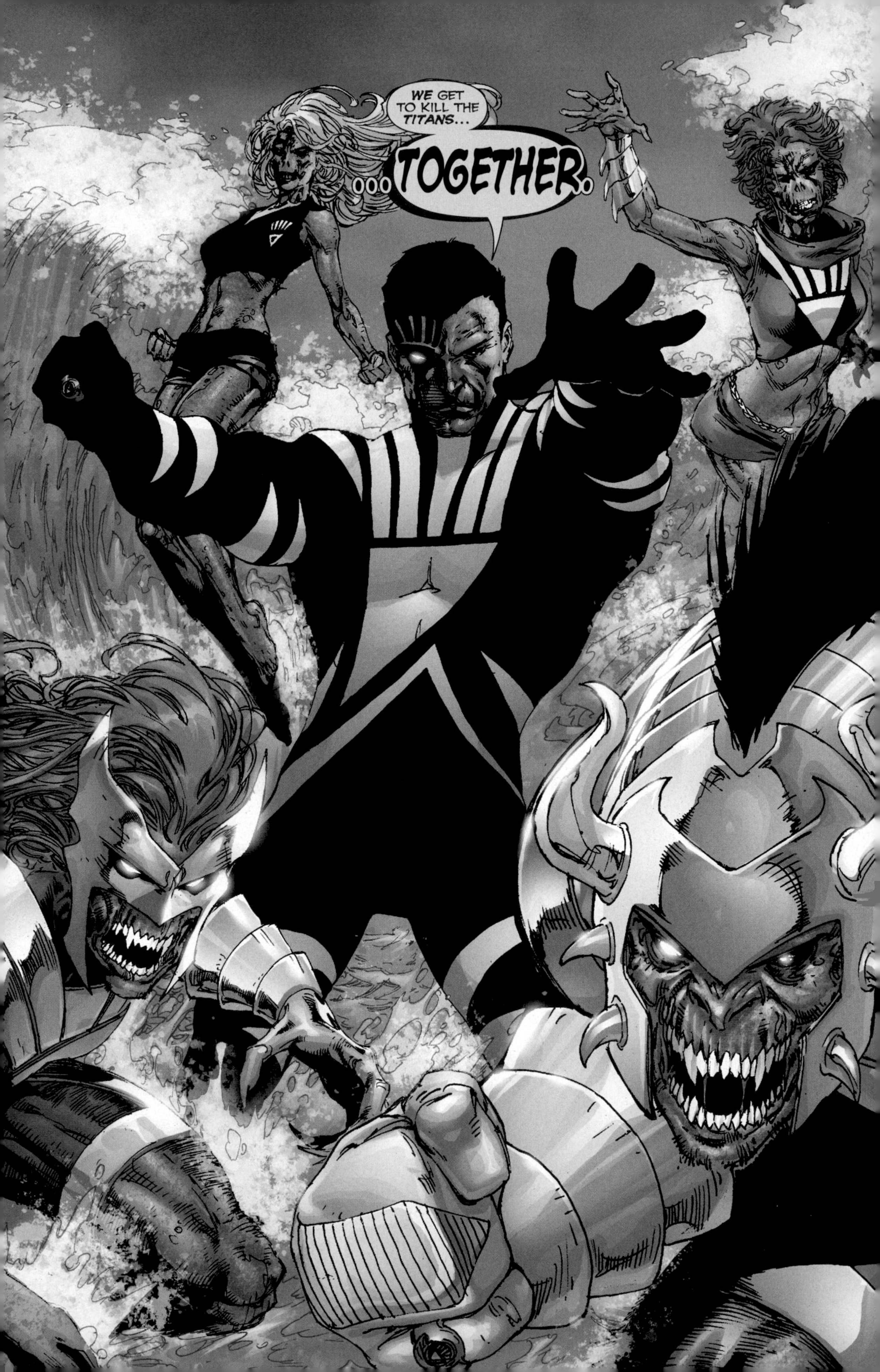
WE GET TO KILL THE TITANS...
...TOGETHER.

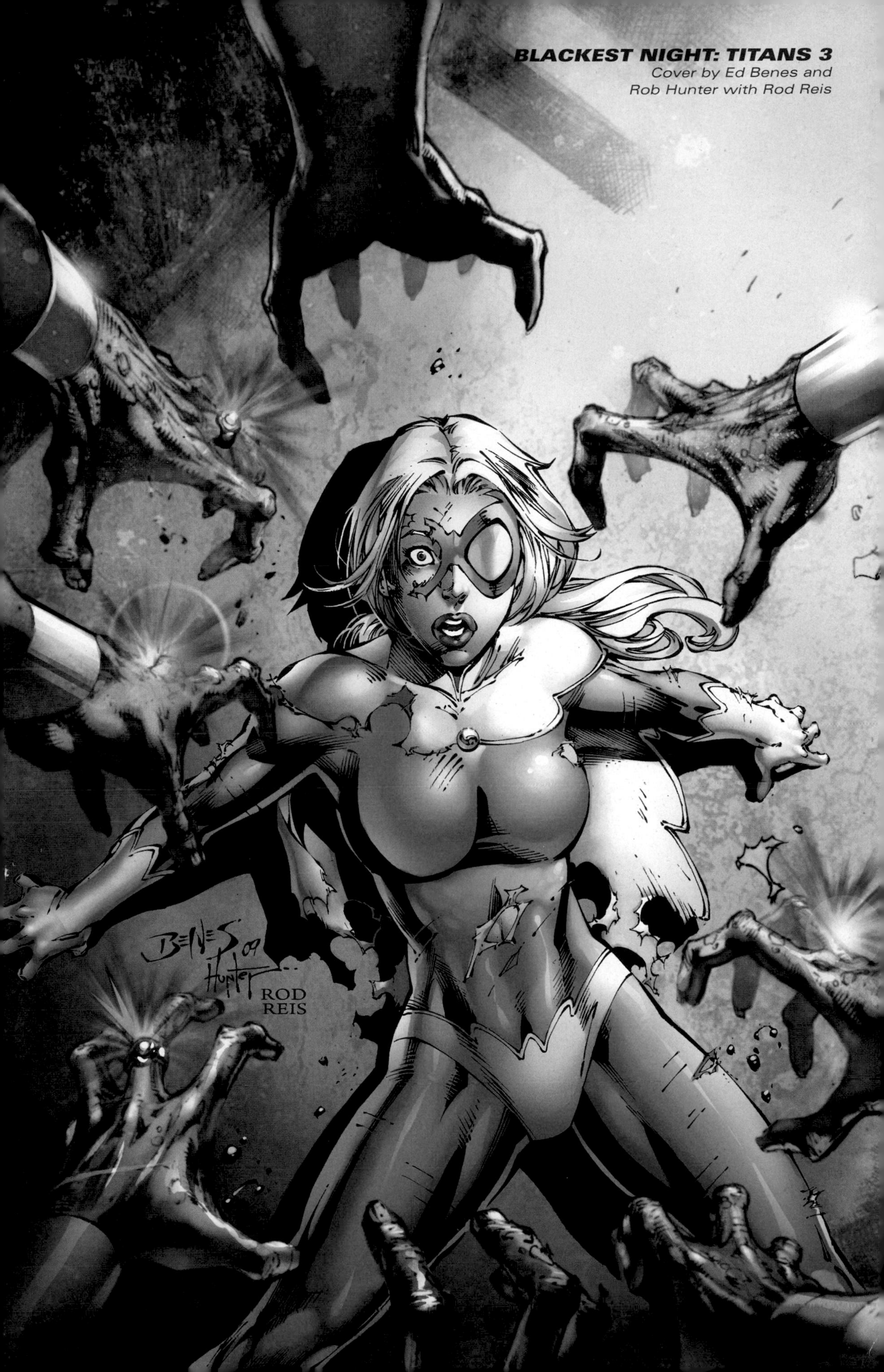
BENES '09
Hunter
ROD
REIS

BLACKEST NIGHT: TITANS 3

Cover by Ed Benes and
Rob Hunter with Rod Reis

WHEN DOVES CRY

J.T. KRUL
WRITER

ED BENES
ARTIST

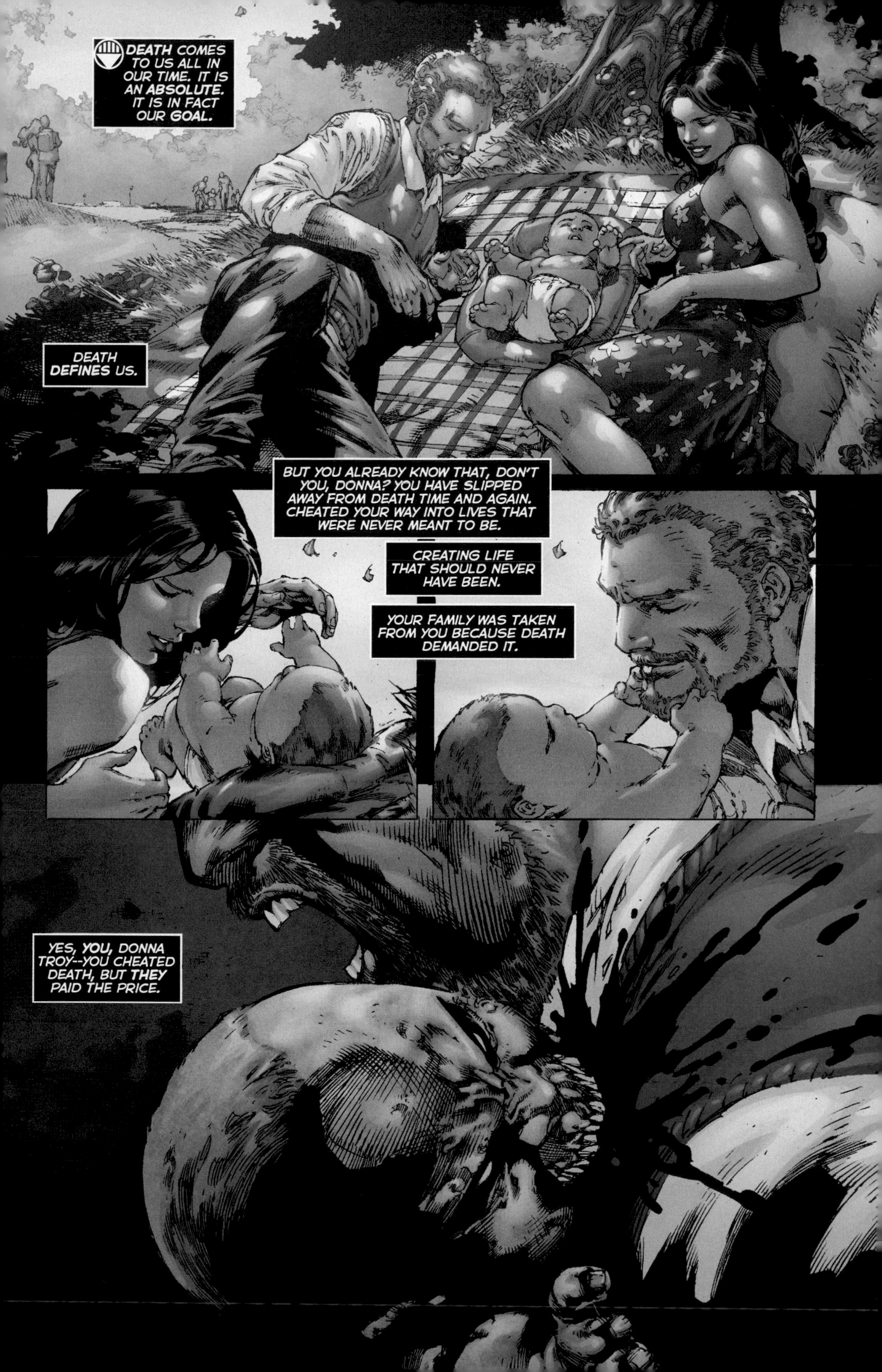
DEATH COMES TO US ALL IN OUR TIME. IT IS AN ABSOLUTE. IT IS IN FACT OUR GOAL.
DEATH DEFINES US.
BUT YOU ALREADY KNOW THAT, DON'T YOU, DONNA? YOU HAVE SLIPPED AWAY FROM DEATH TIME AND AGAIN. CHEATED YOUR WAY INTO LIVES THAT WERE NEVER MEANT TO BE.
CREATING LIFE THAT SHOULD NEVER HAVE BEEN.
YOUR FAMILY WAS TAKEN FROM YOU BECAUSE DEATH DEMANDED IT.
YES, YOU, DONNA TROY--YOU CHEATED DEATH, BUT THEY PAID THE PRICE.

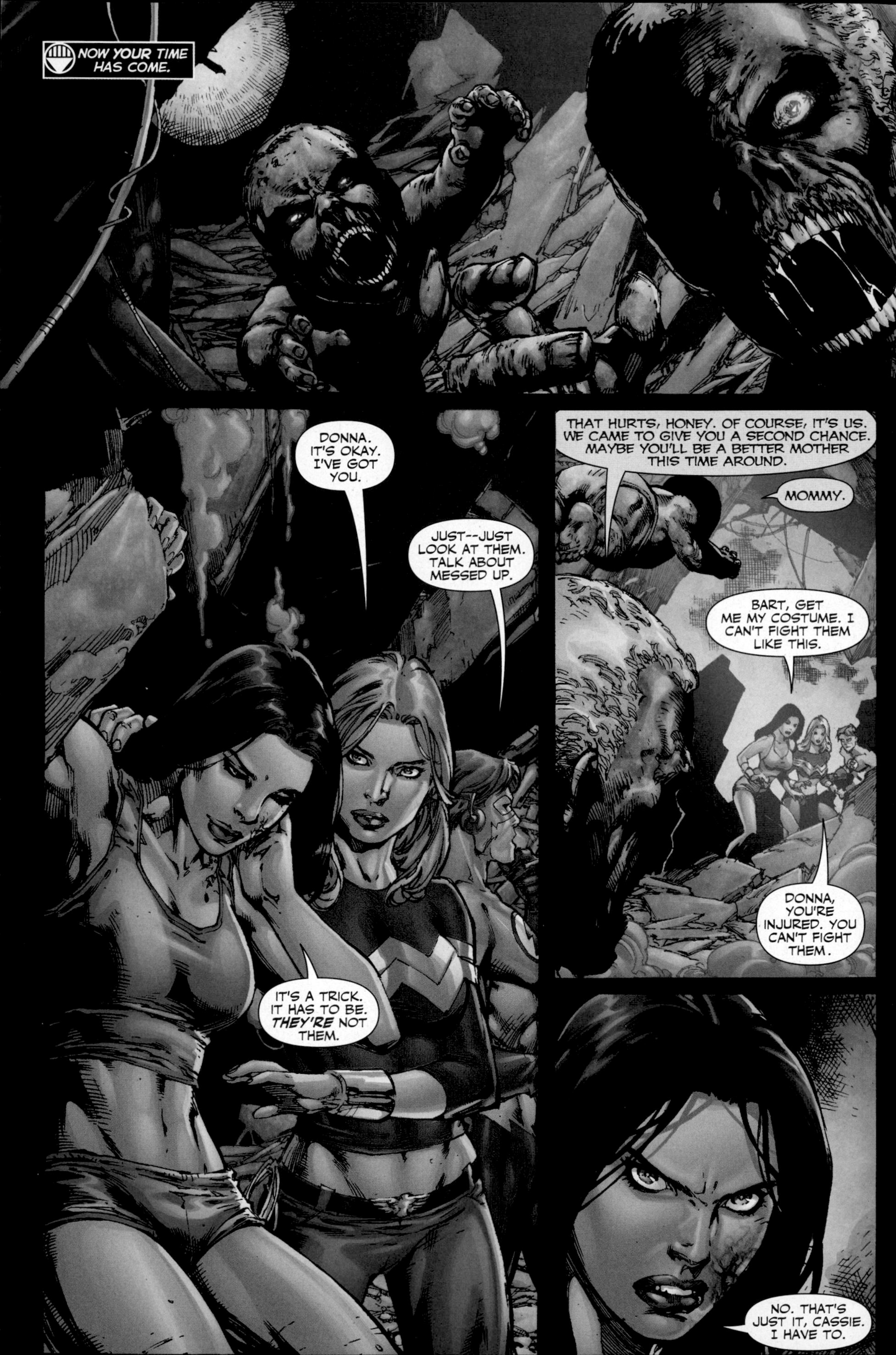
NOW YOUR TIME HAS COME.
DONNA. IT'S OKAY. I'VE GOT YOU.
JUST--JUST LOOK AT THEM. TALK ABOUT MESSED UP.
IT'S A TRICK. IT HAS TO BE. *THEY'RE* NOT THEM.
THAT HURTS, HONEY. OF COURSE, IT'S US. WE CAME TO GIVE YOU A SECOND CHANCE. MAYBE YOU'LL BE A BETTER MOTHER THIS TIME AROUND.
MOMMY.
BART, GET ME MY COSTUME. I CAN'T FIGHT THEM LIKE THIS.
DONNA, YOU'RE INJURED. YOU CAN'T FIGHT THEM.
NO. THAT'S JUST IT, CASSIE. I HAVE TO.

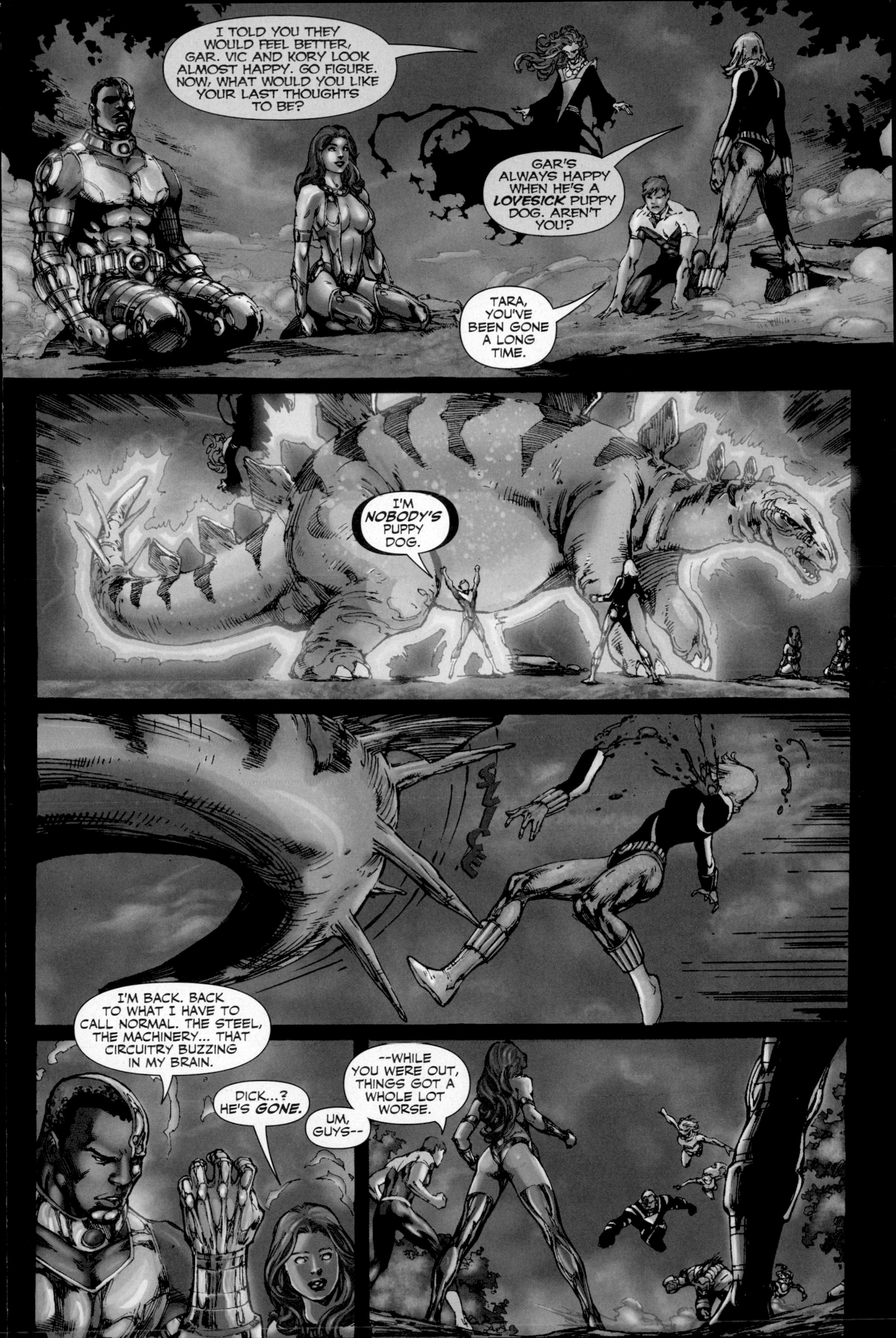

I TOLD YOU THEY WOULD FEEL BETTER, GAR. VIC AND KORY LOOK ALMOST HAPPY. GO FIGURE. NOW, WHAT WOULD YOU LIKE YOUR LAST THOUGHTS TO BE?
GAR'S ALWAYS HAPPY WHEN HE'S A ***LOVESICK*** PUPPY DOG. AREN'T YOU?
TARA, YOU'VE BEEN GONE A LONG TIME.
I'M ***NOBODY'S*** PUPPY DOG.
I'M BACK. BACK TO WHAT I HAVE TO CALL NORMAL. THE STEEL, THE MACHINERY... THAT CIRCUITRY BUZZING IN MY BRAIN.
DICK...? HE'S ***GONE.***
UM, GUYS--
--WHILE YOU WERE OUT, THINGS GOT A WHOLE LOT WORSE.

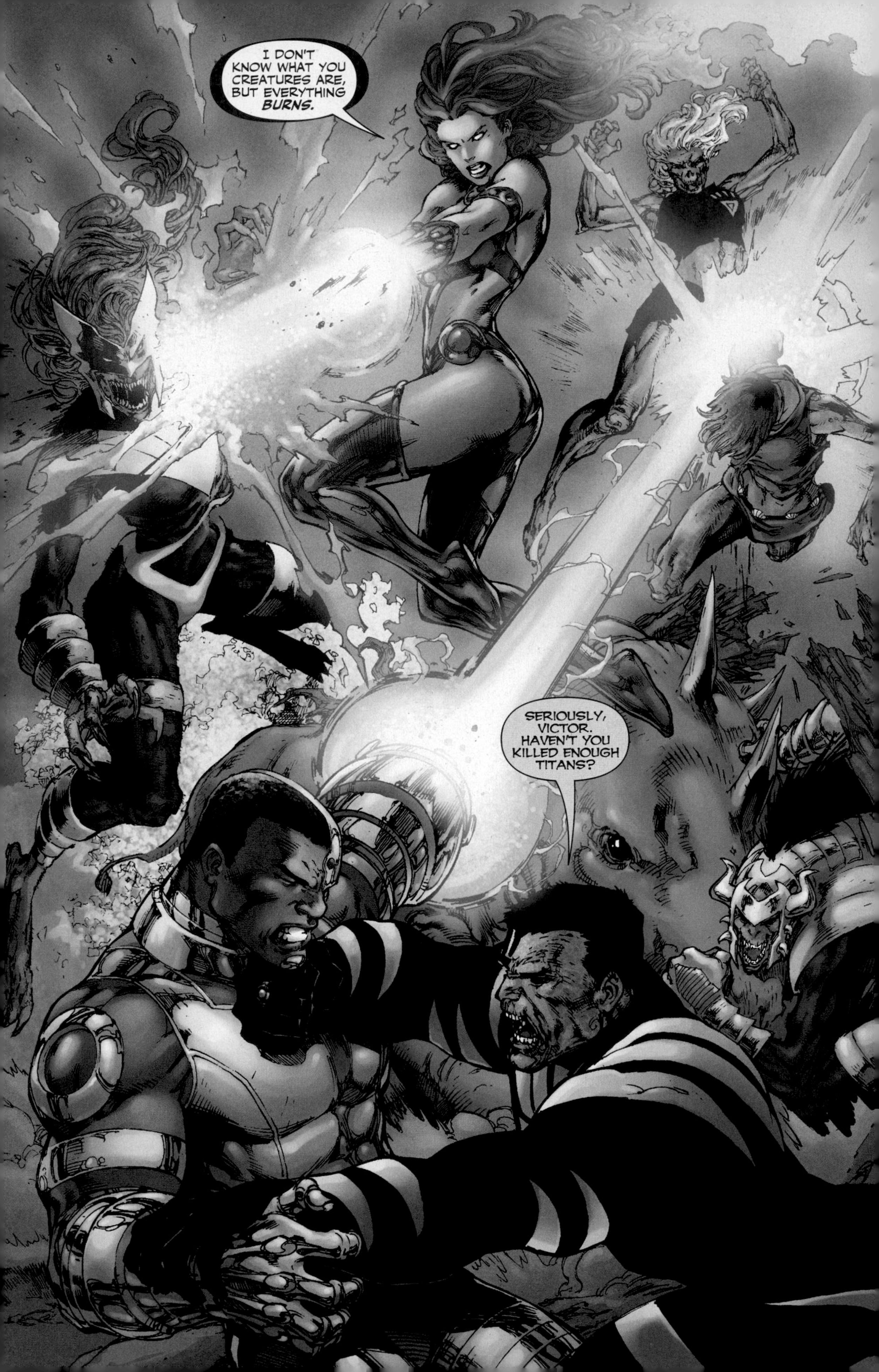
I DON'T KNOW WHAT YOU CREATURES ARE, BUT EVERYTHING *BURNS.*
SERIOUSLY, VICTOR. HAVEN'T YOU KILLED ENOUGH TITANS?

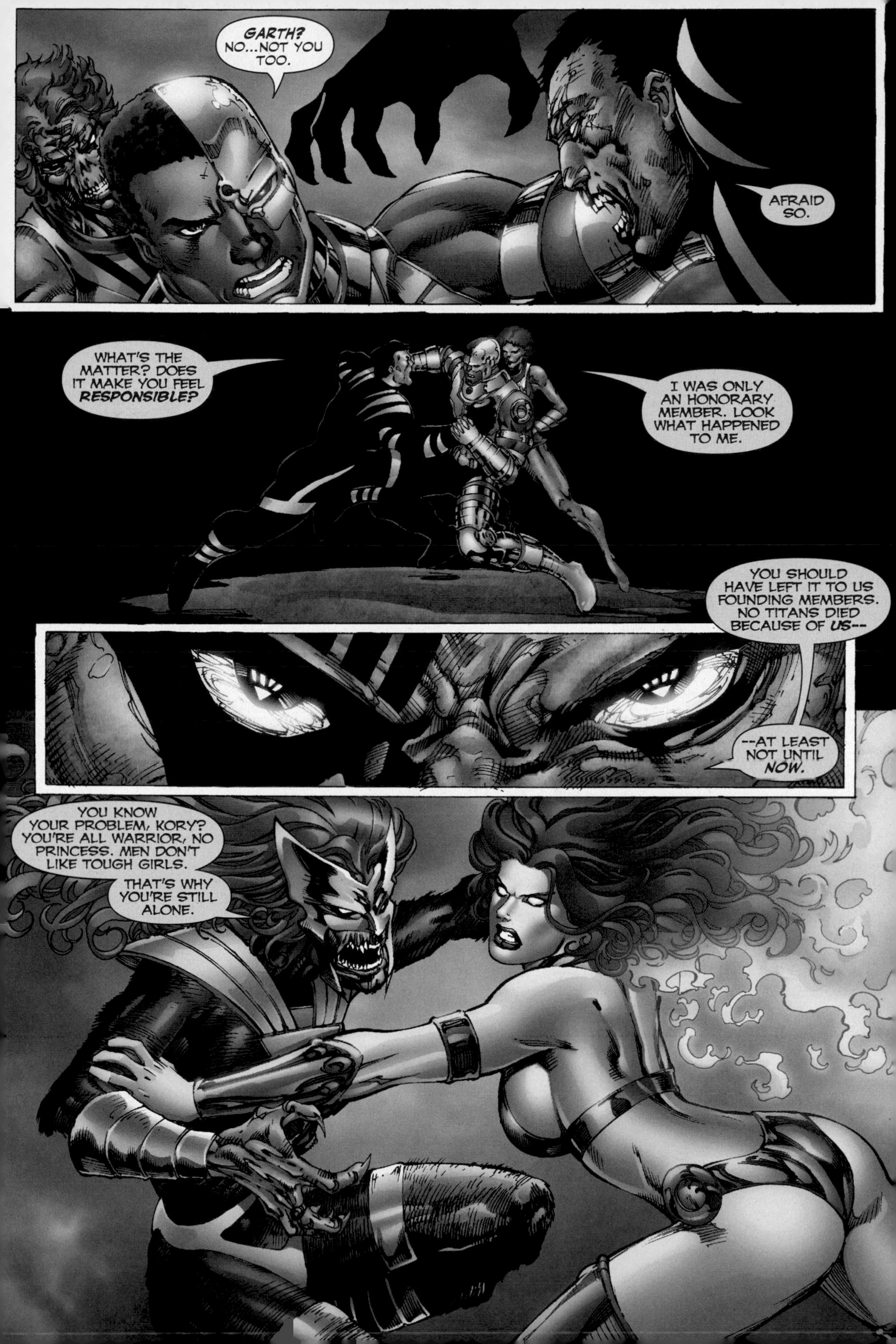
GARTH? NO...NOT YOU TOO.
AFRAID SO.
WHAT'S THE MATTER? DOES IT MAKE YOU FEEL RESPONSIBLE?
I WAS ONLY AN HONORARY MEMBER. LOOK WHAT HAPPENED TO ME.
YOU SHOULD HAVE LEFT IT TO US FOUNDING MEMBERS. NO TITANS DIED BECAUSE OF US--
--AT LEAST NOT UNTIL NOW.
YOU KNOW YOUR PROBLEM, KORY? YOU'RE ALL WARRIOR, NO PRINCESS. MEN DON'T LIKE TOUGH GIRLS.
THAT'S WHY YOU'RE STILL ALONE.

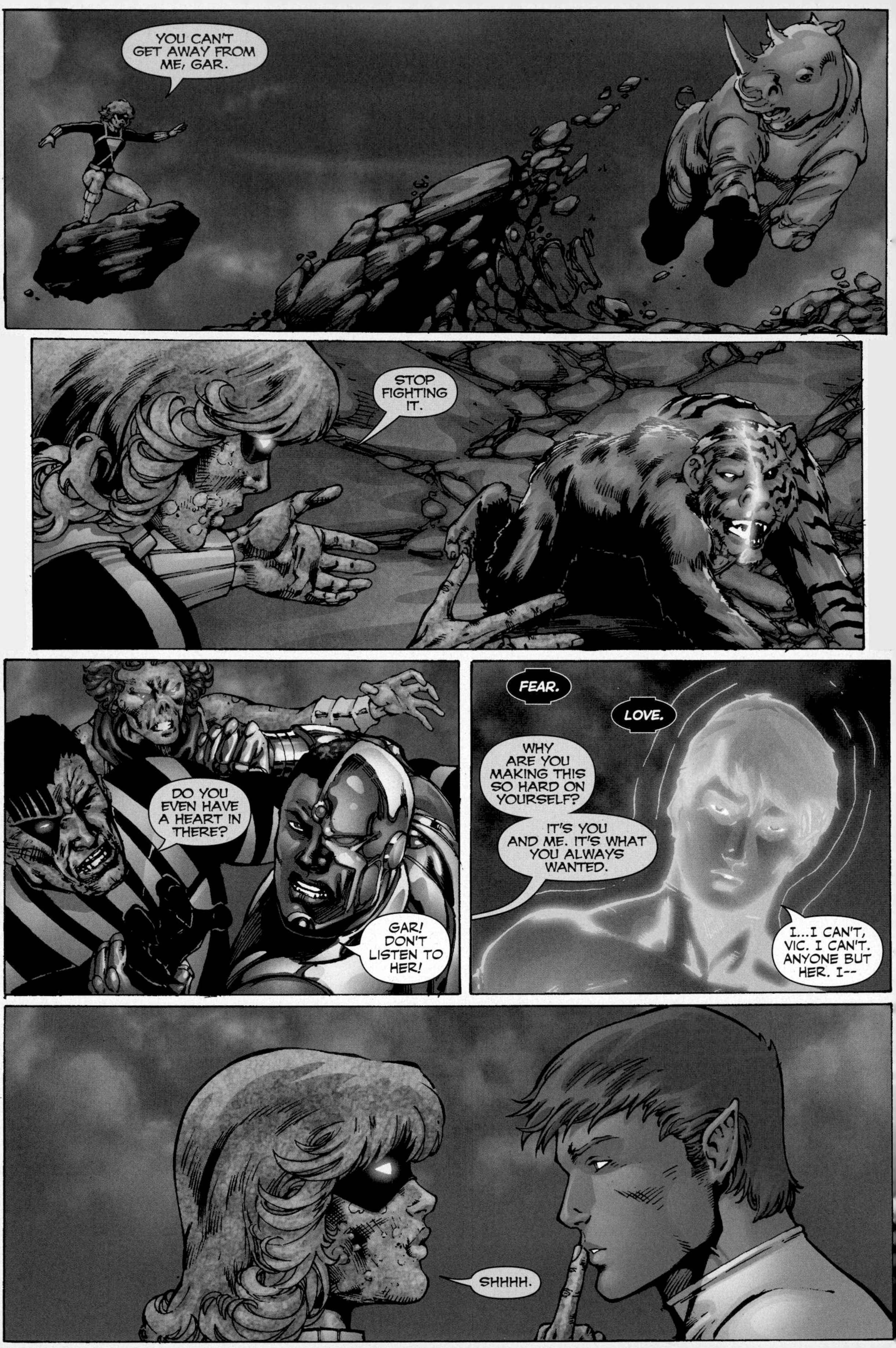

YOU CAN'T GET AWAY FROM ME, GAR.
STOP FIGHTING IT.
DO YOU EVEN HAVE A HEART IN THERE?
GAR! DON'T LISTEN TO HER!
FEAR.
LOVE.
WHY ARE YOU MAKING THIS SO HARD ON YOURSELF?
IT'S YOU AND ME. IT'S WHAT YOU ALWAYS WANTED.
I...I CAN'T, VIC. I CAN'T. ANYONE BUT HER. I--
SHHHH.

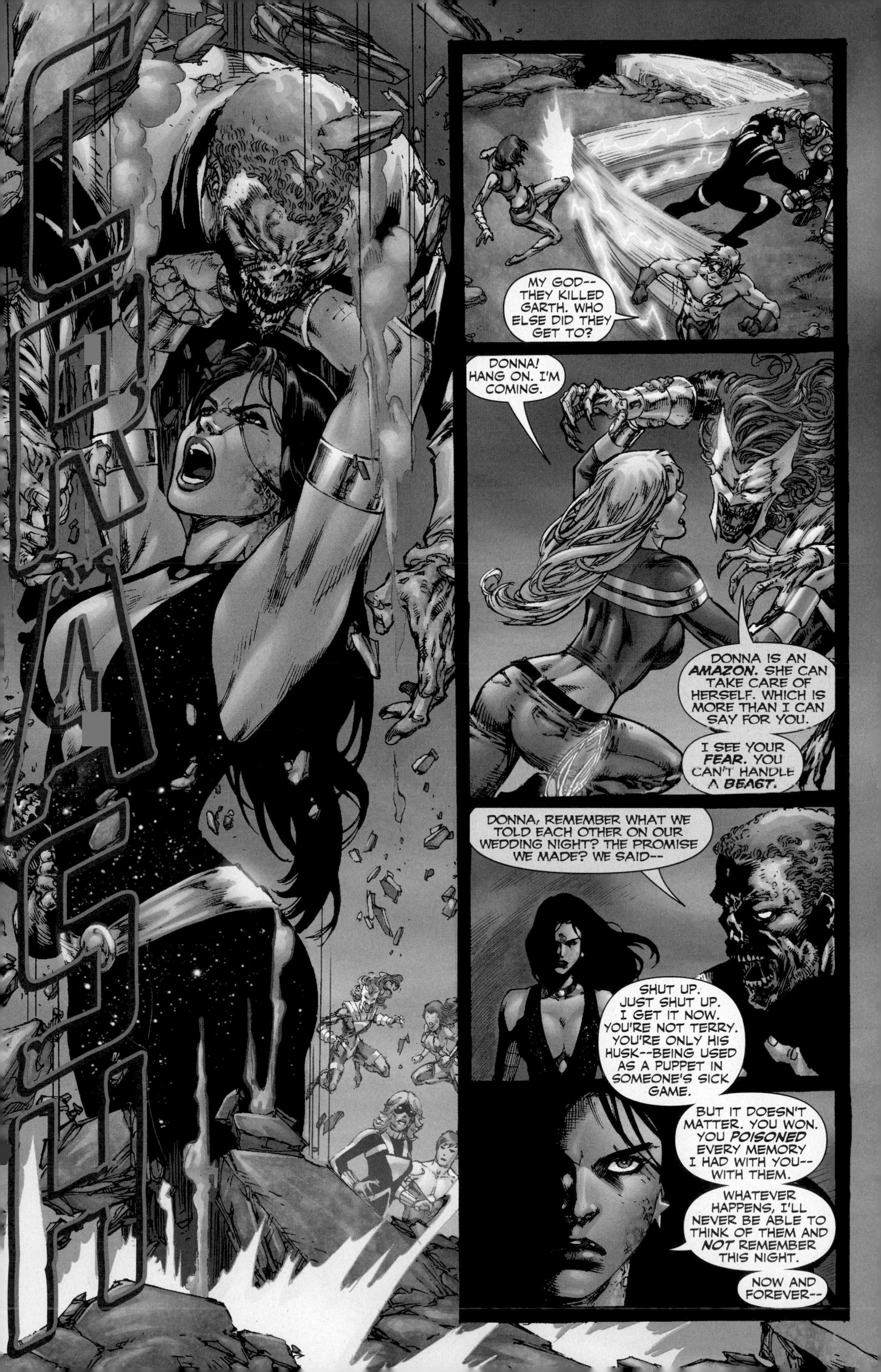
MY GOD-- THEY KILLED GARTH. WHO ELSE DID THEY GET TO?
DONNA! HANG ON. I'M COMING.
DONNA IS AN AMAZON. SHE CAN TAKE CARE OF HERSELF. WHICH IS MORE THAN I CAN SAY FOR YOU.
I SEE YOUR FEAR. YOU CAN'T HANDLE A BEAST.
DONNA, REMEMBER WHAT WE TOLD EACH OTHER ON OUR WEDDING NIGHT? THE PROMISE WE MADE? WE SAID--
SHUT UP. JUST SHUT UP. I GET IT NOW. YOU'RE NOT TERRY. YOU'RE ONLY HIS HUSK--BEING USED AS A PUPPET IN SOMEONE'S SICK GAME.
BUT IT DOESN'T MATTER. YOU WON. YOU POISONED EVERY MEMORY I HAD WITH YOU-- WITH THEM.
WHATEVER HAPPENS, I'LL NEVER BE ABLE TO THINK OF THEM AND NOT REMEMBER THIS NIGHT.
NOW AND FOREVER--

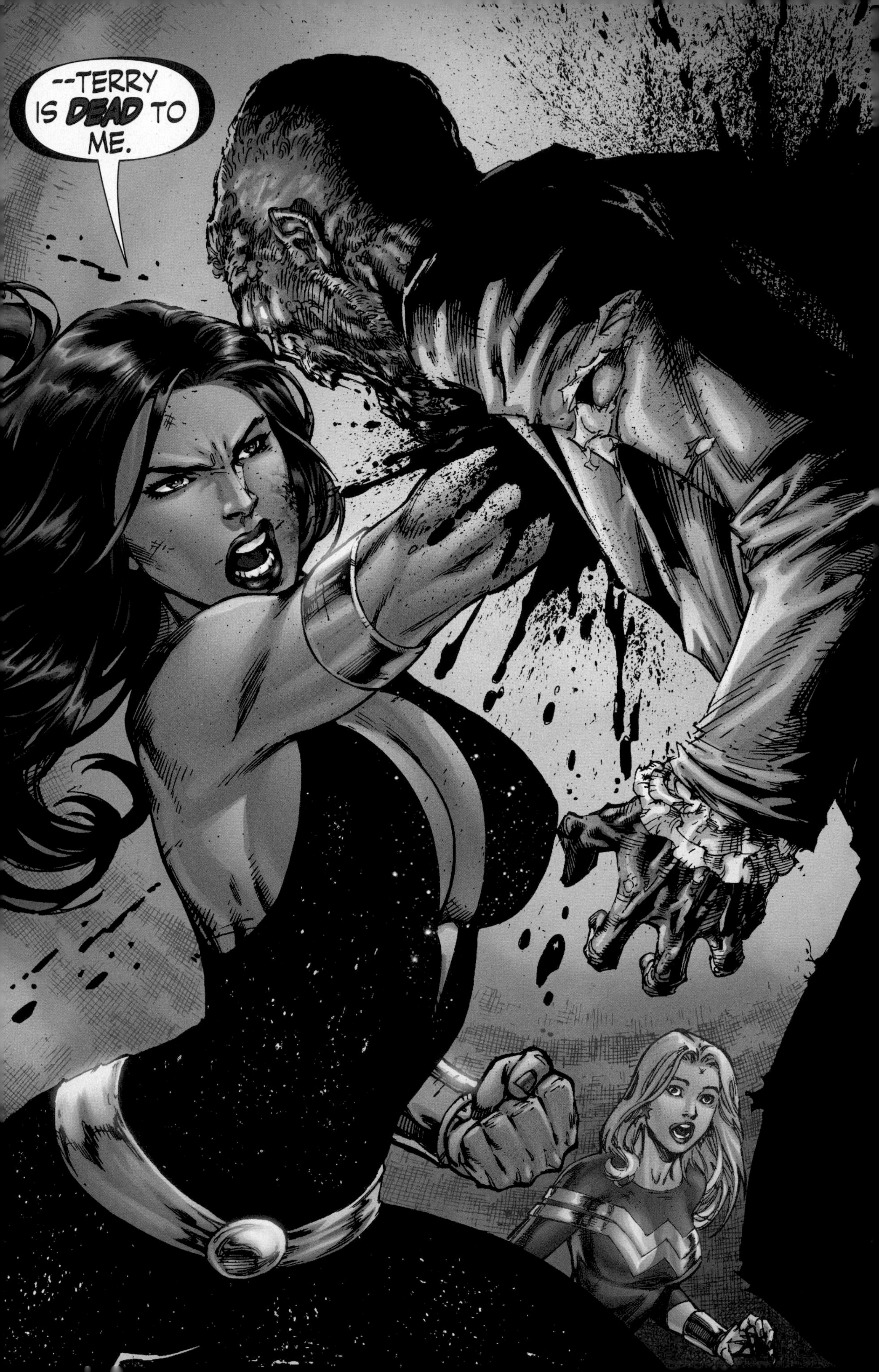
--TERRY IS DEAD TO ME.

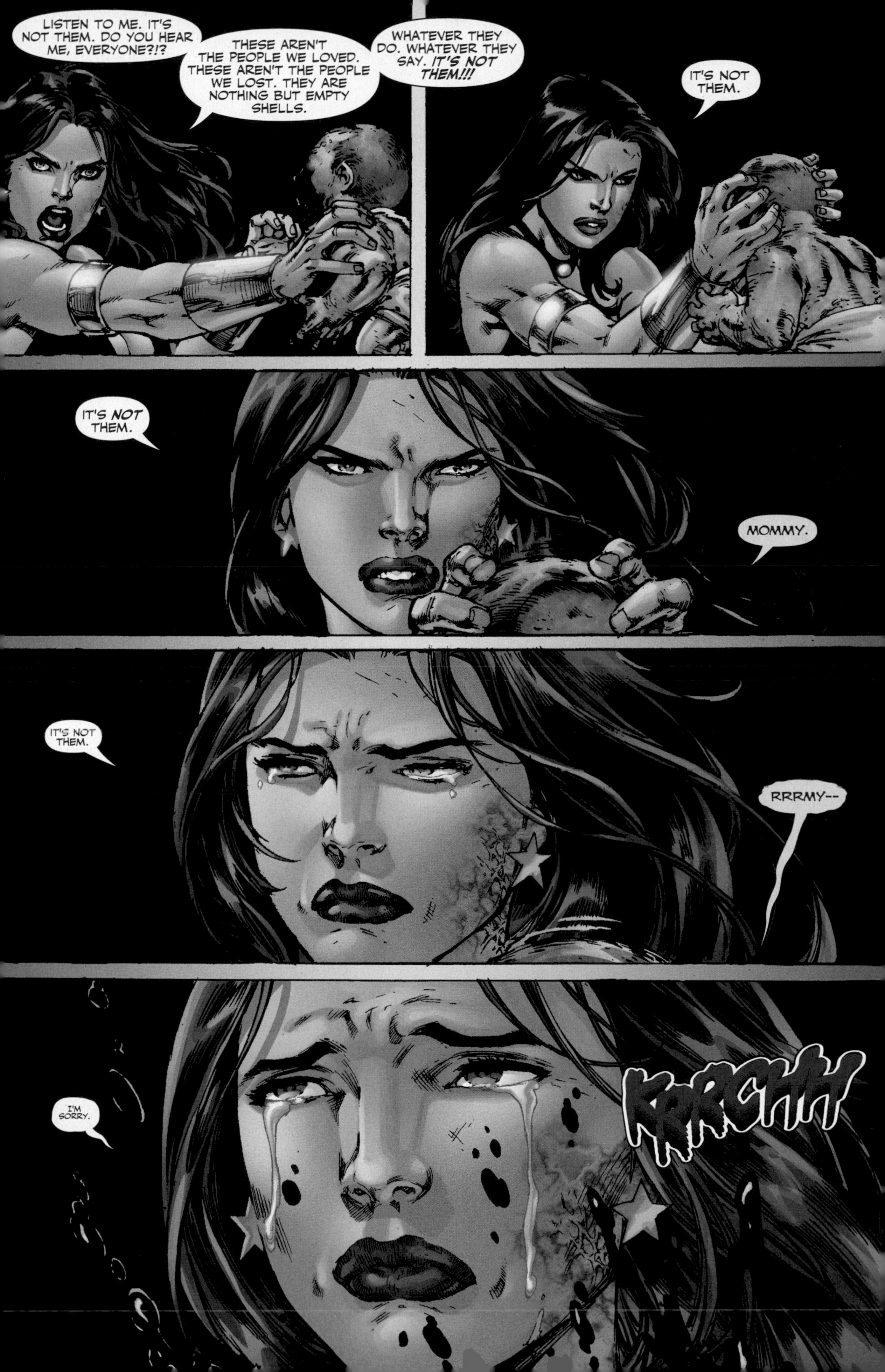
LISTEN TO ME. IT'S NOT THEM. DO YOU HEAR ME, EVERYONE?!?
THESE AREN'T THE PEOPLE WE LOVED. THESE AREN'T THE PEOPLE WE LOST. THEY ARE NOTHING BUT EMPTY SHELLS.
WHATEVER THEY DO. WHATEVER THEY SAY. IT'S NOT THEM!!!
IT'S NOT THEM.
IT'S NOT THEM.
MOMMY.
IT'S NOT THEM.
RRRMY--
I'M SORRY.
KRRCHH

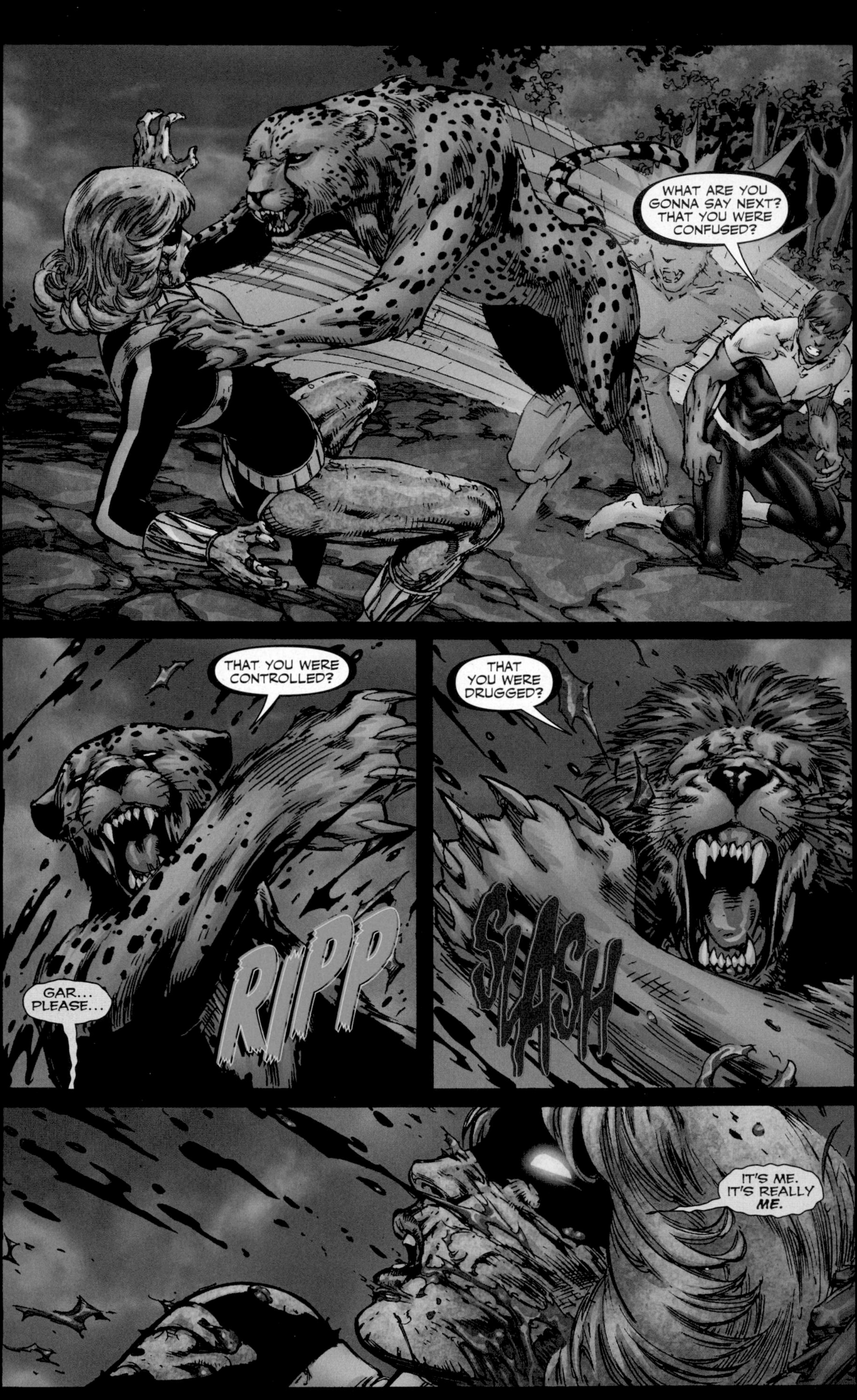
WHAT ARE YOU GONNA SAY NEXT? THAT YOU WERE CONFUSED?
THAT YOU WERE CONTROLLED?
GAR... PLEASE...
RIPP
THAT YOU WERE DRUGGED?
SLASH
IT'S ME. IT'S REALLY *ME.*

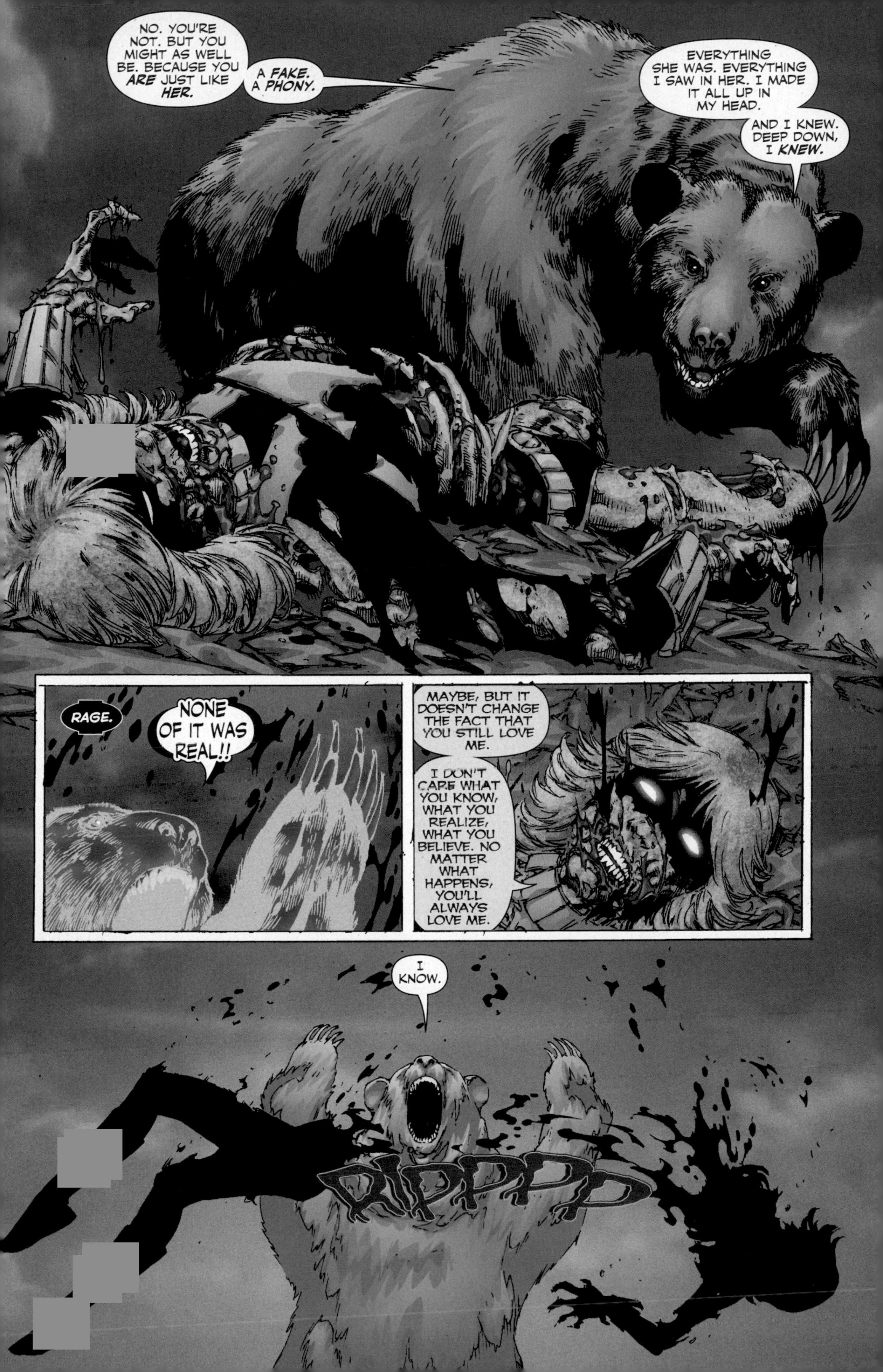
NO. YOU'RE NOT. BUT YOU MIGHT AS WELL BE. BECAUSE YOU ARE JUST LIKE HER.
A FAKE. A PHONY.
EVERYTHING SHE WAS. EVERYTHING I SAW IN HER. I MADE IT ALL UP IN MY HEAD.
AND I KNEW. DEEP DOWN, I KNEW.
RAGE.
NONE OF IT WAS REAL!!
MAYBE, BUT IT DOESN'T CHANGE THE FACT THAT YOU STILL LOVE ME.
I DON'T CARE WHAT YOU KNOW, WHAT YOU REALIZE, WHAT YOU BELIEVE. NO MATTER WHAT HAPPENS, YOU'LL ALWAYS LOVE ME.
I KNOW.
RIPPPP

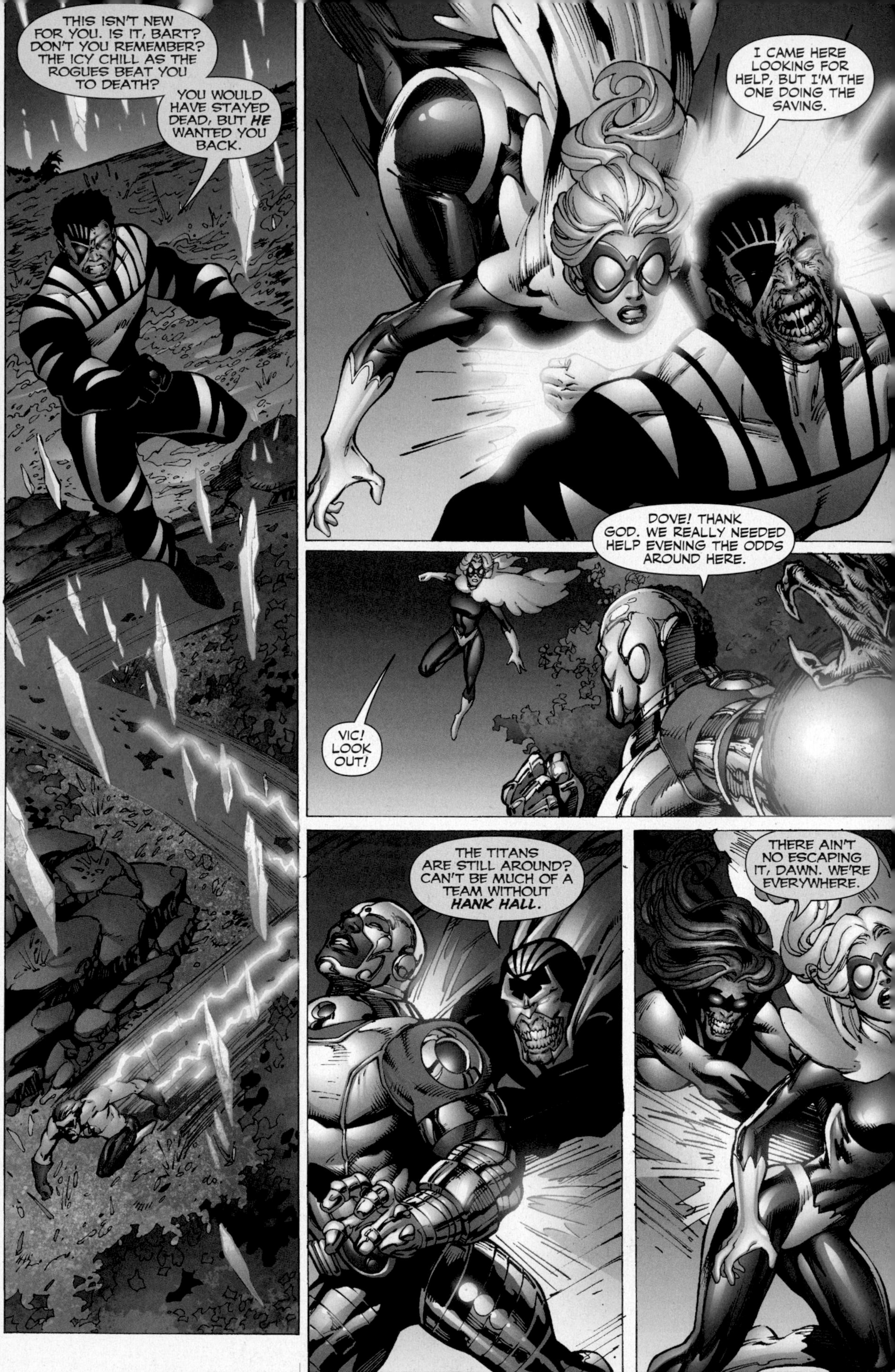
THIS ISN'T NEW FOR YOU. IS IT, BART? DON'T YOU REMEMBER? THE ICY CHILL AS THE ROGUES BEAT YOU TO DEATH?
YOU WOULD HAVE STAYED DEAD, BUT HE WANTED YOU BACK.
I CAME HERE LOOKING FOR HELP, BUT I'M THE ONE DOING THE SAVING.
DOVE! THANK GOD. WE REALLY NEEDED HELP EVENING THE ODDS AROUND HERE.
VIC! LOOK OUT!
THE TITANS ARE STILL AROUND? CAN'T BE MUCH OF A TEAM WITHOUT HANK HALL.
THERE AIN'T NO ESCAPING IT, DAWN. WE'RE EVERYWHERE.

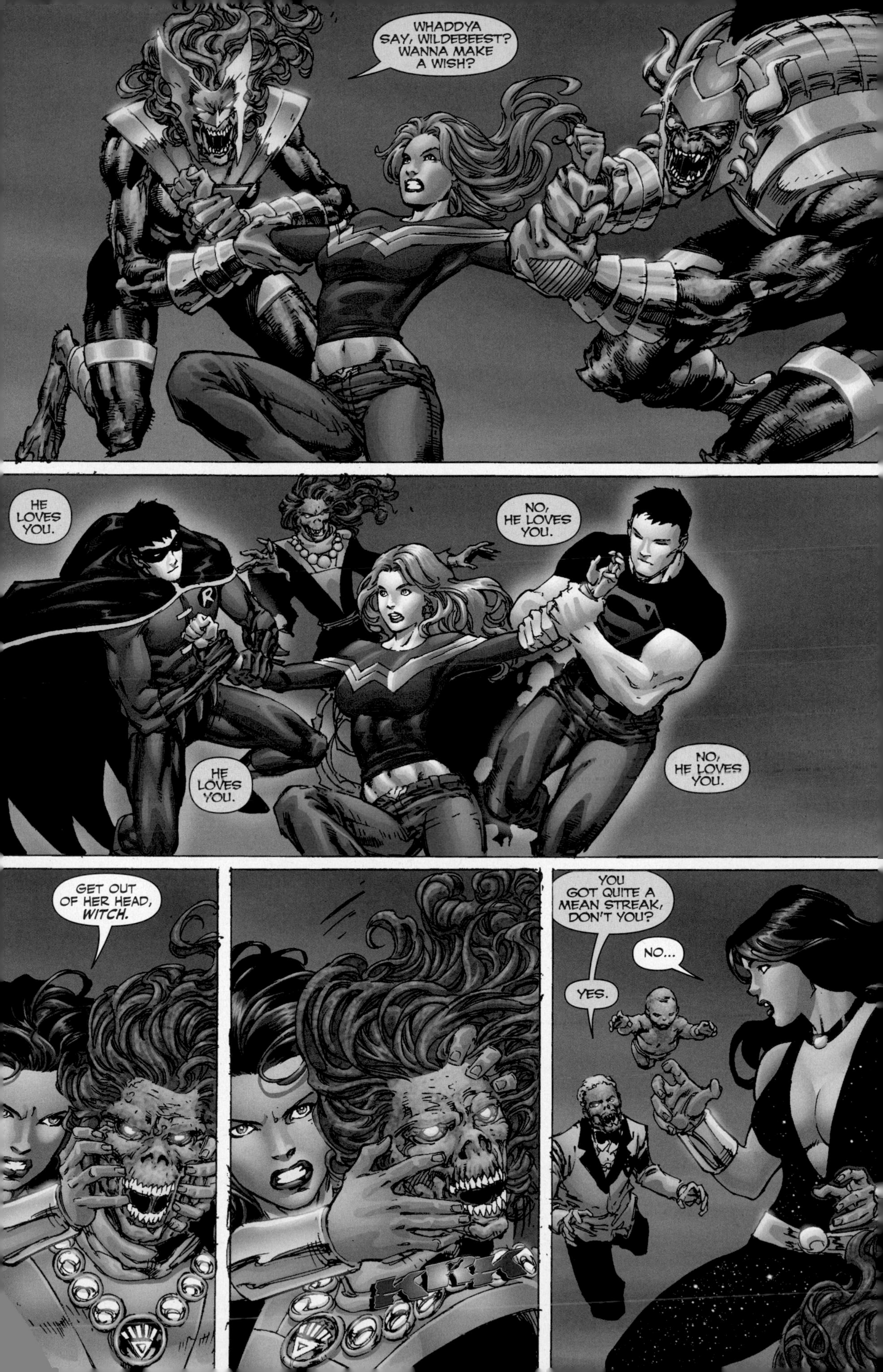
WHADDYA SAY, WILDEBEEST? WANNA MAKE A WISH?
HE LOVES YOU.
NO, HE LOVES YOU.
HE LOVES YOU.
NO, HE LOVES YOU.
GET OUT OF HER HEAD, WITCH.
KRK
YOU GOT QUITE A MEAN STREAK, DON'T YOU?
NO...
YES.

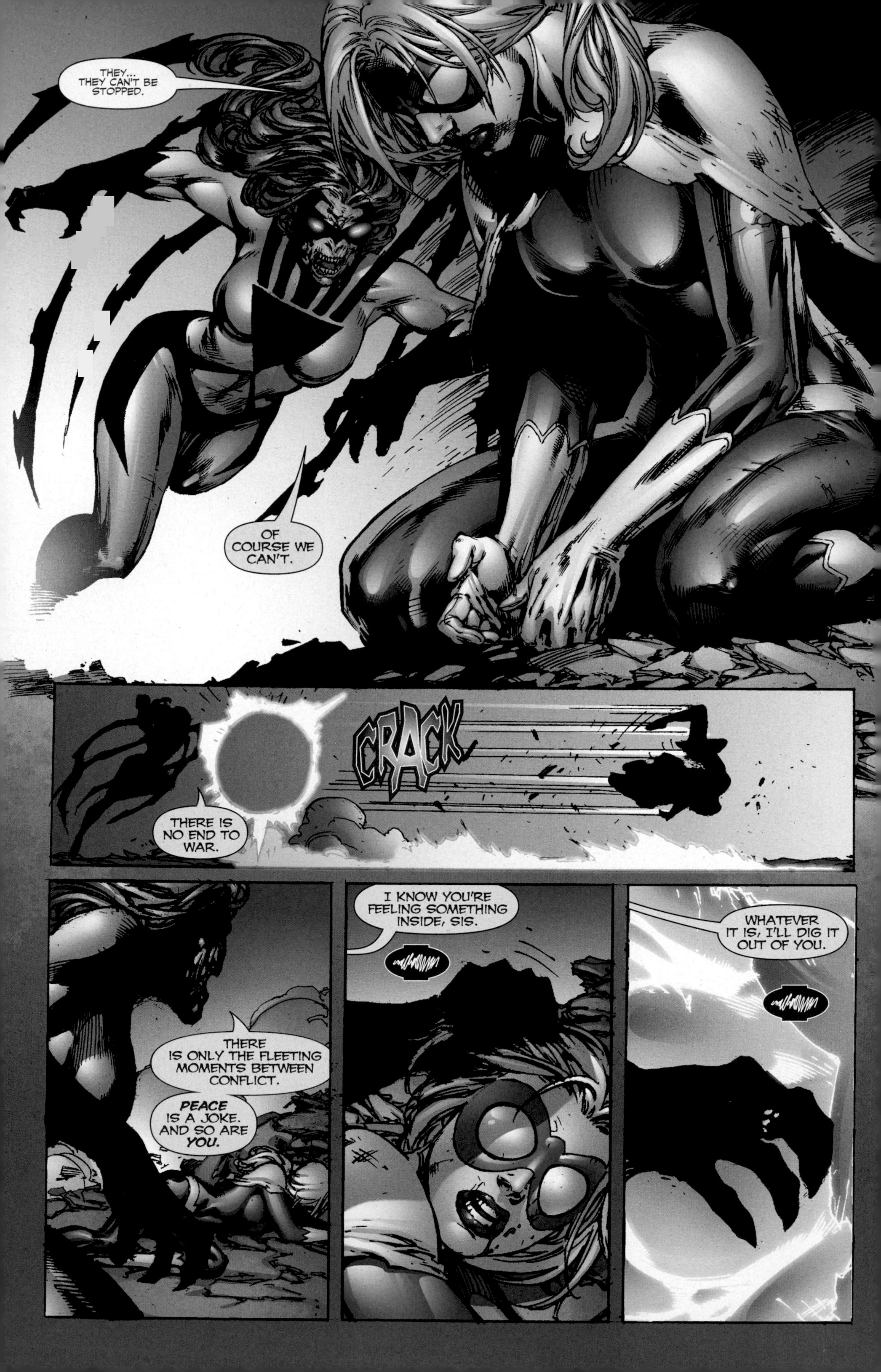
THEY... THEY CAN'T BE STOPPED.
OF COURSE WE CAN'T.
CRACK
THERE IS NO END TO WAR.
THERE IS ONLY THE FLEETING MOMENTS BETWEEN CONFLICT.
PEACE IS A JOKE. AND SO ARE YOU.
I KNOW YOU'RE FEELING SOMETHING INSIDE, SIS.
WHATEVER IT IS, I'LL DIG IT OUT OF YOU.

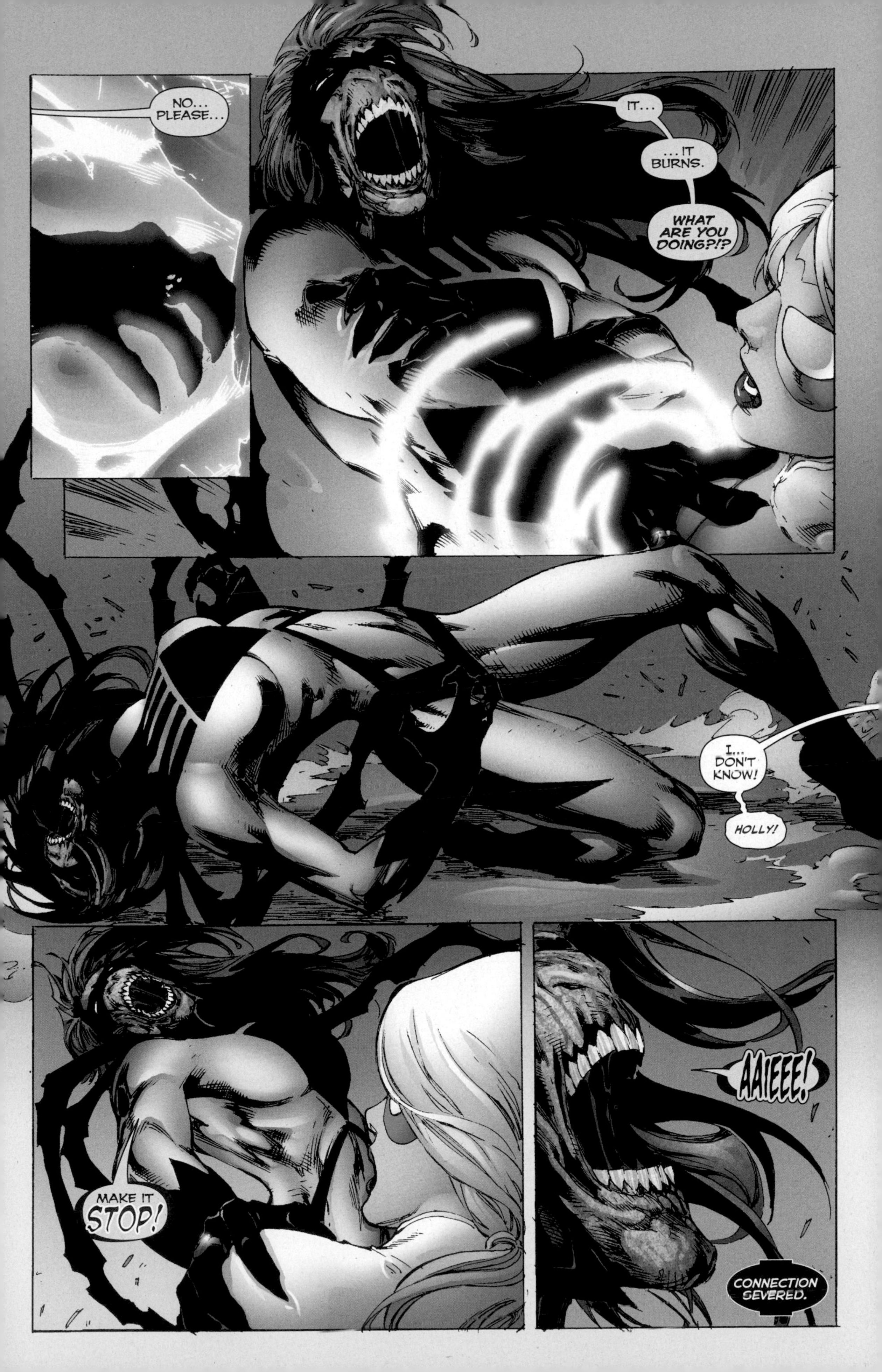
NO... PLEASE...
IT...
...IT BURNS.
WHAT ARE YOU DOING?!?
I... DON'T KNOW!
HOLLY!
MAKE IT STOP!
AAIEEE!
CONNECTION SEVERED.

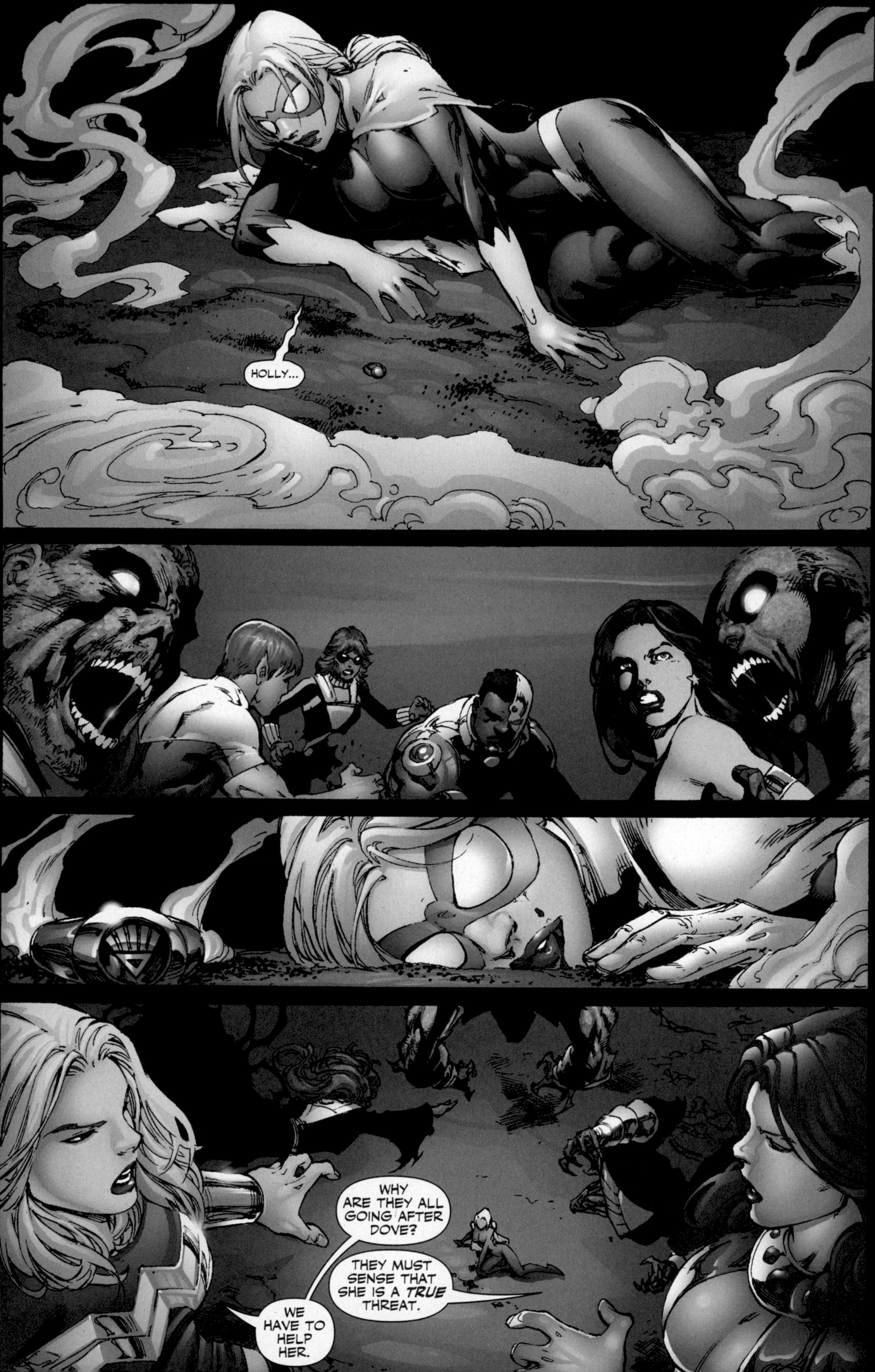
HOLLY...
WHY ARE THEY ALL GOING AFTER DOVE?
THEY MUST SENSE THAT SHE IS A *TRUE* THREAT.
WE HAVE TO HELP HER.

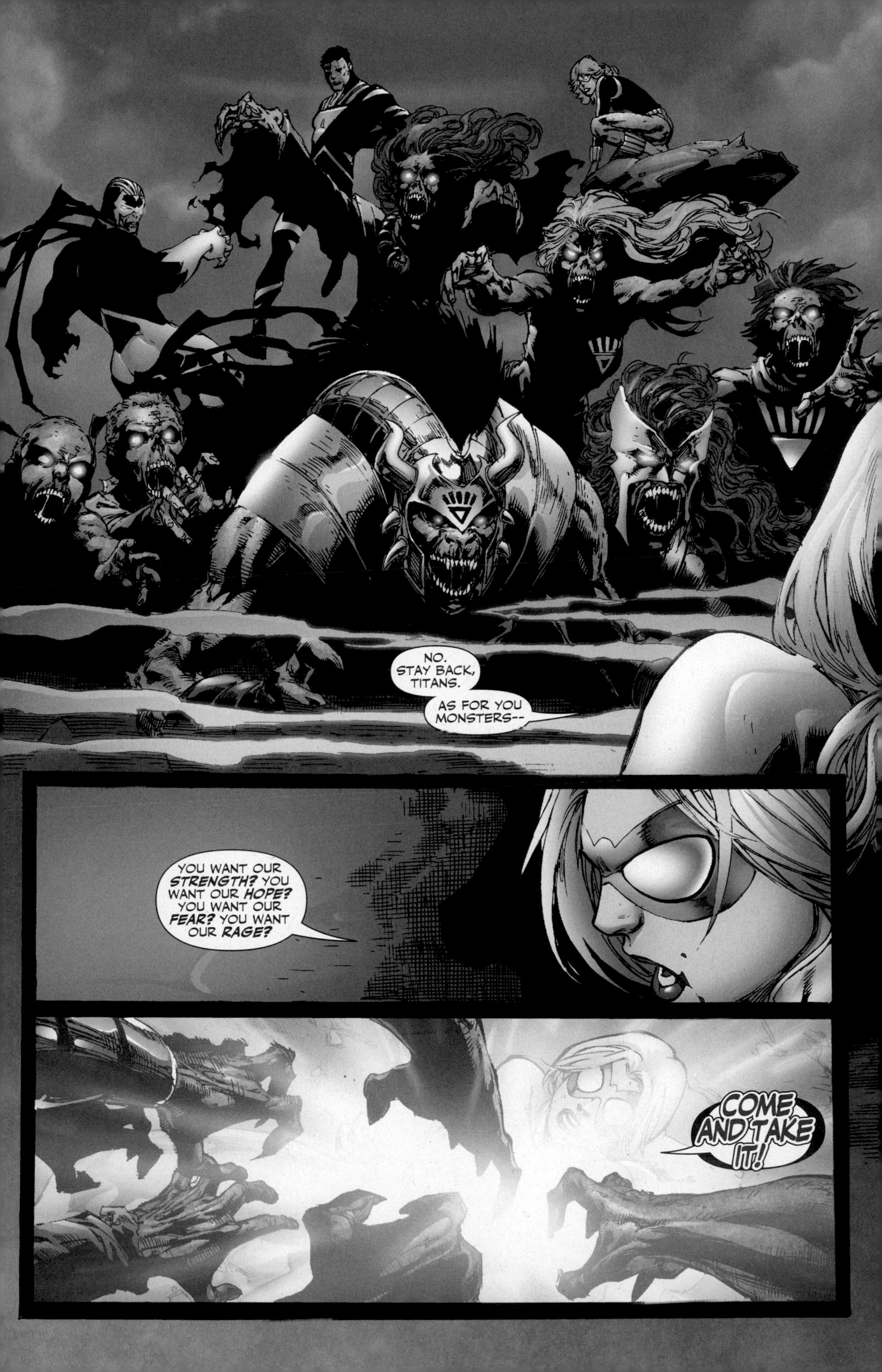
NO. STAY BACK, TITANS.
AS FOR YOU MONSTERS--
YOU WANT OUR *STRENGTH?* YOU WANT OUR *HOPE?* YOU WANT OUR *FEAR?* YOU WANT OUR *RAGE?*
COME AND TAKE IT!

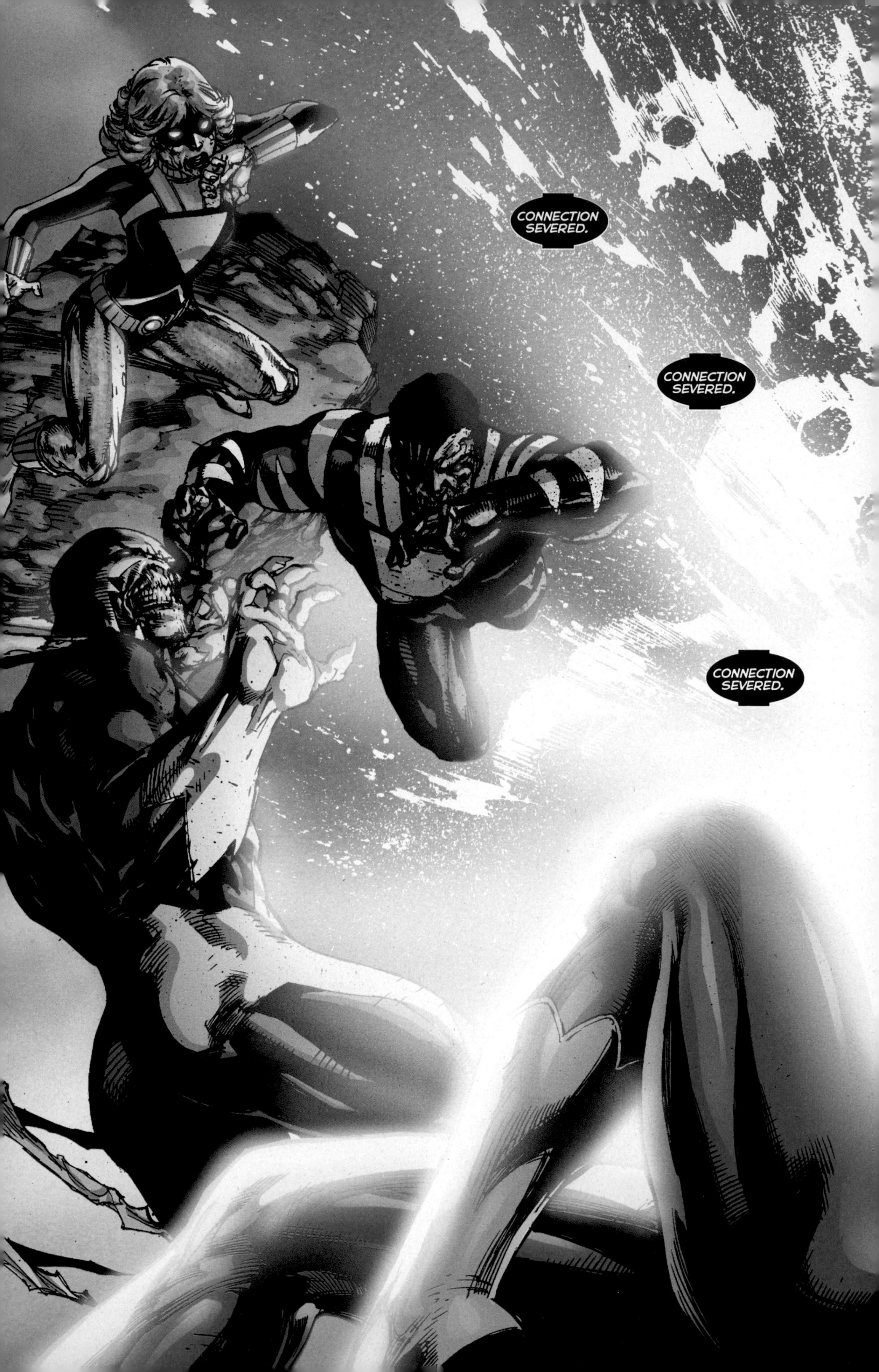
CONNECTION SEVERED.
CONNECTION SEVERED.
CONNECTION SEVERED.

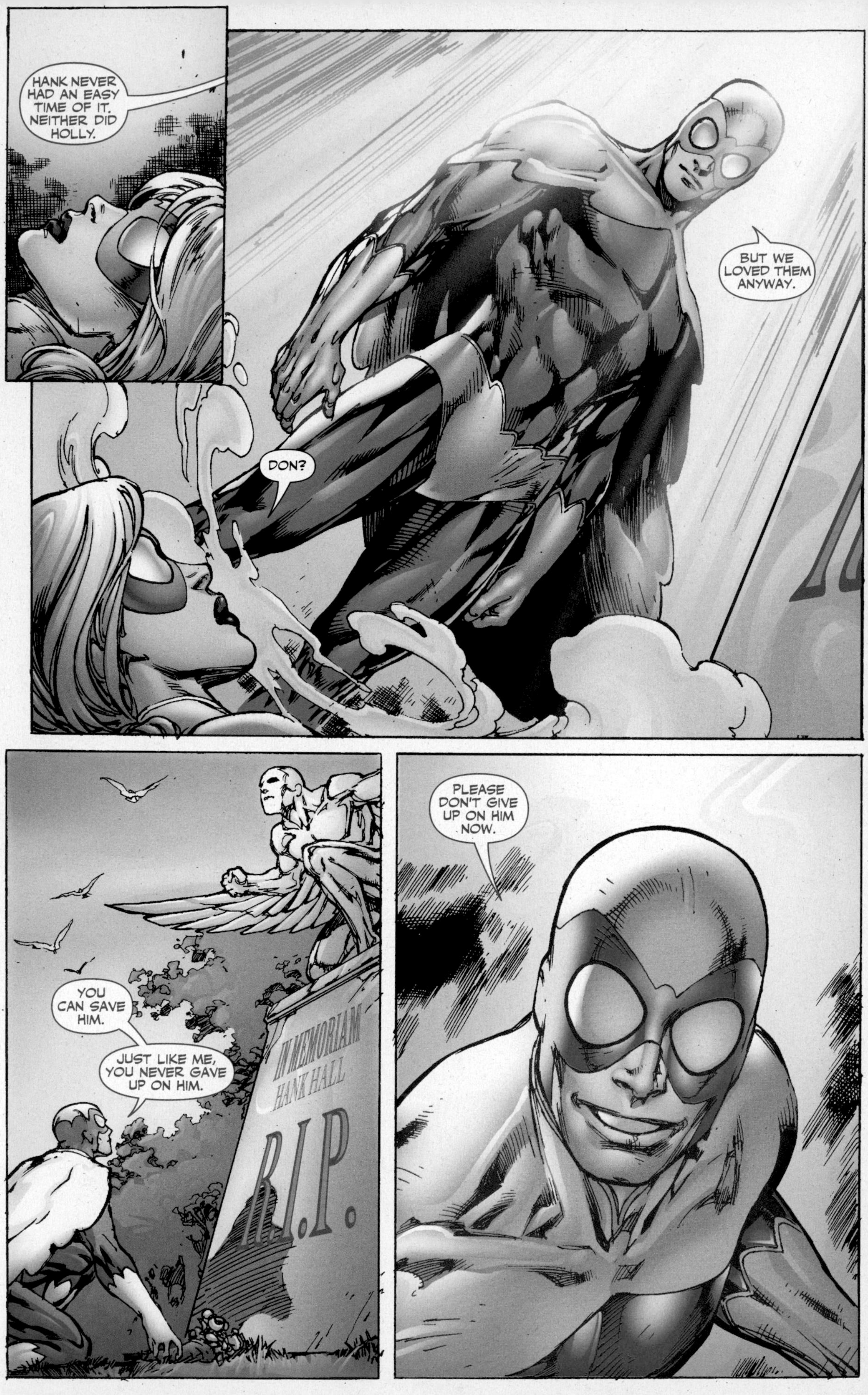
HANK NEVER HAD AN EASY TIME OF IT. NEITHER DID HOLLY.
BUT WE LOVED THEM ANYWAY.
DON?
YOU CAN SAVE HIM.
JUST LIKE ME, YOU NEVER GAVE UP ON HIM.
IN MEMORIAM
HANK HALL
R.I.P.
PLEASE DON'T GIVE UP ON HIM NOW.

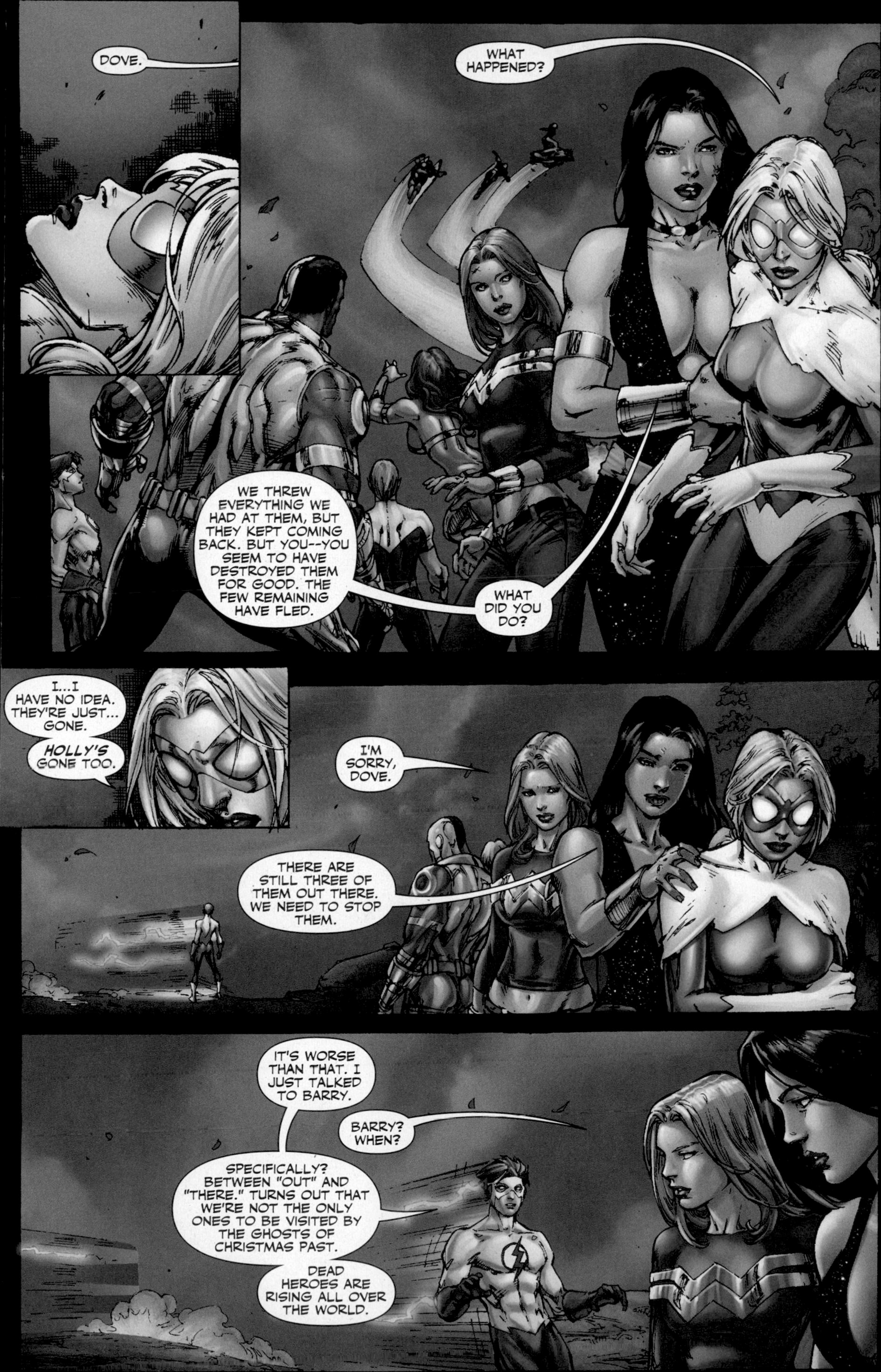
DOVE.
WHAT HAPPENED?
WE THREW EVERYTHING WE HAD AT THEM, BUT THEY KEPT COMING BACK. BUT YOU--YOU SEEM TO HAVE DESTROYED THEM FOR GOOD. THE FEW REMAINING HAVE FLED.
WHAT DID YOU DO?
I...I HAVE NO IDEA. THEY'RE JUST... GONE.
HOLLY'S GONE TOO.
I'M SORRY, DOVE.
THERE ARE STILL THREE OF THEM OUT THERE. WE NEED TO STOP THEM.
IT'S WORSE THAN THAT. I JUST TALKED TO BARRY.
BARRY? WHEN?
SPECIFICALLY? BETWEEN "OUT" AND "THERE." TURNS OUT THAT WE'RE NOT THE ONLY ONES TO BE VISITED BY THE GHOSTS OF CHRISTMAS PAST.
DEAD HEROES ARE RISING ALL OVER THE WORLD.

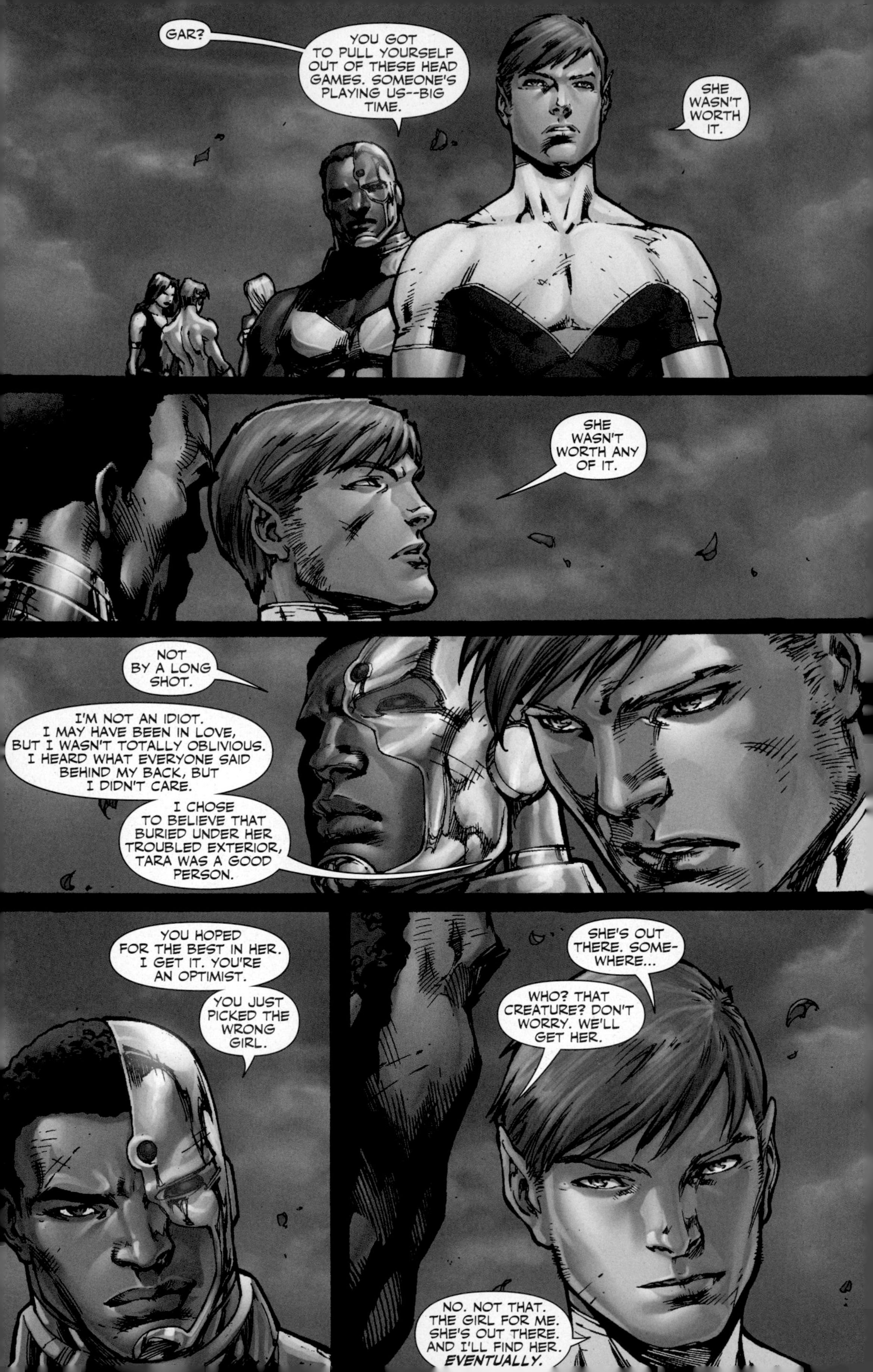

GAR?
YOU GOT TO PULL YOURSELF OUT OF THESE HEAD GAMES. SOMEONE'S PLAYING US--BIG TIME.
SHE WASN'T WORTH IT.
SHE WASN'T WORTH ANY OF IT.
NOT BY A LONG SHOT.
I'M NOT AN IDIOT. I MAY HAVE BEEN IN LOVE, BUT I WASN'T TOTALLY OBLIVIOUS. I HEARD WHAT EVERYONE SAID BEHIND MY BACK, BUT I DIDN'T CARE.
I CHOSE TO BELIEVE THAT BURIED UNDER HER TROUBLED EXTERIOR, TARA WAS A GOOD PERSON.
YOU HOPED FOR THE BEST IN HER. I GET IT. YOU'RE AN OPTIMIST.
YOU JUST PICKED THE WRONG GIRL.
SHE'S OUT THERE. SOME-WHERE...
WHO? THAT CREATURE? DON'T WORRY. WE'LL GET HER.
NO. NOT THAT. THE GIRL FOR ME. SHE'S OUT THERE. AND I'LL FIND HER. *EVENTUALLY.*

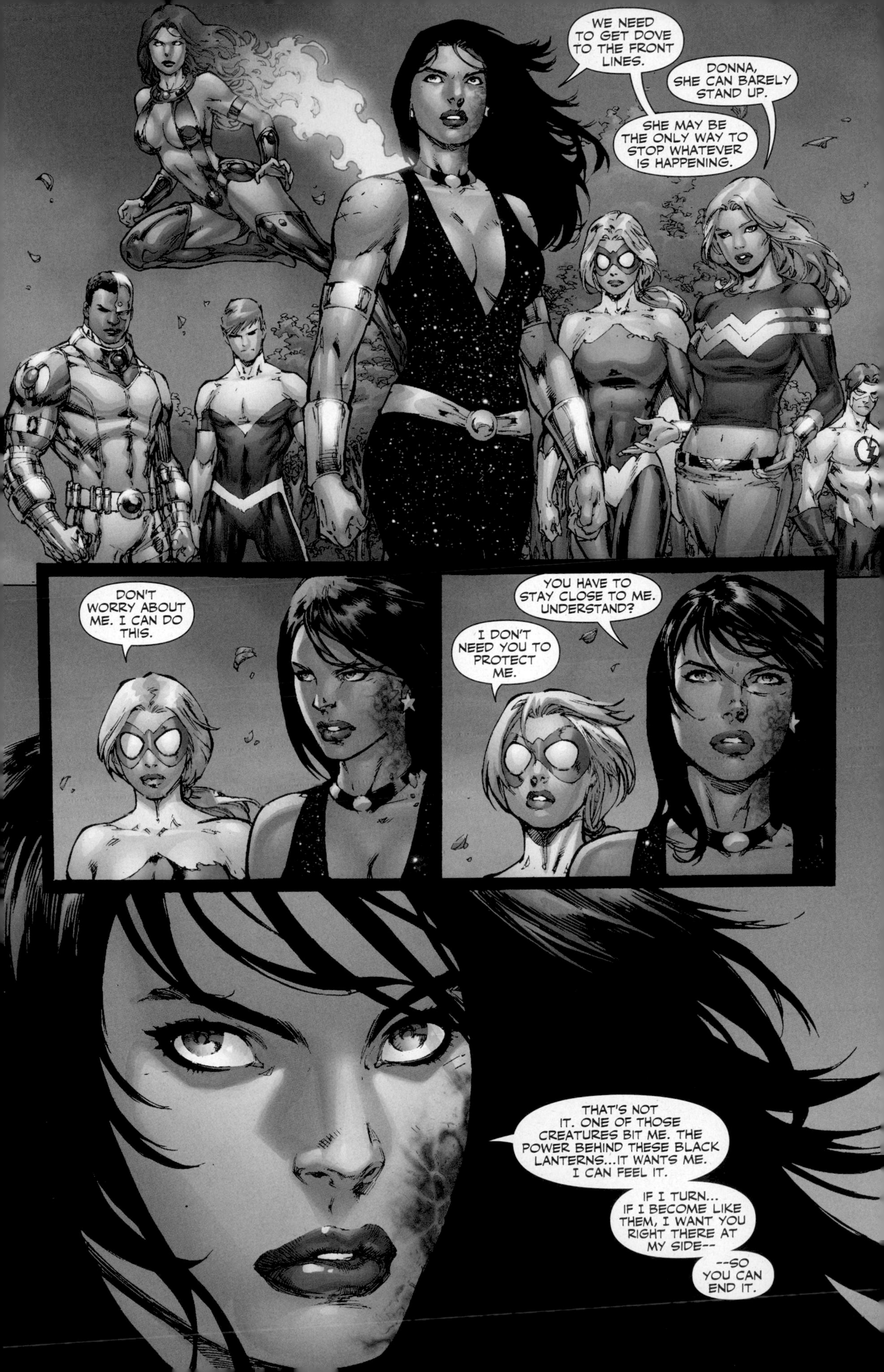
WE NEED TO GET DOVE TO THE FRONT LINES.
DONNA, SHE CAN BARELY STAND UP.
SHE MAY BE THE ONLY WAY TO STOP WHATEVER IS HAPPENING.
DON'T WORRY ABOUT ME. I CAN DO THIS.
YOU HAVE TO STAY CLOSE TO ME. UNDERSTAND?
I DON'T NEED YOU TO PROTECT ME.
THAT'S NOT IT. ONE OF THOSE CREATURES BIT ME. THE POWER BEHIND THESE BLACK LANTERNS...IT WANTS ME. I CAN FEEL IT.
IF I TURN... IF I BECOME LIKE THEM, I WANT YOU RIGHT THERE AT MY SIDE--
--SO YOU CAN END IT.

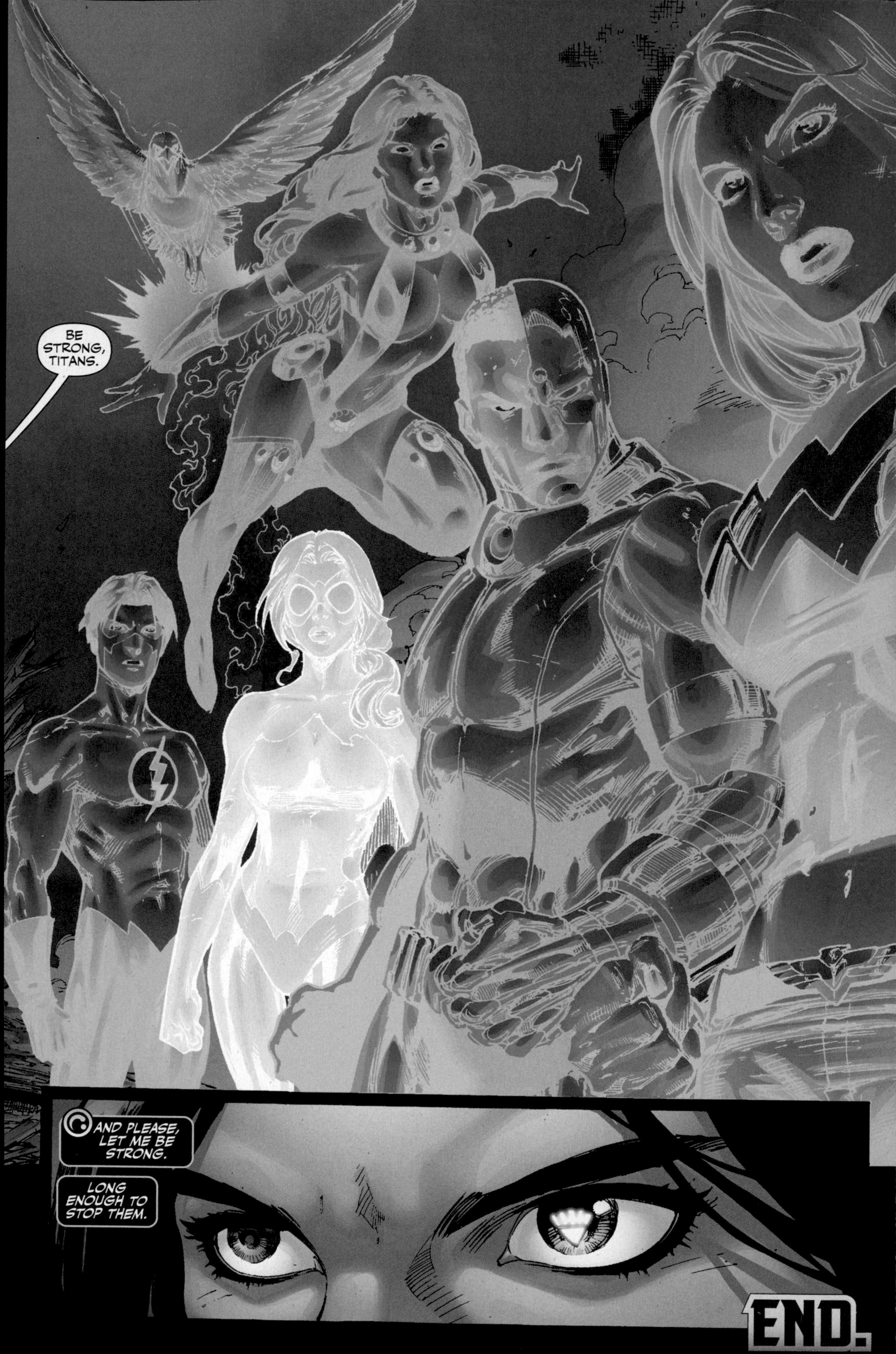
BE STRONG, TITANS.
AND PLEASE, LET ME BE STRONG.
LONG ENOUGH TO STOP THEM.
END.

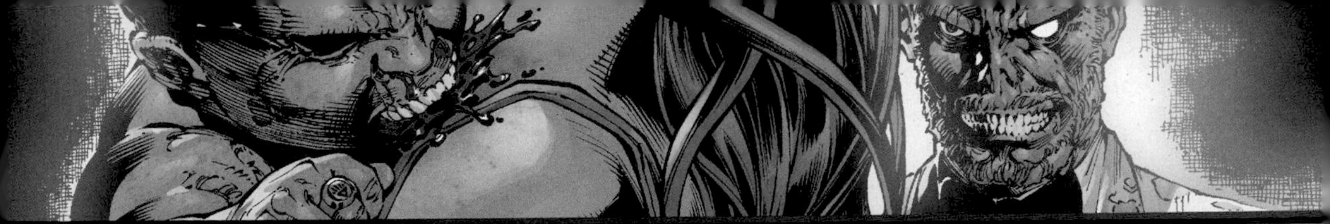

BLACKEST NIGHT
BLACK LANTERN CORPS
VOLUME ONE
VARIANT COVER GALLERY

BLACKEST NIGHT: BATMAN 1–3

Covers by Bill Sienkiewicz

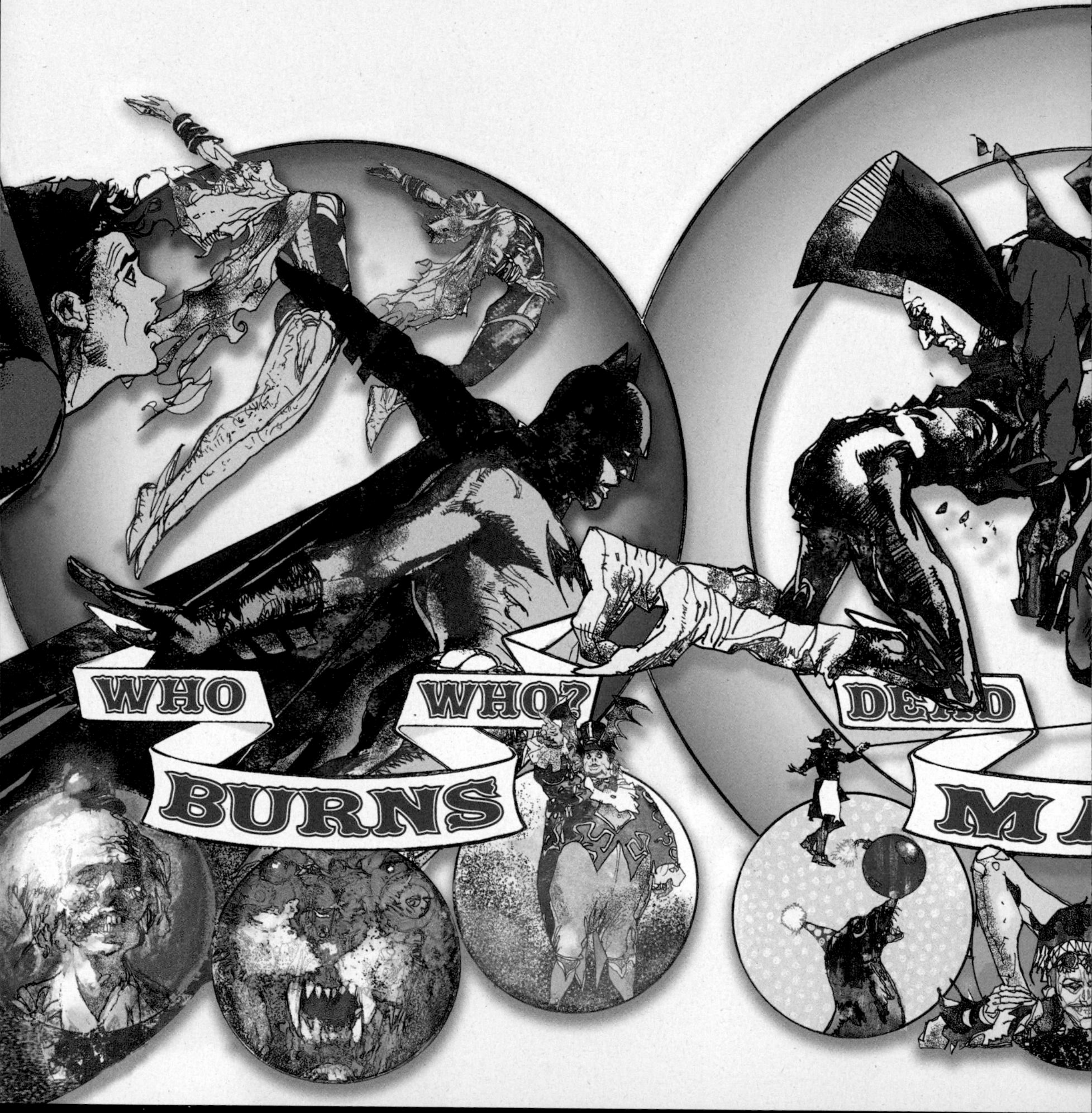
WHO
WHO?
BURNS
DEAD

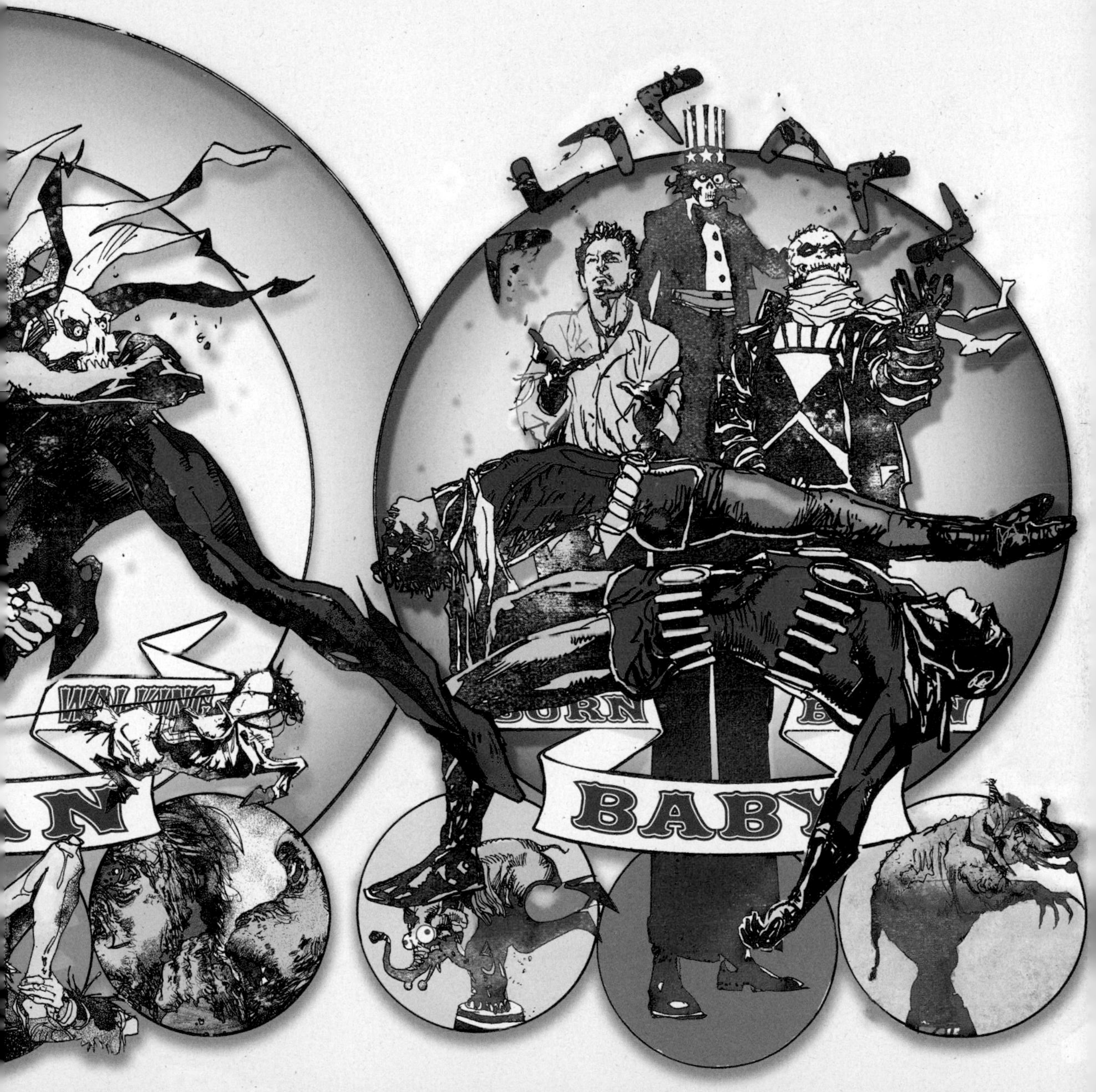
WALKING
BURN
BABY
N

BLACKEST NIGHT: SUPERMAN 1
Cover by Shane Davis and
Sandra Hope with Alex Sinclair

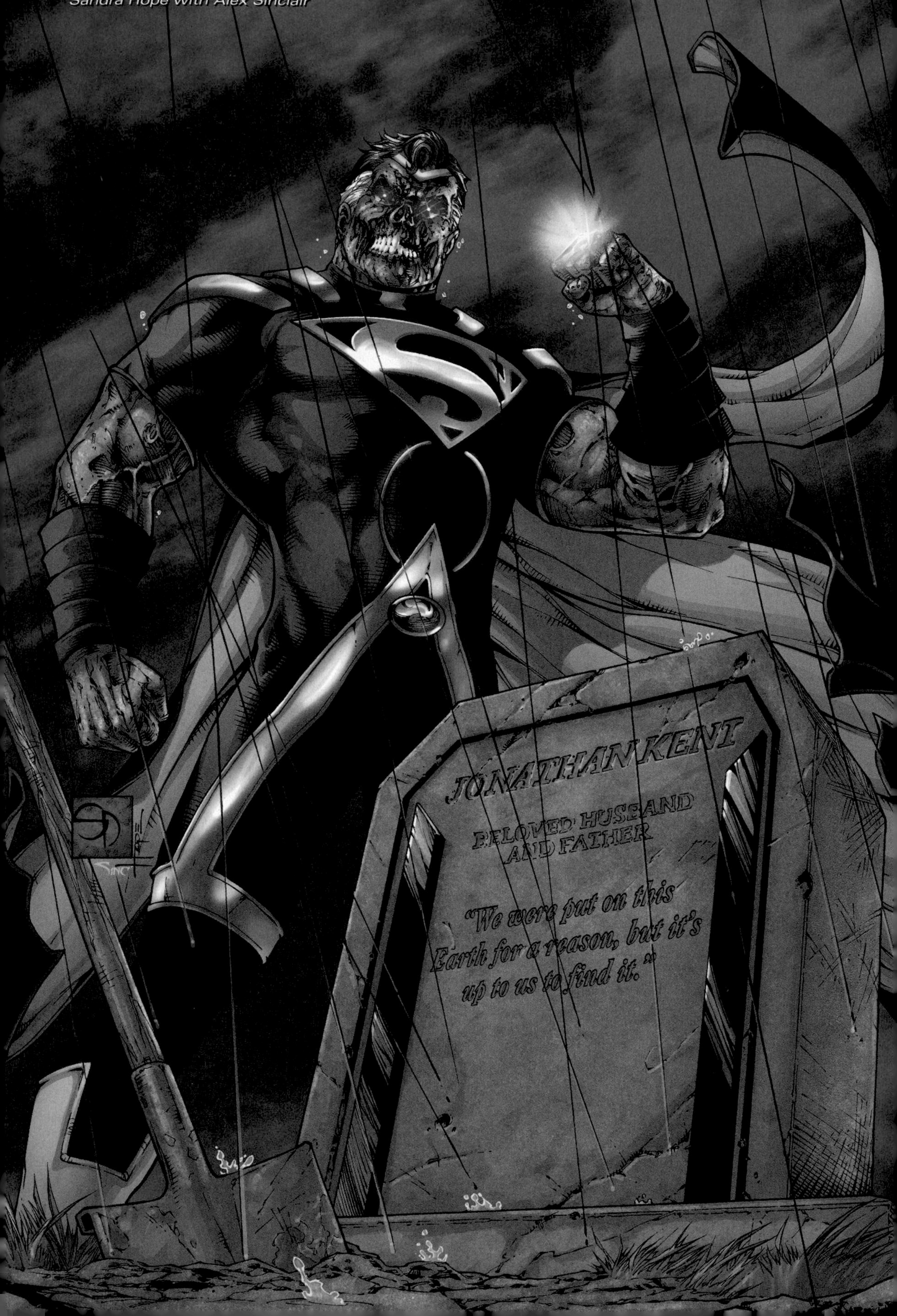
JONATHAN KENT
BELOVED HUSBAND
AND FATHER
"We were put on this
Earth for a reason, but it's
up to us to find it."

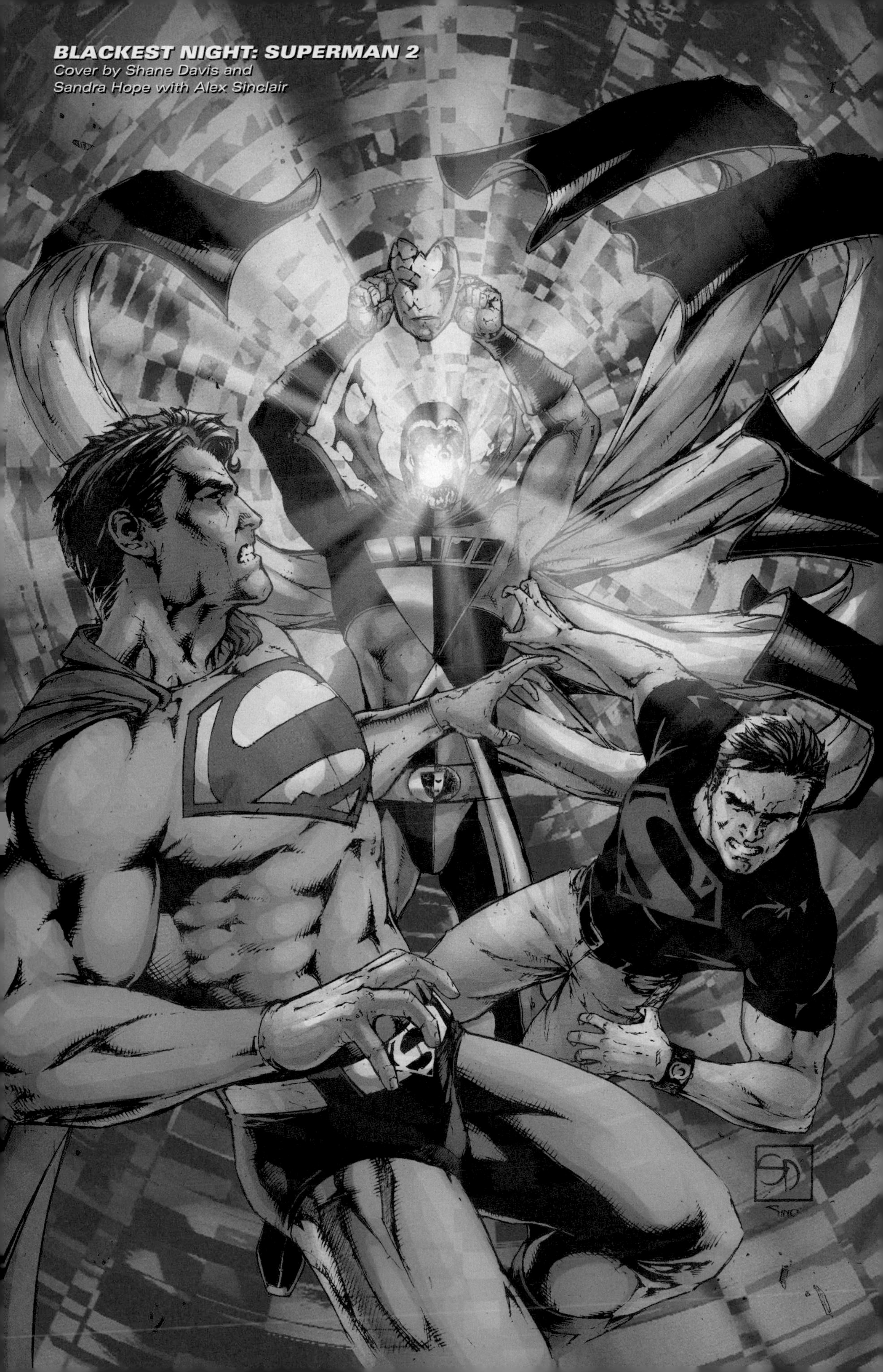

BLACKEST NIGHT: SUPERMAN 2
Cover by Shane Davis and Sandra Hope with Alex Sinclair

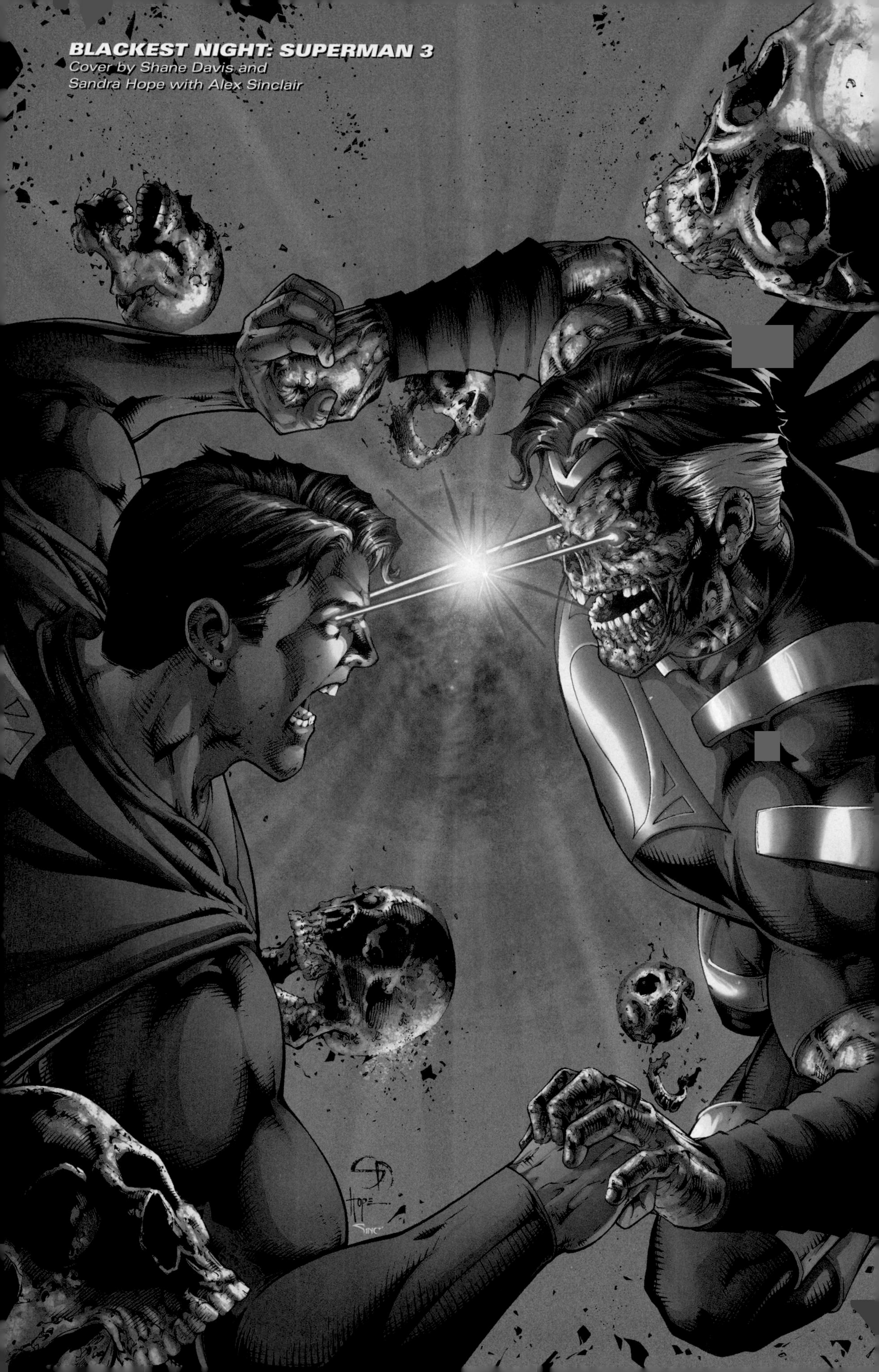

BLACKEST NIGHT: SUPERMAN 3
Cover by Shane Davis and
Sandra Hope with Alex Sinclair

BLACKEST NIGHT: TITANS 1
Cover by Brian Haberlin

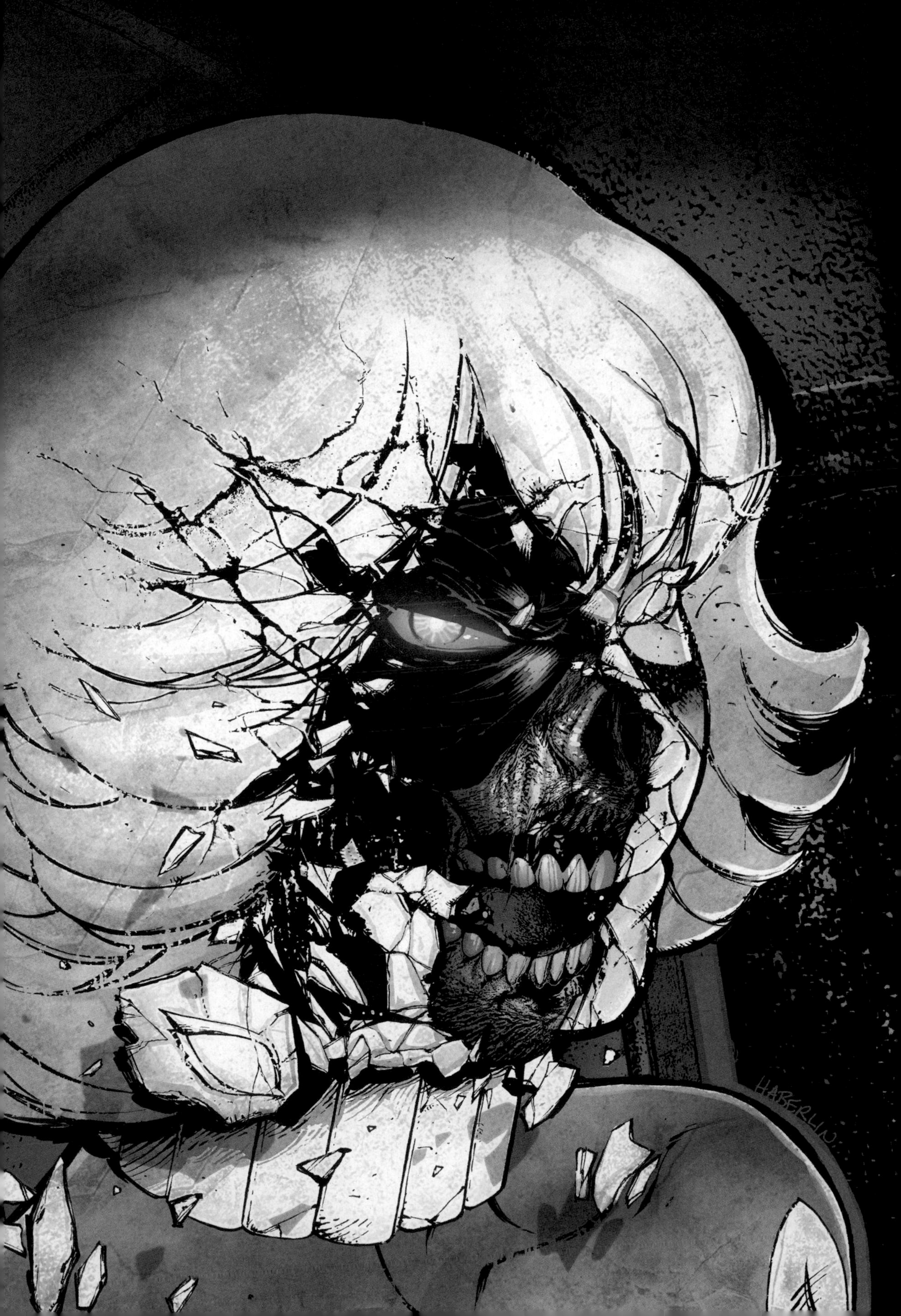
HABERLIN

BLACKEST NIGHT: TITANS 2
Cover by Brian Haberlin

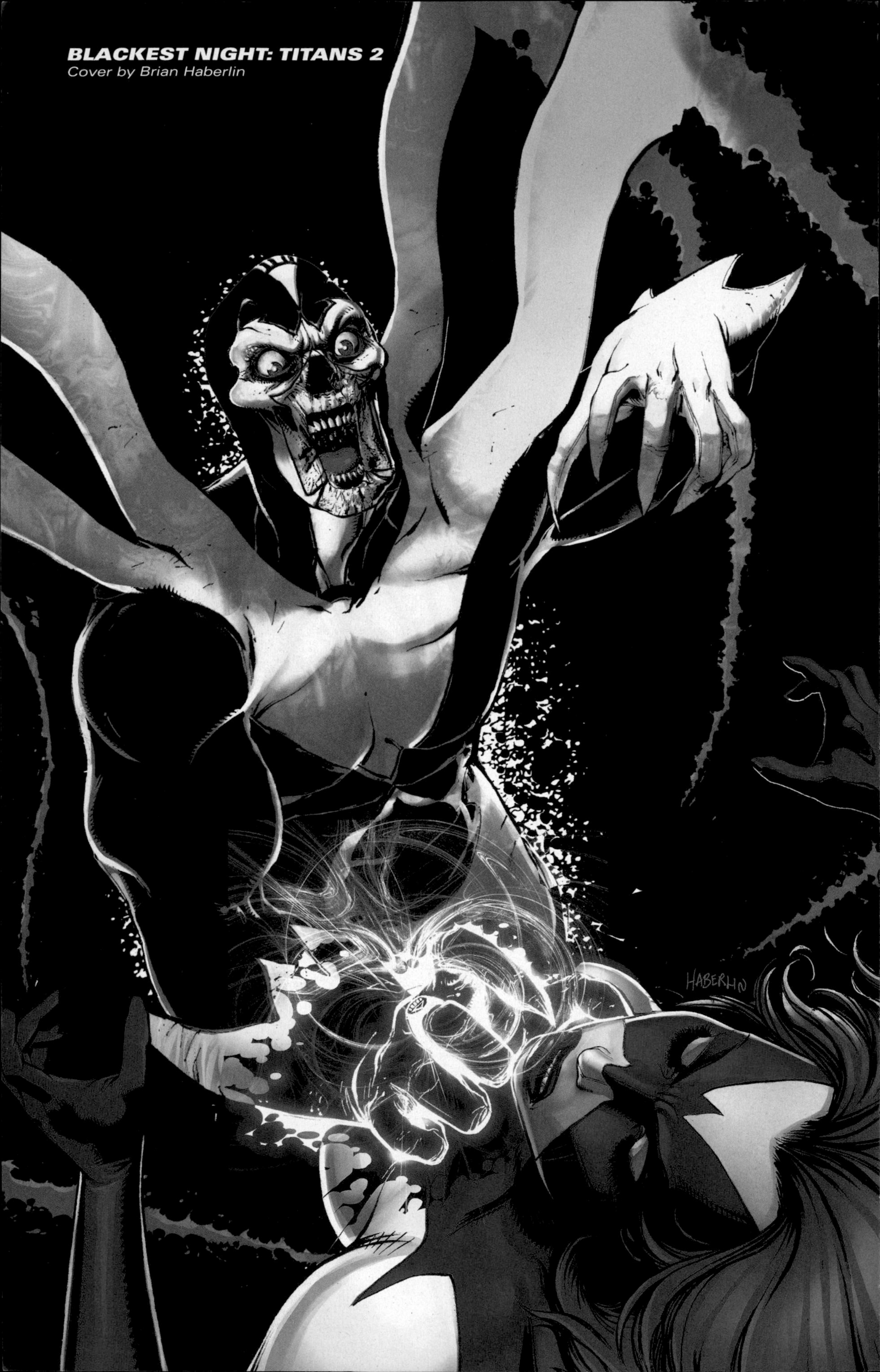
HABERLIN

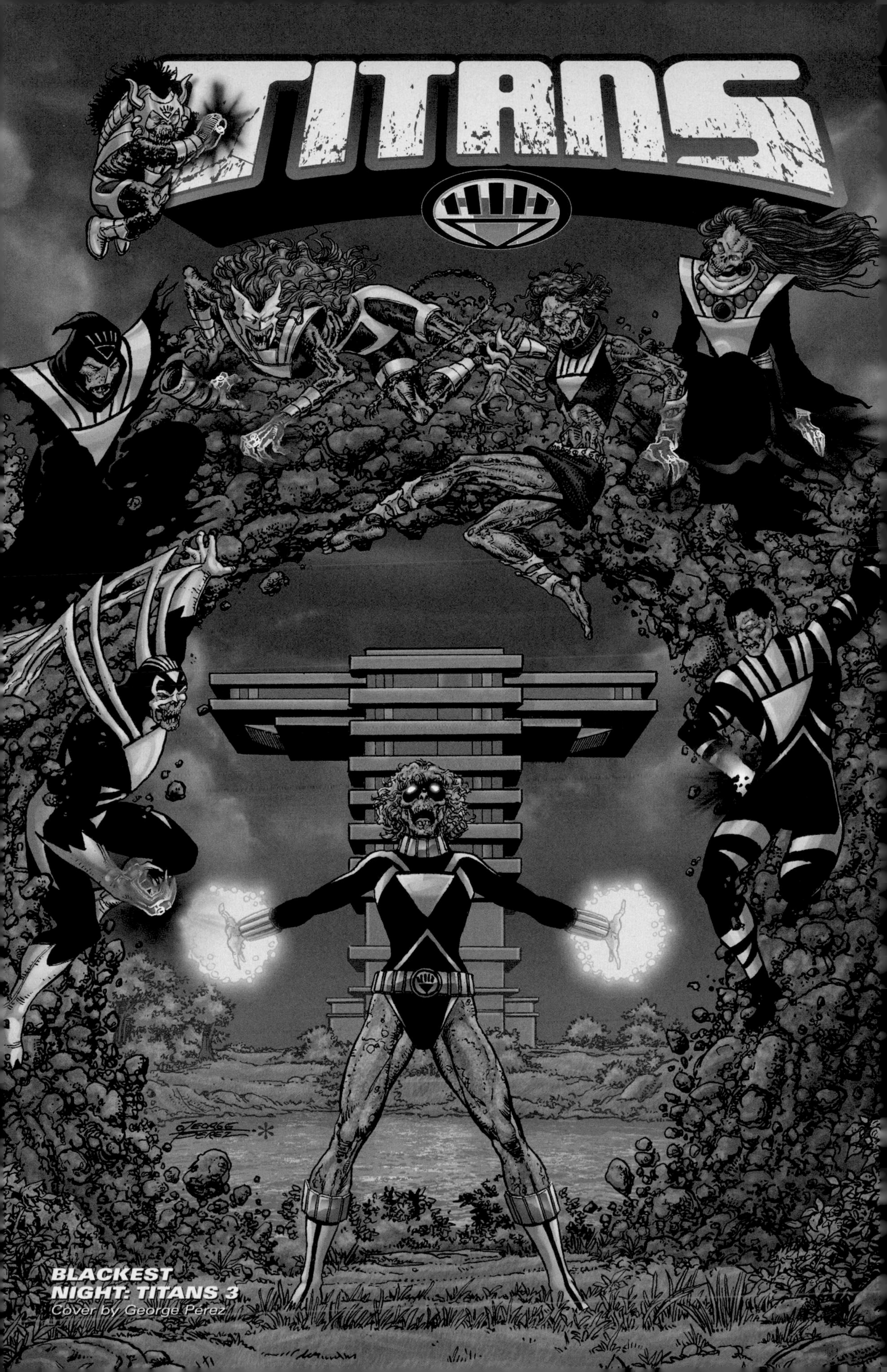
TITANS

BLACKEST NIGHT: TITANS 3
Cover by George Perez

BLACK LANTERN BATMAN VILLAINS

Designs by Joe Prado

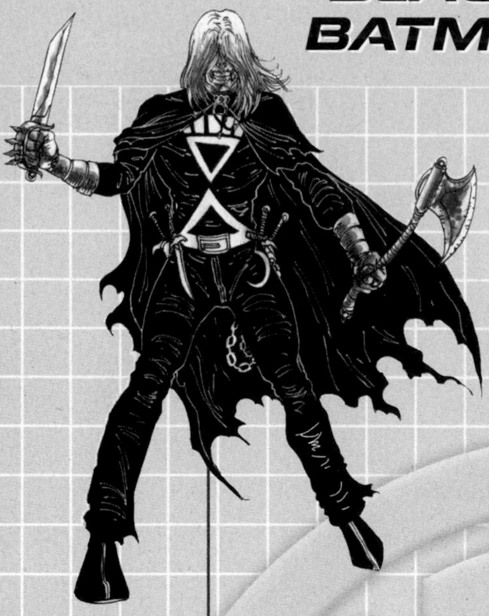

BLACK LANTERN ABATTOIR
ALTER EGO: ARNOLD ETCHISON
A CRAZED SERIAL KILLER, ABATTOIR FELL TO HIS DOOM WHEN JEAN PAUL VALLEY, WHO WAS THEN ACTING AS BATMAN, REFUSED TO ASSIST HIM. AS A BLACK LANTERN HE NOW SEEKS BATMAN, NOT KNOWING THAT DICK GRAYSON IS THE CURRENT ONE.

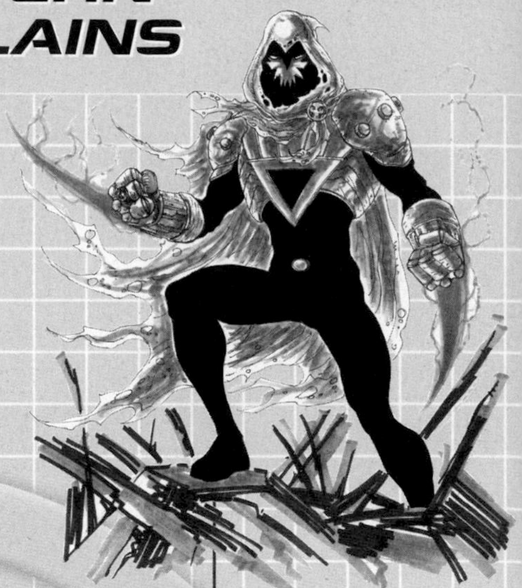

BLACK LANTERN AZRAEL
ALTER EGO: JEAN PAUL VALLEY JR.
HIGHLY INTELLIGENT COMPUTER EXPERT JEAN PAUL DISHED OUT HIS OWN BRAND OF JUSTICE AS THE VIGILANTE AZRAEL, BUT AFTER FACING HIS OWN ULTIMATE JUSTICE IN THE FORM OF TWO BULLETS, BLACK LANTERN AZRAEL CONTINUES DEALING OUT DEATH TO THE RESIDENTS OF GOTHAM CITY.

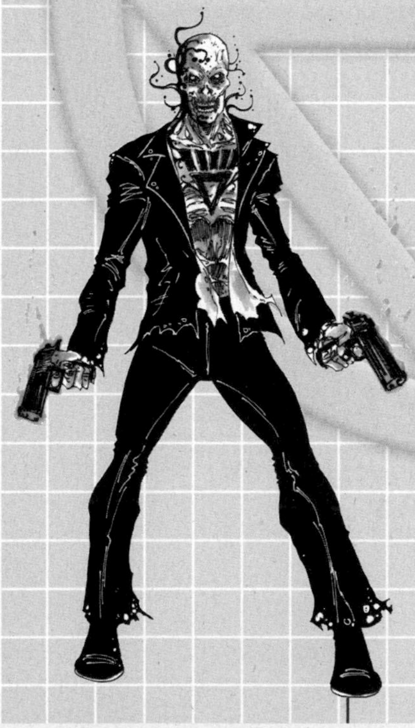

BLACK LANTERN BLACK MASK
ALTER EGO: ROMAN SIONIS
A GENIUS CRIME LORD WHOSE MASK WAS BURNED INTO HIS FACE. HE WAS LATER MURDERED BY CATWOMAN AS RETRIBUTION FOR HIS MANY VICIOUS CRIMES.

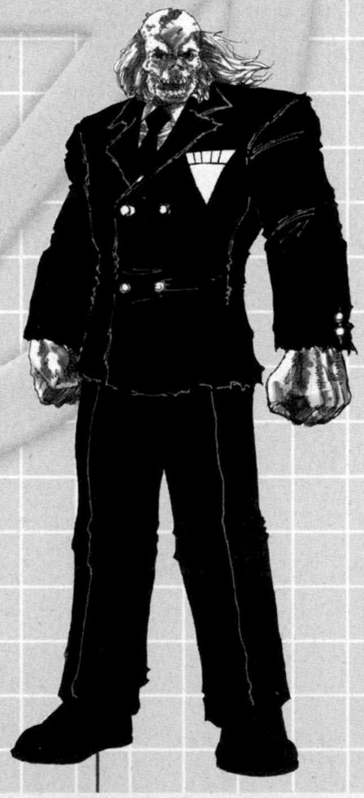

BLACK LANTERN BLOCKBUSTER
ALTER EGO: MARK DESMOND
SUPER STRENGTH AND STAMINA COULD NOT PROTECT BLOCKBUSTER FROM A GUNSHOT TO THE HEAD FROM TARANTULA.

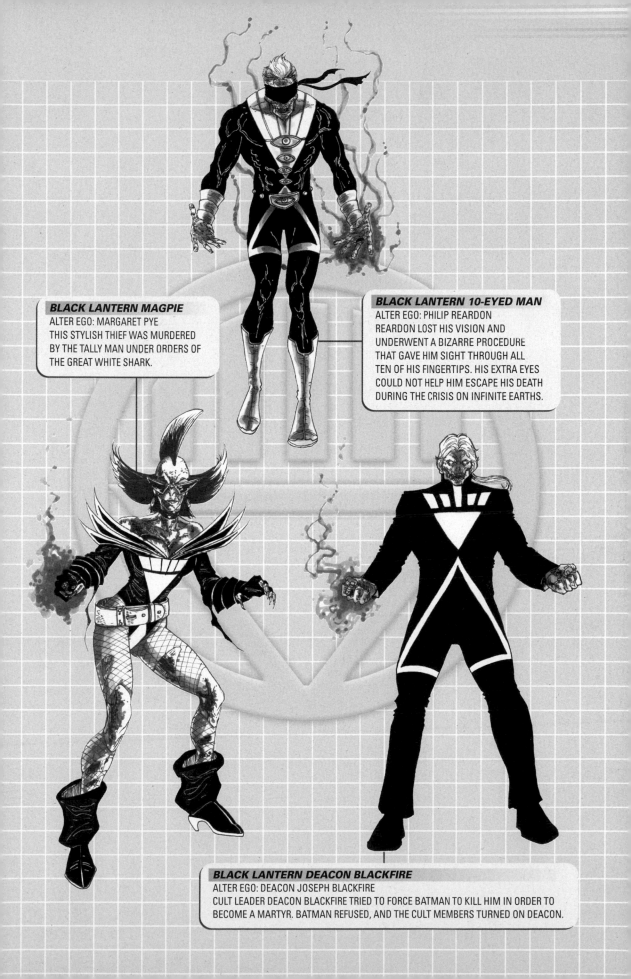

BLACK LANTERN MAGPIE
ALTER EGO: MARGARET PYE
THIS STYLISH THIEF WAS MURDERED
BY THE TALLY MAN UNDER ORDERS OF
THE GREAT WHITE SHARK.

BLACK LANTERN 10-EYED MAN
ALTER EGO: PHILIP REARDON
REARDON LOST HIS VISION AND
UNDERWENT A BIZARRE PROCEDURE
THAT GAVE HIM SIGHT THROUGH ALL
TEN OF HIS FINGERTIPS. HIS EXTRA EYES
COULD NOT HELP HIM ESCAPE HIS DEATH
DURING THE CRISIS ON INFINITE EARTHS.

BLACK LANTERN DEACON BLACKFIRE
ALTER EGO: DEACON JOSEPH BLACKFIRE
CULT LEADER DEACON BLACKFIRE TRIED TO FORCE BATMAN TO KILL HIM IN ORDER TO
BECOME A MARTYR. BATMAN REFUSED, AND THE CULT MEMBERS TURNED ON DEACON.

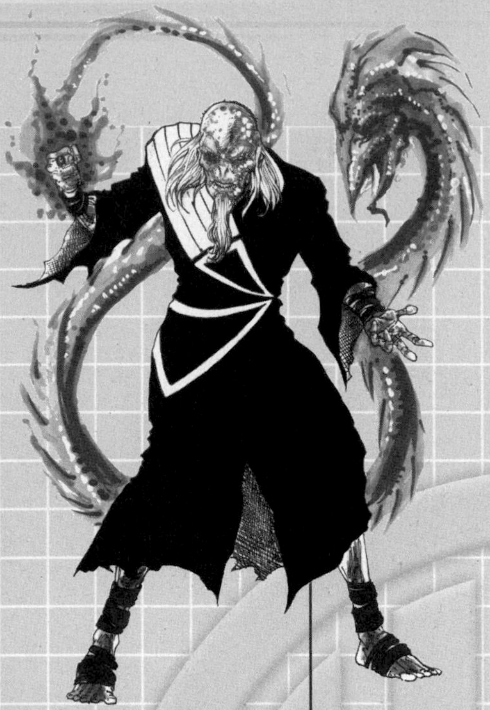

BLACK LANTERN SENSEI
ALTER EGO: UNKNOWN
A MASTER MARTIAL ARTIST WHO WAS ONCE IN CHARGE OF THE LEAGUE OF ASSASSINS, THE SENSEI MET HIS END WHEN HIS CORRUPT SOUL WAS JUDGED UNWORTHY.

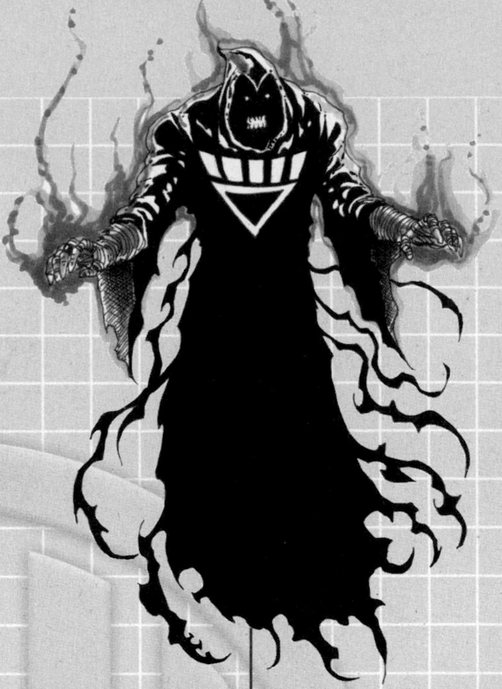

BLACK LANTERN SPOOK
ALTER EGO: VAL KALIBAN
SPOOK, WHO POSSESSED IMPRESSIVE HYPNOTIC SKILLS, WAS DECAPITATED BY DAMIAN WAYNE, THE SON OF BATMAN.

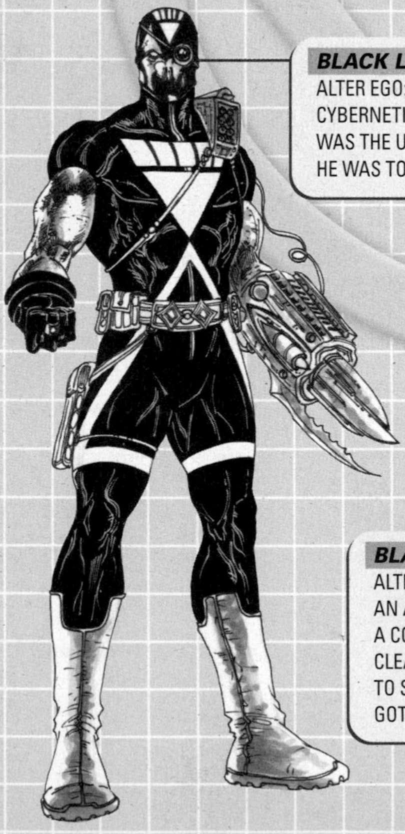

BLACK LANTERN KGBEAST
ALTER EGO: ANATOLI KNYAZEV
CYBERNETICALLY ENHANCED, KGBEAST WAS THE ULTIMATE ASSASSIN UNTIL HE WAS TOSSED FROM A ROOF.

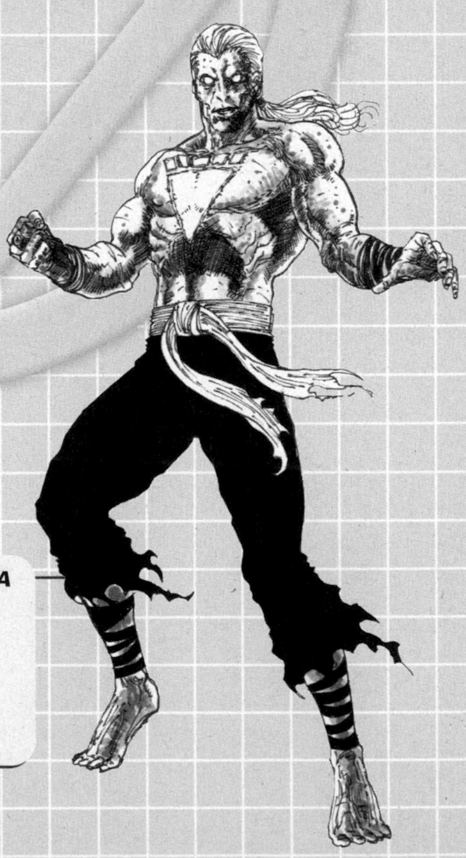

BLACK LANTERN KING COBRA
ALTER EGO: UNKNOWN
AN AVERAGE CRIME LORD WITH A COBRA COSTUME, KING COBRA CLEARLY WASN'T STRONG ENOUGH TO SURVIVE ON THE STREETS OF GOTHAM CITY.

BLACK LANTERN TRIGGER TWINS
ALTER EGO: WALT AND WAYNE TRIGGER
THE TRIGGER BROTHERS WERE EXPERT
MARKSMEN UNTIL THEY BECAME THE BULL'S-EYE.

BLACK LANTERN VENTRILOQUIST
ALTER EGO: ARNOLD WESKER
A PSYCHOTIC CRIMINAL WHO BELIEVES
HIS BOSS IS A DUMMY NAMED SCARFACE,
ARNOLD WAS SHOT AND KILLED, LEADING TO
THE INTRODUCTION OF A NEW VENTRILOQUIST.

BLACK LANTERN TONY ZUCCO
ALTER EGO: BOSS ZUCCO
TONY ZUCCO IS THE MAN WHO HAD
THE FLYING GRAYSONS' TRAPEZE
ROPES CUT, LEADING TO THE BIRTH OF
DICK GRAYSON AS ROBIN. HE WAS
MURDERED BY A RIVAL CRIME BOSS.

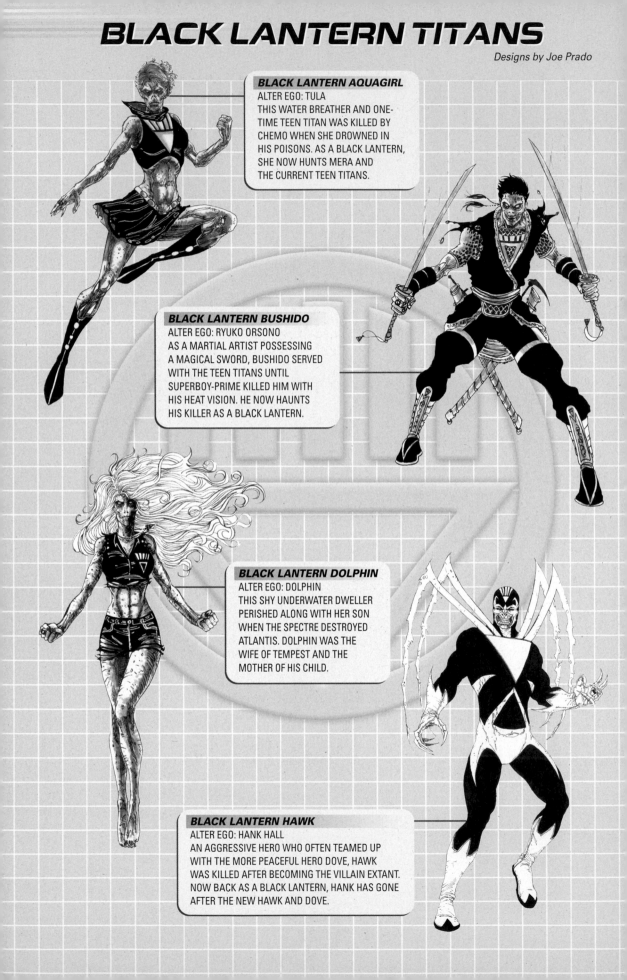

BLACK LANTERN TITANS

Designs by Joe Prado

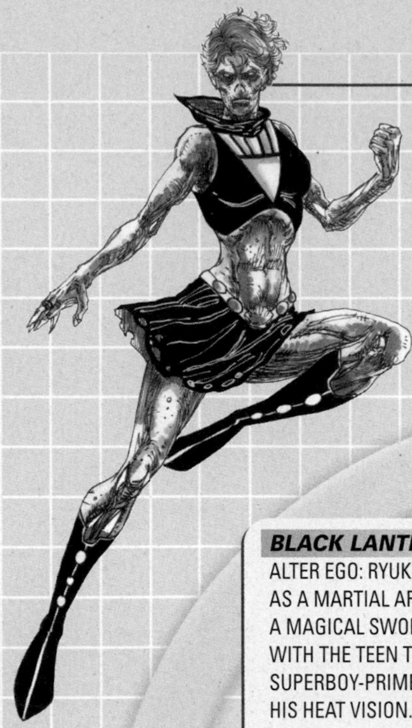

BLACK LANTERN AQUAGIRL

ALTER EGO: TULA

THIS WATER BREATHER AND ONE-TIME TEEN TITAN WAS KILLED BY CHEMO WHEN SHE DROWNED IN HIS POISONS. AS A BLACK LANTERN, SHE NOW HUNTS MERA AND THE CURRENT TEEN TITANS.

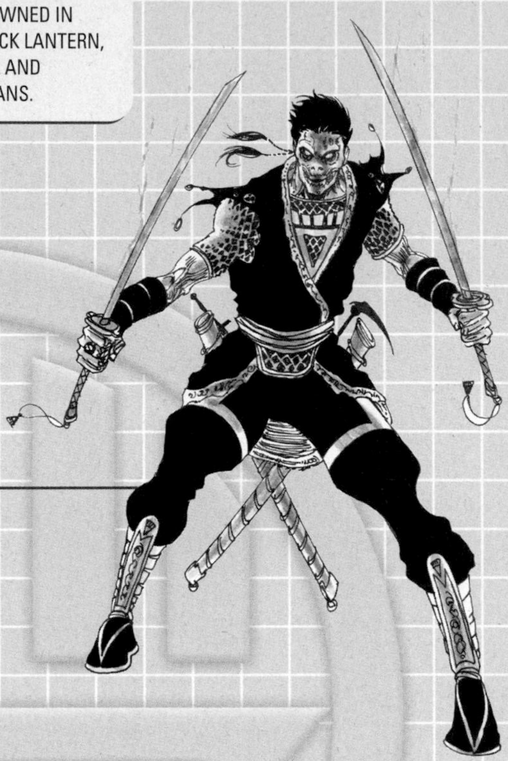

BLACK LANTERN BUSHIDO

ALTER EGO: RYUKO ORSONO

AS A MARTIAL ARTIST POSSESSING A MAGICAL SWORD, BUSHIDO SERVED WITH THE TEEN TITANS UNTIL SUPERBOY-PRIME KILLED HIM WITH HIS HEAT VISION. HE NOW HAUNTS HIS KILLER AS A BLACK LANTERN.

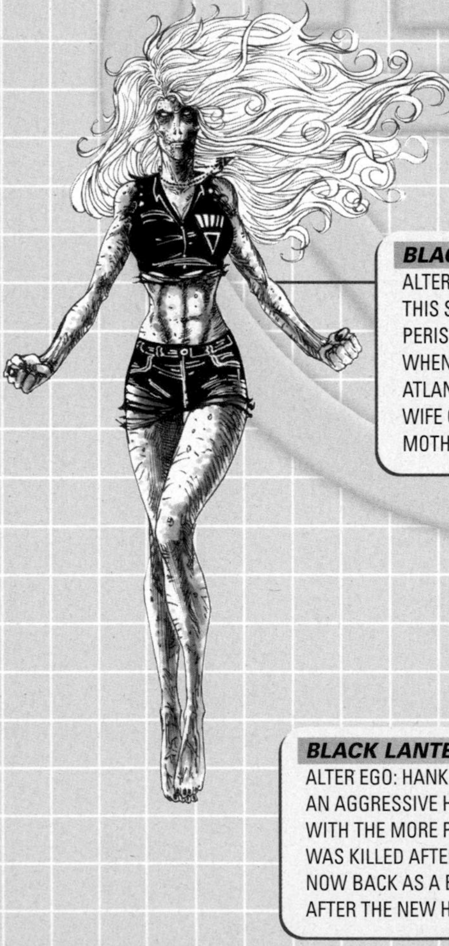

BLACK LANTERN DOLPHIN

ALTER EGO: DOLPHIN

THIS SHY UNDERWATER DWELLER PERISHED ALONG WITH HER SON WHEN THE SPECTRE DESTROYED ATLANTIS. DOLPHIN WAS THE WIFE OF TEMPEST AND THE MOTHER OF HIS CHILD.

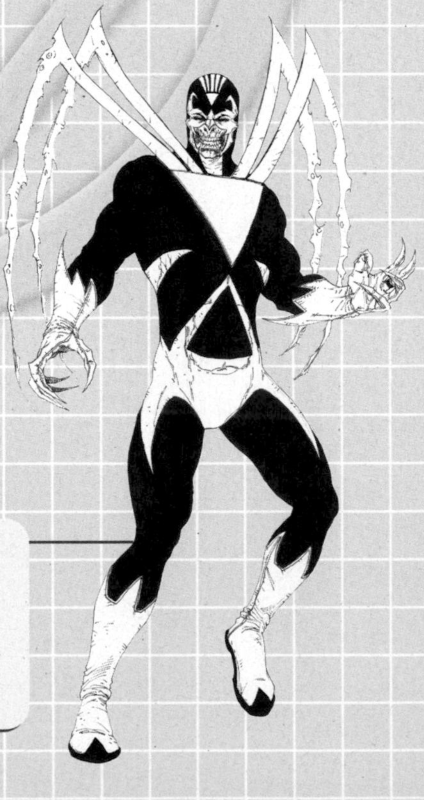

BLACK LANTERN HAWK

ALTER EGO: HANK HALL

AN AGGRESSIVE HERO WHO OFTEN TEAMED UP WITH THE MORE PEACEFUL HERO DOVE, HAWK WAS KILLED AFTER BECOMING THE VILLAIN EXTANT. NOW BACK AS A BLACK LANTERN, HANK HAS GONE AFTER THE NEW HAWK AND DOVE.

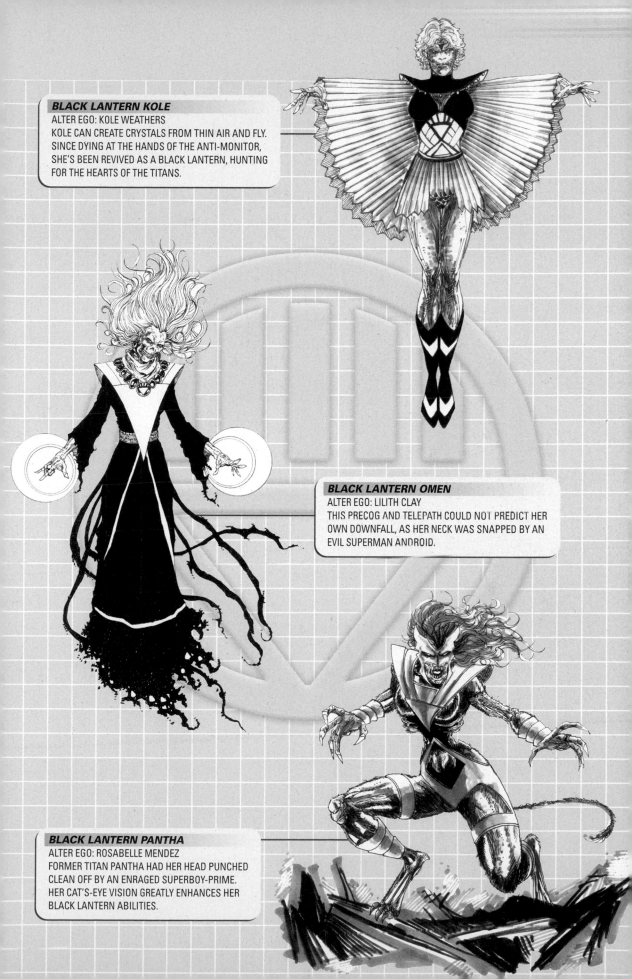

BLACK LANTERN KOLE

ALTER EGO: KOLE WEATHERS
KOLE CAN CREATE CRYSTALS FROM THIN AIR AND FLY. SINCE DYING AT THE HANDS OF THE ANTI-MONITOR, SHE'S BEEN REVIVED AS A BLACK LANTERN, HUNTING FOR THE HEARTS OF THE TITANS.

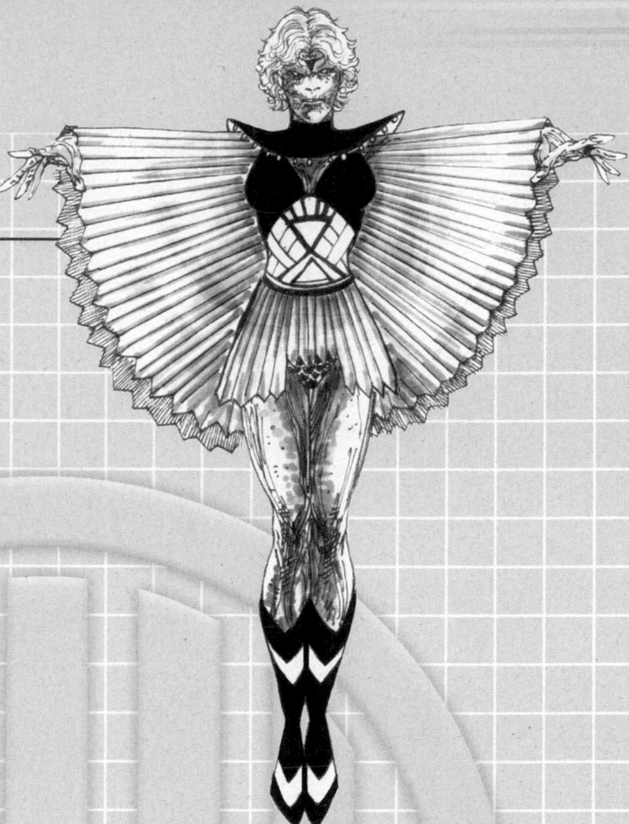

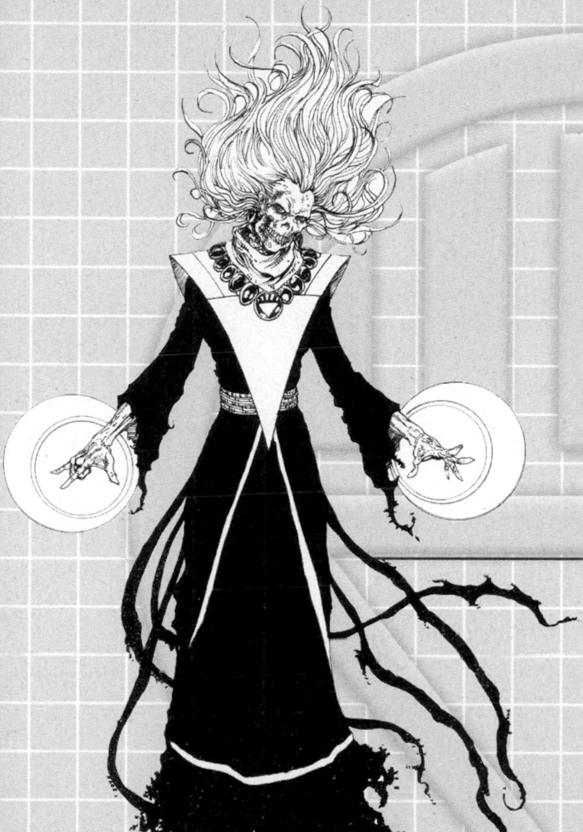

BLACK LANTERN OMEN

ALTER EGO: LILITH CLAY
THIS PRECOG AND TELEPATH COULD NOT PREDICT HER OWN DOWNFALL, AS HER NECK WAS SNAPPED BY AN EVIL SUPERMAN ANDROID.

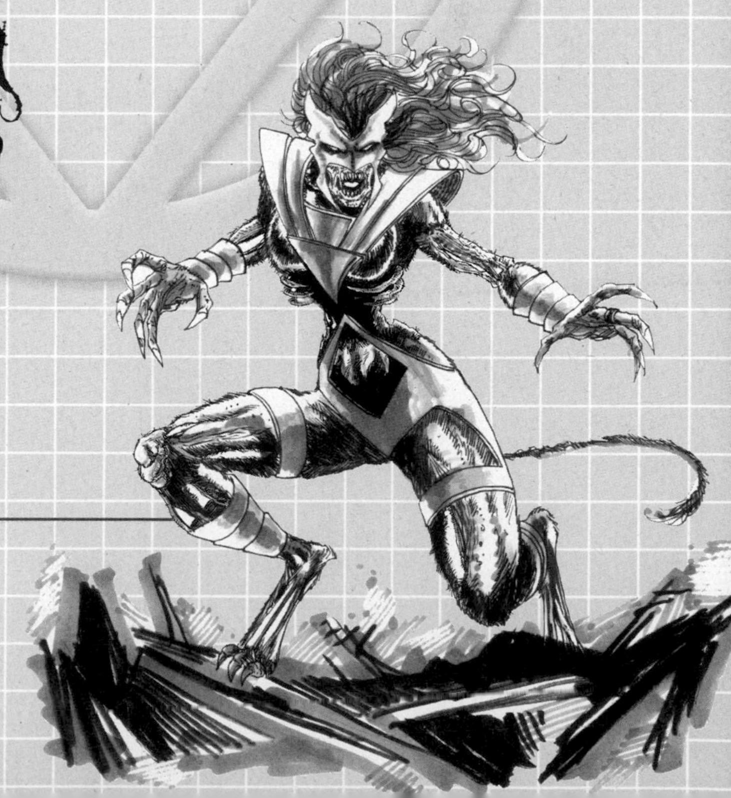

BLACK LANTERN PANTHA

ALTER EGO: ROSABELLE MENDEZ
FORMER TITAN PANTHA HAD HER HEAD PUNCHED CLEAN OFF BY AN ENRAGED SUPERBOY-PRIME. HER CAT'S-EYE VISION GREATLY ENHANCES HER BLACK LANTERN ABILITIES.

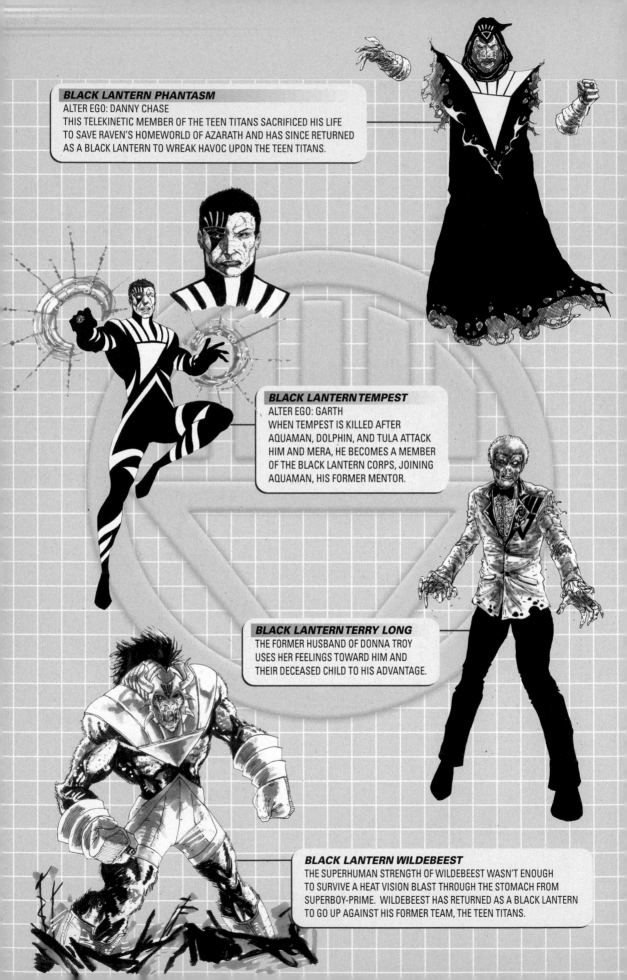

BLACK LANTERN PHANTASM

ALTER EGO: DANNY CHASE

THIS TELEKINETIC MEMBER OF THE TEEN TITANS SACRIFICED HIS LIFE TO SAVE RAVEN'S HOMEWORLD OF AZARATH AND HAS SINCE RETURNED AS A BLACK LANTERN TO WREAK HAVOC UPON THE TEEN TITANS.

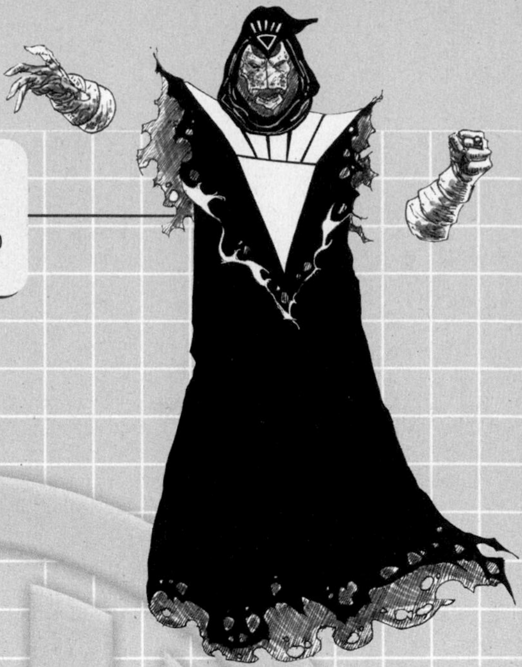

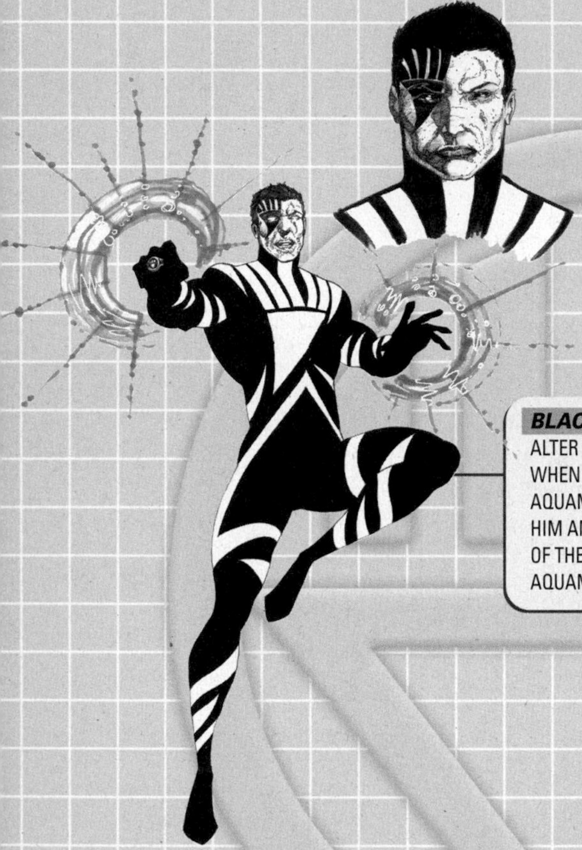

BLACK LANTERN TEMPEST

ALTER EGO: GARTH

WHEN TEMPEST IS KILLED AFTER AQUAMAN, DOLPHIN, AND TULA ATTACK HIM AND MERA, HE BECOMES A MEMBER OF THE BLACK LANTERN CORPS, JOINING AQUAMAN, HIS FORMER MENTOR.

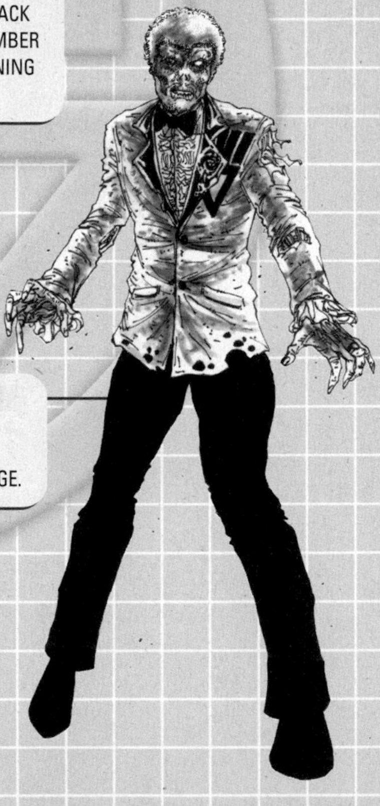

BLACK LANTERN TERRY LONG

THE FORMER HUSBAND OF DONNA TROY USES HER FEELINGS TOWARD HIM AND THEIR DECEASED CHILD TO HIS ADVANTAGE.

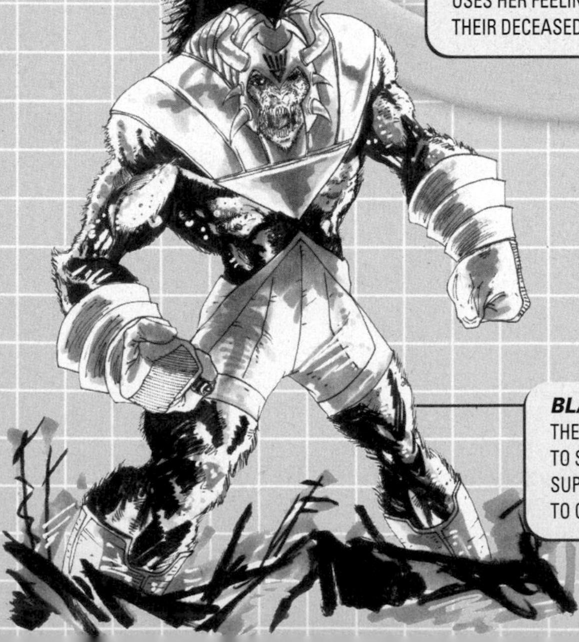

BLACK LANTERN WILDEBEEST

THE SUPERHUMAN STRENGTH OF WILDEBEEST WASN'T ENOUGH TO SURVIVE A HEAT VISION BLAST THROUGH THE STOMACH FROM SUPERBOY-PRIME. WILDEBEEST HAS RETURNED AS A BLACK LANTERN TO GO UP AGAINST HIS FORMER TEAM, THE TEEN TITANS.

BLACK LANTERN TITANS VILLAINS

Designs by Joe Prado

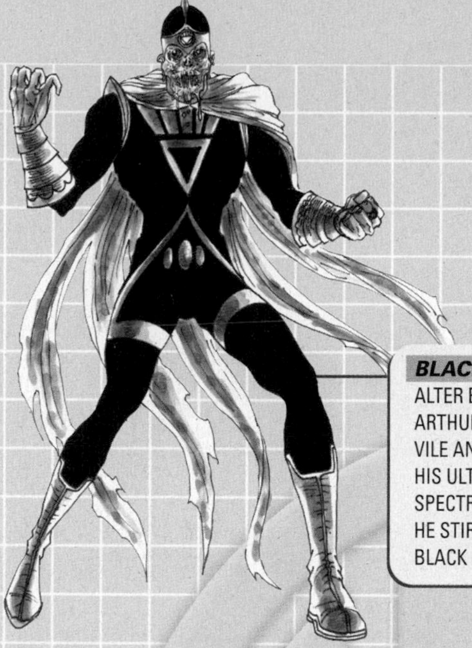

BLACK LANTERN DOCTOR LIGHT

ALTER EGO: ARTHUR LIGHT

ARTHUR LIGHT ALWAYS WAS DISGUSTING, VILE AND PURE EVIL, BUT HE FINALLY FACED HIS ULTIMATE FATE AT THE HANDS OF THE SPECTRE, THE SPIRIT OF VENGEANCE. NOW HE STIRS UP THE EMOTIONS OF THE JLA AS BLACK LANTERN DOCTOR LIGHT.

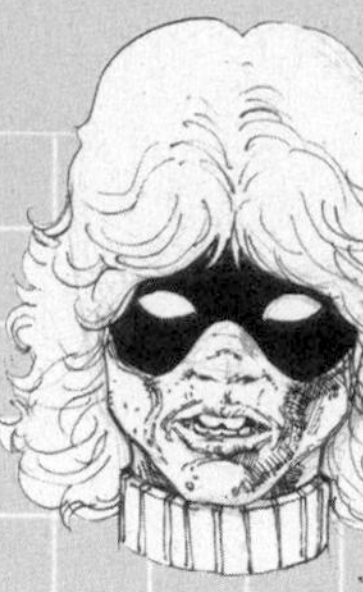

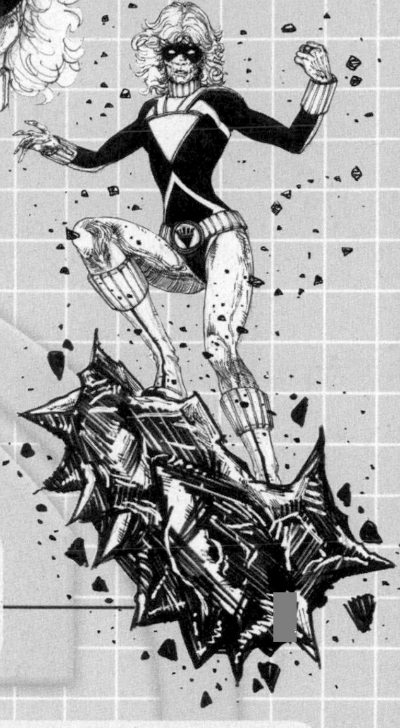

BLACK LANTERN TERRA

ALTER EGO: TARA MARKOV

TERRA ALWAYS PLAYED BOTH SIDES. AS A BLACK LANTERN SHE POSES A TERRIBLE THREAT WITH HER EARTH-CONTROLLING POWERS BUT EVEN MORE AS AN EXCELLENT LIAR.

BLACK LANTERN MADAME ROUGE

ALTER EGO: LAURA DE MILLE

WITH A SPLIT PERSONALITY, MADAME ROUGE IS OFTEN TORN BETWEEN GOOD AND EVIL. WITH HER ELASTIC POWERS, ROUGE HAS PROVEN TO BE A DEADLY THREAT GOING UP AGAINST THE DOOM PATROL AND TEEN TITANS UNTIL ULTIMATELY BEING KILLED BY BEAST BOY. NOW THAT SHE IS A BLACK LANTERN SHE'LL DOUBTLESS CONTINUE TO BE A FORMIDABLE ADVERSARY.

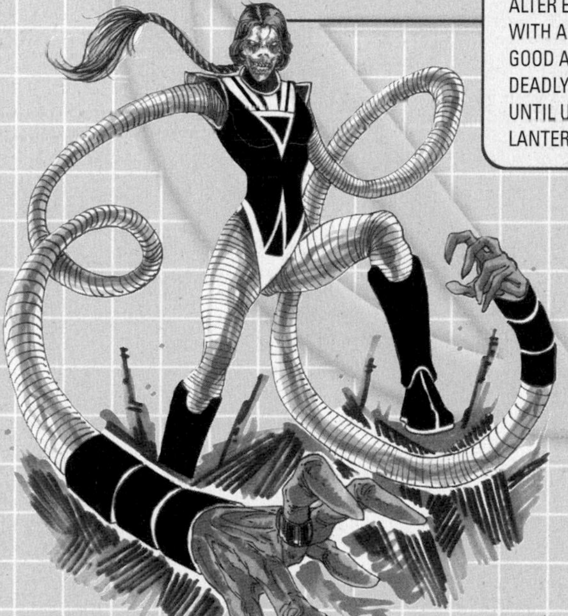

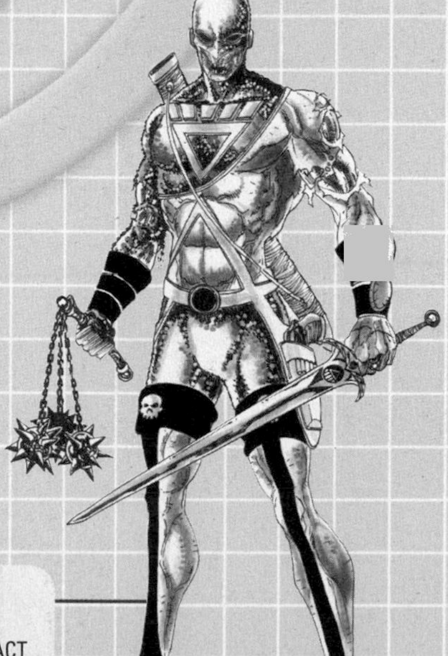

BLACK LANTERN RAVAGER

ALTER EGO: GRANT WILSON

DEATHSTROKE'S SON GRANT WILSON DIED WHILE ATTEMPTING TO COMPLETE A CONTRACT ON THE TITANS. AS A BLACK LANTERN, HIS NEW MISSION IS THE DEATH OF HIS FATHER.

FOLLOW THE COMPLETE

BLACKEST NIGHT

SAGA IN THESE GRAPHIC NOVELS

BLACKEST NIGHT
Geoff Johns & Ivan Reis

BLACKEST NIGHT: GREEN LANTERN
Geoff Johns & Doug Mahnke

BLACKEST NIGHT: GREEN LANTERN CORPS
Peter J. Tomasi & Patrick Gleason

BLACKEST NIGHT: BLACK LANTERN CORPS VOL. 1
Peter J. Tomasi, James Robinson, J.T. Krul, Ardian Syaf, Ed Benes & Eddy Barrows

BLACKEST NIGHT: BLACK LANTERN CORPS VOL. 2
Geoff Johns, James Robinson, Greg Rucka, Scott Kolins, Eddy Barrows & Nicola Scott

BLACKEST NIGHT: RISE OF THE BLACK LANTERNS
Geoff Johns, Peter J. Tomasi, James Robinson & others

BLACKEST NIGHT: TALES OF THE CORPS
Geoff Johns, Peter J. Tomasi & others

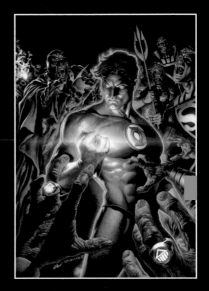

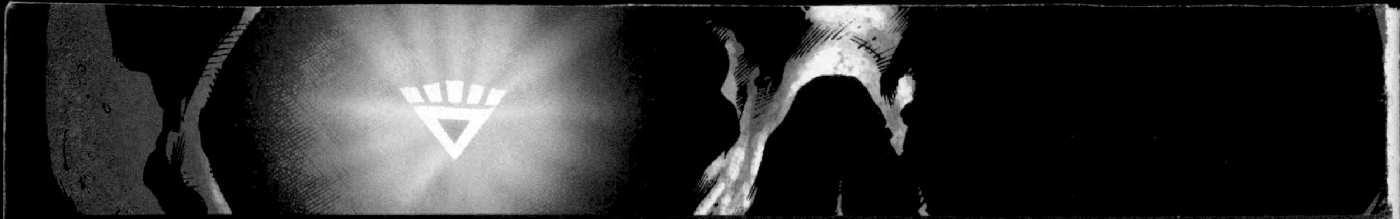